how baking works

works THIRD EDITION

Exploring the Fundamentals of Baking Science

paula figoni

WILEY

JOHN WILEY & SONS, INC.

Library of Congress Cataloging-in-Publication Data:

Figoni, Paula.

How baking works : exploring the fundamentals of baking science / Paula Figoni. -- 3rd ed.

p. cm.

Includes bibliographical references and index.

ISBN 978-0-470-39267-6 (pbk.); ISBN 978-0-470-39813-5 (ebk.)

1. Baking. I. Title.

TX763.F54 2011

641.8'15--dc22

2010006497

Printed in the United States of America

10 9 8 7 6 5 4 3 2 1

Contents

Equipment and Smallwares

1. Baker's or electronic scales
2. Measuring cups and measuring spoons, assorted sizes
3. Sieves or strainers
4. Mixers with 5-quart bowls, three-speed Hobart N50, ten-speed Commercial KitchenAid, or equivalent
5. Flat beater, dough hook, and wire whip attachments for mixers
6. Bowl scrapers
7. Bench scrapers
8. Dough cutters, 2½" (65 mm) or equivalent
9. Thermometers: oven, instant-read, candy
10. Parchment paper
11. Ovens (conventional, reel, deck, etc.)
12. Stovetop burners
13. Half sheet pans
14. Muffin pans (2½" or 3½"/65 or 90 mm size) and paper liners
15. Half hotel pans
16. Silicone (Silpat) pads, to fit half sheet pans
17. Portion scoops, including #8, #16, and #30
18. Timers
19. Rulers
20. Proof box
21. Stainless-steel bowls, especially 2- and 4-quart sizes
22. Mixing spoons, wooden and stainless-steel
23. Spatulas, heat-resistant silicone, rubber, flexible steel, and offset
24. Stainless-steel saucepans, heavy, 2 quart
25. Rolling pins
26. Knives, assorted serrated, paring, etc.
27. Plastic wrap
28. Pastry bags
29. Pastry tips, plain
30. Vegetable peelers
31. Cake pans, 9-inch round
32. Cutting boards
33. Plastic teaspoons for tasting
34. Cups for water
35. Tape and markers for labeling
36. Straight-edge
37. Whisks
38. Plates, 6-inch, or small bowls
39. Pastry brushes
40. Food processors
41. Wooden picks (for testing)
42. Height guides
43. Ceramic custard cups (6 fl. oz./180 ml), or equivalent

Preface

Years ago, there was only one way to become a baker or pastry chef, and that was to apprentice with a master craftsman. The apprentice learned by doing, repeating the necessary skills, year after year, until the skills were mastered. If bakers and pastry chefs understood their ingredients or why they did what they did, it was only after years of experience. Mostly they knew what to do because they did what they had been shown, and it worked.

Today bakers and pastry chefs have more challenges. They must master more skills. They must adapt to faster-changing trends. They must learn to use a wider array of ingredients from different cultures. They must learn to use still more ingredients devised in the chemist's lab. They must learn all this in a shorter length of time.

Baking and pastry programs in colleges and universities are laying the foundation to meet these new challenges. Part of this foundation includes applying the knowledge of science to the bakeshop. The purpose of *How Baking Works, Third Edition* is to help lay this foundation. Yet I'm sure some might wonder if this knowledge is necessary, even helpful. After all, isn't it enough to learn the skills of the bakeshop?

After years of working with experienced bakers and pastry chefs and after years of training students, I am convinced that today, skills are not enough. I have faith that the knowledge of the food scientist can help in facing the challenges in the bakeshop. Finally, I have conviction that this knowledge is useful for the beginner as well as the master.

The food scientist uncovers how different ingredients are processed, views ingredients as made of individual components, and views processes and procedures in the bakeshop in terms of interactions between these components. If ingredients can be viewed in this way, their behavior in the bakeshop begins to make more sense. How they will react under new conditions and new situations can be predicted better, and failures in the bakeshop can be averted. The goal of this book is to share the views of the food scientist with bakers and pastry chefs. Yet I have tried to keep this book focused on the interests and needs of beginning and practicing bakers and pastry chefs. The only theories presented are those necessary to better understand that which will be immediately useful in the bakeshop.

Beyond the practical usefulness of science, there is a beauty to it, a beauty best appreciated when science is applied to the everyday world. I hope that this book allows those who might not yet see this beauty to at least see the possibility of it.

A Note About Temperature and Weight Conversions

Numbers can sound deceptively precise. For instance, the temperature at which yeast cells die is often cited as 140°F (60°C). But was the heat moist or dry? Was the temperature brought up quickly or slowly? What strain of yeast was used, and how much acid, salt, and sugar were present?

The actual temperature at which yeast cells die depends on these and other factors, and that temperature is not necessarily 140°F (60°C). For this reason, many temperatures provided in this text are converted from Fahrenheit to Celsius in ranges of five degrees.

While this may appear inexact, it best reflects the reality of the situation.

Other times, however, temperatures are meant to be precise. For example, it matters when proofing yeast dough whether the temperature is 81°F (27°C) or 85°F (29°C). In this case, temperatures are converted from Fahrenheit to Celsius to the nearest whole degree.

Changes to the Third Edition

While the core format and theme of the text remains the same, several important additions and changes have been made to the third edition of *How Baking Works*. Some of these changes are as follows:

- A new chapter has been added that focuses on baking for health and wellness. This chapter (Chapter 18) includes information on creating pastries and baked goods to improve the general health of all consumers. It also includes information on baking for special diets, including baking for diabetics and those with food allergies and sensitivities.
- The chapter on fats and oils (Chapter 9) was revised and enlarged to reflect changes in the industry, which have been substantial in the few years since the publication of the second edition of this book. Many of these changes were precipitated by the switch away from trans fats across North America and beyond. Besides adding more information on alternatives to trans fats, information was included on the processing of fats and oils in general to increase depth of understanding. By necessity, more chemistry on fats and oils was included in this chapter. The text is still primarily for beginning students, however, so all attempts were made to isolate much of this advanced material in sidebars, separate from the main text.
- The order of chapters was altered slightly, based on the suggestions of readers and reviewers. While each chapter was written to stand alone, some chapters are more meaningful when read in the context of material from earlier chapters. The new ordering of chapters capitalizes on this building of knowledge, and it also better reflects the importance of some ingredients over others in the bakeshop. The chapter

Likewise, weight and volume conversions are not necessarily given to the precise gram or milliliter. In most cases, U.S./imperial units are provided in increments of 0.25 ounce, while metric units are converted in increments of 5 grams or 5 milliliters. This reflects the reality of the bakeshop, where most equipment reads down to these increments.

on eggs, for example, was moved forward, ahead of thickening and gelling agents. Likewise, the chapter on chocolate products was moved ahead of the chapters on fruits and on flavorings.

- Several changes were made to exercises and experiments at the end of each chapter. First, more exercises and experiments were included and many were revised. More important, the formatting of the experiments was improved to make the directions easier to follow and the evaluation of results clearer. Finally, questions at the end of each exercise and experiment were rewritten to better integrate the lessons of the lab with the material in the text. The objective was to reinforce important points made in the text with what is taught in the experiments.
- Many new photos, drawings, charts, and tables were added, and many more revised.
- Sections including those on the tempering of chocolates and the functions of emulsifiers were revised to simplify explanations while still maintaining or even improving on the integrity of the science behind the explanation. As part of this, facts, underlying details, and descriptions were carefully checked, and wording throughout the text was revised accordingly.
- Questions at the end of each chapter were reviewed for clarity and revised as needed; additional questions were added to reflect changes to the text.

An Instructor's Manual (ISBN 978-0470-39814-2) accompanies this book. It can be obtained by contacting your Wiley sales representative. An electronic version of the Instructor's Manual is available to qualified instructors on the companion Web site, at www.wiley.com/college/figoni.

About the Exercises and Experiments

The exercises and experiments in this book are designed to reinforce material from the text in a way that shows rather than tells. Some of the exercises are exclusively paper exercises, with a few involving math. Many more involve the sensory evaluation of ingredients. There are several reasons for including these sensory exercises in the text. First is the narrow objective of learning to identify characterizing traits of ingredients, to better understand the effects that they will have on finished products. Second is the even narrower but very practical objective of learning to identify ingredients that may be unlabeled or accidentally mislabeled. Third is the broad objective of increasing awareness of all the tastes, textures, and sights in the bakeshop, no matter how small or mundane. There is much to be learned in a bakeshop, even when the same items are prepped and baked day after day. The first step to learning is learning to be aware.

While the exercises at the end of each chapter are self-explanatory, the experiments do need some explanation. The experiments allow students to further develop basic bakeshop skills, but that is not the main objective of the experiments. Instead, the emphasis of the experiments is on comparing and evaluating products that vary in some systematic way. The real "products" of these experiments are students' findings, which they summarize in the Results Tables provided at the end of each experiment. There are also specific questions at the end of each experiment, with space provided for students to summarize their conclusions.

The experiments are designed so that one or more can be conducted within a four-hour session by a class divided into five or more groups. Each group in the classroom completes one or more of the products in the experiment. When all products are made and cooled, students evaluate the products, either as a class or individually. Room-temperature water (bottled water, if tap water has a strong taste) should be provided, to cleanse the palate between tastings, and students should constantly return to the control product to make side-by-

side comparisons of it with each test product. Whenever possible, two separate groups should prepare the control product for each experiment, in case one turns out unacceptable.

The key to well-conducted experiments is for the products to be prepared and baked under carefully controlled conditions. This is emphasized by the detail provided in the formulas within each experiment. However, understand that the specific mixing and bake times could change, to adjust to the different equipment and conditions in your classroom bakeshop. What is more important than following the provided methods of preparation exactly as written is that each product made within an experiment by a class be completed exactly as all the others.

Above all else, however, common sense rules when completing experiments. There are times when rigid rules must be forsaken, and chefs and scientists must know when to "work with their ingredients." This means that if it is necessary to make adjustments to products because of the nature of the ingredient, those adjustments should be made. An example of when adjustments must be made to products is in the experiment on preparing rolls with different flours, included in different forms in Chapters 5 and 6. If the same amount of water were used for each type of flour, the gluten in the flour would not be properly hydrated. These adjustments are not made lightly, however, and they must be recorded in a Results Table. Notice that an Additional Comments column is included in each table, for this very purpose.

While any classroom bakeshop can be used, there are certain modifications that might need to be made to efficiently run the experiments. For instance, the bakeshop should be supplied with multiple versions of smaller-scale equipment and smallwares. As an example, multiple five-quart mixers, one per group, are needed in place of one large mixer. A list of equipment and smallwares for outfitting a bakeshop for these experiments follows.

Acknowledgments

I would first like to thank the administration of the College of Culinary Arts at Johnson & Wales University (J&W), who suggested that I write this text, and who continue to support me on this.

The faculty in the baking and pastry program at J&W deserve a special thanks. They let me into their bakeshops, answered my questions, presented me with practical problems, and made me feel like I was one of them. They demonstrated firsthand to the students through their own knowledge and understanding of science that science does indeed belong in the bakeshop. They have made my years at J&W immensely rewarding, challenging, and fun, and that has made all the difference to me. In particular, I would like to thank Chefs Charles Armstrong, Mitch Stamm, Richard Miscovich, Jean Luc Derron, and Robert Pekar for their kind words, their support, their friendship, and their food. They are amazingly sharing and caring, and I am sincerely grateful.

I would like to thank everyone at John Wiley and Sons who worked on this book, especially my editor Christine McKnight, whose unflappable style helped me maintain perspective and stay on track. I would also like to thank the reviewers of the manuscript, whose helpful comments and suggestions strengthened the manuscript. They are Amy Felder of Johnson & Wales University, Virginia Olson of Anne Arundel Community College, Dr. M. Ginger Scarbrough of New Mexico State University, and David Vagasky of Trident Technical College.

As always, I would like to thank my family. My parents, whose memory lives on, and my sisters, who are also my friends. Finally, Bob deserves a special thanks for his support, for his good humor, and for his understanding how important this project was to me. He also deserves a note of congratulations for surviving it all. This book is yours as well as mine.

PAULA FIGONI
Providence, Rhode Island

Introduction to Baking

Introduction

Those who enter the fields of baking and pastry arts do so for a variety of reasons. For some, it is the joy of working with their hands, of creating edible works of art from a few basic ingredients. For others, it is the rush they get from the fast pace of the bakeshop or from its satisfying sights and smells. Still others like the challenge of pleasing and surprising customers. No matter the reason, the decision to work in the field is usually grounded in a love of food, and maybe past experience in a bakeshop or a home kitchen.

Working in a professional bakeshop is different from baking at home, however. Production in a bakeshop is on a larger scale. It takes place day in and day out, sometimes under severe time pressures, in uncomfortably hot and humid conditions, and over long hours. Despite the discomforts and pressures, product quality must remain consistently high, because that is what the customer expects.

It takes specialized knowledge and practiced skills to accomplish these goals successfully. It helps to be attentive to the sights, sounds, and smells of the bakeshop. Experienced bakers and pastry chefs, for example, listen to the sound of cake batter being beaten in a bowl, knowing that changes in sound accompany changes to the batter itself. They push and pummel bread dough to feel how it responds. They use smells from the oven to judge when baking is nearly complete, and they sample their finished products before presenting them to the customer.

Experienced bakers and pastry chefs rely, too, on tools like timers and thermometers, because they know how time and temperature affect product quality. They also rely heavily on accurate scales.

The Importance of Accuracy in the Bakeshop

Most bakery items are made of the same ingredients: flour, water, sugar, eggs, leavening agents, and fat. Sometimes the difference between two products is simply the method of preparation used in assembling the ingredients. Other times the difference is the proportion or amount of each ingredient in a formula. Because small differences in method and in proportion of ingredients can have a large effect on the quality of baked goods, it is crucial that bakers and pastry chefs follow methods of preparation carefully and measure ingredients properly. Otherwise, a product may turn out unexpectedly, or worse, may turn out unacceptable or inedible.

For example, if too much shortening and too few eggs are added to a formula for moist, chewy oatmeal cookies, the cookies will likely turn out crisp and dry. If the same error is made with cake batter, the result will likely be a complete failure, since eggs provide structure and volume. In fact, bakers and pastry chefs require a higher degree of accuracy when measuring ingredients than do culinary chefs in the kitchen.

When the kitchen chef prepares a pot of soup, it doesn't really matter if a little less celery is added or an extra onion is included. The chef still has a pot of soup, and if the flavor is off, adjustments can be made along the way. Bakers and pastry chefs cannot make adjustments along the way. If too little salt is added to bread dough, it will do no good to sprinkle salt onto the bread once it is baked. Instead, ingredients must be weighed and measured accurately at the beginning.

This means that, more so than kitchen chefs, bakers and pastry chefs are chemists in the kitchen. As with chemists, creativity and skill are important for success, but so is accuracy. If a formula calls for two pounds of flour, it doesn't mean around two pounds, more or less. It means two pounds.

Balances and Scales

Formulas used in the bakeshop are in some ways like recipes in the kitchen. Formulas include a list of ingredients and a method of preparation (MOP). Unlike recipes used by the kitchen chef, however, formulas include exact measurements for each ingredient, and these measurements are usually given in weights. The process of weighing ingredients is called *scaling* because pastry chefs use scales to weigh ingredients.

HELPFUL HINT

Baker's scales and their accessories (scoops and weights) must be cared for if they are to remain in balance. They should be wiped regularly with a damp cloth and mild detergent, and they should not be banged or dropped. These precautions are necessary to keep the scale reading accurately.

To determine if a scale is in balance, empty both platforms and move the ounce weight indicator to the far left (that is, to zero). With the scale at eye level, determine whether the platforms are at the same height. If they are not, adjust the weights located beneath the platforms as needed. Repeat this test with a scoop on the left platform and a counterweight on the right. If balancing is needed, do so by adding or removing weight from the counterweight.

The traditional scale used in the bakeshop is a baker's balance scale. It measures ingredients mechanically by balancing them against known weights. It is an investment that should be selected for its durability and its precision. A good baker's scale can weigh amounts as large as 8 pounds (4 kilograms) or more and as small as ¼ ounce (0.25 ounce or 5 grams). This provides the precision needed for most quantity food preparation.

Bakers and pastry chefs sometimes use digital electronic scales. While many affordable electronic scales provide the same or better precision as baker's scales, it is not necessarily the case. The precision of a scale—either mechanical baker's scale or electronic scale—depends entirely on the scale's design and construction, how well the scale is maintained, and whether it has been properly calibrated.

Most digital electronic scales provide information about their precision and capacity on their front or back panels. For example, a scale that is marked *4.0 kg × 5 g* has a capacity of 4 kilograms, meaning it can measure quantities as large as 4 kilograms (about 8.8 pounds). The *readability* of this scale, 5 grams, is the smallest quantity that the scale will display on its digital readout. Readability, sometimes represented as *d* on a scale, is a reasonable indicator of the precision of a scale. Generally, the smaller the readability of the scale, the better it will be at weighing small amounts. Five grams is equivalent to just under 0.2 ounce, which is similar to the 0.25-ounce precision of a good baker's scale.

Consider another electronic scale, one marked *100 oz. × 0.1 oz.* This scale has a capacity of 100 ounces (6.25 pounds or 2.84 kilograms) and a readability of 0.1 ounce (3 grams). The smaller value for readability indicates that this scale likely provides better precision than a typical baker's scale, making it useful for weighing small quantities of spices or flavorings.

More on Scale Readability

The abbreviation for the readability of a scale, *d*, stands for scale division. Readability represents the increments that the scale's weight capacity is divided into. This means that when an item is placed on a scale, the reading on the scale's display panel will be in increments represented by the readability. As weight is added onto a scale with a readability of 5 grams, for example, the reading on the display panel will change from 0 grams, to 5 grams, to 10, 15, 20, and so on. No matter the weight of the ingredient, the scale displays the weight in increments of 5 grams. If a sample in fact weighs 6 grams, the display will read 5 grams. If it weighs 8.75 grams, the display will read 10 grams.

Sometimes a scale fluctuates between readings. Let's say, for example, that the scale in the previous example fluctuates between 5 grams and 10 grams. It is likely that the sample actually weighs about 7.5 grams, which is halfway between 5 grams and 10 grams.

While a scale's readability is an indication of the smallest amount that can be weighed on a scale, it is not the same as the smallest amount that *should* be weighed on a scale. As the amount that you place on a scale approaches the readability of that scale, the uncertainty in the reading increases. A good rule of thumb is that a scale is acceptable for weighing an ingredient as long as the readability of the scale is 10 percent or less than the amount to be weighed. Stated another way as a workable formula:

Smallest quantity to be weighed =
scale readability × 10

Consider a scale where the readability is 0.25 ounce (7 grams). This scale could appropriately weigh quantities as small as 2.5 ounces (70 grams). Likewise, a scale with a readability of 0.1 ounce (3 grams) could adequately weigh quantities as small as 1 ounce (30 grams).

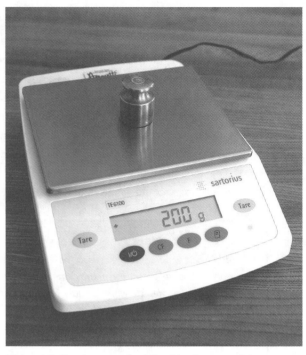

Figure 1.1 Check your scale daily with a known weight to confirm that it is properly calibrated.

Just as baker's scales need to be checked periodically for accuracy, so too must digital scales. Digital scales typically come with a brass weight calibrated for accuracy. Check your scale daily with the brass weight (Figure 1.1). If the scale's reading does not match the mass of the brass weight, follow the manufacturer's instructions to adjust the scale. Because a scale is an important piece of equipment in a bakeshop, it is best to also occasionally check its calibration at two or more different weights (200 grams and 2,000 grams, for example). The scale will need adjustment or repair if either of these two readings is off.

How an ingredient is added to a digital scale can sometimes make a difference in the accuracy of the reading. For example, multiple small additions will sometimes read lower than the identical amount added all at once. This can happen because scales are generally designed so that they don't fluctuate excessively with air movement, and scales cannot necessarily differentiate a very small amount of product from air movement.

Units of Measure

Digital and baker's scales measure in either standard U.S. common units (pounds and ounces; also called imperial units in Canada) or in metric units (kilograms and grams). Some versatile digital scales switch at the touch of a button from U.S./imperial units to metric units. Most countries throughout the world have adopted the metric system. This provides a means of sharing formulas more easily across national borders. More importantly, the metric system is simpler to use once you become familiar with it. With the metric system, for example, fewer math calculations are needed when converting a formula to a new batch size. Since 1 kilogram in metric equals 1,000 grams, you simply move decimal points to convert from one size unit to another. For example, 1.48 kilograms is equal to 1,480 grams, and 343 grams is equal to 0.343 kilograms. Try converting as quickly from pounds to ounces, or ounces to pounds! This ease of use is probably the main reason why more bakers and pastry chefs in North America are adopting the metric system for use in the bakeshop.

Using the metric system consistently, for the most part, does not require tedious math conversions from ounces to grams or pounds to kilograms. This makes it much easier to use the metric system than most people believe. Table 1.1 lists the metric equivalents of a few U.S. common/imperial units, for those times when you do need to convert from one system to another.

It is a common misconception that metric units provide better precision than U.S./imperial units. In fact, metric units are not necessarily more precise, although they are simpler to use. Once again, the precision of measurements depends on the design and construction of the scale, not on the units used.

TABLE 1.1 EQUIVALENCIES BETWEEN U.S. COMMON/IMPERIAL AND METRIC UNITS

WEIGHT	
1 ounce	= 28.4 grams
1 pound	= 454 grams
VOLUME	
1 teaspoon	= 5 milliliters
1 quart	= 0.95 liters

Weight and Volume Measurements

Home cooks in North America use volumetric measurements—measuring cups and measuring spoons—for all ingredients, including dry ingredients. This is a problem when measuring certain ingredients. For example, flour settles over time. When flour settles, there is less air between particles. With less air, density is greater and more flour is needed to fill a container. On the other hand, if flour is sifted before it is measured, there is more air between particles. Density is lower, and less flour is needed to fill a cup (Figure 1.2).

How Can an Ounce Scale Provide the Precision of a Gram Scale?

One gram is a much smaller unit than one ounce (there are 28.35 grams in an ounce), so how is it possible for an ounce scale to provide the same or better precision than a gram scale?

Certainly if the gram scale has a readability of 1 gram and the ounce scale has a readability of 1 ounce, the gram scale will measure more precisely than the ounce scale. But this is rarely the case.

Take, for example, the description of the two electronic scales given earlier. The first scale is a gram scale, with a readability of 5 grams, or 0.2 ounce (5 grams divided by 28.35 grams per ounce). The second scale is an ounce scale with a readability of 0.1 ounce (3 grams). In this particular example, the ounce scale weighs more precisely than the gram scale, because the design and construction of the scale allows it to read smaller amounts.

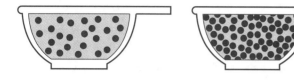

Figure 1.2 A cup filled with sifted flour (**left**) will have fewer flour particles and a lower weight per cup while a cup filled with unsifted flour (**right**) will have more flour particles and a higher weight per cup.

To avoid these inconsistencies, pastry chefs and bakers do not use volumetric measurements for flour and other dry ingredients. Instead, they weigh dry ingredients—and most liquid ingredients—for accuracy. The amount of air in a product or its density does not affect weight measurements the way it affects volume measurements. A pound of sifted flour weighs the same as a pound of unsifted flour, regardless of the density. They both weigh 1 pound!

While some pastry chefs and bakers weigh all ingredients using a scale, others measure some liquids volumetrically, for convenience. They use measuring containers for water and for liquids that have about the same density as water, using one pint of liquid for every pound (or one half-liter for every 500 grams) called for in a formula. While practices vary from one bakeshop to another, ingredients that are often measured volumetrically include milk, cream, and eggs. Table 1.2 indicates why. Notice that the weights per pint (or per half-liter) of cream, milk, and eggs are around the same as that of water. While these ingredients do not weigh exactly 1 pound per pint, they are approximately so (notice, however, that in the metric system, 1 half-liter—500 milliliters—of water at room temperature does weigh exactly 500 grams. This is not a coincidence). Many other liquids, including honey, corn syrup, and oil, have densities much different from water. These liquids are weighed, because 1 pint does not weigh 1 pound.

TABLE 1.2 A COMPARISON OF THE APPROXIMATE WEIGHTS OF 1 PINT AND 1 HALF-LITER OF VARIOUS INGREDIENTS

INGREDIENT	APPROXIMATE WEIGHT PER U.S. PINT (2 CUPS), IN WEIGHT OUNCES	APPROXIMATE WEIGHT PER HALF-LITER (500 ML), IN GRAMS
Splenda	4.0	120
Ginger, ground	6.0	180
Flour, sifted	8.2	245
Flour, unsifted	9.2	275
Sugar, granulated	14.1	420
Oil, vegetable	14.8	445
Cream, heavy	16.4	490
Water	16.7	500
Milk, whole	17.0	510
Eggs, whole	17.2	515
Orange juice	17.4	520
Coffee liqueur	17.5	525
Simple syrup (equal parts sugar and water)	20.6	615
Honey, molasses, and glucose corn syrups	23.0	690

The Difference Between Weight Ounces and Fluid Ounces

Refer to Table 1.3, which lists conversions between U.S. common volumetric measurements. Notice that there are 16 ounces in a pint (2 cups). Recall that there are 16 ounces in a pound. Why, then, did we see from Table 1.2 that a pint does not weigh 1 pound for all ingredients? Likewise, how can there be 16 tablespoons in a cup and 8 ounces in a cup, but 16 tablespoons does not necessarily weigh 8 ounces? These are the problems that result when one word—ounce—is used to represent two different concepts.

The term *ounce* represents a unit of weight or mass. It can also represent volume or capacity. That is, there are weight ounces that measure weight, and there are fluid ounces that measure volume. Notice that Table 1.3 specifies fluid ounces, not weight ounces, in each conversion. While 1 fluid ounce sometimes does weigh 1 ounce, it is not necessarily always so.

Consider feathers and bullets. No one expects 1 cup of feathers to weigh the same as 1 cup of bullets. Likewise, food ingredients vary in how much they weigh per cup. Refer back to Table 1.2, which lists several ingredients—arranged from less dense to more dense—and their weights per pint (2 cups) and per half-liter (500 milliliters). Notice the large range in values. This shows that the expression "a pint's a pound the world 'round" is not only false for feathers and bullets, but it is also false for many common bakeshop ingredients. It is approximately true for water and for ingredients with the same density as water. Because 1 fluid ounce of water (and ingredients with the same density as water) weighs about 1 ounce, and 1 milliliter of water weighs 1 gram, for practical purposes it doesn't matter whether water is weighed on a scale or measured volumetrically.

> **HELPFUL HINT**
>
> *If a formula includes measurements in ounces, be sure to check carefully to determine for each ingredient whether it is to be measured using fluid or weight ounces. Unless you know the density of an ingredient, do not interchange weight measurements with volumetric measurements or vice versa.*

TABLE 1.3 VOLUMETRIC CONVERSIONS FOR U.S. COMMON UNITS

1 tablespoon	= 3 teaspoons
	= 0.5 fluid ounce
1 cup	= 48 teaspoons
	= 16 tablespoons
	= 8 fluid ounces
1 pint	= 16 fluid ounces
	= 2 cups
1 quart	= 32 fluid ounces
	= 4 cups
	= 2 pints
1 gallon	= 128 fluid ounces
	= 16 cups
	= 8 pints
	= 4 quarts

The Difference Between Density and Thickness

Density is a measure of the compactness of particles or molecules in a liquid or solid. If the particles or molecules are loosely packed, the liquid or solid is not dense, and the weight per cup or per liter of that ingredient is low. If the particles or molecules are closely packed, the liquid or solid is dense, and the weight per cup or weight per liter of that ingredient is high. Worded another way, a given weight of a less dense ingredient takes up more space than the same weight of a denser ingredient. Figure 1.3 shows the different volumes taken up by equal weights (7 ounces or 200 grams) of glucose corn syrup, sifted pastry flour, and water. Notice that 7 ounces (200 grams) of glucose corn syrup takes up much less space than the same weight of sifted pastry flour.

Figure 1.3 Equal weights of **(left to right)** glucose syrup, sifted pastry flour, and water take up different volumes.

> **HELPFUL HINT**
>
> *Do not judge the density of a liquid by its appearance. Unless you know for sure that the density of a liquid is close to that of water, assume that it is not; assume that it must be weighed. That is, assume that 1 fluid ounce does not necessarily weigh 1 ounce, and that 1 milliliter does not necessarily weigh 1 gram.*

Viscosity or consistency is a measure of how easily a liquid flows. If a liquid's particles or molecules slide past each other easily, the liquid flows easily and is considered thin. If the particles or molecules bump or tangle with each other, the liquid will not flow easily and is thick. This is the case with fruit purees. Tiny pulp pieces in fruit purees bump and tangle with one another, preventing water and pulp particles from flowing easily past one another. This makes the puree thick.

Some common liquids—honey and molasses, for example—are both dense and thick. The molecules are close together, making these liquids dense, and the molecules do not slide easily past each other, making the liquids thick (Figure 1.4). On the other hand, vegetable oil is thicker than water, yet it is less dense than water, which is why oil floats on water. Notice that the density of a liquid cannot be judged by its appearance.

Figure 1.4 Molasses is thick because molecules do not slide past each other easily.

Honey, molasses, and glucose corn syrups are all quite dense, weighing about 23 ounces per pint (690 grams per half-liter). Why are these liquids so much denser than either sugar or water alone?

Consider, first, a cup of sugar and a cup of water. It is easy to see that dry sugar crystals are separated by empty space, lowering the density of a cup of sugar. What's less obvious is that the molecules that make up water are also separated by empty space. The empty spaces are not visible to the naked eye.

If a cup of sugar is stirred into a cup of water, there is an instant attraction between the sugar and water molecules. This attraction pulls apart the crystals as the sugar dissolves, and the individual sugar molecules fill the empty spaces between water molecules. Because there is less empty space between molecules in a sugar syrup, the syrup is dense. In fact, the cup of sugar and the cup of water, when combined, take up only about 1⅔ cups.

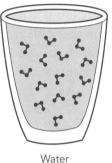
Water

Sugar Dissolved in Water

Baker's Percentages

Formulas, especially bread formulas, are sometimes expressed in terms called *baker's percentages*. With baker's percentages, each ingredient is expressed as the amount of an ingredient compared to the total amount of flour in the formula. Flour is used as the basis for baker's percentages because it is typically the predominant ingredient in most baked goods. Since the total amount of flour is designated as 100 percent, the percentages of all ingredients add up to more than 100 percent. Table 1.4 provides an example of a bread formula expressed in weight and in baker's percentages. Notice that more than one type of flour is included in this formula, but that together the weight of the flours adds up to 100 percent.

TABLE 1.4 WHOLE WHEAT BREAD FORMULA EXPRESSED IN WEIGHT AND IN BAKER'S PERCENTAGES

INGREDIENT	POUNDS	OUNCES	GRAMS	BAKER'S PERCENTAGE
Flour, bread	6		3,000	60%
Flour, whole wheat	4		2,000	40%
Water	5	10.0	2,800	56%
Yeast, compressed		6.0	190	4%
Salt		3.0	95	2%
Total	**16**	**3.0**	**8,085**	**162%**

Note: Metric measures in this table and throughout the text are not necessarily exact conversions of U.S./imperial measures. This is done to avoid the use of awkward numbers. Baker's percentages remain approximately the same regardless of the unit of measure.

For formulas that do not contain flour, each ingredient is expressed relative to the predominant and characteristic ingredient. In the case of a date filling, for example, each ingredient is expressed relative to the amount of dates (Table 1.5). For baked custard, each ingredient is expressed relative to the dairy ingredients—milk and cream.

Baker's percentage—sometimes called *formula percentage* or indicated as "on flour weight basis"—is different from the percentages commonly taught in math classes. Baker's percentages are actually ratios of the amount of an ingredient to the amount of flour. In the more common type of percentage, each ingredient is expressed as a certain percentage of the total batch size. In this case, ingredient percentages add up to 100 percent. Table 1.6 shows the bread formula from Table 1.4, this time expressed as a percentage of the total batch.

Baker's percentages have an advantage over percentages based on total batch size. Baker's percentages require fewer calculations when adding or changing the amount of one ingredient. If percentages used are based on total batch size, then every ingredient percentage will have to be recalculated when any one ingredient is changed, since the total batch size would also change. Needless to say, this is complicated and time consuming and thus, baker's percentages are preferred by some bakers.

Why bother expressing formulas in percentages at all? Percentages allow formulas to be compared easily. Table 1.7 illustrates this point. Compare the two bread formulas in Table 1.7 by looking at the weights of each ingredient. Can you tell quickly which formula is saltier? Before you conclude that Bread #2 is saltier because it contains 6 ounces (190 grams) of salt compared with 3 ounces (95 grams) in Bread #1, notice that the formula for Bread #2 also yields a larger quantity of dough. Unless this difference in yield or batch size is accounted for, weights alone won't reveal which bread is saltier.

When baker's percentages instead of weight are used to compare the two formulas, however, the difference in batch size is accounted for, and it becomes clear that the formula for Bread #1 is saltier. The amount of salt in the formula for Bread #1 is about 2 percent of the weight of the flours compared with 1 percent in Bread #2.

TABLE 1.5   DATE FILLING FORMULA EXPRESSED IN WEIGHT AND IN BAKER'S PERCENTAGES

INGREDIENT	POUNDS	GRAMS	BAKER'S PERCENTAGE
Dates	6	3,000	100%
Sugar	1	500	17%
Water	3	1,500	50%
Total	**10**	**5,000**	**167%**

TABLE 1.6   WHOLE WHEAT BREAD FORMULA EXPRESSED IN WEIGHT AND IN PERCENTAGE OF TOTAL BATCH

INGREDIENT	POUNDS	OUNCES	GRAMS	PERCENTAGE OF TOTAL BATCH
Flour, bread	6		3,000	37%
Flour, whole wheat	4		2,000	25%
Water	5	10.0	2,800	35%
Yeast, compressed		6.0	190	2%
Salt		3.0	95	1%
Total	**16**	**3.0**	**8,085**	**100%**

TABLE 1.7 WHOLE WHEAT BREAD FORMULAS COMPARED BY WEIGHT AND BY BAKER'S PERCENTAGE

BREAD #1

INGREDIENT	POUNDS	OUNCES	GRAMS	BAKER'S PERCENTAGE
Flour, bread	6		3,000	60%
Flour, whole wheat	4		2,000	40%
Water	5	10	2,800	56%
Yeast, compressed		6	190	4%
Salt		3	95	2%
Total	**16**	**4**	**8,085**	**162%**

BREAD #2

INGREDIENT	POUNDS	OUNCES	GRAMS	BAKER'S PERCENTAGE
Flour, bread	22		10,000	60%
Flour, whole wheat	15		6,800	40%
Water	21		9,550	57%
Yeast, compressed		18	500	3%
Salt		6	190	1%
Total	**59**	**8**	**26,965**	**161%**

The Importance of Controlling Ingredient Temperatures

The finest ingredients can be selected, and they can be accurately weighed and properly mixed, but if temperatures are not carefully controlled, there is still a chance for failure. Why? Many ingredients change properties with temperature. Think of fat, especially fats that melt easily, such as butter. Butter must remain within a narrow temperature range (65°–70°F or 18°–21°C) as it is spread onto croissant dough. If it is too cold, it will not spread properly; if it is too warm, it melts into the dough and flakiness is compromised.

Often, ingredients that are at widely different temperatures must be carefully combined to avoid damaging one ingredient with the shock of the heat—or cold—of another. In making vanilla custard sauce, for example, cold yolks cannot be added directly to hot milk, or the yolks could curdle. Instead, in a technique called *tempering*, small amounts of hot milk are stirred into the yolks, diluting and warming them. The tempered yolks can now be safely added to the bulk of the hot liquid.

Tempering is also necessary when stabilizing whipped cream with a gelatin solution. Warmed gelatin hardens into tiny rubbery balls if it is added too quickly to a cold ingredient like whipped cream. The addition of a small amount of whipped cream to the warm gelatin dilutes and slightly cools the gelatin, so it can be added safely to the bulk of the cold whipped cream.

Notice that in the first example of tempering, a small amount of the hot ingredient is added to the cold ingredient, to prevent damage to the cold ingredient. In the second example, a small amount of the cold ingredient is added to the warm ingredient, to prevent damage to the warm ingredient.

Many other examples demonstrate the need for controlling ingredient temperatures and for carefully tempering ingredients. Look for them throughout the text.

The Importance of Controlling Oven Temperatures

Chapter 2 is all about heat transfer and how to control it. Yet the information in the next chapter is of little use if an oven is not calibrated properly. Nor is it of any use if an oven is not allowed to preheat fully before product is added, or if an oven door is opened too often and for too long. Paying attention to these simple points can go far in assuring that products coming from your bakeshop are of consistently high quality.

It is particularly important that oven temperatures be controlled if products are to rise properly. Figure 1.5 shows puff pastry baked at two different oven temperatures. Notice that the puff pastry baked at the lower temperature rose less than the pastry baked at the higher temperature, where a fast burst of steam allowed for more leavening.

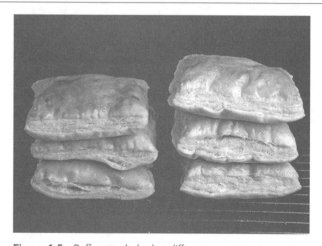

Figure 1.5 Puff pastry baked at different oven temperatures: **Left:** puff pastry baked at 350°F (175°C); **right:** the same pastry baked at 400°F (200°C)

How Important Is Oven Temperature When Baking Cakes?

High-ratio liquid shortening cakes are characterized by high ratios, or baker's percentages, of liquid and sugar to the amount of flour. They are formulated to be mixed in a single step that whips large amounts of tiny air bubbles into the batter. While generally considered to be foolproof, things can go wrong if the oven temperature is off.

When the oven temperature is low, for example, a cake's structure sets later than it should. In the meantime, the batter slowly warms and as it does, it thins out. Air bubbles can rise easily through the thin batter to the surface of the cake, while starch in the flour can sink to the bottom. If the oven temperature is quite low, the baked cake will have a thick rubbery layer of gelatinized starch along the bottom and a low volume overall. Or it could have a series of thin tunnels running from bottom to top, tunnels that follow the trail of escaping bubbles.

Questions for Review

1 Why do bakers and pastry chefs require better accuracy in measuring ingredients than do kitchen chefs?

2 What does it mean for a baker's scale to be out of balance? Describe how to check and adjust a baker's scale for proper balancing.

3 An electronic scale has the following printed on its front display panel: 500 g × 2 g. What does each number refer to?

4 What is the smallest amount that should be weighed on a scale that has 500 g × 2 g on its display panel? (Use the value for the scale's readability in calculating the smallest quantity to be weighed.)

5 What is the main advantage of metric weight measurements (grams and kilograms) over U.S. common or imperial measurements (ounces and pounds)?

6 Explain why weighing ingredients in grams is not necessarily more accurate than weighing in ounces.

7 Why do bakers and pastry chefs prefer weight measurements to volume measurements? (Use flour as an example when answering this question.)

8 When weighing flour to be sifted, does it matter whether the flour is sifted before or after it is weighed? Why or why not?

9 What are the two meanings of the word *ounce*? For which ingredients are they approximately equal?

10 List three ingredients that are sometimes measured using volumetric measures (pints, liters, tablespoons, or milliliters).

11 Why is honey denser than water; that is, why does it weigh more per cup? Why is it thicker?

12 What is the main advantage of using formulas that are expressed in percentages?

13 What is an advantage of baker's percentages over percentages based on total yield?

14 What does it mean to temper ingredients?

15 Explain how to temper hot milk and egg yolks.

Questions for Discussion

1 A friend is preparing a 1-2-3 short dough (which contains, for example, 1 pound sugar, 2 pounds butter, 3 pounds flour, and three eggs). Instead of weighing the ingredients, however, your friend uses measuring cups, measuring 1 cup sugar, 2 cups butter, and 3 cups flour. Why is it unlikely that the cookie dough will turn out properly?

2 You are preparing an orange sauce that calls for 32 fluid ounces of orange juice and 1 ounce of starch. You decide to weigh the 32 ounces on a scale. Using the information from Table 1.2, explain whether you will be adding more or less orange juice than actually required. Will your orange sauce turn out slightly too thick or too thin?

3   Use the information from Table 1.2 to identify which ingredient in each of the following pairs is denser: heavy cream or whole milk; whole eggs or orange juice; oil or water; water or honey. Next, based on your experience, identify which ingredient in each pair is typically thicker. In which pairs of ingredients, if any, were the thicker samples also denser? What do you conclude from this; that is, can the relative weight of an ingredient always be properly judged by its thickness?

4   Explain why whipping air into a custard sauce might make it thicker. Explain what effect the added air will have on the density of the sauce.

5   Explain how to combine warmed melted chocolate and chilled whipped cream together, to prevent bits of chocolate from solidifying into small chips in the cold cream.

Exercises and Experiments

❶ Exercise: Rye Bread Formulas

Use information from these two formulas to answer the questions on page 16.

FORMULA 1

INGREDIENT	POUNDS	OUNCES	GRAMS	BAKER'S PERCENTAGE
Flour, bread	8		3,000	60%
Flour, white rye	2		2,000	40%
Water	6		2,800	56%
Yeast, compressed		6	190	4%
Salt		3	95	2%
Caraway seeds		2.4	75	1.5%
Total	**16**	**11.4**	**8,160**	**163.5%**

FORMULA 2

INGREDIENT	POUNDS	OUNCES	GRAMS	BAKER'S PERCENTAGE
Flour, bread	22		10,000	60%
Flour, white rye	15		6,800	40%
Water	21		9,550	57%
Yeast, compressed		15	425	2.5%
Salt		9	260	1.5%
Caraway seeds		4.75	135	0.8%
Total	**59**	**12.75**	**27,170**	**161.8%**

1 Based on the amount of caraway seeds added to each, which would you expect to have a stronger caraway flavor? Explain your answer.

_____

_____

_____

2 Based on the amount of yeast added to each, which would you expect to rise faster and possibly have a stronger yeast flavor? Explain your answer.

_____

_____

_____

❷ Exercise: Calculating Baker's Percentages

Calculate baker's percentages for the formula below. (Hint: complete the exercise using the metric weights provided; the math is easier and the answers are the same.) Remember that a baker's percentage is really the ratio of the weight of the ingredient divided by the total weight of flour. Use the following formula to complete the exercise. The first two are done for you.

Baker's percentage = 100% × (weight of ingredient) ÷ (total weight of flour)

BROWN SUGAR SPICE COOKIES

INGREDIENT	POUNDS	OUNCES	GRAMS	BAKER'S PERCENTAGE
Flour, pastry	2	8	1,200	= 100% × 1200 ÷ 1200 = 100%
Brown sugar, dark	1	4	600	= 100% × 600 ÷ 1200 = 50%
Butter	1		500	
Eggs		4	125	
Cinnamon		0.7	20	
Salt		0.25	8	
Total	5	4.95	2,453	

③ Experiment: Density and Thickness in Volumetric Measurements

Objectives

- Show how thick samples are not necessarily denser than thin samples.
- Show how different methods of adding flour and other dry ingredients affect density.

Materials and Equipment

- Flour (any type)
- Any starch, such as cornstarch
- Small spoon or scoop
- Dry measuring cup
- Sieve
- Scale

Procedure

1   Prepare a thickened starch solution by cooking any starch with water (about 25 grams cornstarch into 400 grams water) until noticeably thick; cool to room temperature. Or add instant starch to water until noticeably thick, being careful to avoid whisking air into the mixture. *Do not pre-blend instant starch with sugar;* this will increase the density of the solution and alter the results of the experiment.

2   Measure out 1 level cup (250 ml) of each of the following ingredients, then weigh each sample on a scale:
    - Flour lightly spooned into the cup
    - Flour spooned into the cup but shaken after every few spoonfuls to allow flour to settle
    - Flour sifted first, then lightly spooned into the cup
    - Water (room temperature)
    - Thickened starch solution (room temperature)

Results

Record weights for each of the 1 cup samples in the Results Table. Be sure to indicate your units of measure—grams or ounces—in the table.

RESULTS TABLE   DENSITY MEASUREMENTS

PRODUCT	WEIGHT PER CUP
Flour, spooned	
Flour, spooned and shaken	
Flour, sifted then spooned	
Water	
Starch-thickened solution	

Sources of Error

List any sources of error that might make it difficult to draw the proper conclusions from your experiment. In particular, consider if air was trapped in the starch solution as it was prepared and cooled; if cups were properly leveled with a straight-edge; if samples were at room temperature; if scale was used properly.

_____

_____

_____

State what you could do differently next time to minimize or eliminate each source of error.

_____

_____

_____

Conclusions

1   Rank the flour samples—spooned, spooned and shaken, or sifted then spooned—from least dense to densest.

_____

_____

_____

Based on these results, explain why weight, not volume, is best for measuring flour and other dry ingredients.

_____

_____

_____

2   How did the density (weight per cup) of the starch-thickened solution compare with the density of water? How might you explain these results?

_____

_____

_____

Heat Transfer

1. Describe the main means of heat transfer in cooking and baking.

2. Describe ways to control heat transfer in cooking and baking.

3. Describe the advantages and disadvantages of various materials used in cookware and bakeware.

Introduction

We all know that stovetops and ovens generate heat, but how does the heat travel from its source to the food? That is, how is heat transferred? This chapter is all about heat transfer. By understanding heat transfer, bakers and pastry chefs can better control cooking and baking processes and the quality of baked goods.

Methods of Heat Transfer

The three main ways that heat is transferred from its source to food are *radiation*, *conduction*, and *convection*. Most methods of cooking and baking, including simmering, sautéing, frying, and oven baking, rely on more than one means of heat transfer (Figure 2.1). A fourth type of heat transfer, *induction*, takes place on special stovetop surfaces. Each of these means of heat transfer is explained in this section.

Radiation

Radiant heat transfer, or *radiation*, is the rapid transfer of heat through space from a warmer object to the surface of a cooler one. Once molecules on the surface of an object absorb heat rays, they vibrate rapidly. The vibration generates frictional heat within the object. At no time does the radiating body come into direct contact with the object, yet heat energy is transferred from one to the other. Because there is no direct contact, radiation is sometimes described as a form of indirect heat. Examples of appliances that heat primarily by radiation include toasters, broilers, infrared heat lamps, and conventional ovens.

Hot pans also radiate heat. To prove this, place a hand over (not on) the surface of a hot empty pan and feel the heat radiating from its surface. Dark surfaces typically radiate more heat than lighter ones because dark surfaces absorb more heat energy to begin with. Likewise, dull surfaces absorb—and radiate—more heat than shiny surfaces. Not surprisingly, dull black sheet pans bake foods faster than bright shiny ones. Table 2.1 lists the relative amount of heat, called *emissivity*, that radiates or is emitted off several common materials. Dull black materials have an emissivity of 1, the highest amount of heat that a material can radiate. Notice the high amount of heat that radiates off brick, a material used in traditional hearth ovens.

> **HELPFUL HINT**
>
> *Radiant heat transfer is important in oven baking, and a large amount of heat is radiated off hot oven walls. This creates "hot spots" in conventional ovens along the oven walls. If product nearest the walls bakes up dark, it is because of this heat radiation. To prevent uneven baking, place pans in the center of the oven, away from the walls. Or rotate the direction of pans in the oven halfway through baking.*

Radiation is also the means of transferring microwave energy. In a microwave oven, a special tube called a *magnetron* generates microwave energy. Microwave energy passes through many types of cookware and penetrates the surface of food more easily than radiant heat energy. Still, the principles of heat transfer hold, and the absorbed microwaves generate heat because certain molecules throughout the food flip back and forth from the absorbed energy. The flipping motion generates frictional heat, and the food cooks primarily from heat generated from the movement of molecules.

Microwave cooking tends to heat foods unevenly. This is partly because different substances absorb microwave energy differently, but it is also because some substances require less energy, microwave or otherwise, to

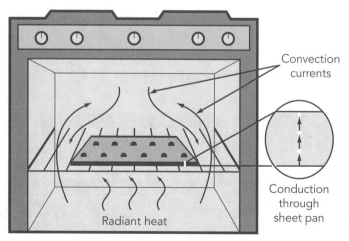

Figure 2.1 Radiation, conduction, and convection in an oven

Convection currents

Conduction through sheet pan

Radiant heat

TABLE 2.1 RADIANT HEAT TRANSFER OF VARIOUS MATERIALS

MATERIAL	RELATIVE RADIANT HEAT TRANSFER
Black body (dull)	1.0
Brick	0.93
Aluminum (dull)	0.2
Aluminum (shiny)	0.04

HELPFUL HINT

If old aluminum sheet pans are pocked with bits of blackened baked-on food, they will radiate heat unevenly. For even cooking and browning, keep cookware and bakeware clean of burned-on food.

heat up. For example, microwave a jelly doughnut and observe that the sugary jelly center will be extremely hot while the outside doughnut will be much less so.

Heating with microwaves is relatively fast because the radiant microwaves penetrate farther into the food (typically 1 to 2 inches) than radiant heat energy, which heats surfaces only. But how does heat from microwave energy spread throughout the food, and how does heat from radiant heat energy penetrate beyond the surface of food? Through two different means: conduction and convection.

Conduction

Conduction occurs when heat passes from a hot area of an object to a cooler area. Heat is passed molecule by molecule. That is, as one molecule absorbs heat and vibrates, it passes heat along to a nearby molecule, which vibrates in turn. Conduction of heat energy continues molecule by molecule, until eventually the entire object is hot. Because direct contact is needed for heat transfer by conduction, it is sometimes described as a form of direct heat transfer.

Heat conduction is important in stovetop cooking, where heat is conducted from the heat source (gas flame or electric coils) directly to the outside of a pan bottom. Conduction continues as heat passes through the pan to the food inside. Even when the pan is removed from the heat, conduction continues until the pan and the food reach the same temperature. This is a source of *carryover cooking*—cooking that occurs after food is removed from its source of heat.

HELPFUL HINT

Water has low heat conductivity, meaning it is slow to conduct heat. This is why it is useful to bake custard and cheesecake, which are best baked slowly and evenly, in a water bath.

Air's heat conductivity is even lower than water's. The use of double sheet pans and double boilers takes advantage of this insulating property of air. When double sheet pans are used for baking cookies, the cookie bottoms are less apt to burn, since the layer of air between the two sheet pans slows heat transfer. With double boilers, the top insert is placed over (not in) boiling water, leaving an insulating pocket of air between the boiling water and the product. Double boilers are useful for gently warming products that are damaged by high heat, such as egg whites, chocolate, and fondant.

How to Bake Crustless Bread

Bread develops a crust during baking because the surface of the dough is exposed to hot radiant heat that crisps and browns it. The rest of the dough is warmed slowly through conduction, with the center of a loaf of bread never getting hotter than 200°F (93°C).

Bread can also be baked in newer-style ovens called *dielectric ovens*, which radiate radio frequency (RF) waves. Heating with RF waves is similar to heating foods with microwaves, but the RF waves penetrate deeper into foods. Bread dough quickly (and expensively) bakes evenly, inside and out, producing bread with the same color and texture throughout. In other words, RF waves can bake bread with no crust. RF ovens are used in the production of Japanese bread crumbs (panko), which are uniformly white, light, and crispy. Japanese bread crumbs are used in preparing tempura and other fried foods.

Heat conduction is important in baking as well. Once radiation heats the surface of a sheet pan of cookies, for example, conduction transfers heat through the pan and through the cookies. Once the cookies are removed from the oven and from the sheet pan, conduction continues until the cookies are the same temperature throughout. The cookies also begin radiating heat to the bakeshop until they cool to room temperature.

Heat conduction is also an important means of cooling products. When hot product is transferred to a cool pan or cool surface, heat is conducted away from the hot product, cooling it quickly. This is why it is common practice to transfer a cooked sauce from a hot saucepan to a cool bowl before placing the bowl in an ice water bath. The cool bowl provides the first round of cooling by conduction; the ice water bath provides the second.

To understand the difference between radiation and conduction, imagine two teams of ten people, each arranged in a line. Each team must pass a ball from the first person to the last. The first team does this quickly by having the first person in the row toss the ball to the last person. The second team passes the ball by handing it from one person to the next, until the ball finally reaches the last person. Think of the first team as radiation and the second team as conduction. Radiation passes the ball (heat) quickly by tossing it through the air. Conduction passes it more slowly by handing it one to the next.

Just as some teams are faster than other teams at passing the ball, some materials pass or conduct heat faster than other materials. Materials that conduct heat fast are described as having high thermal or heat conductivity. In general, solids have higher heat conductivities than liquids and gases, because molecules are closer together in solids than they are in liquids and gases. The closeness of molecules makes it easier to pass the heat from one molecule to the next (remember, the "ball" cannot be tossed with conduction).

Heat conduction can be fast or slow through cookware and bakeware, depending on the heat conductivity of the material used in the construction of the vessel. While metals are not good at radiating heat, they are very good at conducting it. In fact, because of the molecular structure of metals, they are better than most solids at conducting heat. Some metals, however, conduct faster than others. See Table 2.2 for the relative

TABLE 2.2 HEAT CONDUCTIVITIES OF VARIOUS MATERIALS

MATERIAL	RELATIVE HEAT CONDUCTIVITY
Silver	4.2
Copper	3.9
Aluminum	2.2
Stainless steel	0.2
Marble	0.03
Water	0.006
Teflon	0.002
Wood	0.001
Air	0.0003

heat conductivities of different metals and other materials. The higher the number, the faster heat conducts through the material.

Materials that are poor conductors of heat are sometimes called heat *insulators*. Examples of insulators include air, Teflon, and silicone. Insulators can be useful for slowing down heat transfer, important when fast or uneven heating is a problem.

Conduction also varies with the thickness, or gauge, of the material used in a pan's construction. Heavy-gauge material is thicker and conducts heat more slowly than light-gauge material. Although they conduct heat more slowly, heavy-gauge pans are often favored over thin-gauge pans because they transfer heat more evenly. Information about common metals and materials used in the bakeshop follows.

Copper Copper has very high heat conductivity, which means it conducts heat quickly. For this reason, copper is used in cooking sugar, where it is best to reach high temperatures in a relatively short time. Copper is expensive, though, so it is not used for everyday cookware and bakeware. Copper also reacts with food, and it can be toxic at high levels. To prevent its reacting with food, copper cookware is typically coated with a thin protective layer, usually stainless steel or tin, on surfaces that come into contact with food.

Aluminum Aluminum conducts heat only about half as well as copper. This is still quite fast, however, and

Touch a marble surface with one hand and a wood surface with the other, and the marble will feel noticeably cooler to the touch. Yet both the marble and the wood, if they have been in the same room for a while, are at room temperature. How can this be?

Marble has greater heat conductivity than wood, so heat transfers faster from your body to marble than it does to wood. Because the hand touching marble cools more quickly, the marble seems cooler to the touch (when, in actuality, the marble is now slightly warmer, because heat has transferred to it from the hand).

Repeat this demonstration by placing one hand on marble and the other on stainless steel or another metal. Because metals have greater heat conductivity than marble, the stainless steel surface will seem cooler than the marble surface. Again, it seems cooler because heat transfers faster from the hand touching stainless steel than from the one touching marble.

Because of marble's good heat conductivity, marble surfaces are often used in bakeshops to quickly cool hot confectionery products. Why not use a stainless-steel surface instead? Generally, the answer has to do with the price: the cost of stainless steel would be prohibitive. Because a thick stainless-steel table is very expensive to construct, these tables are typically thin, and thus they heat up too quickly. However, special stainless-steel cooling tables are available to confectionery manufacturers. These tables are designed to allow cooling water to circulate within a sandwich of stainless steel. Heat is quickly conducted through the stainless-steel surface to the water, where it is carried away through conduction and convection.

unlike copper, aluminum is inexpensive. Like copper, aluminum reacts with food, especially acidic foods. It discolors fruit products and turns milk and egg mixtures an unattractive gray, limiting its use in stovetop cookware. Aluminum mixer attachments also present a problem with reactive foods, discoloring some products. Since aluminum is a soft metal, it is easily scratched and pitted.

Because of its high conductivity and low cost, though, aluminum is commonly used in bakeware such as sheet pans and cake pans, where discoloration is less an issue. It is easy to burn food cooked or baked on aluminum, especially if the pans are of a thin gauge and oven temperatures are high. To minimize this, purchase heavy-gauge pans and use parchment paper. If necessary, bake delicate items that brown quickly on silicone baking pads placed on aluminum sheet pans, or use a double layer of sheet pans. The layer of silicone or the cushion of air between the two pans acts as an insulator and slows heat conduction to a manageable level.

A newer type of aluminum is called *dark hard-anodized aluminum.* Anodized aluminum has undergone an electrochemical treatment that changes the surface of the aluminum so that it is hard and durable. Anodized aluminum is nonreactive and easy to clean. Although it does not conduct heat as fast as ordinary aluminum, anodized aluminum is dark in color, so some heat is transferred through radiation. Anodized aluminum typically comes in a heavy gauge so it cooks evenly, but it is more expensive than regular aluminum cookware.

Stainless Steel Stainless steel is a type of low-carbon steel (iron alloy) that contains a mix of metals including chromium and often nickel. Stainless steel is not a very good conductor of heat. Yet it is durable, easy to clean, moderately priced, and basically inert; that is, it does not react with food. Stainless steel also has a light-reflective surface that makes it easy to view food as it cooks.

To improve its heat conductivity, lower-quality stainless-steel cookware is manufactured to a thin gauge. However, it is difficult to roll stainless steel (or any metal) to a thin gauge evenly. Because of this, thin-gauge stainless cookware has hot spots where food is likely to burn. While thin-gauge stainless cookware is inexpensive, it is not a good choice for the bakeshop.

A better alternative for stovetop cookware is stainless steel with an aluminum core. The stainless-steel surface provides a nonreactive light-colored surface that makes it easy to view food and is easy to clean; the aluminum core provides improved heat conduction. The best aluminum-core stainless cookware has aluminum extending up the sides of the pan, for even cooking throughout.

Aluminum-core stainless-steel cookware is the best choice for stovetop cooking of fruit mixtures, vanilla custard sauce, and pastry cream.

Cast Iron Cast iron conducts heat reasonably well and, like aluminum, is best when thick and heavy, to slow down and even out heat exchange. Because it is black, cast iron also transfers heat through radiation. However, iron reacts with food, adding a metallic taste and discoloring the food. Because of this reactivity, cast iron is rarely used in the bakeshop. When it is used, it must be well seasoned before its first use so it will not stick or rust. To season cast iron, coat with a thin layer of vegetable oil or shortening and heat in an oven at about 350°F (175°C) for an hour or so. Cast iron is traditionally used to bake cornbread, for a dark, crisp crust.

Tin Tinware is used in traditional French bakeware. It is lightweight, a good conductor of heat, and inexpensive. Tinware rusts easily and darkens with acidic foods, though. If tinware is used in the bakeshop, it must be dried thoroughly as soon as it is washed, to prevent rusting.

Glass, Porcelain Enamel, Ceramic, and Stoneware Glass, porcelain enamel, ceramic, and stoneware all conduct heat poorly. Like most materials that conduct poorly, they retain heat well once they are hot, making them useful for slow cooking. Ceramic ramekins, for example, are ideal for baked custards, which need to bake slowly.

Nonstick Surfaces Nonstick surfaces vary in their durability, but some crack and peel, and most scratch after repeated use. Because they are extremely poor at conducting heat (refer back to Table 2.2), nonstick surfaces such as Teflon act as insulators between the source of heat and any food placed in the pan. This means cooking is slower, making it more difficult to brown foods. However, nonstick saucepans may be acceptable wherever fast heating is not needed.

Silicone Bakeware, Molds, and Sheets Silicone is not a good conductor of heat. For this reason, items bake more slowly and brown more evenly, if they do brown. Professional silicone bakeware, such as Flexipan brand molds, come in many shapes and sizes, and silicone baking mats (Silpat pads) fit half and full sheet pans. Silicone products are nonstick and are able to go from oven (up to 580°F/300°C) to freezer. Because they are flexible, product can be released with a twist.

Convection

Convection is the third way that heat is transferred to—and through—foods. It aids heat transfer through liquids and gases, which otherwise conduct heat slowly. Convection works because warmer liquids and gases are less dense and therefore rise, while colder liquids and gases are denser and therefore sink. The result is the constant movement of cold currents toward warmer ones. It is like having an invisible hand stirring the pot.

Convection currents work without assistance, but the movement of liquid in a pot, for example, can be increased if it is stirred. This is especially important with thick liquids, where fewer convection currents set in. Likewise, convection currents are at work in any oven, but the movement of air in an oven can be increased if the air is forced to circulate. Convection ovens work by doing just that. Some convection ovens have fans that blow hot air, forcing the movement of air throughout the oven. Other ovens, such as reel and rotating ovens, work by moving product through the air. In either case, convection ovens work faster than conventional ovens, as hot air moves more rapidly toward the cooler surfaces of the baked good and colder air moves away. This is why convection, reel, and rotating ovens require lower temperatures and shorter bake times. They also work more evenly, with fewer hot spots.

> **HELPFUL HINT**
>
> *When switching from a conventional to a convection oven, the rule of thumb is to reduce oven temperature by about 25°F (15°C) and to reduce baking time by about 25 percent. When first making this switch, watch products carefully and adjust oven times and temperatures as needed.*

However, convection ovens are not appropriate for all products. They are best for products made from heavy doughs such as cookies. Cakes and muffins, for example, can take on an asymmetric shape if convection

What gets convection currents going? Recall that molecules vibrate when materials and objects are heated. The more they are heated, the faster they vibrate. As they heat up and vibrate faster, they push apart. This movement—this expansion—lowers the density of hot liquids and gases. Less-dense hot liquids and gases rise and move away from the source of heat. As the hot air and hot liquids rise, cold liquids and gases (which are denser) fall, moving closer to the source of heat. Convection currents set in, distributing heat more quickly and more uniformly. Convection currents occur in the air in ovens, in thin batters baking in the oven, within thin liquids in a saucepan, and within fat in a fryer.

currents are too strong or oven temperatures too high. Sponge cakes and soufflés can lose volume, and custards and cheesecakes easily overbake.

Convection currents can work against you; as the oven's door is opened for viewing its contents, convection currents between the cooler air of the bakeshop and the warmer air of the oven quickly set in, cooling the air in the oven and warming the bakeshop. To maintain oven temperatures during baking, minimize the number of times and the amount of time the oven door is opened.

> **HELPFUL HINT**
>
> *To maximize convection currents in any oven, be sure baking pans are placed so that air movement within the oven is unobstructed. To do this, do not overload an oven, and be sure there is space between baking pans for air to circulate.*

Induction

Induction cooking is a newer form of heat transfer. It is popular in kitchens and bakeshops in Europe and is becoming more so in North America. Induction cooking takes place on special smooth-top ceramic surfaces, below which are coils that generate a strong magnetic field. The magnetic field causes molecules in a pan to rapidly flip, generating frictional heat within the pan. The pan heats up almost immediately, and the heat is quickly transferred from the pan to the food via conduction.

For a pan to work on an induction burner, it must have a flat bottom—woks will not work—and it must be made of magnetic material. To determine if a pan is made of magnetic material, place a magnet on its bottom; if it holds, the pan is magnetic. Cast-iron and some stainless-steel pans work on induction burners, but those made of aluminum or copper do not. Many cookware companies sell pans designed specifically for induction cooking.

Induction cooking is gaining popularity because it is fast and more energy efficient than cooking with gas or electric coils. Since the pan heats directly, less heat is lost to the stovetop or into the air, so the bakeshop stays cooler. Heat is also more easily regulated than with gas or electric, and the stovetop surface stays relatively cool, so it is safer. However, keep in mind that some heat is transferred by conduction from the pan, heating the ceramic surface.

Questions for Review

1   What are the three main ways that heat is transferred?

2   How far below the surface does radiated heat penetrate into foods?

3   Why is radiation considered a form of indirect heat?

4   What is the primary means of heat transfer in conventional ovens?

5   How far below the surface does radiated microwave energy typically penetrate into foods?

6   Which bake faster and why: shiny new aluminum sheet pans or dark, dull used ones?

7   Explain how heat conduction works.

8   Which—aluminum or stainless steel—is a better conductor of heat?

9   Which should be used when cooking pastry cream: a stainless steel or an aluminum pot? Why?

10 What are the two main features of cookware that affect how quickly heat is conducted through it?

11 Using the example of two teams passing a ball, explain why heat conduction is slower than radiation.

12 Which—aluminum or air—is a better conductor of heat?

13 What is the definition of a heat insulator? Provide two examples of good insulators.

14 Why might cookies be baked on a double layer of sheet pans?

15 What is the main way that heat energy travels to the interior of solid food? In what two ways does it travel to the interior of a liquid?

16 Provide an example of when it is desirable to slow down heat transfer. Explain one way (besides reducing the heat!) that it can be slowed.

17 What is the main difference between a convection oven and a conventional one?

18 Name an oven that increases convection currents by moving product through the air (rather than by moving the air around the product).

19 Which requires lower baking temperatures and shorter bake times: a conventional or a convection oven? Explain why.

20 Explain how induction cooking works. What are its advantages over cooking with gas or electric coils?

Questions for Discussion

1   Aluminum is known to discolor some food products, so why is it the most common material for sheet pans? That is, why might discoloration be less of an issue with baked goods than with sauces cooked in a pot?

2 Some pastry chefs layer sugar on the bottom of a pan when heating milk for vanilla custard sauce. This prevents the milk from burning onto the pan. Does this make the sugar layer a good heat conductor or a poor one? Explain your answer.

3 Explain why it is faster to cool products in an ice water bath than it is to place them in a refrigerator to chill. For help in answering this question, refer back to Table 2.2.

4 Explain how cookies baking in an oven are heated by radiation, conduction, and convection.

5 Explain how deep-fat frying, in which the frying fat is heated to about 350°F (175°C), is a good example of heat transfer by conduction and convection.

Exercises and Experiments

① Exercise: Heat Transfer

Imagine that you are baking cookies in an oven and you need to slow down heat transfer, so that the cookies don't burn on the outside before they are cooked throughout. Explain the reason that each of the following techniques works to decrease heat transfer. As an example, number 1 is completed for you.

1 Use a lower oven temperature.

Reason: This is the most direct way to decrease heat transfer, since it reduces the amount of heat radiated from the heat source.

2 Use shiny metal sheet pans rather than black matte ones.

Reason: _____
_____
_____

3 Use stainless-steel pans instead of aluminum.

Reason: _____
_____
_____

4 Replace old, stained sheet pans with shiny new ones.

Reason: _____
_____
_____

5 Use thick-gauge pans rather than thin-gauge ones.

Reason: _____
_____
_____

6 Use double sheet pans by placing one sheet pan inside another.

Reason: _____
_____
_____

7 Keep sheet pans away from oven walls.

Reason: _____
_____
_____

8 Place cookies on a silicone pad (Silpat) instead of directly on a sheet pan.

Reason: _____
_____
_____

9 Turn off the fan in a convection oven.

Reason: _____
_____
_____

② Experiment: Hot Spots in a Conventional Oven

It's hard to imagine an oven that heats evenly throughout. The next best thing to having the perfect oven is knowing where the hot spots are in your oven. The fastest and easiest way to "map an oven" is to use an infrared thermometer. Aim the thermometer at various surfaces throughout the preheated oven, and you will learn very quickly where uneven baking might occur.

Another way to find the hot spots is to bake actual product in different locations in the oven and observe where differences occur.

Objectives

Determine if, and where, hot spots exist in an oven.

Products Prepared

Cookies baked in different locations of a conventional or deck oven (no convection fans)

Materials and Equipment

- Scale
- Sieve
- Parchment paper
- Mixer with 5-quart mixing bowl
- Flat beater attachment
- Bowl scraper
- Plain drop cookie dough (see Formula) that makes 24 or more cookies if using full sheet pans, or that makes 12 or more cookies if using half sheet pans

- Two full or half sheet pans (depending on the size of the oven), as nearly identical as possible
- Size #30 (1 fl. oz./30 ml) portion-control scoop or equivalent
- Oven thermometer

Formula

Drop Sugar Cookie Dough

Yield: 48 cookies

INGREDIENT	POUNDS	OUNCES	GRAMS	BAKER'S PERCENTAGE
Flour, bread		8	250	50
Flour, cake		8	250	50
Salt		0.25	8	1.6
Baking soda		0.25	8	1.6
Shortening, all-purpose		13	410	82
Sugar, regular granulated		18	565	113
Eggs		6	185	37
Total	3	5.5	1,676	335.2

Method of Preparation

1 Preheat oven to 375°F (190°C).

2 Allow all ingredients to come to room temperature (temperature of ingredients is important for consistent results).

3 Blend flour, salt, and baking soda thoroughly by sifting together three times onto parchment paper.

4 Combine shortening and sugar in mixing bowl and mix on low for 1 minute. Stop and scrape bowl as needed.

5 Cream shortening-sugar mixture on medium for 2 minutes. Stop and scrape bowl.

6 Add eggs slowly while mixing on low for 30 seconds. Stop and scrape bowl.

7 Add flour to shortening-sugar-egg mixture and mix on low for 1 minute. Stop and scrape bowl.

Procedure

1 Prepare cookie dough using the formula given or using any plain drop cookie formula. To minimize experimental error, use shortening instead of butter.

2 If necessary, clean sheet pans to remove burned-on food. Line the sheet pans with parchment paper.

3 Label parchment paper, indicating which end of pan will be at the front of the oven and sheet pan placement within the oven (top rack, against left wall of oven, etc.).

4 Scoop cookie dough onto prepared sheet pans using #30 scoop or equivalent. Space dough evenly on sheet pans. Place six cookies on half sheet pans and twelve cookies on full sheet pans.

5 Use an oven thermometer placed in center of oven for an initial reading of oven temperature. Record results here: _____.

6 When oven is properly preheated, place both sheet pans in oven and set timer for 19–21 minutes, or according to formula.

7 Bake cookies all for same amount of time (do not rotate pans during baking).

8 Remove pans from oven and cool cookies directly on sheet pans.

9 Check final oven temperature. Record results here: _____.

Results

1 With cookies still on sheet pans, evaluate the amount of browning on each cookie. Use a scale of 1 to 5, 1 being lightest color.

2 Record evaluations for each sheet pan by filling in the drawings of sheet pans in Figures 2.3 and 2.4. See Figure 2.2 for an example of how to record evaluations.

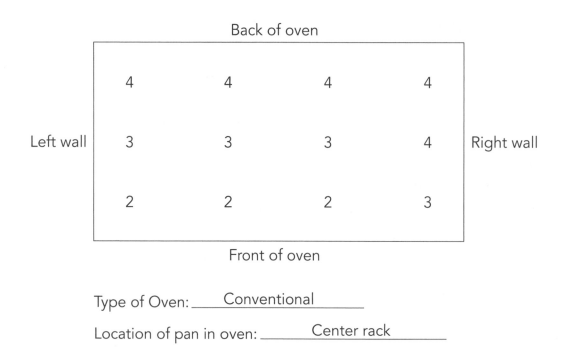

Figure 2.2 Sample results for experiment: full sheet pan placed horizontally on center rack in conventional oven

Type of oven: _____

Location of pan in oven: _____

Figure 2.3

Type of oven: _____

Location of pan in oven: _____

Figure 2.4

Sources of Error

List any sources of error that might make it difficult to draw the proper conclusions from your experiment. For this experiment, note in particular any problems with the pans (uneven bottoms, dents, or baked-on food) and the ovens (was oven temperature stable during baking?).

_____

_____

_____

State what you could do differently next time to minimize or eliminate each of the sources of error.

_____

_____

_____

Conclusions

Select one from the choices in **bold** or fill in the blanks.

1 The difference in color between the cookies nearest the oven walls and those farthest from the walls was **small/moderate/large/no difference**. The darker cookies were **nearest the oven walls/in center of oven/neither**. This is probably because

_____

_____

_____

2 The difference in color between the cookies nearer the back of the oven and those nearer the front was **small/moderate/large/no difference**. The darker cookies were **nearest the back of the oven/nearest the front/neither**. This is probably because

_____

_____

_____

3 What do these results tell you about whether there are hot spots in this oven?

_____

_____

_____

If there were any hot spots, what can you do in the future to compensate for them in this oven, so that they are not a significant source of error in future experiments?

_____

_____

_____

4 Did you notice any other differences in the cookies, or do you have any other comments about the experiment?

_____

_____

_____

3

Overview of the Baking Process

Chapter Objectives

1. Present formulas as a balance of tougheners and tenderizers, moisteners and driers.

2. Discuss the importance of proper mixing technique.

3. Summarize the changes that occur as batters and doughs are mixed, and discuss the importance of water in this process.

4. Provide an overview of the eleven main events that occur as products are baked in the oven.

5. Briefly summarize eight changes that occur as products cool.

Introduction

Three distinct steps or stages occur in baking once ingredients are weighed. First ingredients are mixed into batters or doughs. Next the batter or dough is baked, and finally it is cooled. Many chemical and physical changes occur in products as they pass through each of these three stages. A pastry chef or baker who understands these changes is better able to control them. For example, a pastry chef who understands how mixing, baking, and cooling affect flakiness, tenderness, amount of browning, and crumb structure will be able to control those characteristics in baked goods.

This chapter presents an overview of many important and complex processes that occur in baking. Subsequent chapters address each of these processes in more detail.

Setting the Stage for Success

In Chapter 1, the importance of weighing ingredients properly was introduced. Proper weighing of ingredients is important because successful formulas are carefully balanced mixtures of structure builders (tougheners), tenderizers, moisteners, and driers. *Structure builders* are ingredients that hold the volume and shape of baked goods in place. Structure forms when these ingredients interact, building a framework that holds the product together. A certain amount of structure is necessary in all baked goods, but too much causes toughening. In fact, structure builders are often called tougheners. Examples of structure builders include flour, eggs, cocoa powder, and starch.

While flour is considered a structure builder, it is specific components in the flour—gluten-forming proteins and starch granules, in particular—that provide the structure. Likewise, it is egg proteins that make eggs structure builders.

Tenderizers are the opposite of structure builders. Tenderizers are ingredients in baked goods that interfere with the formation of structure, making the baked goods softer and easier to bite into. A certain amount of tenderizing is necessary in all baked goods so that they are pleasant to eat, but too much tenderizing causes products to crumble and fall apart. Examples of tenderizers include sugars and syrups, fats and oils, and leavening agents.

Moisteners include water (moisture) and ingredients that contain water, such as milk, eggs, cream, and syrups. Moisteners also include liquid fat ingredients such as oil.

Driers are the opposite of moisteners. They are ingredients that absorb moisteners. Examples of driers include flour, cornstarch, dry milk solids, and cocoa powder.

Notice that some ingredients fall into more than one category; for example, oil is both a tenderizer and a moistener, while flour is both a structure builder and a drier.

Once the proper amounts of ingredients are weighed and measured, they must be combined in a specific manner and often at a specific temperature. Changing the manner of mixing or the temperature at which they are mixed can change the product, sometimes quite dramatically. For example, muffins are often mixed using the muffin method, where the fat is melted and stirred into dry ingredients along with other liquids. An alternate method for mixing muffins is to cream the fat first with sugar, then to add liquid and dry ingredients to this. The muffin method produces dense muffins with a coarse crumb. The creaming method produces lighter muffins with the finer crumb of a cake. Table 3.1 lists and briefly describes several common mixing methods used in the bakeshop. Many other methods exist that combine certain features from these methods.

When Are Tender Baked Goods Not Moist?

While some ingredients like oils both moisten and tenderize, moist baked goods are not always tender, nor are tender baked goods always moist. Tender baked goods are easy to bite into, but they are only moist when they also feel somewhat wet, even liquidy, in the mouth. In contrast, some baked goods, like shortbread cookies, are easy to bite into (tender), but dry. Baked goods that are tender yet dry are often described as crumbly or mealy. See Chapter 4 for more on describing the texture of baked goods.

TABLE 3.1 COMMON MIXING METHODS USED IN THE BAKESHOP

METHOD	DESCRIPTION	EXAMPLE OF USE
Straight dough	All ingredients combined and mixed until dough is smooth and well developed	Yeast-raised breads
Sponge and dough	Liquid, yeast, part of flour, part of sugar mixed into a batter or dough (called a *sponge* or *pre-ferment*) and allowed to ferment; added to remaining ingredients and mixed until dough is smooth and well developed	Yeast-raised breads made with poolish (liquid sponge), biga (Italian sponge, usually stiff), levain (naturally fermented sponge), or other sponge or pre-ferment
Creaming or conventional	Shortening and sugar creamed; eggs added, then liquids (if any) added alternately with sifted dry ingredients at low speed	Shortened cakes and coffee cakes, cookies, cake-like muffins
Two-stage or blending	Sifted dry ingredients blended on low speed; softened fat cut in with paddle; liquids added slowly to blend in two stages (eggs added in second stage); beaten to aerate	High-ratio cakes
Liquid shortening	All ingredients blended on low speed, then whipped on high, and finally on medium speed to aerate	High-ratio liquid shortening cakes
Sponge or whipping	Warmed whole eggs (or yolks) and sugar whipped until very light and thick; liquids added; sifted dry ingredients gently folded in, followed by melted butter (if any) or whipped whites (if separated)	Sponge cake (biscuit), genoise, ladyfingers, madeleines
Angel food	Egg whites and sugar whipped until soft peaks form; sifted dry ingredients gently folded in	Angel food cake
Chiffon	Sifted dry ingredients stirred or blended on low speed; oil and other liquid ingredients added and lightly blended until smooth; egg whites and sugar whipped until soft peaks form and folded into flour-oil mixture	Chiffon cake
Muffin or one-stage	Sifted dry ingredients stirred or blended on low speed; liquid fat and other liquid ingredients added in one stage and lightly blended just until moistened	Muffins, quick breads, quick coffee cakes
Biscuit or pastry	Sifted dry ingredients stirred or blended on low speed; solid fat rubbed or cut in by hand or with paddle; liquids stirred in gently	Biscuits, scones, pie pastry, blitz puff pastry

Stage I: Mixing

Mixing distributes ingredients evenly throughout batters and doughs. While this is the obvious reason to mix ingredients, other important events occur during the mixing stage. For example, during mixing, batters and doughs trap pockets of air as paddles and whips push through them. This lightens the batter or dough, making it easier to mix and handle. With continued mixing, large air pockets (or bubbles) are reduced in size to many more smaller ones, providing the "nuclei" that expand during baking into full-sized air cells. This means that batters and doughs must be mixed properly if the baked goods are to rise properly.

Because batters and doughs contain trapped air, they are sometimes referred to as foams. You will soon read that when batters and doughs bake, they transform from foams that trap air to porous sponges that don't. The term *sponge* is used whether the product has a springy, spongy texture or not. It simply refers to the open, porous structure of baked goods, where air and gases move freely in and out.

Throughout the mixing process, the friction of the mixer on the batter or dough wears down large particles, layer by layer, allowing them to dissolve or to hydrate faster in water. As particles such as flour hydrate, water becomes less able to move freely and the batter or dough thickens. The ability of water (sometimes called the *universal solvent*) to dissolve or hydrate particles and molecules is a very important part of the mixing process.

What Is Air?

Air is composed of a mixture of gases: mostly nitrogen (close to 80 percent), oxygen, and a small amount of carbon dioxide. Oxygen is the most important gas in air because it is required for life. Oxygen is also required for many chemical reactions important to the baker, including those that strengthen gluten and whiten flour. Certain destructive reactions, such as the oxidation of fats and oils, also require oxygen, which is why some ingredients such as nuts may be vacuum-packed to exclude air.

The Special Role of Water

All during mixing, water dissolves or at least hydrates many important molecules and particles, both large and small. Even when water is not an ingredient in a formula, it plays a part during the mixing of all batters and doughs, because many ingredients are significant sources of water. Table 3.2 provides information about the amount of water in various bakeshop ingredients. Notice that ingredients do not need to be fluid to contain high amounts of water. Sour cream and bananas, for example, are over 70 percent water, cream cheese over 50 percent, and butter over 15 percent.

Until molecules either dissolve or are hydrated in water, they do not act as expected. For example, undissolved sugar crystals are not able to moisten or tenderize cakes, to stabilize whipped egg whites, or to taste sweet. Undissolved salt is unable to slow yeast fermentation or to preserve food. Undissolved baking powder does not produce carbon dioxide for leavening. Each—the sugar, salt, and baking powder—must first dissolve in water before it can act.

Many larger molecules, such as proteins and starches, do not dissolve completely in water, but they do swell and hydrate. *Hydration* occurs when large molecules—proteins and starches, for example—attract and bond to water. Layers of water form liquid shells around hydrated molecules, swelling and suspending them. Just as sugar, salt, and baking powder must dissolve before they act, so, too, must large molecules hydrate.

Flour contains hard chunks of protein that must hydrate before being transformed into *gluten*, a large, flexible web that is important for proper volume and crumb structure in baked goods. Mixing helps slough off the protein, layer by layer, from the solid chunks in flour, to speed up hydration and formation of gluten. No matter the amount of mixing, without water to hydrate the chunks of protein, gluten would not form.

Besides dissolving and hydrating food molecules, water performs several other important functions that begin during the mixing stage. For example, water activates yeast and allows fermentation to occur. Without sufficient water, yeast cells remain dormant (inactive) or die.

TABLE 3.2 AMOUNT OF WATER IN VARIOUS BAKESHOP INGREDIENTS

INGREDIENT	AMOUNT OF WATER (%)
Strawberries	92
Lemon juice	91
Orange juice	88
Milk, whole	88
Eggs, whole	75
Banana	74
Sour cream	71
Cream cheese	54
Jellies and jams	30
Butter	18
Honey	17
Raisins	15

Water is a convenient means for adjusting the temperature of batters and doughs. Using cold water in pastry dough, for example, keeps fats from melting and ensures a flakier crust. Likewise, carefully controlling water temperature in bread-making ensures that mixed dough is at the proper temperature for fermentation. Heavy doughs, in particular, generate frictional heat from mixing. A small amount of frictional heat is acceptable, even desirable, but with yeast doughs, too much heat warms yeast above the ideal temperature for proper fermentation.

The amount of water in a batter or dough affects its viscosity or consistency. In fact, the consistency of a flour mixture defines whether it is a batter or a dough. *Batters* are unbaked flour mixtures that are relatively high in moisture, making them thin and pourable or scoopable. Examples include cake, crêpe, and muffin batters. *Doughs* are unbaked flour mixtures that are relatively low in moisture, making them thick and moldable. Examples include bread, pie pastry, cookie, and baking powder biscuit doughs. Batter and dough consistency is important for proper shaping and for proper leavening of baked goods.

How to Mix Pie Pastry Dough

Pie pastry dough is mixed in a two-step process. Typically, solid fat is first mixed or rubbed into flour before water is added. The more the fat is rubbed into the flour, the more thoroughly the fat coats the flour particles. Flour particles coated with fat will not easily absorb water. This limits the ability of structure-building gluten to form, and makes for more tender pie pastry. In fact, pie pastries made by rubbing fat thoroughly into flour are considered short or mealy, meaning that they are so tender that they crumble into short, cornmeal-size pieces. Sometimes mealy pie pastry is desirable, especially for bottom crusts of juicy pies. Mealy pie pastry is less likely to absorb pie juices and toughen.

More often, flaky—rather than mealy—pie pastry is considered desirable. Flakiness requires that solid fat remain in chunks; the larger and more solid the chunks, the flakier the pie pastry. To make dough for flaky pastry, solid fat is rubbed into flour just until it is the size of hazelnuts or lima beans. Then the dough is rolled to flatten the lumps of fat and distribute them evenly throughout. Notice how flakiness and tenderness are sometimes at odds: For flakiness, fat is kept as large chunks; for tenderness and mealiness, fat is thoroughly rubbed into flour.

Next, water is added and the dough gently mixed. The water must be ice-cold so the fat remains in solid chunks. If the fat melts from water that is too warm, the pastry will be mealy, not flaky. Mixing distributes water throughout the dough, but it also increases gluten development and toughening. Flaky pie pastry is particularly at risk for toughening because flour particles in flaky pastry are not well coated with fat. To allow time for water absorption without lengthy mixing, pastry chefs often chill pie pastry dough for several hours or overnight before continuing. This allows for water absorption and it firms the fat and keeps it from smearing into the dough, for better flakiness. Overall, for a pie pastry that is both tender and flaky, limit the extent of mixing both before and after water is added, and chill the dough before rolling and baking.

Oil and water don't mix, so what keeps fats and oils from rising to the top of the mixing bowl in cake batter? First, mixing breaks up fat into small chunks and oil into small droplets, both which are less likely to rise. Next, hydrated flour particles and other driers thicken the batter, and this slows fats and oils from rising. Third, emulsifiers help fats, oils, and water coexist. Emulsifiers are present in egg yolks, dairy ingredients, and certain shortenings. They have both a water-loving (hydrophilic) and fat-loving (lipophilic) side, so part of the emulsifier bonds with water while the other part bonds with fats and oils. In doing so, emulsifiers help oil and water "mix."

Emulsions by definition consist of two liquids, with one of the liquids forming droplets that are suspended in the other liquid. If the droplets are very tiny, if they are protected by the right emulsifier or emulsifying protein, or if the suspending liquid is thick, the emulsion can last a very long time. A properly made mayonnaise, for example, is considered a permanent emulsion because it is so stable.

Unlike many ingredients used in baking, fats do not dissolve in water, nor are they hydrated by water. Rather, solid fat breaks into small chunks, and liquid fat (oil) breaks into tiny droplets during mixing to form an emulsion. These small chunks and tiny droplets spread throughout batters and doughs, coating particles that they are attracted to. Anything coated with fat or oil cannot easily absorb water. In fact, that is one reason why fats and oils are effective tenderizers. Fats and oils coat structure builders such as gluten proteins and starches, and interfere with their ability to hydrate and form structure.

It is easy to see why batters and doughs are considered complex. But compared with what is yet to come, the mixing process is relatively simple and straightforward. The next stage, baking, is where the heat of the oven activates additional chemical and physical changes. These changes are described in the next section as eleven separate events, but they are very much interrelated, and many occur simultaneously.

Stage II: Baking

Baking involves the gradual transfer of heat from the surface of cakes, cookies, and breads to their center. As heat travels through, it transforms batters and doughs into baked goods with a firm, dry crust and a softer center.

The soft center of baked goods consists of air cells surrounded by porous cell walls. These *cell walls* consist of a network of egg and gluten proteins embedded with starch granules and other particles. When bakers and pastry chefs refer to the crumb or grain of baked goods, they are referring to the soft inside of baked goods, viewed when sliced (Figure 3.1).

This section describes eleven events that happen during baking. While they are listed as eleven isolated events, in fact they occur concurrently, and in some cases one event influences another. Some of the events that occur during baking, such as starch gelatinization, would not happen at room temperature. Others would eventually happen, but the heat from the oven speeds them up.

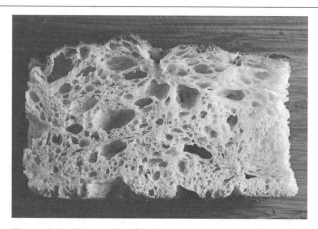

Figure 3.1 The crumb of baked goods is made of air cells surrounded by porous cell walls.

Temperatures are given for some of the events, but they are given only as a guideline because actual temperatures depend on many complex factors. Additionally, there is no upper temperature limit on protein coagulation and on certain other processes such as starch gelatinization and the evaporation of gases. These processes continue as long as the baked good remains in the oven.

1. Fats Melt.

One of the first things that happens when baked goods are placed in the oven is that solid fats melt. The actual temperature at which this occurs varies with the fat and its melting point, with butter melting earlier than all-purpose shortening, for example.

Most fats melt somewhere between 90° and 130°F (30°–55°C). As they melt, trapped air and water escape from the fat. Water evaporates as steam vapor, and the air and steam expand, pushing on cell walls so that baked goods increase in volume. In other words, melting fat contributes to leavening. In general, the later a fat melts, the more it leavens, because the gases escape at about the same time that the cell walls are firm enough to hold their shape. While butter, with its low melting point, provides volume and flakiness when used properly, many fats provide more volume and flakiness than butter because they have higher melting points. An example of fat designed with a very high melting point for maximum volume and flakiness is puff pastry margarine. Fats with too high a melting point can have an unpleasant waxy mouthfeel, though.

Besides melting point, the amount of water and air in a fat affects its ability to leaven. In general, puff pastry margarine, which contains about 16 percent water, provides more leavening than puff pastry shortening, which contains no water. Creamed shortening, which has additional air beaten in, provides more leavening than shortening that has not been creamed. Liquid oil, which contains neither air nor water, does not contribute to leavening at all.

Once melted, fat slithers through batters and doughs to coat gluten strands, egg proteins, and starches. This interferes with these structure builders and prevents them from hydrating and forming structure. In other words, fats tenderize.

The more fats and oils coat structure builders, the more effectively they tenderize. Usually, fats that melt early in baking tenderize more than those that melt late, because they have more time to coat structure builders. Likewise, liquid oil often tenderizes more than solid fat, because the oil begins coating structure builders during the mixing stage.

Finally, as solid fats melt and liquefy, they thin out batters and doughs. Some thinning is desirable, as when cookie dough spreads and cookies bake up thin and crisp. Too much thinning can be undesirable, though, as when cake batter is so thin that it collapses in the oven or forms thin tunnels as it bakes.

2. Gases Form and Expand.

The three most important leavening gases in baked goods are air, steam, and carbon dioxide. Heat from the oven affects these leavening gases in several ways. For example, heat causes water to vaporize into steam. Heat also increases the rate of fermentation in yeast-raised baked goods, so that carbon dioxide gas and alcohol are generated at a faster rate, at least until the yeast dies. Finally, heat helps to dissolve slow-acting baking powders to activate them. Once activated, baking powders release carbon dioxide into the liquid portion of the batter or dough. Depending on the formulation of the baking powder, this may start at room temperature and continue until the temperature reaches 170°F (75°C) or above.

As the temperature rises, steam and carbon dioxide gases move to the air bubbles formed during mixing, enlarging them. Heat also causes the gases themselves to expand. As the air bubbles enlarge and gases further expand, they push on cell walls, forcing them to stretch. The product increases in size and volume; in other words, it leavens. Because cell walls are stretched during leavening, they are thinner, making the baked good easier to bite through; that is, leavening makes baked goods more tender.

With yeast-raised baked goods, much of the leavening happens fairly early in the baking process. This fast expansion of yeast dough during the first few minutes of baking is called *oven spring*. It is the result of water vaporizing into steam, yeast fermenting at a faster rate, and gases expanding in volume and enlarging air bubbles.

3. Microorganisms Die.

Microorganisms are small (microscopic) living entities. Examples of microorganisms include yeast, mold, bacteria, and viruses. Most die by 135°–140°F (55°–60°C), but the actual temperature depends on several things, including the type of microorganism and the amount of sugar and salt present.

Once yeast dies, fermentation stops (meaning the yeast no longer produces carbon dioxide from sugars). This is desirable because overfermented dough has an overpowering sour flavor. Besides killing yeast, heat also kills pathogenic microorganisms such as salmonella. *Pathogenic* microorganisms are those that cause illness or even death. Thus, cooking or baking makes food safer to eat.

4. Sugar Dissolves.

For many batters and doughs, sugar dissolves completely during mixing. However, when batters and doughs are high in sugar or low in moisture—as is the case with most cookie doughs and some cake batters—undissolved sugar crystals are present at the start of baking. These undissolved crystals help thicken and solidify batters and doughs.

When they heat up, however, sugar crystals dissolve in batters and doughs. As they dissolve, sugar crystals pull water from other molecules, such as starches and proteins, to form a sugar syrup that thins out batters and doughs. This thinning becomes significant as temperatures approach 160°F (70°C). As with melted fat, dissolved sugar increases cookie spread. Dissolving sugar also thins out cake batter in the oven, making it more susceptible to collapse or tunneling. To prevent cake batter from collapsing as it heats up, structure builders must begin to thicken and set up.

5. Egg and Gluten Proteins Coagulate.

Egg and gluten proteins are two of the most important structure builders in baked goods. When they are heated, egg and gluten proteins dry out and stiffen, or set. To visualize this for egg proteins, think of the changes that occur as a raw egg cooks and coagulates. The egg turns from clear to opaque, but more important, it turns from liquid to solid. This process typically begins at 140°–160°F (60°–70°C) and continues as temperatures rise.

While the changes that occur in eggs as they are heated are visible, the protein molecules that cause these changes are not—not even under a microscope. If they were visible, raw egg proteins would appear as relatively large coiled molecules surrounded by water. As they are heated, the molecules unfold (denature) and bond with one another to form clusters (Figure 3.2). These clusters of coagulated egg protein trap water and form a continuous network that surrounds air cells. At

the same time, cell walls stretch from the pressure of expanding gases. Eventually, water escapes from the proteins, the bonding proteins become rigid, the cell walls lose their ability to stretch, and the pressure from expanding gases ruptures the rigid cell walls, so they become porous. It is this rigid structure that helps set the final size and shape of baked goods. The process of egg protein coagulation is discussed in more detail in Chapter 10. The changes to gluten proteins are discussed in Chapter 7.

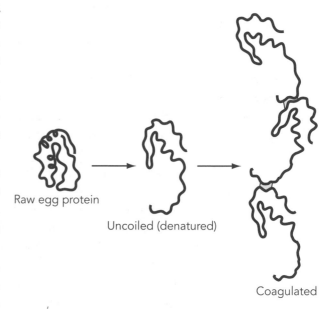

Raw egg protein

Uncoiled (denatured)

Coagulated

Figure 3.2 The process of egg protein coagulation

For best volume, the setting of proteins must be carefully timed with gas expansion. This occurs only if ingredients are correctly weighed and if the oven is set and calibrated to the proper temperature. If timing is off, baked goods could rise and collapse, or not rise at all. As you will see in the next section, however, starch gelatinization contributes to structure in baked goods and also prevents collapse.

6. Starches Gelatinize. 陷粉米糊化

Starch is often the forgotten structure builder in flour, probably because gluten plays such an important and dominant role in raw bread dough. Yet once bread is baked, its structure is built as much on starch, or more, than it is on gluten.

Structure from gelatinized starch is arguably softer and more tender than the structure from egg and gluten proteins. Think of the texture of freshly baked bread. Much of the soft crumb of freshly baked bread is from gelatinized starch. But as with protein structure, too much starch produces toughness and dryness.

Starch gelatinization occurs when starch granules absorb and trap water as they are heated. *Starch granules* are small particles or grains that are tightly packed with starch molecules. They are hard and gritty when raw, but they swell and soften when cooked. As starch granules gelatinize, they grab any water they can get, including water released from gluten and other proteins as they are heated.

Starch granules begin swelling at 120°–140°F (50°–60°C). By 170°F (75°C), gelatinization is well under way, with granules having absorbed a significant amount of water. This causes the batter or dough to thicken considerably and to take on the final shape and crumb structure of the baked product. Gelatinization is not complete, though, until temperatures approach 200°F (95°C) or so, and only if enough water is available. If it

Why Do Bagels Shine When They Are Boiled?

The traditional way to make bagels is to boil them briefly before they are baked. The boiling water gelatinizes starch on the surface of the bagel. The gelatinized starch forms a smooth film, a surface so smooth that light reflects off it in an even shine.

is, granules begin to deform and collapse as starch molecules move out of the granules. Starch gelatinization is discussed in more detail in Chapter 12.

The starch in baked goods rarely has the chance to gelatinize fully, because there is usually not enough water or time available for that to occur. For example, very little starch gelatinization occurs in pie or cookie doughs, because they contain very little water. Instead, the structure of pie pastry relies mostly on gluten, and that of cookies relies on gluten and egg proteins. In contrast, cake batters are high in water, and the structure of baked cakes is highly dependent on gelatinized starch (as well as coagulated egg proteins).

But even when enough water is present, other ingredients, such as sugars and fats, raise the temperature at which starch gelatinizes. This means that starch gelatinizes at a higher temperature in sweet, rich bread dough—dough high in sugar and fat—than it does in lean dough.

As with protein coagulation, once starch gelatinization is well under way, the final volume and shape of baked goods—or of puddings and pie fillings—are set. At this stage in the baking process, the baked good is able to hold its shape, but it still has a wet doughy texture, little color, and an off taste.

> **HELPFUL HINT**
> If your yeast-raised sweet breads or rolls sink back or wrinkle upon cooling, it is likely that the high amount of sugar prevented sufficient starch gelatinization. To stop this from happening, reduce the amount of sugar added, use a stronger flour with a higher gluten content, or extend the bake time, reducing the oven temperature by 25°F (15°C), if necessary.

7. Gases Evaporate.

While the three main leavening gases are air, steam, and carbon dioxide, baked goods contain other gases as well. Many liquids, including vanilla extract and alcohols, evaporate to the gaseous state when heated, and any liquid that evaporates to a gas functions as a leavening gas. Do not underestimate the importance of these other gases to the baking process. Since alcohol is an end product of yeast fermentation, all yeast-raised baked goods contain a measurable amount of alcohol.

Small amounts of carbon dioxide and other gases are lost from batters and doughs as temperatures warm above room temperature. This is because wet cell walls are not completely solid, and they allow slow but steady movement of gases throughout unbaked products. At a certain point, however, cell walls rupture from the pressure of expanding gases, and large amounts of gases escape. Not coincidentally, proteins coagulate and starches gelatinize at about the same time. That is, as the structure of baked goods becomes more rigid, it also becomes more porous to gases. It is transformed from a wet foam that traps air to a porous sponge that does not. With bread, this occurs at around 160°F (72°C). It is at this point that bread dough loses its ability to retain gases and to expand in size. Instead, the gases migrate to exposed surfaces and evaporate.

> **HELPFUL HINT**
>
> *While tools such as kitchen timers are useful, experienced bakers and pastry chefs rely on all their senses, including the sense of smell, when working in the bakeshop. For example, aromas from the oven are an early indicator that a product must soon be checked for doneness.*

As gases escape from baked goods, several important changes occur. First, a dry, hard crust forms on the surface from a loss in moisture. Depending on the formula and oven conditions, the crust may become crisp, as it does in properly made French baguettes, or soft, as it does in breads made with milk. In any case, at this stage in baking, the crust is still pale white.

Besides developing a dry, hard crust, baked goods lose weight as they lose moisture. On average, 18 ounces (510 grams) of dough must be scaled out to yield a typical 1-pound (450 gram) loaf of bread. The third change that occurs as gases evaporate is a loss in flavor. As the bakeshop fills with aromas, like vanilla, it

means that these aromas are escaping from the products as they bake. In most cases, however, there is still enough flavor left in the baked good to be enjoyed by the customer. Other flavor losses during this stage of baking are less obvious but still important. For example, alcohol and carbon dioxide are associated with the taste of raw dough. A significant amount of both have evaporated out of baked goods by about 170°F (75°C). This causes a subtle yet important change in flavor for products high in these gases, such as yeast doughs.

8. Caramelization and Maillard Browning Occur on Crust.

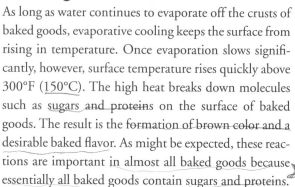

As long as water continues to evaporate off the crusts of baked goods, evaporative cooling keeps the surface from rising in temperature. Once evaporation slows significantly, however, surface temperature rises quickly above 300°F (150°C). The high heat breaks down molecules such as sugars and proteins on the surface of baked goods. The result is the formation of brown color and a desirable baked flavor. As might be expected, these reactions are important in almost all baked goods because essentially all baked goods contain sugars and proteins.

Bakers and pastry chefs do not always differentiate the type of molecule breaking down. Oftentimes, any formation of brown color and baked flavor is called *caramelization.* However, strictly speaking, caramelization is the process of sugars breaking down. Place sugar in a pan on the stove and add heat, and the sugar eventually caramelizes to a fragrant, brown mass.

When sugars break down in the presence of proteins, it is called *Maillard browning.* Because foods contain many different types of sugars and proteins, Maillard browning contributes to the flavor of a wide range of foods, including toasted nuts, roast beef, and baked bread.

Why Is Steam Injected into Ovens During Bread Baking?

Because of the nature of bread formulas, crusts form fairly quickly on many yeast breads. Once a dry, hard crust forms, bread can no longer expand in volume, even if gases within it continue to expand. At best, the gases may crack the surface of the bread as they escape from the product, but they will not provide more leavening.

If steam is injected into the oven during the early stages of baking, the surface of the bread stays moist and flexible. The bread continues to rise for a longer period of time, and the loaf is higher, lighter, and less dense.

Because the formation of a crust is delayed, steam injection promotes formation of a thinner crust. The crust is crispier and glossier because the moist steam facilitates starch gelatinization on the surface of the bread.

Bread that is cooked in a microwave oven does not brown well, and it tastes flat. Unlike oven baking, where the oven is hot and the product heats by conduction from the outside surface to the inside, microwave ovens remain cool and heat a product more evenly throughout. This means that the outside surface of bread does not get very hot in the microwave oven. Without high temperatures, browning reactions do not occur. The crust stays light in color, and the desirable baked flavors from the browning reactions do not form.

While the eight events mentioned previously are the most important ones to bakers and pastry chefs, the following three events also occur during the baking process.

9. Enzymes Are Inactivated.

Enzymes are proteins that act as biological catalysts in plants, animals, and microorganisms. They catalyze, or speed up, chemical reactions without actually being used up in the process. This makes enzymes very efficient, so that a small amount goes a long way. Not only can enzymes speed up chemical reactions; they can cause reactions to occur that might not happen otherwise.

All enzymes, being proteins, are denatured by heat. The process of denaturation inactivates enzymes and stops their activity. Most enzymes are inactivated by temperatures of 160°–180°F (70°–80°C), but they vary in their heat sensitivity. Before they are inactivated, however, rising oven temperatures increase their activity. This increased activity occurs in the early stages of baking only.

Amylase is one example of an enzyme important in yeast-raised baked goods. Amylase is present in a few of the ingredients used in bread doughs, including malted barley flour, diastatic malt syrup, and certain dough conditioners or improvers. Before it is inactivated, amylase (also known as diastase) breaks down starches into sugars and other molecules. A certain amount of starch breakdown is desirable for browning, for softening bread, and to delay staling. If too much starch is destroyed, however, bread darkens from the browning of too much sugar. The bread can also turn to mush, because starch is an important structure builder in bread and other baked goods. It is desirable that amylase is inactivated by heat, as this limits the amount of starch breakdown.

Other enzymes present in baking ingredients include proteases, which break down proteins, and lipases, which break down lipids (fats, oils, and emulsifiers). Notice the suffix -ase in the naming of these enzymes.

10. Changes Occur to Nutrients.

Proteins, fats, carbohydrates, vitamins, and minerals are examples of nutrients in food. Heat changes certain nutrients in very important ways. For example, proteins and starches in flour are more digestible once they are heated. This means that baked foods containing flour are often more nutritious than raw foods. Not all the effects of heat on food are positive, however. Heat destroys some nutrients such as vitamin C (ascorbic acid) and thiamin (vitamin B_1).

11. Pectin Breaks Down.

Pectin is not present in batters or doughs, but many baked goods contain fruit, and pectin is one of the main components holding fruits together (Figure 3.3). When pectin is heated, it dissolves, and fruits soften and lose their shape. While other changes cause fruits to soften when cooked, pectin breakdown is one of the most important.

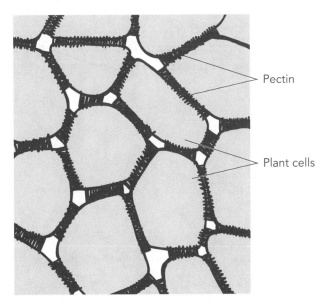

Pectin

Plant cells

Figure 3.3 Pectin is the cement that holds plant cells to one another in fresh fruit.

Stage III: Cooling

When removed from the oven, a baked good continues to cook until its temperature cools to room temperature. This is called *carryover cooking*. Because of carryover cooking, baked goods must be watched carefully during the last few minutes of baking, and must be removed before—not when—they are baked to perfection.

Even when cooled and properly wrapped, baked goods continue to change during storage. The main changes that occur can be summarized as follows.

1   Gases contract and no longer exert pressure on cell walls. Without this pressure, products that do not have porous cell walls and are without sufficient structure (such as soufflés and underbaked items) collapse.

2   Fats resolidify and greasiness decreases. Depending on the fat, however, the product could become hard and waxy, as is the case with puff pastry made with a high-melting fat.

3   Sugars recrystallize on the crusts of low-moisture, high-sugar products, such as cookies and certain cakes and muffins. This gives these products a desirable crunchy crust.

4   Starch molecules bond and solidify, and the structure gets firmer and more rigid. Starch bonding—called *retrogradation*—continues over the next several days, and it is a major cause of staling. Stale baked goods have a hard, dry, crumbly texture.

> **HELPFUL HINT**
> *Each product differs in how much heat it retains and how much cooking continues outside the oven. For example, cream puff shells cool quickly and must be well baked before they are removed from the oven. Baked custards and cheesecakes, however, should still jiggle in the center when they are removed because carryover cooking completes the baking process, firming these products as they cool.*

5   Protein molecules also bond and solidify as the product sets, and likely contribute to staling. Until delicate baked goods cool and structure solidifies, it is best not to cut into them, so they will not crush. A good rule of thumb is to cool products to 100°F (38°C) or below before slicing.

6   Moisture is redistributed within the crumb of baked goods, which may also contribute to staling.

7   In high-moisture products like bread, moisture moves from moist crumb to dry crust, and the crust loses its crispness over the next day, sometimes becoming tough and rubbery.

8   Flavors evaporate, and over the next day or so, wonderful fresh-baked flavors are lost. Some flavor loss occurs because flavors become trapped by starches as they retrograde. Where this is the case, a brief reheating in the oven recovers some lost flavor and softens the structure.

Questions for Review

1 Provide examples of tougheners, tenderizers, moisteners, and driers.

2 Provide an example of how a different mixing method can affect the outcome of a baked good.

3 List and briefly describe seven things that happen as ingredients are mixed into batters or doughs.

4 Describe the two main methods used for mixing bread dough.

5 What products are commonly mixed using the creaming method?

6 Why are unbaked batters and doughs sometimes referred to as foams?

7 Why are baked goods sometimes referred to as sponges?

8 What five functions does water perform in baking?

9 How, and why, can the same pie pastry dough formula result in a tender, mealy crust in one case and a flaky crust in another?

10 How do fats contribute to leavening in baked goods?

11 Which would be expected to provide more leavening: shortening with a melting point of 130°F (55°C) or margarine with a melting point of 130°F (55°C)? Explain why.

12 How do fats and oils tenderize baked goods?

13 Which would be expected to provide more leavening: shortening with a melting point of 105°F (40°C) or shortening with a melting point of 130°F (55°C)? Explain why.

14 Which would be expected to give more tenderness: shortening with a melting point of 105°F (40°C) or shortening with a melting point of 130°F (55°C)? Explain why.

15 How do solid fats increase spread in cookies?

16 How do sugar crystals affect the thickness of batters and doughs? How does dissolved sugar affect thickness?

17 What is oven spring, and what causes it?

18 What are the three main leavening gases in baked goods?

19 How do leavening agents contribute to the tenderness of baked goods?

20 Provide examples of microorganisms. What happens to them during the baking process? Why is this important? Provide two reasons.

21 Describe the process of egg coagulation.

22 Describe the process of starch gelatinization.

23 What causes a dry crust to form on baked goods?

24 What three things result from gases evaporating?

25 Provide an example of an enzyme. What happens to it—and other enzymes—during the baking process?

26 Provide examples of nutrients. For one of the nutrients, briefly explain what happens to it during baking.

27 What happens during baking that would cause apples in an apple pie to soften and lose shape?

28 List and briefly describe eight things that occur as products cool.

29 What is the main cause for the staling of baked goods? What other factors contribute to staling?

Questions for Discussion

1 Explain what could happen if protein coagulation occurs too soon—that is, before gas expansion.

2 Explain what could happen if protein coagulation occurs too late—that is, after gas expansion.

3 What do you think would happen if there were few—or no—structure builders in a baked good?

4 As stated in this chapter, for starch gelatinization to occur, there must be enough water and heat. Think about the amount of liquid in each of the following products. For each pair, state which product relies more on starch gelatinization for its structure. That is, in which will more starch gelatinization occur:
  • Bread or pie pastry?
  • Crisp, dry cookies or muffins?

5 Two of the eight main events that occur in the oven involve gases. Combine the two and describe what happens to gases from the beginning to the end of the baking process and how this affects the product.

Exercises and Experiments

1 Exercise: Tunneling in Cake Batter

Imagine that you are baking cakes or cupcakes using a high-ratio cake formula, and you notice that unsightly tunnels develop during baking. This can be caused by batter that thins too much or stays thin for too long. Explain the reason that each of the following techniques works to increase batter thickness and reduce tunnelling. As an example, number 1 is completed for you.

1 Use cake flour rather than bread or pastry flour.

Reason: Unlike bread flour and pastry flour, the starch in cake flour absorbs more liquids, so cake flour thickens batter more (see Chapter 5 for more information).

2 Increase the amount of flour.

Reason: _____

_____

_____

3 Use a fat that is firmer and has a higher melting point.

Reason: _____

_____

_____

4 Decrease the amount of sugar.

Reason: _____

_____

_____

5 Increase the oven temperature.

Reason: _____

_____

_____

6 Decrease the amount of batter placed in a pan.

Reason: _____

_____

_____

❷ Experiment: How the Mixing Method Affects the Overall Quality of Muffins

Objectives

Demonstrate how the muffin method of mixing ingredients compares with the creaming method in

- Ease in preparation
- Appearance and texture of the muffins
- Overall acceptability of the muffins

Products Prepared

Muffins made by using

- Muffin (one-stage) method of mixing
- Creaming or conventional method of mixing
- Other, if desired (for example, biscuit method or different amounts of creaming)

Materials and Equipment

- Scale
- Muffin pans (2½" or 3½"/65 or 90 mm size)
- Paper liners, pan spray, or pan coating
- Sieve
- Mixer with 5-quart mixing bowl
- Flat beater attachment

- Bowl scraper
- Muffin batter (see Formula), enough to make 24 or more muffins of each variation
- Size #16 (2 fl. oz./60 ml) portion-control scoop or equivalent
- Scale
- Half sheet pans (optional)
- Serrated knife
- Ruler

Formula

Basic Muffin Batter

Yield: 24 muffins (you will have some excess batter)

INGREDIENT	POUNDS	OUNCES	GRAMS	BAKER'S PERCENTAGE
Shortening		7	200	35
Flour, pastry	1	4	570	100
Sugar, regular granulated		8	225	40
Salt (1 tsp)		0.2	6	1
Baking powder		1.2	35	6
Eggs, whole		6	170	30
Milk	1		455	80
Vanilla extract (1½ tsp)		0.2	7	1
Total	**3**	**10.6**	**1,668**	**293**

Method of Preparation

1 Preheat oven to 400°F (200°C).

2 Allow all ingredients to come to room temperature (temperature of ingredients is important for consistent results).

3 Follow instructions for mixing, using either muffin method or creaming method.

For muffin method, mix ingredients as follows:

1 Melt shortening. Cool slightly.

2 Sift flour, sugar, salt, and baking powder together three times into mixing bowl.

3 Beat eggs slightly. Blend in milk, vanilla, and melted shortening.

4 Pour liquids onto dry ingredients in mixing bowl.

5 Using flat beater, blend ingredients together on low speed for 15 seconds or just until moistened. Batter will look lumpy.

For creaming method, mix ingredients as follows:

1 Sift flour, salt, and baking powder together three times.

2 Using flat beater, blend shortening and sugar together on low speed for 30 seconds. Stop and scrape bowl, then blend for another 30 seconds and scrape bowl again.

3 Cream on medium speed for 1 minute. Stop and scrape bowl.

4 Continue creaming for an additional 2 minutes or until light and fluffy.

5 Beat eggs slightly and add vanilla extract.

6 Add the slightly beaten egg mixture in two portions. Stir on low speed for a total of 40 seconds or just until blended.

7 Add the sifted dry ingredients alternately with milk in three parts, while stirring on low for 1 minute or just until blended. Stop and scrape bowl as needed.

Procedure

1 Prepare muffin batter using the given formula or using any basic muffin formula. Prepare one batch using each mixing method.

2 Line muffin pans with paper liners, lightly spray with pan spray, or grease with pan coating. Label pan with mixing method used.

3 Weigh 2 ounces (60 grams) batter into prepared muffin pans. Use #16 scoop as a guide, but volumes will likely be different for the different variations.

4 If desired, place muffin pans on half sheet pans.

5 Use an oven thermometer placed in center of oven for an initial reading of oven temperature. Record results here: _____.

6 When oven is properly preheated, place filled muffin pans in oven and set timer for 20–22 minutes, or according to formula.

7 Bake muffins until they are lightly browned and spring back when center top is pressed lightly. Remove all muffins from oven after same length of time. If necessary, however, adjust bake times for oven variances.

8 Check final oven temperature. Record results here: _____.

9 Remove muffins from hot pans and cool to room temperature.

Results

1 When completely cooled, evaluate average height of muffins from each batch, as follows:
- Slice three cooled muffins from each batch in half, being careful not to compress.
- Measure height of each muffin at its maximum height by placing ruler along the flat edge. Record results for each muffin in ¹⁄₁₆" (1 mm) increments and record results in Results Table 1, which follows.
- Calculate the average muffin height for each batch by adding the heights of the muffins and dividing by 3. Record results in Results Table 1.

2 Evaluate the shape of muffins (even rounded top, peaked top, dips in center, etc.) and record results in Results Table 1.

RESULTS TABLE 1 HEIGHT AND SHAPE OF MUFFINS MIXED USING DIFFERENT METHODS

MIXING METHOD	HEIGHTS OF EACH OF THREE MUFFINS	AVERAGE HEIGHT OF ONE MUFFIN	MUFFIN SHAPES	ADDITIONAL COMMENTS
Muffin				
Creaming				

3 Evaluate the sensory characteristics of completely cooled products and record evaluations in Results Table 2. Consider the following:

- Crust color, from very light to very dark on a scale of 1 to 5
- Crust texture (moist/dry, soft/crisp, etc.)
- Crumb appearance (small uniform air cells, large irregular air cells, tunnels, etc.); also, evaluate color
- Crumb texture (moist/dry, tough/tender, gummy, crumbly, etc.)
- Overall flavor (egg flavor, floury taste, saltiness, sweetness, etc.)
- Overall acceptability, from highly unacceptable to highly acceptable, on a scale of 1 to 5
- Any additional comments, as necessary

RESULTS TABLE 2 SENSORY CHARACTERISTICS OF MUFFINS MIXED USING DIFFERENT METHODS

MIXING METHOD	CRUST COLOR AND TEXTURE	CRUMB APPEARANCE AND TEXTURE	OVERALL FLAVOR	OVERALL ACCEPTABILITY	ADDITIONAL COMMENTS
Muffin					
Creaming					

Sources of Error

List any sources of error that might make it difficult to draw the proper conclusions from your experiment. In particular, consider any problems with the ovens and with properly mixing ingredients.

_____

_____

_____

State what you could do differently next time to minimize or eliminate each source of error.

_____

_____

_____

Conclusions

Select one from the choices in **bold** or fill in the blank.

1   Compared with the muffin method, the creaming method for mixing was **easier/harder/ the same** and took **more/less/the same** amount of time to complete.

2   Muffins made using the creaming method had air cells that were **smaller and more uniform than/larger and less uniform than/the same as** those in muffins made using the muffin method. Overall, the muffins that had more of a cake-like appearance were made using the **creaming/muffin** method.

3   Muffins made using the creaming method were **tougher/more tender/neither tougher nor more tender** than those made using the muffin method.

4   Other noticeable differences between the muffins and the methods of preparation were as follows:

_____

_____

_____

5   The muffins I found more acceptable were made with the **creaming/muffin** method because _____

_____

_____

❸ Experiment: How the Method of Preparation Affects the Quality of Pound Cake

Objectives

Demonstrate how the extent of creaming fat and sifting dry ingredients in pound cake batter affects

- Density of the creamed shortening
- Thickness of cake batter
- Volume of pound cake

- Crumb appearance: coarseness and color of pound cake
- Overall acceptability of pound cake

Products Prepared

Pound cake that has undergone:
- No creaming and no sifting
- 4 minutes of creaming, three siftings (control product)
- Other, if desired (4 minutes creaming, no sifting; no creaming, three siftings; 8 minutes creaming, etc.)

Materials and Equipment

- Scale
- Sieve
- Mixing spoon
- Mixer with 5-quart mixing bowl
- Flat beater attachment
- Bowl scraper
- Pound cake batter (see Formula), enough to make one or more 9-inch cakes of each variation
- Cake pans, 9-inch, one per variation
- Pan coating or pan spray
- Spatula
- Oven thermometer
- Two identical clear 1-cup measuring cups (or similar size clear containers), for measuring density of creamed shortening
- Straight-edge
- Serrated knife
- Ruler

Formula

Shortening Mixture

INGREDIENT	POUNDS	OUNCES	GRAMS
Shortening, all-purpose		10	280
Sugar, regular granulated		20	560
Dried milk solids		1	30
Total	**1**	**15**	**870**

Method of Preparation
(for Control Product)

1   Place shortening in mixing bowl and stir with flat beater to soften, low, 15 seconds. Stop and scrape bowl.

2   Slowly add sugar while creaming on medium for 1 minute. Stop and scrape bowl.

3 Continue creaming on medium for 1 additional minute. Stop and scrape bowl.

4 Slowly add dried milk solids (DMS) while creaming on medium, and continue creaming for 2 additional minutes. Stop and scrape bowl halfway through.

Pound Cake Batter

Yield: *one 9-inch layer*

INGREDIENT	POUNDS	OUNCES	GRAMS	BAKER'S PERCENTAGE
Flour, cake		8	225	100
Baking powder		0.25	7.5	3
Salt		0.1	2.5	1
Shortening Mixture		15.5	435	193
Egg		7	190	84
Water		4.5	125	56
Total	**2**	**3.35**	**985**	**437**

Method of Preparation
(for Control Product)

1 Preheat oven to 350°F (175°C).

2 Allow ingredients to come to room temperature (temperature of ingredients is important for consistent results).

3 Blend flour, baking powder, and salt thoroughly by sifting together three times onto parchment paper.

4 Place 15.5 ounces (435 grams) of shortening mixture into mixing bowl. Set aside the rest for later use.

5 Stir on low with flat beater for 45 seconds, slowly adding slightly beaten eggs. Stop and scrape. Note: Creamed mixture might take on a somewhat curdled look, but it will still be holding a good amount of air. However, do not overmix; if eggs and shortening mixture are well blended before 45 seconds, begin next step immediately.

6 Add dry ingredients alternately with water in three parts, while stirring on low for 1 minute. Stop and scrape bowl.

Method of Preparation
(for Cake with No Creaming or Sifting)

Follow the Method of Preparation for Control Product except:

1 For Shortening Mixture, add sugar and DMS all at once. Stir on low until blended but not creamed, about 1 minute.

2 Do not sift ingredients in step 3; instead, stir gently yet thoroughly with a spoon.

3 Continue with step 4.

Procedure

1   Prepare pound cake batter using the formula given or using any basic pound cake formula. Prepare one batch using the control preparation, and one following the method with no creaming or sifting. To minimize experimental error, use shortening instead of butter or margarine. Note that the Shortening Mixture formula makes double the amount needed for one pound cake layer.

2   Grease cake pans with pan coating or use pan spray. Label each pan with method of preparation used.

3   Weigh batter into prepared cake pans, the same weight for each variation (32 ounces/900 grams per 9-inch pan). Spread batter smooth with a spatula.

4   Evaluate consistency of each batter, from very thin and runny to very thick, on a scale of 1 to 5. Record results in Results Table 1.

5   Use an oven thermometer placed in center of oven for an initial reading of oven temperature. Record result here: _____.

6   When oven is properly preheated, place filled cake pans in oven and set timer for 30–35 minutes, or according to formula. Bake cakes until control product (4-minute creaming and sifted) is light brown and cake springs back when lightly pressed. Remove all cakes from oven after same length of time. If necessary, however, adjust bake times for oven variances.

7   Check final oven temperature. Record result here: _____.

8   Let cakes stand 1 or more minutes, then remove from hot pans and cool to room temperature.

Results

1   Using the extra shortening mixture from each version of the formula, measure density (weight per volume) of mixture from each batch. To measure density:
  • Carefully spoon sample of shortening mixture into tared measuring cup.
  • Visually check cup to confirm that no large air gaps are present.
  • Level the top of the cup with a straight-edge.
  • Weigh the amount of creamed mixture in each cup and record results in Results Table 1.

2   When the cakes are completely cooled, evaluate height and shape as follows:
  • Slice cake from each batch in half, being careful not to compress.
  • Measure height of cake by placing a ruler along the flat edge at the cake's maximum height. Record results in 1/16" (1 mm) increments in Results Table 1.
  • Indicate in Cake Shape column of Results Table 1 whether cake has an even rounded top, or if it peaks or dips in center.
  • Also indicate whether cake is lopsided; that is, if one side is higher than the other.

RESULTS TABLE 1   CAKES MADE WITH DIFFERENT METHODS OF PREPARATION

METHOD OF PREPARATION	CONSISTENCY OF BATTER	DENSITY OF SHORTENING MIXTURE	CAKE HEIGHT	CAKE SHAPE	ADDITIONAL COMMENTS
No sifting, no creaming					
Sifted 3 times, creamed 4 minutes (control product)					

3   Evaluate the sensory characteristics of completely cooled products and record evaluations in Results Table 2. Be sure to compare each in turn to the control product and consider the following:
- Crumb color
- Crumb appearance (small uniform air cells, large irregular air cells, tunnels, etc.)
- Overall acceptability, from highly unacceptable to highly acceptable, on a scale of 1 to 5.
- Add any additional comments, as necessary.

RESULTS TABLE 2   APPEARANCE AND OTHER CHARACTERISTICS OF POUND CAKES MADE WITH DIFFERENT METHODS OF PREPARATION

METHOD OF PREPARATION	CRUMB COLOR AND APPEARANCE	OVERALL ACCEPTABILITY	ADDITIONAL COMMENTS
No sifting, no creaming			
Sifted 3 times, creamed 4 minutes (control product)			

Sources of Error

List any sources of error that might make it difficult to draw the proper conclusions from your experiment. In particular, consider any difficulties in measuring densities of shortening; differences in how batter was mixed and handled; and any problems with ovens.

_____

_____

_____

State what you could do differently next time to minimize or eliminate each of the sources of error.

_____

_____

_____

Conclusions

Select one from the choices in **bold** or fill in the blanks.

1 The density of the shortening mixture used for the control product was **higher than/lower than/the same as** the density of the noncreamed mixture. This is because the amount of air in the shortening mixture **increased/decreased/stayed the same** as creaming time increased. The difference in density was **small/moderate/large**.

2 The batter for the control product was **thicker than/thinner than/the same as** the batter for the noncreamed, nonsifted version. The difference in thickness was **small/moderate/large**.

3 The air cells in the crumb for the control product were **smaller and more uniform than/larger and less uniform than/the same as** the air cells in the noncreamed, nonsifted version, and the crumb color of the control product was **lighter than/darker than/the same as** the crumb color of the noncreamed, nonsifted version. This is because the amount of air in the creamed mixture **increased/decreased** as creaming time increased.

4 Other noticeable differences between the products were as follows:

_____

_____

_____

5 The pound cake I found most acceptable was _____ because:

_____

_____

_____

6 How do you explain the difference in crumb color between the two cakes, given that both were made from the same amount of the same ingredients?

_____

_____

_____

7 Look through cookbooks and the Internet. List two formulas for baked goods that you would expect to be just as affected by improper sifting and creaming as this cake. Explain why you believe so.

_____

_____

_____

Sensory Properties of Food

Introduction

The study of sensory perception is the study of how the sensory organs (eyes, ears, nose, mouth, and skin) detect changes around us, and how the brain senses and interprets these changes. It is receptors on the sensory organs that do the detecting, with receptors on all five organs active during eating. Examples of sensory receptors include taste cells on taste buds throughout the mouth; olfactory cells at the top of the nasal cavity; free nerve endings just beneath the surface of the skin; rods and cones on the retina of the eye; and hair cells in the inner ear. The focus of this chapter is the sensory properties of food (appearance, flavor, and texture) and how to objectively evaluate and describe them. As you read through the chapter, notice how the senses are used individually and together to evaluate these three properties of food. While all five senses are involved when we eat, some are more involved than others. For example, appearance is an important sensory characteristic with essentially all food products, but sound is important with only a few, such as toasted nuts, crisp cookies, and peanut brittle. The evaluation of flavor is further developed in Chapter 17.

Evaluating food is not the same as eating for enjoyment. Sensory evaluation takes practice and deliberate concentration, because the perception of food is complex. Professional bakers and pastry chefs must learn to evaluate food if they are to troubleshoot problems. As professionals, they also must prepare foods that they do not necessarily like, and they must evaluate these foods to confirm that they are prepared properly.

Many factors contribute to an individual's ability to evaluate food objectively, including genetics, gender, and health. However, experience is probably the most important factor: experience at paying attention to the smallest of details. This means that, regardless of your current ability to evaluate food, it can be improved—like any skill—through practice.

Appearance

Appearance creates the first impression customers have of food, and first impressions are important. No matter how appealing the taste, an unattractive appearance is hard to overlook. As humans, we do "eat with our eyes" because our sense of sight is more highly developed than our other senses. This is not the case with many animals. Dogs, for example, depend primarily on smell to explore their world.

The sense of sight is so highly developed in humans that messages received from other senses are often ignored if they conflict with what is seen. Yellow candy is expected to be lemon flavored, and if it is grape flavored, many people cannot correctly identify the flavor. Strawberry ice cream tinted with red food coloring seems to have a stronger strawberry flavor than one that has no added food coloring, even when there is no real difference. While as a professional you must train your senses so that they are not tricked by your sense of sight, it is also important to understand how appearance influences your customers' perceptions.

Appearance has many different aspects. *Color* or *hue*—whether food is yellow or red, for example—is an especially important aspect. Other aspects of appearance include opacity, sheen, shape, and size, and a visual evaluation of texture. *Opacity* is the quality of a product that appears opaque or cloudy. The opposite of opacity is clarity or translucency. An example of an opaque product is milk; an example of a clear or translucent one is water. *Sheen* is the state of a product that appears glossy or shiny. The opposite of glossy or shiny is matte or dull. An example of a product with sheen is honey; an example of a product that is dull is a shortbread cookie.

The Perception of Appearance

When light hits an object, light waves are reflected (bounced off), transmitted (passed through), or absorbed by the object (Figure 4.1). Only light waves that bounce off or pass through food reach our eyes and are seen; the light that is absorbed is not.

Factors Affecting the Perception of Appearance

Three main factors affect the perception of appearance. It is these factors that determine whether two products

Why We See Shadows, but Not Color, in the Dark

When light waves reach our eyes, they pass through the pupil and the lens to the retina, situated at the very back of the eye. The retina is densely packed with millions of receptor cells. There are two main types of receptor cells, rods and cones, named for their shapes. These two photo (light) receptors contain pigments that absorb and react to light, but they react very differently. Rods are exceedingly sensitive, but only to changes in brightness, not to color. This allows us to see shadows moving in the dark. Cones, on the other hand, detect color. They are less sensitive and work only when the light is bright.

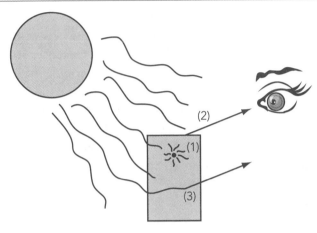

Figure 4.1 Light can be (1) absorbed, (2) reflected, or (3) transmitted through an object.

look the same or not. The first two factors—the nature of the light source and the nature of the object itself—affect how light is absorbed, reflected, and transmitted through foods. The third factor, the nature of the surroundings, is more of an optical illusion.

Nature of the Light Source If the light hitting an object changes, the appearance of the object changes. The appearance changes because the light the object absorbs, reflects, and transmits changes. Both the brightness of

the light source and the type of lighting (for example, fluorescent, incandescent, or halogen) are important to consider (Figure 4.2). Bakers and pastry chefs should be aware that what they see in the bakeshop might not be what the customer sees under dining room lights. Bakeshops often have bright fluorescent lights, while dining rooms tend to have dim incandescent ones. Dim incandescent lights have a warm, yellow cast, which tends to mute the appearance of the product.

Figure 4.2 Fluorescent, incandescent, and halogen lights each change the appearance of foods, especially when they vary in brightness (measured in watts).

What Happens When Light Is Absorbed by Food?

When visible light is absorbed by food or by another object, it vanishes from sight. However, this does not mean that it truly disappears. Light, which is a form of energy, is simply converted to another form of energy (such as heat energy or kinetic energy) when it is absorbed by an object.

Objects absorb light selectively, and different objects absorb light differently. For example, a green leaf contains chlorophyll that absorbs most light except green light. Only the green light is reflected off the leaf and reaches the eyes, which is why the leaf appears green in color. Likewise, red raspberries appear red because they absorb most colors except red, and black objects absorb essentially all light, reflecting little to the eyes. Because white light is composed of all colors of the rainbow (hold a prism up to light to see white light separated into its component colors), an object that appears white does so because it absorbs little, if any, light.

Nature of the Object   Each object has its own characteristic way of absorbing, reflecting, and transmitting light. There are two main reasons that objects might respond differently to light: if they differ in their chemical makeup, and if they differ in their physical structure.

It is logical to expect two products to look different when they differ in their chemical makeup; that is, when they are made from different formulas or when they are made with different raw materials. For example, chocolate icing should look different from vanilla icing because it contains chocolate as an added ingredient. The added chocolate absorbs more light and therefore appears darker than the vanilla icing, which allows more light to be reflected off its surface. Likewise, a pastry cream made with pale yellow yolks should be lighter yellow than another made with dark yellow yolks because the darker yolks are chemically different from the lighter ones. The darker yolks contain a higher amount of *carotenoids*, the yellow pigments in eggs that reflect yellow light and absorb the rest.

When products are baked for different lengths of time or at different temperatures, expect additional differences in appearance. A cake baked for 45 minutes instead of 30 minutes will undergo more browning reactions that cause the surface of the product to darken. Likewise, a cake baked at 425°F (220°C) will undergo more browning reactions than one baked at 300°F (150°C). These browning reactions are chemical changes that affect how light is absorbed, reflected, and transmitted.

When egg whites are beaten, tiny air bubbles are trapped within a network of egg white proteins. This changes the physical structure of the egg whites, and it dramatically alters the appearance of egg whites. The beaten egg whites appear white and opaque instead of clear and translucent, because light no longer easily passes through. Instead, the light bounces off the rounded air cells and scatters in many directions. Scattered light appears opaque.

Likewise, if a cake has small air cells (that is, has a fine crumb), it will look lighter or whiter than the same cake with a coarse crumb. That is why an undermixed white cake, with a coarse crumb, looks slightly yellow. Likewise, an undermixed chocolate cake looks darker and richer than one properly mixed, even if both are made from the same formula.

When fondant is properly handled (warmed to body temperature before use), it forms a smooth, white glaze with an attractive sheen. If it is melted above 100°F (38°C), however, it cools to a rougher, grayer, duller surface. The only difference is that the tiny crystals in fondant melt above 100°F (38°C), then recrystallize to form large, jagged crystals as the fondant cools. There is no chemical difference between the fondants; they both contain the same ingredients. The difference is crystal size, and this affects how light is reflected off the surface and viewed by the eye (Figure 4.3).

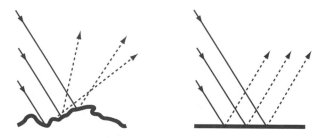

Figure 4.3   Light reflecting off a highly irregular surface appears dull or matte (**left**), while light reflecting off a smooth surface appears shiny or glossy (**right**).

Nature of the Surroundings   Two products can be identical in their chemical and physical makeup, and they can be viewed under the same light, yet if they are placed on different plates, they will likely look different. For example, white cake placed on a black plate will look whiter than the same cake placed on a stark white plate. This is an optical illusion, because it has nothing

Bakers and pastry chefs are in the business of change. Through mixing, heating, cooling, and shaping, they convert common bakeshop ingredients into an array of baked goods, desserts, chocolates, and confections. Some of these changes are physical in nature, some are chemical.

When a physical change is made, no change is made to the material itself. Water (H_2O) can be frozen to ice or evaporated to steam, but it is still water; that is, it still is composed of two parts hydrogen and one part oxygen. Likewise, chocolate can be melted, but it is still chocolate, and large sugar crystals can be pulverized to a fine powder, but it is still sugar. Finally, air can be whipped into cream, yet the cream has the same butterfat, the same milk proteins, and the same lactose. These are physical, not chemical, changes made to ingredients.

When a chemical change is made, the very nature of the material is altered; that is, the material changes into a different substance. This can happen when a substance breaks down in the presence of heat, or when one substance reacts with another. For example, when an acid like cream of tartar reacts with an alkali like baking soda, the result is—among other things—carbon dioxide and water. This is a chemical reaction, since carbon dioxide and water are different substances from cream of tartar and baking soda. Likewise, when sugar is heated on the stove and caramelizes, this is a chemical reaction. The sugar decomposes to completely new and different molecules. As with physical changes to sugar, properties have changed. The difference is that the very chemistry of the material is what caused these changes.

---

to do with any real differences in light reaching the eye. Instead, it has to do with how the brain interprets the strong contrast between white and black, making the white seem whiter still. This difference in color perception is no less real to the customer, and it is as important to consider as any other factor.

Flavor

Appearance may be the first contact customers have with food, but taste (flavor) of food is what they remember. *Taste* is the everyday word for flavor, but to the scientist, taste is only one small part of what is meant by flavor. Flavor includes the basic tastes, smell, and trigeminal effects (chemical feeling factors). These three sensations occur when food molecules (chemicals) stimulate receptors throughout the mouth and nose. Because of the chemical nature of these sensations, the three sensory systems that perceive them are called *chemical sensory systems*. Table 4.1 summarizes information about the three components of flavor and their related sensory systems. Notice that each of these components—basic tastes, smell, and trigeminal effects—is distinctly different. Each is stimulated by different chemicals. Each is detected by different receptors. Yet they occur simultaneously, and they also occur at the same time that the brain evaluates appearance and texture. No wonder sensory evaluation is a challenge, one that requires practice and concentration.

How Chemical Sensory Systems Work

For chemical sensory systems (basic tastes, smell, and trigeminal effects) to work, flavor molecules must first reach receptors that detect their presence. Basic taste molecules (sugars, acids, salts, etc.) must dissolve in saliva to reach the taste buds; odor molecules must evaporate to reach the olfactory cells; and trigeminal factors (menthol, capsaicin, ethanol, etc.) must be absorbed through the top layer of skin to reach nerve endings. Once at the site of the receptors, the flavor molecules interact with (stimulate) receptors in some way, for example by bonding to them. Because these

> **HELPFUL HINT**
>
> *When evaluating food products, be sure to chew solid foods well, and allow time for dry foods to mix with your saliva. This enables flavor molecules to "escape" and reach sensory receptors, allowing you to detect flavors that otherwise would go unnoticed.*

TABLE 4.1   THE THREE COMPONENTS OF FLAVOR

SENSORY SYSTEM	EXAMPLES	RECEPTOR	LOCATION OF RECEPTORS	NATURE OF FLAVOR CHEMICAL
Basic tastes	Sweet, salty, sour, bitter, umami	Taste (gustatory) cells on taste buds	Throughout mouth, but concentrated on tongue	Must dissolve in water (saliva)
Smell	Vanilla, butter, thousands more	Olfactory cells on the olfactory bulb	Top of nasal cavity	Must dissolve in water (nasal mucus); must be volatile
Trigeminal effects	Pungency, burn, numbing, cooling, and others	Nerve endings underneath the surface of the skin	Throughout mouth and nose (and throughout body)	Must be absorbed through skin; must be volatile to be perceived in nasal cavity

What Is a Supertaster?

Just as we are born with differences in eye color and with different heights and weights, so too are we born with different numbers of taste buds. Linda Bartoshuk, a researcher who studies taste perception, and her colleagues measured the number of taste buds on people's tongues by swabbing the tongue with blue dye and measuring the bumps (papillae) that stand out in relief on the tongue as pink spots. Because, on average, five or six taste buds are situated below each papilla, the number of taste buds on a person's tongue can be estimated from this swabbing.

Based on these measurements, Bartoshuk has devised three categories of tasters: supertasters, normal tasters, and nontasters. Most of the population (60 percent) are defined as normal tasters, while 20 percent are supertasters and another 20 percent are nontasters.

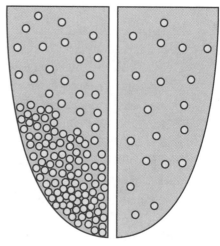

Supertasters have the highest number of taste buds, and it does seem that this affects taste perception. In particular, supertasters seem to be especially sensitive to bitterness. It is not that nontasters cannot perceive any bitterness; it is that bitterness does not seem as strong to them. Being categorized as a supertaster or a nontaster refers only to the number of taste buds on the tongue and does not reflect sensitivities to aroma. Remember, too, that taste perception is influenced by more than the number of taste buds. Experience and training, in particular, are extremely important, because the brain is doing the actual perceiving.

Yet it is important for bakers and pastry chefs to realize that we live in different taste worlds. If others seem to find flavors much weaker or much stronger than you do, you may need to flavor foods differently from your own liking.

Sourness is perceived almost instantly, as soon as food is placed in the mouth, while the perception of bitterness is often slightly delayed and tends to linger as an aftertaste. While taste perception occurs throughout the mouth, sourness often is perceived more toward the sides of the tongue, while bitterness tends to be perceived more toward the back of the throat. If a product is very bitter or very sour, however, it will be perceived throughout the mouth.

A third sensation that is sometimes confused with sourness and bitterness is *astringency*. While sourness causes the mouth to water, astringency leaves a drying sensation that makes the tongue feel rough. Sometimes astringency is described as having a mouthful of cotton balls. Astringency is not a basic taste; the drying is from tannins in foods binding with proteins in saliva. Foods that are predominantly sour include pickles, yogurt, and cultured buttermilk; those that are predominantly bitter include strong black coffee, strong dark beer, and unsweetened chocolate; those that are predominantly astringent include strong black tea and grape skins.

---

receptors are sensitive to different molecules or chemicals and their concentrations, they are called *chemoreceptors*. Once chemoreceptors are excited, electrical impulses are generated that travel through nerve cells to specific regions in the brain, where the information is processed. The organ that actually perceives is the brain, not the eyes, ears, nose, mouth, or skin.

Basic Tastes

Basic tastes include sweet, salty, sour, bitter, and umami. These sensations are perceived on the tongue and throughout the mouth when taste chemicals (sugars, high-intensity sweeteners, salts, acids, caffeine, etc.) bind to receptor taste cells or change them in some way.

Taste cells are clustered on taste buds. Taste buds contain around a hundred taste cells apiece, each taste cell most sensitive to one of the basic tastes. While taste buds are scattered throughout the mouth, most are located on the tongue, hidden in crevices beneath certain papillae, which are small bumps on the tongue.

Saliva, which is mostly water, is important to taste perception because it carries taste molecules (sugars, acids, salts, and bitter compounds) into these crevices and to the taste buds. Figure 4.4 illustrates the location of taste buds on the tongue.

It is easier to correctly identify sweetness and saltiness in foods than sourness and bitterness. Sourness and bitterness are often confused, maybe because some foods that are sour are also bitter, or maybe it is because each contains an element of unpleasantness. Properly distinguishing sourness from bitterness takes practice, but it is an important skill to learn.

While umami is not important in sweet foods, it is important in savory bakeshop items, like quiche, focaccia, and pizza. Figure 4.5 shows food ingredients high in umami.

Figure 4.5 These ingredients provide umami flavor. **Clockwise from top right:** soy sauce, dried mushrooms, dried fish (bonito flakes), dried seaweed, aged blue cheese; **center:** MSG

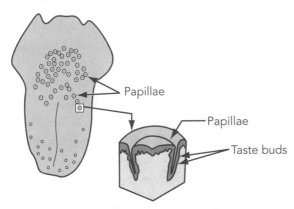

Figure 4.4 Taste buds and the perception of basic tastes

Umami, which means "tastiness" or "savoriness" in Japanese, is today recognized as the fifth basic taste. To get an idea of the taste of umami, dissolve a few crystals of monosodium glutamate (MSG) on your tongue. Better yet, spend a few hours making a rich chicken stock, or prepare a traditional Japanese miso soup using kombu (dried seaweed), bonito (dried fish), dried shiitake mushrooms, and miso (fermented soybean paste). Table 4.2 lists several food sources of umami. Japanese scientists presented the idea of umami as a basic taste in the early 1900s, when monosodium glutamate was first purified from dried seaweed. At that time, many scientists believed that umami was not a basic taste, that it was more likely a blend of other tastes, like sweetness and saltiness. Others classified it as a trigeminal effect (trigeminal effects are discussed in detail in a later section of this chapter). Most scientists today recognize umami as a basic taste, since foods rich in umami stimulate taste cells that do not respond to the other four basic tastes. Researchers are now investigating the existence of additional basic tastes. Taste cells for the perception of fattiness and of a calcium mineral taste were identified in mice, and it is possible that they exist in humans, as well.

TABLE 4.2 NATURAL SOURCES OF UMAMI FLAVOR

Aged cheeses, including Parmesan and Roquefort
Fermented fish products, including anchovy paste, Worcestershire sauce, oyster sauce, and nam pla (Thai fish sauce)
Fermented soy products, including soy sauce, miso (fermented soybean paste), black bean sauce, and hoisin sauce
Dried vegetables, including dried mushrooms, sun-dried tomatoes, and dried seaweed
Dried yeast products, including nutritional yeast, Marmite (British yeast-based spread), and Vegemite (Australian yeast-based spread)
Dried meats and fish, including Serrano ham, prosciutto, chorizo, baccalà (dried cod), and bonito (dried skipjack tuna)
Meat stocks and concentrated meat stocks or extracts, including veal stock and glace de viande (meat glaze)

Smell

Smell—also called *aroma or olfaction*—is often considered the most important of the three components of flavor. It is the most predominant, and is certainly the most complex. Humans perceive only five basic tastes, but they can smell hundreds—even thousands—of distinctly different aromas. Most aromas themselves are complex. For instance, there is no one single coffee molecule. Instead, coffee aroma consists of hundreds of separate chemicals.

To produce smell, molecules must be volatile (that is, they must evaporate and escape from food) to reach the top of the nasal cavity. This is where millions of olfactory cells (smell receptors) are located. The olfactory cells are immersed in mucus, which consists mostly of water, so aroma molecules must be at least partly water soluble as well as volatile. To reach the olfactory cells at the top of the nasal cavity, molecules travel either directly from food through the nose (*orthonasal* pathway) or up the back of the throat (*retronasal* pathway) as food is chewed and warmed in the mouth (Figure 4.6).

Smell is considered the most important component of flavor because, for many foods, most of the flavor comes from its smell. By some estimates, 80 percent of flavor is from smell. It is also through smell that products are best differentiated and described. Imagine, for example, distinguishing between strawberry and cherry juices without the sense of smell. Appearance, even taste (sweetness and sourness, in this case), would

Nothing is more frustrating than sitting down with pencil, paper, and product and smelling . . . nothing. Here are some helpful hints for increasing your sensitivity to smell.

- Move to a quiet area, to focus and concentrate.
- Take several small "bunny sniffs." This pulls flavor molecules up to the olfactory cells.
- Block your nose while you briefly chew food. Then release your nose and breathe in deeply. Your olfactory cells will be bombarded with smells as flavor molecules are pulled up the back of your throat.
- Move the food around in your mouth as you chew it well. This will help to warm and break up the food, allowing molecules to evaporate more easily to the olfactory cells.
- Taste two or more samples side by side. It is easier to describe the flavor of a product when comparing and contrasting it with another sample than it is to taste it on its own.
- Connect smell to memory. Signals from your olfactory cells travel to regions of the brain involved with memory and emotion. Use this part of your brain to help in identifying smells.
- Give your nose frequent breaks. Your olfactory cells—and brain—are easily fatigued. To ease fatigue, move away from what you are smelling and breathe fresh air. By taking breaks, you improve your sensitivity when you return to your evaluations.
- Systematically train yourself to identify smells. For example, learn to identify the spices on your spice rack. Start with a few that are very different from each other, like cinnamon, anise, and ginger. Repeat this exercise until you can clearly identify these spices by smell alone. Then try spices that have similar aromas, such as nutmeg and mace, or allspice and cloves. Once you can identify a small number of spices, increase the number evaluated at one sitting. Next try variations of one spice. For example, compare cinnamons from different regions of the world, or compare aged spices to those freshly purchased.

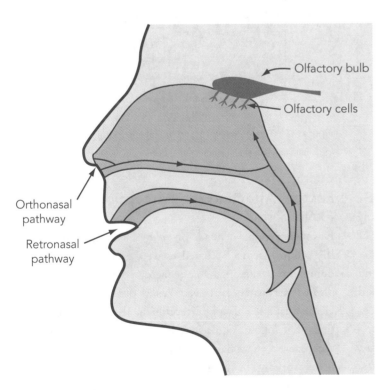

Figure 4.6   Olfactory cells and the perception of smell

hardly provide enough clues. Most of us would need the sense of smell to tell the two juices apart.

Smell is so important to overall flavor that when people have colds, they often say they cannot taste. Strictly speaking, they can still taste the basic tastes, but they cannot smell. This happens because nasal passages are blocked and odor molecules cannot reach the olfactory cells. Since smell makes up most of flavor, flavor seems lost without it.

Although the receptors for smell are at the top of the nasal cavity, it often seems as if smell takes place in the mouth, not the nose. Recall, however, that perception takes place neither in the mouth nor in the nose, but in the brain. Since the brain senses that food is in the mouth, it perceives smell as coming from there as well.

Trigeminal Effects

Trigeminal effects include the pungency of ginger, the burn of cinnamon, the cooling of mint, the heat of hot peppers, the tingling of carbon dioxide, the sting of alcohol, and more (Figure 4.7). The word *trigeminal*

Have you ever felt emotional after smelling a perfume, a flower, or a particular food? If so, then you know first-hand the connection between smell, memory, and emotion.

Aroma is perceived when odor chemicals bind to olfactory cells that are at the top of the nasal cavity. This triggers electrical signals that travel to a part of the brain called the *olfactory bulb*, where the signals converge before traveling along several pathways within the brain. The brain senses and perceives aroma in the cortex of the brain, but on their way, the signals pass the limbic system, an ancient part of the brain involved with emotion and certain types of memory. This is why smell triggers memories and feelings. That is what makes perfume so powerful, and why smells from a bakeshop are good marketing tools for selling product.

Figure 4.7 These ingredients provide trigeminal effects. **Clockwise from top:** mint leaves, black peppercorns, cinnamon sticks, jalapeño peppers, ginger root

refers to the nerve that carries the signal of these sensations from nerve endings in the mouth and nose to the brain. To make matters interesting, this same nerve carries signals of temperature and pressure. Is it any wonder, then, that some trigeminal effects are "hot" or "cooling"?

Trigeminal effects are important to bakers and pastry chefs, even if they never use the term. It is hard to name a spice where the flavor is not dependent on it. Often trigeminal effects go by other names, including *chemical feeling factors*, *pungency*, *chemical irritation*, *chemosensory irritation*, and *chemesthesis*.

Remember that trigeminal effects are part of flavor. As with basic tastes and smell, molecules in food trigger

these sensations. Table 4.3 lists some foods and the predominant molecule (the stimulus) in each food that generates a trigeminal effect. These sensations are perceived by nerve endings located just under the skin throughout the mouth and nose (Figure 4.8). To reach these nerve endings, the flavor chemical must first be absorbed through the skin. For the perception of trigeminal effects in the nose, the flavor chemical must also evaporate. Molecules that dissolve at least partially in fat tend to be absorbed more easily.

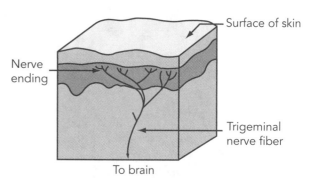

Figure 4.8 The receptors for trigeminal effects are nerve endings just beneath the surface of the skin.

Factors Affecting the Perception of Flavor

Flavor perception depends on many factors related to the product being evaluated as well as to the person doing the evaluating. These factors determine how flavor is ultimately perceived. A few of the important factors that affect flavor perception are listed in the sections that follow. While it is still unclear exactly how these factors affect flavor perception, it is thought that many work by changing the release of flavor molecules from food. If flavor molecules are released differently, flavor will be perceived differently.

TABLE 4.3 FOODS THAT EXHIBIT
A TRIGEMINAL EFFECT

FOOD PRODUCT	STIMULUS
Mint leaves	Menthol
Hot chile peppers	Capsaicin
Ginger	Gingerol
Alcoholic beverages	Ethanol
Carbonated beverages	Carbon dioxide
Black pepper	Piperine

Nature of the Ingredient Different sweeteners provide different qualities of sweetness. Aspartame, also called NutraSweet, may be sweet, but this high-intensity sweetener has a different sweetness from sucrose (table sugar). While sucrose tastes sweet almost immediately, aspartame lags in sweetness. Aspartame also lingers much longer as a sweet aftertaste, and it tastes bitter to many people.

Likewise, malic acid, one of the main acids in apples, has a different sour taste from either citric acid in lemons or acetic acid in vinegar. This is why adding lemon juice or vinegar to mild-tasting apples might not provide the same flavor impact as using apples that are naturally sour.

Product Temperature Product temperature affects flavor perception in several ways. For example, the perception of saltiness decreases as product temperatures rise. This means that warm baking powder biscuits taste less salty than the same biscuits evaluated at room temperature.

Sweetness increases as product temperatures rise. This means that if sorbet mix tastes properly sweetened at room temperature, it will not taste sweet enough when it is frozen. Aroma also typically increases as product temperatures rise. Since molecules evaporate more readily at higher temperatures, more reach the olfactory cells.

> **HELPFUL HINT**
>
> *Because flavor perception changes with product temperature, always evaluate products at their proper serving temperature. If raspberry coulis is to be served cold, evaluate it cold. If it is to be served hot, evaluate it hot.*

Product Texture and Consistency When a product is hard and firm or thick and viscous, it takes a few moments for flavor molecules to dissolve in saliva, to evaporate to the nasal cavity, or to be absorbed through the skin. This affects flavor perception, because if flavor molecules cannot reach receptors, they cannot be perceived.

> **HELPFUL HINT**
>
> *Be careful when adding gelatin to Bavarian creams and chiffon pie fillings. Not only does too much gelatin in these products produce a tough, rubbery dessert, but it also reduces the release of flavor.*

Presence of Other Flavors Add a small amount of acid to a sweet product, and it tastes less sweet. The amount of sugar has not changed, but the presence of acid decreases the perception of sweetness. Likewise, the presence of sugar decreases the perception of sourness in the mix. The same is true of sweetness and bitterness, and sweetness and many trigeminal effects. The job of the pastry chef is often to balance these different flavors and create the most pleasing combination.

Salt and sugar both affect the perception of smell, partly by changing the rate at which molecules evaporate. In general, the more salt or sugar added, the slower aroma molecules are released. The pleasant result is a longer-lasting flavor. Sometimes it takes only a small amount of salt or sugar to change and improve the aroma and overall flavor of food products.

Fat Content Fat-free foods are notorious for having an unappealing taste because fat affects flavor perception, often in unpredictable ways. Many flavor molecules dissolve in fat, so when fat is eliminated, there is a change in how quickly these molecules reach the taste buds, the olfactory cells, and the nerve endings beneath the skin. With this change comes a change in the perception of flavor. Generally, when there is no fat in a food product, flavor is released immediately but lacks staying power. A good strategy for improving flavor is to add just a small amount of fat to help the flavor linger longer. Still, low-fat foods will need additional tweaking for the flavor to be satisfying.

Texture

Texture, like flavor, is complex. Often, texture is ignored unless it is extreme or unpleasant. For example, the texture of breakfast cereal might go unnoticed until it becomes unpleasantly soggy.

The main way texture is evaluated is by touch: how the food feels against the skin, how it feels as it melts from the heat of the mouth, and how it responds to

What Does Sound Tell Us about Crispness?

Sound is just as important as touch (response to pressure) when it comes to evaluating the crispness of foods. Researchers measure the crispness and crunch of food products by setting microphones and recorders to the jaw and measuring the pitch, frequency, and intensity of sound as a person eats crispy or crunchy foods. The louder the sound, the higher-pitched the sound, and the more frequent the sound, the crispier the food. Foods with lower-pitched sounds are more likely described as crunchy.

touch as it is squeezed, bitten, and chewed. Although this is the main way texture is evaluated, other senses come into play. The first—although not necessarily the most accurate—information about texture is based on appearance. A visual evaluation of texture provides the first clues to how soft, firm, gritty, or smooth a product will feel when it is tasted. Sound is important to texture, as well. Tortilla chips and peanut brittle are crunchy because of the sound (or vibration) of the crunch, while thin potato chips and fresh apples are crisp.

As with flavor, an experienced baker or pastry chef uses a full vocabulary to completely describe the texture of food. Table 4.4 lists common food texture terms, with examples. Notice that a cookie can be hard or soft, tough or tender, crumbly or chewy, moist or dry, oily or waxy, and more. Sometimes, one textural characteristic predominates, but for professionals, it is important to practice analyzing food as completely as possible.

Texture terms that refer specifically to how food feels against the inside of the mouth are sometimes called *mouthfeel* terms. Mouthfeel terms include smoothness, creaminess, oiliness, and waxiness.

TABLE 4.4 TEXTURE TERMS FOR DESCRIBING FOOD PRODUCTS

QUESTION	TERM	EXAMPLE
How easily is it pressed or squeezed?	Soft	Fresh Wonder Bread
	Firm; hard	Stale Wonder Bread
How easily can I bite through it?	Tender	Properly mixed pie crust
	Tough	Overmixed pie crust
Does it hold together?	Chewy (hard; holds together)	Tootsie Roll
	Gummy (soft; holds together)	Chewing gum
	Crumbly, short, mealy (tender; breaks apart)	Cornbread
	Brittle (hard; breaks apart)	Peanut brittle
How quickly does it flow?	Thin	Water
	Thick	Molasses
Does it bounce back?	Plastic (solid; doesn't bounce back)	Shortening
	Springy (bounces back)	Jell-O
	Spongy (tough, springy, airy)	Cake made with extra eggs
How does it feel against the soft tissues of the mouth?	Smooth (no particles)	Creamy peanut butter
	Creamy (thick and smooth)	Vanilla custard sauce
	Gritty (small particles)	Curdled custard sauce; flesh of certain pears, especially the Seckel or Clapp varieties
	Chalky (gritty and dry)	High-protein bars
	Coarse (large particles)	Coarse sugar
	Pulpy	Orange juice
What shape are the particles?	Flaky (long, flat layers)	Flaky pie crust
Do they run in the same direction?	Fibrous (long, rope-like)	Celery; rhubarb
How much liquid is present?	Dry	Dry cereal
	Moist	Chewy brownies
	Watery	Water
Is the fat liquid or solid?	Oily (thin)	Oil
	Greasy (thick; coats mouth)	Fat-soaked doughnut
	Waxy (firm or solid)	Wax; puff pastry shortening
How much air is present?	Light, airy	Whipped egg white
	Foamy (light, airy, liquidy)	Steamed milk
	Heavy, dense	Chewy brownies

Questions for Review

1 Why is it that humans often "eat with their eyes"?

2 What three things can happen to light waves as they hit an object? Which two represent light that we see?

3 Why do we perceive limes as green?

4 List the three main factors that affect appearance.

5 Explain why the appearance of an object could be different if it is viewed under different lighting.

6 State which of the following are physical ways of changing the appearance of baked goods, and which are chemical in nature: undermixing cake batter, using bleached flour instead of unbleached, extending bake time by 5 minutes.

7 What causes fondant to dull when it is heated too high?

8 State which of the following are physical ways of aerating baked goods, and which are chemical in nature: whipping egg whites, adding baking powder (contains baking soda and acids), creaming shortening, sifting dry ingredients.

9 Which will appear darker in color: chocolate cake properly mixed, or chocolate cake undermixed? Explain.

10 Explain and provide an example of how a difference in the color of the plate or of sauce on the plate could explain why one piece of a white cake appears whiter than another.

11 What are the three components of flavor? Which receptor senses each component, and where is each receptor located?

12 Why is saliva necessary for the perception of the basic tastes?

13 What is meant by "astringency"? Name two foods that are perceived as astringent.

14 Which is generally considered the most important component of flavor, and why?

15 Provide four helpful hints to follow when evaluating aroma.

16 Why does warm food typically have a stronger flavor than cold food?

17 Why is it difficult to taste when you have a cold?

18 Name four products that have trigeminal effects. Name two that do not.

19 What are other names for trigeminal effects?

20 How does the perception of sweetness change when food is served colder than usual?

21 How does the perception of saltiness change when food is served colder than usual?

22 What happens to the flavor of Bavarian cream when a little extra gelatin is added to firm it up a bit?

23 Name two foods for which sound is particularly important in the perception of texture. Name two foods for which sound is not important.

24 What is meant by "mouthfeel"?

Questions for Discussion

1   Describe how the chemical sensory system works, using the perception of the basic tastes as an example.

2   For each of the five basic tastes, provide two or more examples of food ingredients that are perceived as high in each.

3   As a professional chef, why might it be important to know if you are a supertaster or a nontaster?

Exercises and Experiments

① Exercise: Are You A Supertaster?

Using regular (water-soluble) food-grade blue food coloring, a cotton swab, and a magnifying mirror, apply food coloring to the front half-inch of your tongue. Rinse your mouth with water to remove excess food coloring (spit out or swallow the rinse water). Look in the mirror at the appearance of the tip of your tongue. If necessary, use a flashlight to better see details. Is your tongue mostly blue with a few pink spots, or is it mostly pink with very little blue? The pink spots are the fungiform papillae on your tongue. Fungiform papillae are the only papillae on the front of the tongue where taste buds reside. The smaller bumps on your tongue that dye blue are also papillae, but they are not associated with taste buds. The more pink papillae on your tongue, the more taste buds there are.

To estimate the number of taste buds in a given area on your tongue, place a paper reinforcement sticker on the tip of your tongue or use a hole puncher to punch a hole in a small piece of paper and place the paper on the tip of your tongue. Count the number of pink papillae within the hole. On average, nontasters have fewer than fifteen fungiform papillae in this area; normal tasters have from fifteen to thirty; supertasters have over thirty pink papillae crowded into this small space. Compare the appearance of your tongue with those of your classmates. Can you predict who might be a supertaster and who might be a nontaster?

② Exercise: Ice Cream Storage and Texture

Compare the texture of properly stored (or freshly made) ice cream and ice cream that has been poorly stored (same flavor ice cream, but thawed slightly and refrozen one or more times over the course of several days). Record your evaluations by filling in the Results Table, which follows. Use information from Table 4.4 to help you with texture terms.

RESULTS TABLE A COMPARISON OF THE TEXTURE OF PROPERLY AND IMPROPERLY STORED ICE CREAM

ICE CREAM SAMPLE	VISUAL EVALUATION OF SMOOTHNESS (SCALE OF 1–5, 1 BEING NOT VERY SMOOTH; ICY)	SOFTNESS WHEN SCOOPED (SCALE OF 1–5, 1 BEING SOFT, EASY TO SCOOP)	CREAMINESS WHEN EATEN (SCALE OF 1–5, 1 BEING NOT VERY SMOOTH AND CREAMY; ICY)	ADDITIONAL COMMENTS
Properly stored				
Improperly stored				

Summarize in one sentence the overall texture differences in the ice cream samples:

_____

_____

_____

③ Exercise: Texture

Compare the texture of two products of your choice. Examples include butter and margarine, fresh and stale bread, two different chocolate couvertures, two different types of cake, two pie fillings, two types of dried fruit, ginger snaps and marshmallows, and so forth. Record the names of the two products in the row headings in the following blank Results Table. Decide on the proper sensory characteristics to evaluate and write these in the column headings of the Results Table. Also write a title for your Results Table. Use information from Table 4.4 to help you with texture terms.

RESULTS TABLE _____

PRODUCT				

Summarize in one sentence the overall texture differences between your two samples.

_____

_____

_____

❹ Experiment: Apple Juice Flavor

Apple juice is a relatively mild-tasting juice, which will be made even milder by diluting with water. Next, ingredients will be added to the diluted juice for you to taste. Some samples might taste very strong to you, others might be difficult for you to perceive. This varies from person to person since we live in different taste worlds. If necessary, make up a stronger sample of any ingredient that you cannot taste.

Work slowly through this experiment. You will find that your ability to identify and describe differences between samples will progress as you proceed. Taste samples several times, going back and forth from one to the next as many times as you need.

While diluted apple juice is used to complete this experiment, as you progress through it, think about how the lessons learned using apple juice can be applied to real pastry products such as pie fillings, coulis, ice cream, even chocolate brownies and cheesecake.

Objectives

- Identify and describe differences between sourness, astringency, and bitterness
- Demonstrate how sugar affects perception of sourness
- Demonstrate how acid affects perception of sweetness
- Demonstrate the importance of basic tastes and astringency in overall flavor perception
- Create a good-tasting apple beverage that has a pleasing balance of sweetness, sourness, and astringency

Products Prepared

Diluted apple juice with
- No additions (control product)
- Sugar
- Acid
- Tannin powder
- Caffeine
- Sugar and acid
- Other (sugar and tannin powder, sugar and caffeine, different acid or different sugar, etc.)
- Your choice of additions

Materials and Equipment

- Apple juice, 6 quarts (6 liters) or more
- Water, 2 quarts (2 liters), bottled or tap
- Large bowl or pan, to hold 11 quarts (liters)
- Pitchers, to hold 1 quart (1 liter) of liquid, one per test product
- Scale
- Measuring spoons
- Sugar, regular granulated
- Malic or other acid (citric acid, tartaric acid, or cream of tartar)
- Tannin powder (from wine-making store). If unavailable, use alum (sometimes found in supermarkets, with spices or canning supplies).
- Caffeine tablets, 200 mg, any brand, such as Vivarin or NoDoz Maximum Strength
- Sample tasting cups (1 fl. oz./30 ml soufflé cups or larger)
- Plain unsalted crackers

Procedure

1 Set aside 1 quart (1 liter) apple juice.

2 Dilute 5 quarts (5 liters) apple juice by adding 2 quarts (2 liters) water to it in a large pan or bowl. Add more water if apple juice is very sweet or strong tasting. Set aside 1 quart (1 liter) and label sample "diluted apple juice."

3 Measure out 1 quart (1 liter) diluted apple juice into each of 5 separate containers and prepare samples as described below. (You will have some excess diluted juice.) *Note:* for very small quantities of ingredients, measurements are given in both weight and volumetric measurements. Use measuring spoons with these ingredients, if necessary.

- Add 1 ounce (30 grams) granulated sugar to 1 quart (1 liter) diluted apple juice. Label sample "with sugar."
- Add 0.15 ounce or 1 teaspoon (4 grams or 5 milliliters) malic acid to 1 quart (1 liter) diluted apple juice. Label sample "with acid."
- Add 0.1 ounce or ½ teaspoon (2.5 grams or 2.5 milliliters) tannin powder to 1 quart (1 liter) diluted apple juice. Label sample "with tannin."
- Add 4 caffeine tablets, finely crushed, to 1 quart (1 liter) diluted apple juice. Label sample "with caffeine." *Note:* this is about the same amount of caffeine as in coffee.
- Add 1 ounce (30 grams) granulated sugar and 0.15 ounce or 1 teaspoon (4 grams or 5 milliliters) malic acid to 1 quart (1 liter) diluted apple juice. Label sample "with sugar and acid."

4 Set samples aside at room temperature for about 30 minutes, to allow powders to dissolve completely. Caffeine, in particular, needs time to dissolve.

Results

1 Evaluate the flavor of diluted apple juice samples with added acid, tannin, and caffeine and record results in Results Table 1. Be sure to taste each in turn against the control product (diluted apple juice) and against each other. Block your nose, to focus your attention on sensations throughout the mouth, and cleanse your palate between samples using water and unsalted crackers. Go back and retaste samples as often as needed, and focus on the following:

- What is perceived (puckering, salivating, drying, general unpleasantness, etc.) other than sweetness and aroma.
- When (how quickly) sensation is perceived (immediately, slowly, as an aftertaste, etc.).
- Name other foods with this sensation (unsweetened chocolate, Sour Patch Kids candy, strong black tea, etc.).

RESULTS TABLE 1 SOURNESS, BITTERNESS, AND ASTRINGENCY IN APPLE JUICE

APPLE JUICE	WHAT IS PERCEIVED	WHEN SENSATION IS PERCEIVED	FOODS WITH SIMILAR SENSATION	ADDITIONAL COMMENTS
Diluted				
Diluted, with acid				
Diluted, with tannin				
Diluted, with caffeine				

2 Evaluate the flavor of diluted apple juice samples with added sugar, added acid, and added sugar and acid and record evaluations in Results Table 2, which follows.

a Be sure to compare each in turn with the control product (diluted apple juice, rated as 3 on a scale of 1 to 5) and with each other. Cleanse your palate between samples using water and unsalted crackers. Go back and retaste samples as often as needed, and evaluate the following:
   - Fullness of flavor (a full flavor is one that does not taste watered down or thin)
   - Sweetness
   - Sourness

b Next, compare each of these products with *undiluted* apple juice, to evaluate for acceptability. Record your results in Results Table 2, as you complete the following:
   - Rate each sample as acceptable or unacceptable, and describe what makes it acceptable or unacceptable.
   - Add any additional comments, as necessary.

c Reevaluate the undiluted apple juice, and record results in bottom row of Results Table 2. Be as complete as you can in your evaluation of overall fullness of flavor, sweetness, and sourness. Also evaluate for astringency. If necessary, retaste the diluted apple juice with added tannin powder, if you forget what astringency tastes like.

RESULTS TABLE 2 HOW A COMBINATION OF INGREDIENTS AFFECTS FLAVOR PERCEPTION IN APPLE JUICE

APPLE JUICE	FULLNESS OF FLAVOR (SCALE OF 1–5, 1 BEING VERY LOW)	SWEETNESS (SCALE OF 1–5, 1 BEING VERY LOW)	SOURNESS (SCALE OF 1–5, 1 BEING VERY LOW)	OVERALL ACCEPTABILITY	ADDITIONAL COMMENTS
Diluted apple juice (control product)	3	3	3		
With sugar					
With acid					
With sugar and acid					
Undiluted apple juice					

3 Based on your evaluations above, combine the diluted juice samples or add additional ingredients to either match the undiluted apple juice as closely as possible, or to create a good-tasting apple beverage that balances sweetness, sourness, and astringency.

- Keep track of the samples combined and ingredients added. Label each sample and list them in the first column of Results Table 3.
- Describe the flavor and overall acceptability of each of your apple beverages compared with undiluted apple juice. Record in next two columns in Results Table 3.
- Add any additional comments, as necessary.

APPLE BEVERAGE	DESCRIPTION OF APPLE BEVERAGE FLAVOR	OVERALL ACCEPTABILITY (COMPARED WITH UNDILUTED APPLE JUICE)	ADDITIONAL COMMENTS

Sources of Error

List any sources of error that might make it difficult to draw the proper conclusions from your experiment. Consider, in particular, whether samples were all at the same temperature when evaluated; whether powdered ingredients were fully dissolved; whether a large number of samples made evaluations difficult or confusing for you.

_____
_____
_____

State what you could do differently next time to minimize or eliminate each source of error.

_____
_____
_____

Conclusions

Select one from the choices in **bold** or fill in the blanks.

1 One difference between sourness and bitterness is that **sourness/bitterness** causes you to salivate. Another difference is that **sourness/bitterness** lingers much longer as an aftertaste. An example of a food product that is sour is _____. An example of a food product that is bitter is_____.

2 One difference between sourness and astringency is that **sourness/astringency** makes your mouth dry and your tongue feel rough. An example of a food product that is astringent is _____.

3 Sugar **increased/decreased/did not change** the sourness of the diluted apple juice.

4 Acid **increased/decreased/did not change** the sweetness of the diluted apple juice.

5 Sugar **increased/decreased** the fullness of flavor of the diluted apple juice. What else affected fullness of flavor?

_____

_____

_____

6 Other noticeable differences between the products were as follows:

_____

_____

_____

7 Describe the strategy you used to create a pleasing apple beverage.

_____

_____

_____

8 You make a strawberry coulis (fruit sauce) from fresh pureed strawberries. You taste the coulis and find that it lacks a full, rich, fruity flavor. Based on the results of this experiment, what can you add to improve its flavor?

_____

_____

_____

Wheat Flour

Chapter Objectives

1 Describe the makeup of the wheat kernel and its endosperm.

2 Describe common wheat flour additives and treatments.

3 Classify common flours and other wheat products used in bakeshops and describe their characteristics and uses.

4 List and describe the functions of wheat flour.

5 Describe how to best store and handle wheat flour.

Introduction

Wheat is a cereal grain. Other cereal grains include corn (maize), oats, rice, and rye. Widespread consumption of cereal grains began in the Middle East about 10,000 years ago, when agriculture first began. It was then that wheat was first planted and cultivated.

Today, thousands of different wheat varieties are grown throughout the world. While certain varieties will grow within the Arctic Circle and others near the equator in the Andes mountains, most varieties of wheat require moderate growing conditions. Several locations in North America have ideal conditions for growing wheat, including the midwestern United States and the southern prairie region of Canada. Other major wheat-growing regions include China (where more wheat is grown than in any other country in the world), India, the European Union, and Russia.

Wheat is the most popular cereal grain for use in baked goods. Its popularity stems mainly from the gluten that forms when flour is mixed with water. Without gluten, raised bread is hard to imagine. Wheat is also preferred because of its mild, nutty flavor. Both factors, no doubt, contribute to wheat being the most widely grown cereal grain in the world.

The Wheat Kernel

Wheat kernels are the seeds of the wheat plant, and they are the part of the plant that is milled into flour. Since cereal grains are in the grass family, wheat kernels can be thought of as a type of grass seed. In fact, when a field of wheat starts to grow, it looks like lawn grass.

Wheat kernels, also called *wheat grains*, have three main parts: the endosperm, the germ, and the bran (Figure 5.1). While whole wheat flour contains all three parts of the kernel, white flour is milled from the endosperm. Whole wheat flour is considered a *whole grain product* only when it contains all three parts of the wheat kernel in the same proportions in which they occur in the wheat kernel. In the United States, whole wheat flour is always a whole grain.

The *endosperm* makes up the bulk of the wheat kernel, over 80 percent of it. It is the whitest part, partly because it contains mostly starch. In fact, the endosperm is close

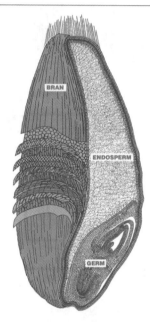

Figure 5.1 Longitudinal section of a grain of wheat

More on Whole Grain Products

Whole grains consist of the entire grain or kernel. If the kernel is cracked, crushed, flaked, or ground, it still must have the same proportions of bran, germ, and endosperm as the original grain to be called whole grain.

Dark-colored products are not necessarily whole grain. Often molasses or caramel coloring is added to baked goods to give them a heartier look. Nor do names of products like "seven-grain bread," "stone-ground," or "organic" guarantee that the product is whole grain.

According to the 2005 Dietary Guidelines for Americans, consuming three or more 1-ounce servings (or the equivalent) of whole grains per day can reduce the risk of several chronic diseases and may help with weight maintenance. Based on recent surveys, only about 10 percent of Americans currently meet this guideline.

Dietary fiber is plant matter that humans cannot digest. It is classified as either soluble or insoluble. Soluble fiber, when placed in water, absorbs the water, thickening or forming a gel. Insoluble fiber will either sink or float in water, but it remains essentially unchanged because it does not absorb water. Just because it is not digested does not mean that dietary fiber is not important in the diet. Both soluble and insoluble dietary fibers are essential for good health, each serving different functions in the body. Insoluble fiber, for example, improves intestinal health and is thought to reduce the risks of certain cancers. Soluble fiber lowers blood cholesterol and may reduce the risk of heart disease. The current recommendation is for healthy North Americans to increase their consumption of dietary fiber to 20–35 grams per day. For many, this means doubling their current intake.

Fiber-rich foods do not necessarily have a fibrous texture. Meats can be fibrous, for example, but those fibers consist of fully digestible proteins and are not dietary fiber. Even fibrous vegetables, like celery, are not necessarily higher in dietary fiber than less fibrous ones. Good sources of fiber, both soluble and insoluble, include most fruits, vegetables, whole grain cereals, nuts and seeds, dried beans, and cocoa powder.

---

to three-quarters starch. The starch is tightly packed in starch granules, which are embedded in chunks of protein. Two important proteins in the endosperm of wheat kernels are the gluten-forming proteins, *glutenin* and *gliadin*. When flour is mixed with water, glutenin and gliadin form a network of gluten, which is important in the structure of baked goods. In fact, wheat is the only common cereal grain that contains sufficient glutenin and gliadin for the formation of good-quality gluten for bread making. Gluten and its unique properties are described in more detail in Chapter 7.

The *germ* is the embryo of the wheat plant. Given the right conditions, the germ sprouts (germinates) and grows into a new plant (Figure 5.2). Wheat germ makes up only a very small part of the wheat kernel (about 2.5 percent), but it is high in protein (about 25 percent protein), fat, B vitamins, vitamin E, and minerals. These nutrients are important to the germ as it sprouts. While germ protein does not form gluten, from a nutritional standpoint, it is of a high quality.

Wheat germ can be purchased and added to baked goods. When bakers add wheat germ to baked goods, it is usually because of the nutritional value of its protein, vitamins, and minerals. Wheat germ is typically sold toasted. The toasting adds a nutty flavor to the wheat germ. It also destroys the enzymes called *lipases* present in wheat germ that break down oils and cause them to oxidize. Because wheat germ is high in polyunsaturated oils that oxidize easily, it is best stored under refrigeration. It does not contain gluten-forming proteins, so wheat germ will not contribute to structure in baked goods.

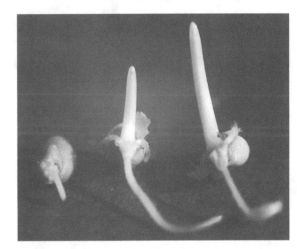

Figure 5.2   Germinating wheat kernel

The *bran* is the protective outer covering of the wheat kernel. It is usually much darker in color than the endosperm, although white wheat, which has a light bran color, is also available. In either case, bran is high in dietary fiber. In fact, the bran is about 42 percent dietary fiber, most of it classified as insoluble fiber. Bran also contains a good amount of protein (about 15 percent), fat, B vitamins, and minerals. As with wheat germ, bran proteins do not form gluten; in fact, you will see later in this chapter that wheat germ and bran actually interfere with gluten development.

Wheat bran can be purchased as small flakes and added to baked goods. The soluble fiber in bran softens and swells in the presence of water, acting as a drier. Additionally, bran particles contribute a dark, rustic appearance, a distinct nutty flavor, and valuable dietary fiber to baked goods.

Makeup of Flour

White flour—the ground endosperm—contains mostly starch, yet other components naturally present in white flour affect its properties. The main components in white flour are listed in the paragraphs that follow, with approximate percentages provided in parentheses. Of these, the two key components are starch and protein. The graph in Figure 5.3 illustrates the major components in flour and the relative amounts of each in typical bread flour.

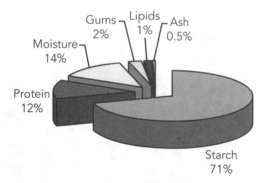

Figure 5.3 The makeup of bread flour

Starch makes up the bulk of flour (68–76 percent). Even bread flour, considered low in starch, contains more starch than all other components combined. Starch is present in flour as small grains or *granules*. Some starch granules are damaged during the milling process or when flour is stored under damp conditions. When this happens, starch is more easily broken down by the enzyme amylase into sugars (glucose and maltose) that are readily fermented by yeast. The amount of sugar naturally present in flour (less than 0.5 percent) is rarely high enough for proper yeast fermentation, which is why most yeast dough formulas include at least some sugar or a source of amylase.

Chunks of *protein* (6–18 percent) act as the cement that holds starch granules in place within the endosperm. Together, glutenin and gliadin, the gluten-forming proteins, make up about 80 percent of the proteins in the endosperm. Other proteins in white flour include enzymes such as amylase, protease, and lipase.

Moisture in flour typically ranges from 11–14 percent. When moisture content rises above 14 percent, flour is susceptible to fungus and mold growth, flavor changes, enzyme activity, and insect infestation. For these reasons, flour must be stored properly covered and in a cool, dry place.

Other carbohydrates in flour besides starch include gums (2–3 percent), primarily *pentosans*. It is easy to overlook the importance of pentosan gums in white flour because they are present at relatively low levels. But they have at least one important function in flour. Because they typically absorb ten or more times their weight in water, a small amount of pentosan gums makes a large contribution to the water absorption value of flour. Pentosans also increase the viscosity or consistency of batters and doughs, which helps hold in air and gas bubbles for leavening. The small amount of pentosans present in wheat flour also appears to interact with gluten, improving its strength and structure. Larger amounts of pentosans have the opposite effect and result in lower volume in baked goods. Pentosan gums are a source of dietary fiber, primarily soluble dietary fiber.

Only a small amount (1–1.5 percent) of *lipids*—oil and emulsifiers—are present in white flour. Some of these lipids, specifically the emulsifiers, are necessary for proper gluten development. Yet because of its nature, wheat oil oxidizes easily and turns rancid, limiting the shelf life of flour. While not dangerous or unsafe, stale flour has a distinct cardboard flavor that is best avoided by storing flour properly and using it promptly.

Ash is composed of inorganic matter (mineral salts) naturally present in wheat kernels, primarily in the bran. It includes iron, copper, potassium, sodium, and zinc. Properly milled white flour is relatively low in ash (less than 0.6 percent) and therefore low in valuable minerals to the diet. Higher amounts of ash could mean that the flour contains too much of the bran and therefore was not properly milled. Ash is measured in flour and grain samples by burning the samples at very high temperatures—over 1,000°F (540°C)—and weighing the remains.

Carotenoid pigments are present in white flour in extremely low amounts (one to four parts per million). They provide the creamy off-white color to unbleached flour. The carotenoid pigments in white flour (xanthophylls) are in the same family as beta-carotene, the orange pigment in carrots.

Some bread labels include "wheat flour" as an ingredient. Wheat flour is not the same as whole wheat flour, although the names are similar. In the United States, whole wheat flour is a whole grain, milled from the whole wheat kernel. Wheat flour is simply another name for white flour, milled from the endosperm. It is called *wheat flour* to distinguish it from rye flour, corn flour, oat flour, or rice flour. This is helpful information for those with allergies to wheat products, but it can mislead consumers into thinking that wheat flour contains all the health benefits of whole wheat

Likewise, wheat bread is not the same as 100 percent whole wheat bread. Wheat bread typically has wheat (white) flour as its main ingredient. A typical wheat bread contains a mixture of 60–75 percent white flour and only 25–40 percent whole wheat flour. A similar bread, called *brown bread*, is sold in the UK. A typical wheat bread label, with ingredients listed in descending order, reads as follows:

INGREDIENTS: ENRICHED WHEAT FLOUR (WHEAT FLOUR, MALTED BARLEY FLOUR, NIACIN, FERROUS SULFATE, THIAMIN MONONITRATE, RIBOFLAVIN, FOLIC ACID), WATER, HIGH FRUCTOSE CORN SYRUP, WHOLE WHEAT FLOUR, YEAST. CONTAINS 2% OR LESS OF EACH OF THE FOLLOWING: VITAL WHEAT GLUTEN, SALT, SOYBEAN OIL, SODIUM STEAROYL LACTYLATE, CARAMEL COLOR.

Classifying Wheat

Bakers generally classify wheat by the hardness of the kernel; that is, by whether the kernel feels *hard* or *soft* to the touch. Hard wheat kernels feel harder than soft ones because the protein in these kernels forms large, hard chunks that hold tightly to the starch granules. Hard wheat kernels are generally high in protein; soft wheat kernels are generally low in protein. As the amount of protein in flour increases, the amount of starch decreases. Hard wheat kernels typically are higher in carotenoids than soft wheat kernels and higher in water-grabbing pentosans and damaged starch granules.

Flours milled from hard wheat kernels are creamy or creamy white in color. They feel slightly gritty and granular because the hardness of the kernels makes them difficult to mill into a fine powder. This coarseness means that hard wheat flours do not pack easily when squeezed and are good for dusting the bench or workspace. Typically, hard wheat flours form "high-quality" (strong) gluten, meaning gluten that stretches well and forms strong, cohesive films that retain gases during fermentation and baking. Because they form strong gluten, hard wheat flours are considered *strong flours*. Strong flours usually are the best driers, meaning that they absorb more water than weak flours. Strong flours require a longer mixing time to fully develop gluten, but they are also more tolerant of overmixing. Strong flours are typically used in yeast-raised products such as breads, rolls, and bagels. They are also used in

While the most common way to classify wheat is to consider the hardness of the kernel, there are other ways. Wheat can be classified by its botanical species, by the time of year it is planted or grown, or by the color of the kernel. In fact, the six major classes of wheat in the United States are described as hard red winter, soft red winter, hard red spring, hard white, soft white, and durum. Except for durum wheat (*Triticum durum*), most wheats milled into flour in North America are varieties of so-called common wheat (*Triticum aestivum*).

The quality of flour within any of the categories can vary greatly. In particular, geographic, climatic, and soil variations affect the composition and quality of wheat. That is why millers typically blend flours from different regions to provide consistent product to their customers, year after year.

making laminated products such as croissants, puff pastry, and Danish.

Flours milled from soft wheat kernels are whiter in color and finer to the touch than hard wheat flours. Because they are so fine, soft wheat flours tend to pack when squeezed and do not flow or dust the bench easily. Soft wheat flours typically form weak gluten that tears easily, which is why they are sometimes called *weak flours*. Weak flours absorb less water than strong flours because they are lower in protein, in pentosan gums, and in broken starch granules. Weak flours are not necessarily less desirable than strong flours. They produce more tender products, and this is desirable for cakes, cookies, crackers, and pastries.

Particle Size

Wheat and other cereal grains can be milled into many different forms, from very fine flour to cracked or whole kernels (Figure 5.4). Small, fine particles absorb water quickly. Large particles such as whole and cracked kernels and coarse meals and flakes often require overnight soaking or gentle heating in liquid before use to allow for proper water absorption and softening. Such a mix of softened grains swollen with water is typically referred to by bread bakers as a *soaker*.

There is evidence that larger particles, such as whole kernels, are absorbed and digested by the body more slowly than fine flours. This is beneficial for diabetics and for others trying to control their blood sugar levels.

Flours

Flours by definition are grains milled to a relatively fine granulation size. Not all flours have the same granulation, though. For example, soft wheat flours are typically ground finer than hard wheat flours because the softness of their kernels makes them easier to mill.

Granular Products

Granular products are coarser than flour. Like flour, they can be whole grain if milled from the whole kernel, or not, if milled from the endosperm. Examples of granular wheat products include farina and semolina. *Farina* is coarsely ground from the endosperm of hard red wheat. Cream of Wheat is an example of a brand of farina. Durum semolina is coarsely ground from the endosperm of durum wheat. *Semolina* is from the Italian for farina. Because durum semolina is yellow in color, it can be easily mistaken for cornmeal.

Meals and grits are available in a variety of sizes, from coarse to fine, with each providing a slightly different texture to baked goods. These terms are more commonly applied to grain products other than wheat, such as corn or rice.

Cracked Kernels

Cracked kernels are whole kernels that have been cracked or cut into fragments. Examples of cracked kernels include cracked wheat or rolled wheat flakes.

Whole Kernels

Grains can be purchased as whole kernels. When whole wheat kernels are purchased, they are generally called *wheat berries*. Whole kernels must be soaked first to soften. They add a contrasting texture and visual appeal to bread.

Figure 5.4 Each of these products is a whole grain. **Left top:** whole wheat pastry flour; **bottom:** regular whole wheat flour. **Right, top to bottom:** cracked wheat, wheat kernels (berries), rolled wheat

Flour and Dough Additives and Treatments

Millers often add small amounts of additives to flour. Some of these additives are also available to bakers for mixing directly into dough. The types and amounts of additives that are allowed are strictly regulated by government agencies. By law, millers must label flour with the additives it contains.

There are several different types of flour additives. Some improve the nutrient content of flour and are required by law. Others improve dough handling or baking properties, or whiten the color of flour. A few of the main flour additives are described in the following sections.

Vitamins and Minerals

Enriched flour is white flour that has iron and B vitamins added in amounts that equal or exceed those in whole wheat flour. Four B vitamins are added to enriched flour: thiamin, riboflavin, niacin, and folic acid. Certain other vitamins and minerals are allowed as optional additives. Essentially all baked goods and pasta products made from white flour in North America are enriched.

Natural Aging

Natural aging occurs when freshly milled "green" flour is exposed to air for several weeks or more. By naturally aging flour, air is added to it. Air is a powerful additive, causing two main changes. First, it whitens the flour. Second, it strengthens the gluten that forms from flour.

Actually, the active ingredient in air is oxygen, which is considered an oxidizing agent. Oxygen oxidizes the carotenoid pigments in flour, changing their chemical structure so that they absorb less light. This makes the flour appear whiter and brighter. Oxygen also oxidizes gluten-forming proteins, allowing them to form stronger gluten. Yeast doughs made from aged flour are easier to handle than those made from green flour, because doughs with stronger gluten are less sticky and less likely to tear when stretched. The ability to stretch without tearing is especially important when gases expand during proofing and baking, resulting in a higher volume and finer crumb in the baked bread.

Natural aging has a few disadvantages. First, it requires time, often several weeks or months. During this time, the flour takes up valuable silo space and is not paying the bills. Besides, the longer flour sits in silos, the more likely it will support mold growth or become infested with insects or rodents. Natural aging also can be inconsistent, and it is not as effective as many chemical bleaching and maturing agents. However, consumers often prefer flours that have been aged naturally over those that contain bleaching and maturing agents. Naturally aged flours are often labeled "unbleached."

Why Is White Flour Enriched?

The milling process involves removing bran and germ from the endosperm. When this is done, vitamins and minerals, dietary fiber, and protein and fat from the bran and germ are removed. It is likely that other important, unidentified nutrients are also removed. Flour enrichment replaces certain vitamins and minerals that are lost from milling. It does not replace the dietary fiber in the bran, the high-quality protein in the germ, or other potentially important yet unidentified nutrients in the bran and germ.

Flour enrichment began in the United States in the early 1940s after government surveys found that a high incidence of disease was caused by certain vitamin and mineral deficiencies. The enforced enrichment of white flour virtually eliminated two of these diseases, beriberi and pellagra.

The U.S. and Canadian governments periodically reevaluate the nutritional needs of North Americans. In the late 1990s, folic acid was added to the list of required vitamins and minerals added to enriched flour. Folic acid prevents certain birth defects, including spina bifida, and can also reduce the risk of coronary heart disease.

Bleaching and Maturing Agents

Maturing agents are additives that change the baking properties of flours. Maturing agents are added to flour by the miller and are found in many dough conditioners that can be added by the baker.

Some maturing agents strengthen gluten, while others weaken it. Because the same term—*maturing agent*—is used to describe additives that have completely opposite functions, it can be confusing. In this text, maturing agents that strengthen gluten, such as potassium bromate and ascorbic acid, will be called *maturing agents that strengthen*, while those that do not will be called *maturing agents that weaken*. In either case, only very small amounts (parts per million) of maturing agents are necessary to cause the desired changes.

One maturing agent that strengthens is potassium bromate. When it is added to flour, the flour is said to be bromated. Potassium bromate has been in use since the early 1900s, and it is the standard against which all other maturing agents are judged. Despite this, potassium bromate is no longer allowed as a flour additive in Canada or in Europe. Potassium bromate is considered a carcinogen because it has been shown to cause cancer in laboratory animals. While still approved for use in the United States, its use is slowly diminishing, and much lower levels are added to flour today than previously. In California, products containing potassium bromate must carry a warning label.

Many companies are searching for bromate replacers to strengthen their flour. While several bromate replacers are available, *ascorbic acid* is one of the most popular. Another name for ascorbic acid is vitamin C. While ascorbic acid is not as effective as potassium bromate and works a little differently, its use is increasing because of concerns over the safety of potassium bromate.

Bleaching agents whiten carotenoids in flour. The most common bleaching agent is benzoyl peroxide. *Benzoyl peroxide* is used in all types of flour because it is extremely effective at whitening and because it contributes no maturing effects. It simply bleaches. Benzoyl peroxide is commonly used to bleach bread, high-gluten, all-purpose, cake, and pastry flours.

Chlorine is a bleaching agent that is used almost exclusively on cake flour. It was introduced in the 1930s and continues to be used in a few countries including the United States, Canada, Australia, New Zealand, and South Africa. Besides whitening, chlorine improves the baking properties of soft wheat flour. It does this mainly by oxidizing starch in flour, causing starch granules to absorb water and swell more readily. In other words, chlorinated flours are better driers, and they form thicker batters and stiffer doughs. Chlorine also increases the ability of starch to bind with fats, helping to distribute fats evenly throughout batters and doughs for a finer crumb. While chlorine substantially weakens gluten, this is of lesser importance than its effects on starch.

Notice that chlorine's action on gluten is very different from the action of natural aging or maturing agents like potassium bromate. Chlorine is a maturing agent that weakens, and it is used on soft wheat flour. Potassium bromate and ascorbic acid are maturing agents that strengthen, and they are used on hard wheat flour. Table 5.1 summarizes some of the different effects of these and other flour additives on flour.

TABLE 5.1 FLOUR ADDITIVES AND THEIR EFFECTS ON FLOUR

TYPE	ADDITIVE	CAROTENOIDS	GLUTEN	STARCH	PRIMARY USE
Natural aging	Air (oxygen)	Whitens	Strengthens	No effect	All flours
Maturing agents that strengthen	Potassium bromate	No effect	Strengthens	No effect	High-gluten flour
	Ascorbic acid	No effect	Strengthens	No effect	High-gluten flour; some bread flours
Bleaching agent	Benzoyl peroxide	Whitens	No effect	No effect	All flours
Bleaching and maturing agent that weakens	Chlorine	Whitens	Weakens	Increases ability to absorb water and swell	Cake flour

How Do Maturing Agents That Strengthen Work?

Maturing agents that strengthen gluten simulate natural aging. That is, they oxidize portions of glutenin and gliadin molecules, altering them so that more bonds form when gluten forms. The more bonds there are, the stronger, drier, and more elastic the dough becomes. When gases expand during final proof and oven spring, this stronger gluten stretches without breaking. Gases don't escape, so loaf volume is higher and the crumb is less coarse. Many maturing agents are more effective than natural aging at strengthening gluten. For the most part, maturing agents that strengthen do not whiten flour.

While potassium bromate and bromate replacers all work in a similar manner, they work at different times in the bread-making process. That is why commercial dough conditioners often contain a combination of maturing agents to strengthen dough throughout the process. For example, some bromate replacers are fast-acting, oxidizing gluten as soon as water is added to the flour. In contrast, potassium bromate is slow-acting and works primarily during final proof and the early stages of baking (oven spring), when strength is needed most. Ascorbic acid works consistently throughout bread production as long as oxygen (air) is present, just not as effectively as potassium bromate.

Does the Source of Amylase Matter?

The source of the amylase (more specifically, alpha-amylase) added by the miller makes a surprising difference in the quality of baked bread. This is because not all amylases are alike. In particular, different amylase enzymes are inactivated at different oven temperatures. Since amylase can have its greatest activity on bread dough during baking, its heat stability is extremely important.

Fungal amylase, for example, is typically inactivated before starch granules gelatinize—that is, before the granules are most susceptible to its action. If the only reason for the amylase is to improve fermentation, it is acceptable, even desirable, for amylase to stop working early on during baking. After all, fermentation stops once the dough warms to 140°F (60°C) or so. However, if the enzyme is added to soften the crumb and delay staling, fungal amylase will hardly be effective, since the heat will inactivate the enzyme before it has a chance to break down a good amount of starch granules.

Early versions of bacterial amylase, on the other hand, were inactivated very late in baking, or sometimes not at all. With these enzymes, starch breakdown could be so extensive that bread became gummy. Newer versions of bacterial amylase are inactivated at temperatures that are intermediate to regular fungal amylase and to these early bacterial amylases. In fact, these newer bacterial amylases are most similar to cereal amylases in their heat stability. They provide just enough starch breakdown so that staling is delayed, but not so much that the bread bakes up gummy.

You can always tell from the label whether flour has been bleached, but you cannot necessarily tell which bleaching agent was used. Ask the manufacturer if you would like to know.

Amylase

Amylase is one of several enzymes important in bread making. Recall from Chapter 3 that amylase breaks down starch in bread dough into sugars and other products. This provides food for yeast fermentation, increases browning during baking, softens the crumb, and slows staling during shelf life.

During fermentation, amylase acts primarily on starch from damaged granules. During baking, amylase activity increases when starch granules gelatinize and become more susceptible to its action. Enzyme activity stops when amylase is inactivated by the heat.

While white flour does contain some amylase, the level is typically too low to be of much benefit. To make up for this deficiency, amylase is sometimes added to flour by the miller. The amylase is from either bacteria or fungi. If amylase is not added by the miller, the baker can add any of several ingredients that are rich sources of amylase, including malted flour, sprouted wheat berries or soaked grain particles, diastatic malt syrup, rye flour, untoasted soy flour, or any number of dough conditioners that contain this starch-breaking enzyme.

Malted Flours

Malted flours can be thought of as flours with enzyme activity. The main enzymes in malted flours are amylases, but proteases (enzymes that break down proteins) are also present. While any grain can be malted, barley is the most common grain made into malted flour. Malted barley flour is often referred to as *malted flour*, *dry malt*, or more simply as *malt*.

Certain brands of flour for yeast dough production have added malted barley flour, or the baker can purchase dry malt flour separately and add it to yeast dough at around 0.25–0.5 percent (baker's percentage).

Malted wheat and malted rye flours are also available. They differ from malted barley flour in flavor and in enzyme activity. Malt syrups (also called *malt extracts*) and dried malt syrups are related products. They are discussed in Chapter 8.

Dough Conditioners

Dough conditioners are also called *dough improvers*. They are off-white, dry, granular products that look similar to flour. Dough conditioners are used in the production of yeast-raised products. Because they contain a mix of ingredients, dough conditioners perform

---

What Is Malting?

To malt means to sprout or germinate whole grain kernels under controlled conditions, as one might sprout beans or seeds. Malted grains are used in beer making as well as in baking.

There are three main steps to malting grains for flour: steeping, germination, and drying. To steep grains, whole kernels are gently stirred in a tank of cool water and allowed to soak. After they gain close to half their weight in water, the swollen kernels are transferred to a flat bed to germinate. Germinating kernels produce a mix of active enzymes, including amylases that break down starches, and proteases that break down proteins. After about four to five days germinating in a cool, humid environment, the sprouted kernels are transferred to an oven and gently dried to their original moisture (less than 14 percent). This stops germination but leaves the active enzymes intact. The final step is to grind the dried malted kernels into flour.

What Is in Dough Conditioners?

While many brands of dough conditioners are available, most contain a mixture of the following ingredients:
- Emulsifiers such as DATEM and calcium stearoyl-2-lactylate, to increase water absorption and gluten strength. (DATEM stands for diacetyl tartaric acid esters of mono- and diglycerides.)
- Salts and acids such as calcium carbonate or monocalcium phosphate, to optimize gluten development by adjusting water hardness and pH. Calcium carbonate increases both water hardness and pH; monocalcium phosphate increases water hardness while it decreases pH. Monocalcium phosphate, an acid salt, is also present in many baking powders.
- Maturing agents that strengthen, such as potassium bromate, ascorbic acid, potassium iodate, and azodicarbonamide (ADA), to increase gluten strength.
- Yeast foods such as ammonium salts, to improve yeast fermentation.
- Enzymes such as amylase, to improve yeast fermentation and browning, to soften crumb, and to delay staling.
- Reducing agents such as L-cysteine, which break bonds in gluten or block them from forming. These agents increase the extensibility and reduce the strength of doughs. They are the opposite of maturing agents that strengthen. Pizza dough, for example, can benefit from the addition of L-cysteine, so that it stretches, handles easily, and doesn't shrink.

many functions. They are particularly useful when good gluten development is necessary for high volume and a fine crumb, especially when flour quality is poor or when dough undergoes rigorous conditions. Rigorous conditions can occur in large-scale bakery operations, where doughs are roughly handled in automated equipment. Or they may occur when dough is frozen and ice crystals damage gluten structure. Sometimes, however, bakeries rely on dough conditioners to eliminate the need for bulk fermentation. While this saves time, it alters the flavor of the bread by reducing its development, which arises from a lengthier fermentation.

Dough conditioners should not be overused. Too much of a good thing yields poor texture and volume—and can be illegal. Both the United States and Canada regulate many of the additives present in dough conditioners.

Vital Wheat Gluten

Vital wheat gluten is a dry powder that contains a high amount (up to 75 percent) of protein that is vital; that is, protein that forms gluten when mixed with water. It is purchased as a creamy yellow powder. Vital wheat gluten is added to yeast-raised doughs to improve flour

> ### HELPFUL HINT
>
> *If your bakery is short on dry storage space, it can help to reduce the number of flours that are kept in inventory. For example, instead of purchasing two strong flours—one for baguettes and another for bagels—consider using the same flour for both products. When preparing bagels, which require more strength, add a small amount of vital wheat gluten. A good starting point is to add 2–5 percent vital wheat gluten, or about ¼–¾ ounce for every pound of flour (20–50 grams for every kilogram of flour). Depending on your needs and on the quality of the starting flour, this amount might need to be adjusted higher or lower.*

quality, to increase mixing and fermentation tolerances, to improve volume, and to result in a finer crumb. The addition of vital wheat gluten requires an increase in water in a formula, for full hydration. This additional water and the higher volume achieved with added gluten can extend shelf life by keeping the bread softer longer. Care must be taken, however, not to overdo the amount of wheat gluten added to bread formulas. Too much gluten can make a product tough and chewy.

Commercial Grades of White Flours

Recall that the endosperm is the whitest part of the kernel and that it is the part of the kernel milled into white flour. Recall, too, that the endosperm contains all the gluten-forming proteins. It's no wonder then that in North America commercial grades of white flour are defined by how much is pure endosperm. Flour that is very high in endosperm must be carefully milled, though, and this makes it higher in price. High-endosperm flours are whiter in color because they are relatively low in bran and germ impurities. So while these so-called high-quality flours are high in baking quality, they are lowest in nutritional quality.

Since wheat bran is naturally high in ash, the traditional way for manufacturers to confirm the grade of flour is to measure its ash content. While ash content is also affected by wheat variety and soil conditions, it does provide some indication of the amount of bran in flour and, therefore, of the flour's commercial grade. The following grades of flour apply to rye flour as well as wheat.

Patent Flour

Patent flour is the highest quality of all commercial grades of white flour. Bakers often use the term *patent flour* to mean patent bread flour, but most flours sold today—whether bread, pastry, or cake—are patent flours. Patent flour is made by combining the first few streams of flour from the milling process. It consists of the innermost part of the endosperm and is essentially free of bran and germ. This makes patent flour lowest in ash, whitest in color, and best able to form gluten without the interference of bran or germ impurities. Different grades of patent flours are available, depending on which streams of flour from the milling process are blended. The highest-quality patent flour is called *extra short* or *fancy patent*.

Clear Flour

Clear flour is the lowest quality of all commercial grades of flour. It is milled from the outer part of the endosperm, made from flour streams that remain after

Flour milling has two objectives: First, it is a process that separates the endosperm from the bran and germ. Second, it involves grinding the grain to fine flour. Ideally, milling separates out as much endosperm as possible without damaging starch granules, but this is difficult to do. In fact, commercial milling operations are able to extract only an average of 72 pounds of flour for every 100 pounds of wheat, for a so-called extraction rate of 72 percent, even though the endosperm makes up 85 percent of the wheat kernel. To accomplish these objectives, the modern milling operation:

1 Cleans the kernels to remove dirt, weed seeds, stones, and other debris.

2 Tempers the kernels by adjusting moisture content. Tempering toughens the bran and makes the germ more pliable, so the endosperm is easily separated from the bran and germ.

3 Breaks or crushes the kernels between corrugated (fluted) rollers, loosening chunks of endosperm from the bran and germ.

4 Separates, or purifies, the endosperm from the bran and the germ, using sieves and air currents. The resulting farina-size endosperm chunks are called *middlings*.

5 Grinds the endosperm middlings into flour between a series of smooth reduction rollers that look like large pasta rollers. The closer the rollers are set, the finer the flour. Through this process, flour particles are gradually reduced in size and removed as a stream of flour.

These last three operations are repeated several times, producing streams of flour in which each progressive stream that has gone back through the corrugated rollers contains less endosperm and more bran and germ "impurities" than the last. These streams are selectively combined and sifted to produce commercial grades of flour. The flour is then naturally aged or treated with bleaching and maturing agents. Other approved additives may be blended in before the flour is packaged and sold.

patent flour is produced (Figure 5.5). While different grades are available, all clear flours are relatively high in bran, high in protein and ash, and slightly gray in color. This is because clear flour contains the *aleurone*, the part of the endosperm closest to the bran layer. The aleurone is rich in enzyme activity, dietary fiber, and minerals (ash). While it is nutrient rich, the aleurone is low in gluten-forming proteins.

A high grade of clear flour, called *first clear*, remains after the production of hard wheat first patent flour.

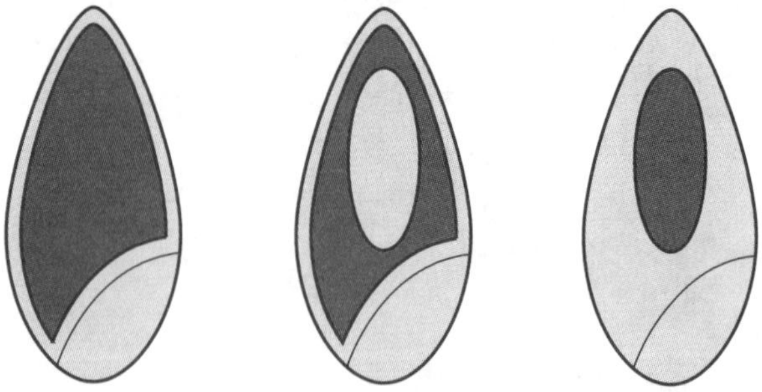

Figure 5.5 **Left to right:** straight flour, milled from the entire endosperm; clear flour, from just inside the bran layer; and patent flour, from the heart of the endosperm

Most clear flour sold to bakers is first clear from hard wheat flour and typically has a protein content of 13–15 percent and an ash content of about 0.8 percent.

Clear flour is less expensive than patent flour. While it is higher in total protein, the gluten formed from clear flour is typically weaker than that from patent flour.

First clear is commonly added to rye and whole grain breads. Its protein provides needed strength to low-gluten grains, while its slightly gray cast is hidden by the dark color of the rye or whole grain. Lower, darker grades of clear flour are used in the manufacture of vital wheat gluten.

Straight Flour

Straight flour (Figure 5.5) is milled from the entire endosperm. It is made by combining all usable streams of flour from the milling process and contains bran and germ particles that are not easily separated from the endosperm. Straight flour is not commonly used by the baking industry in North America. French bakers, however, use a type of straight flour in breads.

Traditional gristmills of the mid-1800s had difficulty milling the hard kernels of Midwestern and Canadian spring wheat. A new process using granite millstones was imported from Hungary and greatly improved the ability to process these hard kernels into white flour. But it wasn't until a Frenchman named LaCroix developed a purifier, which improved the yield and quality of white flour, that hard spring wheat was more easily milled into white flour. In 1865, the U.S. Patent Office granted a patent for the purifier. This was followed by hundreds more patents for refining white flour. These new patented processes, used in the mills of Minnesota, revolutionized the milling industry. Consumer demand for midwestern patent flour continued to rise in both North America and Europe, and the center of the milling industry in the United States moved from eastern cities to the upper Midwest, which became an internationally renowned center of milling. Today, the term *patent flour* still refers to highly purified white flour.

Types of Patent Wheat Flours

Most flours purchased by the baker and pastry chef today, whether bread, pastry, or cake, are patent flours, milled from the heart of the endosperm. There are many differences among the various patent wheat flours. Some of these differences are due to the type of wheat used in producing the flour. Others occur because of differences in milling practices or additives.

Bread

Bread flours are milled from either hard red spring or hard red winter wheat. They are high in protein (typically 11.5–13.5 percent protein) that forms good-quality gluten, essential for high volume and fine crumb in yeast-raised baked goods. Because they are from hard wheat kernels, bread flours are difficult for the miller to grind. This is why bread flours are coarser in texture than pastry flours, and why they contain a higher percentage of broken and fragmented starch granules. These damaged starch granules absorb more water than intact granules, which slows staling. Damaged granules are also more susceptible than intact ones to breakdown by amylase, which further slows staling. Additionally, as the amylase breaks down starches into sugars, yeast fermentation can increase.

Bread flours can be purchased unbleached or bleached (generally with benzoyl peroxide). Some bread flours contain added malted barley flour to boost amylase activity and provide for better yeast fermentation, dough

Most specifications for strong flours, whether bread, high-gluten, or clear flour, include a value called the *falling number* that indicates amylase activity.

The falling number of flour is measured by heating the flour with water in a tube while it is stirred with a rod. As the starch gelatinizes, it is liquefied by the action of amylase enzymes in the flour. This thins out the flour mixture, and the stirring rod drops to the bottom of the tube. The time it takes (in seconds) for the stirring rod to fall to the bottom of the tube is referred to as the flour's falling number. The higher the falling number, the less amylase activity in the flour.

Falling number values greater than about 200 seconds are generally acceptable for bread making. Flours with much lower values might exhibit too much enzyme activity, yielding a dark crust, sticky crumb, and weak bread structure. So that the flour you purchase tomorrow acts the same as what you purchased today, millers adjust amylase activity in flour by blending different streams of flours or by adjusting the amount of amylase or dry malt added to the flour. This way, the falling number and the amylase activity in a brand of flour is the same from one year to the next.

handling, and shelf life. Bread flours are typically used for pan breads, rolls, croissants, and sweet yeast doughs.

Artisan Bread Artisan bread flours, which are milled from hard red winter wheat, resemble French bread flour; that is, they are relatively low in protein (11.5–12.5 percent) and often higher in ash than other bread flours. The lower protein content of winter wheats provides for a crisper crust (less water absorption) and a crumb with desirable irregular holes. In other words, these flours are ideal for French baguettes and other crusty lean yeast breads.

Although artisan bread flours are lower in protein than other bread flours, the quality of the protein must be high. High-quality protein forms gluten with a good balance between strength and extensibility. If gluten is not strong enough, it tears as dough is stretched, and the dough collapses from the rigors of long fermentations typical of artisan breads. These doughs need to be handled gently, as they are more easily overmixed. Because they produce soft, stretchy doughs, artisan flours are also a good choice for use in flat breads such tortillas and pita bread.

Artisan bread flours often have a slightly higher ash content than other patent flours. The higher ash content indicates that a greater fraction of the wheat kernel is included in the flour. The flour will contain more minerals, more pentosans, and more active enzymes. This can create a grayish cast on the flour but is thought to improve yeast fermentation and flavor. Artisan bread flours typically do not contain bleaching or maturing agents and are more likely than other flours to be organic.

High-Gluten

High-gluten flours are milled from hard wheat, generally hard red spring wheat. They are naturally high in protein (typically 13.5–14.5 percent protein) and often have potassium bromate or a bromate replacer added for even stronger gluten. High-gluten flours require a high amount of water to form acceptable doughs, because of their high protein content and the high degree of damaged starch granules generated during milling. They require extra mixing to fully develop gluten, but they can withstand overmixing better than regular bread flours. Like bread flours, high-gluten flours sometimes are bleached and can contain added malted flour. They are used almost exclusively for yeast-raised baked

HELPFUL HINT

If bread has a wet, sticky crumb, weak structure, and a dark crust, the dough might benefit from less amylase activity. To reduce amylase activity, consider the following:

- *Reduce the amount of dry malt, sprouted kernels, diastatic malt syrup, or other ingredients that contain active enzymes.*
- *Use a flour with a higher falling number, which is an indication of lower amylase activity.*
- *Increase the amount of added salt, if possible. Salt slows enzyme activity.*
- *Increase the oven temperature, if possible, to speed up the baking process. This way, the dough spends less time exposed to temperatures that accelerate enzyme activity.*
- *If allowing for long fermentation times, provide conditions for the growth and fermentation of lactic acid bacteria over yeast, so pH will be lowered quickly (amylase is less active at low pHs). For example, retard (refrigerate) the dough to lower the fermentation temperature.*

If bread has poor volume, a pale crust, and a dry crumb that stales too quickly, try increasing amylase activity. To increase amylase activity, do the opposite of what is stated in the items above.

goods, particularly those requiring maximum strength and structure. Use high-gluten flours in bagels, hearth breads, thin crust pizzas, and hard rolls.

Do not confuse high-gluten flour with vital wheat gluten, which looks like flour but is best thought of as a flour additive. As with vital wheat gluten, be careful not to overuse high-gluten flour so that breads are not too tough or chewy.

Pastry

Pastry flours are milled from soft wheat, generally from soft red winter wheat, but they can be milled from soft white wheat, as well. In either case, they are low in protein—typically 7–9.5 percent—and are easily milled to a fine granulation. Pastry flour is not usually bleached, but bleached pastry flour is available. Because it is typically low in protein, in water-grabbing pentosans, and in damaged starch granules, it has a low capacity to absorb water. Batters and doughs made with pastry flour remain relatively soft and fluid during the early stages of baking. This allows cookie dough to spread farther and cakes to rise higher than with a stronger flour.

If bread is made from pastry flour, it will not look or taste the same as bread made from bread flour. First, the dough will be softer, even though less water is required in the mixing. It will readily break and tear and be over-mixed more easily.

Once the bread is baked, it will have lower volume. The crust will not brown as readily, and the crumb will be whiter. Air cells in the crumb will tend to be larger and more irregular. Expect a different flavor, and if the bread is stored over several days, it will become stale faster.

Many of these differences are due to the lower amount and quality of protein in pastry flour compared with bread flour.

Cake

Cake flours are milled from soft wheat, generally from soft red winter wheat. They are short, or fancy, patent flours, meaning that they are milled from the absolute heart of the endosperm. This gives cake flour a finer granulation because the wheat is easy to mill, and has whiter and brighter color, lower protein content (6–8 percent), and a slightly higher starch content than other flours. Cake flours are typically bleached with both chlorine and benzoyl peroxide, yielding a stark white color and a distinctly changed flavor. They are some-times called *chlorinated* or *high-ratio flours*.

Recall that chlorine is a maturing agent that weakens gluten and increases the ability of starch granules to swell as they absorb water (and oils). Cookie dough made from cake flour instead of pastry flour is stiff and dry, and the lack of free liquid prevents much, if any, spread during baking. Cookies made from cake flour hold their shape better than those made from pastry flour, but they brown very little, and they have a cake-like texture (Figure 5.6).

Figure 5.6 Different flours in cookie dough result in differences in height and spread. **Left:** cookies made with pastry flour; **right:** the same cookies made with cake flour

The importance of chlorine on the properties of cake flour cannot be overstressed. It is as much the chlorine treatment as the low protein content and fine granulation that defines cake flour—if not more. Researchers are exploring alternatives to chlorination, which is no longer allowed in the European Union. Some promising alternative treatments include the use of dry heat, enzymes, and additives such as xanthan gum.

> **HELPFUL HINT**
>
> *Some cookies are really more like small cakes, just richer and drier. Cake flour is the ideal flour for this type of cookie. Consider holiday cookie cutter cookies, for example. Cut-out sugar cookies look best if they retain their shape and stay white throughout baking. The color on these cookies best comes from the icings used to decorate them, not from browning in the oven.*

All-Purpose

All-purpose (AP) flour is not typically used by professional pastry chefs. However, it is sold in the foodservice industry as H&R flour, which stands for *hotel and restaurant* flour. AP flour typically has between 9.5 and 11.5 percent protein, but this can vary with the brand. While AP flour is often made from a blend of hard and soft wheat, this is not always the case. Some brands, such as King Arthur flour, are made entirely from hard wheat. Other brands, such as White Lily, are made entirely from soft wheat. AP flour comes bleached (with benzoyl peroxide or chlorine) or unbleached, is typically enriched with vitamins and minerals, and may contain added malted barley flour.

How Important Is Cake Flour When Making Cakes?

Many cakes can be made successfully with pastry or bread flour, but light, sweet, moist, and tender high-ratio cakes cannot. High-ratio cakes are made from formulas that contain a high ratio of liquid and sugar to flour. Without cake flour, these cakes would not rise, or more likely they would rise and then collapse during baking and cooling. Here's why.

Recall that chlorine modifies the starch in flour so that starch granules swell and thicken batters, even as large amounts of water and sugar are added. Thick batters are good at holding tiny air and gas bubbles during mixing and baking, and cake flour provides for a thicker batter than either bread or pastry flour. Because leavening gases are held in the cake batter for a longer time during baking, the cake batter expands higher, and the baked cake has a lighter texture, higher volume, and finer, softer crumb.

What If a Formula Calls for All-Purpose Flour?

Not all professional bakeshops stock all-purpose flour. What should be used if a formula calls for all-purpose flour and none is available? The standard substitute for AP flour is generally given as a blend of bread and cake flour, usually a 60/40 or 50/50 blend. This works well with some products, including many cookie formulas. Yet a blend of bread and cake flours is not always the best substitute for AP flour.

For yeast-raised products, bread flour is a better choice. Additional water will be needed to form the dough, and longer mixing will be needed to develop the gluten. The dough will handle more easily, the product will be higher than if it was made from all-purpose flour, and it will have a finer crumb.

For fine-textured high-ratio cakes, use cake flour instead of AP flour. For most other cakes such as gingerbread and carrot cake, and for many other products including pie dough and baking powder biscuits, use bread or pastry flour.

Other Wheat Flours

Whole Wheat

Whole wheat flour is sometimes called *graham* or *entire wheat flour* in North America and *wholemeal flour* in Great Britain and other countries. It is a whole grain product because it contains all three parts of the kernel (bran, germ, and endosperm) in the same proportions as they occurred in the original kernel. Its high ash content (over 1.5 percent) indicates the presence of the mineral-rich bran. The bran—and to a lesser degree, the germ—is high in both insoluble and soluble dietary fiber, primarily from pentosan gums. This is the main reason why whole wheat flour is a better drier than white flour. Whole wheat flour has a shorter shelf life than white flour because the bran and the germ are high in oil, an oil which easily oxidizes to produce rancid, off flavors. (In Canada, some whole wheat flour has most of the oily germ and some of the bran removed to help reduce rancidity. While legally called whole wheat flour, it cannot be declared as a whole grain).

Whole wheat flour comes in different granulations, from coarse to fine. This is true of both stone-ground flour and conventionally (roller) milled flour. Because coarse flour particles absorb water more slowly than finer ones, they do not form gluten as quickly. Surprisingly, though, the finer the bran particles in whole wheat flour, the worse the fermentation tolerance of bread dough. The end result is that bread made with finely ground bran will have a lower volume than bread made with coarse bran.

It is a common misconception that graham flour is whole wheat flour with a different particle size. When Reverend Sylvester Graham first created graham crackers in 1829, he used coarsely ground whole wheat flour. However, in both the United States and Canada

Early man made the first stone-ground flour by crushing and pounding whole grains between stones. Over the centuries, the process evolved to the use of stone, or grist, mills. A gristmill consists of two rotating circular granite millstones that rub or crush the grain sandwiched between them. Grinding can be combined with sifting to separate bran particles from the white flour. Before roller mills revolutionized the milling industry in the late 1800s, there were over 22,000 neighborhood gristmills across the United States, mostly run by windmills or water wheels.

Today, stone grinding is mostly used to mill whole grain flours and meals rather than white flour. While the miller can make some adjustments to the millstones, stone-ground flour is generally characterized by an even distribution of germ oil throughout the flour, and often by smaller bran particles than are present in roller-milled flours. When bran particles are small, protein and other nutrients in them are more completely available for digestion. It is for this reason that stone-ground flour manufacturers sometimes advertise the digestibility and higher nutritional value of their products.

Old gristmills grind slowly, generating relatively little heat as the grain is crushed to flour. This can prevent the destruction of active enzymes and the oxidation of oils. The presence of active enzymes in stone-ground flour is a mixed blessing, though. While the low heat of gristmills might not oxidize wheat germ oils, enzymes can. This is probably why stone-ground flours can have a short shelf life, and it is probably why they can have a stronger flavor than roller-milled flour.

Roller mills are the primary means for milling flour today. They were invented in Europe as early as the 1500s but did not have widespread use in North America until the late 1800s. Roller mills consist of a sequence of paired iron rollers, some grooved and some smooth, that rotate inwards. Because one roller is set to spin at a faster rate than the other, the grains caught in the middle are twisted and chopped. This flattens the bran into large flakes and breaks the endosperm into chunks. This is different from the rubbing and crushing that generally takes place in gristmills.

Whole wheat flour from roller mills is usually made by recombining the endosperm, bran, and germ in the proportions in which they were present in the original kernel. Often the endosperm is ground fine but the bran particles are kept large, for best gluten development and least interference from bran particles. Because the germ is flattened in this process and not rubbed throughout the flour, its valuable oils remain in the germ. This is said to minimize oxidation of the oils in the flour. It is also likely that the higher heat of roller milling destroys lipase enzymes, which helps prevent off flavors and extends shelf life.

today, there are no regulations that differentiate graham flour from whole wheat flour based on particle size. The two terms are essentially interchangeable.

Whole wheat flour is typically milled from hard red wheat, although whole wheat pastry flour, milled from soft red wheat, is available. In either case, whole wheat flour is higher in protein than white flour milled from the same wheat. Despite this higher protein content (11–14 percent or more), whole wheat flour does not form as much gluten as white flour with the same or even lower protein content. There are several reasons for this:

- Sharp bran particles in whole wheat flour literally cut through gluten strands as they form.
- Bran is high in pentosan gums, which interfere with gluten formation.
- Much of the protein in whole wheat flour is from the bran and the germ, which do not form gluten.
- Wheat germ contains a protein fragment (glutathione) that interferes with gluten development.

This means that yeast-raised doughs and baked goods made with whole wheat flour will be different from those made from white flour. Specifically, whole wheat bread dough is less cohesive and resilient than dough made with bread flour and therefore has lower gas-retaining properties. Because of this, 100 percent whole wheat bread typically is denser and coarser than white bread.

Durum wheat is commonly sold either as finely ground flour, called *durum flour*, or as a coarser granular product, called *durum semolina* or simply *semolina*. The particles in durum semolina are about the same size as those in farina. Today, the term *semolina flour* is sometimes used to mean durum flour.

Baked goods made from 100 percent whole wheat flour are of course darker in color and stronger in flavor than those made from white flour. To satisfy customers who are unaccustomed to the strong taste of bread made from whole wheat flour, bakers often blend about one-quarter to one-half part whole wheat flour to one part bread or high-gluten flour. As consumers become aware of the positive health benefits of whole grain baked goods, they will likely learn to appreciate the nutty flavor and denser texture of 100 percent whole wheat bread.

Whole White Wheat Whole white wheat flour is made from either soft or hard white wheat, two newer classes of wheat grown in North America. Farmers began growing more white wheat to satisfy the Asian market, where white wheat is preferred to red wheat flour for noodle making. Although it is less hardy than red wheat, increasing amounts of white wheat are now being grown as North Americans become interested in increasing their consumption of whole grains. Whole white wheat flour is light in color (golden, not white) and has a sweeter, milder taste than whole wheat flour made from red wheats. This makes it more acceptable to consumers who prefer lighter, milder-tasting breads and pastries. Because it is a whole grain, whole white wheat flour is just as high in dietary fiber as regular whole wheat flour. For this reason, whole white wheat flour is being used in many whole grain breakfast cereals and baked goods.

Durum

Durum flour is made from the endosperm of durum wheat. Durum wheat is not the same as common wheat, which is used in white and whole wheat flours. Durum wheat has a very hard kernel (harder than so-called hard wheat kernels) and it is very high in protein (12–15 percent). Because it is extremely hard, durum wheat is difficult to reduce to a flour, and when it is, the flour is high in damaged starch granules.

Durum flour is high in yellow carotenoid pigments, which provide a desirable golden color to pasta products. Besides being used in pasta, durum products are used in specialty baked goods such as Italian semolina bread.

Because it is ground from the endosperm only, durum flour is not a whole grain, but whole durum flour is available. Whole durum flour and whole durum semolina contain the bran, germ, and endosperm of durum wheat and are therefore whole grains. They are used in the production of whole wheat pasta.

Functions of Flour

Providing Structure

Flour is one of two main bakeshop ingredients that contribute to the toughening or structure building in baked goods (eggs being the other). Structure allows products to hold a new, larger size and shape as gases expand and leaven. It prevents products from collapsing during baking and cooling. Besides its importance in baked goods, flour provides structure—thickening, really—to pastry creams and certain pie fillings.

Gluten and starch are responsible for much of the structure-building ability of flour. Gluten is formed from two proteins in flour, glutenin and gliadin, when the flour is mixed with water. The unique structure of gluten is especially important in yeast-raised doughs, and this will be discussed in more detail in Chapter 7.

While not as important in wheat flours as gluten and starch, pentosan gums can contribute to structure. These gums appear either to form their own structure or to interact with gluten. As you will see in Chapter 6, pentosans are especially important to the structure of dough made from rye flour.

By one estimate, almost half the water in bread dough is held by starch, about one-third by flour proteins, and close to one-quarter by the small amount of gums in white flour. Starch absorbs most of the water in doughs because there is so much of it. Yet the best way to predict which of two wheat flours will absorb more water is by comparing the amount of protein each contains. Proteins, including gluten-forming proteins, absorb fully one to two times their weight in water, while undamaged starch granules absorb only about one-quarter to one-half their weight in water. This means that a small increase in protein has a noticeable increase in the amount of water absorbed in doughs. High-gluten flour absorbs more water than bread flour, and bread flour absorbs more than pastry flour.

Besides protein to absorb more water, high-protein flours, being from hard wheat, contain more pentosans and more damaged starch granules. Damaged granules take up three to four times as much water as intact granules.

Predicting water absorption from protein values works as long as the wheat flour is not bleached with chlorine. Recall that chlorine changes starch granules so that they absorb much more water and swell without heat. This is the main reason why chlorinated cake flour absorbs as much water as it does. Another reason is that cake flour is milled finer, and finer particles always absorb water faster.

Which of these structure builders (gluten, starch, or gums) is most important to a particular baked product depends on the type of flour and the formula used. For example, little, if any, gluten forms from cake flour or from nonwheat flours. Instead, starch—or starch and gums—becomes the main structure builder. On the other hand, products low in moisture, like pie crust and crisp cookies, inevitably rely on gluten alone for structure, because starch gelatinization does not occur in the absence of sufficient water.

Even with flours that contain gluten, gluten is not necessarily the only—or the most important—structure builder. Take yeast-raised baked goods, for example. Gluten and starch share the role of structure building in these products. Gluten structure is most important in unbaked dough, but starch is arguably more important as baking progresses.

Absorbing Liquids

Ingredients such as flour that absorb liquids are also called *driers*. Starches, proteins, and gums are the three main components in flour that absorb moisture (water) and oil, helping to bind ingredients together. Notice that the same components that form structure are also driers.

The absorption value of flour is an important quality factor in bread baking. It is defined as the amount of water absorbed by flour when forming bread dough. High absorption values are desirable in bread baking because the added moisture slows staling. Higher water absorption also means that less flour is needed to make a loaf of bread, so if cost is a factor, this is an important point.

Water absorption values of most bread flours range around 50–65 percent, meaning that 1 pound (450 grams) of flour absorbs over 0.5 pound (225 grams) of water. While several factors affect the absorption value of flour, flours that absorb more water typically have a higher protein content.

Contributing Flavor

Wheat flours have a relatively mild, slightly nutty flavor that is generally considered desirable. Each has a different flavor, though. Expect clear flour, for example, with its higher protein and ash content, to have a stronger flavor than a soft patent flour like pastry flour. Expect cake flour to have a different flavor because of the chlorine treatment it has undergone. Expect whole wheat flour to have the strongest flavor of all, because it also contains the germ and the bran.

Contributing Color

Flours vary in color for various reasons. For example, regular whole wheat has a nut brown color from pigments in the bran, while whole white wheat flour has a golden color because its bran layer is much paler in color. Durum flour has a pale yellow color because it is high in carotenoids, while unbleached white flour has a creamy color because it is relatively low in carotenoids. Cake flour has a bright white color because bleaching oxidizes its carotenoids. These color differences carry over to the baked goods.

Flour also contributes protein, small amounts of sugar, and starches for Maillard browning (the breakdown of sugars and proteins) to provide a dark color on crusts. High-protein flours typically undergo more Maillard browning than low-protein flours. So, for example, expect a browner crust when bread flour is used instead of pastry flour in pie crust.

Adding Nutritional Value

Essentially all flours and grain products contribute complex carbohydrates (starch), vitamins, minerals, and protein. However, the protein in wheat is low in lysine, an essential amino acid. This means that wheat protein is not as nutritionally complete as egg or milk protein and is best supplemented with other protein sources for good health.

White flour is a poor source of fiber, but whole wheat flour and whole white wheat flour, being whole grain products, are good sources of dietary fiber, primarily from the pentosans in the bran. Less well known but no less important are many other health-promoting substances in flour that are concentrated in the bran and the germ. While these substances have not all been identified or studied, the important message is that whole grain foods offer protection against a wide range of diseases, including coronary heart disease, cancer, and diabetes.

Storage of Flours

All flours, even white flour, have a limited shelf life. In fact, millers recommend that flours, especially whole grain flours, be stored for no more than six months. The main change that occurs is the oxidation of oils when flour is exposed to air. The result is rancid, cardboard-like off flavors. While whole wheat flour, wheat germ, and bran are most likely to oxidize because of their high oil content, even the small amount of oil present in white flour—about 1 percent—eventually causes flavor changes. To avoid problems, rotate stock by following the FIFO rule (first in, first out) and do not add new flour to old. Flour should be stored covered and in a cool, dry area, particularly in the hot, humid days of summer. This prevents the flour from absorbing moisture and odors and from attracting insects and rodents. Whole grain flours, being more nutritious than white flours, are most susceptible to infestation from insects and rodents. Wheat germ and whole wheat flour are

> **HELPFUL HINT**
>
> *If you see silky cobwebs in your flour bin or around the bakeshop, you have flour moths. The webs form as newly hatched worm-like larvae of flour moths feed on flours and grains. Because whole grains are more nutritious, these are usually the first flours to be infested. Discard the flour immediately, before the larvae mature to adult flying moths and the problem spreads. Call in a pest control professional if the problem persists.*
>
> *To prevent this problem in the future, sweep up food spillage as soon as it happens. Be sure to clean hard-to-reach places and places that rarely get cleaned. Dismantle storage racks, if necessary. Rotate stock using the FIFO rule, and be especially vigilant with whole grain products.*

ideally stored under refrigeration, if not used within a few months.

Questions for Review

1 Why is wheat so commonly used in the bakeshop? Why not flour from another cereal grain?

2 Identify the three main parts of a wheat kernel. Which is/are milled into white flour? Which is/are milled into whole wheat flour?

3 What is another name for wheat flour?

4 Which of the following are not necessarily whole grains: Nine-grain bread, stone-ground flour, organic flour, graham flour?

5 What are the two main types of dietary fiber? What are the primary health benefits of each?

6 What components are naturally present in white flour? That is, what is the makeup of the wheat endosperm?

7 Which component in white flour (in the wheat endosperm) is present in larger amounts than all other components combined?

8 What is ash composed of? How is it measured in flour?

9 Which of the three main parts of the wheat kernel is highest in ash?

10 What are the main differences between flours milled from hard wheat and those milled from soft wheat?

11 What is the difference between flour and meal?

12 What is added to flour to enrich it? What is lost from milling wheat kernels into white flour that is not replaced with enrichment?

13 What is meant by "green flour"?

14 What are the two main changes brought about by naturally aging flour?

15 What are the disadvantages of naturally aging flour?

16 Provide an explanation for the advantages of maturing agents that strengthen.

17 What is the standard maturing agent for hard wheat flours, the one that all others are judged against?

18 Which maturing agent has been shown to be a carcinogen?

19 Name a bromate replacer. How does it act differently than potassium bromate?

20 Are potassium bromate and bromate replacers more likely to be added to bread flour or to cake flour? Why?

21 Name the most common bleaching agent for flour.

22 Name three effects of chlorine on flour. Which appears to be the most critical function of the three?

23 Is chlorine more likely to be added to bread flours or to cake flours? Why?

24 Why might flour contain a small amount of added amylase or malted barley flour?

25 What is meant by "patent flour"?

26 How does clear flour differ from straight flour? What is the main use for clear flour?

27 How much higher in protein is the typical high-gluten flour compared with the typical bread flour? What additives are commonly added to high-gluten flour to further increase the structure-building and water-absorption abilities of the flour?

28 How is artisan bread flour different from regular bread flour? How do these differences affect the qualities of baked bread?

29 How much lower in protein is the typical cake flour compared with the typical pastry flour? What else is different between cake flour and pastry flour that can explain their different properties?

30 What is used instead of chlorination to treat flour for use in cakes in countries that do not allow the chlorination of flour?

31 Which of the following are whole grains: cracked wheat, whole wheat flour, wheat berries, wheat flour, durum flour, durum semolina, whole white wheat flour, clear flour?

32 What are the differences in color, flavor, and dietary fiber between regular whole wheat flour and whole white wheat flour?

33 Why does whole wheat flour have a shorter shelf life than white flour?

34 Which of the following are usually milled from hard wheat and which from soft wheat: high-gluten flour, bread flour, artisan bread flour, pastry flour, cake flour, all-purpose flour?

35 Which contains more carotenoids: bread flour or durum flour? How does the amount of carotenoids affect the appearance of flour?

36 One function of flour is to provide structure or toughening. What structure builder forms from glutenin and gliadin when flour is mixed with water? What else in flour provides structure?

37 One function of flour is that it is a drier. What three components in wheat flour absorb water and function as driers?

38 What is meant by the "absorption value" of flour? How can you generally predict which of two flours will absorb more water?

39 You normally use regular bread flour in a formula and switch to high-gluten flour. Will you need more water or less water to fully develop the gluten? Explain your answer.

40 Why does bread flour absorb more water than pastry flour?

41 Why does cake flour absorb more water than pastry flour?

42 Why does flour have a limited shelf life? That is, why should it be stored for no longer than six months?

43 Are you more likely to find silky cobwebs in whole wheat flour or in white flour? What causes these webs to form, and what should you do about it?

Questions for Discussion

1   Assume that two samples of wheat flour contain the same amount of protein, yet one forms more gluten than the other. Provide three explanations for why this could be. Assume that the differences are in the flours and their treatments only and not in the formulas or the methods of preparation for making the dough. Be sure to explain your reasons.

2   Assume that a sample of whole wheat flour and one of white flour contain the same amount of protein. Provide three explanations for why less gluten forms from the whole wheat flour than from the white flour. Be sure to explain your reasons.

3   Why does bread flour typically contain more broken and fragmented starch granules than pastry flour? How does the extent of this damage affect the flour's water absorption value and its susceptibility to amylase action? Why is this desirable for bread baking?

4   Why does pastry flour typically absorb less water than cake flour? Why is this desirable when making thin, crisp cookies?

5   In what way is flour treated with potassium bromate or ascorbic acid similar to naturally aged flour? In what way is it different?

6   In what way is flour treated with chlorine similar to naturally aged flour? In what ways is it different?

7   How can you tell that the dough you used in baking a batch of bread underwent too little amylase activity? Name four ways that you could increase amylase activity the next time you make bread.

8   You have two bread flours available to you. The first is milled from hard spring wheat, is bleached, and has added ascorbic acid and malted barley flour. The other is made from a hard winter wheat, is unbleached, and also has malted barley flour added. First, identify which flour is likely designed for artisan bread. Second, which is the better choice to use in preparing a sweet yeast dough like brioche? Which is the better choice for baguettes? Explain your answers.

9   How might a high-ratio cake made with chlorinated cake flour differ from one made with pastry flour? Consider appearance, flavor, texture, and height.

Exercises and Experiments

① Exercise: Sensory Characteristics of Wheat Flours

Use your textbook to fill out the first two columns of the Results Table on page 103. Next, fill in the Description column with the brand name of each flour. Include additional information that further describes and differentiates the flour from others of the same kind (stone-ground, bromated, enriched, etc.). Identify from the package if the flour is bleached or not. Next, use fresh samples to evaluate the appearance, particle size, and ability to pack of each of the wheat flours or wheat ingredients. To evaluate particle size, rub a thin layer of flour between your fingertips and describe in your own words how fine or coarse it feels. To evaluate whether flour packs or holds together, scoop up a fistful of flour in your hand and squeeze (Figure 5.7). If it holds together in one piece, it packs. If it doesn't hold together completely, record if there is slight packing, or none at all. Use this opportunity to learn how to identify flours from their sensory characteristics alone. Add any additional comments or observations that you might have to the last column in the Results Table, such as an ingredient listing. Three rows are left blank, for the evaluation of additional wheat flours, if desired.

Figure 5.7 **(a)** Bread flour does not pack well when squeezed; **(b)** pastry flour packs.

Use information from the table and from your textbook to answer the following questions. Select one from the choices in **bold** or fill in the blanks.

1 The hard wheat flours are **higher/lower** in protein than the soft wheat flours. The flour with the highest amount of protein is **high-gluten/bread/durum flour**.

2 Soft wheat flours pack **better/worse** than hard wheat flours when squeezed in a fist because they consist of **coarser/finer** particles that feel **silky/granular** when rubbed between fingertips. This is related to their **higher/lower** protein content, which makes them **easier/more difficult** for the miller to pulverize finely.

3 Was your bread flour **bleached/unbleached**? Was your bread flour **more/less** creamy yellow in color than your pastry flour? Some bread flours are unbleached and some are bleached. When unbleached, bread flour is more creamy yellow in color than pastry flour because hard wheats are higher in **bran/carotenoid** pigments. When bread flour is bleached, however, it likely will be **more/less** creamy yellow in color than pastry flour, which is usually unbleached.

4 Because bread flour can be either more or less creamy colored than pastry flour, the best way to tell the difference between bread flour and pastry flour is:

_____

_____

_____

TYPE OF FLOUR/ FLOUR INGREDIENT	KERNEL HARDNESS	TYPICAL PERCENT PROTEIN	DESCRIPTION	BLEACHED (YES/NO)	APPEARANCE	PARTICLE SIZE	PACKING	ADDITIONAL COMMENTS
Bread								
Pastry								
Cake (chlorinated)								
High-gluten								
Whole wheat								
Whole wheat pastry								
Whole white wheat								
Durum flour								
Durum semolina								

5 The fastest and easiest way to tell the difference between cake flour and pastry flour is

_____

_____

_____

6 The whole wheat flours **were/were not** enriched because

_____

_____

_____

7 The whole white wheat flour was **bleached/unbleached**. Its color is best described as

_____

_____

_____

8 The main difference between durum semolina and durum flour is that durum semolina is **finer/coarser** than durum flour. Durum wheat is difficult for the miller to grind because durum wheat kernels are **harder/softer** than any other wheat.

9 Durum wheat kernels are **higher/lower** than other wheats in carotenoid pigments, making durum semolina and durum flour desirable for their yellow color. Durum semolina and durum flour are specialty products used in the production of _____

_____

_____

❷ Exercise: Wheat Flours as Driers

Use the instructions below to prepare and evaluate dough prepared from each of the flours used in Exercise 1 above. The same amount of water will be added to each flour, so the dough's consistency will be a good indication of the water absorption value of the flour; that is, how effective a drier it is.

1 Add 500 grams flour and 250 grams room temperature water into mixing bowl.

2 Using dough hook, mix on low speed for 60 seconds.

3 Stop and scrape bowl, then slowly add an additional 50 grams water, mixing on low speed for 60 seconds.

4 Mix on medium speed for 5 minutes. If necessary, cover bowl and beater with parchment paper or dry towel while mixing, to prevent flour from flying out of mixing bowl.

5 Shape dough into a ball. Lay all dough balls side by side on parchment paper, for easy comparison. Label each ball by flour type. Let rest for at least 15 minutes.

6 Compare doughs for firmness, stickiness, and shape. Notice that some balls hold their shape and feel firm and dry to the touch. Other balls will slump or spread and feel soft or sticky. Add these comments to the last column of the Results Table in Exercise 1.

7 Based on the shape and feel of the dough balls, rank the flours in order of their apparent water absorption values.

Answer the following questions, based on your evaluation of the dough balls. Select one from the choices in **bold** or fill in the blanks:

1. When comparing pastry flour with bread flour, pastry flour produced **softer/firmer** dough that held its shape **more/less** than bread flour. This means that pastry flour is a **more/less** effective drier than bread flour. The difference appeared **small/moderate/large**. Pastry flour has these properties because it is milled from a **hard/soft** flour and is therefore **lower/higher** than bread flour in water-absorbing proteins, pentosan gums, and damaged starch granules.

2. When comparing cake flour with pastry flour, cake flour produced **softer/firmer** dough that held its shape **more/less** than pastry flour. This means that cake flour is a **more/less** effective drier than pastry flour. The difference appeared **small/moderate/large**. Cake flour has these properties primarily because it is treated with _____, a bleaching and maturing agent that oxidizes starch granules and causes them to swell **more/less** than the intact starch granules in pastry flour.

3. When comparing high-gluten flour with bread flour, high-gluten flour produced a **softer/firmer** dough that held its shape **more/less** than bread flour. This means that high-gluten flour is a **more/less** effective drier than bread flour. The difference appeared **small/moderate/large**. High-gluten flour has these properties primarily because it is made from hard **winter/spring** wheat and is typically **higher/lower** than bread flour in water-absorbing proteins, pentosan gums, and damaged starch granules.

4. When comparing whole wheat flour with bread flour, whole wheat flour produced a **softer/firmer** dough that held its shape **more/less** than bread flour. This means that whole wheat flour is a **more/less** effective drier than bread flour. The difference appeared **small/moderate/large**. Whole wheat flour has these properties primarily because it contains all three parts of the wheat kernel, not just the **bran/germ/endosperm** that bread flour is milled from. The bran, in particular, is high in water-soluble **starches/pentosans**, which can absorb up to ten times their weight in water.

5. Did you notice any other differences between doughs? _____
   _____
   _____

③ Experiment: Different Wheat Flours in Lean Yeast Rolls

One way to learn about an ingredient, such as flour, is to make product—for example, yeast bread—from different types of that ingredient. Because lean dough used in making bread contains little else besides flour and water, it's perfect for learning about the properties of flours, even if some of those flours would never be used in making yeast bread.

Objectives

Demonstrate how the type of flour affects
- Height of rolls
- Crispness and browning on the crust of rolls
- Crumb color and structure
- Overall flavor and texture of rolls
- Overall acceptability of rolls

Products Prepared

Lean yeast rolls made with

- Bread flour (control product)
- High-gluten flour
- Pastry flour
- Cake flour
- Whole wheat flour
- Other, if desired (all-purpose flour, artisan bread flour, white whole wheat flour, etc.)

Materials and Equipment

- Proof box
- Scale
- Sieve
- Parchment paper
- Mixer with 5-quart mixing bowl
- Flat beater attachment
- Bowl scraper
- Dough hook attachment
- Lean dough (see Formula), enough to make 12 or more rolls of each variation
- Muffin pans (2½" or 3½"/65 or 90 mm size)
- Pan spray or pan coating
- Oven thermometer
- Serrated knife
- Ruler

Formula

Lean Dough

Yield: *12 rolls*

INGREDIENT	POUNDS	OUNCES	GRAMS	BAKER'S PERCENTAGE
Flour	1	2	500	100
Salt		0.25	8	1.5
Yeast, instant		0.25	8	1.5
Water, 85°F (30°C)		10	280	56
Total	**1**	**12.5**	**796**	**159**

Method of Preparation

1   Preheat oven to 425°F (220°C).

2   Set proof box to 85°F (30°C) and 85 percent relative humidity.

3   Weigh an additional 5 ounces (140 grams) water (at 85°F/30°C) and set aside. (This will be used for adjusting dough consistency in step 7.)

4 Combine flour and salt thoroughly by sifting together three times onto parchment paper. *Note:* if all particles (for example, bran particles in whole wheat flour) do not fit through sieve, stir them back into mixture.

5 Place flour/salt mixture, yeast, and water into mixer bowl.

6 Blend on low for 1 minute with flat beater. Stop and scrape bowl.

7 Add additional water (from step 3) slowly and as needed, to adjust consistency. Record amount of water added to each dough in Results Table 1, which follows.

8 Mix using dough hook on medium for 5 minutes, or as needed.

9 Remove dough from mixer; cover loosely with plastic and label with flour type.

Procedure

1 Prepare lean dough using the formula above or using any basic lean bread dough formula. Prepare one batch of dough for each flour type.

2 Place doughs in proof box for bulk fermentation until doubled in bulk, about 45 minutes.

3 Punch down doughs to distribute carbon dioxide into smaller air pockets.

4 Divide each batch of dough into 2-ounce (60 gram) pieces and round into rolls.

5 Lightly spray muffin pans with pan spray or grease with pan coating.

6 Place rolls in greased muffin pans and label. If desired, save a piece of each dough, unbaked, to evaluate later for its properties.

7 Place rolls in proof box for about 15 minutes, or until control product is nearly doubled in volume and light and airy to touch.

8 Use an oven thermometer placed in center of oven to read initial oven temperature. Record results here: _____.

9 When oven is properly preheated, place filled muffin pans in oven and set timer according to formula.

10 Bake rolls until control product (made with bread flour) is properly baked. Remove *all* rolls from oven after same length of time, even though some will be paler in color or not have risen properly. If necessary, however, adjust bake times for oven variances. Record bake times in Results Table 1.

11 Check final oven temperature. Record results here: _____.

12 Remove rolls from hot pans and cool to room temperature.

Results

1 When rolls are completely cooled, evaluate height as follows:
- Slice three rolls from each batch in half, being careful not to compress.
- Measure height of each roll by placing a ruler along the flat edge at the roll's maximum height. Record results for each of three rolls in ¹⁄₁₆" (1 mm) in Results Table 1.
- Calculate the average roll height by adding the heights of the rolls and dividing this by 3. Record results in Results Table 1.

2 Enter information from textbook on average protein content of each flour in Results Table 1.

3 If desired, evaluate saved dough pieces for elasticity and extensibility; that is, for how easily each stretches, how well each resists tearing, and how well each bounces back when pressed. Describe your evaluations as Additional Comments in Results Table 1.

RESULTS TABLE 1 YEAST ROLLS MADE WITH DIFFERENT WHEAT FLOURS

TYPE OF FLOUR	ADDITIONAL WATER ADDED TO DOUGH (OUNCES OR GRAMS)	BAKE TIME (IN MINUTES)	HEIGHTS OF EACH OF THREE ROLLS	AVERAGE HEIGHT FOR ONE ROLL	AVERAGE PROTEIN CONTENT OF FLOUR	ADDITIONAL COMMENTS
Bread (control product)						
High-gluten						
Pastry						
Cake						
Whole wheat						

4 Evaluate the sensory characteristics of completely cooled products and record evaluations in Results Table 2. Be sure to compare each in turn with the control product and evaluate the following:

- Crust color, from light to dark, on a scale of 1 to 5
- Crust texture (thick/thin, soft/hard, moist/dry, crispy/soggy, etc.)
- Crumb appearance (small/large air cells, uniform/irregular air cells, tunnels, etc.)
- Crumb texture (tough/tender, moist/dry, spongy, crumbly, chewy, gummy, etc.)
- Flavor (yeasty, floury, sweet, salty, sour, bitter, etc.)
- Overall acceptability, from highly unacceptable to highly acceptable, on a scale of 1 to 5
- Any additional comments, as necessary.

RESULTS TABLE 2 SENSORY CHARACTERISTICS OF YEAST ROLLS MADE
WITH DIFFERENT WHEAT FLOURS

TYPE OF FLOUR	CRUST COLOR AND TEXTURE	CRUMB APPEARANCE AND TEXTURE	FLAVOR	OVERALL ACCEPTABILITY	ADDITIONAL COMMENTS
Bread (control product)					
High-gluten					
Pastry					
Cake					
Whole wheat					

Sources of Error

List any sources of error that might make it difficult to draw the proper conclusions from your experiment. In particular, consider any problems properly adjusting the amount of water added to each dough, determining appropriate mix times, or any problems with the oven.

_____

_____

_____

State what you could do differently next time to minimize or eliminate each source of error.

_____

_____

_____

Conclusions

Select one from the choices in **bold** or fill in the blanks.

1 Rolls made with pastry flour were **shorter than/taller than/the same height as** those made with bread flour. This is likely because pastry flour is milled from a **soft/hard** wheat and therefore contains **more/less/the same amount of** gluten than bread flour, which is milled from a **soft/hard** wheat. The difference in height was **small/moderate/large**.

2 Rolls made with cake flour were **paler than/darker than/the same color as** those made with bread flour. This is partly because cake flour contains **more/less/the same amount of** protein than bread flour and therefore the rolls underwent **more/less/the same amount of** Maillard browning. The difference in browning was **small/moderate/large**.

3 Rolls made with high gluten flour were **tougher/more tender/neither tougher nor more tender** than those made with bread flour. A likely reason for this is:

_____

_____

_____

4 Compare rolls made with whole wheat flour with those made with bread flour. What were the main differences in appearance, flavor, and texture? Explain the main reasons for these differences.

_____

_____

_____

5 Explain why whole wheat bread sold in North America is often made with a blend of whole wheat flour and hard wheat flour.

_____

_____

_____

6 Which rolls did you feel were acceptable overall, and why?

_____

_____

_____

7 Based on the results of this experiment, which flours are not acceptable for use in yeast-raised products? Explain your answer.

_____

_____

_____

8 Rank flours in roll height from the one that produced the tallest roll to the shortest. How can you explain these differences in roll height?

_____

_____

_____

9 Rank flours in roll toughness from the flour that produced the toughest roll to the most tender. How can you explain these differences in toughness?

_____

_____

_____

❹ Experiment: Different Flours Used in Rolled Cookies

There are many types of cookies, and each reacts differently to the type of flour used. This experiment uses a formula similar to one used by millers and manufacturers for evaluating the quality of soft flours. High-quality soft flour should be low in protein, in damaged starch granules, and in gums. If it is low in these three driers, cookie dough will thin out when heated, and the cookies will spread to a larger size.

Objectives

Demonstrate how the type of flour affects

- Consistency and handling of cookie dough
- Height and spread of cookies
- Appearance of cookies
- Flavor and texture of cookies
- Overall acceptability of cookies

Products Prepared

Rolled sugar cookies made with

- Pastry flour (control product)
- Bread flour
- Cake flour
- Whole white wheat flour (soft)
- Other, if desired (all-purpose flour, whole wheat pastry flour, blend of 60 percent bread flour and 40 percent cake flour, etc.)

Materials and Equipment

- Scale
- Sieve
- Parchment paper
- Mixer with 5-quart mixing bowl
- Flat beater attachment
- Bowl scraper
- Rolled sugar cookie dough (see Formula), enough to make 12 or more cookies of each variation
- Silicone pads or parchment paper
- Cutting board, size of silicone pad or larger
- Height guides, for rolling dough to approximately ¼" (7 mm)
- Size #16 (2 fl. oz./60 ml) portion-control scoop or equivalent
- Rolling pin
- Circular dough cutter, 2½" (65 mm), or similar size
- Sheet pans, full or half
- Oven thermometer
- Serrated knife
- Ruler

Formula

Rolled Sugar Cookie Dough

Yield: *12 cookies*

INGREDIENT	POUNDS	OUNCES	GRAMS	BAKER'S PERCENTAGE
Flour	1	8	700	100
Salt		0.25	7	1
Baking soda		0.25	7	1
Shortening, all-purpose		7	200	29
Sugar, regular granulated		14	400	58
Milk, whole		5	150	21
Total	**3**	**2.5**	**1,464**	**210**

Method of Preparation

1 Preheat oven to 400°F (200°C).

2 Allow all ingredients to come to room temperature (temperature of ingredients is important for consistent results).

3 Blend flour, salt, and baking soda thoroughly by sifting together three times onto parchment paper. *Note:* if all particles (for example, bran particles in whole white wheat flour) do not fit through sieve, stir them back into mixture.

4 Combine shortening and sugar in mixing bowl and mix on low with paddle attachment for 1 minute. Stop and scrape bowl, as needed.

5 Cream shortening and sugar on medium for 1 minute. Stop and scrape bowl.

6 Slowly add half the milk while mixing on low; mix for a total of 1 minute. Stop and scrape bowl.

7 Add flour and mix on low for 1 minute. Stop and scrape bowl.

8 Add remaining milk and mix on low for an additional 1 minute.

Note: Flours vary in their water content and water absorption values. If dough does not hold together well enough to roll, add small amounts of water as needed and record amount added in Additional Comments column of Results Table 1.

Procedure

1 Prepare cookie dough using the formula above or using any basic rolled sugar cookie formula. Prepare one batch of dough for each flour type.

2 Place silicone pad on cutting board and place gauge strips along sides of pad.

3 Scoop dough onto silicone pad using #16 scoop (or equivalent).

4 Flatten each dough mound lightly with palm of hand.

5 Using height guides, roll to thickness of ¼" (7 mm) with one forward rolling pin stroke and one return (backward) stroke.

6 Cut dough with circular cutter and remove excess scraps from silicone pad.

7 Slide silicone pad with cookie dough onto sheet pan.

8 Use an oven thermometer placed in center of oven to read initial oven temperature. Record results here: _____.

9 When oven is properly preheated, place filled sheet pans in oven and set timer for 10–12 minutes, or according to formula.

10 Bake cookies until control product (made with pastry flour) is light brown. Remove *all* cookies from oven after same length of time, even though some will be paler in color or have not spread as much. If necessary, however, adjust bake times for oven variances.

11 Record bake times in Results Table 2.

12 Check final oven temperature. Record results here: _____.

13 Remove cookies from hot pans and cool to room temperature.

Results

1 Evaluate each dough for its consistency and record results in Results Table 1. In your evaluation, consider how soft/firm the dough is by how much force is required to roll it out.

2 Evaluate dough for its ease in handling and record results in Results Table 1. In your evaluation, consider:
- How well the dough holds together (dough cohesion)
- How sticky the dough is (dough adhesion)

RESULTS TABLE 1   SUGAR COOKIE DOUGH CONSISTENCY AND HANDLING

TYPE OF FLOUR	DOUGH CONSISTENCY (SOFTNESS/FIRMNESS)	EASE OF HANDLING	ADDITIONAL COMMENTS
Pastry (control product)			
Bread			
Cake			
Whole white wheat pastry			

3 When cookies are completely cooled, measure spread (width, or diameter) as follows:
- Slice three cookies from each batch in half, being careful not to compress them.
- Measure spread of each cookie in ¹⁄₁₆" (1 mm) increments. Record results in Results Table 2.
- Calculate the average cookie spread by dividing the total width by 3. Record results in Results Table 2.

4 Measure cookie height as follows:
- Measure height of sliced cookie by placing a ruler along the flat edge at the center of the cookie. Record results for each of three cookies in ¹⁄₁₆" (1 mm) increments in Results Table 2.
- Calculate the average cookie height by adding the heights of the cookies and dividing this by 3. Record results in Results Table 2.

RESULTS TABLE 2   SPREAD AND HEIGHT OF ROLLED SUGAR COOKIES

TYPE OF FLOUR	BAKE TIME (IN MINUTES)	WIDTHS (SPREAD) OF EACH OF THREE COOKIES	AVERAGE WIDTH (SPREAD) OF ONE COOKIE	HEIGHTS OF EACH OF THREE COOKIES	AVERAGE HEIGHT FOR ONE COOKIE	ADDITIONAL COMMENTS
Pastry (control product)						
Bread						
Cake						
Whole white wheat pastry						

5 Evaluate the sensory characteristics of completely cooled products and record evaluations in Results Table 3. Be sure to compare each in turn to the control product. *Note:* to evaluate crumb, break (rather than cut) cookies in half, so crumb is not compressed by knife edge. Consider the following:
- Surface color and appearance (smooth, crinkled, etc.)
- Crumb appearance (small uniform air cells, large open air cells, etc.)
- Texture (hard/soft, moist/dry, crispy, chewy, gummy, cake-like, etc.)
- Flavor (sweetness, saltiness, floury flavor, fatty/shortening flavor, etc.)
- Overall acceptability.
- Add any additional comments, as necessary.

RESULTS TABLE 3   SENSORY CHARACTERISTICS OF ROLLED SUGAR COOKIES

TYPE OF FLOUR	SURFACE COLOR AND APPEARANCE	CRUMB APPEARANCE AND TEXTURE	FLAVOR	OVERALL ACCEPTABILITY	ADDITIONAL COMMENTS
Pastry (control product)					
Bread					
Cake					
Whole white					
Wheat pastry					

Sources of Error

List any sources of error that might make it difficult to draw the proper conclusions from your experiment. In particular, be aware of differences in the amount of mixing and rolling dough, and any problems with ovens.

_____

_____

_____

State what you could do differently next time to minimize or eliminate each source of error.

_____

_____

_____

Conclusions

Select one from the choices in **bold** or fill in the blanks.

1   The cookie that was the driest (before any extra water was added) was made with **bread/ cake/pastry** flour. This is probably because _____. The differences in dough consistency were **small/moderate/large**.

2   The cookies that stayed whitest were made from **bread/cake/pastry** flour. These cookies stayed white partly because the flour used was a bleached flour, and also because it was the **highest/lowest** in protein. The difference in browning was **small/moderate/large**.

3   The cookies with the most cake-like texture were made from **bread/cake/pastry** flour. These cookies were cake-like because the flour used was chlorinated, allowing starch granules to form its characteristic soft structure as it absorbed water **more easily/with much difficulty**.

4 The cookies that spread the most were made from **bread/cake/pastry** flour. This was probably because this flour was the **most effective/least effective** drier of the three, so the dough held its shape **better/worse** when it was heated.

5 The cookies that rose the highest were made from **bread/cake/pastry** flour. The cookies that rose the highest spread **more/less** than the other cookies. This is probably because

_____

_____

_____.

6 Compare cookies made with whole white wheat pastry flour to those made with regular pastry flour (the control product). What were the main differences in appearance, flavor, and texture? Explain the main reasons for these differences.

_____

_____

_____

7 Rank flours from the one that produced the toughest cookies to the most tender.

_____

_____

_____

8 Which of these differences in toughness can be explained solely by percent protein in flour?

_____

_____

_____

9 For those differences in toughness that cannot be explained by the percent protein in the flour, how can the differences be explained?_____

_____

_____

10 Which cookies were acceptable overall and which were not? Explain your answer.

_____

_____

_____

11 Would you expect that certain flours would be more acceptable for certain uses, for example, for decorated gingerbread men, or for traditional shortbread?

_____

_____

_____

12 Based on the results of this experiment, do you think the type of flour is as important in making cookies as it is in making breads and rolls? Explain your answer.

_____

_____

_____

6

Variety Grains and Flours

Chapter Objectives

1 Classify common variety grains and flours used in the bakeshop.

2 Describe the makeup, characteristics, and uses of common variety grains and flours.

Introduction

Wheat is the only common cereal grain with a good amount of gluten-forming proteins, making it the most popular grain for baked goods in North America and in many other parts of the world. Yet other grains and flours are available to the baker. Each has a distinctive flavor and color that contributes to its value. Many also have specific health benefits. Bakeshops that limit their products to those made from common wheat miss the opportunity to provide variety to their customers.

Many variety flours contain as much protein as wheat, or more. However, because the proteins in these flours do not form gluten (except for triticum grains, to a degree, and possibly rye), protein content is not a useful indicator of quality, other than nutritional quality. Figure 6.1 compares the amount of protein in various flours, including whole wheat flour. As with wheat, most cereal grains are low in the essential amino acid lysine.

This chapter discusses many variety flours available to the baker. These flours are classified into three main

Figure 6.2   Left to right: amaranth, spelt, quinoa

categories: cereal grains, alternative wheat grains, and cereal-free grains and flours. Those classified by botanists as cereal grains, such as rye and corn, are the edible seeds of agricultural grasses. Cereal grains are high in starch. Figure 6.2 displays spelt, which looks similar to common wheat kernels, and two cereal-free grains, amaranth and quinoa, often used in multigrain breads.

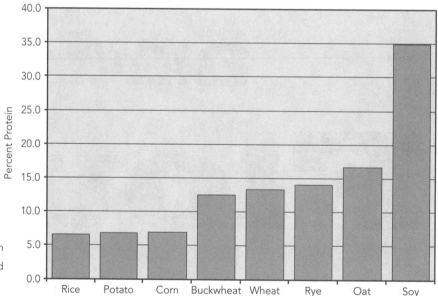

Figure 6.1   The amount of protein in whole grain variety flours compared with whole wheat flour

Cereal Grains

Rye

Rye grass is tolerant of poor soil and cold climates—climates such as those of Russia, Eastern Europe, and Scandinavia—where wheat cultivation is difficult. Not surprisingly, rye bread consumption is high in these regions, although rye represents only about 1 percent of the world's production of cereal grains.

Breads made from rye flour tend to be dense and gummy, and they have a strong flavor. Although rye is as high in protein as wheat, rye flour has, at best, a

Check out a traditional European rye bread formula and it's a good bet that it's a sourdough. Sourdough bread is typically made by adding some "old dough" from a previous batch. The old dough contains active yeast and bacteria that produce acids during fermentation. This, of course, gives sourdough breads a distinctive sour taste. But the acids do more. They lower the pH of the dough to a level where the pentosans absorb more water, swelling and stiffening the dough. Stiffer doughs are better at holding in gases during fermentation, proofing, and baking. Since rye doughs start off poor at retaining gases, this is an important benefit.

The lower pH also decreases amylase activity. Rye flour is typically high in amylase activity, much higher than wheat flour. If amylase is allowed to aggressively break down starches into sugars, the dough thins out and the baked bread is dark, dense, and soggy.

While a low pH decreases amylase activity, it increases the activity of another enzyme, phytase, that breaks down phytates. Phytates are notorious for tying up minerals, making them unavailable. With phytase, the minerals are released and the bread is more nutritious. This is particularly important with rye breads made from medium, dark, and whole ryes, which are high in phytate-bound minerals.

Besides these benefits, the presence of acids and the lower pH in sourdoughs helps prevent mold growth. Since rye bread typically has a high moisture content, it would otherwise mold easily. With the added acid, sourdough ryes often have an even longer shelf life than wheat breads.

limited ability to form gluten. While it contains sufficient gliadin, rye flour is low in glutenin, which forms the backbone of gluten. In addition, rye flour is very high in pentosan gums (8 percent or more) that interfere with what little gluten could form. The pentosans themselves, however, do provide a type of cohesive structure in rye dough.

Because of its high pentosan gum content, rye flour absorbs noticeably larger quantities of water than does wheat flour. For this and other reasons, doughs made from rye flour are gummy and sticky. They are also easily overmixed and have poor fermentation tolerance; that is, they do not retain gases well during fermentation, proofing, and the early stages of baking. As Figure 6.3 shows, rye dough releases most of its gases earlier in baking than does wheat dough, before starches have a chance to gelatinize and structure sets. The result is less leavening, with a lower volume and dense crumb.

Rye bread formulas in North America generally include hard wheat flour (clear, high-gluten, or bread flour) to supply needed gluten and to balance flavor. Standard commercial rye bread formulas generally contain about one-quarter to one-half part rye flour to one part wheat flour. Caraway seed, an ancient spice native to many of the same regions as rye grass, is a common addition to rye bread formulas.

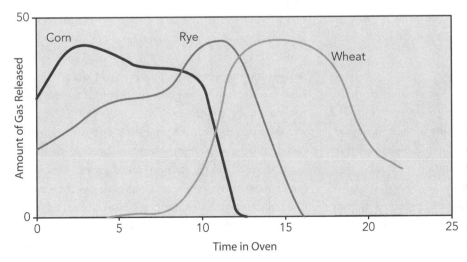

Figure 6.3 Gases evaporate from rye dough earlier in the baking process than they do from wheat dough, and they evaporate even earlier from dough made with all corn flour. The earlier the gases evaporate, the less they are able to contribute to bread rising.

Rye flour is not significantly higher in oil than wheat flour. However, because it is higher in polyunsaturated fatty acids, rye oil oxidizes more easily, producing rancid off flavors. To ensure that rye flour is always fresh, purchase it in quantities needed for no more than a three-month period.

As with wheat, a range of commercial rye products is available to the baker. *Light* or *white rye* is patent rye flour, sometimes bleached, from the heart of the rye endosperm. It is the mildest tasting, most common rye flour used in North America and is used in rye or sour rye breads. Unlike the wheat endosperm, rye endosperm is high in dietary fiber, notably soluble dietary fiber from pentosan gums.

Medium rye is straight flour from the whole endosperm, and *dark rye* is clear flour left from the production of light rye (Figure 6.4). Of light, medium, and dark rye flours, dark rye has the darkest color and strongest flavor, and produces the lowest bread volume. *Whole rye flour*, also called *pumpernickel*, is made from the whole rye kernel. Like whole wheat flour, whole rye flour contains the bran, germ, and endosperm. Pumpernickel is sometimes coarsely ground as meal or cut into flakes.

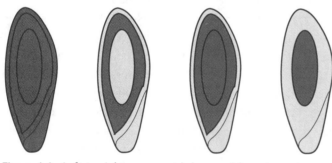

Figure 6.4 Left to right: pumpernickel, ground from the entire rye kernel; dark rye, from the outer part of the endosperm; medium rye, from the entire endosperm; light rye, from the heart of the endosperm

Corn

Corn, or maize, is typically sold as ground cornmeal, but it is also available as a coarser grit or finer flour. The size of the granule affects the quality of the baked good. Coarse-textured cornmeal, for example, makes a slightly gritty bread, one that is denser and more crumbly than cornbread made from fine cornmeal.

Corn contains a good amount of protein but none of it is gluten forming. (However, corn protein is sometimes confusingly called corn gluten.) For this reason, wheat flour is usually added to baked goods that contain cornmeal. Wheat flour provides structure and gas-retaining properties to the baked good, while cornmeal provides an appealing crumbliness, flavor, and color.

Corn products are typically white or yellow, but blue corn products are also available. Yellow cornmeal, because of its high carotenoid content, provides an attractive golden color to baked products such as cornbread and corn muffins. Carotenoids are valuable phytonutrients, plant-based (*phyto*) foods that have special health-promoting or disease-preventing properties. Carotenoids act as antioxidants, destroying damaging compounds that our body produces.

Most corn products sold today are not whole grain. That is, they are milled from the corn endosperm, since corn germ is extremely large and high in oil (30–35 percent), and becomes rancid very quickly. Cornmeal milled from the endosperm is sometimes called *degerminated*. Degerminated cornmeal is enriched to replace vitamins and minerals lost in milling. It has a milder flavor than whole grain cornmeal, but it lasts significantly longer.

Traditional Mexican corn flour used in making corn tortillas is called *masa harina*. Masa harina is made by soaking dried corn in limewater or another alkaline solution. This softens the kernels, making it easy to grind them into flour. Soaking also removes the bran layer, changes the properties and flavor of the corn, yellows the color, and substantially increases its nutritional value. In fact, if untreated corn becomes a dietary staple, as it has in certain cultures, this results in protein or niacin deficiencies (pellagra).

Oats

Oat products used in baked goods include rolled oats and quick-cooking rolled oats. Steel-cut oats are also available. Oats are most commonly used in cookies, streusel toppings, muffins, and breads. Oats are somewhat higher than most grains in protein, but the protein does not form gluten.

Oat products including oat flour and oatmeal, also called rolled oats, are whole grain because they are made from whole oat kernels, called *groats*. *Groats* are the kernels of any cereal grain that have had their inedible hulls removed. Regular rolled oats, also called *large flake* or *old-fashioned rolled oats*, are whole groats that have been steamed, then flattened between rollers. The

Limewater, used in the production of masa harina, has nothing to do with the citrus fruit lime. Instead, it is a dilute solution of calcium hydroxide (a moderately strong alkali) in water. While it is not the same thing as limestone, a common rock used in building construction, it is related. Besides being used in the production of masa harina, calcium hydroxide is important in sugar processing, since it traps impurities from sugar beet or sugar cane juice.

What's So Good About Oats?

If you've ever made oatmeal cereal for breakfast, you likely have experienced the gummy, gluey nature of oats. The gumminess comes from beta-glucan, a gum in oats that functions as dietary fiber in our bodies. While all whole grain cereals, including whole wheat, contain dietary fiber, oatmeal is higher than most in this soluble particular dietary fiber. Soluble fiber in oat products has been shown to lower cholesterol, which can lower the risk of coronary heart disease. In fact, in the United States, food products made from rolled oats, oat bran, and oat flour that contain enough soluble fiber and are low in fat can make legal claims that they may reduce the risk of heart disease. The only other common grain with a high level of beta-glucan is barley. Baked goods high in barley's beta-glucan can also make the claim that they may reduce the risk of heart disease.

steaming makes it easy to flatten the oats. Steaming also inactivates powerful lipase enzymes that could cause the oil in oats to oxidize and produce off flavors. Quick-cooking rolled oats (quick oats) are made by cutting each groat into several thin pieces before steaming and rolling. Quick oats (Figure 6.5) require less cook time because water penetrates the thin pieces faster.

Steel-cut or Irish oats are chopped into small chunks rather than rolled. They are chewier and often have a stronger flavor than rolled oats, because they are usually not steamed. The stronger flavor is from active lipase enzymes breaking down oils. Because of their chunky shape and the fact that they have not been previously cooked, steel-cut oats take longer to cook than rolled oats.

Regular rolled oats and quick oats are often used interchangeably in baking formulas. Regular rolled oats, because of their larger size, have a coarser, chewier texture. Cookies made with regular rolled oats may spread excessively if the formula specifies quick oats. The addition of a small amount of white flour may be needed to absorb the free liquid that causes excessive spread.

Rice

There are many different varieties of rice, each exhibiting different textures. If using rice in a rice pudding

Figure 6.5   Different cuts of oatmeal absorb water differently. **Clockwise from top left:** old-fashioned, quick-cooking, and steel-cut oats

or pie, decide the texture you prefer, and select the rice product accordingly. For example, long-grain white rice holds its shape well, especially if parboiled by the manufacturer. Medium- and short-grain white rice both cook into a creamy, clingy texture. Whole grain rice is called *brown rice*, for the color of the bran layer. Brown rice cooks up to a chewier texture than white rice.

Rice flour, milled from the endosperm of the rice kernel, can be purchased in specialty shops. It is not a standardized product, and often you will not know what type of rice it was ground from. It is a low-protein flour that contains no gluten, making it a common ingredient in gluten-free baked goods. Flours from medium- and short-grain rice are best for use in gluten-free breads and cakes, while flours from long-grain rice are best added to shortbread cookies or wherever a dry, sandy texture is desirable. Rice flour is also used in certain Middle Eastern and Asian cakes and cookies.

Pearl Millet

Pearl millet (*Pennisetum glaucum*) is the most common of thousands of millet varieties grown throughout the world. These tiny tear-shaped cereal grains originated in Africa thousands of years ago, but once introduced into India, pearl millet became widely grown there as well.

Millet grows despite hot, dry climate conditions and poor soil, making it a valuable staple in countries where little else will grow. Unless first cooked in water, millet retains a crunchy texture in baked goods. Once ground, pearl millet must be used immediately, or it must be refrigerated, to prevent off flavors from developing in the oils. Because it does not contain gluten, pearl millet flour must be combined with wheat for leavened baked goods. In India, pearl millet flour is used in flatbreads (*roti*). Grains of pearl millet pop like popcorn.

Teff

Teff has been grown in Ethiopia for thousands of years, and it is still the most plentiful cereal grain grown there. Teff grains are probably the smallest of any cereal grain. They are traditionally ground into flour, fermented, and made into a mildly sour, spongy pancake called *injera*. Teff, in the form of injera and many other baked goods, is eaten daily in Ethiopia by those who can afford it. As Ethiopian restaurants have become popular in both Europe and North America, the cultivation and use of teff have spread to these areas.

Alternative Wheat Grains

Several variety grains are actually distant ancestors or close cousins to common wheat (*Triticum aestivum*). Each is indeed a type of wheat and each contains gluten. Despite the common misconception that these grains are acceptable for those with celiac disease or wheat allergies (see Chapter 18), this is not necessarily the case. In fact, food products sold in the United States that are made with any of the following grains must declare on the label that they contain wheat as an allergen. However, people do vary in their sensitivities to gluten and to allergens, and some who must avoid common wheat can tolerate one or more of these grains.

Spelt

Spelt (*Triticum spelta*) is considered an ancestor to modern wheat. In the United States, spelt has been grown for years, mostly in Ohio, as animal feed, but small amounts are now grown for specialty and health food stores. Europe is also showing renewed interest in spelt. Germany and surrounding regions grow significant amounts of spelt, locally called *dinkel*.

Like wheat, spelt can be milled into whole grain or into white flour. Spelt proteins form gluten, but the gluten is weak and easily overworked. Spelt bread dough should be mixed for only a short period of time, to avoid overworking the gluten and reducing its ability to retain leavening gases. Spelt has a lower water absorption value than wheat, so less water is needed when forming batters and doughs. It is best used in place of soft, rather than hard, wheat.

Kamut

Kamut (*Triticum turgidum*) is considered to be an ancient relative of modern durum wheat. Kamut seeds were first brought to the United States from Egypt only about fifty years ago. The seeds were propagated unchanged (not cross-bred with other wheat species) from the ancient seed. Kamut, which is an early Egyptian word for wheat, is a trademarked name licensed to those who grow the grain as certified organic. The grain grows well in dry regions of the Great Plains of Montana and in the Canadian provinces of Saskatchewan and Alberta.

Kamut kernels, which are two to three times the size of common wheat kernels, are high in protein like durum wheat. Like spelt, Kamut has been successfully marketed to consumers as a health and specialty food product. Whole grain Kamut has a sweeter, milder taste than common wheat, probably because its large size means it has less bran for the amount of endosperm. Kamut products are especially popular in Europe. Because it forms strong gluten, similar to durum wheat, it is most commonly used in whole grain pastas, breads, hot cereals, bulgur, and couscous.

Triticale

Triticale was developed by plant breeders looking to combine the grain quality of wheat (*triticum*) with the hardiness of rye (*secale*). The name triticale comes from a combination of the Latin names of each grain. Because of its superior nutritional quality compared to wheat, there were high expectations in the 1960s and 1970s that triticale would provide the means of feeding growing populations in countries such as India, Pakistan, and Mexico. Today, triticale is used primarily as animal feed in North America and many other places around the world. It is used instead of soft wheat especially in Mexico, in tortillas, crackers, and cookies.

Einkorn and Emmer (Farro)

Ancestors of today's cultivated varieties of einkorn (*Triticum monococcum*) and emmer (*Triticum dicoccum*) originated around the Fertile Crescent of the Tigris and Euphrates Rivers in what is Iraq today. Einkorn is considered the very first wheat grain cultivated by man, starting about 10,000 years ago. Before that, einkorn was gathered wild.

Emmer has some similarities to spelt, but it is much older, predating spelt by thousands of years. Spelt is often mistakenly identified as emmer. Emmer fell out of favor thousands of years ago when people switched to durum wheat. Like einkorn and spelt, emmer is not free threshing, meaning that the kernels do not easily fall out of their husks or hulls. Cereal husks are acceptable as feed for livestock but not as food for humans. However, the very thing that made harvesting these grains difficult in preindustrial times has turned into an advantage. The close-fitting husk protects the kernel from insects and fungus, so these grains are easier to grow organically.

Einkorn and emmer were made into porridge by the earliest civilizations before they were made into bread and beer. Einkorn has a high ratio of gliadin to glutenin, which results in a soft, sticky dough that is not particularly suitable for bread. Emmer, on the other hand, makes satisfactory dough but a heavy-textured bread. Emmer is very likely the wheat that was used by the Egyptians when they first made bread. Today, emmer is grown primarily in the Tuscan region of Italy, where it is known as *farro*.

Cereal-Free Grains and Flours

The following seeds, legumes, and tubers are often ground into flours and used in baked goods. For this reason, they are included in this chapter. None contain gluten, so all can be consumed by those with celiac disease (gluten intolerance; see Chapter 18).

While not classified by botanists as cereals (they are not members of the grass family), amaranth, buckwheat, and quinoa in particular are similar to cereal grains in composition and use. These three grains are sometimes called *pseudocereals*. When ground whole, they are classified as whole grains; flaxseed, soy, and potato are not.

Amaranth

Amaranth is an ancient seed that was a staple crop of the Aztecs and Maya of South and Central America. Amaranth plants are green herbs, and the seeds are small and light brown. Although not as popular as quinoa, there has been resurgence of interest in amaranth. Like quinoa, amaranth is high in lysine and is used in multigrain breads. Amaranth seeds can be popped like popcorn.

Buckwheat

Despite its name, buckwheat is not wheat at all. Buckwheat kernels have many similarities to cereal grain kernels. They can be ground into whole grain flour or more coarsely into grits. Or the endosperm can be separated and milled into a lighter, milder flour. Buckwheat

Flaxseed contains a high amount of lignan, an important compound known as a *phytoestrogen*. In fact, flaxseed contains significantly more lignan than any other plant source. Phytoestrogens are antioxidants that appear to have health benefits. While it is still being researched, lignan is showing promise in preventing certain diseases such as breast cancer.

Flaxseed is over 40 percent oil, approaching the amount of oil found in peanuts and pistachios. Unlike peanuts and pistachios, however, the oil in flaxseed is particularly high in alpha linolenic acid (ALA), an essential omega-3 fatty acid. Just as flaxseed contains more lignan than any other plant source, so too does it contain more ALA. ALA and other omega-3 fatty acids are important because they appear to reduce the risk of coronary heart disease.

Flaxseed can be ground into flour using a blender or food processor. Unground, flaxseed will keep for a year or more, protected by its hard coating. Once ground, it must be used immediately or refrigerated. ALA, the oil in flaxseed, is a highly polyunsaturated fatty acid, meaning that it oxidizes rapidly. Oxidized ALA has a strong off flavor, reminiscent of paint or turpentine. This is really not too surprising, since the industrial name for flaxseed is linseed. Boiled linseed oil is one of the main ingredients in oil-based paints.

---

is also sold as whole kernels or groats. Roasted buckwheat groats are called *kasha* and are consumed in parts of Eastern Europe and Russia.

Because of its strong, distinct flavor, dark color, and lack of gluten, buckwheat flour is typically used in combination with wheat flour, usually one-quarter to one-half part buckwheat flour to one part wheat flour. Buckwheat is not higher in protein than wheat, but the protein it contains has a more nutritionally balanced profile than wheat. Russian pancakes (*blini*) are traditionally made from buckwheat, as are Breton crêpes in the north of France and soba noodles in Japan.

Flaxseed

Flaxseeds are small, oily seeds, typically dark brown in color. Canada is the world's largest producer of flaxseed, exporting it primarily to the United States, Europe, Japan, and South Korea.

Flaxseeds are oval like sesame seeds, but they are very hard and should be ground into fine flour before use. Unground flaxseed can pass through the body undigested. If it is not digested, the flaxseed will not provide any nutritional benefits. Yet it is because of its nutritional benefits that flaxseed use has increased dramatically in just a few years.

Flaxseed flour can be added to batters and doughs in small amounts (less than 10 percent flour weight) without much change in flavor. Often the amount of fat in the mix can be lowered because of the high amount

of oil in flaxseed. Flaxseed is also high in a particular vegetable gum, called a *mucilage*, that gives it a gummy, gooey consistency when it is added to water. This mucilage is an excellent source of soluble dietary fiber. Because of the water absorption capacity of mucilage, the amount of water generally needs to be increased when flaxseed flour is added to batters and doughs.

Potato

The potato is a tuber, not a cereal grain, but it can be cooked, dried, and cut into flakes or milled into flour. Potato products are valued in yeast doughs and other baked goods for the starch they contain. The starch in potato flakes, cooked potatoes, and the water from cooked potatoes is already gelatinized. Gelatinized potato starch is easily broken down by amylase into sugar and other products. This increases water absorption of doughs and improves fermentation. Breads and other baked goods containing potato products are soft and moist and they resist staling.

Quinoa

Quinoa has many of the same characteristics of cereal grains and was a staple crop of the ancient Inca empire; it still grows best in the very high elevations of the Andes Mountains in South America. Quinoa is a seed, not a cereal grain. Quinoa seeds, which are small like sesame seeds, are very high in healthful unsaturated fatty acids. Unlike wheat and most other cereal grains, quinoa is high in lysine, an essential amino acid. When used in multigrain breads, quinoa compensates for their amino acid deficiencies.

Because of its high level of unsaturated fatty acids, quinoa seeds can oxidize fairly quickly, especially once the seeds are ground. It is best to refrigerate quinoa seeds if they are to be kept for a time.

Soy

The soybean is a legume, not a cereal grain. Its composition and characteristics are quite different from wheat and other cereal grains. Compared to wheat, dried soybeans are high in protein (about 35 percent), high in fat (about 20 percent), and low in starch (15 to 20 percent). Soy flour used in baking is typically defatted, which means that some or all of the fat is removed. Soy flour comes toasted or untoasted.

Untoasted soy flour contains powerful active enzymes useful in yeast breads. An enzyme in untoasted soy flour, lipoxygenase, oxidizes carotenoids, whitening flour without the use of chemical bleaching agents. This is the main reason untoasted soy flour is added to bread dough. Only a small amount—0.5 percent flour weight—of enzyme-active soy flour is needed; in fact, higher amounts have a detrimental effect on bread flavor and texture. Amylase is another active enzyme present in untoasted soy flour. Recall that amylase breaks down starch into sugars, improving fermentation, crust color, and bread softness, and delaying staling. Other enzymes in untoasted soy flour, proteases, act on proteins to improve dough mixing and gluten development. In these ways, untoasted soy flour is a bleaching and maturing agent (see Flour and Dough Additives and Treatments, in Chapter 5).

Soy flour has quite different functions when it is toasted. Toasted soy flour no longer contains active enzymes and has a more appealing flavor, so it can be used at higher levels than enzyme-active soy flour. Soy flour does not contain gluten-forming proteins, but it does provide good nutrition. Soy protein is high in the essential amino acid lysine, so it can be used in breads to improve their protein quality. Soy protein has also been shown to lower the risk of heart disease. In fact, in the United States, food products that contain a certain amount (6.25 grams) of soy protein per serving and are low in fat, saturated fat, cholesterol, and salt can now make legal claims that they may reduce the risk of heart disease.

Like flaxseed, soy contains antioxidant phytoestrogens. While the phytoestrogens in flaxseed are called lignans, those in soy are isoflavones. Like lignans, isoflavones are thought to reduce the risk of certain cancers.

Soy flours have other uses in baked goods. They increase water absorption of doughs and reduce fat absorption in doughnuts. Soy flours sometimes function as milk and egg substitutes.

Questions for Review

1 Name four cereal grains besides wheat that are milled into flours or meals.

2 What component in rye flour, besides starch, absorbs a large quantity of water as dough forms?

3 What component in rye flour replaces gluten as the main source of a cohesive structure, with an ability to hold in gases during proofing and baking?

4 How does rye bread dough compare to wheat dough in consistency and in its ability to resist overmixing and overfermenting?

5 Which type of rye flour is patent flour, made from the heart of the rye endosperm?

6 Why does white rye flour have a shorter shelf life than white wheat flour?

7 What are the advantages of using a sourdough when preparing rye bread?

8 Which of the following are whole grains: degerminated cornmeal, quick-cooking oats, pumpernickel, kasha, white rye flour, rice flour?

9 What is masa harina and how is it produced?

10 How are quick-cooking rolled oats processed differently than regular rolled oats? How does this affect their use in baked goods?

11 What is spelt? What is it used for?

12 What is Kamut? What is it used for?

13 Which two grains were crossed by plant breeders to produce triticale?

14 Why are spelt, emmer, and einkorn easier to grow organically than other grains?

15 Which cereal grains contain high amounts of soluble dietary fiber?

16 What is ALA and what are its benefits? In which seed is it found?

17 What is a phytoestrogen? Name one found in flaxseed and another in soybeans.

18 Why should flaxseed be ground into flour before use? How is this best done?

19 What is the main reason for adding untoasted soy flour to yeast breads?

20 What is the main reason for adding toasted soy flour to baked goods?

21 What effect does potato flour or potatoes have on the quality of baked goods? Why does it have this effect?

Questions for Discussion

1 How might a bread made with rye flour differ from one made with wheat flour? Consider flavor, density, and texture.

2 Which variety grains are related to wheat (triticum) and why might this be important to a person with celiac disease or wheat allergies?

3 In general, how does the amount and the nutritional quality of protein in wheat flour compare to other flours?

Exercises and Experiments

❶ Exercise: Different Variety Grains

Use your textbook to fill out the first column of the following Results Table. Next, use fresh samples to evaluate the appearance (color), aroma, and particle size of each of the flours or meals. To evaluate particle size, rub a thin layer of flour or meal between your fingers and rate how fine or coarse it feels. Use this opportunity to learn how to identify different flours from their sensory characteristics alone. Add any additional comments or observations that you might have to the last column in the Results Table. Use the two blank rows at the bottom of the Results Table to evaluate additional flours and meals, if desired.

RESULTS TABLE   VARIETY FLOURS AND MEALS

TYPE OF FLOUR/ INGREDIENT	CONTAINS GLUTEN-FORMING PROTEINS? (Y/N)	APPEARANCE	AROMA	PARTICLE SIZE	ADDITIONAL COMMENTS
White rye flour					
Whole rye flour (pumpernickel)					
Corn flour					
Corn meal					
Oatmeal, old-fashioned					
Oatmeal, quick					
Rice flour					
Buckwheat flour					
Soy flour					
Quinoa flour					
Spelt flour					

② Experiment: Different Variety Flours in Lean Yeast Rolls

Many of the flours used in this experiment contain no gluten. For this reason, doughs include bread flour as an ingredient. Otherwise, this experiment is identical to the one in Chapter 5.

Objectives

Demonstrate how the type of flour affects
- Height of rolls
- Crispness and browning on the crust of rolls
- Crumb color and structure
- Overall flavor of rolls
- Overall texture of rolls
- Overall acceptability of rolls

Products Prepared

Lean yeast rolls made with
- Bread flour, 100 percent (control product)
- White rye, 40 percent and bread flour, 60 percent
- Corn flour, 40 percent and bread flour, 60 percent
- Oat flour, 40 percent and bread flour, 60 percent
- Other, if desired (100 percent spelt; 100 percent white rye; 40 percent pumpernickel, cornmeal, oatmeal, buckwheat, or soy, etc.)

Materials and Equipment

- Proof box
- Scale
- Sieve
- Parchment paper
- Mixer with 5-quart mixing bowl
- Flat beater attachment
- Bowl scraper
- Dough hook attachment
- Plastic wrap
- Lean Dough (see Formula), enough to make 12 or more rolls of each variation
- Muffin pans (2½" or 3½" /65 or 90 mm size)
- Pan spray or pan coating
- Oven thermometer
- Serrated knife
- Ruler

Formula

Lean Dough

Yield: *12 rolls*

INGREDIENT	POUNDS	OUNCES	GRAMS	BAKER'S PERCENTAGE
Bread flour		11	300	60
Variety flour (or additional bread flour for control)		7	200	40
Salt		0.25	8	1.5
Yeast, instant		0.25	8	1.5
Water, 85°F (30°C)		10	280	56
Total	**1**	**12.5**	**796**	**159**

Method of Preparation

1   Preheat oven to 425°F (220°C).

2   Set proof box to 85°F (30°C) and 85 percent relative humidity.

3   Weigh an additional 5 ounces (140 grams) water (at 85°F/30°C) and set aside. (This will be used for adjusting dough consistency in step 7.)

4   Combine flour and salt thoroughly by sifting together three times onto parchment paper. *Note:* if all particles (for example, bran particles) do not fit through sieve, stir them back into mixture.

5   Place flour-salt mixture, yeast, and water in mixing bowl.

6   Blend on low with flat beater for 1 minute. Stop and scrape bowl.

7   Add additional water (from step 3) slowly and as needed, to adjust consistency. Record amount of water added to each dough in Results Table 1.

8   Mix using dough hook on medium for 5 minutes, or as needed.

9   Remove dough from mixer; cover loosely with plastic and label with flour type.

Procedure

1   Prepare lean doughs using the formula above. Prepare one batch of dough for each flour type.

2   Place doughs in proof box for bulk fermentation until doubled in bulk, about 45 minutes.

3   Punch down doughs to distribute carbon dioxide into smaller air pockets.

4   Divide each batch of dough into 2-ounce (60 gram) pieces and round into rolls.

5   Lightly spray muffin pans with pan spray or grease with pan coating.

6   Place rolls in greased muffin pans and label; if desired, save a piece of each dough, unbaked, to evaluate later for its properties.

7 Place rolls in proof box for about 15 minutes, or until control product is nearly doubled in volume and light and airy to touch.

8 Use an oven thermometer placed in center of oven to read initial oven temperature. Record results here: _____.

9 When oven is properly preheated, place filled muffin pans in oven and set timer according to formula.

10 Bake rolls until control product (made with bread flour) is properly baked. Remove *all* rolls from oven after same length of time, even though some will be paler in color or have not risen properly. If necessary, however, adjust bake times for oven variances. Record bake times in Results Table 1.

11 Check final oven temperature. Record results here: _____.

12 Remove rolls from hot pans and cool to room temperature.

Results

1 When rolls are completely cooled, evaluate height as follows:
  - Slice three rolls from each batch in half, being careful not to compress.
  - Measure height of each roll by placing a ruler along the flat edge at the roll's maximum height. Record results for each of three rolls in ¹⁄₁₆" (1 mm) increments in Results Table 1.
  - Calculate the average roll height by adding the heights of the rolls and dividing this by 3. Record results in Results Table 1.

2 If desired, evaluate saved dough pieces for elasticity and extensibility; that is, for how easily each stretches, how well each resists tearing, and how well each bounces back when pressed. Describe your evaluations as Additional Comments in Results Table 1.

RESULTS TABLE 1   YEAST ROLLS MADE WITH VARIETY GRAINS

TYPE OF FLOUR	ADDITIONAL WATER ADDED TO DOUGH (OUNCES OR GRAMS)	BAKE TIME (IN MINUTES)	HEIGHTS OF EACH OF THREE ROLLS	AVERAGE HEIGHT FOR ONE ROLL	ADDITIONAL COMMENTS
Bread flour, 100% (control product)					
White rye, 40%; Bread flour 60%					
Corn, 40%; Bread flour 60%					
Oat, 40%; Bread flour 60%					

3 Evaluate the sensory characteristics of completely cooled products and record evaluations in Results Table 2. Be sure to compare each in turn to the control product and evaluate the following:

- Crust color, from light to dark, on a scale of 1 to 5
- Crust texture (thick/thin, soft/hard, moist/dry, crispy/soggy, etc.)
- Crumb appearance (small/large air cells, uniform/irregular air cells, tunnels, etc.)
- Crumb texture (tough/tender, moist/dry, spongy, crumbly, chewy, gummy, etc.)
- Flavor (yeasty, floury, sweet, salty, sour, bitter, etc.)
- Overall acceptability, from highly unacceptable to highly acceptable, on a scale of 1 to 5
- Any additional comments, as necessary

RESULTS TABLE 2 SENSORY CHARACTERISTICS OF YEAST ROLLS MADE WITH VARIETY GRAINS

TYPE OF FLOUR	CRUST COLOR AND TEXTURE	CRUMB APPEARANCE AND TEXTURE	FLAVOR	OVERALL ACCEPTABILITY	ADDITIONAL COMMENTS
Bread flour, 100% (control product)					
White rye, 40%; Bread flour 60%					
Corn, 40%; Bread flour 60%					
Oat, 40%; Bread flour 60%					

Sources of Error

List any sources of error that might make it difficult to draw the proper conclusions from your experiment. In particular, consider any problems properly adjusting the amount of water added to each dough, determining appropriate mix times, or any problems with the ovens.

_____

_____

_____

State what you could do differently next time to minimize or eliminate each source of error.

_____

_____

_____

Conclusions

Select one from the choices in **bold** or fill in the blanks.

1 Rolls made with white rye required **more/less/same amount of** water to form an acceptable dough than those made entirely with bread flour. This is because rye flour contains more **pentosan/beta-glucan/mucilage** gums than bread flour. The difference in water absorption was **small/moderate/large**.

2 Rolls made with white rye flour were **shorter than/taller than/the same height as** those made entirely with bread flour. This is because white rye flour contains **more/less/the same amount of** gluten than bread flour and has a **lower/higher/same** fermentation tolerance than bread flour. The difference in height was **small/moderate/large**.

3 The differences in texture between rolls made with white rye flour and those made entirely with bread flour was **small/moderate/large**. The differences in texture were as follows:

_____

_____

_____

4 Compare rolls that were made with corn flour with those made entirely with bread flour. What were the main differences in appearance, flavor, and texture?

_____

_____

_____

How do you explain these differences?

_____

_____

_____

5 Compare rolls that were made with oat flour with those made entirely with bread flour. What were the main differences in appearance, flavor, and texture?

_____

_____

_____

How do you explain these differences?

_____

_____

_____

6 Which rolls did you feel were acceptable overall, and why?

_____

_____

_____

7 Based on the results of this experiment, which flours are not acceptable for use in yeast-raised products? Explain your answer.

_____

_____

_____

8 Rank flours in roll height from the one that produced the shortest roll to the tallest. How can you explain these differences in roll height?

_____

_____

_____

9 Rank flours in roll toughness from the flour that produced the toughest roll to the most tender. How can you explain these differences in toughness?

_____

_____

_____

10 Based on the results of this experiment, which flours do you think could be used at a higher level than 40 percent without sacrificing quality?

_____

_____

_____

11 Based on the results of this experiment, which flours do you think should be used at a lower level than 40 percent so they are acceptable?

_____

_____

_____

12 Explain why variety breads (those made with rye, oats, corn, etc.) sold in the United States typically contain a hard wheat flour in their formulas.

_____

_____

_____

Gluten

Chapter Objectives

1 Describe the formation and development of gluten from flour and water.

2 Describe the importance of gluten to various baked goods.

3 List and explain ways to increase or decrease gluten development.

4 Differentiate between gluten development and relaxation.

Introduction

Gluten is one of three main structure builders in baked goods. The other two are egg proteins and starch. While all three are important, gluten, which forms and develops when flour is mixed with water, is probably the most complex of the three and can be the most difficult to control. In fact, a seemingly small change in a formula or mixing method can have a large effect on gluten development. This is especially true with bread and other yeast doughs, which rely heavily on gluten for unbaked dough structure.

While it is true that yeast doughs depend on gluten for structure more than most other baked goods, it is important with any baked good to know when to increase gluten, when to decrease it, and how to make these changes. This chapter is all about gluten: what it is, how it forms, and, most important, how to control it.

Recent advances have been made in the preparation of gluten-free breads and other baked goods. For information on gluten-free baked goods, go to Chapter 18.

The Formation and Development of Gluten

Flour itself does not contain gluten. Instead, flour contains two proteins (glutenin and gliadin) that form gluten when water is added. Besides water, gluten requires mixing to form a strong, continuous network.

Gluten is a dynamic system, constantly changing as it is handled, but overall, it becomes strong and stretchy as it is mixed. Glutenin is thought to provide most of the strength, also called *tenacity*, to gluten, while gliadin provides its stretchiness, or *extensibility*. Glutenin also provides *elasticity* to gluten; that is, its ability to bounce back once it is stretched or pressed.

Although glutenin and gliadin molecules cannot be seen, changes to gluten are reflected by what is seen in the bakeshop. That is, batters and doughs become

What Does Gluten Look Like?

Gluten cannot be seen with the naked eye, but scientists are making progress in understanding its structure. The backbone of the gluten network likely consists of the largest glutenin molecules, called *subunits*, lined up and tightly linked to one another. These tightly linked glutenin subunits come together more loosely with gliadin into larger gluten aggregates. While the complex structure of gluten is not completely understood, portions of glutenin are thought to loop, making gluten stretchy and flexible. Gluten is further made flexible by the presence of compact, coiled gliadin molecules interspersed throughout.

Gliadin

Glutenin subunit

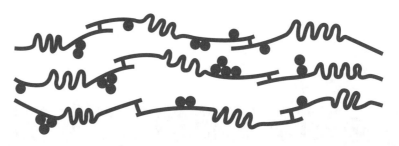

At the next level of gluten structure, gluten aggregates interact to form a tangled network of larger gluten particles that loosely interact with starch granules, fats, sugars, and gums. It does seem that gluten structure is held together by some very strong bonds and many more weak ones that break and reform easily. Many weak bonds break, in particular during mixing, only to reform around the surfaces of expanding air bubbles during proofing and the early stages of baking. It is this combination of strong and weak forces breaking and reforming that contributes to the unique nature of gluten.

Gluten's makeup and structure are responsible for its unique nature, which scientists describe as viscoelastic. Viscoelasticity is the ability of a material to stretch and easily change shape—like a thick or viscous liquid—without breaking or tearing, and to partly bounce back to its original shape, like an elastic or rubber band. Viscoelastic products can be thought of as part liquid, part solid. Few food products exhibit this dual nature as clearly as gluten in dough that has reached maturity, which is why it is difficult, although not impossible, to make bread without using wheat flour. Consider the following products that are not viscoelastic.

Corn syrup is not viscoelastic because it does not have elasticity or rubberiness. That is, corn syrup cannot bounce back to its original shape once it flows. Corn syrup is also not strong and solid enough to capture and hold expanding gases.

Shortening is not viscoelastic because it cannot stretch or flow like a liquid. While it is soft enough to change shape yet solid enough to hold its shape, shortening cannot stretch and hold expanding gases.

Peanut brittle is not viscoelastic because it is too firm and rigid. While it holds its shape quite nicely, peanut brittle will not stretch or change shape easily. If gases were able to expand at all in peanut brittle, the brittle would not expand. Instead, it would crack and shatter from the buildup of pressure.

Figure 7.1 Dough visibly becomes smoother, drier, and less lumpy as mixing hydrates and develops the gluten into a strong, cohesive network. **Left:** dough optimally mixed. **Right:** dough undermixed

smoother, stronger, drier, and less lumpy as they are mixed and gluten develops. Fully developed yeast-raised dough has a dry, silky appearance, while dough still at the *cleanup stage* forms a ball that is coarse and rough looking (Figure 7.1).

Bakers typically determine if dough is fully developed by performing the windowpane test. To make a windowpane, pull off a piece of dough about 1 inch or so in diameter. Roll it between your hands to shape into a ball, and then gently pull the dough between your hands. Rotate the dough as you do this, so that you are pulling it in all directions, forming a paper-thin sheet of dough. Fully developed dough should form a uniformly thin, smooth film without tearing (Figure 7.2).

Gluten in yeast dough continues to change during bulk fermentation and proofing. Once the dough has the proper balance of strength and stretchiness, it has reached dough maturity. Mature dough is easy to handle and shape, and it will rise properly during baking.

When batters and doughs are baked, most of the moisture evaporates or is absorbed by gelatinizing starch granules. With this loss of moisture and in the presence of heat, gluten sets into a firm and rigid yet porous structure that holds its shape. While not unique to gluten (egg proteins, when heated, also set into a firm, rigid structure), this is nonetheless an important feature of gluten.

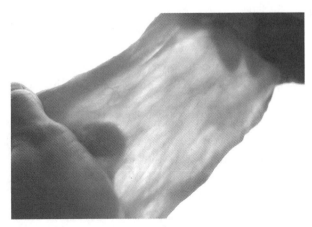

Figure 7.2 Flour dough optimally mixed, in stretched windowpane

There are several tests used by cereal chemists, grain millers, and bakeries to evaluate the quality of wheat flour. One test, especially popular in France, uses an instrument called the *Chopin alveograph*. The alveograph blows air into dough made from flour, water, and salt, forming an expanding bubble. This mimics the fermentation process, in which gas cells expand in a similar way. It is not unlike blowing bubbles with bubble gum.

Three values from this test are particularly useful. The first value is a measure of how resistant the dough is to stretching, also called *tensile strength*, or *tenacity*. Dough tenacity, often designated as P, measures the maximum pressure reached as a bubble is inflated. Consider the tenacity of bubble gum. Bubble gum that requires you to blow hard to form a bubble would have high tenacity. Bread dough with very high tenacity will be bucky. Bucky doughs are most often made from flours with a high gluten content, such as a high-gluten flour. These flours absorb a large amount of water, since they are typically high in gluten, and they might not stretch well during fermentation.

A second value, L, represents dough extensibility. Dough extensibility is a measure of how far the dough bubble stretches before it breaks. Once again, we can relate this to bubble gum. Bubble gum that blows into a big bubble before popping would have a high L value. With flour, the greater the L value, the higher the dough will rise during fermentation.

Often, the P and L value are expressed as a ratio, P/L, which provides a combined index of gluten behavior. It captures the relative amount of tenacity to extensibility in dough. Notice how the alveograph measures similar characteristics that bakers evaluate when they produce a windowpane from developed dough.

A final value, W, measures the total energy used to inflate the dough bubble. It is an indication of how well dough will hold up during proofing and baking. In Europe, flours are often described by their W value. Flour with a very low W value is inappropriate for use in bread baking: pastry flours have low W values. Flour with a very high W is good for doughs that undergo long fermentation times, or for sweet doughs. Flours with a moderate W work well in doughs that undergo a shorter rise.

Determining Gluten Requirements

It is tempting to generalize and say that, for bread, the more gluten the better, and for pastries, the less gluten the better. But this is oversimplifying the matter. Different types of bread have different gluten requirements (Figure 7.3). Even when gluten requirements are high, bread dough can have too much strong gluten. Breads with too much gluten tend to be tough and chewy, have low volume because they cannot stretch, and develop soft and thin crusts. Just as bread can have too much gluten, pastries can have too little. Pie crusts with too little gluten break and crumble easily, cakes collapse, and baking powder biscuits slump.

Still, yeast-raised baked goods require the most gluten of all bakeshop products. Gluten is so important to bread that when bread bakers speak of flour quality, they are typically referring to the amount and quality of gluten that forms from the flour. Bread dough made from high-quality flour will expand easily and is best at retaining gases generated during fermentation and oven

Figure 7.3 Different types of yeast breads have different gluten requirements. Artisan bread, top, with its flattened shape, large open grain, and crisp crust requires less gluten, while white Pullman sandwich bread (*pain de mie*), bottom, requires more.

Balancing Glutenin and Gliadin

When yeast-raised dough is properly developed or matured, it has the right balance of glutenin and gliadin for that particular product. If there is too much glutenin for the amount of gliadin, the dough will be bucky. That is, the dough will be so strong and tenacious that it will be difficult to stretch (Figure 7.4). Bucky doughs don't rise well, producing low-volume loaves with a tight crumb. Bucky doughs are also difficult to shape, since they bounce back too readily. Pizza prepared from dough that is too strong and bucky is most apt to shrink during shaping and baking.

If there too little glutenin for the amount of gliadin, however, the dough will be slack. Slack doughs are soft and easy to stretch, but they don't bounce back or hold their shape (Figure 7.5). They will rise easily, but they don't retain gases during long fermentations and instead can collapse. That is, slack doughs have poor *fermentation tolerance*. Breads made with very slack doughs will have low volume, and they tend to have large air cells. Some thin-crust pizzas, tortillas, and artisan breads such as ciabatta are made with relatively slack doughs.

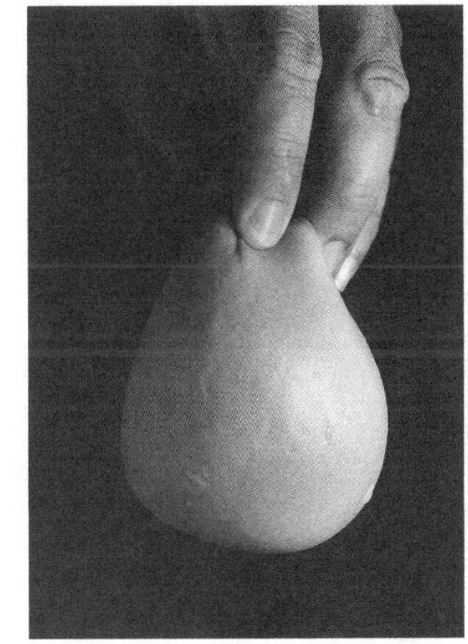

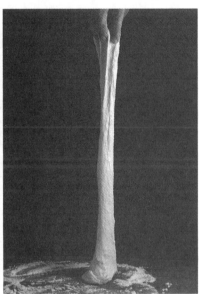

Figure 7.4 Left: Bucky dough, with too much glutenin for the amount of gliadin, holds its shape but doesn't stretch easily.

Figure 7.5 Right: Slack dough, with too little glutenin for the amount of gliadin, is soft and extensible but doesn't hold its shape well.

spring. The baked bread typically has large loaf volume and a fine crumb, because cell walls are less apt to tear.

Of common yeast doughs, sandwich breads, with their high volume, fine crumb, and added sugar and fat, require a relatively high amount of gluten. Traditional boiled bagels, with their chewy texture, have even higher gluten requirements. Hearth breads—those that are baked directly on sheet pans or baking stones—also require a high amount of gluten, but only if high volume and a fine crumb are desired. Without sufficient gluten (and without a pan) to hold them in shape, hearth breads flatten under their own weight. This flattening is desirable with some rustic artisan breads, however, such as ciabatta. Ciabatta is well-named, since the word means "slipper" in Italian, and soft, wet ciabatta dough takes on the shape of a flat slipper as it slumps on the baking stone. Ciabatta also has a large, open grain and crisp crust characteristic of bread made with low amounts of gluten. With less gluten, the dough breaks and tears more readily as gases expand, forming the desired large air pockets characteristic of this type of product.

While it is easy to say that pastries require less gluten than breads do, it is often difficult to compare the gluten requirements of various pastries, since they are complex mixtures of tougheners and tenderizers, moisteners and driers. It is probably safe to say, however, that products containing significant amounts of other structure builders, including eggs and starch, require the least amount of gluten for their structure. Liquid shortening cakes, which rely on the soft structure of gelatinized starch, and sponge cakes, with their high egg content, both require very little gluten.

Controlling Gluten Development

There are three main ways that gluten develops and doughs mature during bread making. One way is by mixing, sometimes called *mechanical dough development*. A second way is by *chemical dough development*, through the use of ascorbic acid and other maturing agents that strengthen. Finally, gluten is developed over time during bulk fermentation and final proof. Of the three, this last means of gluten development is the most complex and least understood, because many other chemical and physical changes happen as dough undergoes fermentation. While they act in different ways, all three means of gluten development encourage the alignment and bonding of glutenin subunits into a large, cohesive network.

While these are the main ways that gluten develops, there are many ways to control gluten development, whether to increase it so that dough is stronger and more elastic, or alternatively, to decrease it so that dough is softer, slacker, and more extensible. The following list includes the most common ingredients and processes that can be adjusted or changed as a means of controlling gluten development. Many were introduced in Chapters 5 and 6. They are included again here to present a comprehensive list that can be helpful with problem solving in the bakeshop.

- Type of flour
- Amount of water
- Water hardness
- Water pH
- Mixing and kneading
- Batter and dough temperature
- Fermentation
- Maturing agents and dough conditioners
- Reducing agents
- Enzymes
- Tenderizers and softeners
- Salt
- Other structure builders
- Milk
- Fiber, bran, fruit pieces, spices, and the like

Some of these items, such as dough conditioners and heat-treated milk, apply exclusively to yeast-raised doughs. Others apply to all baked goods. Even so, most items on the list tend to have their greatest effect on baked goods that rely heavily on gluten—and not on eggs and starch—for structure.

Besides yeast doughs, pie pastry relies heavily on gluten for structure. Expect pie pastry quality to suffer noticeably when too much or too little gluten develops, and expect it to be affected by many items on the list.

In contrast, high-ratio liquid shortening cakes and other baked goods made from cake flour contain very little gluten to begin with. Only those items on the list—such as fats, sugars, and water pH—that also affect other structure builders like eggs and starch will have a large effect on the structure of liquid shortening cakes.

Type of Flour

One way to control gluten development is through proper flour selection. For example, the *type of grain* is an extremely important consideration because wheat flour is the only common grain with the potential for forming a good amount of gluten. Rye flour has about the same amount of protein as wheat, but recall that very little rye protein forms gluten. Any gluten that forms from rye flour is of such poor quality that, except for certain specialty rustic loaves, most formulas for rye bread in North America contain added wheat flour. Other flours, such as oat, corn, buckwheat, and soy, do not form gluten at all. Baked goods made from these flours do not have good gas-retaining or structure-building properties and are dense and compact if no wheat flour is added.

Different *varieties of wheat* vary in the amount and quality of gluten that form from them. Recall from Chapter 5 that currently thousands of different varieties of wheat are grown throughout the world, but that they are generally classified as either soft wheats or hard wheats. Soft wheats are low in protein, and the protein quality is typically poor (from the standpoint of gluten development), meaning that there is a lower amount of glutenin for the amount of gliadin, and the glutenin subunits tend to be smaller in size. Soft wheat flours form gluten that is weak and tears easily.

Hard wheats are high in protein and contain a higher percentage of glutenin for the amount of gliadin, and the glutenin subunits tend to be large in size. Strong wheat flours form gluten that is strong, cohesive, and elastic. While the quality of protein in flour depends mostly on which variety of wheat is grown, the amount

Flour quality should be judged by its intended use. Historically, however, certain flours—typically those high in gluten-forming proteins, low in ash, and having a sufficient amount of damaged starch granules—were commonly described as "high-quality." These flours (which are relatively high in alveograph P and W values) are great for general bread baking because the gluten that forms retains gases well through mixing, proofing, and baking. This does not mean that so-called high-quality flour is best for all baked goods, or even for all breads. Pastry chefs would argue that the qualities required for the best cookies and cakes are quite different. That is, high-quality pastry flour typically is low in gluten (has a low alveograph P and W), has a very fine granulation, is relatively low in pentosans and other gums, and has few damaged starch granules.

Bread bakers also are not necessarily looking for the highest gluten content in their flour. To achieve a soft, open crumb in their products, artisan bread bakers typically use flour with a lower amount of gluten than is in traditional bread or high-gluten flours. A high-quality artisan bread flour typically forms a softer, more extensible dough (has a moderate alveograph P and W) than does a high-gluten flour.

Nor are high-quality flours particularly high in nutritional quality, even when enriched. Because they are white flours, they contain no bran or germ particles. This means that they are not a good source of dietary fiber. It also means that they will be low in lysine, an essential amino acid, and, therefore, their protein will not be nutritionally complete. In contrast, wheat germ in whole wheat flour contains protein that is more nutritious—but of course, wheat germ proteins do not form gluten.

of protein is highly dependent on environmental conditions such as climate, soil quality, and the amount of fertilizer applied.

Whole wheat flour is typically the same or higher in protein than white flour. But this does not translate into more gluten development. Recall that the bran and germ interfere with gluten development, and that the proteins from these components do not form gluten. Glutenin and gliadin are found exclusively in the endosperm; these gluten-forming proteins are not present in the bran nor the germ.

Amount of Water

Recall that gluten is not actually present in flour itself. Glutenin and gliadin, which are present in flour as solid chunks of protein, form a gluten network as they hydrate and swell with up to two times their weight in water.

Water hydration is absolutely essential for gluten development. In fact, one way to control gluten development is by adjusting the amount of water in a formula. For example, gluten in pie and biscuit doughs is starved for water; that is, it is not fully hydrated. Because it is not fully hydrated, gluten in these products does not develop completely and the product remains tender.

If a small amount of water is added to gluten that is not fully hydrated, more gluten develops and the dough toughens. This will not happen with most cake batters. Cake batter usually contains excess water. Since the gluten is already fully hydrated, adding more water to most cake batters does not increase gluten development. Instead, adding more water dilutes out proteins, weakening gluten.

Water is sometimes added as an ingredient in its own right. More often, however, water is added as a part of other liquids or other ingredients such as milk or eggs. Liquid oil, however, contains no water at all, and it does not contribute to gluten development. In fact, oil—being a tenderizer—interferes with gluten development.

Water Hardness

Water hardness is a measure of the amount of minerals such as calcium and magnesium in water. Hard water is high in minerals, while soft water is low in minerals. If you ever see hard white mineral deposits, called *scale*, on equipment surfaces, you know the water is hard.

Because minerals strengthen gluten, yeast doughs prepared from hard water can be too strong and elastic; that is, too bucky. They do not stretch when gases expand, or they stretch only to quickly bounce back. Doughs prepared from soft water can be too soft, slack, and sticky. Ideally, water for bread baking is neither too hard nor too soft.

When Should "Too Much" Water Be Added to Bread Dough?

If you've ever wondered how coarse-grained rustic breads get their appealing large, irregular holes, it helps to understand that they form when gluten is weak and tears relatively easily. Artisan bakers use several approaches to achieve this. First, they use flour with a relatively low protein content. Second, they may add excess water, so that the amount of water is sometimes over 70 percent (baker's percentage), compared with 50–60 percent for regular lean dough. This produces a well-hydrated dough, one that is soft and slack—almost a cross between batter and dough. Although messy to work with, superhydrated doughs can produce fine artisan breads. Not only is the grain coarsened by the additional water, but a longer bake time is needed to dry out the bread, resulting in a thicker, crisp crust.

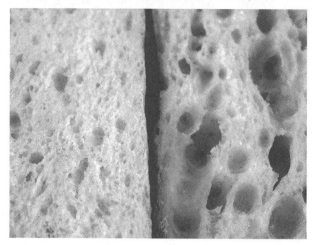

The baguette on left is made from regular lean dough; the baguette on the right from a well-hydrated lean dough.
Photo by Richard Miscovich

Why Are Some Waters Hard and Some Soft?

Water becomes hard as it picks up minerals from contact with the earth. Ground water, which percolates through soil on its way to water wells, is usually harder than surface water from lakes and reservoirs. Since the earth varies in composition from one location to another, water hardness also varies. For example, parts of Florida, Texas, and the Southwest have hard water, while the water in New England and the Southeast is soft.

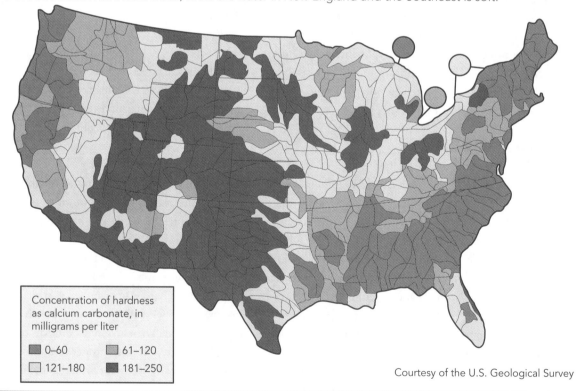

Concentration of hardness as calcium carbonate, in milligrams per liter

- 0–60
- 61–120
- 121–180
- 181–250

Courtesy of the U.S. Geological Survey

If water is too hard or too soft, there are several ways to compensate. First, there are dough conditioners designed specifically for soft water and others designed for hard water. Dough conditioners for soft water contain calcium salts such as calcium sulfate to increase the mineral content. Dough conditioners for hard water contain acids that prevent minerals from interacting with gluten.

Probably the best way to deal with water that is too hard or too soft is to adjust other ingredients and processes. For example, if water is hard and doughs are too strong and elastic, use more water in mixing the dough, to dilute the gluten and slacken the dough. Or use a softer flour or less mixing. If necessary, however, hard water can be treated with a water softener system. Water softeners remove calcium and magnesium from the water. Not only does this prevent the effects of minerals on gluten, it also eliminates damage to equipment from scale buildup. Water that is treated with a water softener, however, is high in sodium, which in some people can contribute to high blood pressure.

Water pH

Just as water hardness is a measure of the amount of minerals, pH is a measure of the acidity or alkalinity of water. The pH scale (Figure 7.6) runs from 0 to 14. At pH 7, water is neutral—neither acidic nor alkaline (basic). If acid is present, pH falls below 7. If base or alkali is present, it rises above 7. Water supplies rarely have a neutral pH. Areas of North America plagued by acid rain—Canada and the United States along the Atlantic coast, for example—typically have water with a low pH.

The ideal pH for maximum gluten development is slightly acidic, at a pH of 5 to 6. This means that adding acid so that the pH falls below 5, or adding alkali so it rises above 6, will reduce gluten strength. It is easy to adjust pH by adding acids or alkalis, and bakers and pastry chefs do this all the time. Examples of acids commonly added to baked goods include cream of tartar, fruits and fruit juice, cultured dairy products, and vinegar. For example, vinegar or another acid is added to strudel dough to dissolve gluten and reduce its strength, so that the dough is more extensible and easier to stretch without tearing. An example of an alkali is baking soda. Adding a small amount of baking soda to cookie dough provides for a porous, open, and more tender crumb.

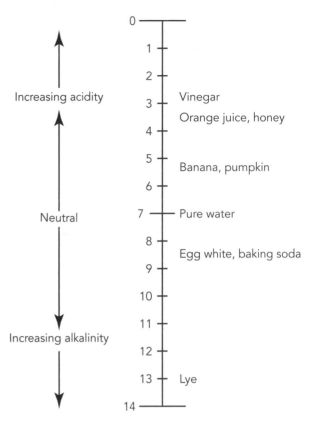

Figure 7.6 The pH scale ranges from 0 to 14, with most foods neutral to acidic.

pH is often adjusted indirectly, as when a yeast dough is allowed to ferment for a longer time. As dough ferments, especially under conditions that encourage bacteria fermentation, acids are produced and the pH drops. Just from a change in pH alone, dough becomes softer and more extensible.

Although water hardness and water pH are completely different concepts, they can influence each other. For example, certain minerals, like calcium carbonate, that increase water hardness also increase pH. Some acids that decrease pH also decrease the effects of water hardness. Just the same, it is helpful to keep these two concepts—water hardness and water pH—separate in your mind.

Mixing and Kneading

Besides water, gluten requires mixing or kneading for development. Mixing promotes gluten development in several ways. First, it speeds up hydration (absorption of water) by exposing new surfaces of flour particles to water. This continues until flour particles are worn down in size and no longer spherical. Mixing also

Cookie dough spreads across a cookie sheet if the dough is thin enough to spread. When most cookie doughs heat up in the oven, their consistency thins and the dough spreads. At a certain temperature, heat sets the gluten and egg proteins so that the dough thickens and stops spreading.

Whether this is desirable or not depends on what kind of cookie you wish to bake, but often some spread is desirable. There are many ways to increase cookie spread. One way is to add a small amount of baking soda, as little as 0.25 to 0.5 ounce (5 to 15 grams) for 10 pounds (4.5 kilograms) of cookie dough. This increases the pH of the dough, and it raises the set temperature of the gluten and egg proteins. With more free water and less structure for a longer time, cookies that contain baking soda spread more and have a coarser, more porous crumb. Since moisture evaporates more easily from a porous crumb, baking soda often provides for a crisper crumb, as well.

Measure baking soda carefully. Baking soda increases browning significantly, and if used at too high a level, it leaves a distinct salty-chemical off flavor. Too much baking soda also causes eggs in baked goods to turn grayish green.

When working at high altitudes, omit baking soda from cookie dough. The lower air pressure at high altitudes already encourages spread.

---

incorporates oxygen from the air into dough, which oxidizes and strengthens gluten. Finally, mixing distributes the particles evenly throughout the dough, so that ultimately a strong, continuous gluten network forms.

Too much mixing can develop too much gluten. For all products except yeast-raised doughs, overmixing refers to toughening from too much gluten development. Products vary in their susceptibility to overmixing. Baking powder biscuits, for example, require a certain amount of light kneading to develop some gluten. Too little kneading, and biscuits slump during

Figure 7.7 The more baking powder biscuit dough is mixed and kneaded, the less it spreads and slumps and the higher it rises, but the tougher the biscuits. **Left to right:** not kneaded; lightly kneaded; heavily kneaded biscuit dough

> **HELPFUL HINT**
> *Because gluten strands align in the direction that they are mixed, be sure that dough is evenly mixed in all directions. When using a mixer, this is generally not a problem, since dough moves around the mixing bowl as it is mixed. If kneading dough by hand, however, dough must be turned 90 degrees with every knead. Likewise, when laminated doughs are folded or sheeted, the dough is rotated with each fold or with each run through the sheeter. Otherwise, gluten strands align in one direction. This becomes especially evident when dough is not allowed to relax before it is shaped and baked. The dough will tend to shrink in the direction that the gluten strands are oriented.*

baking from a lack of structure. Too much, and they hold their shape but are tough. The right amount of mixing and kneading allows biscuits to remain tender yet still hold their shape (Figure 7.7).

It is hard to imagine certain batters developing much, if any, gluten from mixing. Consider high-ratio liquid shortening cakes made with cake flour. Despite several minutes of mixing, the use of cake flour and of a high amount of water and tenderizers practically eliminates any concern over gluten development. High-ratio liquid shortening cakes should still be mixed no longer than recommended, though. They rely on proper mixing for adequate air incorporation and leavening.

Recall that Chapter 3 discussed the reasons for the formation of tunnels in high-ratio cake batters. Traditional muffin batter is much lower in tenderizing fats and sugars than cake batter, and it develops tunnels during baking for very different reasons.

To keep them from toughening, traditional muffins are mixed just long enough to dampen flour. Even the slightest amount of overmixing produces tough muffins pocked with tunnels. Tunnels are a defect that occurs when overmixing develops too much gluten in muffins. When overmixed batter is baked, evaporating gases have difficulty escaping from the product. Thick gluten-reinforced cell walls prevent muffins from slowly letting off steam. Instead, gases build up until finally enough pressure forces them to escape upward, much as volcanoes erupt. On their way out, the gases bore tunnels through the batter, marking their escape route.

One way to prevent this toughening and tunneling, of course, is to not overmix. Another way is to use soft flour and to add tenderizers to the formula, making it difficult to overmix. Today, many muffin batters are made with cake or pastry flour and contain high amounts of tenderizing fats and sugar. While this solves the tunnel problem, today's muffins often resemble tender cupcakes more than they do the coarse-grained, rustic muffins of yesterday.

With yeast-raised doughs, adequate mixing is required to disperse glutenin particles well enough so that a strong continuous network of gluten forms, one that can trap and hold gases. Undermixed doughs are sticky and lack smoothness, and when baked, the bread has low volume and a coarse crumb from tearing.

The longer or more vigorously bread doughs are mixed, the more mechanical dough development takes place—at least up to a point. If dough is mixed beyond that point, the gluten network breaks down (Figure 7.8). This is sometimes called the *letdown stage* of mixing, and it is what is meant by "overmixed" yeast dough. The dough becomes soft and sticky, it tears into stringy pieces when stretched, and it no longer retains water or gas. Bread made from overmixed dough suffers from poor loaf volume and a coarse crumb. Doughs most susceptible to overmixing are those that do not develop strong gluten to begin with.

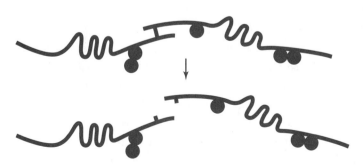

Figure 7.8 Extreme mixing breaks down gluten structure.

Knowing when yeast dough is adequately mixed is an art as well as a science, since many factors affect the amount of mixing needed for proper dough development. First, different flours require different mixing times, with strong flours that are high in glutenin tolerating—even requiring—longer mix times than weak flours. Rye flour, which contains little glutenin, is very easily overmixed. Different formulas also have different mixing requirements. Rich yeast doughs, which are high in tenderizing sugars and fats, require more mixing to fully develop, yet are susceptible to overmixing. A mixer's design and speed must be considered as well. Finally, dough that will undergo a long bulk fermentation should be mixed for less time, since fermentation also contributes to gluten development. The knowledge that is required to properly mix yeast dough comes from both proper training and practical experience.

Batter and Dough Temperature

Batter and dough temperature is also a factor in gluten development. The warmer the temperature, the faster flour particles hydrate and the faster gluten proteins oxidize. Faster hydration and oxidation mean faster gluten development and dough maturation. Faster gluten development does not necessarily mean more gluten development, but it could, if mix times are short.

Practically speaking, however, bakers seldom, if ever, control gluten development by controlling dough temperature. That is because dough temperature is

No-time dough is yeast-raised dough that does not undergo bulk fermentation. Instead, the dough undergoes a simple 10- or 15-minute bench rest before being divided. This saves an hour or sometimes several hours of time, depending on the type of bread produced. But how can an important step like bulk fermentation be eliminated?

Gluten develops and matures through mixing, through fermentation, and through the use of maturing agents such as ascorbic acid. If dough undergoes mechanical dough development by intensive high-speed mixing, or if it undergoes chemical dough development through the use of chemical maturing agents and dough conditioners, less fermentation time is needed for the dough to properly mature.

While intensive high-speed mixing requires special equipment, any bakeshop can use chemical maturing agents and dough conditioners to shorten or eliminate bulk fermentation. Because no-time doughs undergo a final proof, carbon dioxide needed for proper leavening is not sacrificed, despite the elimination of the bulk fermentation step.

Before trying no-time doughs, however, the baker should consider the pros and cons. Certainly, no-time doughs take less time to prepare, and time is money. And, while there is the added cost of the chemicals, this is somewhat offset by a higher amount of water absorbed by the doughs. However, breads develop a good amount of flavor during bulk fermentation. When this step is eliminated, bread may lack the subtle flavors that are the pride of the baker.

controlled for other reasons. For example, in yeast-raised doughs, proper dough temperature is important for controlling yeast fermentation. The ideal dough temperature for fermentation is typically somewhere between 70° and 80°F (21°–27°C), although this varies from one formula to the next. If dough temperatures are too high, fermentation occurs too rapidly and flavor does not develop properly.

In products such as pie pastry dough, the use of cold water prevents solid fat in the dough from melting. While this reduces tenderness, fat must remain solid in pie pastry dough if the pie is to be flaky.

Maturing Agents and Dough Conditioners

Recall that maturing agents are generally added to flour to affect baking qualities. Maturing agents do this partly or exclusively through their effects on gluten. Some maturing agents, primarily chlorine gas, weaken gluten. (Don't forget that chlorine also whitens carotenoids and changes starch granules so that they swell more easily.) Others, such as ascorbic acid and potassium bromate, strengthen gluten.

The main role of dough conditioners is to increase gluten strength, contributing to *chemical dough development*. This is especially important when dough undergoes extreme conditions, as when it is run through high-speed commercial equipment. Recall from Chapter 5 that dough conditioners contain a mix of ingredients. The main ingredients in dough conditioners are maturing agents that strengthen, but other ingredients important for strengthening gluten include emulsifiers as well as salts and acids that adjust water hardness and pH. The amount of dough conditioner to use varies with the brand, but it is typically 0.2–0.5 percent of the weight of the flour.

Fermentation and Proofing

During fermentation, yeast in dough converts sugars into carbon dioxide and alcohol. This typically occurs in two separate stages—bulk fermentation and final proofing—and can take several hours to complete. Many events occur during fermentation and proofing, and these are discussed in more detail in Chapter 11. For now, it is helpful to understand that the three main events are (1) the production of leavening gases, (2) the development of flavor, and (3) the development and strengthening of gluten.

It is partly the action of expanding air bubbles pushing on gluten that helps strengthen it. At the same time, bonds that were broken during mixing slowly reform around these expanding bubbles, so that bread ultimately develops higher volume and a finer crumb.

Just as too much mixing tears gluten strands and weakens gluten strength and elasticity, so does too much fermentation and proofing. The end result of overproofed dough is similar to that of overmixed dough—softness, stickiness, and a loss of gas-retaining ability.

Some of this softening occurs from excessive amylase and protease activity, which break down starch and gluten structure, respectively, or from the action of glutathione and other reducing agents on gluten. The softening effects of reducing agents and of protease enzymes are discussed in the next two sections.

Reducing Agents

Reducing agents have the opposite effect of maturing agents that strengthen. While maturing agents like ascorbic acid oxidize gluten-forming proteins, allowing them to form more bonds that hold gluten together more strongly, reducing agents alter ("reduce") gluten-forming proteins so that they form fewer bonds and hold together more weakly. The most common reducing agent used by large-scale commercial bakeries is L-cysteine. L-cysteine is an amino acid found in proteins throughout nature. It is a common ingredient in dough conditioners. L-cysteine and other reducing agents are sometimes added to dough in large-scale commercial operations so that the dough mixes faster and more easily and generates less frictional heat. The softening and slackening effect of the reducing agent is later counteracted with maturing agents like potassium bromate, which help rebuild gluten structure during proofing and baking, when structure is needed most.

Probably the most potent reducing agent is not necessarily added intentionally. This reducing agent is called *glutathione*. Glutathione is a protein fragment found in fluid milk and many milk products; in active dry yeast and other yeast products that contain dead yeast cells; and in wheat germ. Glutathione works slowly during bulk fermentation of doughs.

When active dry yeast is used improperly—that is, when water or dough temperature is low—a significant amount of glutathione leaks out of dead yeast cells, reducing and weakening gluten. For this reason, professional bakers seldom use active dry yeast. Most prefer compressed or instant yeast, which does not contain as many dead yeast cells.

Interestingly, so-called nonleavening yeast is sold that intentionally contains a high amount of glutathione. This is sometimes used for pizza and tortilla production, so that doughs will stretch more easily and not shrink when baked.

Glutathione is also found in whole wheat flour, in particular in the wheat germ. Recall that weaker gluten develops from whole wheat flour than from white flour, and one reason for this is the glutathione in wheat germ. Wheat germ can be purchased raw or toasted. Toasted wheat germ will not have the same high glutathione activity as raw wheat germ, since glutathione is inactivated by heat.

Enzyme Activity

Recall that amylase is an enzyme that breaks down starches. Likewise, proteases are enzymes that break down proteins, including gluten. When gluten is broken down into smaller pieces by protease, it is weakened and the dough becomes softer, smoother, and more extensible. Like reducing agents, proteases are sometimes added to dough by large-scale commercial bakeries so that the dough mixes faster and more easily and is easier to stretch and shape.

There are small amounts of protease enzymes naturally present in all flours, even white flour, but under normal conditions, these enzymes are not active. Artisan bread bakers have found ways, sometimes unknowingly, to activate the protease naturally present in flour. Table 7.1 summarizes some potential sources of protease activity in bread baking.

TABLE 7.1 SOURCES OF PROTEASE ACTIVITY IN BREAD BAKING

Malted flours, including malted barley flour (dry malt)
Sprouted wheat berries
Soakers
Whole wheat flour
Rye flour
Autolysed doughs
Liquid levains (sourdoughs)
Poolish and other pre-ferments

An autolyse is a rest period that follows a brief, slow mixing of the flour and water used in yeast dough. The rest period lasts 15–30 minutes. During this time, water continues to hydrate proteins and starches, and gluten further develops. A short period of mixing continues after the rest period, just enough to complete dough development.

Enzymes are active during the autolyse period. Protease enzymes, in particular, improve the extensibility (stretchiness) of dough, and this is one of the reasons why bread bakers autolyse. Undoubtedly, amylase enzymes are also active during an autolyse.

Because an autolyse reduces the total mixing time, it reduces the dough's exposure to the oxygen in air. While some exposure to oxygen is desirable for dough development, some bakers believe that too much oxidation causes the flavor of the bread to deteriorate and the color to bleach excessively.

An autolyse is most commonly used when making baguettes or a similar lean bread, especially if a liquid pre-ferment is not used.

Flours and grains that have been malted (sprouted), for example, contain protease in addition to amylase and other enzymes. Rye flour naturally contains more protease activity than wheat flour, and whole grains contain more than white flour, because whole grains include the protease-rich aleurone layer, the part of the endosperm closest to the bran layer and highest in enzyme activity. Because clear flour also contains the aleurone, clear flour is higher in protease activity than patent flour.

Autolysed dough—that is, yeast dough that undergoes a rest period after a brief, slow mixing—experiences a certain amount of protease activity. This is especially true if salt is withheld at this stage, since salt slows enzyme activity.

Protease activity can be especially high in sourdoughs. Sourdoughs, as the name suggests, are acidic and have a low pH, and wheat protease is particularly active at low pH. Additionally, certain bacteria (lactic acid bacteria) flourish in sourdoughs, and these bacteria contribute active protease activity. Protease activity is also high in pre-ferments, especially a poolish. A poolish is a pre-ferment made of equal parts flour and water, so it is watery. Because it is allowed to ferment for hours and because salt is withheld, enzyme activity is especially high.

Protease activity weakens gluten but also makes it more extensible, so bread dough made with a poolish or one that has been autolysed will stretch easily for better volume and a large, open crumb. The breakdown of protein from protease activity also releases amino acids that are valuable for the flavor of bread and can contribute to Maillard browning.

If not controlled, however, protease enzymes can weaken gluten to the point where the dough tears too easily and has little fermentation tolerance. If this occurs, gases will escape from the dough, bread volume will be low, and the dough could collapse during proofing or baking.

All enzymes increase in activity when temperatures are warm, and all become more active when more water is available and salt is omitted. Some enzymes, like wheat proteases, are more active at an acidic low pH, while others, like amylases, are more active when the pH is closer neutral. By controlling time, temperature, dough hydration, salt levels, and pH, bakers can control the activity of protease and other enzymes. In this way, they can control the flavor, texture, and color of their breads.

Tenderizers and Softeners

Some tenderizers, such as *fats, oils,* and certain *emulsifiers,* work by coating gluten strands (and other structure builders). This reduces gluten development in at least one way. Proteins coated with fat cannot absorb water and properly hydrate. Unless they hydrate, glutenin and gliadin proteins cannot adequately bond and form a large gluten network. Short gluten strands form instead, and the product is tenderized. The use of the term *shortening* to mean "*fat*" is derived from this ability of fats to shorten gluten strands.

Besides fat, another important tenderizer in baked goods is sugar. Sugars tenderize by interacting with both water and gluten proteins, keeping the gluten proteins from properly hydrating and interacting. Rich

Can Overworking Pie Pastry Dough Produce a Tender Crust?

The first stage in making pie pastry dough is to cut fat into the dry ingredients. For the flakiest pie crust, fat chunks should be kept fairly large, about the size of a hazelnut. If fat is worked into the flour until it is the size of cornmeal, will too much gluten develop?

Before answering this question, recall that two things—water and mixing—are needed for gluten to develop. As long as water is not present, gluten cannot form and there is no risk that dough will toughen, no matter how much mixing occurs. Instead, overmixing fat into flour distributes the fat more completely, thoroughly coating flour particles. The result is less water absorption, less gluten development, and more tenderness. In fact, working the fat into flour is one way to produce a tender, mealy pie crust. It is only after water is added to pie crust dough that mixing develops gluten and toughening.

Does Salt Bleach Flour?

When bread is made without salt, the crumb takes on an off-white cast. At first glance, it appears that salt bleaches flour, much as chlorine and benzoyl peroxide do. However, this is not the case. Instead, salt acts by strengthening gluten, preventing it from tearing when it stretches from the pressure of expanding gases. The result is a fine, even crumb. Light bounces off a fine crumb more evenly than it does off a coarser crumb. This makes the bread appear whiter, even when the flour has the same amount of carotenoids—the pigments that color flour—as the coarser, off-white bread.

sweet doughs, such as brioche, contain large amounts of both fat and sugar. If flour containing too little gluten is used in these doughs, they could collapse and lose volume during proofing or the early stages of baking. That is why rich sweet dough formulas sometimes call for high-gluten flour.

Leavening gases also tenderize baked goods through their action on gluten strands. As leavening gases expand during baking, they stretch gluten strands. Stretched gluten strands form thin, weaker cell walls that are easily broken. With the right amount of leavening gases, baked goods are weak enough to be pleasantly tender, yet strong enough to keep from collapsing.

Salt
Salt is added to bread dough at approximately 1.5–2 percent or so of the weight of flour. Salt has several functions in baked goods. It modifies flavor, increases crust color, and slows the rates of yeast fermentation and enzyme activity. This is especially important with dough containing rye flour, since rye flour is relatively high in enzyme activity and in the rate that it ferments. Salt also strengthens gluten, improving its cohesiveness and making it less sticky. This means that salt prevents

excessive tearing when gluten stretches, so bread is easier to handle and has better volume and a finer crumb.

Because salt noticeably strengthens gluten, bread bakers sometimes delay the addition of salt to dough made from strong flour, adding it late in the mixing process. The dough mixes faster and cooler, because there is less resistance and frictional heat generated during mixing. Once salt is added, the dough tightens and is more difficult to stretch, but it will stretch further without tearing.

Other Structure Builders
Starches, including corn, rice, and potato starches, sometimes partially replace flour in cakes, cookies, and pastries. For example, genoise sponge cake is often made with up to half the flour replaced with cornstarch, for tenderness. This works best in products with a limited amount of water. With limited water, only a limited amount of starch gelatinizes. Unlike gelatinized starch, which contributes structure to baked goods, ungelatinized starch granules act as inert fillers that interfere with gluten forming its network. With today's soft cake flour, however, it is probably unnecessary to use starch to tenderize baked goods, except in special circumstances.

Eggs are also structure builders. Even with the fat in egg yolks, adding eggs to baked goods provides more structure once the eggs coagulate. But raw eggs in bread dough interfere with gluten development during mixing and fermentation. The final baked bread might be tougher than if eggs were not added, but the added toughening is due to coagulated eggs, not gluten.

> **HELPFUL HINT**
>
> *Rich sweet doughs contain several ingredients—namely sugar, fat, and eggs—that interfere with gluten development. These doughs can collapse during proofing and baking unless precautions are taken. One way to develop enough gluten so that these doughs don't collapse is to develop sufficient gluten before adding these ingredients. For example, all or part of the eggs in brioche are sometimes withheld until the last minute of mixing, to allow gluten structure to properly develop.*

Milk

Fluid milk is, above all else, a source of water. In fact, it is primarily water—about 85–89 percent water. This means that any time milk is added to baked goods, water—which is necessary for gluten development—is also being added.

Fluid milk also contains glutathione, the reducing agent that softens dough. This becomes important in the production of yeast-raised baked goods, where the effects become noticeable during fermentation. If glutathione is not first destroyed, bread dough softens and becomes slack, and oven spring decreases. The result is lower loaf volume and coarser texture.

Heat denatures, or destroys, glutathione. Pasteurization, a heat process applied to essentially all milk sold in North America, is not enough heat to inactivate it. This is why bakers sometimes scald fluid milk before using it in yeast doughs. To scald milk, heat it in a saucepan until it reaches a simmer (180°F/82°C), then cool.

Likewise, not all dry milk solids (DMS) have been exposed to sufficient heat to destroy glutathione. Only DMS labeled as "high-heat" have been heated sufficiently. The milk used in high-heat DMS has been held at 190°F (88°C) for 30 minutes prior to drying. High-heat DMS are most commonly used in yeast doughs. They are also perfectly acceptable for use in other baked goods.

Fiber, Bran, Grain Particles, Fruit Pieces, Spices, and the Like

Any particle that physically gets in the way of gluten strands from forming will decrease gluten development. For example, cracked wheat particles, bran flakes, or flaxseeds added to bread dough create gaps in the gluten structure, shortening and weakening the gluten. Surprisingly, even spice particles interfere with gluten formation.

Dough Relaxation

To rest or relax dough means to allow it to sit awhile. For example, bread dough requires a short bench rest before it is shaped. Laminated doughs, including croissants, Danish, and puff pastry doughs, usually rest in the refrigerator between folds. This rest period is important. It makes it easier to shape, roll, and fold the dough properly, because the dough becomes less elastic and more extensible.

Bread, croissant, and Danish doughs need to rest because the gluten is well-developed, meaning that it is very strong and elastic. Doughs that are strong and elastic—those with high alveograph P/L ratios—require more relaxation time than softer, slacker doughs with lower P/L ratios. Elasticity—the tendency of dough to shorten up or bounce back—can be a problem when dough is rolled and shaped. The further dough is stretched and the more it is worked, the more stressed it is. By relaxing dough once it has been worked, gluten strands have a chance to adjust to the new length or shape, and will not bounce back before baking.

Bread dough will continue to relax for up to 45 minutes or longer after mixing, depending on the dough. Softer, slacker doughs, including most pastry doughs, relax in less time. Once dough has relaxed, it is easier to shape, and it will shrink less upon baking.

Do not confuse dough relaxation with yeast dough bulk fermentation or proofing. During fermentation and proofing, yeast continues to produce carbon dioxide gas, slowly stretching gluten strands. The stretching helps to further develop the gluten and mature the

More on Dough Relaxation

To understand why worked dough needs a relaxation period, it helps to view gluten at the molecular level. Recall from earlier in this chapter that gluten consists of a three-dimensional tangled network held together with a mix of both strong and weak bonds. As dough is rolled and shaped, weak bonds are apt to break, allowing particles to slide past one another. Once rolling and shaping stops, new weak bonds form and the dough takes on its new shape.

When dough is stretched and pulled quickly, it doesn't stretch as far as when it is stretched and pulled more slowly. Instead, the dough resists stretching and is apt to tear. If the dough is pulled slowly, it has time to make small adjustments along the way. It is as if the gluten strands in the dough are acting like a bowl of noodles. If you try to pull on one noodle in the bowl quickly, it will likely break. If instead you pull on it slowly and evenly, it will wiggle its way out without breaking.

---

dough. During dough relaxation, gluten strands are not necessarily stretched. The dough rests, and gluten strands adjust to a new length or shape.

Pie pastry dough benefits from a rest period after mixing, to make it easier to roll and shape. Some pastry chefs also relax rolled and shaped pie dough before baking, so it will not shrink during baking. As with laminated doughs, pie pastry dough is usually chilled during the rest period. Chilling solidifies fat, allowing for flakier pastry.

There is yet a third reason to allow pie pastry dough to rest for at least several hours before use. Recall that pie dough contains very little water, to keep gluten development at a minimum. If water is not mixed in properly, the dough may become crumbly in some spots and soggy in others. On the other hand, if dough is mixed thoroughly to assure even distribution of water, gluten overdevelops. If, instead, dough rests for several hours, water distributes itself evenly throughout the dough. This is important in pie pastry doughs, which are barely mixed and contain little water. It is also important when working with grains having large particles, such as durum semolina.

In summary, the main thing that happens as doughs relax is that gluten strands have time to adjust to their new length or shape. This makes them easier to roll and shape and less likely to shrink during baking. Some doughs rest to allow time for gluten and starch to properly absorb water. Finally, when refrigerated during resting, the fats in dough harden, for better lamination and flakiness.

Questions for Review

1 Which protein, glutenin or gliadin, provides the backbone structure to gluten, imparting strength and tenacity?

2 What are the three main ways that gluten is developed during bread making?

3 What is the difference between extensibility and elasticity? Which protein, glutenin or gliadin, is primarily responsible for each?

4 What is meant by fermentation tolerance? How does fermentation tolerance affect bread loaf volume and crumb structure?

5 What are the characteristics of a high-quality flour used in bagels? In cookies?

6 Will a small increase in the amount of water added to pie pastry dough be likely to increase or decrease gluten development? Explain your answer.

7 Will a small increase in the amount of water added to superhydrated bread dough be likely to increase or decrease gluten development? Explain your answer.

8 How would you describe the difference between water hardness and water pH? How does each affect gluten development?

9 Will a small amount of baking soda added to cookie dough increase or decrease cookie spread? Why might baking soda have this effect?

10 Describe how mixing promotes the development of gluten.

11 How does too little mixing affect the quality of baking powder biscuits? How does too much mixing affect them?

12 What is meant by the letdown stage of mixing yeast-raised doughs?

13 Which is more likely easily overmixed: dough containing a blend of rye and bread flour, or one containing only bread flour? Dough made with regular bread flour or one made with a lower-protein artisan bread flour?

14 What is one cause of tunnels in muffins? How can using a formula high in sugar and fat reduce the likelihood that tunnels will form?

15 Why should doughs that undergo longer fermentation or proofing times be mixed for a shorter time than those that undergo just a short proof?

16 How does dough temperature affect gluten development? What else does dough temperature affect in pie pastry doughs? In bread doughs?

17 What three events occur during dough fermentation? Which of these three can also be accomplished by intensive high-speed mixing or by chemical maturing agents?

18 What is meant by "no-time dough"? What is the main advantage of no-time dough? What is the main disadvantage?

19 What is meant by a "reducing agent"? When might reducing agents be beneficial?

20 What is glutathione and where is it found?

21 What are proteases and how do they affect gluten?

22 Which of the following in each pair is likely to have more protease activity: rye flour or wheat flour; white flour or whole wheat flour; liquid pre-ferment, with a high amount of water, or a firmer pre-ferment with a lower amount of water; a pre-ferment with added salt, or a pre-ferment with no added salt?

23 Why might a rich sweet dough call for high-gluten flour?

24 Why will pie pastry dough bake up more tender when the fat is well worked into the flour (before water is added) than when it is left in larger chunks?

25 How does salt affect gluten in yeast-raised doughs?

26 Why might bread made with salt have a whiter crumb than bread made without salt?

27 Why is fluid milk usually scalded before it is used in yeast-raised doughs? Why might you not want to scald milk before use?

28 What is meant by "high-heat DMS"? What is it used for?

29 You are shaping pizza dough, but it shrinks before you have a chance to add toppings and bake. What should you do?

30 What is the difference between gluten development and gluten relaxation?

31 What are the three reasons why pie pastry dough might be chilled and allowed to rest several hours or overnight before use?

Questions for Discussion

1 Since high-ratio liquid shortening cakes are made with cake flour that contains very little gluten, how is it that the amount of fat and sugar in liquid shortening cakes can have a large effect on the tenderness of these cakes?

2 Explain why developing the maximum amount of gluten is not necessarily desirable in bread baking.

3 Explain why developing the minimum amount of gluten is not necessarily desirable with pastries.

4 Why is the careful selection of flour more important with breads than with muffins?

5 You are making a laminated dough, such as a croissant or puff pastry dough, with two bread flours to choose from: one with a high alveograph P/L ratio, the other with a low ratio. Which flour should you use? Explain.

6 A baker moves from New York (where water is very soft) to Texas (where water is very hard). How might changes be made to the type of flour, the amount of water, and the amount of mixing, so that the bagels made in Texas have the same texture as those made in New York?

7 Explain why the use of cake flour and of a high amount of water and tenderizers in high-ratio liquid shortening cakes practically eliminates any concern over gluten development.

8 A brioche dough rose beautifully only to collapse during the early stages of baking. What changes might be needed in the method of preparation? Consider changes that might be needed in mixing, fermentation, pretreating milk, and so forth. Note: brioche is made from a sweet, rich dough that generally contains eggs, butter, sugar, and fluid milk (as well as bread flour, yeast, and salt).

Exercises and Experiments

❶ Exercise: Increasing Gluten Development in Batters and Doughs

In the spaces that follow, list all the ways you know that will increase gluten development in batters and doughs. For the purposes of this exercise, focus entirely on gluten structure, not on structure in general. Don't be concerned about other changes that might make your product less desirable in other ways. Be specific and be practical; that is, think of changes you could tell an assistant to execute. Be sure to start each line with an action word such as the following: add, increase, decrease, change, omit, include, use. While each item might not apply to all types of products, each should work in at least one. Follow the format used in the first two, which are done for you, and see if you can add at least ten more ways.

1 Use bread flour instead of pastry flour.

2 Increase the amount of water in dough where gluten is not fully hydrated.

3 _____

4 _____

5 _____

6 _____

7 _____

8 _____

9 _____

10 _____

11 _____

12 _____

_____

_____

13 _____

_____

_____

14 _____

_____

_____

15 _____

_____

_____

❷ Exercise: Functions of Ingredients in Bread

On a sheet of paper, copy the name of each ingredient listed on the label of any brand of bread from the supermarket. State what the ingredient is (flour, variety grain, sweetener, fat or oil, emulsifier, maturing agent, etc.), then briefly explain its function in the bread. Use your entire textbook, not just this chapter, as a reference. For the flour, state whether it is bleached or unbleached; if it is bleached, state which bleaching agent you believe was likely used. Also state whether the flour is enriched, why it is enriched, and which vitamins and minerals were added for enrichment. Attach the original label to the assignment.

❸ Experiment: Amount and Quality of Gluten in Different Flours

Objectives

Gain an increased understanding of different flours and the gluten they contain by
- Kneading doughs by hand
- Separating out the gluten contained in each flour
- Measuring the size of the gluten ball from each flour
- Evaluating the qualities of gluten from each flour

Products Prepared

Gluten balls made from
- Vital wheat gluten
- High-gluten flour
- Bread flour
- Pastry flour
- Cake flour
- Whole wheat flour
- White rye flour
- Corn flour
- Other, if desired (all-purpose flour, artisan bread flour, white whole wheat flour, whole wheat pastry flour, durum flour, etc.)

Materials and Equipment

- Scale
- Stainless-steel bowls, 4-quart (4-liter) or larger, one per gluten ball
- Sieves or strainers, one per gluten ball

Procedure

1 Prepare dough from each flour by combining 8 ounces (250 grams) flour with 4 ounces (125 grams) water. Set aside a small amount of the 8 ounces (250 grams) of flour to use to dust the table surface.

2 Add more water to each flour, as necessary, until dough is able to be kneaded. You do not need to keep track of the amount of water added to the dough.

3 Knead each dough by hand for 5–7 minutes, or until gluten is fully developed. Use flour set aside to prevent dough from sticking; do not add any additional flour unless necessary. If additional flour is necessary, weigh the amount of flour. Record the total weight of flour (8 ounces/250 grams plus any additional flour) in Results Table 1, which follows.

4 Place dough in bowls and fill bowls with cool water. Time permitting, let gluten balls soak in water for 20 minutes.

5 Knead and tear apart each dough by hand while it is submerged (Figure 7.9), until the water is very cloudy (cloudiness is primarily from the starch, bran particles, and gums coming from the flour). For flours that have little or no cohesive gluten (rye flour, cake flour, corn flour), the dough will fall apart easily when placed in water; for these flours, swish the bits of dough through water to remove starch.

Figure 7.9 In back, rinsing and kneading a gluten ball. In front, gluten balls made from bread, pastry, and cake flours.

6 Gather bits of dough into a ball or allow particles to settle to the bottom of the bowl and drain off cloudy water, replacing it with fresh cool water. For cake flour, use a fine sieve (chinois) to prevent loss of dough and bits of gluten. If desired, also use sieve or strainer to retrieve bran particles from whole wheat flour. Set aside bran particles and display with whole wheat gluten ball.

7 Continue this process until water squeezed from gluten ball is clear; this will take 20 minutes or more of continuous kneading and tearing for most doughs, longer with cake flour.

8 When water is completely clear, drain off and squeeze the gluten ball to remove as much excess water as possible. For rye and corn flour, no gluten ball will form. Instead, save a small amount of partially washed dough. Be sure that these are clearly labeled as bits of partially washed dough and not as gluten balls.

9 Pat gluten balls dry.

10 Find information on the typical percent protein content for each flour from this textbook and record information in Results Table 1.

11 Allow the gluten balls to relax for a minimum of fifteen minutes before evaluating. This allows time for gluten network to recover from the washing process.

Results

1 Weigh each gluten ball on scale and record results in Results Table 1. Use the two blank rows to record results for any other types of flours tested. Do not weigh partially washed dough from rye and corn flours; these are not gluten balls. Gluten balls do not form from these flours.

2 Estimate the percent of gluten in flour as follows, and record results in Results Table 1:

$$\text{Percent Gluten in Flour} = \frac{100 \times \text{Weight of Gluten Ball}}{3 \times \text{Weight of Flour}}$$

This calculation is based on the assumption that gluten absorbs two times its weight in water, meaning that every ounce (30 grams) of the gluten ball is ⅓ ounce (10 grams) gluten. This calculation also assumes that the gluten ball is only gluten. In fact, lipids, ash, and some starch and gums are trapped in gluten balls.

Where the total amount of flour is 8 ounces, the formula can be simplified to 4.2 × weight of gluten ball. For 250 grams flour, the simplified formula is 0.13 × weight of gluten ball.

RESULTS TABLE 1   AMOUNT OF GLUTEN IN FLOURS

TYPE OF FLOUR	WEIGHT OF FLOUR (OUNCES OR GRAMS)	WEIGHT OF GLUTEN BALL (OUNCES OR GRAMS)	ESTIMATED PERCENT GLUTEN IN FLOUR (FROM CALCULATION)	TYPICAL PERCENT PROTEIN IN FLOUR (FROM TEXT)	ADDITIONAL COMMENTS
Vital wheat gluten					
High-gluten					
Bread					
Pastry					
Cake					
Whole wheat					
White rye					
Corn flour					

3   Evaluate each relaxed gluten ball for the quality of its gluten and record results in Results Table 2. To do this, gently pull each ball between your hands, much as you pull bread dough to form a windowpane. Rotate the ball as you do this, so that you are pulling it in all directions. Next, gently poke the stretched dough with your fingertips, to test its ability to withstand tearing. Be sure to compare each in turn with the gluten ball made from bread flour and evaluate for strength and cohesiveness, using the following guidelines.

- Strength (tenacity): The harder it is to stretch, the stronger the gluten. If the gluten ball falls apart and is not cohesive enough to stretch, record that it does not stretch.
- Cohesiveness (ability to resist tearing): The better it forms a thin film that resists tearing when poked, the more cohesive it is.
- If desired, also evaluate for extensibility (how far dough stretches) and elasticity/ springiness (how well the gluten ball springs back when pressed or stretched) and record in Additional Comments column.

4 Evaluate the partially washed rye and corn doughs. While these are not gluten balls, they do have properties that are important to note. Evaluate the doughs for strength and cohesiveness; that is, do they hold together when pressed, if not stretched? Also record an appropriate description of the consistency of each in the Additional Comments column. For example, record if washed dough feels slick and slimy, if it is more like wet sand and crumbles, if it is pasty, etc.

RESULTS TABLE 2 QUALITY OF GLUTEN FROM DIFFERENT FLOURS

TYPE OF FLOUR	STRENGTH AND COHESIVENESS	ADDITIONAL COMMENTS
Vital wheat gluten		
High-gluten		
Bread		
Pastry		
Cake		
Whole wheat		
White rye		
Corn		

Sources of Error

List any sources of error that might make it difficult to draw the proper conclusions from your experiment. In particular, consider whether kneading was complete; whether gluten balls were thoroughly rinsed and water squeezed from final gluten ball ran clear; whether bits of gluten were lost during the rinse; whether bran was completely separated from whole wheat dough.

_____

_____

_____

State what you could do differently next time to minimize or eliminate each source of error.

_____

_____

_____

Conclusions

Select one from the choices in **bold** or fill in the blanks.

1   The gluten ball made from pastry flour was **smaller/larger** than the gluten ball made from bread flour. This is because pastry flour is from a **soft/hard** wheat that is **lower/higher** in protein than bread flour. The difference in size was **small/moderate/large**.

2   When stretched, the gluten ball made from pastry flour tore **more easily than/less easily than/the same amount as** the gluten ball made from bread flour. This is because the gluten that forms from pastry flour is **stronger than/weaker than/the same as** gluten that forms from bread flour. The difference in strength between the gluten balls was **small/moderate/large**.

3   The gluten ball made from cake flour was **larger/smaller** than the gluten ball made from pastry flour. This is partly because cake flour is generally slightly **higher/lower** in protein than pastry flour. It is also because cake flour has been treated with **potassium bromate/benzoyl peroxide/chlorine**, a bleaching agent that **weakens/strengthens** gluten. The difference in size between the gluten balls was **small/moderate/large**.

4   When stretched, the gluten ball made from cake flour **fell apart/held together** well. This is largely because the bleaching agent **potassium bromate/benzoyl peroxide/chlorine** has been added to cake flour.

5   The gluten ball made from whole wheat flour was **larger than/smaller than/the same size as** the gluten ball made from bread flour. It also formed gluten that was **stronger than/weaker than/the same as** the gluten that formed from bread flour. This is primarily because _____.

6   The flour that formed the largest gluten ball was_____. This flour formed the largest gluten ball because _____
_____.

7   While neither rye nor corn form gluten, **rye/corn** flour formed dough that had some strength and cohesiveness; that is, that held together somewhat. The dough held together because the flour is high in soluble pentosan **gums/starch**, which also gave the dough a slick, slimy feel.

8   How do you explain why whole wheat bread typically is denser than white bread?

_____
_____
_____

9   How do you explain why rye bread typically is denser than white bread?

_____
_____
_____

10 For which flours did the calculated percentage of gluten match the typical percentage of protein listed in the text?

_____

_____

_____

11 In general, how did the size of the gluten balls change with the amount of protein present in each flour?

_____

_____

_____

12 For which flours did the calculated percentage of gluten not match the typical percentage of protein listed in the text? Can you explain these discrepancies?

_____

_____

_____

13 How do you think forming a gluten ball from flour can help predict the suitability of the flour for use in bread baking?

_____

_____

_____

8

Sugar and Other Sweeteners

Chapter Objectives

1. Present the basic chemistry of sugars.

2. Describe the production and makeup of various sweeteners.

3. Classify common sweeteners and describe their characteristics and uses.

4. List the functions of sweeteners and relate these functions to their makeup.

5. Describe how to best store and handle sweeteners.

Introduction

While granulated sugar is the most common sweetener in the bakeshop, many other sweeteners are available to the baker and pastry chef. Successful bakers and pastry chefs have a clear understanding of the advantages and disadvantages of each sweetener. They know when they can substitute one for another, and they know how to do it. The first challenge in understanding sweeteners is sorting through the terminology.

Sweeteners

Sweeteners can be divided into two main categories: dry crystalline sugars and syrups. A third category, specialty sweeteners, covers sweeteners that do not fit neatly into either of the first two categories. Although less commonly used and often expensive, specialty sweeteners fulfill needs that cannot easily be met by the common sweeteners. Before discussing each category of sweeteners, it will help to cover some general points.

Sugar generally means sucrose, the most common sugar in the bakeshop. Other sugars include fructose, glucose, maltose, and lactose. Any of these can be purchased as dry white crystals, although except for sucrose, it is more common to purchase them in syrup form.

All sugars are classified as simple carbohydrates, molecules that consist of carbon (C), hydrogen (H), and oxygen (O) atoms arranged in a specific way. Sugars are further classified as monosaccharides or disaccharides. *Monosaccharides* consist of one (*mono*) sugar unit (*saccharide*) and are considered simple sugars. The two main monosaccharides are glucose and fructose, although there are others. These two sugars are naturally present in many ripened fruits and are important in the makeup of certain syrups.

The skeletal molecular structure of the monosaccharide glucose is sometimes shown as a hexagon, while fructose is sometimes shown as a pentagon (Figure 8.1). Understand that these skeletal figures overlook the true complexity of sugar molecules. For one, they do not show the carbon, hydrogen, and oxygen atoms that form the structure of the molecules.

Figure 8.2 does show the atoms that make up glucose and fructose molecules. If you count the number of carbon, hydrogen, and oxygen atoms on each molecule, you will notice that glucose and fructose have the same molecular formula ($C_6H_{12}O_6$). But because the atoms are arranged differently, glucose and fructose are different molecules having different properties. This chapter discusses some of the different properties of these and other sugars.

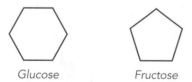

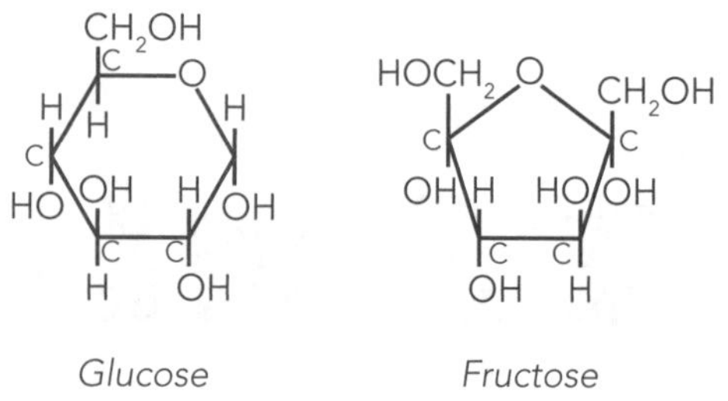

Glucose   *Fructose*

Figure 8.2 Detailed representation of the monosaccharides glucose and fructose

Disaccharides consist of two sugar units bonded together (Figure 8.3). Maltose (malt sugar) is one example of a disaccharide. It consists of two glucose molecules. Maltose is commonly found in glucose corn syrup and malt syrup. Lactose (milk sugar) is a disaccharide found only in dairy products. Sucrose, the most common sugar in the bakeshop, is also a

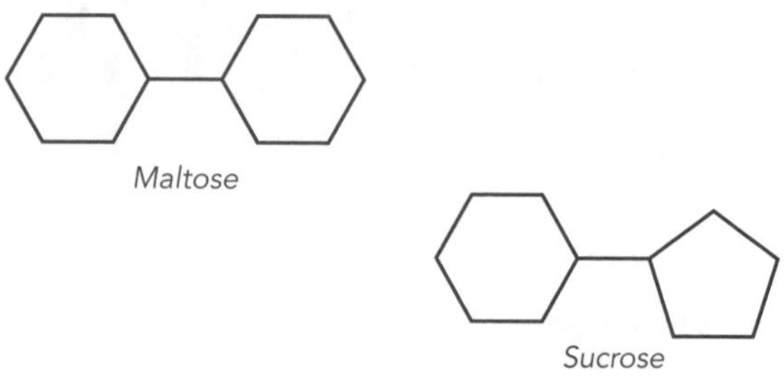

Maltose

Sucrose

Figure 8.3 Typical representation of the skeletal structures of the disaccharides maltose and sucrose

Glucose   *Fructose*

Figure 8.1 Typical representation of the skeletal structures of the monosaccharides glucose and fructose

The most abundant sugar in nature, glucose has an abundance of names. For example, glucose is typically called *dextrose* when purchased as dry crystalline sugar. Dextrose is added to processed food products, including cake mixes, chocolate chips, sausages, and hot dogs. It provides many of the properties of sugar with less of the sweetness. Commercially, the main source of crystalline dextrose is corn, so dextrose is sometimes called *corn sugar*.

Glucose is present in nearly all ripened fruit, but its presence in grapes is essential to the fermentation of grapes to wine. This is why winemakers call glucose *grape sugar*.

Another name for glucose is *blood sugar*, because it is the sugar that flows through the bloodstream. People with diabetes tend to have high blood sugar levels unless they control it through diet and/or medication.

Glucose is also shorthand for glucose syrup, commonly called *corn syrup* in the United States (because it is usually derived from cornstarch). To minimize confusion, this text refers to the syrup as *glucose corn syrup*. While glucose corn syrup does contain a certain amount of the monosaccharide glucose, it generally contains significant amounts of other components as well, so the name is somewhat misleading. Historically, however, glucose corn syrups were manufactured for the glucose they contained, so while misleading, the name is logical. Many other syrups contain the monosaccharide glucose, including honey, molasses, invert syrup, and malt syrup.

disaccharide. It consists of one molecule of glucose bonded to fructose.

In addition to monosaccharides and disaccharides, two other main classifications of carbohydrates are oligosaccharides and polysaccharides. *Oligosaccharides* are made up of a few (*oligo*) sugar units, usually three to ten, bonded into a chain. Oligosaccharides, which are called *higher saccharides* or sometimes *dextrins* by the sweetener industry, are present in many syrups used in the bakeshop. Figure 8.4 shows the skeletal structure of two higher saccharides.

Polysaccharides are very large carbohydrate molecules made up of many (*poly*)—often thousands—of sugar units. Two polysaccharides discussed in this chapter are *starch* and *inulin* (not to be confused with insulin, the hormone that controls blood glucose levels in our bodies). The sugar units in starch are glucose; those in inulin are primarily fructose.

Sugar crystals are highly ordered arrangements of sugar molecules bonded together. They form because sugar molecules of the same type are attracted to one another. Crystal growth can be desirable, as when making rock candy, or it can be unwanted, as when making nut brittle, caramel, or pulled sugar. Smooth and creamy fondants and icings require the smallest of crystals for the best appearance and mouthfeel.

For the most part, sugar crystals are pure. This means, for example, that crystals of sucrose consist entirely of sucrose, even when they form from syrups that contain a mix of sugars. The mix just makes it more difficult for crystals to form, because it makes it difficult for molecules of the same type to come together. Because they are pure, sugar crystals are naturally white in color and do not need to be chemically bleached. When crystals are off color, as they are in semirefined and brown sugars, it is because "impurities" are trapped between the crystals.

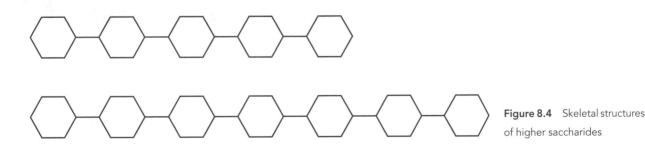

Figure 8.4 Skeletal structures of higher saccharides

Boiled confections encompass a wide range of sweets that all start with sugar dissolved in water, then boiled to concentrate. *Crystalline* boiled confections include rock candy, maple sugar candy, fondant, fudge, penuche, and Southern pralines. *Noncrystalline* (or glassy) boiled confections include poured and cast sugar, hard candy (for example, lollipops), and nougatine or nut brittles. The following are also classified as noncrystalline confections:

- Taffy and other forms of pulled sugar
- Cotton candy and other forms of spun sugar
- Blown sugar
- Toffees and soft caramels
- Marshmallows, nougats, divinity, and other aerated confections
- Jams, jellies, and jelly candies

The challenges in making boiled confections are many, but one of the greatest challenges is determining when the right amount of water has boiled off. A reliable thermometer or refractometer is needed for the task, leaving the second challenge, that of controlling crystallization, to the use of a reliable formula and the experience and expertise of a skilled confectioner. Look for helpful hints throughout this chapter on ways to control sugar crystallization in boiled confections and cooked sugar solutions.

The Hygroscopic Nature of Sugar

All sugars are *hygroscopic*, at least to some degree, meaning that they attract and bond to water. Because sugars are strongly attracted to water, they can pull water away from other molecules including proteins, starches, and gums. When this occurs in batters and doughs, the batters and doughs soften and thin out as sugar is added. The proteins, starches, and gums become less hydrated, so they trap less water. The water is released to sugar, forming a thin syrup as part of the batter or dough. Figure 8.5 shows this, where a seemingly dry powder made from starch and water is liquefied by the addition of dry sugar.

Highly hygroscopic sugars such as fructose readily pick up water from moist air. The hygroscopic nature of sugars is considered desirable when soft, moist cookies must stay soft and moist, or when icings must not dry, crack, or dull. When used in this manner, hygroscopic sugars are sometimes called *humectants*.

The hygroscopic nature of sugars is sometimes undesirable, as when a dusting of powdered sugar on a doughnut liquefies; when the surface of cookies, cakes, and muffins becomes gummy or soggy; or when spun or pulled sugar becomes sticky and collapses.

Figure 8.5 Sugar pulls water from starch granules. **Bottom left:** dry starch with an equal weight of water; **bottom right:** same weight of granulated sugar; **top:** liquid prepared by adding the granulated sugar to the starch-water mix.

Dry Crystalline Sugars

Sucrose is naturally present in maple tree sap, palm tree sap, dates, ripe bananas, and many other ripened fruits. Commercial production of sucrose involves removing and purifying natural sucrose from sugarcane or sugar beets. Various forms of dry crystalline sugar are available, each differing primarily in granulation or particle size. Some contain additional ingredients such as cornstarch or molasses. Most have more than one name. Sometimes the name refers to particle size (or grain) of the crystals (extrafine, superfine); other times, it refers to use (sanding sugar) or to user (confectioners' sugar, baker's special sugar). Going from largest to smallest in particle size:

coarse > regular > superfine > 6X powdered > 10X powdered > fondant sugar

The particle size of sugar crystals is traditionally given in microns. A micron, also called a *micrometer*, is one-millionth of a meter, or less than 0.00004 inches. In other words, a micron is a very small unit. Particles that are less than about 45 microns are not easily felt on the tongue. As the size of sugar crystals approaches 45 microns, the crystals start to feel gritty. Figure 8.6 graphically shows the typical range of particle sizes for several crystalline sugars. The sizes are given in microns.

While there are many different sugars, one is not necessarily better than another. Like flours, fats, and other bakeshop ingredients, there are simply differences among the sugars, with each being good for some applications and not for others.

Regular Granulated Sugar

Regular granulated sugar is also called fine or extrafine sugar. In Canada, granulated sugar is mostly purified from sugarcane; in Europe, it is mostly purified from sugar beets; in the United States, about half is from sugarcane, the other half from sugar beets.

Regular granulated sugar from either cane or beets is typically greater than 99.9 percent pure sucrose, meaning that both are extremely pure and highly refined. For most practical applications, sugar refined in North America from either source can be used interchangeably. However, even very small amounts of impurities can cause undesirable crystallization and browning in sugar confectionery. When this occurs, it is often necessary to add a small amount of cream of tartar. Cream of tartar and other acids prevent both crystallization and browning by lowering pH.

Today there is a trend towards using sugars that have not gone through the complete refining process. The best description of these sugars is probably *dried cane syrup*, but they go by many different names, including *unrefined milled sugar*, *evaporated cane juice*, or *natural cane juice crystals*. These sugars have been refined through one, rather than three, washings and centrifuge cycles. They also have not been filtered to decolorize. Sometimes called *first crystallization sugars*, these sugars retain a small amount of lightly colored refiners' syrup (generally

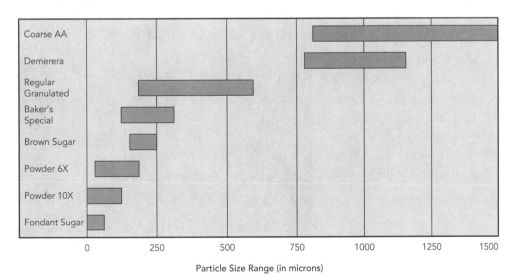

Figure 8.6 Sugar particle size ranges for different sugars

Particle Size Range (in microns)

Sugarcane is a tall, reedy grass that was first cultivated in the South Pacific at least eight thousand years ago. It migrated west to India, then to China and Persia (Iran), countries that have extracted and purified sugar from the cane—either as syrup or as crystals—for the past two or three thousand years.

Europeans were relatively late in using cane sugar, relying on more available sweeteners such as honey and ripened fruit. When cane sugar was eventually introduced to Europe during the Crusades in the eleventh and twelfth centuries, it was considered so precious that it was used mostly in medicines.

Sugarcane is a tropical crop that does not grow well in much of Europe, so for years sugar was under the control of Arab traders. However, once the Spanish and Portuguese brought the cultivation of sugarcane into Africa and the New World, sugar became readily available throughout Europe. Although still a luxury, by the 1600s sugar was used in confectionery and in coffee, tea, and hot chocolate. As demand grew, slaves were brought from Africa to the New World to work the sugar plantations. Still, it wasn't until the 1800s, when sugar refining methods were improved, that prices came down and sugar became readily available to the middle class.

The use of beets for sugar manufacture was a more recent development, first commercialized by a Prussian (German) chemist in the 1700s. The process was adopted and refined by the French in the early 1800s, when the Napoleonic Wars created a need for a domestic source of this important ingredient. The antislavery movement in Europe and the Americas further drove interest in sugar beet cultivation, because sugar beets grow in temperate climates without extensive labor. Over the years, sugar beets have been selectively bred to contain high amounts of sucrose. Today they contain about 17 percent sucrose, over twice the amount in beets from the 1700s, and slightly more than that in sugarcane. Sugar beets remain the predominant source of sugar in Europe today.

---

less than 2 percent). They have a pale blond or gold color and a very mild flavor, much closer to regular granulated sugar than to brown sugar. They will function in baked goods as regular granulated sugar, except for a slight off-white cast they give to light-colored products.

These semirefined sugars are marketed as a substitute for granulated sugar to the natural foods industry and can be made to various granulation sizes, just like regular granulated sugar. Organic cane sugars (that is, sugars made from sugarcane grown organically) are often sold semirefined. Organic cane sugars typically are appropriate for use in vegan products, since bone char (an animal product commonly used to refine cane sugar) is not allowed in any USDA certified organic product.

When deciding on the best sweetener for your particular needs, make an informed decision. Do not consider these sugars—including the organic versions—to have improved health or nutritional benefits, and keep in mind that they can be two to three times the price of regular granulated sugar.

Coarse Sugars

Coarse sugars have larger crystals than regular granulated sugar. They are useful as a garnish on muffins and other baked goods (Figure 8.7). Because of their large size, coarse crystals do not readily dissolve, and they have an attractive sparkle. One example of a coarse crystalline

Figure 8.7 Sugars for garnish. **Left:** pearl sugar; **right:** coarse confectioners AA

The manufacture of white sugar involves two basic steps that often take place at separate locations: the production, or *milling*, of raw sugar from sugarcane or sugar beets, and the *refining* of this inedible, molasses-coated raw sugar into pure white sugar, less-refined golden sugar, and brown sugar. The specifics in producing cane sugar are somewhat different from those for beet sugar. In both cases, however, the sucrose is not changed chemically during the process. Instead, through a series of steps (filtration, crystallization, washing, and centrifugation), sucrose is physically separated from impurities naturally present in the sugarcane or sugar beet. The following is a general description of cane sugar milling and refining.

The first step in milling cane sugar is crushing freshly harvested sugarcane and extracting the juice with water. Next, lime (calcium hydroxide, an alkali) and carbon dioxide are added to this cloudy juice to trap impurities. The impurities (field debris, fiber, waxes, fats, etc.) settle to the bottom and the liquid is strained to remove them from the clear juice. Water is evaporated from the clear juice until it is a thick golden syrup. The syrup is filtered, then concentrated by gently heating it in vacuum pans. As water evaporates and the syrup becomes supersaturated, sugar crystals form. The crystallized mixture is centrifuged (spun, as in a salad spinner) to separate crystals from the dark, thick syrup (molasses). The crystals are washed and recentrifuged. The light brown crude raw sugar is ready to be refined into pure white sugar.

In the meantime, the molasses from the centrifuging of sugar cane syrup is recycled, often two or three times, by heating and recentrifuging until no more sucrose crystals can be easily extracted. With each extraction, the amount of sugar in the molasses decreases while the color, flavor, and ash increase. Final-extraction molasses has little easily extracted sucrose. While so-called first, second, and third extractions of cane molasses are sometimes blended and sold for food use, final-extraction molasses is generally not. It is considered too dark in color and too harsh in flavor for use by humans.

The crude raw sugar—considered unclean and inedible in North America—is sent to a sugar refinery, where it undergoes a series of processes involving more washing, centrifuging, clarifying, and filtering. The sugar syrup is also decolorized, meaning that it is passed through an ion exchange or activated carbon filter, much as you might pass water through a water filter. Decolorizing removes the last bits of golden-colored material from the syrup. Some cane—but no beet—sugar manufacturers still use bone char from cattle for decolorizing, which strict vegetarians find unacceptable.

Finally, the pure sugar is crystallized for the last time, then dried, screened through wire meshes, packed, and sold. The remaining syrup, commonly called molasses, is referred to as *refiners' syrup* by the sugar industry. This differentiates it from molasses syrup left from the milling operation of sugar manufacture.

sugar is sometimes called *sanding sugar*, although that term also refers to a different product called *pearl sugar*. For added sheen, coarse sugars are sometimes polished with a coating of edible carnauba wax. *Carnauba wax* is a hard natural wax from a Brazilian palm tree. The shiny waxed coarse sugars are particularly attractive as a garnish, and the wax coating further prevents the crystals from picking up moisture and dissolving into batters or doughs.

Coarse white sugars are often best for the whitest fondants and confections and the clearest syrups, because they have the fewest impurities of all granulated sugars. Being pure, coarse sugars are significantly more expensive than regular granulated sugar. The high purity—often exceeding 99.98 percent—is necessary if large, sparkling crystals are to form. One coarse sugar designed for the whitest confections is called *confectioners AA*. Do not confuse this pure, very-large-grained translucent sugar with finely pulverized powdered confectioners' sugar.

Powdered Sugar

Powdered sugar is often called *confectioners' sugar* in the United States and *icing sugar* in Canada. It consists of sucrose crystals finely pulverized into powder, and is available in various degrees of fineness. The fineness of

Pearl sugar consists of opaque white rounded granules that do not dissolve readily. Pearl sugar is used much like coarse crystalline sugar, to provide a crunchy decorative topping on sweet baked goods, but it has a very different look from the clear, glistening crystals of coarse crystalline sugar. Pearl sugar is sometimes called sanding sugar, decorative sugar, or nibs.

What's in a Name?

Each of the following sugars is similar in particle size to superfine granulated. It is interesting to see that each name says something about the sugar and how it is used. For practical purposes, these sugars can be used interchangeably, although they vary slightly in particle size.

- **Fruit sugar:** dissolves quickly when sprinkled on fresh fruit (do not confuse this with fructose, also called fruit sugar because it is found in fruit).
- **Baker's sugar:** used by bakers to produce the finest crumb in certain cakes; it also produces greater spread in cookies and is good for sugaring doughnuts.
- **Bar sugar:** dissolves quickly in cold beverages.
- **Caster or castor sugar:** named for the small container used for serving sugar in British homes.

grind is sometimes indicated by a number before an X; the higher the number, the greater the fineness. Two common powdered sugars are 6X and 10X. Of the two, 10X is best for the smoothest uncooked icings and confections, where anything coarser would be too gritty. For decorative dustings on desserts, 6X powdered sugar is the better choice, since its coarser grind means it is less likely to cake or liquefy.

Powdered sugars typically contain about 3 percent cornstarch, which absorbs moisture and prevents caking. Cornstarch also stiffens and stabilizes meringues and whipped cream sweetened with powdered sugar. However, you might notice a raw starch taste when using powdered sugar in certain applications.

Fondant and Icing Sugars

Fondant and icing sugars are extremely fine powdered sugars, having the smallest grain size (less than 45 microns) of any sugar. They are designed for quickly preparing the smoothest fondant, glaze, or cream praline centers, with no cooking necessary. These sugars are sometimes processed ("agglomerated") into special porous particles that dissolve easily and do not cake, even when no cornstarch is added. This means that some fondant and icing sugars do not have the raw starchy taste characteristic of powdered confectioners' sugars.

Additionally, some fondant and icing sugars contain 3–10 percent invert sugar, which improves sheen and prevents drying of prepared products. Others designed specifically for preparing fondant glazes contain maltodextrin, which reduces stickiness and improves the ability of the glaze to adhere to doughnuts and other baked goods. Examples of fondant sugars include Easy Fond and Drifond.

Superfine Granulated

Superfine sugar has crystals that are intermediate in size between powdered sugar and regular granulated sugar. Superfine sugar (also called *ultrafine*) dissolves more quickly in liquids than regular granulated sugar. It also allows the incorporation of smaller air cells into batters and creamed shortenings, and is good for sugaring baked goods.

While not all bakeshops stock superfine sugar, those that do find that it produces a finer, more uniform crumb in certain cakes; it reduces beading in common meringues; and it increases spread in cookies.

Regular (Soft) Brown Sugar

Brown sugar generally refers to fine granulated sugar with a small amount—usually less than 10 percent—of molasses or refiners' syrup. Because some, or all, of the molasses is near the surface of the tiny sugar crystals, brown sugar is soft, sticky, and tends to clump. Depending on the color and flavor of the molasses used in its production, brown sugar is considered light brown (yellow or golden) or dark brown. Sometimes, but not always, dark brown sugar has caramel coloring added for an even darker color. In North America, there is very little, if any, difference in the amount of molasses added to regular light and dark brown sugars.

Brown sugar is commercially made one of two ways. The first way is to boil semirefined sugar with molasses or refiners' syrup, allowing the sugar to recrystallize with the molasses syrup and other "impurities." Another way is to blend cane sugar molasses with granulated white sugar, coating ("painting") the crystals with molasses. Both methods are common. The first method is typically used when brown sugar is made from sugar cane. The second is always used when brown sugar is made from sugar beets.

Brown sugar is used primarily for its color and distinct molasses flavor; the small amount of molasses in brown sugar has little, if any, effect on the moistness of baked goods or on its nutritional value. Use light or dark brown sugar in cookies, cakes, confections, and breads, replacing regular granulated sugar pound for pound. Brown sugar is soft and tends to clump because it is higher in moisture (3–4 percent) than regular granulated sugar, so it must be stored in an airtight container.

If brown sugar is unavailable, substitute about 1 pound (or 1 kilogram) molasses and 9 pounds (or 9 kilograms) sugar for every 10 pounds (or 10 kilograms) brown sugar in a formula. The color, flavor, and overall quality of the final product will depend on the color, flavor, and quality of the added molasses.

Specialty Brown Sugars

There are several brown sugars available to the baker in addition to regular light and dark brown sugars (Figure 8.8). Many were developed and introduced to the market within the last twenty years. Since the processes used in making these products vary with the manufacturer, they can be described in general terms only. All brown sugars retain small amounts of vitamins and minerals from the molasses they contain, but none is a significant source of either.

Muscovado sugar is the darkest, richest-tasting brown sugar, having a uniquely fruity flavor reminiscent of

Figure 8.8 Brown sugar. **Clockwise from top:** regular light brown, dark muscovado, Demerara, and Sucanat

caramel and raisins. It is soft and moist, consisting of powdery-fine crystals enrobed in molasses. Muscovado sugar is sometimes called Barbados sugar, after the island in the Caribbean where it was produced in the 1700s. It was originally made by draining excess molasses from crystallized raw unrefined sugar before shipping the sugar to England for refining. The word *muscovado* is derived from the Spanish word for unrefined. The term historically is used to refer to any unrefined noncentrifugal brown sugar (see "Noncentrifugal Sugars: Artisan Sugars from Around the World," next page).

Today muscovado sugar is just as likely made by boiling molasses, often strong, dark third-extraction molasses, and seeding it with sugar to crystallize. This is similar to how regular light and dark brown cane sugar—but not beet sugar—is made. The thick syrup is stirred slowly as it cools to prevent it from hardening into a solid block.

Think of muscovado as a richer version of regular soft dark brown sugar with a higher level of molasses. Its strong flavor and dark color are especially good in gingerbread, fruit cakes, and rich chocolate baked goods. Light muscovado is also available. Light muscovado contains less molasses and has a correspondingly lighter color and flavor.

Sucanat is the trademarked name (SUgar CAne NATural) for a free-flowing, organically grown,

In some areas of the world, sugarcane juice is still evaporated in open pans until it is dry to produce a crude, unrefined brown sugar, much as it was made thousands of years ago. These unrefined raw sugars are sometimes called *noncentrifugal sugars*, since they have not been centrifuged (spun) to remove molasses at any stage in the process.

Unrefined sugars retain the rich, hearty flavor of molasses; in fact, they can be thought of as crystallized molasses or whole cane sugars, with nothing removed at any stage. Each is unique because of differences in regional practices. Most come in varying degrees of color, from golden to dark brown, depending on how they are boiled and what clarifying agents and additives are used. The sugar is generally consumed where it is produced, but quantities are available through specialty distributors as interest in the unique flavor of each region's sugar has grown.

Jaggery, made in the villages of India where it is often called *gur*, is one common example of an unrefined sugar. Jaggery is made by boiling and stirring sugarcane juice until it evaporates to a thickened crystallized syrup. The hot fudge-like mixture is cast in cylindrical molds or formed into cakes and cooled to harden. Sometimes jaggery is grated from hardened blocks and sold as powdery crystals, called *shakkar* (Hindi for sugar). When it is washed with water, centrifuged, and crumbled into grains, the resulting semirefined product is called *khandsari*. About one-third to one-half of the sugar consumed in India is still in the form of jaggery, shakkar, and khandsari. Jaggery is also used throughout Southeast Asia.

Other examples of unrefined sugar include *panela*, made in Colombia and sold as rectangular or round flat loaves throughout South America; *rapadura*, from Brazil; cone-shaped *piloncillo* from Mexico; and *panocha* from the Philippines.

A refined artisan sugar made in Japan is called *wasanbon toh*. Wasanbon toh, made from a special variety of sugarcane, is refined by repeatedly mixing sugar crystals with water, kneading the mix by hand, and pressing it with stones to remove molasses syrup. When the process is completed, the sugar takes the form of a fine, ivory-white powder. Wasanbon toh is said to have a delicate flavor that is important in traditional Japanese sweets.

---

unrefined brown sugar. It is made from sugar cane juice concentrated to a thick golden brown syrup (molasses), then slowly stirred as it cools and dries. Since nothing is added or removed, Sucanat—which is formed into dry, porous granules rather than crystals—is generally described as a whole cane sugar. Sucanat can be used instead of light or dark brown sugar in baking, but its large porous granules do not dissolve as readily, so Sucanat sometimes acts differently in baking.

Turbinado sugar is similar in taste and color to light brown sugar, but it is dry and free flowing rather than soft and moist. Turbinado sugar is sometimes called *raw, washed raw,* or *unrefined sugar,* but these terms are somewhat misleading. A better description might be to call turbinado sugar partially or semirefined. To make turbinado sugar, crude raw sugar is first cleaned by steaming. It is then washed and centrifuged to remove surface molasses before it is crystallized and dried. These refining steps turn crude raw sugar into an edible light golden brown sugar that typically retains about 2 percent molasses. The name "turbinado" comes from the use of the centrifuge, also called a turbine, in the refining process of this and all sugars except artisan noncentrifugal ones. Sugar In The Raw from Hawaii and Florida Crystals are two brands of turbinado brown sugar.

Demerara sugar is a type of turbinado sugar. It is a light brown sugar with large, golden crystals. It is popular in Great Britain as a sweetener in coffee or on cereal. Because its crystals are large, crunchy, and glistening, Demerara is also used as a decorative sanding sugar on muffins and other baked goods. Demerara sugar is named after a region in Guyana, the country in South America where quantities of it were first made. Today, much of the Demerara and muscovado sugar sold is produced on the island of Mauritius, off the coast of Africa and exported to Europe and North America.

Syrups

Syrups are mixtures of one or more sugars dissolved in water, usually with small amounts of other components including acids, colorants, flavorants, and thickeners. Although these other components are present in small amounts, they are extremely important because they provide the unique character of each syrup.

Most syrups contain about 20 percent water, but there are exceptions. For example, invert syrup typically contains from 23 to 29 percent water; maple syrup has about 33 percent water; and simple syrup often contains 50 percent water.

Sometimes, the thicker the syrup, the less water it contains. Usually, however, syrups are thick because they contain higher saccharides in addition to sugar. The larger size of higher saccharides makes them slower to move and more apt to bump and tangle, which is why they thicken. Higher saccharides are present in glucose corn syrups and other thick syrups such as honey and molasses.

Sometimes syrups can be used interchangeably, but often one syrup, because of its makeup, excels over others at a particular function. For example, most syrups tend to sweeten, moisten, and brown when used in baked goods. But syrups high in fructose (such as invert syrup, high fructose corn syrup, agave syrup, and honey) excel at these functions. As the makeup and functions of syrups are described in the following sections, notice how these syrups are similar in other ways. Table 8.1 summarizes and compares the typical composition of various syrups and other sweeteners. Actual values can vary, depending on the brand or the source of sweetener.

Simple Syrup

The simplest syrup is called *simple syrup*. Bakers and pastry chefs typically make simple syrup by heating equal parts by weight of granulated sugar and water, although other ratios of sugar to water can be used. The ratio of sugar to water in simple syrup should not go above 2:1, or the sugar is likely to crystallize. Often a small amount of lemon juice or sliced lemon is added to simple syrup. The acid in lemon can help prevent darkening and crystallization, especially in syrups high in sugar. It can also prevent the growth of spoilage microorganisms.

TABLE 8.1   COMPOSITION OF COMMON SWEETENERS (%)

SWEETENER	TOTAL SOLIDS	SUCROSE	FRUCTOSE	GLUCOSE	MALTOSE	HIGHER SACCHARIDES
Brown sugar, light	96	95	2	3	0	0
Brown sugar, dark	96	95	2	3	0	0
Maple syrup	67	90	5	5	0	0
Molasses, premium	80	54	23	23	0	0
Invert, medium	77	50	25	25	0	0
HFCS-42	77	0	42	50	2	6
Invert, full	77	6	47	47	0	0
Honey	83	2	47	38	8	5
Agave syrup	71	0	80	14	0	6
Glucose syrup, low-conversion	80	0	0	7	45	48
Glucose syrup, high-conversion	82	0	0	37	32	31
Malt syrup	78	0	0	3	77	20

Syrups are sometimes described by their solids content. For example, a typical glucose corn syrup contains about 80 percent solids and 20 percent water. Such a syrup is described as having 80° Brix. Brix, named after Adolf Brix, the German scientist who created the scale, is a measure of the percentage of soluble solids (primarily sugar) in syrups and other products, including fruit juices.

Just as temperature is measured in Fahrenheit or Celsius, the solids content of syrups can be measured in Brix or Baumé units. Baumé (Bé) units, named after Antoine Baumé, the French scientist who created the scale, are familiar to many pastry chefs. Brix and Baumé units can both be measured using a hydrometer, sometimes called a *saccharometer*, meaning "sugar meter." A hydrometer actually measures specific gravity, which is related to density. Syrups having a high Brix or Baumé reading have a higher specific gravity, are denser, and therefore contain more soluble solids and less water than those having a lower reading.

A typical glucose corn syrup with a Brix of 80 will have a Baumé reading of about 43. A typical simple syrup (one used in sorbets) has a Brix just over 50 and a Baumé of 28, while most sorbet mixes have a Brix of 27 and a Baumé of 15. Brix units can be converted to Baumé units using a formula or a special conversion chart. For the range of syrups typically used by pastry chefs, the following formulas provides a good estimate of the relationship between the two:

Baumé = 0.55 × Brix

Brix = Baumé ÷ 0.55

While pastry chefs have traditionally used hydrometers (Figure 8.9) and Baumé units, many have switched to Brix units. They are also using different devices, called refractometers, to measure Brix (Figure 8.10). Refractometers are more expensive than hydrometers, but they are faster and easier to use, and they require a much smaller sample.

Figure 8.9   A hydrometer measuring the sugar concentration (Brix) of a syrup

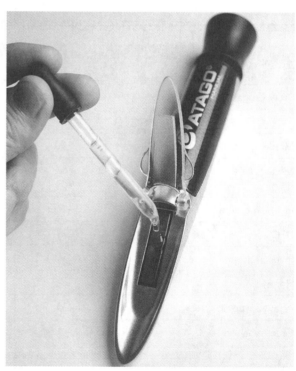

Figure 8.10   A drop of liquid being placed on a refractometer for measuring its sugar concentration (Brix)

Simple syrup has many uses. For example, it is used for moistening cake layers, glazing fresh fruit, thinning fondant, poaching fruit, and preparing sorbets. Simple syrup is the only syrup made by bakers and pastry chefs. All others, including invert syrup, molasses, glucose corn syrup, maple syrup, honey, and malt syrup, are purchased.

Invert Syrup

The term *invert syrup* is sometimes used by bakers and pastry chefs to describe any liquid syrup, including glucose corn syrup, maple syrup, honey, and molasses. The term has a more specific meaning, however. It refers to a type of syrup that contains approximately equal amounts of fructose and glucose.

While invert syrup is not as commonly used in the bakeshop as, for example, glucose corn syrup, it is still important to understand what it is and what its properties are. By learning about invert syrup, you will learn about sugars in general and how they function.

To produce invert syrup (Figure 8.11), the manufacturer typically adds acid to sugar (sucrose) syrup, heats it, then filters, refines, and concentrates it. Recall that sucrose is a disaccharide consisting of fructose and glucose bonded together. The combination of heat and acid breaks (hydrolyzes) the bond between the two monosaccharides, releasing them. The process is sometimes called *inversion*, and what remains is invert syrup: equal parts fructose and glucose dissolved in water, with a small amount of residual acid. The acid helps reduce the growth of spoilage microorganisms, including yeast and mold.

There are two main types of invert syrup commonly used in bakeshops. The first is called total or *full invert syrup*, and it contains little, if any, remaining sucrose. The second, called *medium invert syrup*, has only half

its sugar inverted into glucose and fructose. Both syrups are available in a range of sugar solids, from 71 to 77 percent solids (corresponding to 29 to 23 percent moisture).

Invert syrup is also sometimes called *invert sugar*, or simply invert. It generally comes as a clear, light-colored liquid or a thicker opaque cream that contains tiny crystals of sugar suspended in syrup. Several brands are available to bakers and pastry chefs, including Nulomoline, Trimoline, and FreshVert.

Invert syrup is only slightly more expensive than sucrose, but like all syrups, it is messier to use and has a shorter shelf life. This means that syrups like invert should be used only if they have properties that sugar cannot provide.

Several properties of invert syrup make it valuable in bakeshops and pastry shops. One is that it keeps baked goods soft and moist longer. Another is that it keeps icings, fondants, and confections smooth, shiny, and free from cracking and drying. A third is that it prevents the formation of ice crystals in frozen desserts, keeping them softer while frozen. Soft frozen desserts are easier to scoop, slice, and eat straight from the freezer.

Invert syrup is sweeter than sugar and browns much faster. When it is used in baked goods, oven temperatures should be lowered by about 25°F (15°C), to prevent excessive browning. Even with a lower oven temperature, no more than 25 percent of the sugar in a formula should be replaced with invert syrup. Too much invert tends to make baked goods dark, dense, gummy, and too sweet. Use even less invert syrup, if any, in white cake so the cake stays white. If necessary, a small amount of cream of tartar can be added to lower pH and slow browning.

Because of its hygroscopic nature, invert syrup is more effective than sugar at tying up water, making

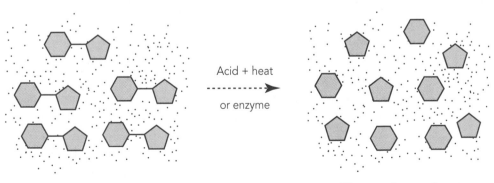

Acid + heat

or enzyme

Sucrose in water

Glucose + fructose in water

Figure 8.11 The inversion of sucrose to invert syrup

What Is Golden Syrup?

Golden syrup, also known as light treacle, is popular with consumers in Great Britain. It is cane sugar syrup with a golden color and a mild caramelized sugar flavor. Golden syrup is a refiners' syrup (that is, a by-product of the cane sugar refining process) or it can be made directly by boiling and concentrating cane juice.

Golden syrup contains a moderate amount of invert sugar, so it is essentially a medium invert syrup, one that has not been highly filtered or refined. In fact, golden syrup is sold to manufacturers in North America as straw-colored medium invert syrup. Golden syrup is used in cooking and baking, as pancake syrup, and as ice cream topping.

The Secret behind Chocolate-Covered Cherries

Chocolate-covered cherries contain candied cherries surrounded by liquid fondant, all encased with chocolate (Figure 8.12). What is the secret to coating these very liquid centers in chocolate?

The secret is invertase. When a small amount of the enzyme invertase is added to a hard fondant, the sugar in the fondant begins to slowly invert, or break down, into glucose and fructose. As this happens, the sugar crystals dissolve and the fondant liquefies. Because it takes several days or weeks for this to happen, the fondant is still firm when the fondant-coated candied cherries are coated or dipped in chocolate. By the time the fondant liquefies, the chocolate has long since set up as a protective coating.

Figure 8.12 The fondant center in chocolate-covered cherries liquefies from the action of the enzyme invertase.

water less available for the growth of microorganisms. That is, invert syrup can lower *water activity*. By replacing some sugar with invert syrup, for example, fondant cream centers in chocolates not only stay soft and creamy, but they are less likely to spoil.

Although bakers and pastry chefs do not produce invert syrup in bulk in the pastry shop, small amounts are produced in the normal course of creating many boiled confections. For example, when acid (such as cream of tartar or tartaric acid) is added to boiling sugar, a certain amount of sugar is inverted to fructose and glucose. The longer the sugar is heated and the more acid added, the more sugar inverts to fructose and glucose. This helps reduce sugar crystallization in the same manner as adding invert syrup directly. Because sugar inversion makes it difficult for large sugar crystals

to form, the cooled confection is smoother, shinier, and less apt to crack and dry than if no acid were added.

It can be difficult for a pastry chef to control the amount of sugar inversion when acid is added directly to boiled confections. In particular, the cook time and the amount of acid added must be carefully controlled. If too much sugar inverts, confections may be sticky or not set up properly. If too little sugar inverts, confections might crystallize or be too firm and dry.

Recall that a small amount of lemon juice is sometimes added to simple syrup. Depending on the amount added and the length of time the syrup is heated, the acid allows a certain amount of sucrose to invert to fructose and glucose. This inversion continues, although more slowly, after the syrup cools. Again, the mix of sugars helps prevent concentrated syrups from crystallizing.

At first glance, it might appear that the water in invert syrup gives it its special properties. After all, one of the main properties of invert syrup is keeping baked goods and confections soft and moist. But adjust formulas for water or compare invert syrup with most other syrups, and invert would still be superior at moistening and at certain other functions.

In fact, it is the monosaccharides in invert syrup—the fructose and the glucose—that give it different properties from sucrose. While sucrose is made up of fructose and glucose, in sucrose they are bound to each other as a disaccharide. In full invert syrup, they are not.

Recall that fructose is particularly hygroscopic, meaning it is better than most sugars, including sucrose, at moistening. Recall, too, that a mixture of sugars crystallizes more slowly than pure sugar. When a small amount of invert syrup is added to icings, fondants, and confections, the mix of sugars keeps them from crystallizing. This means more softness, creaminess, and shine. Additionally, monosaccharides such as fructose and glucose, being smaller in size, are better at lowering the freezing point of water and lowering water activity. Fructose and glucose are also more reactive, meaning that they break down and brown faster than sucrose.

Molasses

Molasses is the concentrated juice of sugarcane. It is used primarily for color and flavor, although the moderate amount of invert sugar in molasses provides moistness and softness to baked goods, much as medium invert syrup does. While sweeteners are not considered particularly good sources of nutrients, molasses is among the highest of all sweeteners in many essential minerals, some B vitamins, and health-promoting polyphenolic compounds.

Many grades of molasses are available to the baker and pastry chef. The highest grades are sweetest, lightest in color, and mildest in flavor. They are more expensive than lower-grade molasses, but are not necessarily better for baking. Strong flavors from spices and whole grains can easily overwhelm the mild, sweet flavor of premium imported molasses. A darker lower-grade molasses might be more suitable. Canada has mandatory standards for molasses, while the United States has voluntary grading. Any grade of molasses can be sulfured (that is, can have sulfur dioxide or sulfites added) but premium molasses is most apt to be unsulfured.

Several factors affect molasses grading. Molasses made by directly boiling and concentrating sugarcane juice in an open kettle, with no sugar crystals removed, is considered premium grade or fancy molasses. The best premium-grade molasses is imported from the Caribbean. An example of premium imported molasses is Home Maid.

Lower grades of molasses are by-products of cane sugar milling, often blended from first-, second-, and third-extraction molasses. Because some of the sugar has been removed and the molasses has undergone more processing, lower-grade molasses is darker in color, less sweet, more acidic, and more bitter than premium molasses. Lower-grade molasses is also higher in nutrients. In Canada, two lower grades of molasses are table and cooking molasses. Lower-grade cooking molasses can be an excellent choice when a hearty, robust flavor and dark color are desired.

In the United States, *blackstrap molasses* usually refers to inedible final-extraction molasses, extremely bitter and not very sweet. In Canada, blackstrap is another name for cooking molasses.

> **HELPFUL HINT**
>
> If the batch size of a boiled confection or cooked sugar solution is changed, the amount of acid added should be changed as well. For example, if a batch of cooked sugar is increased in size, it will take longer for the batch to reach its final temperature. With longer heat exposure, more sugar will break down into glucose and fructose. More glucose and fructose means the cooked sugar will be softer, more likely to discolor, and more susceptible to absorbing moisture and becoming sticky. To compensate for this, when a batch is increased in size, use less acid, or add the acid later in the process. Likewise, when a batch is reduced in size, the batch will cook faster and therefore require more acid to achieve the same amount of sugar inversion. Otherwise, less sugar will invert, and the cooked sugar will be too firm and more likely to crystallize.

Treacles are dark cane syrups sold in Great Britain. In other words, treacles are food-grade molasses or refiners' syrups. Just as molasses varies in color and flavor, so do treacles. Black treacle is equivalent to a low-grade edible blackstrap molasses, very dark in color and bitter in taste. Medium brown treacles are made by refining black treacle or blending it with higher-grade refiners' syrups.

Molasses from the processing of sugar beets is not food grade. Instead, it is used as animal feed; it is also used in the production of baker's yeast and in other fermentation processes.

Glucose Corn Syrups

Glucose syrups—glucose, for short—are clear syrups produced from the hydrolysis (breakdown) of starch. By far the most common starch used in the production of glucose syrup in North America is cornstarch, but any starch, including potato, wheat, or rice, can be used. In the United States, glucose syrup made from cornstarch is commonly called corn syrup. Throughout this text, however, the term "glucose corn syrup" is used to refer generically to syrups derived from any starch. Keep in mind that the syrups made from noncorn starches (such as potato starch) are properly called glucose syrup (or potato syrup, for example), but not corn syrup.

Starch is a carbohydrate that consists of hundreds, even thousands, of glucose molecules bonded together. To produce glucose corn syrup, the manufacturer typically heats starch in the presence of water and acid and treats it with enzymes (Figure 8.13), hydrolyzing the large starch molecules into smaller units. The syrup is filtered and refined through a series of steps to remove color and flavor. The more refined the syrup, the cleaner its flavor, the clearer its appearance, and the less likely it will darken over time.

The manufacturer controls the acid, heat, enzymes, and refining processes, producing a range of glucose corn syrups, each best for a particular use.

Whatever the process, all glucose corn syrups contain a certain amount of sugar (primarily glucose and maltose) that sweetens, browns, moistens, and tenderizes. The rest remains as larger fragments, called higher saccharides. Higher saccharides do not have the properties of sugar; that is, they do not sweeten, brown, moisten, or tenderize. However, because of their larger size, they thicken and add body and pliability to products. Their large size also makes them superior at interfering with the movement of molecules, so sugars are less likely to crystallize and water molecules are less likely to form ice in their presence.

Glucose corn syrups are often classified by the amount of conversion to sugar that the starch has undergone. High-conversion syrups undergo a high amount of hydrolysis and are high in sugars (and low in higher saccharides); low-conversion syrups undergo a low amount of hydrolysis and are low in sugars (and high in higher saccharides). Medium-conversion syrups fall between the two extremes. There are other differences among glucose corn syrups, but the degree of conversion is one that is important to bakers and pastry chefs. Table 8.1 compares the composition of high- and low-conversion glucose corn syrups with other common sweeteners.

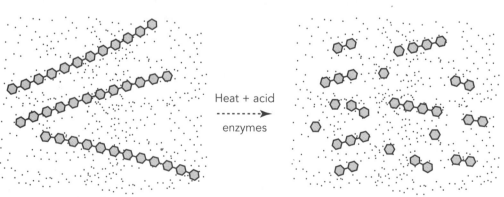

Starch in water   Heat + acid enzymes →   Glucose + maltose + higher saccharides in water

Figure 8.13

Hydrolysis of starch into glucose corn syrup

The History of Glucose Corn Syrup

The history of glucose corn syrup is tied to the political history of Europe. In the early 1800s, when the Napoleonic Wars were being fought in Europe, England set up blockades around France. These blockades prevented imported items, including food, from entering France. Needing to feed his army and his country, Napoléon offered cash rewards for new ways to produce and preserve food domestically.

One cash reward was given for the production of sugar from native plants. Starch sugar was originally produced by treating potato starch with acid. The resulting starch sugar was not as sweet as cane sugar, so when the blockade was lifted, France stopped producing it. Production began again in the mid-1800s, this time in the United States. Shortly thereafter, Americans began producing starch sugar from cornstarch instead of potato starch, and the corn syrup industry was born. Today more than half of the sweeteners consumed annually by each American come from corn.

What Is DE?

DE stands for dextrose equivalent. It is a measure of the degree of conversion of starch to sugar in glucose corn syrups. Pure cornstarch has a DE of 0, while pure dextrose has a DE of 100. Low-conversion syrups have DEs between 20 and 37; medium-conversion syrups are between 38 and 58; high-conversion have DEs between 58 and 73; and very-high-conversion syrups have DEs greater than 73. When the DE is less than 20, the syrup is no longer called a glucose corn syrup. Instead, it is called *maltodextrin*.

While many different glucose corn syrups are available to bakers and pastry chefs, most bakeshops stock two or three at most. Regular glucose corn syrup—a medium-conversion syrup (DE of 42)—is a good all-purpose glucose corn syrup. The sugar in regular glucose corn syrup provides some tenderness and sweetness to baked goods (although not as much as sucrose), and it moistens and browns (although not as well as invert syrup). While it is never used as the only sweetener in baked goods, regular glucose corn syrup is sometimes added along with granulated sugar. It is used, along with brown sugar or molasses, in pecan pie filling. Karo light corn syrup is most similar to regular glucose corn syrup, although it also contains fructose, salt, and vanilla for added sweetness and flavor.

Low-conversion glucose corn syrups (DE of 20 to 37) are ideally suited for use in candies and confections. They are very thick, barely sweet, and unlikely to brown or crystallize. They are best for the whitest, smoothest, shiniest icings, confections, and fondants. They are also useful for increasing the pliability and strength of pulled and spun sugar, for thickening fruit coulis and other sauces, and for preventing ice crystallization in frozen desserts. Glucose Crystal is one example of a low-conversion glucose syrup made from wheat starch. Glucose Crystal is imported from France and is also highly refined, giving it a crystal clear appearance and a premium price.

Dark corn syrup is regular light glucose corn syrup with added molasses or refiner's syrup, caramel coloring, and flavoring. An example of dark glucose corn syrup is Karo dark corn syrup, which also contains salt and an antimicrobial agent. Dark glucose corn syrup can be used as an inexpensive substitute for molasses in baked goods and confections, although it is much milder tasting than most molasses syrups.

High Fructose Corn Syrup High fructose corn syrup is one of the newer corn syrups. Called *glucose-fructose* in Canada and *isoglucose* in the European Union, it was first popularized in the 1970s and 1980s, when high sugar prices and improved syrup quality made it the standard sweetener in the United States for carbonated beverages and many other food products.

The name glucose-fructose is particularly appropriate, since one of the most common high fructose corn syrups (HFCS-42) contains approximately equal parts fructose and glucose (see Table 8.1), making it

Perfect fudge is smooth and creamy. Like fondant and other crystalline or "grained" confections, fudge consists of many microscopic crystals suspended in a thin layer of syrup. The crystals provide body and bulk while the syrup provides a smooth creaminess and shine. If too few crystals form, fudge is soft and sticky. If they grow too large, the fudge feels gritty.

There are several tricks to preparing the smoothest, creamiest fudge. One is to use a thermometer to best determine when fudge is properly cooked (238°-240°F/114°-116°C). Another is to properly use key ingredients. A key ingredient in many fudge formulas is cream of tartar. Cream of tartar is an acid, and the combination of heat and acid breaks down a certain amount of sucrose into invert sugar—equal parts fructose and glucose. Fructose and glucose are considered doctoring or interfering agents because their very presence interferes with the growth of large, gritty crystals of sucrose. The result is smoother, shinier fudge.

The disadvantage of relying on acid to invert sugar is that the process is difficult for pastry chefs to control. Too little inversion and the fudge is dull, hard, and gritty; too much and the fudge may not crystallize and set up. This guesswork is eliminated, however, by simply adding a measured amount of invert syrup or, even better, glucose corn syrup.

Low-conversion glucose corn syrup—one that is low in sugar and high in the higher saccharides—is best to use as a doctoring agent in fudge and other confections. Higher saccharides thicken the sugar mixture, greatly slowing crystallization. Figure 8.14 compares the crystal size in fondant or any grained confection without a doctoring agent added and with one added.

Doctoring agent

Figure 8.14 Crystal size in fondant and other confections is affected by the addition of glucose corn syrup and other doctoring agents that interfere with sugar crystallization. **Left:** a microscopic view of coarse crystals in fondant made with no additive; **right:** smaller crystals in a fondant made with added doctoring agent

Low-conversion glucose corn syrup is particularly ideal for fondant and other confections that are prized for their white appearance, because it does not contain large amounts of sugars that brown. Avoid adding too much glucose corn syrup, though. Especially when they are low-conversion syrups, too much glucose corn syrup prevents so much crystallization that fudge takes on the consistency of chewy icing.

very similar to full invert syrup in composition and in properties. While bakers and pastry chefs do not commonly use high fructose corn syrup, it is useful to know that it is a high-quality, low-price substitute for invert syrup.

Rice Syrup Rice syrup is glucose syrup made from rice starch, much as corn syrup is made from cornstarch. Although rice syrup could be refined and used interchangeably with other glucose syrups, it typically is not. Instead, the most common rice syrup sold in North America is brown rice syrup, which undergoes

less refining so it can be marketed as a sweetener to the health food industry. Besides having a brown color and a distinct flavor, brown rice syrup is often sold as certified organic. Because brown rice syrup is less refined, it retains some of the vitamins and minerals from the rice.

As with all glucose corn syrups, rice syrup contains a mix of glucose, maltose, and higher saccharides. According to one manufacturer, their brown rice syrup contains 3 percent glucose, 45 percent maltose, and 50 percent "soluble complex carbohydrates" (higher saccharides). By definition, this particular rice syrup is a low-conversion glucose syrup.

How Safe Is High Fructose Corn Syrup?

In 2004, a simple hypothesis circulated on the role high fructose corn syrup might play in the increase in obesity in the United States. The hypothesis focused on the fructose in high fructose corn syrup and how it is metabolized in the body differently than, for example, glucose. Since then, isolated studies and hypotheses have surfaced on the role HFCS might play in other health problems including diabetes and cardiovascular disease. Still more attention has focused on the presence of so-called reactive dicarbonyls that were found in samples of HFCS-sweetened carbonated beverages. The end result is that HFCS-containing food products and beverages are now avoided by many consumers, and sugar (sucrose) is perceived as a more natural, safer, and healthier sweetener.

In reality, the common types of high fructose corn syrup used in North America have about equal amounts of fructose and glucose and are metabolized in a similar manner as other common sweeteners, including honey and invert syrup. Likewise, reactive dicarbonyls are found throughout our food supply, since they are products of Maillard browning. Not surprisingly, toast and roasted coffee are much higher in these substances than are carbonated beverages. The unfortunate result of this controversy is that it distracts from more likely causes of obesity and other health problems in the United States, such as the overconsumption of calories regardless of the source.

Substituting Honey for Granulated Sugar

The National Honey Board recommends the following substitution for using honey in place of granulated sugar. This substitution accounts for both the amount of water in honey and for its intense sweetness: Use 1 pound honey in place of 1 pound granulated sugar and reduce water (or other liquid) in the formula by 2.5–3 ounces. Or use 500 grams honey in place of 500 grams granulated sugar and reduce water (or other liquid) in the formula by 80–95 grams.

Honey

Honey—flower nectar collected and processed by honeybees—was probably the first sweetener. An early cave painting shows Neolithic man collecting wild honey from a hive. Honey remained the primary sweetener in Europe for thousands of years until the use of sugar became widespread in the 1700s.

Today honey is an expensive ingredient, used primarily for its unique flavor. After it is collected from beehives, it is separated from the waxy honeycomb, heated to dissolve crystals and destroy spoilage yeast, and filtered to remove impurities. Honey is sold mostly as syrup, but honey cream is also available, consisting of tiny crystals suspended in concentrated syrup.

Honey is sometimes called a natural invert syrup, because enzymes in the honeybee invert the sucrose in the nectar to fructose and glucose. Like invert syrup, honey is very sweet, browns easily, and has the ability to keep baked goods and icings soft and moist.

While all syrups are slightly acidic, honey is one of the most acidic, with a pH as low as 3.5. Despite this, honey does not taste sour, partly because its acids are very mild tasting.

Honeys are named for the flower that the nectar is collected from. The most common honey throughout the world is sweet clover honey, but others—orange blossom and tupelo, to name two—are also popular. Many expensive specialty honeys are available, but they should be considered flavoring agents and not be used in general baking. Either clover honey or baker's honey is appropriate for baking. *Baker's honey* is a relatively inexpensive blend that has a darker color and stronger flavor than straight clover honey.

Maple Syrup

Maple syrup is made by boiling and evaporating the sap of the sugar maple tree, which begins to flow in

During fermentation, yeast breaks down sugars and in the process generates carbon dioxide gas. If there is an adequate supply of carbon dioxide throughout fermentation and proofing, bread leavens properly. For this to occur, it is best to have sugars available throughout the entire fermentation process.

Sucrose, fructose, and glucose are all quickly broken down and fermented by yeast in the early stages of bulk fermentation. Lactose is generally not fermented at all, while maltose is fermented slowly. By including maltose in yeast-raised formulas, yeast food is available through final proof, and this ensures adequate gassing during this critical stage. The result is properly leavened bread. Besides malt syrups, good sources of maltose include malted barley flour and certain glucose corn syrups.

early spring. It is produced throughout the northeastern United States and southeastern Canada, where over 80 percent of the world's supply of maple syrup is produced. Like jaggery and other unrefined noncentrifugal sugars, maple syrup is boiled in open pans, often over a wood fire. Because sap is only 2 or 3 percent sugar, about 40 gallons (151 liters) of sap are needed to produce 1 gallon (4 liters) of maple syrup. This makes maple syrup an extremely expensive sweetener. It is prized for its unique and very sweet aroma, which develops from the Maillard reactions that occur as sap is boiled over high heat.

Do not confuse maple-flavored pancake syrup with real maple syrup. Pancake syrup is made from inexpensive glucose corn syrup, with added caramel coloring and maple flavoring.

While flavor is important, maple syrup is graded primarily by color. Usually, lighter-colored syrups are produced early in the season and darker ones later. Darker-colored syrups have a stronger flavor, lower grade, and lower price. An all-purpose maple syrup is Grade A Medium Amber in the United States (Canada No. 1 Light). A lighter, more delicate-flavored maple syrup, U.S. Grade A Light Amber (Canada No. 1 Extra Light), may be more appropriate for use in candies and confections, while stronger-flavored, darker ones such as U.S. Grade A Dark Amber (Canada No. 1 Medium) or Grade B (Canada No 2. Amber) may be best for baking.

The sugar solids in maple syrup are almost entirely sucrose, with a small amount (usually less than 10 percent) invert sugar. Because it is low in invert sugar, do not expect much more added moistness and softness from maple syrup than you would get from sugar and water. Instead, enjoy maple syrup for its flavor.

Malt Syrup or Extract

Malt syrup is produced by malting (sprouting) cereal grain, extracting it with water, then concentrating the resulting mixture to a syrup. The malting process initiates many biological processes in the cereal, including the breakdown of large starch molecules to sugars. Malt syrup, like malted flour, can be made from any cereal, but barley and wheat are most commonly used.

Malt syrup, which is also called *malt extract*, has a distinct flavor and color that is somewhat similar to molasses. Unlike molasses, malt syrup is very high in maltose. Maltose and, to a lesser degree, trace amounts of protein and ash, improve yeast fermentation, one reason why malt syrup is often used in bread, bagels, biscuit, and cracker production. Malt syrup is also often added to the water used for boiling bagels, for added sheen.

The two main types of malt syrup are diastatic and nondiastatic. Diastatic malt syrup contains a small amount of enzymes, primarily amylase (diastase) from the malting process. Nondiastatic malt syrup has been heated to eliminate all active enzymes, but it still contains the distinct flavor and the maltose that is characteristic of all malt syrups.

Specialty Sweeteners

Agave Syrup

Agave syrup is made from the sap of the agave, a succulent plant farmed in Mexico. To make agave syrup, the core of the agave is heated and sap pressed from the plant. The sap contains the polysaccharide inulin, along with smaller amounts of glucose and fructose. Heat and/or enzymes hydrolyze (break down) inulin to fructose, much as starch is hydrolyzed to glucose in the making of glucose corn syrup. Enzymes can also convert the glucose in agave to fructose in the same way that high fructose corn syrup is made from glucose corn syrup. The sap can be clarified, filtered, and concentrated, much as glucose and invert syrups are processed.

There are several brands of agave syrup, also called *agave nectar*, on the market. Some are dark in color and strong in flavor because they are less processed, while others are highly refined and pale in color. Some are made from organically grown agave and marketed as a raw food, which means they have not been heated above 120°F (50°C) or so. Raw foods retain their heat-sensitive nutrients and natural enzyme activity.

Like high fructose corn syrups, agave syrups vary in the amount of fructose that they contain. This variability can occur because of differences in how the sap is processed or because of differences in the amount of fructose-containing inulin naturally present in the agave. For example, the blue agave, which is also the only agave plant allowed in the making of tequila, is naturally high in inulin.

There are few, if any, higher saccharides present in the various brands of agave syrups, making them easy to use because they are very thin and pourable. Besides containing 50–90 percent fructose, agave syrups contain varying amounts of the monosaccharide glucose. The more fructose and less glucose in agave syrup, the less likely the syrup will crystallize and the sweeter it will be. Agave syrups, especially those highest in fructose, are said to have a low glycemic response (see Chapter 18).

Dextrose

Dextrose is another name for glucose, the monosaccharide. It is the name used when the monosaccharide is purchased as dry sugar. Dextrose is sold as crystals or as pulverized powder. It is less sweet than sucrose and is useful when the properties of sugar are desired but the sweetness is not. For example, dextrose provides bulk without much sweetness in some chocolates and chocolate products. Dextrose also improves the shelf life of confections, because it is more effective than sucrose at lowering water activity and inhibiting microbial growth.

Doughnut Sugar

Doughnut sugar, also called *dusting sugar*, looks like confectioners' sugar, but it is made from finely pulverized dextrose. Dextrose, even when finely pulverized, does not easily dissolve, so doughnut sugar is less likely than confectioners' sugar to liquefy when exposed to heat and humidity. Besides being used to dust and coat doughnuts, doughnut sugar can be used to dust plated desserts.

Expect a different flavor from dextrose, especially when it is undissolved. Dextrose is less sweet than sucrose, and dextrose crystals provide a cooling sensation when they melt in the mouth. Doughnut sugar may contain other ingredients besides dextrose, such as vanilla or cinnamon flavoring and vegetable oil. Vegetable oil helps the sugar adhere to doughnuts and baked goods, but it changes the mouthfeel and produces an off flavor as it ages and oxidizes. Of all the dry sugars, doughnut sugar has the shortest shelf life because of the oil it contains.

> **HELPFUL HINT**
>
> *Purchase only as much doughnut sugar as you will use within three months or so, and store it, covered, in a cool, dry spot. Be sure to taste and smell the sugar before you use it, and discard it if you detect a cardboard-like or other rancid flavor.*

Dried Glucose Syrup

Dried glucose syrup, also called *corn syrup solids* or *glucose solids*, is glucose corn syrup with most of its water removed (only 7 percent or less water remaining). Just as there are many different types of glucose corn syrups, so are there many types of dried glucose syrups. Dried glucose syrup is used wherever the functionality of glucose corn syrup is desired without the added water. For example, dried glucose syrup can provide added body to the mouthfeel of ice cream and other frozen desserts.

Why Does Dextrose Cool the Tongue?

Dextrose crystals require a relatively large amount of energy to dissolve because they are held together with strong bonds. When dextrose crystals are placed in the mouth, the energy needed to break the bonds and dissolve the crystals comes from the heat of the mouth. So much heat is needed that the temperature inside the mouth drops briefly, creating a cooling sensation.

What Are Polyols?

Polyols are also known as *sugar alcohols*, although they are neither sugars nor alcohols. Like sugar, polyols are carbohydrates. Just as there are many different types of sugars, so too are there many different types of polyols. Some are purchased as dry crystals, others as liquid syrups. Examples of polyols include sorbitol, glycerine (glycerol), maltitol, erythritol, and xylitol.

In general, polyols provide sweetness and bulk and certain other functions of sugar except browning. They are lower in calories than sugar and do not promote tooth decay. Products sweetened exclusively with polyols can be labeled "sugar-free." Because they are not readily absorbed by the body, polyols can be useful in products for diabetics and for those on reduced-calorie diets. However, most polyols have a laxative effect, which can cause diarrhea when consumed in large quantities. Of all the polyols, erythritol has the lowest laxative effect.

Maltitol is the closest to sugar in taste and other properties and can be used as a one-to-one replacement for sugar in confections and baked goods. Glycerine and sorbitol, which are both hygroscopic, have been used by confectioners and pastry chefs for years, to provide softness and moistness to confections. Xylitol, like dextrose, provides a cooling sensation when used in crystalline form. Its most common application is in sugar-free gum.

Some polyols, such as isomalt, are not found in nature, while others are. Dried plums (prunes), for example, contain about 15 percent sorbitol, according to the California Dried Plum Board. This high amount of sorbitol, in addition to even higher amounts of glucose and fructose, make dried plums—and the baked goods that they are added to—soft and moist.

Prepared Fondant

Prepared fondant is sold as soft cream or as firm sheets or rolls (Massa Ticino is a Swiss brand). Although it can be made from scratch, fondant requires time and skill to prepare. Cream fondant, warmed and thinned, is used for glazing doughnuts, petit fours, and other baked goods. It also serves as a base for cream praline centers and for uncooked icings. Rolled fondant is used primarily on wedding cakes.

To use prepared cream fondant as a simple icing or glaze, warm it gently to 98°–100°F (37°–38°C). Add simple syrup, pasteurized egg white, flavored liqueur, or any other liquid to thin it before use. To maintain a soft, smooth consistency and an attractive sheen, do not heat fondant above the recommended temperature. Otherwise, small sugar crystals melt, only to reform as large, coarse crystals on cooling.

Isomalt

Isomalt is a relatively new sweetener made by chemically modifying sucrose. Isomalt is not found in nature. It has been approved for use in the United States since 1990. Isomalt is purchased as a white powder or in small beads, and while it is expensive, it has some advantages over sucrose when used in making decorative sugar pieces and garnishes from spun, poured, and pulled sugar. Isomalt does not easily brown, pick up moisture, or crystallize and grain, so sugar work

> **HELPFUL HINT**
> *When warming prepared fondant, always do so in a double boiler, and stir while warming. This way, the fondant will soften without exceeding the critical 98°–100°F (37°–38°C), which is necessary to maintain its consistency and sheen.*

No food, natural or synthetic, is perfectly safe. Even pure water is toxic at some level. The question is not whether a new food ingredient is safe, but whether it is safe at the level at which it is commonly consumed.

Studies used to make these evaluations include animal studies, human epidemiological studies, evaluations of breakdown products from digestion, and sometimes human volunteer behavioral studies. Some of these studies are funded by the federal government, while others are funded by the very companies that plan to manufacture the ingredient. While this does not necessarily mean that the studies are biased, it can place a cloud of doubt over the research.

Animal studies typically evaluate the occurrence of cancer in laboratory rats or other animals fed extremely high levels of the added ingredient. High levels are used in cancer studies to compensate for the relatively few test animals (usually no more than a few hundred) used in these studies. Results must be carefully interpreted because of the high levels used and because the metabolism of rats, while similar to humans, is not identical.

Epidemiological studies look at human populations and the rate of disease and try to make connections between the two. For example, studies have compared bladder cancer patients with otherwise similar people to determine if there was a difference in their use of saccharin (which has been shown to cause bladder cancer in rats). These studies showed no connection between the two.

Blood and urine can be evaluated for the presence of high-intensity sweeteners and their metabolites—that is, the substances they break down into during digestion. Sucralose is not metabolized by the body at all, while aspartame breaks down to aspartic acid, phenylalanine, and methanol. While all three of these substances are present in many common foods that we eat and are safe if consumed at "normal" levels, some scientists believe that the rate at which aspartame breaks down is much faster, making it unsafe. Human volunteer studies have been conducted in which volunteers consumed high amounts of aspartame, sometimes for up to twenty-four weeks, and blood samples were analyzed or neurological and behavioral problems were evaluated. While the researchers concluded that aspartame was safe, others have questioned whether these studies were too short or whether the test designs were adequate.

---

remains relatively dry and white. In fact, isomalt picks up essentially no moisture unless the relative humidity in the room approaches 85 percent. However, isomalt does not have the same melt-in-the-mouth sensation as sucrose, because it does not easily dissolve. Besides being used for decorative sugar pieces, isomalt serves as a bulking agent in low-calorie and "sugar-free" hard candies and confections.

Isomalt is about half as sweet as sucrose. Although it sweetens and is derived from sugar, isomalt is not chemically a sugar. It is classified as a polyol, a type of sugar replacer.

Fructose

Fructose is sometimes called *levulose* or *fruit sugar*. While it is present in many syrups, including honey, molasses, invert syrup, and high fructose corn syrup, fructose can be purchased as dry, white crystals. Crystalline fructose is expensive, but it has a clean, distinct sweetness that complements fruit flavors. It is most commonly used in fruit-based desserts, sorbets, and confections. Commercially, fructose is produced from high fructose corn syrup. It is considered sweeter than sugar, so generally less is needed than sucrose.

High-Intensity Sweeteners

High-intensity sweeteners, sometimes called *low-calorie, nonnutritive,* or *artificial sweeteners,* are typically 200 or more times sweeter than sugar. They provide only one function in baked goods: sweetness. High-intensity sweeteners are largely unsuitable as the only sweetener in pastry and bakery products, which rely on sugar for many functions besides sweetness.

The four most common high-intensity sweeteners in the United States are saccharin, the sweetener in Sweet 'N Low; aspartame, also known as NutraSweet and Equal; acesulfame potassium, more commonly known by its brand names Sunett and Sweet One; and sucralose, also known as Splenda. A fifth sweetener, neotame, was approved for use in the United States in 2002, but it is not yet in general use.

The most recent sweetener to be approved in the United States is a natural sweetener called rebiana or Reb A (short for rebaudioside A). Rebiana is a highly refined white powder extracted and purified from stevia leaves, a sweet herb that grows wild in South and Central America. Stevia leaves have been used for centuries by people in Paraguay and Brazil to sweeten beverages. Because it is not synthesized, rebiana is the first all-natural high-intensity sweetener. It is sold under the brand names PureVia and Truvia. Rebiana can be used in baking, but like other high intensity sweeteners, it has a delayed sweetness and aftertaste, and it provides none of the functions of sugar besides sweetness (erythritol, a bulking agent added to both PureVia and Truvia,

provides some of sugar's functions). As a starting point, use 6.5 ounces Truvia for every pound of sugar, or 40 grams Truvia for every 100 grams sugar.

Of these high-intensity sweeteners, Splenda is probably the best choice for baking and other applications. Unlike aspartame, sucralose does not lose its sweetness from the heat of the oven. Its safety is also less in question by consumers and consumer advocacy groups.

Besides containing sucralose, Splenda contains maltodextrin as a bulking agent. The maltodextrin-sucralose blend in Splenda can substitute one for one for sucrose (by volume, not weight). Start with the one-for-one replacement of Splenda for sugar, but expect some differences in appearance, taste, and texture in the finished product. By adjusting levels of Splenda and other ingredients, an acceptable, if not identical, product can usually be made.

Functions of Sweeteners

As with other important ingredients in baked goods, sweeteners provide many functions. Some of the functions of sweeteners are related to their hygroscopic properties—their ability to attract and hold water.

Main Functions

Sweetening   All sugars and syrups sweeten, but not to the same degree. Fructose is generally considered sweeter than sucrose. The other common sugars are less sweet. While the following rankings for sugars and syrups are only approximate (relative sweetening power depends on concentration, pH, and other factors), they indicate how substituting one sweetener for another can change a product's sweetness. Figure 8.15 shows this graphically.

Sugars: fructose > sucrose > glucose > maltose > lactose

Syrups: clover honey > invert > medium-conversion glucose corn syrup

Tenderizing   Once dissolved, sugars interfere with gluten formation, protein coagulation, and starch gelatinization. In other words, sugars delay the formation of structure, and in doing so, they tenderize. At least some of the tenderizing effect of sugars is related to

their hygroscopic nature. Since gluten, egg, and starch structure all require the presence of water, sugar's strong ability to attract water keeps the water from the structure builders. It is also likely that sugar interacts with the structure builders themselves. In either case, sugar increases the temperature at which proteins coagulate and starches gelatinize, which delays structure formation.

The more sugar added, the more delayed the structure formation, and the more tender the baked good. If too much sugar is added to a product, too little structure forms, and the product will never rise, or more likely it will rise but collapse as it cools. Figure 8.16 shows how too much sugar causes a cake to spread over the liner and to collapse in the center, from a lack of structure. Notice, too, how the cake made with too little sugar formed structure too early, before steam expanded from the heat of the oven. The result is a compact cake with a peaked, ruptured surface, presumably from steam forcing its way through the crust.

While most tender products are also soft and moist, some are not. Shortbread cookies, for example, are tender yet dry and crumbly. Sugar contributes to this form of tenderness, as well.

Retaining Moistness and Improving Shelf Life
The hygroscopic nature of sugars increases the softness and

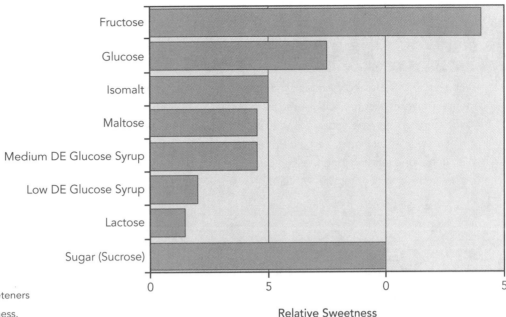

Fructose
Glucose
Isomalt
Maltose
Medium DE Glucose Syrup
Low DE Glucose Syrup
Lactose
Sugar (Sucrose)

0   5   0   5

Figure 8.15 Sweeteners vary in their sweetness.

Relative Sweetness

moistness in freshly baked products. It also extends shelf life by keeping baked goods from drying and staling.

In general, fructose, being the most hygroscopic of common sugars, provides more moistness and a longer shelf life than other sugars. Syrups containing a significant amount of fructose, such as invert syrup, honey, high fructose corn syrup, and agave syrup, provide more moistness than other syrups or granulated sugar. Differences are particularly noticeable after several days of storage.

Contributing Brown Color and a Caramelized or Baked Flavor

While some sweeteners, such as brown sugar, molasses, malt syrup, and honey, have a brown

Figure 8.16 The amount of sugar affects the volume, shape, and color of pound cakes. **Left to right:** low amount of sugar, regular amount of sugar, and high amount of sugar

color, most sweeteners contribute brown color and a pleasant caramelized or fresh-baked flavor through the processes of caramelization and Maillard browning.

Because caramelization and Maillard browning have similar end results, the distinction between the two is often overlooked. Strictly speaking, caramelization is the process that sugars undergo when heated to a high temperature. Maillard browning is a similar process but proteins, in addition to sugars, take part in the reactions. With proteins present, browning happens faster and at a lower temperature. Proteins in flours, eggs, and dairy products all take part in Maillard browning. Only a small amount of protein is needed to greatly speed up the process, and the more protein, usually the more browning. This is why baked goods made with bread flour brown faster than those made with pastry or cake flour.

The more heat a product is exposed to, the more browning. For baked goods, this means that, logically, higher oven temperatures increase browning on crusts. Paradoxically, for boiled confections, higher temperatures typically *decrease* the extent of browning. This is true because boiled confections are usually cooked until the right amount of water has boiled off. If the temperature is low, the time it takes to boil off the right amount of water is long, and the total amount of heat that the confection is exposed to is high. Many formulas for boiled confections call for high heat and a rolling boil, to minimize heat exposure and the extent of browning.

When sugars are heated, a series of complex chemical reactions occur that break down sugars into smaller fragments. These smaller molecules evaporate easily and trigger our sense of smell, providing the wonderful aromas associated with caramelized sugar. With continued heating, the fragments react with one another and form large molecules called polymers. Large polymers do not evaporate, but they do absorb light, imparting a brown color. With continued heating, bitter-tasting polymers form. That is why it is important not to overheat sugars.

Similar reactions occur with Maillard browning—that is, when sugars and proteins react together.

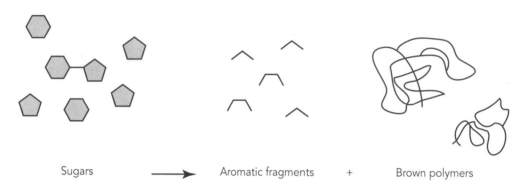

Sugars   ⟶   Aromatic fragments   +   Brown polymers

If enough time is allowed, Maillard browning occurs at room temperature. For example, sucrose must be heated to 320°–340°F (160°–170°C) before it caramelizes, but dry milk solids undergo Maillard browning and develop off flavors after a year or so of storage at room temperature. Table 8.2 compares the processes of caramelization and Maillard browning.

Another distinction between caramelization and Maillard browning is the flavor that each provides. While caramelized flavor is best described as that of cooked sugar, the flavors of Maillard browning are as diverse as roasted cocoa, roasted coffee, roasted nuts, toffee, maple syrup, and molasses (maple tree sap and sugarcane provide small amounts of protein for Maillard browning). Much of the flavor and color in the crust of baked goods also comes from Maillard browning.

Maillard browning is generally considered desirable, but it sometimes causes brown discoloration and the development of off flavors during storage. For example, the browning of dry milk solids at room temperature is undesirable, as is the browning that occurs when white chocolate is stored for a year or more. Notice that dry milk solids and white chocolate both contain dairy ingredients. Products that contain dairy ingredients are particularly susceptible to Maillard browning because they contain milk proteins and lactose, a sugar that browns relatively quickly.

Monosaccharides brown faster than most disaccharides. This is true with both caramelization and Maillard browning, and it is why invert syrup, which contains the monosaccharides fructose and glucose, browns faster than granulated sugar. In fact, for sucrose to brown, it

TABLE 8.2 COMPARISON OF CARAMELIZATION AND MAILLARD BROWNING

BROWNING REACTION	REACTING MOLECULES	TEMPERATURES REQUIRED	EXAMPLES
Caramelization	Sugars (and certain other carbohydrates)	Very high	Caramelized or burnt sugar
Maillard browning	Sugars (and certain other carbohydrates) and proteins	Lower temperatures; can occur at room temperature	Roasted cocoa, coffee, nuts; crust on baked goods; discoloration of white chocolate during storage

must first be broken down into glucose and fructose, which then take part in caramelization and Maillard browning. Intact sucrose does not brown. Isomalt, the polyol used in pulled, poured, and spun sugar, hardly browns at all. Roughly, the rate of browning of the various sweeteners, from fastest to slowest, is as follows:

fructose > glucose > lactose > maltose > sucrose > isomalt

The browning of sugar increases in the presence certain minerals, including copper and iron. All that is needed is a very tiny amount—parts per million—of minerals for browning to be significantly increased. Minerals are present in some water supplies, in unrefined syrups (malt, molasses, maple, honey, rice), and in salt.

Acids and alkalis also affect browning by their effect on pH. A small amount of baking soda, which increases pH, is often added to baked goods to increase browning. Buttermilk, which is acidic and lowers pH, slows browning, as does cream of tartar. Since water often contains minerals, acids, and alkalis, it can be a factor in the extent of browning, especially with confections.

Assisting in Leavening   There is air between sugar crystals, which are irregular in shape, while there is little or no air in syrups. Whenever dry sugar is added to batters and doughs, air—one of the three main leavening gases in baked goods—is added. This is also true when fats are creamed with sugar. Only dry sugars, not

syrups, assist in adding air to creamed fats and to batters and doughs, lowering their density and providing for additional leavening.

Providing Bulk and Substance to Fondant and Sugar-Based Confections   Sugar crystals provide bulk and substance to fondant, confections, and certain other products. To understand what this means, consider that fondant contains 90 percent or more crystallized sugar. Without these solid sugar crystals, fondant would consist of liquid syrup.

While sugar is not considered a structure builder in baked goods (remember, the more sugar, the more tender the baked good), in fondant and other products that contain sugar crystals, the solid crystals do provide substance. This substance defines the size and shape of these products. In this sense, solid sugar crystals do provide a type of structure.

Stabilizing Whipped Egg Foams   Sugar, if added properly, stabilizes whipped egg whites, meaning that sweetened whipped whites (meringue) will be less likely to collapse and weep. Sugar also stabilizes whipped whole egg and whipped yolk in foam-type cakes such as genoise and chiffon. More on sugar's ability to stabilize whipped egg whites will be discussed in Chapter 10.

Providing Food for Yeast Fermentation   All common sugars except lactose are fermented by yeast. Through yeast fermentation, these sugars provide carbon dioxide gas for leavening doughs. Sucrose, fructose, and glucose are fermented quickly, maltose more slowly.

Additional Functions

Adding Flavor   All sweeteners provide sweetness, of course, but certain sweeteners are also valued for the distinctive flavor they provide. This is true for brown

Many traditional gingerbread formulas do not contain baking powder as a chemical leavener. Instead, they rely on molasses (a source of acid) and baking soda (an alkali) to react and produce carbon dioxide. Because this reaction happens at room temperature, some formulas also include a small amount of baking powder, so that additional carbon dioxide is generated in the oven, where it is needed most.

sugar, honey, maple syrup, malt syrup, rice syrup, dark agave syrup, molasses, and dark glucose corn syrup. Other sweeteners are more neutral in flavor, providing mostly sweetness. Examples of sweeteners that are neutral in flavor include granulated sugar, powdered sugar, light glucose corn syrup, and invert syrup.

Reducing Iciness and Hardness in Frozen Desserts

Sugars lower the freezing point of frozen desserts by holding on to water and interfering with the formation of ice crystals. Increasing the amount of sugar in frozen desserts makes them softer and less icy. The monosaccharides—fructose and glucose—are more effective at lowering freezing point than disaccharides.

Thick syrups, such as low-conversion (low DE) glucose corn syrups, are also extremely effective at preventing iciness, but they do so in a different manner from monosaccharides. The large higher saccharides in low-conversion glucose corn syrups interfere with ice crystal formation by preventing water molecules from easily moving around. This limits water's growth into large, sharp ice crystals.

> **HELPFUL HINT**
>
> *When preparing ice cream, add a small amount (5 percent or less) of a low-conversion glucose corn syrup to the mix. The ice cream will be smoother and creamier, and it will last longer in the freezer without getting icy. Do not add more than 5 percent syrup, though, or the ice cream could become too firm and chewy.*

Providing a Source of Acid for Leavening

Most syrups contain some acid, while most dry sugars do not. The acid in syrups, when combined with baking soda in baked goods, produces carbon dioxide for leavening. For example, the pH of honey is typically 3.5–4.5, meaning that it is quite acidic. The National Honey Board recommends the use of ½ teaspoon (1.2 milliliters) baking soda to neutralize the acid in one cup—approximately

12 weight ounces (340 grams)—of honey. This provides about the same amount of carbon dioxide as 1 teaspoon (5 milliliters) baking powder.

Preventing Microbial Growth

When used at low levels, sugars are a source of food for microorganisms, encouraging their growth. At very high levels, however, sugars have the opposite effect. By lowering water activity, sugar acts as a preservative, preventing the growth of microorganisms. That is why the yeast in rich, sweet doughs ferments and proofs more slowly than in lean doughs, and why sugar-free cakes (those made with a high-intensity sweetener) mold within days. The high sugar content of jams, jellies, sweetened condensed milk, candied fruit, and many candies and confections in part explains their ability to resist microbial growth.

Adding Sheen to Icings

Syrups, in particular, add a glossy sheen to icings and many confections. They do this by forming a smooth, mirror-like surface over the jagged irregularity of sugar crystals.

Promoting a Crisp Crust on Certain Baked Goods

Often, baked goods develop a desirable crisp crust as they cool. The crisp crust forms when moisture evaporates during baking. Sugar promotes this crispiness as it recrystallizes during cooling. This is particularly noticeable with cookie, brownie, and pound cake formulas that are especially high in sugar and low in moisture.

> **HELPFUL HINT**
>
> *If your soft, moist cookies become dry, hard, or crisp within a few days, replace a small amount of the sugar (10–25 percent of the weight of sugar) with invert syrup, sorbitol, or fructose. These sweeteners are particularly effective at preventing the crystallization of sugar that causes a change in texture, and they do so without adding a flavor of their own.*

Hygroscopic sweeteners such as fructose, sorbitol, invert syrup, molasses, and honey prevent moisture loss and also interfere with sugar crystallization. In doing so, these sweeteners promote the formation of soft, moist baked goods.

Some cookie doughs form an attractive surface cracking as they bake (Figure 8.17). This happens when the surface dries and sugars recrystallize before the cookie itself expands in height and spread. Cracking happens best when the amount of sugar is high and when coarse sugars are used. Hygroscopic sweeteners reduce cracking by preventing moisture loss and by interfering with sugar recrystallization.

Figure 8.17 Recrystallizing sugar forms cracks on cookies during baking.

Promoting Spread in Cookies Sugar, once dissolved, promotes spread in cookies. The sugar pulls water from proteins and starches as it dissolves, turning cookie dough into more of a sugar syrup. At the same time, sugar delays the coagulation of proteins and the gelatinization of starches. This means that the cookie dough spreads across the cookie sheet as it warms from the heat of the oven. This continues until proteins coagulate and set the structure.

The more sugar in cookie dough, the more the cookie spreads. Sugars with a finer granulation spread more because they dissolve sooner, and only dissolved sugars tenderize and thin out doughs. Powdered sugar, which contains cornstarch, prevents spread in cookies, despite its finer grind.

Providing Energy for the Body Sugars—like most carbohydrates—provide energy for the body. This is another way of saying that they provide calories. Since most sweeteners are pure and consist almost entirely of carbohydrates, few nutrients besides calories are provided. Molasses is an exception; although it is low in most nutrients, it can be a good source of calcium, potassium, and iron.

Storage and Handling

All sweeteners should be stored covered to prevent them from picking up odors. Covering also prevents dry sugars from absorbing or losing moisture. This is particularly important for powdered and brown sugars, which cake when they pick up and lose moisture. If powdered sugar does cake or clump, pass it through a sieve before use. If this occurs to brown sugar, warm it gently in the oven or microwave before passing it through a sieve.

Except for doughnut sugars, which contain oils that oxidize, properly covered dry sugars have an unlimited shelf life. Certain syrups—invert syrup and some glucose corn syrups, for example—darken when stored for too long, particularly when temperatures are warm. If light syrups darken, do not discard them. Instead, use them in dark products such as brownies or whole wheat bread.

Syrups high in moisture, such as maple syrup and simple syrup, must be refrigerated to prevent yeast and mold growth. It is best not to refrigerate other syrups. Refrigeration causes syrups high in glucose to crystallize. This occurs with honey, invert syrup, and high fructose corn syrup. If syrup does crystallize, stir well to distribute the crystals evenly throughout. While it is generally unnecessary to heat the syrup to dissolve crystals, you may do so. Be sure to heat gently, especially with delicate syrups like honey. Honey's flavor may be damaged when the syrup is heated above 160°F (70°C).

On occasion, osmophilic yeast (that is, yeast that grows in high-sugar environments) will ferment in molasses, honey, or glucose corn syrups. When this happens, you will likely see small bubbles of carbon dioxide trapped in the syrup, and you might smell a yeasty aroma. Other times, mold will grow on the surface of syrups. To be safe, discard these syrups, and purchase only the amount needed for six months to a year.

Substituting Syrup for Sugar

Recall that syrups contain one or more sugars and water. Most syrups contain about 80 percent sugar and 20 percent water. This means that 1 pound (or 1 kilogram) of syrup typically contains 0.8 pound (or 0.8 kilogram) sugar and 0.2 pound (or 0.2 kilogram) water. Because a 1:1 substitution of granulated sugar with syrup changes the amount of sugar solids in a product by about 20 percent, it is sometimes desirable to calculate and adjust the amount of syrup and liquid when making a substitution. Starting guidelines for changing between granulated sugar and many syrups (those that are 80 percent sugar and 20 percent water) are as follows. *Note:* The following calculations do not adjust for differences in sweetness or other properties of sweeteners. Recall, for example, that the Honey Board recommends substituting honey 1:1 for sugar while reducing the amount of water.

- *To substitute syrup for granulated sugar:* Divide the weight of sugar by 0.80 to determine the weight of syrup to use. Reduce the amount of water or other liquid by the difference between the two. For example, for 1 pound (16 ounces) of sugar, use 20 ounces of syrup and reduce the amount of liquid by 4 ounces. For 500 grams of sugar, use 625 grams of syrup and reduce the amount of liquid by 125 grams.

- *To substitute granulated sugar for syrup:* Multiply the weight of syrup by 0.80 to determine the weight of granulated sugar to use. Increase the amount of liquid by the difference between the two. For example, for 1 pound (16 ounces) of syrup, use 12.8 ounces of sugar and increase the amount of liquid by 3.2 ounces. For 500 grams of syrup, use 400 grams of sugar and increase the amount of liquid by 100 grams.

Questions for Review

1　Draw and label the skeletal structures of two monosaccharides and two disaccharides. Which of these represents the structure of regular granulated sugar?

2　What are other names for glucose, the monosaccharide?

3　How would you describe sugar crystals?

4　Which is more likely to crystallize sooner: syrup containing only one type of sugar molecule, or syrup that is identical in every way except that it contains two or more types? Explain your answer.

5　What does it mean to say that sugars are hygroscopic? Which of the common sugars is most hygroscopic?

6　Provide an example of when using a highly hygroscopic sweetener is desirable; provide an example of when using a highly hygroscopic sweetener is undesirable.

7　What is the main difference between extrafine, coarse, and superfine sugars? What is another name for each?

8　How does dried cane syrup compare to regular granulated sugar in color, flavor, and crystal size?

9　Coarse sugar is more expensive than regular granulated sugar. In fact, it can be three times the price of regular granulated sugar. Why use it?

10　What is another name for powdered sugar? Why might powdered sugar have a different flavor and sweetness than regular granulated sugar?

11　What is the difference between 6X and 10X powdered sugar? What is each best used for?

12　Below what size particle, in microns, do sugar crystals feel smooth and not gritty? Which dry sugar has most particles below this level?

13　What are the main reasons for using brown sugar in baked goods?

14　About how much molasses is in regular light brown sugar? About how much is in regular dark brown sugar?

15　What is the main difference between regular dark and light brown sugars? That is, what makes dark brown sugar darker than light brown?

16　Which is the brown sugar equivalent of coarse sugar?

17　Provide an example of an unrefined noncentrifugal sugar. How are noncentrifugal sugars made?

18　Which of the following sugars are refined, which are unrefined, and which are semirefined: evaporated cane juice, light brown cane sugar, dark brown beet sugar, Demerara, Sucanat, jaggery.

19　How would you define "syrup"?

20　How can two syrups contain the same amount of water, but one be much thicker than the other?

21 What is the makeup of full invert syrup? What is the makeup of medium invert?

22 Draw the process for the commercial production of invert syrup.

23 What are the advantages of invert syrup over sucrose in baked goods? In icings, confections, and fondants?

24 What are the characteristics of premium-grade molasses? Why is it not necessarily the best molasses for baking?

25 Draw the process for the commercial production of glucose corn syrups.

26 What are the differences in makeup between a high-conversion glucose corn syrup and a low-conversion one?

27 What is meant by the DE of glucose corn syrup?

28 What are the properties of high-conversion glucose corn syrups; that is, what functions do they perform well? What are the properties of low-conversion glucose corn syrups?

29 Which corn-derived syrup is most similar in composition to invert syrup?

30 What sugar makes up doughnut sugar? Why is this better than powdered sugar for dusting doughnuts and plated desserts?

31 What is the difference between glucose corn syrup with a DE of 42 and dried glucose syrup with the same DE?

32 What is isomalt? Why is it sometimes used instead of sugar?

33 Which polyol is closest to granulated sugar in taste and in other properties? How does it—and other polyols—compare to sugar in caloric content?

34 What are the most common uses for crystalline fructose?

35 What ingredient, besides sucralose, is added to Splenda? What is its function?

36 Which high-intensity sweetener is natural?

37 What are the eight main functions of sweeteners? Which one of these is the only function that high-intensity sweeteners typically provide?

38 Why might granulated sugars assist in leavening while syrups do not?

39 What are the two components in milk that allow it to undergo Maillard browning?

40 Why might white chocolate darken and develop off flavors as it ages?

41 Explain the proper procedures for handling and storing honey.

Questions for Discussion

1 Rank the following sugars from highest amount of molasses to lowest: Demerara, regular granulated sugar, evaporated cane juice, regular dark brown sugar, muscovado.

2 What might happen to the quality of white cake if too much invert syrup is added? When answering this question, assume that you've adjusted your formula for the amount of water in the syrup.

3 You prepare simple syrup from two parts sugar to one part water. After several days of refrigeration, the syrup becomes cloudy as the sugar crystallizes. What could have been added to the syrup to prevent sugar crystallization?

4 You want to make soft, moist cookies. Which syrup will be best to add to your formula: regular glucose corn syrup or invert syrup? Why?

5 For each of the following syrups, state whether it is best described as a medium invert, full invert, or not an invert syrup at all: premium molasses, honey, golden syrup, low DE glucose corn syrup, high DE glucose corn syrup, high fructose corn syrup, maple syrup.

6 You're substituting glucose corn syrup for 8 pounds (or 8 kilograms) of sucrose in a formula. How much glucose corn syrup should you add and how should you adjust the water so that you end up with the same amount of sweetener and water as in the original formula? Show your work.

7 You're substituting 8 pounds (or 8 kilograms) of sucrose in a formula with maple syrup, which is 67 percent—not 80 percent—sugar solids. What adjustments should be made to this formula?

Exercises and Experiments

① Exercise: Decreasing Browning in Baked Goods and Confections

In the spaces that follow, list all the ways you know that will decrease browning in baked goods and in confections. For the purposes of this exercise, focus entirely on decreasing the browning, and don't be concerned about other changes that might make your product less desirable in other ways. Be specific and be practical; that is, think of changes you could tell an assistant to execute. Be sure to start each line with an action word such as the following: add, increase, decrease, change, omit, include, use. While each item might not apply to all types of products, each should work in at least one. Follow the format used in the first, which is done for you, and see if you can add at least five more ways.

1 Use water instead of milk in an egg wash, or omit the wash altogether.

2 _____

_____

_____

3 _____

_____

_____

4 _____

_____

_____

5 _____

_____

_____

6 _____

_____

_____

7 _____

_____

_____

8 _____

_____

_____

9 _____

_____

_____

10 _____

_____

_____

❷ Exercise: How Sugar Concentration Affects the Boiling Point of Water

The boiling point of pure water at sea level is 212°F. When sugar—or any substance—is dissolved in water, the boiling point increases above 212°F. This is because sugar molecules take up space, including space near the top of a pot, and gets in the way of water molecules escaping from a pot into the atmosphere. As the concentration of sugar increases (as it does when water evaporates from a sugar syrup), the boiling point also increases.

When sugar syrup is boiled, as when preparing boiled confections, water evaporates off but the sugar remains behind. The boiling point increases as this occurs because the sugar concentration also increases, making it more difficult for water to evaporate. That is why thermometers are used to determine if confections (and jams and jellies) have been boiled long enough to set properly. The thermometer is being used to determine if the correct sugar concentration has been reached.

Instructions: Enter the data from the following table onto the graph, and draw the best curve through the points. Your graph shows the relationship between the amount of sugar in a syrup and the syrup's boiling point. Next, answer the questions that follow.

% SUGAR CONCENTRATION	BOILING POINT, °F
0	212
20	212.5
40	214
50	215
60	217
70	221
80	229
85	236
90	247
95	265
98	280

Relationship Between Sugar Concentration and Boiling Point

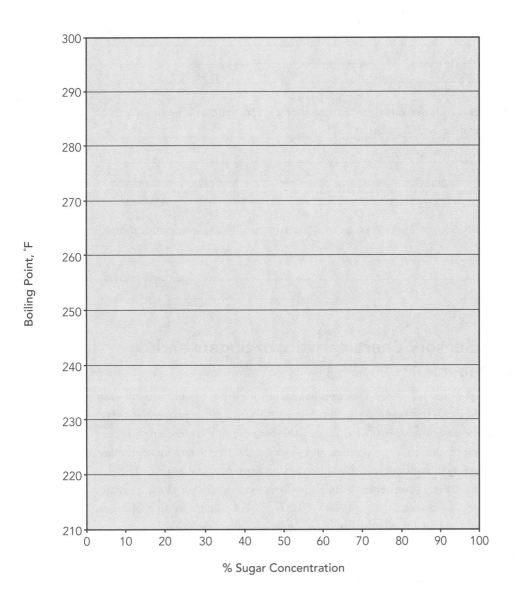

Boiling Point, °F

% Sugar Concentration

1 Compare the change to the boiling point when going from 40 to 50 percent sugar to the change when going from 80 to 90 percent. Which 10 percent increase in concentration has the larger change in boiling point?

_____

_____

_____

2 Do you think this makes it easier or harder to accurately use a thermometer for judging sugar concentration when the value is low (as when making a simple syrup made with 50 percent sugar)? Explain why.

_____

_____

_____

3 Estimate from the graph the boiling point of a sugar syrup that contains 65 percent sugar (about the amount in jams and jellies).

_____

_____

_____

4 Estimate from the graph the sugar concentration of a syrup that has a boiling point of 240°F, the approximate boiling point of fondant.

_____

_____

_____

5 Why might the actual concentration of sugar in fondant be different from your estimate?

_____

_____

_____

❸ Exercise: Sensory Characteristics of Sugars and Other Sweeteners

Using the Results Table, first fill in the Description column with the brand name of each sweetener. Include additional information that further describes and differentiates the sweetener from others of the same kind (granulated sugar, for example, could be identified as cane or beet sugar, fine or extrafine). Next, compare and describe the sweeteners in appearance and flavor (besides sweetness, consider sourness, bitterness, astringency, and aroma). Use this opportunity to identify different sweeteners from their sensory characteristics alone. Add any additional comments or observations that you might have to the last column in the table, such as an ingredient listing and how quickly the dry sweeteners dissolve in your mouth.

Use information from the Results Table and from your textbook to answer the following questions. Select one from the choices in **bold** or fill in the blanks.

1 Coarse sugar dissolved in the mouth **faster/more slowly** than regular granulated sugar, primarily because the crystals are **larger/smaller** than regular granulated sugar.

2 What ingredient is sometimes added to coarse sugars for sheen, and to keep the crystals from dissolving during baking? _____. Was this ingredient added to your coarse sugar? _____

3 The main sensory differences between powdered sugar and doughnut sugar are _____

_____

_____

4 Fructose dissolved in the mouth **faster/more slowly** than granulated sugar, primarily because it is **very/not very** hygroscopic. Fructose was also **sweeter/less sweet** than granulated sugar.

TYPE OF SWEETENER	DESCRIPTION	APPEARANCE	SWEETNESS/ FLAVOR	ADDITIONAL COMMENTS
Regular granulated				
Dried cane syrup				
Coarse				
Powdered				
Doughnut				
Crystalline fructose				
Isomalt				
Splenda				
Invert syrup				
Glucose syrup, medium DE				
Glucose syrup, low DE				
Light brown				
Dark brown				
Molasses				
Dark corn syrup				
Honey				

5 Isomalt dissolved in the mouth **faster/more slowly** than granulated sugar, primarily because it is **very/not very** hygroscopic. Isomalt was also **sweeter/less sweet** than granulated sugar.

6 Splenda tasted **sweeter than/less sweet than/the same in sweetness as** regular granulated sugar. Other differences between Splenda and sugar are _____

_____

_____

7 How would you describe the flavor of invert syrup?

_____

_____

_____

8 The low DE glucose syrup was derived from **corn/wheat/other** starch. The medium DE glucose syrup was derived from **corn/wheat/other** starch.

9 The glucose syrup that was sweeter was **low/medium** DE because it was **lower/higher** in sugars. It was also **thicker/thinner** because it was **lower/higher** in higher saccharides.

10 The low DE glucose syrup had **better clarity than/worse clarity than/the same clarity as** the medium DE glucose syrup. This means that it was refined **more/less/about the same** and will darken and brown **faster/slower/about the same** as the medium DE syrup. This makes it **better/worse/about the same** for use in white sugar confections and showpieces.

11 The dark brown sugar had **stronger/weaker/the same** flavor as the light brown sugar. How do you explain these results?

_____

_____

_____

12 How would you describe the flavor of molasses?

_____

_____

_____

13 How would you describe the difference in flavor between dark corn syrup and molasses?

_____

_____

_____

14 Honey has a pH that is typically **lower/higher** than most other syrups, indicating the presence of acids. The flavor of honey **was/was not** particularly sour. Explain.

_____

_____

_____

❹ Experiment: How the Amount of Sugar Affects the Quality of Pound Cake

Objectives

Demonstrate how the amount of sugar affects
- The size and shape of pound cake
- The amount of browning on the crust of pound cake
- The flavor and texture of pound cake
- The overall acceptability of pound cake

Products Prepared

Pound cake made with
- Full amount of sugar (control product)
- No sugar
- Half the amount of sugar
- One and a half times the amount of sugar
- Double the amount of sugar
- Other, if desired (three-quarters the amount of sugar, one and one-quarter the amount of sugar, etc.)

Materials and Equipment

- Scale
- Sieve
- Parchment paper
- Mixer with 5-quart mixing bowl
- Flat beater attachment
- Bowl scraper
- Whisk
- Pound cake batter (see Formula), enough to make 24 or more cakes of each variation
- Muffin pans (2½" or 3½" /65 or 90 mm size)
- Paper liners, pan spray, or pan coating
- Size #16 (2 fl. oz./60 ml) portion-control scoop or equivalent
- Half sheet pans (optional)
- Oven thermometer
- Wooden pick (for testing)
- Serrated knife
- Ruler

Formula

High-Ratio Pound Cake

Yield: *24 cakes for control product, full amount of sugar; yield will vary with other amounts of sugar*

INGREDIENT	POUNDS	OUNCES	GRAMS	BAKER'S PERCENTAGE
Flour, cake		12	350	100
Dried milk solids		1.4	40	11
Salt		0.2	7	2
Baking powder		0.4	10	3
Sugar, regular granulated		14	400	115
Shortening, high-ratio plastic		8	230	66
Water		6	175	50
Eggs, whole		8	230	66
Total	**3**	**2**	**1,442**	**413**

Method of Preparation
(for control product, full amount of sugar)

1 Preheat oven to 375°F (190°C).

2 Allow all ingredients to come to room temperature (temperature of ingredients is important for consistent results).

3 Blend flour, dried milk solids, salt, and baking powder thoroughly by sifting together three times onto parchment paper.

4 Place sifted dry ingredients and granulated sugar in bowl; add shortening and half the water (3 ounces or 87 grams).

5 Mix on low for 30 seconds using flat beater. Stop and scrape bowl and beater.

6 Continue mixing on low for an additional 4 minutes, stopping once a minute to scrape the bowl and beater. Batter should be smooth.

7 Combine the remaining water (3 ounces or 88 grams) and lightly beaten eggs with a whisk.

8 Add half the water-egg mixture to batter and mix on low for 4 minutes. Stop and scrape bowl.

9 Add the remaining water-egg mixture and mix on low for 5 minutes.

10 Scrape bowl and set aside batter until ready to use.

Method of Preparation
(for cakes with varying amounts of sugar)

Follow the Method of Preparation for the control product (full amount of sugar), except use the following amounts of sugar in step 4:

1   For no sugar, omit sugar entirely.

2   For half the amount, use 7 ounces (200 grams) sugar.

3   For one and a half times the amount, use 1 pound, 5 ounces (600 grams) sugar.

4   For double the amount, use 1 pound, 12 ounces (800 grams) sugar.

Procedure

1   Prepare cake batter using the high-ratio pound cake formula above, or using any basic high-ratio pound cake formula. Prepare one batch of batter for each variation.

2   Line muffin pans with paper liners, lightly spray with pan spray, or grease with pan coating. Label with amount of sweetener to be added to cake batter.

3   Scoop batter into prepared muffin pans using #16 scoop (or equivalent).

4   If desired, place muffin pans onto half sheet pans.

5   Use an oven thermometer placed in center of oven for an initial reading of oven temperature. Record results here: _____.

6   When oven is properly preheated, place filled muffin pans into oven and set timer for 32–35 minutes, or according to formula.

7   Bake cakes until control product pulls away slightly from sides of pan, cake springs back when center top is lightly pressed, and wooden pick inserted into center of cake comes out clean. Control product should be lightly browned. Remove *all* cakes from oven after same length of time, even though some will be paler in color or have not risen properly. If necessary, however, adjust bake times for oven variances.

8   Record bake times in Results Table 1, which follows.

9   Check final oven temperature. Record results here: _____.

10   Remove cakes from hot pans and cool to room temperature.

Results

1   When completely cooled, evaluate average weight of cakes from each batch, as follows:
   • Measure weight of each of three typical cakes. Record results for each cake in Results Table 1.
   • Calculate the average cake weight by adding the weights and dividing by 3. Record results in Results Table 1.

2 Evaluate average height as follows:

- Slice three cakes from each batch in half, being careful not to compress.
- Measure height of each of three typical cakes by placing a ruler along the flat edge at the cake's center point. Record results in ¹⁄₁₆" (1 mm) increments in Results Table 1.
- Calculate the average cake height by adding the heights and dividing by 3. Record results in Results Table 1.

3 Evaluate the shape of cakes (even rounded top, peaked top, dips in center, etc.) and draw shape or describe shape in words in Results Table 1.

RESULTS TABLE 1 SIZE AND SHAPE OF HIGH-RATIO POUND CAKES MADE WITH DIFFERENT AMOUNTS OF SUGAR

AMOUNT OF SUGAR	BAKE TIME (IN MINUTES)	WEIGHTS OF EACH OF THREE CAKES	AVERAGE WEIGHT OF CAKE	HEIGHTS OF EACH OF THREE CAKES	AVERAGE HEIGHT OF CAKE	CAKE SHAPE	ADDITIONAL COMMENTS
Full amount (control product)							
None							
Half the amount							
One and a half times the amount							
Double the amount							

4 Evaluate the sensory characteristics of completely cooled products and record evaluations in Results Table 2. If possible, allow cakes to age for one or more days before evaluating, to accentuate differences. Be sure to compare each in turn to the control product and consider the following:

- Crust color, from very light to very dark, on a scale of 1 to 5
- Crumb appearance (small/large air cells, uniform/irregular air cells, tunnels, etc.; also, evaluate color)
- Sweetness, from not sweet at all to extremely sweet, on a scale of 1 to 5
- Flavor (egg flavor, floury taste, saltiness, etc.)
- Crumb texture (tough/tender, moist/dry, gummy, spongy, crumbly, etc.)
- Overall acceptability, from highly unacceptable to highly acceptable, on a scale of 1 to 5
- Add any additional comments, as necessary

RESULTS TABLE 2 SENSORY CHARACTERISTICS OF POUND CAKES MADE WITH DIFFERENT AMOUNTS OF SUGAR

AMOUNT OF SUGAR	CRUST COLOR	CRUMB APPEARANCE	SWEETNESS	FLAVOR	TEXTURE	OVERALL ACCEPTABILITY	ADDITIONAL COMMENTS
Full amount (control product)							
None							
Half the amount							
One and a half times the amount							
Double the amount							

Sources of Error

List any sources of error that might make it difficult to draw the proper conclusions from your experiment. In particular, consider difficulties in mixing and handling batters, and any problems with the ovens.

_____

_____

_____

State what you could do differently next time to minimize or eliminate each source of error.

_____

_____

_____

Conclusions

Select one from the choices in **bold** or fill in the blanks.

1   As the amount of sugar increased in the pound cakes, the sweetness tended to **increase/ decrease/stay the same**. This is because sugar is the major source of sweetness in pound cake.

2   As the amount of sugar increased in the pound cakes, the color **lightened/darkened/ stayed the same**. This is because the reaction between sugars and proteins, called _____, increases as the amount of sugar increases. This was noticeable, for example, when comparing the control product (1× sugar) to the pound cake made with no sugar. The control product was **lighter/darker**.

3   As the amount of sugar increased in the pound cakes, the moistness tended to **increase/ decrease/stay the same**. This is because sugars are _____, meaning that they attract and bond to water, essentially forming a sugar syrup in the cake. By bonding with water, the sugar, for example, prevents the _____ in flour from gelatinizing and acting as a drier. The driest of all the pound cakes was the one made with **no sugar/1× sugar/1½× sugar/2× sugar**.

4   As the amount of sugar increased in the pound cakes, the texture tends to become **tougher/ more tender/neither tougher nor more tender**. This is partly because sugar **speeds up/ delays** the formation of structure from the coagulation of _____ and the gelatinization of _____.

5   As the amount of sugar increased from none to the amount in the control product, the density of the batter and therefore the weight per cake **increased/decreased/stayed the same**. This is probably because _____

_____

_____

6   As the amount of sugar increased from the amount in the control product to 2×, the height of the cake **increased/decreased/stayed the same**. This is probably because _____

_____

_____

7 As the amount of sugar increased from none to the amount in the control product, the flavor (besides sweetness) of the cake changed in the following ways: _____

_____

_____

8 Did you notice any other differences in the cakes or their batters? _____

_____

_____

⑤ Experiment: How Different Sweeteners Affect the Quality of Pound Cake

Objectives

Demonstrate how different sweeteners affect
- The size and shape of pound cake
- The amount of browning on the crust of pound cake
- The flavor of pound cake
- The texture of pound cake
- The overall acceptability of pound cake

Products Prepared

Pound cake made with
- Regular granulated sugar (control product)
- Dark (or light) brown sugar
- Honey (formula adjusted for amount of water in honey)
- Invert syrup (formula adjusted for amount of water in syrup)
- Splenda (formula adjusted so that Splenda is substituted for sugar 1:1 *by volume*)
- Other, if desired (half sugar/half honey, glucose corn syrup, malt syrup, molasses, maltitol, agave, etc.)

Materials and Equipment

- Scale
- Sieve
- Parchment paper
- Mixer with 5-quart mixing bowl
- Flat beater attachment
- Bowl scraper
- Whisk
- Pound cake batter (see Formula in previous experiment), enough to make 24 or more cakes of each variation
- Muffin pans (2½" or 3½" /65 or 90 mm size)
- Paper liners, pan spray, or pan coating
- Size #16 (2 fl. oz./60 ml) portion-control scoop or equivalent
- Half sheet pans (optional)
- Oven thermometer
- Wooden pick (for testing)
- Serrated knife
- Ruler

Procedure

1 Prepare cake batter using the high-ratio pound cake formula given in the previous experiment, or using any basic high-ratio pound cake formula. Prepare one batch of batter for each variation.

2 Line muffin pans with paper liners, lightly spray with pan spray, or grease with pan coating. Label with type of sweetener to be added to cake batter.

3 Scoop batter into prepared muffin pans using #16 scoop (or equivalent).

4 If desired, place muffin pans onto half sheet pans.

5 Use an oven thermometer placed in center of oven for an initial reading of oven temperature. Record results here: _____.

6 When oven is properly preheated, place filled muffin pans into oven and set timer for 32–35 minutes, or according to formula.

7 Bake cakes until control product (made with regular granulated sugar) pulls away slightly from sides of pan, cake springs back when center top is lightly pressed, and wooden pick inserted into center of cake comes out clean. Control product should be lightly browned. Remove *all* cakes from oven after same length of time, even though some will be paler or darker in color or have not risen as high. If necessary, however, adjust bake times for oven variances.

8 Record bake times in Results Table 1, which follows.

9 Check final oven temperature. Record results here: _____.

10 Remove cakes from hot pans and cool to room temperature.

Method of Preparation
(for cakes made with different sweeteners)

Follow the Method of Preparation for the control product (regular granulated sugar, see page 202), except make the following adjustments when using these sweeteners:

1 For cake made with brown sugar, substitute brown sugar for granulated sugar in step 4.

2 For cake made with honey (80° Brix), measure 17.5 ounces (500 grams) honey and add it in step 4 along with the dry ingredients and shortening; omit sugar and water in this step and reduce water in step 7 to 2.5 ounces (75 grams).

3 For cake made with invert syrup (75° Brix), measure 18.7 ounces (533 grams) invert syrup and add it in step 4 along with the dry ingredients and shortening; omit sugar and water in this step and reduce water in step 7 to 3.3 ounces (42 grams).

4 For cake made with Splenda, measure 1.75 ounces (50 grams) Splenda and add it in step 4 along with the other dry ingredients, shortening, and water; omit sugar in this step.

Results

1 When completely cooled, evaluate average weight of cakes from each batch, as follows:
   • Measure weight of each of three typical cakes. Record results for each cake in Results Table 1.

- Calculate the average cake weight by adding the weights and dividing by 3. Record results in Results Table 1.

2 Evaluate average height as follows:
- Slice three cakes from each batch in half, being careful not to compress.
- Measure height of each cake by placing a ruler along the flat edge at the cake's center point. Record results for each of three cakes in ¹⁄₁₆" (1 mm) increments in Results Table 1.
- Calculate the average cake height by adding the heights of the cakes and dividing this by 3. Record results in Results Table 1.
- Evaluate the shape of cakes (even rounded top, peaked top, dips in center, etc.) and draw shape or describe in words in Results Table 1.

RESULTS TABLE 1 SIZE AND SHAPE OF HIGH-RATIO POUND CAKES MADE WITH DIFFERENT TYPES OF SWEETENER

TYPE OF SWEETENER	BAKE TIME (IN MINUTES)	WEIGHTS OF EACH OF THREE CAKES	AVERAGE WEIGHT OF CAKES	HEIGHTS OF EACH OF THREE CAKES	AVERAGE HEIGHT OF CAKES	CAKE SHAPE	ADDITIONAL COMMENTS
Granulated sugar (control product)							
Brown sugar							
Honey							
Invert syrup							
Splenda							

3 Evaluate the sensory characteristics of completely cooled products and record evaluations in Results Table 2. If possible, allow cakes to age for one or more days before evaluating, to accentuate differences. Be sure to compare each in turn to the control product and consider the following:

- Crust color, from very light to very dark, on a scale of 1 to 5
- Crumb appearance (small/large air cells, uniform/irregular air cells, tunnels, etc.; also, evaluate color)
- Sweetness, from not sweet at all to extremely sweet, on a scale of 1 to 5
- Flavor (egg flavor, floury taste, saltiness, molasses, caramelized, etc.)
- Crumb texture (tough/tender, moist/dry, gummy, spongy, crumbly, etc.)
- Overall acceptability, from highly unacceptable to highly acceptable, on a scale of 1 to 5
- Add any additional comments, as necessary

RESULTS TABLE 2 SENSORY CHARACTERISTICS OF POUND CAKES MADE WITH DIFFERENT SWEETENERS

TYPE OF SWEETENER	CRUST COLOR AND TEXTURE	CRUMB APPEARANCE AND TEXTURE	SWEETNESS	OVERALL FLAVOR	OVERALL ACCEPTABILITY	ADDITIONAL COMMENTS
Granulated sugar (control product)						
Brown sugar						
Honey						
Invert syrup						
Splenda						

Sources of Error

List any sources of error that might make it difficult to draw the proper conclusions from your experiment. In particular, consider difficulties in mixing and handling batters, and any problems with the ovens.

_____
_____
_____

State what you could do differently next time to minimize or eliminate each source of error.

_____
_____
_____

Conclusions

Select one from the choices in **bold** or fill in the blanks.

1   Overall, pound cakes made with honey or invert syrup weighed **more than/less than/the same as** those made with granulated sugar. This is probably because syrups **do/do not** assist with the creaming process and **do/do not** help increase the amount of air incorporated into batters and doughs.

2   Overall, pound cakes made with honey or invert syrup exhibited **more/less/the same** leavening as those made with granulated sugar. This is probably because **more/less/the same amount of** air was incorporated into batter made with syrup compared with batter made with granulated sugar.

3   Overall, pound cakes made with honey or invert syrup browned **more than/less than/ the same as** those made with granulated sugar. This is probably because honey and invert syrup both contain substantial amounts of the monosaccharides _____ and _____, two sweeteners that brown **more than/less than/the same as** sucrose.

4   The adjustments made to the pound cake formula made with invert syrup were as follows:
_____
_____
_____

5   This means that any differences in moistness and tenderness in the pound cakes made with invert syrup compared with those made with granulated sugar **are/are not** due to the water in invert syrup.

6   The main differences between the pound cakes made with honey and those made with invert syrup were in **color and flavor/moistness and tenderness/height and crumb structure**. This suggests that honey **can/cannot** be successfully used in place of invert syrup in baked goods without making additional adjustments (except for minor adjustments for differences in water content).

7 The main differences between the pound cakes made with brown sugar and those made with regular granulated sugar were in **color and flavor/moistness and tenderness/height and crumb structure**. This suggests that brown sugar **can/cannot** be successfully used in place of regular granulated sugar in baked goods without making additional adjustments.

8 Compared with pound cakes made with granulated sugar, the pound cakes made with Splenda were **more sweet/less sweet/the same in sweetness.** Based on sweetness alone, I would **increase/decrease/not change** the amount of Splenda in this formula, if I were to make it again.

9 Compared with pound cakes made with granulated sugar, the pound cakes made with Splenda were **more moist/less moist/the same in moistness**, **more tender/less tender/the same in tenderness**, and had **more/less/the same** open crumb and leavening. This suggests that Splenda **can/cannot** be successfully used in place of regular granulated sugar in baked goods without making additional adjustments.

10 Go to www.splendafoodservice.com, a Web site by the manufacturer of Splenda, and read tips for using Splenda in cooking and baking. Which of their suggestions might be worthwhile trying, to improve the quality of the pound cake made with Splenda? Explain your answer.

_____

_____

_____

11 Select one sweetener from those tested (besides Splenda) that did not produce the "perfect" pound cake. If you could change anything in the formula or the method of preparation, what would you change to make the product more acceptable?

_____

_____

_____

12 Did you notice any other differences in the pound cakes or their batters?

_____

_____

_____

Fats, Oils, and Emulsifiers

9

Introduction

High-quality baked goods require a balance between tougheners and tenderizers, moisteners and driers. Any good formula will already contain the proper balance of ingredients, but it is still helpful to understand the ingredients that most contribute to this balance.

Fats, oils, and emulsifiers are indispensable moisteners and tenderizers. Yet recommendations for a healthful diet include reducing intake of certain fats, namely saturated fats and trans fats. North Americans are aware of these recommendations and have health and diet concerns about fat. While most baked goods cannot be made without fats, it is important to use them properly and to understand the concerns of your customers.

Chemistry of Fats, Oils, and Emulsifiers

Lipids are loosely defined as substances that do not dissolve in water. Fats, oils, emulsifiers, and flavor oils (peppermint oil and orange oil, for example) are all classified as lipids. Flavor oils are discussed in Chapter 17.

Fats are, strictly speaking, lipids that are solid at room temperature. The term *fat* is also commonly used to refer to any lipid, whether fat, oil, or emulsifier. For example, the amount of fat listed on food labels includes the amount of solid fat, liquid oil, and emulsifier present in the food product (Figure 9.1).

Oils are lipids that are liquid at room temperature. Oils are typically from vegetable sources such as soybean, cottonseed, canola, and corn. *Tropical oils* such as coconut, palm, and palm kernel oil are solid at room temperature (70°F/21°C), but they melt quickly in a warm room.

Emulsifiers can be either liquid or solid, just like fats and oils. There are many different emulsifiers, but they all have one thing in common: part of the molecule is attracted to, and dissolves in, water, while another part of the molecule is attracted to, and dissolves in, fats and oils. By dissolving in both water and fats/oils, emulsifiers hold the two together as an emulsion. This ability to hold oil and water together is one of the most important functions of emulsifiers in baked goods.

Chemically speaking, fats and oils—but not emulsifiers—are *triglycerides*. Triglycerides consist of three (*tri-*) fatty acids attached to a three-carbon glycerol (glycerine) molecule. Figure 9.2 is a simplified representation of a fat or oil molecule with its three fatty acids. *Fatty acids* are made of carbon chains that have anywhere from four to twenty-two carbon atoms. Because they are important to the makeup of fats and oils, it is worthwhile to study the chemistry of fatty

Nutrition Facts
Serving Size 1 Tablespoon (14g)
Servings Per Container 64

Amount Per Serving	
Calories 120	Calories from Fat 120

	% Daily Value*
Total Fat 14g	**22%**
Saturated Fat 1g	5%
Trans Fat 0g	
Cholesterol 0mg	0%
Sodium 0mg	0%
Total Carbohydrate 0g	0%
Dietary Fiber 0g	0%
Sugars 0g	
Protein 0g	

Vitamin A 0%	•	Vitamin C 0%
Calcium 0%	•	Iron 0%

*Percent Daily Values are based on a 2,000 calories diet. Your daily values may be higher or lower depending on your calorie needs:

		Calories:	2,000	2,500
Total Fat	Less than		65g	80g
Saturated Fat	Less than		20g	25g
Cholesterol	Less than		300mg	300mg
Sodium	Less than		2,400mg	2,400mg
Total Carbohydrate			300g	375g
Dietary Fiber			25g	30g

Calories per gram:
Fat 9 • Carbohydrate 4 • Protein 4

Figure 9.1 Nutrition Facts label for pure canola oil uses the term *fat* to describe the amount of total lipids—that is solid fat, liquid oil, and emulsifiers—contained in the product

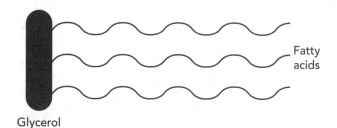

Glycerol

Figure 9.2 A triglyceride

The Importance of Omega

Omega-3 fatty acids are polyunsaturated fatty acids that have their last double bond three carbons in from the last (omega) carbon on the fatty acid chain. The last carbon atom is called the omega carbon because omega is the last letter in the Greek alphabet. The polyunsaturated fatty acid in Figure 9.4 is an omega-3 fatty acid.

Omega-6 fatty acids have their last double bond six carbons in from the omega end of the carbon chain. A diet with no more than twice the amount of omega-6s to omega-3s (2:1 ratio) is thought to be ideal from the standpoint of health. Western diets, however, are characterized by a ratio of about 15:1, too high in omega-6s and too low in omega-3s. A diet with an excessively high ratio of omega-6s to omega-3s is thought to contribute to cardiovascular disease, cancer, and certain inflammatory diseases such as arthritis. Most oils, like corn, peanut, safflower, and cottonseed oil have extremely high ratios of omega-6 to omega-3. The most common oil used worldwide, soybean oil, has a more reasonable ratio of about 7:1, while canola oil has a healthful 2:1 ratio. Foods that are high in omega-3s relative to omega-6s include salmon, flaxseed, and walnuts.

acids in more detail. As you go through the next few paragraphs, notice how terms commonly used by consumers (saturated, monounsaturated, polyunsaturated, trans fats, omega-3s) are based on the chemical structures of fatty acids.

Fatty acids can be short or long, saturated or unsaturated. Figure 9.3 shows a saturated fatty acid and an unsaturated fatty acid in some detail. Carbon atoms on *saturated fatty acids* are fully saturated with hydrogen atoms; that is, they cannot hold more hydrogen, and all bonds between carbon atoms are single. *Unsaturated fatty acids* contain two or more carbon atoms that are not fully saturated with hydrogen atoms. Carbon atoms that are not saturated form double bonds. The unsaturated fatty acid in Figure 9.3 is called a *monounsaturated fatty acid* because it has only one (*mono*) double bond between carbon atoms. (While the monounsaturated fatty acid in Figure 9.3 contains a second double bond, that double bond is between a carbon atom and an oxygen atom, not between two carbons.) Unsaturated

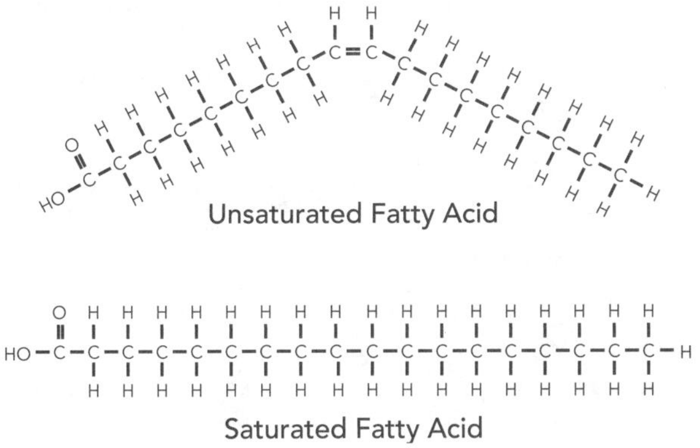

Figure 9.4 A polyunsaturated fatty acid. This is an omega-3 fatty acid, with the last double bond three carbons in from the omega end of the carbon chain.

fatty acids are either monounsaturated or polyunsaturated (having more than one double bond between carbon atoms). Notice the bend in the molecule at the double bond. Fatty acids bend at every double bond between carbon atoms, so polyunsaturated fatty acids can be quite curled (Figure 9.4).

The triglycerides that make up food fats and oils are considered *mixed triglycerides* because they contain a mix of different fatty acids, some short, some long, some straight, some bent (Figure 9.5). All common food fats have been analyzed for the mix of fatty acids

Unsaturated Fatty Acid

Saturated Fatty Acid

Figure 9.3 Unsaturated and saturated fatty acids

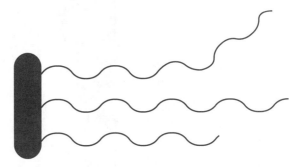

Figure 9.5 A mixed triglyceride, with short, long, straight, and bent fatty acids

Solid fats contain many tiny fat crystals. Fat crystals consist of fat molecules arranged in an orderly fashion, bonded one to the next. For solid fat to melt, these bonds must break, just as bonds must break between water molecules for ice to melt.

Unlike pure water, which consists of identical molecules of H_2O, fats contain a mix of different fatty acids. While identical water molecules melt at the same temperature (32°F/0°C), each fatty acid melts at its own distinct temperature.

When fats soften, it is because some fat crystals have melted while others have not. For example, butter noticeably softens at around 80°F (27°C) because many of the bonds between shorter fatty acids have broken. It is not until about 94°F (34°C) that bonds break between the longer fatty acids in butter and the butter liquefies completely. The temperature at which there are no solid fat crystals visible and a fat appears as a completely clear liquid is defined as its *final melting point*. It is at this point that essentially all the fat crystals have melted to liquid. However, the fat has been melting all along.

Fats such as butter, which melt quickly and completely from body heat, have a pleasant mouthfeel. Fats that melt slowly or incompletely, such as all-purpose shortening, tend to have a less pleasant, often waxy mouthfeel.

---

that they contain. Figure 9.6 shows the fatty acid profiles of various food fats and oils. Notice how each contains a distinct mix of saturated, monounsaturated, and polyunsaturated fatty acids.

Typically, the higher a fat is in saturated fatty acids, the more solid the fat. That is why animal fats, tropical oils, and cocoa butter, which are all naturally high in saturated fatty acids, are solid at room temperature. Most vegetable oils are liquid at room temperature because they are low in saturated fatty acids. Dietary guidelines for North Americans recommend that intake of saturated fatty acids be limited because they have been shown to raise blood cholesterol and increase the risk of coronary heart disease.

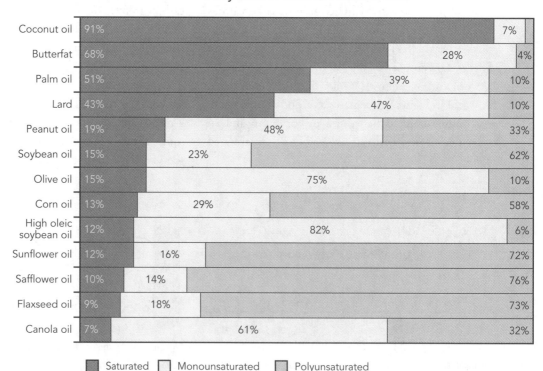

Fatty Acid Profiles of Fats and Oils

	Saturated	Monounsaturated	Polyunsaturated
Coconut oil	91%		7%
Butterfat	68%	28%	4%
Palm oil	51%	39%	10%
Lard	43%	47%	10%
Peanut oil	19%	48%	33%
Soybean oil	15%	23%	62%
Olive oil	15%	75%	10%
Corn oil	13%	29%	58%
High oleic soybean oil	12%	82%	6%
Sunflower oil	12%	16%	72%
Safflower oil	10%	14%	76%
Flaxseed oil	9%	18%	73%
Canola oil	7%	61%	32%

Figure 9.6 Fatty acid profiles of different fats and oils

All solid fats contain a certain amount of solid fat crystals. Like all crystals, fat crystals are highly ordered arrangements of molecules bonded one to the next. Saturated fatty acids are more apt to form solid fat crystals because they are straight molecules (refer back to Figure 9.3). Straight molecules easily line up in an orderly fashion, bonding and packing tightly into crystals. Unsaturated fatty acids are bent, and it is more difficult for bent molecules to line up and bond. Instead, unsaturated fatty acids arrange themselves loosely, and while they might tangle, they do not tightly bond into solid crystals, at least at room temperature. The more unsaturated the fatty acid, the more bent the molecule, and the harder it is for the fatty acid to crystallize into a solid fat.

Left: saturated fatty acids easily line up to form solid crystals; **right:** unsaturated fatty acids do not

Trans fatty acids are unsaturated fatty acids in which the two hydrogen atoms of a double bond are on opposite sides of the double bond (Figure 9.7). Most naturally occurring unsaturated fatty acids—"cis" fatty acids—have the two hydrogen atoms on the same side of the double bond. This seemingly small difference in structure has a big effect on health. This effect will be discussed later in this chapter.

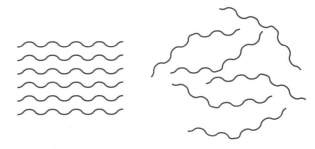

Figure 9.7 Close up of a naturally occurring cis fatty acid and a trans fatty acid

Processing of Fats and Oils

Most fats and oils used in the bakeshop are highly refined, meaning that they are composed of almost 100 percent triglycerides with almost everything else removed. In fact, the only unrefined fat commonly used in the bakeshop is butter.

Once refined, fats and oils are further processed to increase their functionality. They can be fractionated, hydrogenated, and aerated, for example. This section discusses some of the processes that turn crude vegetable oils into refined designer fats.

Extraction and Refining
Oils are extracted from soybeans and other oilseeds, nuts, and fruit primarily through the use of solvents. Hexane is the solvent of choice, since it is very efficient, and once the oil is extracted, the hexane can be separated out and reused. Because hexane is highly volatile, traces of it are easily removed by heating the oil.

Once the "crude" oil is extracted, it is refined in two main steps. The first refining step, *degumming,* is when naturally present emulsifiers, primarily lecithin, are physically removed by centrifuging (spinning) the oil with water. The emulsifiers are spun out with the water, and the lecithin can be purified and sold separately. Soybean oil, being high in emulsifiers, is in fact the main commercial source of lecithin.

After it is degummed, the crude oil undergoes an *alkali refining* step, in which a strong alkali (lye) is added to the oil. The alkali forms complexes (soaps) with free fatty acids (that is, fatty acids that are not tied up as triglycerides). The alkali also causes proteins and other impurities to settle out of solution, where they are easy to centrifuge out.

After refining, oil is *bleached* by passing it through filtering material such as bentonite clay, which attracts and adsorbs most coloring agents. The final step in purifying

Before solvent extraction became the standard means of removing oils from oilseeds and other sources, oils were mechanically extracted by pressing. A machine called an *expeller press* was commonly used. In an expeller press, high pressure forces oil out of seeds, nuts, or fruits. The oil seeps through a perforated screen and the refuse stays behind. If the nut or seed is hard, high pressure is needed to extract the oil, and the oil heats up. The heat can damage delicate flavors and nutrients. If the oily material is soft, though, like olives, and it is gently pressed, the oil does not heat up and delicate flavors and nutrients are preserved. When pressed gently in this manner, the oil is sometimes marketed as "cold-pressed expeller oil." Expeller-pressed oils are more expensive than regular oils because the process is not as efficient at removing oils as solvent extraction.

crude oils is called *deodorization*, in which steam and heat are used to evaporate off trace amounts of odor-causing molecules. At this point, the oil is relatively colorless and bland tasting and is considered refined, bleached, and deodorized, or RBD. It can be sold as is, or further processed in several different ways.

Hydrogenation

Check the ingredient labels of fats and oils used in the bakeshop and you will notice that some of them—including many all-purpose shortenings, high-ratio shortenings, margarine, lard, even liquid oils—have been hydrogenated.

Hydrogenation converts unsaturated fatty acids to saturated ones through the addition of hydrogen (Figure 9.8). Fats and oils are hydrogenated by exposing them to hydrogen gas in the presence of high heat, pressure, and a catalyst such as nickel. Catalysts speed up chemical reactions without actually being used up in the reaction. The nickel is removed before the hydrogenated fat is packaged and sold.

As fats and oils become hydrogenated, they become more saturated and therefore more solid. Fully hydrogenated fats are so solid that they are hard to work with, so fats have traditionally been partially hydrogenated. Partial hydrogenation leaves some fatty acids unsaturated, so the fat is soft and plastic. The manufacturer

Figure 9.9 The manufacturer controls the hydrogenation process to achieve the desired consistency. **Clockwise, from top:** partially hydrogenated liquid shortening, partially hydrogenated plastic shortening, and fully hydrogenated shortening.

controls the process to achieve the desired degree of hydrogenation for the desired consistency (Figure 9.9).

Notice that hydrogenation is not the same as adding air to fats. Hydrogenation is a chemical process that changes the fatty acid molecule by forcing hydrogen onto it. *Aeration* occurs when air is whipped into solid fat, as when fat is creamed. For fats to be properly aerated, however, they must have a soft, plastic consistency. The process of hydrogenation is one way to create soft, plastic fats from liquid oils so that they are suitable for aerating.

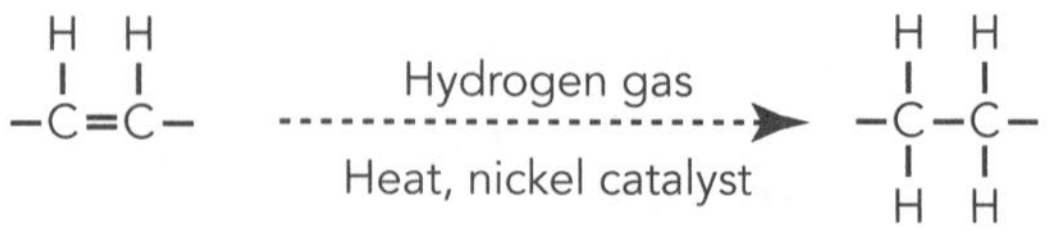

Unsaturated liquid oil

Saturated solid fat

Figure 9.8 Hydrogenation of liquid oil into a solid fat

Are Plastic Fats Edible?

Plastic fats are not made from plastic. Rather, they are edible fats that have a plastic consistency, meaning that they are soft, moldable solids, like Play-Doh. Plastic fats are part liquid and part solid; that is, they consist of liquid oil trapped in a network of solid fat crystals. Examples of fats that are plastic at room temperature (70°F/21°C) include all-purpose shortening, lard, and butter. Fats that are not plastic at room temperature include vegetable oils, which are liquid at room temperature, and cocoa butter, which is a hard solid.

Plasticity depends on temperature. Butter is plastic at room temperature, but it is rock solid in the freezer and completely liquid in a hot bakeshop. All-purpose shortening is plastic when refrigerated and is still plastic when the bakeshop warms. That is one of the advantages of all-purpose shortening: it keeps its soft, workable consistency over a wide range of temperatures.

Why Hydrogenate?

There are two main reasons to hydrogenate fats and oils. The first, as already mentioned, is to increase the solidity of a fat or oil. Solid fat is desirable, for example, for flakiness and volume in pastry or to decrease the greasiness in doughnuts and cookies.

The second reason to hydrogenate fats and oils is to increase stability against oxidative rancidity. *Oxidative rancidity* is the breakdown of fatty acids into smaller fragments that have rancid off flavors. Because double bonds are the weakest bonds on a fatty acid, the more double bonds on a fatty acid (that is, the more unsaturated the fatty acid), the faster it breaks down and undergoes oxidative rancidity. This means that monounsaturated fats oxidize faster than saturated ones, and polyunsaturated fats oxidize fastest of all. In fact, highly polyunsaturated fats can oxidize 100 times faster than highly saturated ones.

Hydrogenation reduces oxidative rancidity by converting unsaturated fatty acids into saturated ones and highly reactive polyunsaturated fatty acids into less unsaturated ones. Even a small amount of hydrogenation helps delay rancidity. That is why vegetable oils, which remain liquid and therefore don't appear hydrogenated, sometimes are.

Regular soybean oil, in particular, is highly polyunsaturated (refer back to Figure 9.6). By hydrogenating the polyunsaturated fatty acids, soybean oil is much less likely to oxidize to an unpleasant beany, fishy, or painty smell. Today, because of its use in shortenings, margarines, and vegetable oil, soybean oil is the most common vegetable fat in the bakeshop. In fact, soybeans are the second largest crop in the United States, second only to corn. Figure 9.10 shows mature soybeans in a pod. Standard mature, dried soybeans contain about 20 percent oil, over half of it polyunsaturated.

Figure 9.10 Mature soybeans in pod

An unfortunate downside of hydrogenation is that it generates saturated fatty acids. A diet high in saturated fat is thought to increase blood cholesterol and the risk of coronary heart disease. A greater downside is that the process of partial hydrogenation typically generates trans fatty acids. While small amounts of trans fatty acids (sometimes called *trans fats*) occur naturally in butter, by far the greatest source of trans fats in the Western diet is from partial—but not total—hydrogenation of fats and oils. Since January 2006, food manufacturers are

Hydrogenation is the traditional way to reduce the amount of polyunsaturated fatty acids in oils so that they are more stable. There are other ways to do this, however, so that the oil is also trans fat–free. For example, soybeans and other oilseeds can be specially bred or genetically modified to be naturally low in polyunsaturated fatty acids. Because they are naturally low in polyunsaturated fatty acids, oils extracted from these oilseeds are less likely to oxidize and turn rancid. These stable oils are called *low-lin oils* or *high-oleic oils*, to distinguish them from regular oils. Low-lin oils are low in alpha linolenic acid (ALA), an omega-3 polyunsaturated fatty acid (see Figure 9.4) that is highly susceptible to rancidity. High oleic oils are low in all polyunsaturated fatty acids (not just ALA) and high in oleic acid, a monounsaturated fatty acid. High oleic oils are sometimes marketed as "omega-9 oils," since oleic acid is classified as an omega-9 fatty acid. Figure 9.6 includes the fatty acid profile for a high-oleic soybean oil. Notice how much lower it is in highly reactive polyunsaturated fatty acids compared with regular soybean oil.

While it is relatively easy to replace regular cooking oils with trans fat–free ones, it is more difficult to replace partially hydrogenated plastic fats. Many trans fat–free shortenings and margarines are made from palm oil or other fats that are naturally saturated. While naturally saturated and therefore somewhat solid, palm oil does not have the best plastic consistency. To improve on its plasticity without adding trans fats, manufacturers can do one of two things. First, they can blend palm oil with a fully hydrogenated solid fat. Since full hydrogenation, unlike partial hydrogenation, does not generate trans fats, any amount of a fully hydrogenated fat can be blended with palm oil to achieve the desired plastic consistency, without trans fats. This same technique can be used with any oil. For example, canola oil can be combined with a fully hydrogenated fat to produce a canola-based shortening.

Another way to produce trans fat–free plastic shortenings is through the process of interesterification. *Interesterification* uses an enzyme—lipase—or other means to rearrange or change the order of fatty acids on a triglyceride, altering how the fat solidifies and melts. The result is a fat with improved properties over other trans fat–free shortenings, often with a lower saturated fat content. Interesterification is also used for improving the plastic properties of lard. Because the structure of the fat has been changed, these fats are sometimes called *structured fats*.

required by law to disclose on food labels the amount of trans fat present in their products. Many municipalities have banned the use of trans fats in restaurants and bakeries. New York City, for example, has banned trans fats in all foodservice establishments, including bakeshops, since 2008. The state of California will ban trans fats in bakeshops statewide starting in 2011.

Trans fatty acids from partial hydrogenation are of concern because they tend to increase bad (LDL) cholesterol in the blood while also decreasing good (HDL) cholesterol. In doing so, trans fats are thought to increase the risk of coronary heart disease even more than naturally saturated fatty acids. Trans fats have also been implicated in increasing damage to blood vessel walls.

In response to these concerns, people are reminded to minimize their intake of fats, especially saturated and trans fats. Bakers and pastry chefs cannot replace all saturated fats with unsaturated ones in the bakeshop, despite the concerns of their customers. But it is still important to understand that baked goods and fried foods have been implicated as the two major sources of saturated and trans fats in our diet, and that there are options available for improving the healthfulness of baked goods through the proper selection of fats. These options are explored in the next section and in Chapter 18.

Trans Fat–Free Shortenings and Oils

New versions of vegetable fats and oils have been developed that are without trans fats yet have stability and functions approaching those of regular fats and oils. While this is done for health reasons, many trans fat–free shortenings and margarines are still quite high in saturated fat (some as high as 50 percent saturated fat), so they are still not the healthiest of fats. Without

Palm kernel oil and palm oil are two different tropical oils that have one thing in common: they both come from the same plant, the oil palm tree (*Elaeis guineensis*). Palm kernel oil comes from the inner seed, or kernel, of the fruit of the oil palm, while palm oil comes from the bright orange oily pulp (the mesocarp) that surrounds the kernel. Palm kernel oil and palm oil are not interchangeable, since they do not have the same properties. While both are saturated, palm oil is more suitable for use as a plastic shortening. Palm kernel oil is more like coconut oil. It is more highly saturated, has a faster melt, and it is often used as a cocoa butter substitute in confectionary coatings (see Chapter 15) or as a creme filling in cookies.

the trans fats, they also do not function the same as standard partially hydrogenated ones. For example, trans fat–free shortenings tend to be more sensitive to changes in temperature; that is, they do not have as wide a plastic working range. This means that they will cream differently, and they will soften and melt more easily during storage. It also means that pie crusts might be less flaky, because trans fat–free shortenings tend to soften and seep into dough more easily, and icings made with them might not spread as smoothly or pipe as easily. Many trans fat–free shortenings (those that are also low in saturated fats) oxidize more easily, so these fats are more likely to turn rancid faster than normal, even if they contain antioxidants. Trans fat–free shortenings must be stored carefully so they don't lose their soft, smooth consistency and fresh flavor.

Cooling and Aeration of Plastic Fats

Once oils are partially hydrogenated or otherwise processed to be soft solids, they are cooled and aerated, in one step, until smooth and creamy. The equipment used for cooling and aerating fats is similar to a commercial ice cream machine, where the fat is agitated inside a chilled cylindrical drum.

> **HELPFUL HINT**
>
> *If you are having difficulty creaming with a trans fat–free shortening, consider storing the shortening in a different location to adjust its temperature. Because many have a narrower plastic range than traditional (partially hydrogenated) shortenings, even a small difference in temperature can cause the shortening to become too hard or too soft.*

Depending on the source of fat, how it is processed, and how it is cooled, fats solidify into one of several different crystalline structures. The three main crystalline structures are called alpha, beta prime, and beta. Each has its own distinct features, which are discussed throughout this chapter, but all-purpose shortenings are typically solidified into tiny beta prime crystals. The needle-like crystals are so tiny (about 1 micron) that shortening feels smooth and creamy.

Shortening manufacturers aerate with nitrogen instead of air. Air contains oxygen, which causes fats to undergo oxidative rancidity. Since air itself is almost 80 percent nitrogen, nitrogen is perfectly safe in foods.

Fats and Oils

Fats and oils differ from each other in cost, flavor, consistency, amount of fat, amount of air, amount of water, and melting point. Some contain additives such as emulsifiers, antioxidants, salt, colors, flavors, antimicrobial agents, milk solids, and more (Table 9.1). These differences affect how each fat functions in the bakeshop.

Butter

Butter is made from heavy cream. While some of the fat in chilled cream is in the form of liquid globules, a large amount consists of tiny solid fat crystals, so tiny that cream seems totally liquid in the mouth. Butter manufacturing involves the separation of this fat, both solid fat crystals and liquid globules, from much of the remaining liquid, or buttermilk.

TABLE 9.1   COMMON ADDITIVES TO FATS AND OILS

ADDITIVE	DESCRIPTION	COMMON USE IN FATS AND OILS
Annatto	Natural coloring from the seed of the annatto (achiote) shrub	Color for butter
Beta-carotene	A form of vitamin A	Color for margarine
BHA	Synthetic antioxidant; butylated hydroxyanisole	Minimizes oxidative rancidity
BHT	Synthetic antioxidant; butylated hydroxytoluene	Minimizes oxidative rancidity
Citric acid	Organic acid, especially high in citrus fruits	Minimizes oxidative rancidity, especially in lard and other fats that contain small amounts of iron or other destructive minerals
Cottonseed oil, hydrogenated	From seed of cotton plant	Added to plastic shortening to encourage formation of proper beta prime crystal structure for creaming
Dimethylpolysiloxane	Silicone derivative	Added to frying fats to reduce foaming and to delay the degradation of fats exposed to high heat
Lactic acid esters of monoglycerides	Emulsifier	Added to high-ratio liquid shortenings to encourage formation of proper alpha crystal formation for aeration
Lecithin	Emulsifier	Added to margarine to minimize spattering during pan sautéing; added to pan release sprays, to prevent baked goods from sticking
Mono- and diglycerides such as glyceryl monostearate	Emulsifier	Added to high-ratio shortenings to increase aeration, moistness, and tenderness, and especially to prevent staling of baked goods
Polyglycerol esters (PGE)	Emulsifier	Prevents clouding in salad oil by inhibiting fat crystallization
Polysorbate 60	Emulsifier	Added to high-ratio shortening, to aid creaming and for stabilizing cake batters and icings.
Potassium sorbate	Potassium salt of sorbic acid, a natural organic acid	Added to margarine to prevent microbial growth
Propyl gallate	Synthetic antioxidant	Minimizes oxidative rancidity
Propylene glycol monoesters (PGME), such as propylene glycol monostearate (PGMS)	Emulsifier	Added to high-ratio liquid shortenings. Alpha-tending emulsifier that is highly effective at aerating cake batters; also good at distributing and holding fat, for moistness and tenderness
Salt	Sodium chloride	Flavoring and preservative in butter and margarine
Sodium benzoate	Sodium salt of benzoic acid, a natural organic acid	Added to margarine to prevent microbial growth
Stearic acid	Natural saturated fatty acid	Added to high-ratio liquid shortening. Assists emulsifiers in aerating cake batters and distributing and holding fat, for moistness and tenderness
TBHQ	Synthetic antioxidant; tert-butylhydroquinone	Minimizes oxidative rancidity
Tocopherols	Mixture of vitamin E and related molecules; antioxidant	Minimizes oxidative rancidity
Vitamin A palmitate		Added to margarine as a vitamin
Vitamin D		Added to margarine as a vitamin

At one time, cream was agitated in wooden butter churns. Today, butter is manufactured in large batches or even larger continuous commercial operations. Either way, the first step in butter manufacture is to pasteurize cream, then cool it to 60°F (16°C). If butter is made from cultured cream, a bacteria culture is added, and the cream is allowed to ripen and develop flavor as the bacteria convert lactose into lactic acid. Next, the cream is aged under carefully controlled conditions that encourage the growth of the proper crystalline structure. This aging step is similar to the tempering of chocolates, which is discussed in Chapter 15. It is an important step for achieving the right butter consistency. If desired, small amounts of natural yellow annatto color may be added before the cream is vigorously agitated, or churned.

Churning first produces whipped cream, as air is whipped in and fat droplets (globules) begin to clump around air bubbles. Continued violent agitation creates an extensive three-dimensional network of clumped liquid globules, stiffened and reinforced with tiny solid fat crystals. Eventually, large pools of liquid buttermilk seep out and chunks of butter granules form, as the whipped cream collapses. After churning, the butter chunks are salted, if desired, then worked or kneaded, to shape them and to remove excess water. Because kneading also softens butter, this process is sometimes called *work softening*. What remains is butter, a smooth emulsion of solid fat crystals and liquid butterfat, with droplets of water, air bubbles, and milk solids trapped throughout.

Butter flavor and consistency varies from one brand to the next, partly because of the cows' diet. Cream that is high in short fatty acids, for example, tends to be stronger in flavor and produces softer butter than cream that is high in longer fatty acids. Other differences in butter flavor and consistency have to do with how the butter is processed. Slow pasteurization of cream produces butter with a nuttier, cooked flavor than cream that is ultrapasteurized. How the cream is chilled, how it is churned and washed, how much air is incorporated into it, and how much fat it contains all affect consistency.

As with other fats, butter provides many important characteristics in baked goods, including moistness, tenderness, flakiness, and volume. But this does not explain the widespread use of butter in quality bakeshops, because butter does not excel at any of these functions. Instead, butter's two main advantages are its flavor and its mouthfeel. No other fat can match butter in these two attributes. Margarine may contain natural butter flavor and have a low final melting point, but it still does not have the superior flavor and texture of butter.

Butter has many disadvantages. For example, it is expensive. Butter can be several times more expensive than margarine, and its price fluctuates with the seasons and with supply. Butterfat is an undesirable fat from a health standpoint. It is the highest of common bakeshop fats in saturated fat—even higher than lard—and it contains cholesterol.

Butter is also one of the most difficult fats to work with, because it has a narrow plastic range. It is too hard when used directly out of the refrigerator, and it melts quickly from the heat of hands or a warm bakeshop. In fact, the best temperature for creaming butter is generally within the narrow range of 65°–70°F (18°–21°C). Its low melting point also means that oven temperatures must be set properly and the butter must be well-chilled to achieve the best flakiness and volume for puff pastries and other laminated baked goods.

Butter spoils faster than other fats, especially if it is unsalted. It is susceptible to bacterial spoilage if it is not refrigerated for the short term or frozen for the long term. Butter that has undergone bacterial spoilage has either a sour milk or rancid off flavor.

Classifying Butter Butter can be classified by the type of cream used in its production. The two types of butters are cultured butter and sweet cream butter. *Cultured butter* is made from sour cream, in which bacteria have converted lactose to lactic acid. Cultured butter, also called *ripened butter*, has a distinct sour flavor similar to sour cream. It is rarely, if ever, salted. *Sweet cream butter* has a milder flavor than cultured butter. It is called "*sweet cream*" because the cream has not been soured, not because it contains a sweetener.

While both types are available worldwide, there are regional preferences. Sweet cream butter is traditional

The very act of making butter—of churning cream and removing buttermilk—is a form of food preservation, because buttermilk supports bacterial growth. But butter still contains some buttermilk, which is rich in nutrients, so it can still spoil. This was a problem in the days before refrigeration.

Where salt was available, it was used as a preservative in butter. Salt is a very powerful antimicrobial agent, and salted butter could contain a fairly high amount of buttermilk and not spoil.

In countries where salt was not readily available, other means were needed for preservation. As milk sat out for cream to slowly rise to the surface, the milk and cream would sour before the cream was churned. The "friendly" bacteria in sour or ripened cream slow the growth of undesirable spoilage bacteria. Since this is not as effective as salt in preventing bacterial growth, a higher amount of buttermilk often was removed in the production of cultured butter. This may explain why some European butters are higher in butterfat.

Some countries, notably India, simmer butter to destroy bacteria and to remove water. The resulting liquid butterfat, called *ghee*, has a distinctive nutty flavor from the Maillard reaction that occurs when milk proteins and milk sugar (lactose) are heated. Since it contains essentially no water, ghee lasts longer than butter.

Today, refrigeration is more readily available, yet many people still prefer butter made in the traditional style of their culture. In North America, more than 95 percent of butter sold is salted sweet cream butter.

---

throughout North America and Great Britain. Cultured butter is traditional in certain countries in Europe, particularly France, Germany, and Switzerland. *European-style butter* made and sold in North America is either cultured butter or sweet cream butter with an added cultured cream flavor. Plugrá is an example of a European-style butter that has a delicate tang from an added cultured cream flavor.

Makeup of Butter The minimum amount of butterfat required in butter in the United States and in Canada is 80 percent, slightly lower than the 82 percent minimum required in most European countries. European-style butters, like European butters, typically contain a minimum of 82 percent butterfat. While 82 percent is the minimum allowed in Europe, it is not uncommon for European butters to have as much as 86 percent butterfat, or more. Butter containing a higher percentage of butterfat typically has a smoother, creamier mouthfeel. Because it is also lower in water, higher-fat butter is often firmer in consistency and slower to melt.

Butterfat consists mostly of triglycerides with a small amount of natural emulsifiers. The emulsifiers, which make up about 2–3 percent of butterfat, include mono- and diglycerides and lecithin. Butterfat also contains cholesterol and vitamin A, a fat-soluble vitamin.

The remaining 20 percent of butter's makeup includes water (typically 16–18 percent), milk solids, and salt, if added. Milk solids consist of proteins, lactose, and minerals. Proteins and lactose in milk solids contribute to Maillard browning in baked goods. Water and a small amount of air in butter provide for leavening.

A few optional ingredients are allowed in butter in the United States and Canada. For example, natural butter flavor and annatto, a natural coloring, can be added. Salt can be added for flavor, and bacterial cultures can be added if the butter is cultured.

Bakers and pastry chefs generally use unsalted butter in the bakeshop, for good reason. First, the amount of salt added to butter can be unpredictable, as it varies from one brand to the next. Second, the amount of salt in butter may be too high for certain products, such as buttercream. Finally, it is easier to detect off flavors in unsalted butter than in salted butter. While butter in

HELPFUL HINT

High-fat butter is useful when preparing laminated doughs including croissant and puff pastry dough. High-fat butter maintains a firm yet workable consistency over a wider range of temperatures. It is less likely than regular butter to melt into dough or seep out, so it gives a better rise and more flakiness. If high-fat butter is unavailable when preparing laminated dough, add flour to butter to firm it up to the consistency of the dough, or use a roll-in or puff pastry margarine.

In the United States, there are three grades of butter: Grades AA, A, and B. U.S. Grade AA and Grade A are the quality ratings most often seen, but some U.S. Grade B butter is available. The grading of butter is a voluntary system administered by the U.S. Department of Agriculture (USDA).

Flavor is considered the most important attribute of butter, and a preference in the United States for mild-tasting butter is reflected in the USDA scoring system. Of the three grades, USDA Grade AA butter is made from the freshest cream. It has a mild butter flavor with minimal flavor defects. USDA Grade A butter has a stronger, slightly sour but still pleasant flavor. Grade B butter has a flavor that is more like cultured butter, a flavor that some prefer.

A lesser part of butter's score is related to its body or consistency and its color. U.S. Grade AA butter must have a smooth, creamy consistency and uniform color. The cow's diet strongly influences butter consistency, as does the season of the year that the cow is milked. The manufacturer, however, has control over other factors that influence butter consistency. These factors include the percentage of fat and milk solids in butter, the heating and cooling of cream, and how the butter is churned and worked.

Canada has one grade for butter, Canada 1. Canada 1 butter can be mild-flavored or sour, depending on whether it is made from sweet cream or cultured cream. Other characteristics of Canada 1 butter are similar to USDA Grade AA or A.

HELPFUL HINT

The proteins and lactose in butter may be browned deliberately to make browned butter, or beurre noisette. Noisette is French for "hazelnut," and browned butter has an appealing nutty flavor and the rich color of hazelnuts. To brown butter, cook it in a sauté pan until the water evaporates and the butter has a golden brown color. Remove from heat and strain the clear liquid beurre noisette from the solids. Discard the solids.

If butter is heated just until the water evaporates and is skimmed and strained before milk solids brown, it is called clarified butter. Clarified butter is a staple on the line in restaurant kitchens. Because milk solids have been removed, clarified butter is less likely to scorch, smoke, or burn when foods are sautéed under high heat.

North America will be free of off flavors when initially graded, it can pick up odors if stored improperly. If salted butter is used in the bakeshop, formulas must be adjusted accordingly (assume the amount of salt added to butter is about 2.0–2.5 percent).

Unsalted butter is sometimes confusingly called sweet butter. It is best to stay away from this term because it is easily mistaken for sweet cream butter, which is butter made from sweet cream. Sweet cream butter can be either salted or unsalted.

Lard

Lard, rendered from hog fat, is a by-product of the meat industry. It was once a common ingredient in cooking and baking in North America, Great Britain, Spain, and other countries around the world. The highest grade lard, called *leaf lard*, surrounds the kidneys and abdomen of the animal. Other grades of lard include hard fat from the back; soft fat from around muscle tissue; and caul fat from around the stomach and intestines. Because it is a pork-based product, lard is not kosher (permitted under Jewish dietary laws) or halal (permitted under Islamic dietary laws).

Lard's unique crystalline structure makes it valuable for providing flakiness to pastries and pie crusts. It is also prized for its mild meaty flavor, characteristic of certain traditional ethnic pastries. Except for these uses, lard has largely been replaced by shortening in North America. However, there has recently been a small resurgence in interest in the use of lard in pastries.

Today's lard is more like all-purpose shortening. It is highly refined, bleached, and deodorized for a mild flavor, white color, and better uniformity. It is 100 percent fat, usually with small amounts of antioxidants added to protect it from developing rancidity. To improve its ability to trap air, lard is often hydrogenated and otherwise processed to give it a less greasy feel, a less grainy texture, and to improve its creaming

Lard naturally solidifies into large beta crystals, which give it a translucent appearance and a coarse, grainy texture. Unlike the small beta prime crystals in all-purpose shortening, large beta crystals do not hold air well, so unmodified lard does not cream well and is not good for producing fine-textured cakes. Instead, lard's large beta crystals are ideal for separating layers of dough in laminated products. In other words, large beta crystals are what make unmodified lard uniquely suited for making flaky pie crusts and other pastries.

ability. While this allows lard to produce fine-textured cakes, it is at the expense of providing flakiness to pastries and pie crusts.

Margarine

Margarine is imitation butter. While great improvements have been made over the years in margarine quality, it is still not the real thing, and it does not have the superior flavor and mouthfeel of butter. But margarine has several advantages over butter, and this probably explains why sales volume of margarine in North America has exceeded that of butter since the late 1950s.

One advantage of margarine is its lower price. Another advantage is that margarine contains no cholesterol, and soft margarines are lower in saturated fats than butter, although they may contain trans fats. A third advantage of some margarines is their stronger flavor. While this might sound like a contradiction since butter is prized for its flavor, margarine flavor can be more assertive, if less refined. Finally, margarines are designer fats, and like shortenings, features can be built into them, so that they are easier to use and more functional in certain applications.

> ### HELPFUL HINT
>
> *Margarine, or a blend of margarine and butter, can in theory be used instead of butter in just about any product, but it is best to use butter wherever mouthfeel or butter flavor is especially important. For example, while margarine, or a blend of margarine and butter, might be acceptable in chocolate brownies, butter alone is best in shortbread cookies and in buttercream, if butter flavor and a melting mouthfeel are of prime importance.*
>
> *Don't forget to adjust a formula for salt if salted margarine is used in place of unsalted butter. Assume that salted margarine contains about 2.5–3.0 percent salt.*

Makeup of Margarine   Most margarines that are partially hydrogenated are made from soybean oil, but they can be made from any vegetable or animal fat. For example, trans fat–free margarines are often made from naturally saturated palm oil. True margarine has a similar composition to butter; that is, it contains a minimum of 80 percent fat and about 16 percent water, and a similar amount of air is trapped in margarine as in butter. This means that margarine has the same number of calories as butter. While low-fat and fat-free "margarines" (called *spreads*) do exist, these products do not generally work well in baking. Low-fat and fat-free spreads contain a high amount of water. They rely on gums and starches to provide a butter-like consistency.

Margarine made without coloring and flavoring would be white and bland tasting, like shortening. That is why margarine contains coloring (usually beta-carotene) and butter flavoring, either natural or artificial. Margarine, like butter, can be purchased salted or unsalted.

Besides salt, several other optional ingredients can be added to margarine, including milk solids, lecithin, and antimicrobial agents. When margarine contains salt and antimicrobial agents and does not contain milk solids, like shortening it does not need refrigeration.

Classifying Margarine   Margarines are designer fats, meaning that the manufacturer blends or hydrogenates them to any degree of firmness and plasticity. One way to classify margarine is by firmness and final melting point. The following four types of margarines are listed with approximate final melting points. These four categories are somewhat arbitrary, and one company's baker's margarine is another's roll-in. Still, fitting a large number of products into categories can be helpful as an introduction to and overview of the range of products available.

Table margarine is designed primarily to be easily spread on bread and to melt completely at body temperature (typical melting point: 85°–95°F/32°–38°C).

On occasion, consumer recipes call for oleo. Oleo is just another name for margarine. The French chemist who invented margarine in the 1860s made it from beef fat and gave it the full name oleomargarine. Beef fat consists primarily of oleic acid and two saturated acids (palmitic and stearic acids), which, in the 1800s, was called margaric acid.

The U.S. Food and Drug Administration (FDA) shortened the official name of oleomargarine to margarine in 1951, but some people—mostly those who remember the days before 1951—still refer to margarine as "oleo."

It is what we think of as margarine, sold by the pound in supermarkets next to butter. Unlike butter, table margarine is soft enough to be used right out of the cooler. Of all the margarines, table margarine has the best mouthfeel for use in icings—be sure to use one that is unsalted—but the icing will not hold up well on warm days. It can be creamed for use in cookies and cakes, although it is not the best margarine for the job. While table margarine melts completely in the mouth, it does not have the same mouthfeel as butter. Instead, it can leave a greasy or oily slick on the tongue.

Baker's margarine (typical melting point: 95°–110°F/ 35°–41°C), also called all-purpose or cake margarine, can be thought of as a soft all-purpose shortening with butter flavor and color added. Because it is ideal for creaming, baker's margarine is the margarine of choice for making cookies and cakes, and for icings that need to hold up to warm weather. The mouthfeel of baker's margarines range from slightly greasy and oily to firm and sometimes chewy.

Roll-in margarine has a higher final melting point (typically 105°–115°F/41°–46°C) and firmer consistency than baker's margarine. Roll-in margarine is used in Danish pastries, and it provides a good amount of flakiness and volume in puff pastries and croissants, but with some waxiness.

Puff pastry margarine has an extremely high final melting point (typically 115°–135°F/ 47°–57°C) and a firm, waxy consistency. Although firm, puff pastry margarine is still plastic, so it is easy to evenly roll in and fold with puff pastry dough. While puff pastry margarine is excellent for picture-perfect, light and flaky pastries, the pastries tend to have an unpleasant waxy mouthfeel.

Mouthfeel is complex and is related to the total melting behavior of a fat, not just its final melting point. Figure 9.11 graphically compares the melting

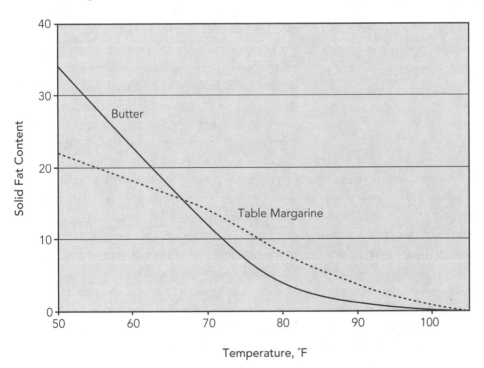

Figure 9.11 Melting curves for butter and table margarine

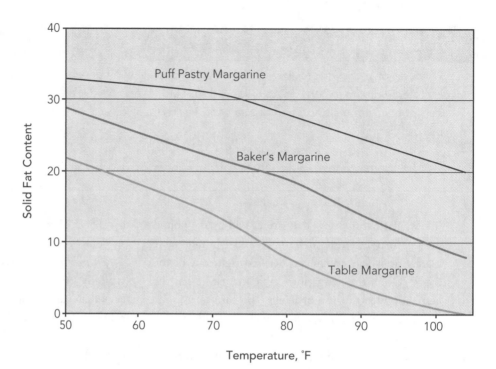

Figure 9.12 Melting curves for puff pastry, baker's, and table margarines

behavior of butter and table margarine. Notice that both are completely melted by body heat, but that butter has a much steeper curve than margarine; that is, butter melts faster. This is partly what gives butter a more pleasant mouthfeel than table margarine.

Figure 9.12 compares the melting behavior of three different margarines. Notice that the puff pastry margarine has the most solid fat over the entire range of temperatures, from room temperature (70°F/21°C) to above body temperature (100°F/38°C). The chewy, waxy mouthfeel of puff pastry margarine can be explained by the high percentage of solid fat crystals (over 20 percent) that still remains at body temperature.

Shortenings

The main difference between shortening and margarine is that shortening is 100 percent fat and contains no water. Most shortenings are also white and bland tasting, but some are butter flavored and colored with beta-carotene or another yellow color. Shortenings range in consistency from creamy liquid to solid flakes.

Shortening was originally developed as a replacement for lard. Like margarine, shortenings are designer fats, so many types are available to the baker and pastry chef. The three main types of shortenings used in the bakeshop are all-purpose shortening, high-ratio plastic shortening, and high-ratio liquid shortening. Other shortenings are available, too, including ones designed specifically for frying; for the softest, lightest icings; for the flakiest pastries; or for breads with a soft crumb and long shelf life (delayed staling).

Classifying Shortening *All-purpose (AP) shortening* contains no added emulsifiers. It contains about 10 percent air trapped in the fat, important for leavening, and is designed for use in products where it is creamed, such as cookies, or where it is rubbed into flour, such as pie dough and biscuits. Through hydrogenation, blending, or other processes, AP shortening is made plastic and workable over a wide temperature range, making it easier than butter to cream or otherwise work. Final melting point varies with the brand, but it is typically anywhere from 110° to 120°F (43°–50°C).

Although all-purpose shortening appears solid at room temperature, it contains a large amount of liquid oil. In fact, AP shortening can be up to 80 percent liquid oil. The remaining 20 percent or so consists of a honeycomb network of tiny solid fat crystals that give AP shortening its soft solid consistency. The solid fat crystals in AP shortening are tiny beta prime crystals, which not only are effective at trapping oil, but also allow the best incorporation of air during creaming.

As with margarines, the most common fats used in manufacturing all-purpose shortenings are soybean oil and palm oils. Soybean oil, and other fats that tend to form large, coarse beta crystals, must be blended with a small amount of another fat that forms tiny beta prime crystals, to initiate proper fat crystallization. Fats that tend to form these desirable beta prime crystals include palm oil and hydrogenated cottonseed oil.

AP and other plastic shortenings look different if allowed to melt and resolidify. Instead of being smooth, creamy, and white, resolidified shortening appears hard, translucent, and somewhat gritty, with liquid oil sometimes pooling around pockets of hardened fat. This is the first clue that things have changed. In fact, the small beta prime crystals that formed the original honeycomb network have not reformed. Instead much larger, more stable beta crystals have formed. The shortening will no longer cream well, since only small fat crystals can stabilize small air bubbles in creamed shortening and in cake batters. Melted and rehardened shortening is acceptable for use in muffins made with melted fat, however, or for frying.

Fried pastries, such as doughnuts and beignets, will be less greasy when fried in shortening than when fried in oil. However, AP shortening contains saturated fat, so there is a nutritional downside to using it for frying. Many AP shortenings contain small amounts of antifoaming agent, to prevent fat from foaming excessively in a fryer, and to prevent them from degrading too quickly. An example of an antifoaming agent is dimethylpolysiloxane, a silicone additive added to many fats and oils designed for frying and sautéing.

HELPFUL HINT

To keep your frying fat from degrading too quickly, lower its temperature and cover it when not in use. This minimizes exposure to damaging heat and ultraviolet (UV) light. Also, filter the fat frequently to remove bits of food. Because fresh fat lacks a "fried food" flavor, avoid replacing used fat with completely new fat. Instead, top off old fat in the fryer with fresh fat, as needed. When the fat does darken or thicken excessively, however, replace it with fresh fat, or your food will taste and feel heavy and greasy.

High-ratio plastic shortening looks and feels like all-purpose shortening, but it has emulsifiers added. The most common emulsifiers added to high-ratio shortenings are mono- and diglycerides. High-ratio shortenings—sometimes called *emulsified* or *cake and icing shortenings*—are best used in cakes, icings, and fillings, or in any product that includes a relatively high amount of liquid or air. They are also used in breads and other baked goods, where the emulsifiers soften the crumb and help delay staling. Emulsified shortenings should never be used in frying, because the emulsifiers break down and smoke under high heat. While high-ratio plastic shortening can be used in pie dough, there is no advantage to this. Pie dough contains very little liquid or air and it has little tendency to stale, so emulsifiers are unnecessary. In fact, emulsifiers assist the fat in blending into the flour, so it can be difficult making flaky pie crusts with emulsified shortenings.

The emulsifiers in high-ratio shortenings provide plain icings with a lighter, fluffier texture that holds more liquid ingredients without breaking (eggs provide the same function in richer buttercreams). These same emulsifiers help to distribute fat and air bubbles more evenly throughout cake batters. This means that cakes and other baked goods made with high-ratio shortenings are generally lighter, more tender, have a finer crumb, and stale more slowly than those made with butter or AP shortening.

High-ratio liquid shortening, like high-ratio plastic shortening, has added emulsifiers. The high level of emulsifiers in high-ratio liquid shortening, however, is extremely effective at incorporating and holding air into batters as they are whipped, rather than into shortening that is creamed. High-ratio liquid shortening is much less solid than high-ratio plastic shortenings, so it is lower in saturated fat. While it is fluid and can be poured, it does contain small amounts of important solid fat crystals, giving it an opaque, creamy look at room temperature.

High-ratio liquid shortening is primarily used in liquid shortening cakes, where it provides by far the highest volume, most moistness, most tender crumb, and the longest shelf life of any fat or oil. High-ratio liquid shortenings are so effective at moistening and tenderizing that manufacturers often recommend that the amount of shortening be reduced by about 20 percent when switching from a plastic shortening to a liquid one.

High-ratio liquid shortenings are extremely effective at incorporating air into cake batters. This, of course, makes for a lighter, more tender product, but it does more. It lowers costs, and it has changed the way cakes are made in this country. Instead of creaming shortening

Procter & Gamble first added emulsifiers to shortenings in the 1930s. Cakes made with these new shortenings were moister, more tender, and had a finer crumb and longer shelf life because of the emulsifiers.

Cake batters made with emulsified shortenings also held a higher ratio of water to flour because emulsifiers are effective at holding oil and water together. Since the batters held more water, they also held more sugar, which dissolves in water. A higher ratio of water and sugar meant that the ability of emulsified shortenings to increase moistness, tenderness, and shelf life went well beyond the abilities of the emulsifiers themselves. It also meant that the cost of making cakes was lowered, since water and sugar are both inexpensive ingredients. No wonder the importance of the higher ratio of water and sugar in cake was reflected in the name of the shortening itself.

---

as a first step in cake making, liquid shortening cake batters are mixed in a simple one-step process.

Substituting Between Shortening and Butter

Recall that shortening and lard are 100 percent fat, while butter and margarine are only 80 percent or so fat. In many formulas, one fat can be substituted directly for another, one for one. Products made with the 80 percent fat will be slightly different in texture—generally less moist and tender—and they will have the characteristic flavor of the fat. While it is generally acceptable to substitute one plastic fat for another, oils should be used only in recipes developed for their use.

Because a one-for-one substitution of shortening and butter, for example, changes the amount of fat in a product by about 20 percent, it is sometimes desirable to calculate and adjust the amount of fat and liquid when making these changes. Starting guidelines for changing between butter (or margarine) and shortening (or lard) are as follows.

- *To substitute butter for shortening:* Divide the weight of shortening by 0.80 to determine the weight of butter to use. Reduce the amount of liquid (milk or water) by the difference between the two. For example, for 1 pound (16 ounces) of shortening, use 20 ounces of butter and reduce the amount of liquid by 4 ounces. For 500 grams of shortening, use 625 grams of butter and reduce the amount of liquid by 125 grams.

- *To substitute shortening for butter:* Multiply the weight of butter by 0.80 to determine the weight of shortening to use. Increase the amount of liquid by the difference between the two. For example, for 1 pound of butter, use 12.75 ounces of shortening and increase the amount of liquid by 3.25 ounces. For 500 grams of butter, use 400 grams of shortening and increase the amount of liquid by 100 grams.

Oil

Even though it is liquid, oil contains no water; it is 100 percent fat, high in monounsaturated and polyunsaturated fatty acids that do not easily solidify. Oil used in the bakeshop is sometimes called *vegetable oil* because it is extracted from a vegetable source such as soybeans or cottonseed. Vegetable oils are sometimes labeled "salad oils" if they are appropriate for use in salad dressings (that is, when they do not become cloudy or solidify when refrigerated). The most common vegetable oil worldwide is soybean oil, but others are available, including corn, canola, sunflower, and peanut. While these oils vary slightly in flavor and color, they can be used interchangeably in baking.

Oil is the only common lipid that does not contribute to leavening in baked goods. Unlike plastic fats, oil does not contain trapped air or water. Unlike high-ratio liquid shortenings, it does not contain emulsifiers that allow batters to trap and hold large volumes of air. In fact, oils can destabilize the aeration of cake batters, especially when they contain antifoaming agents, which is generally the case with oils designed for frying.

Oil is used in quick breads, muffins, and chiffon cake for a distinctively moist yet dense, coarse crumb. Oil is also sometimes used in pie crusts, especially the bottom crusts of juicy pies. Oil crusts are not flaky. While they are not flaky, crusts made with oil do not absorb as much water when they are mixed, so they bake up tender. Once baked, they are resistant to soaking up wet, juicy fillings. They do not become soggy or

When salad oil is refrigerated, it remains crystal clear and liquid, even when fully chilled. Do the same with olive oil and it becomes cloudy and hardens as some of its fatty acids crystallize. That is because salad oils have been winterized while most olive oils have not.

Winterizing is a process in which oil is stored at cold temperatures to allow higher-melting triglycerides to crystallize. The chilled oil is filtered to physically remove these solid fat crystals. What is left is salad oil, which consists of triglycerides that stay liquid at cold temperatures.

toughen, as happens with flaky bottom crusts. Mealy pie crusts also do not splinter like flaky crusts, so they cut more cleanly.

Olive Oil Olive oil is the most expensive of all oils used in the bakeshop. It can be refined like other oils to be mild flavored and light in color, but then it would lack its attractive green-gold color and fruity flavor. Refined olive oil is sometimes labeled "*light*" in the United States. Light olive oil is light in color and flavor only; olive oil, refined or not, has the same amount of fat (100 percent) and the same number of calories as any oil. Because olive oil is high in desirable monounsaturated fatty acids, it is often considered the fat of choice for a healthful diet.

Olive oil is most often sold unrefined, or virgin. Most countries follow the grades set by the International Olive Oil Council (IOOC) in defining olive oil products. Virgin olive oil is squeezed and separated from crushed olives without the use of heat and without altering the natural oil in any way. While virgin olive oil is commonly described as cold pressed, today virgin olive oil is not so much pressed as it is centrifuged or spun to separate it out.

The quality of virgin olive oil is defined by the quality of its flavor and by the amount of free fatty acids present in the oil. Free fatty acids are fatty acids that are not part of a triglyceride molecule. The amount of free fatty acids is an indication of the level of care taken in handling and processing the olives. Extra virgin olive oil is the highest-quality virgin olive oil, with a fine, fruity aroma and the lowest level of free fatty acids.

Within the world of extra virgin olive oils, there is a wide range of flavor characteristics and prices. In all cases, however, extra virgin olive oils become bitter and lose their fine flavor when they are exposed to high heat. Extra virgin olive oils are best used where there is minimal heat exposure. For applications that involve high heat, less expensive virgin or refined olive oil may be more appropriate. Olive oil is most commonly used in savory flatbreads, focaccia, pizza, and yeast-raised doughs, but it also shows up in regional Mediterranean specialty desserts.

Emulsifiers

Emulsifiers have been mentioned throughout this chapter and in previous chapters, and many are listed by name in Table 9.1. From this table, it is evident that emulsifiers provide a wide range of functions in baked goods. Because they are so important in baking, they deserve more consideration.

In all cases, emulsifiers function by interacting with other ingredients. For example, emulsifiers interact with fats and oils, helping to disperse them more evenly throughout batters and doughs. Better distribution of fats means more tender, better-textured baked goods. Emulsifiers also stabilize air bubbles creamed into shortening or whipped into liquid batters, and they keep air bubbles evenly dispersed throughout the batter during baking (Figure 9.13).

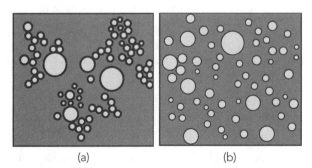

(a)   (b)

Figure 9.13 Emulsifiers help disperse air throughout cake batter. **(a)** Butter without added emulsifier **(b)** Butter with added emulsifier

What Do Emulsifiers Look Like?

While some emulsifiers have pretty complicated molecular structures, mono- and diglycerides, the emulsifiers added to high-ratio shortenings, have relatively simple structures. Mono- and diglycerides consist of a mixture of molecules of monoglycerides and molecules of diglycerides. *Mono* means one and *di* means two. Instead of having three fatty acids, like triglycerides (fats and oils), monoglycerides have one fatty acid (FA) attached to glycerol, and diglycerides have two. The fatty acid part of the molecule is *lipophilic*; that is, it is attracted to fats, oils, and air, while the rest of the molecule is attracted to water (*hydrophilic*).

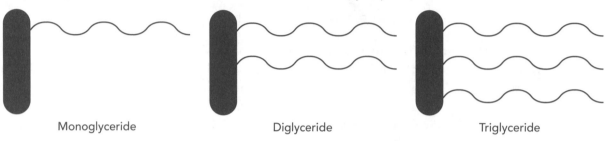

Monoglyceride   Diglyceride   Triglyceride

Emulsifiers are able to stabilize both oil droplets and air bubbles because part of the molecule is attracted to water, while the rest of the molecule is repelled by it. The part of the molecule that is attracted to water dissolves in the water, milk, and eggs that make up the bulk of batters and doughs. The part of the molecule that is repelled by water gravitates towards oil droplets and air bubbles. That is why emulsifiers situate themselves around oil droplets and air bubbles, keeping the oil droplets and air bubbles intact and helping to disperse them throughout batters and doughs. By surrounding each oil droplet, emulsifiers seal off the oil so it can't interfere with aeration of cake batter. Figure 9.14 shows how molecules of emulsifiers orient themselves so that the water-loving (hydrophilic) head of the molecule dissolves in liquid batter, while the fat-loving (lipophilic) tail dissolves in oil droplets or juts into air bubbles. Because emulsifiers often situate themselves at the surfaces of liquids or air bubbles, they are sometimes called *surfactants*.

Emulsifiers interact with proteins, improving their strength and flexibility so they stretch without breaking. Stronger, more flexible proteins in cake batters hold air exceptionally well, which means better-textured baked goods. Emulsifiers interact with starch molecules, preventing them from retrograding or bonding with one another, which is a primary cause of staling. This, too, translates to better-textured baked goods.

Emulsifiers can be purchased separately and added with fats to batters and doughs; however, it is not

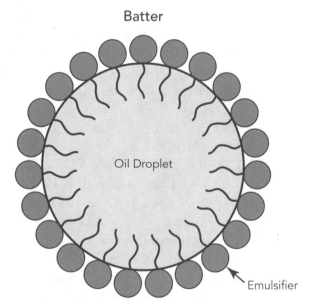

Batter

Oil Droplet

Emulsifier

Figure 9.14 Emulsifiers orient themselves around oil droplets and air bubbles, so that the water-loving head of the molecule dissolves in liquid batter, while the fat-loving tail sticks into oil droplets and air bubbles.

common for bakers and pastry chefs to do so. Instead, the main sources of emulsifiers in the bakeshop include:

- Dough conditioners used in yeast-raised doughs
- High-ratio shortenings
- Dairy ingredients and egg yolks, which naturally contain complex mixtures of emulsifiers, lecithin being the best known

Functions of Fats, Oils, and Emulsifiers

Main Functions

Providing Tenderness Fats, oils, and emulsifiers tenderize by coating structure builders—gluten proteins, egg proteins, and starch granules—and preventing them from hydrating and forming structure. Tenderness is the opposite of toughness. A tender product is easy to break, chew, squeeze, or crumble because it lacks a strong structure.

Tenderness is usually considered a good thing. After all, baked goods that are tender are pleasantly easy to bite. Tenderizers, however, must be balanced with structure builders (tougheners). Too much tenderness is undesirable because overly tender products collapse, break apart, or are excessively crumbly or mealy.

Another name for tenderness is *shortness*. Lipids literally shorten gluten strands by interfering with the formation of a large, extended gluten network. This is reflected in the shorter (crumbly or mealy) texture of baked goods that are high in fat, especially if they are also low in moisture. Shortbread cookies, for example, have a characteristically crumbly texture because they are both high in fat and low in moisture. The ability of fats to tenderize by shortening gluten strands is so important that when all-purpose shortening was first created, it was called shortening for its effectiveness at shortening gluten strands. While all-purpose shortening is named for this ability to provide shortness, all fats, oils, and emulsifiers serve this function. Not all lipids provide shortness (tenderness) to the same degree, however.

Pound for pound, butter and margarine, having only 80 percent fat (and containing water besides), tenderize less effectively than shortening and lard, which contain 100 percent fat. This is true unless formulas are adjusted when converting between fats, as described earlier.

The softer or more fluid the fat, the more easily it mixes into batters and doughs, coating flour particles and egg proteins. In other words, all else being equal, the softer or more fluid the fat, the more it tenderizes. This explains why pie crust made with oil is tender, short, and mealy. It also partly explains why plastic fats that are softened by creaming tenderize better than ones not creamed. Finally, it explains why highly saturated, very hard cocoa butter in chocolate does little to tenderize baked goods.

In the case of pie pastry dough and certain other products, tenderness increases the more fat is worked into flour before water is added. The more it is incorporated, the smaller the piece size of the fat, and the more it coats structure-building flour particles. This is why French pie crust (*pâte brisée*) is short and mealy. French chefs achieve this texture through *fraisage*, a process in which fat and flour are kneaded with the heel of the hand until they are thoroughly blended.

Emulsifiers, like those added to high-ratio shortenings, are extremely effective at providing tenderness. They accomplish this in at least two ways. First, emulsifiers help fats and oils disperse throughout baked goods, so the fats and oils coat structure builders more completely. Second, emulsifiers themselves are extremely effective at coating structure builders. In fact, the amount of fat in baked goods can be reduced when emulsifiers are added. Check the labels of low-fat baked goods and you will see that many are high in emulsifiers such as mono- and diglycerides.

> **HELPFUL HINT**
>
> *For tender, cake-like muffins, use a plastic fat and cream it to lighten. For firm, dense yet moist muffins, use liquid oil or melted fat, lightly blended into dry ingredients (muffin method; see Table 3.1).*

Finally, the more leavening provided by the fat, the more it tenderizes, because leavening stretches and thins cell walls, weakening them. This is why oil, which does not leaven, might excel at tenderizing pie pastry, but it makes cakes and muffins that are firm, because they are dense.

In summary, the shortening or tenderizing abilities of fats depend on the following:

- The amount present; the more fat, oil, or emulsifier, the more tenderizing
- How soft and fluid it is; the more soft and fluid the fat, the more tenderizing
- Piece size; the smaller the piece size of the fat (from more mixing) or the better it is distributed through the batter or dough, the more tenderizing
- The presence of emulsifiers, such as mono- and diglycerides
- The ability of the fat, oil, or emulsifier to leaven

Providing Flakiness in Pastries *Flakiness* refers to the tendency of pastry to form thin, flat, often crisp layers. Flakiness requires that flattened chunks of solid fat separate bits of dough. Flaky pastries include those in which fat is repeatedly rolled and folded (laminated) with dough, as in puff pastry, croissant, and Danish pastry doughs. It also includes pastries in which chunks of fat are cut into dough, as in pie dough (Figure 9.15) and blitz puff pastry. Whether the fat is layered with dough or remains as chunks, the later the fat melts in the oven, the greater the flakiness and also the leavening.

With pie pastry and blitz puff pastry doughs, to keep layers distinct, chunks of fat should be kept large. If using butter in a warm bakeshop, be sure the butter is slightly chilled yet still workable, so it won't blend into the dough. Whenever possible, work the fat into the dough with your fingertips instead of using a mixer, since mixers quickly overblend fat with flour. Be sure water added is chilled, so it doesn't melt the fat, and

Figure 9.15 Pastry made with chunks of solid fat is flaky, top, while pastry made with oil is mealy, bottom.

The Rise of Puff Pastry

Puff pastry consists of many discrete and intact layers of dough separated by equally discrete and intact layers of plastic fat. When heated in the oven, the layers of fat melt. As temperatures rise, water in the dough evaporates into steam, and the steam expands into the gaps left by the melted fat. The melted fat prevents the steam from escaping, at least at first, and the dough layers push apart from steam pressure. Finally, structure sets in the dough layers, and the result is flaky puff pastry.

Notice that the leavening occurs in the gaps between the dough layers; the dough itself remains relatively unleavened. Wherever dough layers touch, however, leavening and flakiness is reduced. This can happen inadvertently when fat is unevenly rolled between the dough, when the dough tears, or when it is cut with a dull tool or while soft. To make it easier to roll fat evenly, be sure that the fat is plastic and workable and matches the firmness of the dough. If using butter, it helps to have it slightly chilled, and to blend it with a small amount of flour before rolling. To prevent dough from tearing, use a relatively strong flour, but be sure to let the dough relax (rest) between folds.

Sometimes dough is intentionally docked, or pierced, to prevent excessive puffing. Puff pastry dough is also sometimes pressed on its edges, to keep layers from flaking off completely. Figure 9.16 shows puff pastry that is flaky through the center, but pressed along its edges.

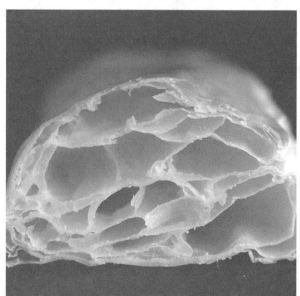

Figure 9.16 Puff pastry rises when water in dough evaporates into steam, expanding into gaps between dough layers. Flakiness is inhibited along the pressed edges of this puff pastry.

How to Make Flaky Pie Crust Tender

The perfect pie crust is both tender and flaky. It is tender enough to bite easily, and it is also flaky, so that distinct layers of dough are clearly visible. To create pie crust that is both tender and flaky, keep the chunks of fat large for flakiness, and use other means besides piece size to achieve tenderness. For example, to maximize tenderness, be sure the protein content in the flour is low, and keep the amount of flour dusted on the work surface to a minimum. Increase the amount of fat in the formula, if necessary, and be sure only a minimum amount of water is added. Do not overwork the dough once water is added, and if necessary, chill the dough for several hours or overnight, to allow water to passively migrate throughout dough.

chill the dough before rolling. Notice how flakiness can be at odds with tenderness, which is greatest when fat is worked well into the dough.

In summary, the ability of fats to provide flakiness depends on the following:

- How solid it is: in general, the more solid the fat and the higher its melting point, the more flakiness
- Piece size: the larger the piece size of the fat, the more flakiness

Assisting in Leavening   As with eggs, fats help incorporate air into baked goods and, in doing so, contribute to leavening and additional tenderizing. Fats are not leaveners themselves—air, steam, and carbon dioxide are the leaveners—but fats play an important role in the leavening process. The four main ways that fats assist in leavening have been discussed elsewhere in this chapter but are recapped here.

The leavening that occurs in flaky pastries was just discussed, when layers of solid fat create gaps upon melting, gaps that expand from steam pressure. Additionally, all plastic fats contain some entrapped air. The air is distributed throughout the fat as very tiny bubbles. Some fats—butter and margarine—contain water droplets as well. Both air bubbles and water droplets contribute to leavening in baked goods, and this is the second way that fats assist with leavening.

Additional air bubbles are incorporated into plastic fats when they are creamed. The air bubbles are surrounded and protected by many tiny solid fat crystals that keep the bubbles intact. Creaming is facilitated when sharp-edge sugar crystals are added to the fat as it is mixed. The sugar must be crystalline; liquid syrups and round-edged powdered sugar are not effective in adding air bubbles. Cookies and cakes made by the creaming method rely on plastic fats for the bulk of

> **HELPFUL HINT**
>
> *When creaming butter or shortening for cookies, be sure not to overmix. For dense cookies that hold their shape, blend fat and sugar on low speed, just to a smooth paste. For light, tender, crumbly cookies that spread thin, cream the fat and sugar on medium speed until light.*

their volume and fine crumb. This is true even when baking powder is added.

The fourth way for fats to assist in leavening is related to the ability of certain emulsifiers to trap and hold large volumes of air. Some emulsifiers function during creaming, working with plastic fats to trap air bubbles, keeping them small, intact, and well-dispersed throughout the fat and, later, the batter or dough. Other emulsifiers work in liquid systems, such as liquid shortening cake batters. These emulsifiers function partly by surrounding oil droplets, sealing them off. This way, the proteins in eggs can whip more easily. High-ratio liquid shortening cakes rely on this means of leavening for their light, airy texture.

In summary, the four main ways that fats contribute to leavening in baked goods are as follows:

- By providing gaps and spaces upon melting, gaps where steam can expand and leaven flaky pastries
- By the air and water trapped in plastic fats, which get incorporated into batters and doughs
- Through the incorporation of additional air during the creaming of plastic fats
- Through the assistance of emulsifiers in high-ratio shortenings

Contributing Moistness   Moistness is a characteristic of all fluid ingredients because moistness is the sensation of something being liquid. Both moisture (water) and liquid oil provide moistness. Notice the distinction made between moistness and moisture. Liquid oil provides moistness but not moisture. Butter, which contains moisture, usually contributes less moistness than oil does.

Moistness is not the same as tenderness, but the two can be related. Often, anything that is moist is also tender. However, chewy foods are moist but not tender, and crisp, crumbly cookies are tender without being moist.

Not all fats contribute significantly to moistness; only those, like oil, that are fluid at body temperature do. Emulsifiers also contribute to moistness. Interestingly, fats often contribute more moistness to baked goods than does water. This is probably because much of the water in baked goods is either driven off or becomes tightly bound to proteins and starches.

In summary, the moistening ability of fats depends on the following:

- How fluid it is; the more fluid the fat at body temperature, the more moistening
- The presence of emulsifiers, such as mono- and diglycerides

Preventing Staling Lipids—especially emulsifiers such as mono- and diglycerides in high-ratio shortenings—interfere with the process of retrogradation of gelatinized starch. One way that lipids prevent the retrogradation of starch is by preventing starch granules from gelatinizing in the first place. Lipids also bond directly with starch molecules so that they cannot bond with each other. Since starch retrogradation is a major cause of staling in baked goods, lipids prevent the hard, dry, crumbly texture and loss of flavor associated with staling.

Contributing Flavor A major reason for using butter is for its unsurpassed flavor. Other fats that contribute a distinct flavor include lard, olive oil, and margarine. While margarine does not have the fine flavor of butter, it can be an acceptable substitute in certain situations.

Even neutral fats contribute to flavor because all fats add a certain richness. And, in the case of fried foods, desirable fried flavor comes from the breakdown of fats and oils exposed to high heat.

Additional Functions

Contributing Color Some fats—butter and margarine, in particular—provide a distinct golden yellow color to baked goods. Fats that contain milk solids (butter and certain margarines) undergo Maillard browning on the surfaces of baked goods, contributing further to color. All fats increase the rate of heating of baked goods, and in doing so allow for faster browning. This is especially noticeable when comparing low-fat baked goods to regular baked goods. The low-fat baked goods inevitably are paler in color.

Providing a Fine Crumb to Baked Goods Plastic fats and emulsifiers provide a finer, less coarse crumb to baked goods. There are probably several reasons for this, including the ability of plastic fats and emulsifiers to allow the incorporation of many tiny air cells into batters and doughs.

Adding Creaminess to Sauces, Custards, Confections, and Frozen Desserts Many sauces, confections, and frozen desserts are emulsions of liquid fat droplets in milk or another liquid. For example, vanilla custard sauce, ganache, and ice cream are all emulsions. The microscopic droplets of liquid fat are like very tiny balls that roll over the tongue, giving the perception of a rich, creamy texture.

Conducting Heat Fats and oils conduct heat from the oven, pan, or fryer directly to food. Fats and oils can be heated to a much higher temperature than water—350°F (177°C), compared to 212°F (100°C)—before they evaporate or break down. This high heat allows for the formation of a dry, crisp, brown crust in deep-fried foods and often in baking.

Providing Bulk and Substance to Icings and Fillings Solid fat crystals provide bulk and substance to icings, fillings, and certain other products. To understand what this means, consider that icings contain anywhere from 30 to 50 percent solid fat. Without this solid fat, icings would consist of loose sugar crystals or of crystals dissolved or suspended in egg white or another liquid.

While fats are not considered structure builders in baked goods (remember, the more fat, the more tender the baked good), in icings and other products that contain solid fat, the solid crystals do provide substance. This substance defines the size and shape of these products. In this sense, solid fat does provide a type of structure.

Promoting Smoothness in Confections   Fats, oils, and emulsifiers interfere with sugar crystallization, providing a desirable smoothness to confections.

Blending Flavors and Masking Off Flavors   When fats are removed from baked goods, flavors become disjointed and the baked good doesn't taste as rich and full flavored. Fats probably affect taste perception because many flavors dissolve in them.

Acting as a Release Agent   Lipids, either applied to grease the pan or added to a formula, help ensure that baked foods are easily removed from their pans. The emulsifier lecithin is extremely effective at this and is a major ingredient in most pan release sprays. Not surprisingly, low-fat baked goods tend to stick to pans and paper liners, so the use of pan release sprays is particularly important with these products.

Increasing the Softness and Extensibility of Doughs   Lipids "lubricate" particles by coating them so they slide past each other more easily. In particular, lipids lubricate gluten strands, making them softer, more flexible, and less likely to break as they stretch. This is advantageous while mixing doughs, since it reduces friction, making it easier to mix without generating excessive heat. It is also advantageous during yeast fermentation since it allows

for a higher volume. Certain emulsifiers in particular are used for this purpose, including sodium stearoyl-2-lactylate and DATEM. You will often see one or both of these emulsifiers in dough conditioners for use in yeast doughs.

Water and other moisteners also provide a certain amount of lubrication and softening to doughs. Both water and lipids are sometimes called *plasticizers* because they make doughs softer and more workable—that is, more plastic. When the amount of lipids added to batter or dough is increased, often the amount of water and other moisteners must be reduced to maintain the proper consistency of the batter or dough. Likewise, when the amount of lipids is reduced, the amount of other moisteners must be increased accordingly.

Thinning Out Melted Chocolates and Couvertures   Fats, oils, and emulsifiers, especially lecithin, coat and lubricate solid particles in melted chocolates and couvertures, allowing the particles to slide past each other more easily. This thins the consistency of the coating, allowing it to be applied in a thin, even layer over pastries and confections. Pastry chefs typically use cocoa butter to thin out chocolate couvertures because of its pleasing mouthfeel. Melted butter and other fats can be used, but the chocolate, when cooled, will not harden as well and will have less snap.

Increasing Spread in Cookies   Fats, oils, and emulsifiers coat and lubricate solid particles in cookie doughs, reducing mixing time and thinning the doughs. This allows for more spread when the cookie bakes. The more fat, usually the more spread, and the more liquid the fat, the more spread.

HELPFUL HINT

When making pie pastry dough, adjust the amount of water according to how the fat is added. For example, when fat is worked into the flour until it forms small cornmeal-size pieces, the flour particles become well-lubricated by the fat. Less water is needed to form a soft, workable dough than when the fat is kept in larger chunks. This is why formulas for mealy pâte brisée contain less water than formulas for flaky pie crusts.

HELPFUL HINT

To reduce excessive spreading and thinning of cookies during baking, be sure the dough is well-chilled and the sheet pans are not warm before baking. This is especially important when cookie dough contains butter, which melts easily.

Storage and Handling

Two properties of fats that must be protected during storage are flavor and texture (plasticity). Fats and oils develop off flavors primarily from three sources: oxidative rancidity, which occurs with exposure to heat, light, air, and metal catalysts; bacterial spoilage, which occurs only in butter and those margarines that contain milk solids; and absorption of odors from the bakeshop.

The more unsaturated a fatty acid, the faster it will oxidize and develop a stale, rancid flavor. Expect oils that are relatively high in polyunsaturated fatty acids (such as flaxseed oil) to oxidize many times faster than oils that are higher in monounsaturated fatty acids (such as olive oil). Likewise, expect most plastic fats, which are typically low in unsaturated fatty acids, to oxidize slowest of all. However, because oilseeds today are bred and processed in ways that affect the oil's stability, it is no longer possible to generalize and say, for example, that all soybean oils are highly susceptible to oxidation (although years ago that was the case). No matter the fat or oil, however, all should be stored properly to minimize oxidative rancidity. This means covering them when not in use and storing them in a cool, dark place.

Fats and oils sometimes contain antioxidants to slow oxidative rancidity. Examples of antioxidants include

HELPFUL HINT

An easy way to predict how quickly a fat or oil will oxidize is to consider its fatty acid profile. Specifically, the higher it is in polyunsaturated fatty acids, the faster the fat or oil will oxidize and produce rancid off flavors. You can find this information for most common fats and oils in Figure 9.6.

BHA, BHT, TBHQ, and vitamin E (tocopherols). Microbial spoilage is slowed by the addition of antimicrobial agents, including sodium benzoate and potassium sorbate, salt, or friendly lactic acid bacteria, as when cream is cultured before use in butter.

To prevent changes in flavor and texture, cover the fat or oil tightly. This will keep out moisture, air, light, and strong odors. It is acceptable to store fats and oils in a cool, dry place, but butter must be stored at 40°F (4°C) or below. Do not expose fats to light, and do not allow plastic fats to melt. Melting changes the crystalline structure of fats, altering their texture and ability to cream. It also reduces the amount of air in fat, lowering its ability to assist in leavening. As with all ingredients, follow the FIFO (first in, first out) system to rotate stock.

Questions for Review

1   What is a triglyceride? What is a fatty acid?

2   What is the difference between the chemical structure of a saturated fatty acid and an unsaturated fatty acid? Which is more likely to increase risk of coronary heart disease? Which are liquid oils high in?

3   Which oils are solid at room temperature? What makes them solid at room temperature, when most oils are liquid?

4   Which of the following are solid because they are naturally high in saturated fatty acids, and which must be hydrogenated or otherwise treated to make them solid: butter, soy margarine, palm oil shortening, lard?

5   Draw the process of hydrogenation, starting with an unsaturated fatty acid. Provide two reasons why fats and oils are hydrogenated.

6   Why might liquid oils oxidize faster than solid fats?

7   Why might vegetable or salad oil be partially hydrogenated?

8   How would you define a plastic fat? Which of the following fats are plastic at room temperature (70°F/21°C): vegetable oil, high-ratio liquid shortening, all-purpose shortening, butter, lard, cocoa butter?

9   How does hydrogenation affect the healthfulness of fat?

10 Where are trans fatty acids typically found in our food supply? Why are trans fats considered undesirable?

11 What is meant by "low-lin vegetable oil"? What is meant by "high-oleic oil"? What is the main advantage of these two oils?

12 Name three ways that shortening and margarine processors are able to manufacture trans fat–free plastic shortenings.

13 Why might palm oil–based shortenings cream differently than partially hydrogenated soybean shortenings? What can you do to improve its ability to cream properly?

14 Which of the following fats and oils are considered 100 percent fat: vegetable oil, high-ratio liquid shortening, all-purpose shortening, butter, margarine, high-ratio plastic shortening, lard? Which are only around 80 percent fat? Which contain air? Which contain water?

15 What are the two main advantages of using butter in baked goods? That is, what does butter excel at compared with other fats? What are four disadvantages?

16 How do European butters differ from North American butters in butterfat content?

17 Classify the two main types of butters by the type of cream used in their production. Which is the most common in North America? Which is common in Europe?

18 What does it mean to say that lard is not kosher and not halal?

19 What is the advantage of the coarse, grainy texture of unmodified lard?

20 What are the advantages of margarine over butter?

21 List the four main types of margarines. In what way are they different from each other? What are the main uses for each, and why?

22 When does margarine not require refrigeration?

23 Will margarine with the same final melting point as butter have as desirable a mouthfeel? Why or why not?

24 What is the main difference between margarines and shortenings?

25 What is in high-ratio shortening that is not in all-purpose shortening?

26 Which—all-purpose or high-ratio plastic shortening—is the best choice for each of the following: light, fluffy icing; pie dough; baking powder biscuits; cookies; fine-textured light cake.

27 What are two differences between a high-ratio plastic shortening and a liquid one?

28 Which baked goods are traditionally made with liquid oil?

29 Why is oil sometimes used instead of shortening or butter for the bottom crusts of juicy pies?

30 Why will muffins made with oil be denser than those made with all-purpose shortening?

31 What are mono- and diglycerides and where are they found?

32 Why is too much tenderness in baked goods undesirable?

33 What are the two main ways that emulsifiers contribute to tenderness in baked goods?

34 Why does oil result in a more tender but less flaky pie crust than plastic shortening? Why might oil result in a less tender cake than shortening?

35 What is the difference between moistness and tenderness?

36 Why might low-fat baked goods bake up paler than regular baked goods?

37 What is oxidative rancidity? How should fats and oils be stored, to delay rancidity?

38 What do antioxidants prevent in fats and oils? Name two antioxidants.

Questions for Discussion

1 List the pros and cons of local communities banning trans fats from use in restaurants and bakeshops.

2 Besides being more tender, what else is different about a cake made with high-ratio liquid shortening from one made with other fats, such as an AP shortening?

3 Describe three reasons why butter might give you a less tender cake than a high-ratio shortening. In answering this question, assume formulas for each cake are identical except for the type of fat.

4 How can you tell that the following ingredient label is for margarine and not shortening? *Soybean oil, fully hydrogenated soybean oil, water, salt, soy lecithin, mono & diglycerides, sodium benzoate, natural flavors, beta-carotene, Vitamin A palmitate.* Would you expect the above fat to contain trans fats? Why or why not?

5 Explain how fats are involved in the leavening of each of the following products: puff pastry; cake made with high-ratio plastic shortening; cake made with high-ratio liquid shortening.

6 You have two sunflower oils with very different fatty acid profiles. One has 69 percent polyunsaturated fatty acids; the other has 9 percent. Which will oxidize and taste rancid sooner, and why?

7 A biscuit formula calls for 7 pounds 8 ounces (3.75 kilograms) of shortening, but you wish to use butter instead. It also contains 12 pounds (6.0 kilograms) water. Show your calculations for determining how much butter should be used in place of the shortening, so that the amount of fat stays the same. Also show how the amount of water added will change.

Exercises and Experiments

❶ Exercise: How to Increase Flakiness in Pie Pastry

Recall that flakiness results from dough being layered with bits of fat that melt in the oven, leaving gaps that expand from the heat. Imagine that you have a formula but the pastry is not as flaky as you wish. Explain why each of the changes listed as follows could work to increase flakiness. The first is completed for you.

1 Increase the amount of fat.

Reason: The more fat, the more layers can be formed between layers of dough.

2 Switch to a higher melting fat.

Reason: _____
_____
_____

3 Refrigerate fat before use and chill dough before rolling and shaping.

Reason: _____
_____
_____

4 Minimize the extent that the fat is worked into the dry flour.

Reason: _____
_____
_____

5 Increase oven temperature.

Reason: _____
_____
_____

6 Switch to a fat that contains water.

Reason: _____
_____
_____

❷ Exercise: How to Decrease Tenderness in Pie Pastry

Recall that tenderness in pastry is achieved primarily by minimizing the development of a strong gluten structure. Imagine that you have a formula for making pastry that is too tender; that is, that falls apart too easily. Explain why each of the changes listed as follows could work to decrease tenderness. The first is completed for you.

1　Decrease the amount of fat or increase the amount of flour.

Reason: The less fat for the amount of gluten in flour, the more gluten structure can form.

2　Switch to a higher-melting fat.

Reason: _____
_____
_____

3　Refrigerate fat before use and chill dough before rolling and shaping.

Reason: _____
_____
_____

4　Minimize the extent that the fat is worked into the dry flour.

Reason: _____
_____
_____

5　Increase the amount of water.

Reason: _____
_____
_____

6　Increase the amount of kneading and rolling.

Reason: _____
_____
_____

7　Switch to stronger flour, for example, switch some or all of the pastry flour to bread flour.

Reason: _____
_____
_____

③ Exercise: Sensory Characteristics of Different Fats and Oils

In the Results Table for this exercise, use your textbook to fill in the percent fat for each fat and oil. Next, record from its package the brand name and list of ingredients for each. Finally, use fresh samples brought to room temperature to evaluate the appearance (color, clarity) and consistency as well as the aroma of each fat and oil. Use this opportunity to identify different fats and oils from their sensory characteristics alone. Two rows are left blank, for the evaluation of additional fats and oil, if desired.

RESULTS TABLE DIFFERENT FATS AND OILS

TYPE OF FAT	PERCENT FAT	BRAND NAME	INGREDIENT STATEMENT	APPEARANCE	CONSISTENCY	AROMA
All-purpose shortening						
High-ratio plastic shortening						
High-ratio liquid shortening						
Vegetable oil						
Butter, sweet cream						
Butter, cultured cream (European or European-style)						
Margarine, regular baker's						
Margarine, roll-in or puff pastry						

(continues)

TYPE OF FAT	PERCENT FAT	BRAND NAME	INGREDIENT STATEMENT	APPEARANCE	CONSISTENCY	AROMA
Lard						
Pan spray						

Use information from your textbook and from the table above to answer the following questions. Select one from the choices in **bold** or fill in the blanks.

1 An emulsifier that is often added to high-ratio plastic shortening is actually a blend of emulsifiers called mono- and _____. This emulsifier blend **is/is not** in the high-ratio plastic shortening evaluated in this exercise. Other fats and oils that contain this emulsifier blend, if any, include the following:

_____

_____

_____

2 High-ratio liquid shortening is **more/less** solid than high-ratio plastic shortening because it is **higher/lower** in saturated fats. While it is fluid and can be poured at room temperature, it contains small amounts of solid fat crystals, giving it a **creamy and opaque/thin and clear** appearance.

3 List the ingredients that are in the high-ratio liquid shortening, then briefly list the function of each ingredient. Use Table 9.1 for assistance.

_____

_____

_____

4 An antifoaming agent that is often added to fats and oils designed for use in the fryer and for other high-heat applications is called _____.
The fats and oils that contain this antifoaming agent, if any, include the following:

_____

_____

_____

5 You want to prepare baked goods with no preservatives (preservatives include BHA, BHT, TBHQ, tocopherols, potassium sorbate, and sodium benzoate). The fats and oils that contain preservatives and therefore could not be used in preservative-free baked goods are as follows:

_____

_____

_____

6 The main differences in appearance, flavor, and mouthfeel between sweet cream butter and regular margarine are the following:

_____

_____

_____

Overall, these differences are **small/moderate/large**.

7 The main difference between the roll-in (or puff pastry) margarine and the regular margarine is in **color/flavor/mouthfeel** and can best be described as follows:

_____

_____

_____

This difference is **small/moderate/large** and it **is/is not** reflected in any differences in the ingredients listed on the labels of the two margarines.

8 Lard is sometimes hydrogenated so that _____. The lard evaluated **was/was not** hydrogenated. Compared with all-purpose shortening, lard had the following differences in appearance, texture, and flavor:

_____

_____

_____

Overall, these differences are **small/moderate/large**.

❹ Experiment: How the Type of Fat Affects the Yield and the Overall Quality of Liquid Shortening Sponge Cake

High-ratio liquid shortening can be used to make a light and airy sponge cake using a one-step mixing method. While it is usually not recommended that the method of preparation specifically designed for one fat be used for very different fats, we will do just that in this experiment. In doing so, you will experience how differences in consistency, fat content, and the presence of emulsifiers affects the function of various fats in baked goods.

Objectives

Demonstrate how the type of fat affects
- The lightness and volume of cake batter
- The moistness, tenderness, crumb structure, and lightness of cake
- The overall flavor of cake
- The overall acceptability of cake

Products Prepared

Sponge cake, liquid shortening type, made with
- High-ratio liquid shortening (control product)
- High-ratio plastic shortening
- All-purpose shortening
- Vegetable oil (without dimethylpolysiloxane or other antifoaming agent)
- Butter, unsalted, melted
- Other, if desired (olive oil, margarine, puff pastry shortening, all-purpose shortening, all-purpose vegetable oil with dimethylpolysiloxane, one-half or three-quarters the full amount of liquid shortening, mixture of butter and high-ratio liquid shortening, etc.)

Materials and Equipment

- Scale
- Sieve
- Mixer with 5-quart mixing bowl
- Wire whip attachment
- Bowl scraper
- Muffin pans (2½" or 3½"/65 or 90 mm size), two per variation
- Paper liners or pan spray
- Cake batter (see Formula), enough to make 24 or more cakes of each variation
- Size #16 (2 fl. oz./60 ml) portion-control scoop or equivalent
- Half sheet pans (optional)
- Oven thermometer
- Wooden pick (for testing)
- Clear 1-cup (250 ml) measuring cups, one for each variation (optional)
- Straight-edge (optional)
- Serrated knife
- Ruler

Formula

Sponge Cake Using Liquid Shortening

Yield: 30 or more for control product; yield will vary with other types of fat

INGREDIENT	POUND	OUNCE	GRAMS	BAKER'S PERCENTAGE
Flour, cake		10	300	100
Baking powder		0.8	24	8
Salt (1 tsp, 5 ml)		0.2	6	2
Sugar, regular granulated		13.3	400	133
Fat or oil		6	180	60
Milk		5.3	160	53
Eggs, whole		15	450	150
Total	**3**	**2.6**	**1,520**	**506**

Method of Preparation

1 Preheat oven to 350°F (220°C).

2 Have ingredients at room temperature (except melted butter; cool slightly before use), for best aeration.

3 Sift dry ingredients together three times.

4 Place milk, eggs, and fat or oil in mixing bowl; add sifted dry ingredients on top.

5 Using whip attachment on mixer, blend on low for 30 seconds. Stop and scrape whip and bowl.

6 Whip for 3 minutes on high. Stop and scrape.

7 Whip for 2 minutes on medium; do not overwhip.

8 Use batter immediately.

Procedure

1 Line muffin pans with paper liners or spray with pan spray; label with the type of fat to be used in cake.

2 Prepare cake batter using the formula for sponge cake above, or using any basic sponge cake formula designed for high-ratio liquid shortening. Prepare one batch of batter for each variation.

3 Scoop batter into prepared muffin pans using level #16 scoop (or any scoop that fills cup one-half to three-quarters full). Save excess batter.

4 If desired, place muffin pans onto half sheet pans.

5 Use an oven thermometer placed in center of oven for an initial reading of oven temperature. Record results here: _____.

6 When oven is properly preheated, place filled muffin pans in oven and set timer for 27–30 minutes.

7 Bake cakes until control product (made with high-ratio liquid shortening) is light brown, springs back when center top is lightly pressed, and wooden pick inserted into center of cake comes out clean. Remove all cakes from oven after same length of time, even though some will be paler or darker and will not have risen as high. If necessary, however, adjust bake time for oven variances and record bake time in Comments column of Results Table 1.

8 Check final oven temperature. Record results here: _____.

9 Remove cakes from hot pans and cool to room temperature.

Results

1 If desired, measure the density (weight per volume) of the batter to evaluate the relative amount of air incorporated into each variation. To measure density:
- Carefully spoon batter into tared measuring cup (8 fl. oz. or 250 ml).
- Visually check cup to confirm that no large air gaps are present.
- Level the top surface of the cup with a straight-edge.
- Weigh the amount of batter in each cup and record results in Additional Comments column of Results Table 1.

2 Scoop out excess batter using #16 scoop; discard or bake off batter. Record total number of cakes per batch in Results Table 1.

3 Examine batter; note in Additional Comments column of Results Table 1 if batter has a curdled, separated appearance or if air bubbles are rising to the surface.

4 When completely cooled, evaluate average weight of cakes from each batch, as follows:
- Measure weight of each of three typical cakes. Record results for each cake in Results Table 1.
- Calculate the average cake weight by adding the weights and dividing by 3. Record results in Results Table 1.

5 Evaluate average height as follows:
- Slice three cakes from each batch in half, being careful not to compress.
- Measure height of each of three typical cakes by placing a ruler along the flat edge at the cake's maximum height. Record results in 1/16" (1 mm) increments in Results Table 1.
- Calculate the average cake height by adding the heights and dividing by 3. Record results in Results Table 1.

6 Note in Cake Shape column of Results Table 1 whether cakes have evenly rounded tops or if they peak, flatten, or dip in center. Also note whether cakes are lopsided; that is, if one side is higher than the other.

RESULTS TABLE 1 SIZE, SHAPE, AND NUMBER OF CAKES MADE WITH DIFFERENT FATS AND OILS

TYPE OF FAT	NUMBER OF CAKES PER BATCH	WEIGHTS OF EACH OF THREE CAKES	AVERAGE WEIGHT FOR ONE CAKE	HEIGHTS OF EACH OF THREE CAKES	AVERAGE HEIGHT FOR ONE CAKE	CAKE SHAPE	ADDITIONAL COMMENTS
High-ratio liquid shortening (control product)							
High-ratio plastic shortening							
All-purpose shortening							
Vegetable oil							
Butter, melted							

7 Evaluate the sensory characteristics of completely cooled products and record evaluations in Results Table 2, which follows. Be sure to compare each in turn to the control product and consider the following:
- Crust appearance (light/dark, smooth/mottled from escaping air bubbles, etc.)
- Crumb appearance (small/large air cells, uniform/irregular air cells, tunnels, etc); also, evaluate color
- Crumb texture (tough/tender, moist/dry, spongy, crumbly, etc.)
- Overall flavor (butter, egg, sweetness, saltiness, flour taste, etc.)
- Overall acceptability, from highly unacceptable to highly acceptable, on a scale of 1 to 5
- Add any additional comments, as necessary

RESULTS TABLE 2 SENSORY CHARACTERISTICS OF SPONGE CAKES MADE WITH DIFFERENT FATS AND OILS

TYPE OF FAT	CRUST APPEARANCE	CRUMB APPEARANCE AND TEXTURE	OVERALL FLAVOR	OVERALL ACCEPTABILITY	COMMENTS
High-ratio liquid shortening (control product)					
High-ratio plastic shortening					
All-purpose shortening					
Vegetable oil					
Butter, melted					

Sources of Error

List any sources of error that might make it difficult to draw the proper conclusions from your experiment. In particular, consider any differences in ingredient and batter temperatures, how batter was mixed and handled, any difficulty in dispensing equal volumes of batter into muffin pans, and any problems with ovens.

_____

_____

_____

State what you could do differently next time to minimize or eliminate each source of error.

_____

_____

_____

Conclusions

Select one from the choices in **bold** or fill in the blanks.

1 Of the following fats, the number of cakes (the volume of batter) was greatest for the cake made with **high-ratio liquid shortening/melted butter/oil**. This is primarily because this fat contains a high amount of **antifoaming agents/emulsifiers/antioxidants** that are extremely effective at allowing cake batter to incorporate and hold in air.

2 Of the following fats, the number of cakes (the volume of batter) was lowest for the cake made with **high-ratio liquid shortening/high-ratio plastic shortening/oil**. This is partly because this fat does not contain emulsifiers, but it also **does/does not** contain leavening gases, like air or water.

3 The cakes that weighed the least **were/were not** made with the fat that produced the highest number of cakes, while the cakes that weighed the most **were/were not** made with the fat that produced the least number of cakes. Explain these results.

_____

_____

_____

4 The cakes made with all-purpose shortening **were/were not** as tender as those made with high-ratio plastic shortening. This is because the **all-purpose/high-ratio plastic shortening** contains emulsifiers that help tenderize and aerate.

5 In general, the lighter, airier cakes were **tougher/more tender** than the heavier, denser cakes. This is partly because the lighter cakes have **thicker/thinner** cell walls that are **easier/harder** to bite through.

6 While oil, being a **liquid/solid** fat, is often extremely effective at tenderizing baked goods, it is not as effective as the other fats in tenderizing this cake. This is probably because there is **more/less** aeration and leavening with oil than with the other fats, resulting in **thinner/ thicker** cell walls that are **easier/harder** to bite through.

7 The main reason for using butter instead of another fat in this cake formula is for maximizing **tenderness/moistness/flavor/leavening**.

8 Cakes made with melted butter **were/were not** acceptable overall. Compared with cakes made with high-ratio liquid shortening, those made with high-ratio plastic shortening have the following differences in appearance, texture, and flavor:

_____

_____

_____

Overall, these differences are **small/moderate/large**.

9 Cakes made with high-ratio plastic shortening **were/were not** acceptable overall. Compared with cakes made with high-ratio liquid shortening, those made with high-ratio plastic shortening have the following differences in appearance, texture, and flavor:

_____
_____
_____

Overall, these differences are **small/moderate/large**.

10 Cakes made with all-purpose shortening **were/were not** acceptable overall. Compared with cakes made with high-ratio liquid shortening, those made with all-purpose shortening have the following differences in appearance, texture, and flavor:

_____
_____
_____

Overall, these differences were **small/moderate/large**.

11 Cakes made with oil **were/were not** acceptable overall. Compared with cakes made with high-ratio liquid shortening, those made with oil had the following differences in appearance, texture, and flavor:

_____
_____
_____

Overall, these differences are **small/moderate/large**.

12 Did any batter(s) appear unstable? Signs of an unstable batter include a curdled look, in which the fat and moisture separate, or air bubbles escaping from the surface.

_____
_____
_____

How do you explain these results?

_____
_____
_____

13 Other comments I would like to add about differences in the batters, baked cakes, or about the experiment:

_____
_____
_____

⑤ Experiment: How the Type of Fat Affects the Overall Quality of a Simple Icing

Objectives

Demonstrate how the type of fat affects

- The lightness and volume of icing
- The appearance, flavor, and mouthfeel of icing
- How easy icing is to spread
- The overall acceptability of icing for various uses

Products Prepared

Simple icing made with

- Butter, unsalted, sweet cream (control product)
- Butter, cultured cream, higher fat (European or European-style)
- All-purpose plastic shortening
- High-ratio plastic shortening
- Margarine, unsalted
- Half butter, half high-ratio plastic shortening
- Other, if desired (salted butter, salted margarine, icing shortening, three-quarters butter/one-quarter shortening, one-quarter butter/three-quarters shortening, etc.)

Materials and Equipment

- Scale
- Mixer with 5-quart mixing bowl
- Flat beater attachment
- Whip attachment
- Bowl scraper
- Simple icing (see Formula), enough to make about 1 pound (500 grams) or more of each variation
- Clear 1-cup (250 ml) measuring cups, one for each variation
- Straight-edge
- Cakes, cupcakes, or plates, for spreading icing onto
- Flexible steel spatula or palette knife

Formula

> ### Simple Icing
>
> **Yield:** *About 2 cups (one-half liter)*

INGREDIENT	POUND	OUNCE	GRAMS	BAKER'S PERCENTAGE
Fat		6	180	60
Sugar, powdered		10	300	100
Egg whites, pasteurized		2	60	20
Total	**1**	**2**	**540**	**180**

Method of Preparation

1 Allow all ingredients to come to room temperature (temperature of ingredients is important for consistent results).

2 If two fats are used, soften the firmer of the two first by mixing it using the flat beater attachment on low speed.

3 Cream the fat(s) on low for 3 minutes, or until smooth and light.

4 Add powdered sugar and blend on low for 1 minute. Stop and scrape bowl and beater.

5 Switch to whip attachment and whip on high for 6 minutes. Stop and scrape bowl and beater after every 2 minutes.

6 Add egg whites and whip on high for 5 additional minutes or until smooth and light.

7 Cover, label, and hold at room temperature until ready to evaluate.

Procedure

1 Prepare icings using the formula for simple icing above, or using any simple buttercream icing. Prepare one batch of icing for each variation.

2 Be sure icings are all at room temperature.

3 Measure density (weight per volume) of icings to evaluate the relative amount of air incorporated into each variation. To measure density:
   - Carefully spoon each creamed icing into tared measuring cup (8 fl. oz./250 ml).
   - Visually check cup to confirm that no large air gaps are present.
   - Level the top surface of the cup with a straight-edge.
   - Weigh the amount of icing in each cup and record results in Results Table 1.

4 Calculate specific gravity from density measurements. *Specific gravity*, also called *relative density*, is a measure of a product's density relative to water. Unlike density, specific gravity does not depend on the size of the container used to take the measurements. To calculate specific gravity, divide the density (weight per volume) of each icing by the weight of the same volume of water. Specific gravity is a unitless value.

Results

1 Evaluate how well icing can be spread on a cake. To do this, spread icing on cooled cupcakes, cake, or the back of a plastic or paper plate. Rate the softness, smoothness, and overall ease of spreading the icing and record evaluations in Results Table.

2 Evaluate the sensory characteristics of icings and record evaluations in Results Table. Be sure to compare each in turn to the control product and consider the following:
   - Appearance (smoothness and color)
   - Mouthfeel (light/heavy, oily/waxy, etc.)
   - Flavor (butter, egg, sweetness, saltiness, etc.)
   - Add any additional comments, as necessary

RESULTS TABLE EVALUATION OF LIGHTNESS (DENSITY), EASE IN SPREADING, AND SENSORY CHARACTERISTICS OF ICING MADE WITH DIFFERENT TYPES OF FAT

TYPE OF FAT	DENSITY (WEIGHT/ VOLUME)	SPECIFIC GRAVITY	EASE IN SPREADING	APPEARANCE	MOUTHFEEL	FLAVOR	ADDITIONAL COMMENTS
Butter, sweet cream, unsalted							
Butter, European							
All-purpose plastic shortening							
High-ratio plastic shortening							
Margarine, unsalted							
Half butter, half high-ratio plastic shortening							

Sources of Error

List any sources of error that might make it difficult to draw the proper conclusions from your experiment. In particular, consider differences in temperature of fats, how icings were mixed, and whether there were large air pockets present when icing densities were measured.

_____

_____

_____

State what you could do differently next time to minimize or eliminate each source of error.

_____

_____

_____

Conclusions

Select one from the choices in **bold** or fill in the blanks.

1   The icing made with European (or European style) butter differed from the icing made with sweet cream butter in the following ways:

_____

_____

_____

The differences were **small/moderate/large**.

2   The lower the specific gravity of an icing, the **lighter/heavier** it is because **more/less** air is whipped into it. The fat that whipped up into the lightest icing with the lowest specific gravity was **butter/AP shortening/high-ratio shortening/margarine**. This is probably because it contains emulsifiers such as _____ that help to incorporate air.

3   The icing with the heavier mouthfeel was made with **AP shortening/high-ratio shortening**. This difference is primarily because of differences in **specific gravity/melting point**. This made it **more/less** pleasant to taste.

4   The icing made with unsalted margarine melted **faster/slower** than sweet cream butter. In my opinion, this gave it a **more/less** pleasant mouthfeel. Other differences between these two icings were as follows:

_____

_____

_____

The differences were **small/moderate/large**.

5   Summarize the main differences in appearance, flavor, and mouthfeel between the icing made with high-ratio plastic shortening and the icing made with butter (the control product).

_____

_____

_____

The differences were **small/moderate/large**.

6   The icing(s) that would be acceptable for use on a white wedding cake could be made with _____ because_____

7   The icing(s) that would be acceptable as a flavorful buttercream could be made with _____ because_____

8   The icing(s) that would be acceptable as a butter-flavored icing during hot summer months could be made with _____ because_____

9   Which icing did you prefer overall, and why?

_____

_____

_____

10

Eggs and Egg Products

Introduction

Because of eggs' versatility, nearly all baked goods contain them. This, in turn, partly explains why the production of eggs in North America has evolved to become a large commercial operation. Today in the United States, most eggs come from companies having flocks of 75,000 hens or more, with some companies having five million hens or more. The average hen lays 250 to 300 eggs per year, over twice as many as fifty years ago. This increase is the result of improvements in breeding, nutrition, housing, and management practices. In turn, the price of eggs has remained steady over the years.

The Makeup of an Egg

Eggs have six distinct parts: thin white, thick white, yolk, shell, air cell, and chalazae (Figure 10.1). About two-thirds of the weight of the edible part of an egg is egg white; about one-third is the yolk. Overall, most of the whole egg is moisture, with smaller but important amounts of protein, fat, and emulsifiers (Figure 10.2).

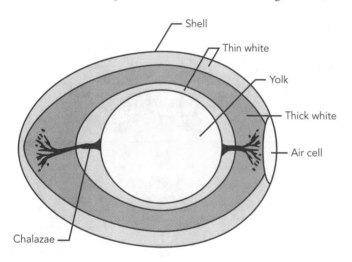

Figure 10.1 The parts of an egg

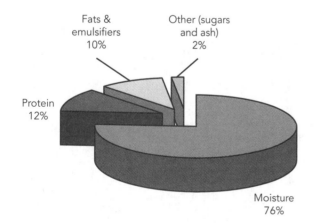

Figure 10.2 The makeup of an egg

White

Another name for egg white is *egg albumen*. Other than small amounts of mineral ash and glucose, egg white consists entirely of protein and water. There are more than six different types of proteins in egg white, and it is this mix of proteins that is responsible for most of the functions of egg whites, including its two main functions: structure building and aeration.

While the special mix of proteins in egg white is extremely important to its functionality, egg white is actually mostly water, about 90 percent water and only 10 percent protein (Table 10.1).

Compared to the yolk, fresh egg white has very little flavor or color. As it ages, however, egg white develops a slight sulfury aroma when it is cooked, especially when the pH is high. The smell comes from the release of sulfur from the egg proteins as they are heated.

Egg white has both thick and thin portions, with the thick portion thinning as the egg ages. As it thins, egg white loses its ability to form foams that are stable.

Yolk

Egg yolks are about half moisture and half yolk solids. The solids in egg yolks consist of proteins, fats, and emulsifiers (Table 10.1), with small amounts of mineral ash and yellow-orange carotenoids. Egg yolk proteins are not the same as egg white proteins, but like egg white proteins, they are important structure builders in baked goods. Many egg yolk proteins are *lipoproteins*, proteins bound to lipids—that is, fats and emulsifiers. It is because of these lipoproteins and emulsifiers that egg yolks are superior at emulsifying foods.

The lipoproteins in egg yolk form microscopically small granules that are suspended in the liquid portion of the yolk. Also suspended in the yolk are emulsified fat

What Are Proteins?

Proteins are very large molecules made of many amino acids linked together into long chains. Often thousands of amino acids form a single protein. Because there are more than twenty different amino acids in nature, with each having its own unique properties, proteins can become quite complex. What distinguishes one protein from another is the number and arrangement of amino acids within the molecule.

Proteins fall into two major classes based on their shape: fibrous and globular proteins. *Fibrous proteins* have a roughly linear shape. They excel at thickening and forming structure. Glutenin, which forms the backbone of gluten, is an important fibrous protein in baked goods. Ovomucin is a fibrous protein in egg whites.

Most proteins, however, are classified as globular proteins. *Globular proteins* have a spherical shape, at least in their native state. Heat, acid, and salt can change their shape, however, and in doing so, they can change how these proteins function. Enzymes are globular proteins, as are most of the proteins in eggs.

Ovomucin, an Egg White Protein

Egg whites contain a mix of more than six different proteins, with each having a different size, shape, and function. For example, the largest-size protein in egg white by far is ovomucin. Because of its large size and its fibrous structure, ovomucin provides thickness to egg whites. While ovomucin is in both the thick and thin portions of the white, not surprisingly, thick egg white contains about four times as much ovomucin as thin egg white. As the egg ages, ovomucin breaks down and dissolves, causing the egg white to thin. While ovomucin, because of its thickness, is important in foaming and helping to stabilize meringue, it plays only a minor role in the heat coagulation of eggs.

While large for a protein, ovomucin fibers are not visible to the naked eye. However, add two or three parts water to egg white in a dark-colored cup, stir to dissolve, and set aside for a few minutes. You will soon see delicate white fibers form out of solution, fibers composed primarily of ovomucin.

TABLE 10.1 THE MAKEUP OF WHOLE EGGS, EGG WHITES, AND EGG YOLKS

COMPONENT	WHOLE	WHITE	YOLK
Moisture	76%	88%	50%
Protein	12%	10%	17%
Fat and emulsifiers	10%	0%	30%
Other (sugars and ash)	2%	2%	3%

droplets (globules). In other words, egg yolks not only stabilize emulsions, they are emulsions themselves.

As eggs age, yolks pick up moisture from the white. Crack an aged egg onto a smooth surface, and you will see the yolk thin out and flatten. The yolk has a protective membrane that weakens as it ages, making it more difficult to separate the yolk from the white. The weakening of this membrane also increases the possibility that bacteria will pass into the nutrient-rich yolk, where they can multiply if the egg is not kept cold.

The most well-known emulsifier in egg yolk is lecithin. Egg yolk contains a surprisingly high amount of lecithin, about 10 percent. Like most of the lipids in egg yolk, lecithin is bound as lipoproteins. The emulsifying lipoproteins perform many functions in foods, most notably bonding to both water and oil. By bonding to both, emulsifiers and emulsifying lipoproteins hold together (bind) complex mixtures of ingredients such as cake batters. Figure 10.3 shows how a small amount of lecithin is able to hold together an emulsion made of oil and water. The lecithin was first added to the oil, then water was slowly added using an immersion blender. The creamy look of the emulsion is from light bouncing off the microscopically small droplets of oil and trapped air dispersed throughout the water.

Lecithin is not a single substance. It is a complex mixture of emulsifying lipids widely found in nature. Besides egg yolks, lecithin is found in dairy ingredients, cereal grains, soybeans, and peanuts. Lecithin is sold as a dark, oily liquid or sometimes as powder or granules.

The emulsifying lipids in lecithin are classified as phospholipids. Phospholipid molecules look something like triglyceride molecules—that is, like fats and oils. Recall from Chapter 9 that triglycerides consist of three fatty acids attached to glycerol. Phospholipids consist of two fatty acids attached to glycerol. Instead of the third fatty acid, phospholipids contain a so-called phosphate group. The fatty acids are attracted to fats and oils (lipids) in food, while the phosphate group is attracted to water. It is this ability to attract both lipids and water that allows phospholipids such as lecithin to act as emulsifiers.

Figure 10.3 Lecithin is an emulsifier in egg yolk that bonds to both water and oil, holding them together. **Left:** an emulsion of oil, water, and lecithin; **right:** oil and water alone

An important factor in the color of egg yolk is the hen's feed. The more carotenoids in the feed, the more yellow-orange the yolk. Alfalfa and yellow corn, which are both high in carotenoids, produce deeply colored yolks. Wheat, oat, and white corn produce lighter yolks. When feed is naturally low in carotenoids, marigold petals—a rich source of carotenoids—can be added for color.

The hen's feed also affects the flavor of the yolks. This explains why some brands of eggs taste different from others. Sometimes, for example, organic eggs taste different from regular eggs. It isn't that being organic necessarily gives them a different flavor; more likely, the growers are using a particular feed that—organic or not—has a distinct flavor that passes into the egg.

Omega-3 fatty acids are sometimes added to feed for hens so that the eggs are high in this healthful oil. Eggs that contain omega-3 fatty acids will have a different flavor from regular eggs.

Shell

Eggshell represents about 11 percent of the weight of an egg. Although it serves as a hard protective covering, the eggshell is porous. This means that odors penetrate eggshells, and moisture and gases (primarily carbon dioxide) can escape. In commercial practice, shell eggs are washed with a detergent and sanitized to remove dirt and to reduce the likelihood of salmonella contamination. In the past, eggshells were lightly coated with mineral oil to delay moisture loss. Because eggs move from farm to market quickly and are refrigerated throughout distribution, moisture loss is no longer a problem. For this reason, few egg processors oil eggs today.

Eggshell color can be either brown or white, depending on the breed of hen. Hens with white feathers and white earlobes lay white eggs; hens with red feathers and red lobes lay brown eggs. While most (95 percent) commercial breeds produce white eggs, hens bred in parts of New England produce brown eggs. Shell color has no effect on flavor, nutrition, or functionality of eggs.

Air Pocket

Eggs contain two protective membranes between the shell and the white. Soon after an egg is laid, an air cell forms between the membranes at the egg's larger end. As the egg ages, loses moisture, and shrinks, the air pocket increases in size. This is why older eggs float in water while fresh ones sink.

The use of organic eggs in the United States more than doubled during the 1990s and continues to grow at an annual rate of about 15 percent a year. In response to the growing popularity of organic products, the United States initiated the National Organic Program in 2002 to unify the use of the term organic across the country. Organic growers must now be certified or they cannot use the term *organic* to describe their products.

Organic food is produced by farmers who use renewable resources and conservation to enhance environmental quality. Organic eggs come from animals that are given no antibiotics or growth hormones. The hens are fed organic feed, which is produced without using most pesticides, synthetic fertilizers, irradiation, or genetic engineering. Before a product can be labeled organic, a government-approved certifier inspects the farm where the food is grown to make sure the farmer is following all the rules necessary to meet USDA organic standards. The safety and nutritional quality of organic eggs is not necessarily different from those of standard eggs.

Chalazae

The chalazae are twisted white cords that hold the yolk to the center of the egg. They disintegrate as the egg ages. Chalazae are an extension of the egg white and are similar in composition to ovomucin, the fibrous protein that thickens egg white. The chalazae are completely edible, although pastry chefs typically use a chinois or sieve to strain them from certain products, such as custards.

Commercial Classification of Shell Eggs

Shell eggs are eggs purchased in their shells, either by the dozen or in *flats*. One flat holds 2½ dozen or 30 eggs. There are 12 flats in a case, which means that one case contains 30 dozen or 360 eggs.

Shell eggs are sometimes called fresh eggs, but this is misleading. Shell eggs might be several weeks or months old, so they are not necessarily fresh. Shell eggs are sorted and classified according to grade (quality) and size. The U.S. Department of Agriculture (USDA) and Agriculture and Agri-Food Canada (AAFC) offer programs to classify and label eggs with both a grade and a size classification. In Canada, the program is mandatory; in the United States, it is voluntary, with about 30 percent of all eggs sold in the United States graded by the USDA.

Grade

The three USDA grades for acceptable shell eggs are U.S. Grades AA, A, and B. Canada has two acceptable grades, A and B. Quality grades do not reflect product safety or nutritional quality, and Grade B eggs, stored properly, are safe to eat and will have the same nutritional quality as higher-grade eggs.

Usually, USDA-graded eggs are washed, packed, and graded within a day to a week of being laid, but they can be legally graded for up to 30 days. They must be labeled with the date that they were packed and graded; often they will also have a sell-by or expiration date. The pack date must be displayed as the Julian date, where the number 001 represents January 1 and the number 365 represents December 31. The sell-by date is defined as no more than 45 days from the time the eggs are packed and graded. This means that USDA-graded eggs can theoretically be sold for more than two months after they are laid, although most will be sold within days of being packed. Certain states in the United States also regulate the grading and labeling of shell eggs for those packers who do not take part in the USDA's voluntary grading program.

Prior to 1998, eggs that were nearing their expiration date could be returned to the packer to be washed, packed, and graded a second time, extending their usable life. This is no longer allowed in the United States, for safety reasons.

Grades A and AA are the most common eggs purchased for the bakeshop. The main difference between

How Are Eggs Graded for Quality?

Candling is the primary method used for measuring the quality of eggs. In candling, a bright light passes through the egg still in its shell and exposes the size of its air pocket, thickness and clarity of the white, the position and stability of the yolk, the presence of blood spots or a developing embryo, and more.

USDA Grade AA and Grade A eggs is in the firmness of the white and the size of the air cell. Only eggs with the firmest whites and the smallest air cells can be labeled USDA Grade AA. Firm whites—and yolks—are particularly important when frying or poaching eggs because they hold their shape best (Figure 10.4). They are less important for baking.

Grade B eggs may have one or more of the following defects: stained shells, large air cells, watery whites, small blood spots in the white, or an enlarged, flattened yolk. Grade B eggs are acceptable for general baking, but whites from Grade B eggs may not whip properly if they are watery.

While the quality grade of eggs does not necessarily reflect age, quality does decline over time. Even properly refrigerated eggs stored in their carton will decline from Grade AA to Grade A in about one week. In about another five weeks, they will drop from Grade A to Grade B, as the whites thin and the air pockets enlarge. However, a properly handled and refrigerated egg will retain its nutritional value and wholesomeness for a considerably longer time.

Size

Size classifications for eggs are different from quality classifications. The six size classifications for shell eggs in North America are based on minimum weights per dozen; they do not refer to the dimensions of an individual egg or how large it is. The most common size classifications for eggs used in the bakeshop are large, extra large, and jumbo; the three other classifications are medium, small, and peewee. Because the size classifications are based on minimum weights for an entire dozen, individual eggs themselves will vary in weight.

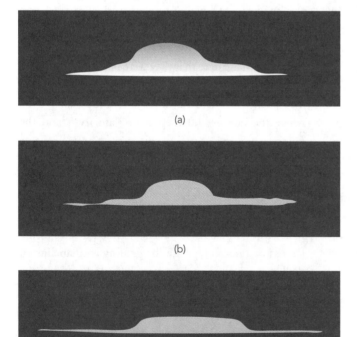

(a)

(b)

(c)

Figure 10.4 Egg grades: **(a)** Grade AA **(b)** Grade A **(c)** Grade B

Egg Products

Egg products include various forms of eggs that are sold removed from their shells. The range of products includes egg whites, egg yolks, and whole egg products sold refrigerated, frozen, or dried. Liquid and dried egg products have been available since the late 1800s, but quality was generally poor. Today, however, about one-third of the eggs used in the United States are egg products.

Changes in processing have improved over the years so that frozen and refrigerated liquid egg products can be used in place of shell eggs in most bakeshop applications. While the viscosity of frozen products changes somewhat over time, for the most part this does not affect their properties. Dried egg products are less popular in the bakeshop than liquid egg products, although they, too, can be used successfully in many applications.

Advantages of Egg Products

Egg products are steadily replacing shell eggs in the bakeshop, and there are several reasons for this. The main one is safety. By law, egg products must be pasteurized so that they are free from salmonella bacteria. This means that it is safe to use egg products in uncooked items such as buttercream and sorbet. USDA inspection of the processing of egg products is mandatory in the United States.

TABLE 10.2 MAIN ADVANTAGES OF EGG PRODUCTS

Safety, because by law, they must be pasteurized
Time saved in cracking and separating eggs; potentially reduced labor costs
Space saving (storage)
No loss due to breakage
Longer shelf life, as long as products remain dry or frozen
No leftover whites or yolks from separating shell eggs
Uniformity in quality

There are other advantages to egg products besides food safety (Table 10.2). Cost, however, is not usually one of them, because egg products can be expensive. However, egg products save time, so if labor is expensive they can save money in the long run.

Types of Egg Products

Frozen Whites Frozen egg whites often contain an added thickener such as guar gum. A small amount of guar gum protects egg whites from ice crystal damage. Guar gum also increases viscosity, improving the ability of frozen whites to foam. Whipping agents such as triethyl citrate are sometimes added to frozen whites so that thawed frozen egg whites often whip up faster and higher than whites from the shell.

Frozen egg whites can be used in most applications requiring egg whites, including meringue and angel food cake. In some cases, however, frozen egg whites do not form as firm or as stable a foam as whites from fresh shell eggs. This seems to be the case with the making

---

Automated Egg Breaking

As many as 162,000 eggs per hour (45 eggs per second) can be broken on modern automated egg-breaking machines. According to the American Egg Board, this is because technology for these machines has improved dramatically in recent years.

How Are Eggs Pasteurized?

Pasteurization is a process that eliminates pathogenic (disease-causing) microorganisms such as salmonella in food products. The most common means of pasteurizing food is to apply heat for a specific period of time. The higher the heat, the less time is needed to ensure food safety. With most food products, high pasteurization temperatures are desired because the shorter heating time inflicts less quality damage to the food. Eggs, however, cannot be pasteurized at high temperatures or the egg proteins coagulate. A typical commercial pasteurization process for liquid whole eggs is to heat the eggs for 3.5 minutes at 140°F (60°C). Other pasteurization processes exist. For example, dried egg whites can be pasteurized by holding them at 130°F (54°C) for seven days or more. For the most part, pasteurization does not affect the properties of the eggs.

What Causes a Gray-Green Color to Form in Eggs?

You may recall seeing a gray-green ring surrounding the yolk in hard-boiled eggs, or the graying of scrambled eggs left on a steam table too long. While harmless, this discoloration is unattractive. It is caused by a chemical reaction that occurs when eggs, especially old ones, are heated for extended periods.

Proteins in egg whites are high in sulfur. You cannot see or smell sulfur in fresh eggs, but as eggs are heated, some of the sulfur is released. When sulfur from egg white combines with iron from egg yolk, an iron sulfide forms. This iron sulfide has a gray-green color.

Iron sulfide is especially likely to form when eggs are heated for too long, or when they are heated in water that is high in iron. High pH also favors this reaction. The pH of an egg increases as it ages, so not surprisingly, old eggs are more likely to discolor than fresh ones.

The formation of iron sulfide in the presence of high pH explains why baked goods with too much added baking soda—which raises pH—can have a slight greenish tinge.

---

of Swiss meringue, for which egg whites and sugar are warmed together in a double boiler before whipping. When this is a problem, fresh or dried whites can be blended with frozen whites to assure better whipping.

Like all egg products, frozen whites are pasteurized and are preferred to shell whites in uncooked products. In fact, in many areas, laws mandate that raw egg not be used in uncooked or undercooked products.

Separation of thick and thin whites may occur upon thawing, so be sure to shake or stir thawed whites before use.

Frozen Sugared Yolks Frozen yolks contain added sugar or glucose corn syrup, generally 10 percent. Frozen yolks for use in unsweetened products (mayonnaise, hollandaise sauce, Caesar salad dressing) have added salt instead of sugar. The added sweetener or salt lowers the freezing point, preventing excessive ice crystal damage that causes yolk proteins to gel irreversibly to a thick gummy solid. Even then, frozen sugared yolks thaw to a thicker consistency than yolks that have not been frozen. However, this should not negatively affect functionality. In fact, thicker yolks can assist in the formation of stable emulsions.

For general use, replace regular yolks directly with sugared yolks. For products that contain a high amount of yolk, such as vanilla custard sauce, you may wish to adjust the amount of sugar and yolks in the formula. To make this adjustment for sugar, replace each pound of yolks with 1.1 pounds (about 1 pound, 1.5 ounces) of sugared yolks and reduce the amount of sugar in the formula by 0.1 pounds (about 1.5 ounces). Using metric units, replace each kilogram of yolks with 1.1 kilograms of sugared yolks and reduce the amount of sugar in the formula by 0.1 kilograms (100 grams).

Refrigerated Liquid Yolks Unlike yolks sold frozen, refrigerated liquid yolks do not contain additives to lower the freezing point and protect the yolks from gelling. Since excessive gelling reduces the ability of egg yolks to aerate, emulsify, and mix well with other ingredients, it is best not to freeze liquid yolks sold for refrigerated storage. This is especially important if the yolks are to be used in biscuit (sponge cake), French buttercream, or bombe mixtures, which rely on whipped egg yolks for volume.

Frozen Whole Eggs Frozen whole eggs contain whites and yolks in their natural proportion. While whole eggs will thicken when frozen, the thickening is typically minimal. Often frozen whole eggs contain a small amount of added citric acid. The citric acid prevents a gray-green discoloration from occurring when whole eggs are heated. If citric acid is not added, you can add lemon juice, which contains citric acid, or sour cream, which contains lactic acid. Only a small amount is needed to lower the pH to the point where discoloration is prevented.

Liquid Whole-Egg Substitutes Whole-egg substitutes such as Egg Beaters are made from egg whites. They generally contain over 99 percent egg white, making them fat-free and cholesterol-free. Whole-egg substitutes are available for those interested in lowering the amount of fat and cholesterol in their diet.

Whole-egg substitutes often contain added beta-carotene for a yellow color. Other optional ingredients include dry milk solids, vitamins and minerals, gums, salt, and seasonings. Be sure to read ingredient labels before using whole-egg substitutes. Some contain onion, garlic, and other seasonings that are inappropriate for use in sweet baked goods.

Instead of using whole-egg substitutes in low-fat baked goods, consider using egg whites. Egg whites work quite well, often at a substantially lower price and with better flavor. If necessary, add a small amount of yellow-orange food coloring to your batter or dough for the look of whole egg.

Dried Eggs   Pasteurized dried whole eggs, egg yolks, and egg whites are also available for use in the bakeshop.

They are dried until less than 5 percent moisture remains and can be conveniently stored in a cool dry place until reconstituted. Drying can reduce the acceptability of eggs in certain applications because of changes to color and flavor. Egg yolks are sometimes dried with sugar because the sugar protects the lipoproteins from losing their ability to emulsify.

While not commonly used in the bakeshop, dried egg products are perfectly acceptable for use in baked goods such as muffins, breads, cookies, and some cakes. Follow the manufacturer's instructions for reconstituting dried egg products, or sift the egg powder with other dry ingredients and add a measured amount of water with the liquids.

Because of their heat sensitivity, dried egg whites are processed differently than dried whole eggs and egg yolks. First, the liquid whites are treated with an enzyme to remove the small amount of glucose naturally present in egg whites. If this glucose is not removed, dried egg whites darken through Maillard browning to an unattractive tan color during drying, storage, and baking. Once dried, the egg white powder is typically held for a week to ten days in a hot room at 130°F (54°C). The heat pasteurizes the egg whites, but it does more: it improves the egg white's gel strength and its whipping ability.

Pastry chefs sometimes add dried egg whites to liquid egg whites to increase body and improve the stability of meringue. Because they are glucose-free, dried egg whites are sometimes used in baked meringue shells to minimize browning. Finally, dried egg whites are often used instead of liquid egg whites when making royal icing, an uncooked icing that dries to a glossy hard finish.

Functions of Eggs

Eggs provide many complex functions in baked goods, some of which overlap. For example, the ability of eggs to bind ingredients is related to their ability to emulsify and to form structure.

Main Functions

 Providing Structure   Coagulated egg proteins in both egg whites and egg yolks are important structure builders in baked goods. For example, eggs are as important as flour—sometimes more so—in building structure in cakes. In fact, without eggs, most cakes collapse. Eggs also contribute to structure in quick breads, cookies, muffins, and certain yeast breads.

Coagulated egg proteins also provide thickening and gelling (a form of structure) in pastry cream, crème anglaise, cream pie, and custards. Because egg coagulation is so important to the structure of custards and related products, it will be discussed in more detail later.

Eggs are considered tougheners because of their ability to provide structure. Eggs are probably the

What Would Happen If Eggs Were Left Out of Muffins?

Traditional muffins and quick breads rely as much—or more—on eggs as on flour for their coarse, crumbly structure. They are typically made with pastry flour or a combination of pastry and bread flour. If eggs were left out of muffin batter and replaced with milk or water, the muffins would be more tender and have a lower volume, but the gluten and starch in the flour would likely prevent the muffins from collapse. The muffins would lack a richness and be white in color and bland in flavor. In fact, eggless muffins taste more like sweet and tender baking powder biscuits than flavorful muffins.

If Egg Yolks Contain Tenderizers, Why Are They Not Called Tenderizers?

Actually, sometimes egg yolks are referred to as tenderizers. When they are, it is usually when the yolks are compared with whole eggs. And it is true that baked goods made with egg yolks generally have a more tender crumb than those made with the same weight of whole eggs. However, this is not the same as saying that egg yolks are true tenderizers. They are still tougheners; they simply produce a more tender structure than whole eggs.

Here's another way of looking at it: Add more of a tenderizer, such as sugar or fat, to batters and doughs, and baked goods will be more tender. Add more yolks, and baked goods toughen, just less so than if the same amount of whole eggs were added. Think of it as a tug of war between tougheners and tenderizers in yolks—and the tougheners win.

only common bakery ingredient containing significant amounts of both tougheners (proteins) and tenderizers (fats and emulsifiers). The tenderizers in eggs are concentrated in the yolk.

Because of the tenderizing fats and emulsifiers in the yolk, egg yolks often contribute less toughening (and less structure) than an equal weight of egg whites. The proteins in yolk, bound as lipoproteins, do not coagulate as quickly as egg white proteins and produce a shorter, more tender structure.

A ranking of the structure-building abilities of eggs is as follows:

whites > whole > yolks

Notice that despite containing tenderizers, egg yolks are classified as tougheners or structure builders. Egg yolks are not tenderizers. Figure 10.5 shows the difference between cake made with egg yolks and cake made without any eggs at all. While the cake made without eggs collapsed and cracked, the cake made with egg yolks held its shape as well as if whole eggs had been used. The cake made without eggs contained water, oil, and milk solid in place of the egg.

Figure 10.5 **Background:** cake made with egg yolks has sufficient structure to hold its shape; **foreground:** cake made without eggs collapsed and cracked from too little structure

What Would Happen If Egg Yolks Replaced Whole Eggs in Cakes?

If egg yolks replaced whole eggs in a liquid shortening cake, the cake baked with egg yolks would be richer in flavor, more yellow in color, and likely crumbly and dry.

Baked goods become crumbly when they are so tender and dry that they break into tiny pieces when cut or chewed. Cakes made with egg yolks can be crumbly because the yolks are lower in moisture, making the cake drier. Because egg yolks are also higher than whole eggs in lipids, the cake will likely be more tender, too.

Because egg yolks contain a good amount of structure-building proteins, cakes rarely collapse when yolks are used. In some cake formulas, however, direct substitution of whole eggs with egg yolks produces a denser, tougher product. This happens if water is so limited that there is much less steam produced to both leaven and tenderize the cake.

Aerating Eggs are unique because they are especially good at aerating, producing a relatively stable foam. Foams consist of tiny bubbles of air or another gas surrounded by a liquid or solid film. By aerating, eggs assist in the leavening process. The actual leavener is air. Eggs simply form the foam that allows air to be incorporated into baked goods. Examples of baked goods that rely heavily on the foaming ability of eggs for leavening include sponge, genoise, chiffon, and angel food cakes.

The foaming power of eggs refers to how high they can be whipped. Egg whites, which have a very high foaming power, can whip up to eight times their volume. However, whites whipped this high have extremely thin cell walls consisting of overstretched protein films. When placed in a hot oven, these protein films stretch even more and are likely to break and collapse. There are ways to prevent the overwhipping of eggs and egg whites so that baked goods don't collapse in the oven. These are discussed later in this chapter.

Whole eggs and egg yolks also foam, just not as well as egg whites. The foaming of whole eggs is important, for example, in the leavening of genoise, while egg yolks contribute to the lightness of many sponge cakes. A ranking of the foaming power of eggs is as follows:

whites > whole > yolks

The foaming of egg whites will be discussed in more detail later in this chapter, when meringues are discussed.

Emulsifying Egg yolks are effective emulsifiers, meaning that they can keep oil and water in emulsions from separating. Egg yolks are particularly effective at emulsifying because of their lipoproteins and emulsifiers, including lecithin. Without this ability, eggs would not be effective at binding ingredients in batters and doughs.

Eggs are generally added to creamed butter or shortening. This emulsifies and stabilizes the mixture, and helps to blend it with the rest of the ingredients. Care must be taken when adding eggs to creamed shortening. If eggs are added too quickly or while still cold, the emulsion breaks. While the subsequent addition of flour and other ingredients appears to bind the emulsion back together, a poorly emulsified batter bakes into a cake that may not rise properly and that has a coarser crumb.

Contributing Flavor The rich flavor of eggs comes mostly from egg yolk, partly because that is where the fat is concentrated.

Contributing Color Yellow-orange carotenoids in yolk provide a rich yellow color to baked goods, creams, and sauces. Once highly variable from season to season, egg producers now control yolk color through feed supplements such as marigold petals.

Eggs also contain protein (and a small amount of glucose) that contributes to the brown color from Maillard reactions.

> **HELPFUL HINT**
> *Do not use aluminum bowls, beaters, or saucepans when working with egg mixtures such as pastry cream or crème anglaise. Use stainless steel instead. The eggs discolor aluminum—and worse, aluminum discolors egg mixtures to a dull gray.*

Sorbets are smooth frozen ices made without milk or other dairy products. The mark of a fine sorbet is a soft texture, free of large ice crystals. While any good ice cream freezer can make a smooth sorbet, the addition of egg white helps sorbets stay smoother during storage. Egg whites affect other qualities of sorbets, too, and whether these differences are desirable comes down to personal preference.

For example, sorbets made with added egg white are lighter and airier than ones made without. This is because the whites are aerated in the ice cream freezer as the mix is stirred and frozen. Because of their airiness, they also have a paler color and milder flavor than sorbets made without egg white.

If you choose to add egg white to sorbet, be sure the whites are pasteurized. If you do not have access to pasteurized egg whites, it is best to leave egg whites out of sorbet.

Adding Nutritional Value   Egg proteins in both the yolk and the white are of the highest nutritional quality. Eggs also contribute vitamins and minerals. The yellow-orange carotenoids in egg yolks, like all carotenoids, are antioxidants important to health. In particular, these carotenoids (specifically one called lutein) are thought to reduce the risk of macular degeneration, the leading cause of severe vision loss in people over the age of fifty.

While hens today are bred and fed to produce yolks that are lower in fat and cholesterol, egg yolks are still a significant source of both. Fat, in particular, is considered a contributing factor to many diseases. Both fat and dietary cholesterol are thought to increase the risk of high blood cholesterol and coronary heart disease. While health guidelines for the consumption of eggs have been relaxed in recent years, health authorities still recommend limiting egg consumption.

Additional Functions

Preventing Staling   Fats, emulsifiers, and proteins in eggs interfere with the process of starch retrogradation, which is a major cause of staling in baked goods.

Adding Shine to the Surface of Baked Goods   Egg proteins dry to a glossy brown film when egg wash is applied to the surface of doughs. Egg wash can be made with eggs diluted with water or, for additional browning, eggs diluted with milk. Any part of the egg can be used, with egg yolk wash providing the most browning and sheen.

A small amount of salt added to an egg wash thins it out. It takes a few hours for this to happen, but it does make the egg wash easier to apply evenly. The egg thins out because the egg proteins are neutralized by the salt and are no longer attracted to one another. This allows the proteins to be better hydrated by water, even to dissolve in it. Biochemists have a term for the ability of salt to dissolve proteins in water. They call it the *salting in* effect.

Serving as an Edible Glue   Eggs help nuts, seeds, spices, and sugar crystals adhere to baked goods. Eggs also allow batters to adhere to foods that are fried.

Promoting Smoothness in Icings, Confections, and Frozen Desserts   Fats, emulsifiers, and proteins in eggs interfere with sugar and ice crystallization, promoting a velvety smooth texture in icings, confections, and frozen desserts. French-style ice cream is ice cream that contains added egg yolks for creamy smoothness and richness.

Adding Moisture   Whole eggs contain approximately 75 percent moisture. Any time eggs are added to batter or dough, a good amount of moisture is also added. Remember that baking involves balancing moisteners with driers. If eggs are increased in a formula, other liquids—milk or water, for example—must be decreased.

Do not confuse adding moisture with adding moistness. Because eggs also contain structure-building proteins, the use of eggs often makes a product taste tougher and drier.

Increasing Softness in Raw Dough   Eggs interfere with gluten development in raw dough, even as they provide structure of their own once baked. Gluten proteins bond with other gluten proteins, and egg fats, emulsifiers, and proteins interfere with this bonding.

Some people like their brownies dense and fudgy, others like them light and cakey. Everybody has their favorite brownie formula, which can vary widely in the proportion of chocolate to sugar, fat, and other tenderizers, and to flour, eggs, and other structure builders. Brownie formulas also vary in mixing methods.

Sometimes, however, the difference is as simple as the number of eggs added. Eggs can provide aeration and structure, and cake-like brownies are lighter and hold their shape better than fudgy ones. But the added lightness from cake-like brownies is as likely from the moisture in the eggs as it is from aeration. Moisture converts to steam when heated, and steam is very powerful leavening gas, important in lightening the texture of baked goods. The moisture in eggs also allows starch to more fully gelatinize, and gelatinized starch is essential for a cake-like crumb.

More on Coagulation: Basic Egg Custard

A basic egg custard is an egg-based cream consisting of eggs, milk or cream, sugar, and flavoring. The mixture is thickened or gelled through the heat coagulation of egg proteins. Examples of egg custards include crème caramel, crème brûlée, and crème anglaise (vanilla custard sauce). Many other products have a custard base. For example, pumpkin pie filling, cream pie filling, bread pudding, rice pudding, pastry cream, quiches, and even cheesecakes are variations on the basic egg custard.

A properly cooked custard-based product is a moist, tender gel or a smooth, creamy sauce. The thickening and gelling occur over time as the temperature of the mixture increases and the eggs coagulate.

A Description of the Process of Egg Coagulation

As eggs are heated, proteins in both the whites and the yolks gradually denature or unfold (Figure 10.6). The unfolded proteins move through the liquid and bond (aggregate) with one another. In fact, protein coagulation is sometimes called *protein aggregation*. Properly aggregated egg proteins form a strong yet often flexible network that traps water and other liquids.

The more eggs are heated, the more egg proteins aggregate, and the tighter, firmer, and more rigid the protein network becomes. Eventually, the proteins overcoagulate, shrinking and squeezing out liquids, much as a sponge shrinks and releases water when it is wrung. Overcoagulation is sometimes called *curdling*, and it results in *weeping* or *syneresis*, where bits of tough gel float in pools of squeezed-out liquid.

Often, however, water that is released from overcoagulated proteins evaporates or it is absorbed by other ingredients. This happens in cakes and other baked goods, where gelatinizing starches absorb water that is squeezed from overcoagulated egg proteins. However, the protein network and the cake still shrink to a dry, rubbery toughness.

In general, it is beneficial to slow down coagulation. This reduces the risk of overcoagulation and provides the highest-quality custard or baked product—one that is soft, moist, and tender.

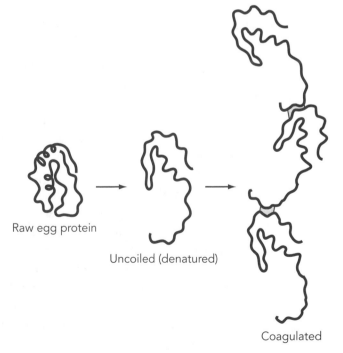

Raw egg protein

Uncoiled (denatured)

Coagulated

Figure 10.6 The process of egg coagulation

How Does Sugar "Cook" Egg Yolks?

When sugar is placed on egg yolks and not stirred in, the yolks gel and appear to cook. Sugar, being hygroscopic, pulls water from the egg yolks (recall that yolks are about 50 percent water) and dries them. Without water, proteins in the yolk are closer together and quickly aggregate as if heat was applied.

To avoid this, never add sugar to yolks without stirring the two together. The yolks will thicken, but they will not solidify.

Tempering Eggs into Hot Mixtures

An important technique in the bakeshop is the tempering of ingredients: the careful addition of one ingredient to another when two ingredients start at different temperatures. The goal of tempering is to avoid damaging either ingredient.

Tempering is important when adding eggs to hot mixtures. If eggs are added directly to hot milk, for example, heat from the milk prematurely cooks the eggs, and bits of coagulated egg form in the mixture. Avoid this by slowly adding a small amount of hot milk to the eggs before they are added to the bulk of the milk. This dilutes the eggs without significantly raising their temperature. Once they are diluted, the eggs are much less likely to be heat damaged as they are added to the rest of the milk.

Some formulas call for other ingredients, such as sugar, to be added to eggs before they are tempered with hot milk. Adding sugar or another room temperature ingredient is yet another way to dilute and protect eggs from the effects of heat.

While heat is the most common means of coagulating proteins, proteins are also coagulated by acid, salt, freezing, whipping, and drying.

Factors Affecting Egg Coagulation

There are several ways to slow down coagulation and reduce the risk of overcoagulation. When coagulation is slowed, it takes a higher temperature to bring it about. Following is a discussion of the main factors that affect the rate of egg protein coagulation, the temperature at which it occurs, and the risk of overcoagulation. Temperatures given are approximate.

Amount or Proportion of Egg

Proteins in an undiluted egg properly coagulate by about 160°F (70°C). Dilute the egg with milk, water, or other ingredients, and the coagulation temperature increases. For example, the coagulation temperature for most vanilla custard sauce formulas is between 180° and 185°F (82°–85°C). The dilution of egg proteins with milk, sugar, and cream makes it more difficult for the proteins to bump into one another and bond. This reduces the risk of overcoagulation. When bonding does

eventually occur, expect a softer, more tender product as the additional liquid is trapped in the coagulated protein network.

Rate of Cooking

Egg coagulation does not happen instantaneously. It requires time, and the faster the rate of cooking, the less time it takes. However, when eggs coagulate too quickly, the egg proteins do not unfold properly and are less likely to thicken or gel as well. For

> **HELPFUL HINT**
>
> *Water baths are good for baking egg custard, bread pudding, and cheesecake. Water baths rarely exceed simmering (180°–190°F/82°–88°C), even when the oven is set at 325°F (165°C) or more. This slows the process and evens out baking so that the outside of the custard does not become tough, rubbery, and curdled before the inside bakes.*
>
> *To use a water bath, place filled containers to be baked in a pan. Place the pan in the oven and fill with hot water at least halfway up the sides of the containers. Do not fill so high that water sloshes into your product.*

The predominant protein in egg white is called *ovalbumin*. While poultry scientists are unsure of the function of ovalbumin to the egg (it might simply serve as a source of food to a growing chick embryo), they are more certain of how it functions during cooking and baking. As with all proteins, ovalbumin's molecular structure determines how it functions.

Ovalbumin's structure is considered globular because in its normal state, it is folded into a spherical shape. Ovalbumin forms a spherical shape because it contains a large number of hydrophobic amino acids, which are amino acids that dislike water. Since egg white contains a lot of water (it is almost 90 percent water), ovalbumin curls up in a ball, with the hydrophobic amino acids tucked away inside the molecule.

When ovalbumin is heated, the molecule unfolds (denatures), exposing the previously hidden hydrophobic regions. It is the attraction of the hydrophobic region of one protein to the hydrophobic region of another that causes denatured ovalbumin molecules to aggregate into clusters. In this way, the hydrophobic amino acids remain hidden from water.

While the hydrophobic amino acids might dislike water, they love fats and oils. So it is easy to see why fats and oils interact with proteins like ovalbumin, "coating" them, and interfering with their aggregation.

example, vanilla custard sauce cooked over high heat is not only more likely to curdle and burn, it is also less likely to fully thicken. To maximize thickening, use a low heat setting while stirring constantly.

Part of Egg Used   Egg yolks coagulate at a higher temperature (150°–160°F/65°–70°C) than egg whites (140°–150°F/60°–65°C), making them less likely to weep and curdle. Recall that egg yolk proteins are lipoproteins, bonded to fats and emulsifiers. The fats and emulsifiers make it more difficult for proteins to aggregate. Ranking the parts of the egg from highest to lowest in the rate of coagulation and the tendency to overcoagulate:

whites > whole > yolks

Sugar   Besides diluting protein molecules, sugar slows egg protein coagulation in custards and baked goods by preventing the proteins from unfolding. If the proteins are slow to unfold, they will be slow to coagulate, unless temperatures are raised. This means that sugar helps prevent curdling. It is one reason why quiches, which are essentially egg custard made without sugar, are more apt to curdle and weep than egg custard itself.

It is no surprise that sugars are considered tenderizers in baked goods; by slowing coagulation, sugars slow the formation of egg structure. (Sugars also slow the formation of gluten structure and starch structure.) If enough sugar is present, coagulation is stopped

completely, and the baked good appears undercooked, even after extended baking.

Lipids   Like sugars, lipids (fats, oils, and emulsifiers) interfere with coagulation of egg proteins and so tenderize custards much as they tenderize baked goods. Lipids likely slow coagulation by interacting directly with egg proteins, just as they tenderize gluten structure by interacting with gluten proteins.

Actually, custards made with a high amount of lipids from either cream or egg yolk are more than just soft and tender. Cream and egg yolks provide an added dimension, a smoothness and creaminess not seen in custards made without these ingredients. This creamy texture is the hallmark of well-made crème brûlée, which is custard prepared from heavy cream and egg yolks, topped with a crisp burnt sugar crust.

Acid   Acid speeds up egg coagulation, lowering the temperature of coagulation. The acid comes from added lemon or other fruit juice, raisins or other fruits, or cultured dairy products. When using acidic ingredients in custard products, be sure to carefully monitor baking times.

Starch   Starch increases the temperature of egg coagulation by interfering with the process. To understand how effective starch is at slowing the process and increasing the temperature of egg coagulation, compare the cooking of pastry cream with that of vanilla custard sauce. Pastry cream is essentially custard sauce with added cornstarch or flour. Pastry cream is—must be—brought to a boil and boiled for 2 or more minutes. Vanilla custard sauce could not survive 2 minutes of boiling. In fact, custard sauce generally curdles before it reaches 185°F (85°C). While other differences between the two formulas exist, the main reason pastry cream can be boiled without curdling is because it contains added starch.

Other Factors   Salts in hard water and in dairy ingredients, or the addition of a small amount of table salt (sodium chloride), speed up and strengthen the coagulation of egg proteins. Dairy proteins also likely interact with egg proteins, firming up the gel. Imagine egg custard made with water instead of milk. The custard would be very soft and barely set. Using hard water and a small amount of salt to replace the milk restores much of the lost gel strength—but none of the rich dairy flavor.

Protease enzymes break down egg proteins much as they break down gelatin protein. Try to make baked custard with added uncooked pineapple, which contains active protease, and the custard will not set. Cook the pineapple first, inactivating the enzyme, and the intact egg proteins in the custard will coagulate.

Stirring eggs as they are heated also affects coagulation. Compare baked egg custard, for example, with vanilla custard sauce, stirred as it is cooked on the stovetop. Custard sauce is typically made with egg yolks and part heavy cream, while baked custard is made with whole eggs and whole milk. From this alone, you would expect a softer set from the custard sauce than from the baked custard. But there is also a striking difference in procedure. Custard sauce is stirred in a saucepan as the eggs are heated, while baked custard is not. Constant stirring keeps egg proteins from aggregating into a solid mass, so the sauce thickens instead of gelling into a firm solid (and, if not stirred, custard sauce would burn the bottom of the pan).

More on Aeration: Meringue

Meringue is egg white whipped with sugar. It is used for lightness and volume in mousses, soufflés, angel food and sponge cakes, and icings. It can also be baked in a low-temperature oven for macaroons, cake layers, and tartlet shells.

Meringue could not form without the unique combination of proteins that are present in egg white. Several egg white proteins, including *ovalbumin, conalbumin, globulin, ovomucin,* and *lysozyme* work together for maximum foaming power and foam stability during whipping and during baking.

A Description of the Process of Egg Foam Formation

As eggs are whipped, two things happen simultaneously. Air bubbles are beaten into the liquid, and certain egg proteins denature or unfold. The unfolded proteins quickly move through the liquid to the surface of the bubbles (Figure 10.7). Once there, neighboring proteins bond or aggregate around the bubbles, forming a filmy network. Surrounded by these strong, flexible films, air bubbles are less likely to collapse, so more bubbles can be beaten in, even as the walls of the film thin out.

A useful way to classify meringue is by the ratio of sugar to egg whites. Using this means of classification, the two main types of meringue are hard meringue and soft meringue. Hard meringue uses about two parts sugar for every part egg white, by weight. This means that about 2.4 ounces (66 grams) of sugar is needed for every large egg white (about 1.2 ounces or 33 grams). Soft meringue uses equal weights of sugar and egg white.

Hard meringue is denser and less tender than soft meringue, but it is more stable and it can be easily piped. Use a hard meringue for baked torte layers or for baked meringue shells or cookies. Use a soft meringue for a light-textured topping on a lemon meringue pie, for example, but only if it is to be served fairly soon after production.

Hard meringue is more common in the bakeshop because of its stability.

Notice that what happens to egg proteins during whipping is similar—but not identical—to what happens to egg proteins when they are heated. In both cases, protein molecules unfold and bond, forming a type of structure.

Factors Affecting Meringue Stability

Stability in a meringue is important. Stable meringue is firm yet flexible and resilient, so it can hold up to folding, piping, and baking. Often, the very things that increase stability decrease volume and tenderness. As always, the goal of the pastry chef is to balance opposite features. In this case, the goal is to balance stability with volume and tenderness.

Following is a discussion of the main factors that affect meringue stability.

Sugar Sugar greatly stabilizes meringues even as it slows whipping and decreases volume slightly. For a common meringue—one in which room temperature egg whites are whipped with granulated sugar—sugar stabilizes best if it is added slowly, and only if the proper amount is added. Sugar should be added slowly to provide time for crystals to dissolve and not weigh down

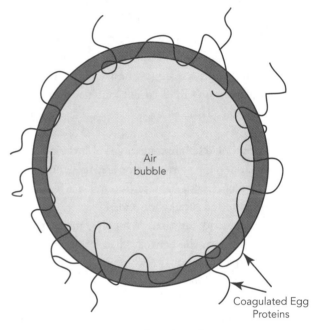

Figure 10.7 The process of egg foam formation

the foam. In addition, if sugar is added too quickly, protein molecules may not unfold properly. The result is a softer meringue or, in extreme cases, whites that will not whip.

Sugar stabilizes meringue by slowing the unfolding and aggregation of protein molecules. This aids stability because it protects against overwhipping. There is another way that sugar stabilizes meringue. As it dissolves in meringue's liquid film, sugar forms a thick, viscous syrup that is slow to drain. This protects the bubbles from collapse. The sugary syrup also adds a satiny sheen to the appearance of meringue.

Lipids Lipids (fats, oils, and emulsifiers) interfere with aeration. Depending on the type and the amount, lipids either slow down aeration or prevent it from happening

> ### HELPFUL HINT
>
> *Undissolved sugar crystals weigh down meringue, weakening it. Once baked, these crystals attract moisture and sometimes form unattractive beads of syrup. To minimize beading and volume loss, use sugar with a fine grind, such as superfine sugar, so sugar dissolves fast. Or sift sugar first, to remove lumps, and add it slowly, allowing it to dissolve between additions. Because sugar slows whipping, be sure to add sugar only after egg whites have already begun to foam.*

at all. This is especially true of egg yolk lipids—lecithin in particular—more so than of shortening or vegetable oil. Even a small amount of yolk can prevent whites from whipping.

Lipids interfere with aeration by coating proteins, preventing them from unfolding and aggregating. But they do more. Lipids compete with proteins for a spot at the foam's bubble surface. Since lipids themselves cannot form a strong, cohesive network the way egg proteins can, lipid-coated bubbles expand rapidly, only to collapse.

Acid   Acid stabilizes meringue by lowering pH. Cream of tartar is the most common acid used, but lemon juice and vinegar also stabilize. Too much acid leaves a sour, off taste and should be avoided.

Add acid early on. Whipping might take longer, but the protein network that forms will be flexible and stable against overwhipping, folding, piping, and baking. The meringue will also be whiter.

Temperature of Whites   Egg whites right out of the refrigerator will not whip well. The ideal temperature to whip a common or French meringue is room temperature, about 70°F (21°C).

Besides making common meringues, bakeshops also prepare Swiss and Italian meringues. Any of these three can be made soft or hard; that is, made with equal parts sugar to whites or with two parts sugar to whites. Swiss meringue is made by warming sugar with egg whites in a double boiler prior to whipping. This process dissolves sugar crystals, and the higher temperature—to

110°–120°F (40°–50°C)—undoubtedly has an effect on the unfolding of egg proteins. Swiss meringue is used more often in the bakeshop, and when properly prepared, is more stable than common meringue.

Probably because frozen egg whites have already been heated to pasteurize them, care must be taken when using them in Swiss meringues. Warm the whites just until sugar crystals dissolve, then immediately remove from heat.

An Italian meringue is essentially a cooked meringue. Hot sugar syrup, heated to 248°–250°F (120°–121°C), is slowly added to whipped egg whites. The hot syrup coagulates the whipped egg proteins. An Italian meringue is the most stable of the three types of meringue. However, an Italian meringue has the lowest volume and the most dense, least tender mouthfeel.

Thickness of Whites   Thin older whites whip more easily to a higher volume than thick, fresh ones. But once whipped, the foam from thin whites is less stable, because the liquid film drains more easily from the bubbles. If volume is more important than stability, older eggs are better.

For the most part, however, eggs purchased through normal channels have already aged, sometimes by several weeks. For better stability, a good rule of thumb is to use fresher eggs for meringues, saving older ones for general baking.

Whipping Time   Both underwhipped and overwhipped egg whites are unstable. If underwhipped, proteins are not fully aggregated to form a strong film. In time, underwhipped whites weep.

When whipped too quickly or for too long, proteins denature and aggregate extensively, and the protective film that surrounds each air bubble becomes overstretched and rigid. The whites eventually collapse, forming tightly bonded, inflexible clumps of protein floating in squeezed-out liquid. In other words, too much whipping has a curdling effect on egg protein structure similar to the effect of too much heat. Over-whipped whites should be discarded.

Other Factors Other factors that affect the stability of meringue include the presence of copper or salt, and the type of whisk used. Whipping in a copper bowl increases meringue stability in much the same way that cream of tartar works; that is, it improves the flexibility of a protein network so that it is stable against overwhipping, folding, piping, and baking. With copper bowls, tiny particles of copper are whipped into the whites each time the whisk hits the bowl. Egg whites whipped in copper have a slight golden color.

Salt appears to decrease meringue stability, so it is best left out of whites when they are whipped. Large wires or blades on a whisk produce larger, less stable air cells than thinner ones. When choosing a whisk, it is best to use a finer piano whisk for whipping whites.

Storage and Handling

The U.S. Food and Drug Administration (FDA) classifies shell eggs as a potentially hazardous food, even if the eggs are clean, whole, and uncracked. Dry eggs that have been reconstituted and frozen egg products that have been thawed are also potentially hazardous.

The following guidelines should be followed when working with eggs to ensure microbiological safety.

Receiving and Storing Eggs and Egg Products

- Check the temperature of a shipment of whole shell eggs by breaking one or two into a small cup and immediately measuring the temperature with an accurate thermometer. The temperature of an incoming shipment of eggs should be 45°F (7°C) or below, by law.
- Evaluate one or two eggs from a shipment for freshness. Check for cleanliness of shell, thickness of white and yolk, and odor.

- Refrigerate or freeze eggs and egg products immediately upon delivery. Store dry egg products at room temperature in a cool dry area. Store shell eggs in their original containers. The ideal storage conditions for shell eggs is 38°–40°F (3°–4°C) with 75–85 percent relative humidity. This helps maintain the overall quality of eggs. At the very least, be sure to refrigerate shell eggs, reconstituted dry eggs, and thawed frozen egg products at temperatures at or below 45°F (7°C).
- Unopened refrigerated liquid egg products can be held for up to 12 weeks, if kept at or below 40°F (4°C). Once opened, use within a few days. To keep track of product age, label cartons with thaw dates. Always rotate stock: first in, first out (FIFO).
- Treat opened thawed frozen liquid egg products as you would refrigerated products. Refrain from refreezing unused product, since it is freezing and thawing that causes the most damage to frozen foods, including egg products.

What Is Salmonellosis?

Salmonella is a type of bacteria that causes one of the most common foodborne infections, salmonellosis. An estimated 118,000 illnesses per year in the United States are caused by the consumption of eggs contaminated with salmonella. Cracked or dirty eggs are a clear risk factor for salmonella contamination, but even clean, intact eggs can be contaminated. Symptoms of salmonellosis include diarrhea, fever, intense abdominal pain, and vomiting. Mild cases often last two to three days. Severe cases last longer and can be fatal, especially for young children, the elderly, or those with weak immune systems.

Since salmonella cannot be completely eliminated from raw foods of animal origin, it must be carefully controlled by the food preparer. Eggs and dairy products are two common bakeshop ingredients that are potential sources of salmonella and must be handled properly. Because salmonella does not grow below 40°F (4°C) and it is destroyed when heated to 160°F (71°C), it is clear that properly cooking and storing eggs and products that contain eggs are important means for assuring food safety in the bakeshop.

Alkalinity of Egg Whites

Egg white is one of the few foods that is naturally alkaline. Fresh egg whites have a pH approaching 8, and this increases to 9 or 10 as eggs age and carbon dioxide evaporates through eggshells. While the natural alkalinity of egg whites helps reduce bacterial growth, salmonella bacteria could still be present, so egg whites should still be cooked or pasteurized before consumption.

Lysozyme, an Egg White Protein

The first line of defense an egg has against the invasion of bacteria is its eggshell, and the second is the egg white itself. While the egg white has several weapons of defense, one of its most effective is the protein lysozyme. Lysozyme is appropriately named. It is an enzyme that lyses, or breaks down, the cell walls of certain bacteria, including salmonella bacteria. In destroying the bacteria's cell wall, lysozyme destroys the bacteria. Lysozyme is not unique to egg white; it is also found in human tears and saliva. While lysozyme makes it difficult for salmonella and other bacteria to grow in egg white, it is not impossible for them to do so. The USDA has estimated that one in twenty thousand eggs harbors salmonella bacteria.

Usage

- Discard eggs that have even the smallest of cracks or that have a strong off odor.
- Do not wash eggs before use; eggs have been washed and sanitized by the packer.
- Do not crack and pool large amounts of eggs for later use, since eggs out of the shell are particularly susceptible to growth of bacteria.
- Do not crack an egg directly into a bowl containing other ingredients or other eggs; crack into a small cup or bowl, inspect for shell pieces, then add to batch.
- When breaking eggs, do not allow shell to come in contact with egg contents. Although sanitized by the egg processor, eggshells could subsequently pick up dirt or microorganisms. *Hint:* Use a metal spoon and not a piece of shell to remove yolk inadvertently dropped into whites.
- Do not thaw frozen eggs at room temperature; follow the guidelines given in the following section.
- To avoid cross contamination, be sure to sanitize equipment, utensils, and countertops that have come in contact with eggs and wash hands thoroughly after handling raw eggs and before handling other foods.
- Minimum cook time for shell eggs: hold at or above 140°F (60°C) for at least 3.5 minutes.
- Use pasteurized egg products whenever eggs are needed for products that are not heated and held at 140°F (60°C) for at least 3.5 minutes.

- If a cooked product, such as a vanilla custard sauce, is to be cooled before service, cool quickly in an ice water bath and hold at or below 40°F (4°C), to minimize time in temperature danger zone; use within one day.

How to Thaw Frozen Egg Products

There are two acceptable ways to thaw frozen egg products. The first is to thaw frozen eggs under refrigeration. This method is preferred, but it requires planning ahead.

The second acceptable way to thaw frozen egg products is to place unopened containers under cold running water. Do not thaw containers under hot water. This could cook the eggs, destroying their functionality. Do not thaw containers at room temperature; the time it takes for the inner core to thaw exposes the outer area to potentially dangerous temperatures for too long.

How to Use Dried Eggs

There are two ways to use dried eggs in baked goods. The easiest way is to blend dried eggs with other dry ingredients, being sure to increase the amount of water in your formula accordingly.

The second way to use dried eggs is to reconstitute with cool water before use. Allow time for reconstituted egg to stand, refrigerated, before use. Wait at least 1 hour for reconstituted yolks, 3 hours for whites. This allows time for eggs to hydrate properly.

Questions for Review

1 How much (in fractions or a percentage) of the edible part of an egg is egg white? How much is egg yolk?

2 How many dozen eggs are in a flat?

3 How do egg whites and egg yolks compare in moisture, lipids (fat and emulsifiers), and protein content?

4 What is another name for egg white?

5 Name an emulsifier present in egg yolks.

6 Which component in egg yolk provides yellow color? Why might the color of yolk vary from one egg producer to another and throughout the season?

7 Which component in whole eggs (fats, emulsifiers, proteins, water, minerals, etc.) provides structure or toughening? Which two components are considered tenderizers? Where is each of these components located (white, yolk, or both)?

8 Explain how egg yolks can be considered structure builders, even though they contain tenderizers.

9 Why do the FDA and the American Egg Board call eggs purchased in the shell "shell eggs" and not "fresh eggs"?

10 What is meant by an "egg product"? What are the advantages of egg products over shell eggs?

11 Why should egg products be used instead of shell eggs in uncooked buttercream or sorbet?

12 Why is citric acid often added to frozen pasteurized whole eggs?

13 Why is guar gum often added to frozen pasteurized egg whites?

14 Why is sugar often added to frozen pasteurized egg yolks?

15 Rank egg whites, egg yolks, and whole eggs from highest to lowest in each of the following functions: structure building and toughening, leavening, color, flavor, and emulsification.

16 Why will the addition of extra egg whites (which are about 90 percent water) to cake batter sometimes produce a drier, rather than a moister, cake?

17 How do sugars and fats affect the process of egg coagulation? That is, do they speed it up and increase the likelihood of curdling and toughening due to overcooking, or do they slow it down and decrease the likelihood of curdling and toughening?

18 Which is better for producing the highest-quality baked custard: using an oven temperature that is slightly too high, or using one that is slightly too low? Explain.

19 Besides producing softer and more tender custards, how else do fats (from cream and egg yolks, for example) affect the texture of custards?

20 How is the volume of freshly whipped foam affected when steps are taken to increase stability? That is, as you increase the stability of whipped egg whites, will volume most likely increase, decrease, or stay the same?

21 What is the difference between a hard meringue and a soft meringue? When is one used instead of the other?

22 Briefly describe differences in the preparation of common, Swiss, and Italian meringues. Which is the most stable? Which is the least stable?

23 What happens to the thickness of an egg white (and yolk) as it ages? How does this affect its ability to whip?

24 How does sugar affect the stability of whipped egg whites? What happens when sugar is added too fast or too soon to whipping eggs?

25 How do fats and egg yolks affect the ability of a meringue to form?

26 How does acid affect the stability of whipped egg whites?

27 What is the name of the acid that is most commonly added to egg whites as they are whipped?

28 Provide six safety guidelines to follow when using eggs and egg products, and explain why each is important.

Questions for Discussion

1 A formula calls for 35 whole eggs. How much whole egg should you weigh out?

2 A formula calls for 10 egg yolks. How much egg yolk should you weigh out?

3 A formula calls for 6 egg whites. How much egg white should you weigh out?

4 Why might a slightly greenish cast develop in baking powder biscuits that contain eggs? How can it be prevented?

5 Draw the process of the heat coagulation of egg proteins. Include in your drawing what happens when eggs receive too much heat. Explain in words what is happening at each step, and be sure to properly label all your squiggles.

6 You need to temper room temperature eggs with hot milk to avoid coagulating the eggs. Explain how you will do this, and explain how it prevents coagulation of eggs.

7 You have extra egg yolks and decide to use them instead of whole eggs in a cake. You use 1 pound (or kilogram) egg yolk for each pound (or kilogram) of whole eggs called for in the formula. What differences might you expect in the cake baked with egg yolks compared with the cake baked with whole eggs?

8 Describe the process of egg foam formation.

9 List steps to follow when receiving and storing eggs and egg products, and explain why each is important.

Exercises and Experiments

① Exercise: Sensory Characteristics of Egg Products and Egg Replacers

In the Results Table, fill in the Description column with the brand name of each egg product and replacer. Include additional information that further describes and differentiates the product from others of the same kind. Next, identify from the package if the product is pasteurized or not, and list the ingredients for each egg product or egg replacer. Next, use fresh samples brought to room temperature to evaluate the appearance (color, clarity, and consistency) as well as the aroma of each. Use this opportunity to identify different egg products and egg replacers from their sensory characteristics alone. Two rows are left blank, for the evaluation of additional egg products, if desired.

RESULTS TABLE   EGG PRODUCTS AND REPLACERS

EGG PRODUCT	DESCRIPTION	PASTEURIZED (YES/NO)	LIST OF INGREDIENTS	APPEARANCE	AROMA
Frozen whole eggs					
Frozen egg whites					
Dried egg whites					
Frozen egg yolks					
Refrigerated egg yolks					
Liquid whole-egg substitute (e.g., Egg Beaters)					
Powdered egg replacer					

Use information from your textbook and from the preceding table to answer the following questions. Select one from the choices in **bold** or fill in the blanks.

1   The only egg product/replacer that is *not* labeled as pasteurized is _____
    _____. This product is probably not pasteurized because _____
    _____
    _____.

2   Frozen whole eggs sometimes have _____ added to keep them from discolor-
    ing when heated. This ingredient **was/was not** added to the frozen whole eggs evaluated.

3   Frozen egg whites sometimes have _____ added, a natural vegetable gum
    that thickens the whites and prevents ice crystal damage. This gum **was/was not** added to
    the frozen egg whites evaluated.

4   Frozen egg whites sometimes have _____ added as a whipping agent. This
    whipping agent **was/was not** added to the frozen egg whites evaluated

5   Frozen egg yolks sometimes have _____ or _____ added
    to keep them from denaturing and coagulating into a thick gel. The frozen egg yolks
    evaluated has the following ingredient(s) added to prevent gelling:

    _____
    _____
    _____

6   The ingredient in the whole egg substitute that provides a yellow-orange egg color is ___
    _____
    _____.

7   Since one of their main uses is in making scrambled eggs and omelets, whole egg sub-
    stitutes often contain added salt and seasonings. The seasonings added to the whole egg
    substitute evaluated are as follows:

    _____
    _____
    _____

8   You want to prepare baked goods with no preservatives (preservatives include sodium
    benzoate, potassium sorbate, and calcium proprionate). The egg products/replacers that
    do not contain preservatives and therefore could be used in preservative-free baked goods
    are as follows:

    _____
    _____
    _____

9   The main ingredient in liquid whole-egg substitute that provides structure is _____
    _____
    _____.

10 The main ingredient(s) in the powdered egg replacer that provides structure is/are _____

_____

_____.

11 You have a customer who is allergic to eggs. When preparing a cake for this customer, you could use **whole-egg substitute/powdered egg replacer**.

❷ Exercise: How to Minimize Weeping and Curdling in a Custard Sauce (Crème Anglaise)

Imagine that you have a custard sauce formula that tends to weep and curdle during cooking. You can make any change to the formula or to the method of preparation. You list the following changes that could decrease weeping and curdling because each decreases the rate of egg coagulation. While some of these changes will not work in every situation, and some work better than others, each is a possibility. Explain the reasons that each could work. The first is completed for you.

1 Use lower cooking temperature.

Reason: This is the most direct way to slow the rate of coagulation, since it reduces the rate of heat that reaches the custard. When eggs are heated slowly, there is more time for egg proteins to properly unfold and coagulate without curdling.

2 Use cream instead of milk.

Reason: _____

_____

_____

3 Increase amount of sugar.

Reason: _____

_____

_____

4 Cook custard in double boiler (bain marie), above simmering water.

Reason: _____

_____

_____

5 Decrease amount of egg.

Reason: _____

_____

_____

❸ Experiment: How Different Eggs and Liquids Affect the Overall Quality of Baked Custard

Objectives

Demonstrate how different eggs and liquids affect
- Firmness of baked custard
- Appearance, flavor, and mouthfeel of baked custard
- Overall acceptability of baked custard

Products Prepared

Baked custard made with
- Whole egg/whole milk (control product)
- Egg white/whole milk
- Egg yolk/whole milk
- Whole egg/cream
- Whole egg/soy milk
- Whole egg/water
- Other, if desired (liquid whole egg substitute/whole milk; whole egg/low-fat milk; whole egg/whole milk with added raw pineapple juice; frozen pasteurized whole egg/whole egg; etc.)

Materials and Equipment

- Scale
- Stainless-steel saucepans
- Stainless-steel bowls
- Whisk
- Custard (see Formula), enough to make 8 or more custard cups of each variation
- Ceramic custard cups (6 fl. oz./180 ml), or equivalent
- Size #8 (4 fl. oz./120 ml) portion-control scoop or equivalent
- Oven thermometer
- Hotel pans, for water baths
- Instant-read thermometer (optional)

Formula

Baked Custard

Yield: *eight ½-cup servings*

INGREDIENT	POUNDS	OUNCES	GRAMS	BAKER'S PERCENTAGE
Milk, whole	1		450	100
Eggs, whole		7.2	200	45
Sugar, regular, granulated		4	112	25
Vanilla extract		0.3	8	2
Total	**1**	**11.5**	**770**	**172**

Method of Preparation

1 Preheat oven to 325°F (160°C).

2 Bring milk to a boil in saucepan. Remove from heat.

3 Whisk egg, sugar, and vanilla extract in bowl.

4 Gently whisk hot milk into egg mixture.

Procedure

1 Label custard cups or ovens with type of egg and liquid to be used in each batch of baked custard.

2 Prepare custard mixture using the above formula or using any basic baked custard formula. Prepare one batch for each variation.

3 Fill ceramic custard cups using #8 scoop (or any scoop that fills cup about three-quarters full).

4 Use an oven thermometer placed in center of oven for an initial reading of oven temperature. Record results here: _____.

5 When oven is properly preheated, place filled custard cups in shallow hotel pan and place in oven. Pour about ½ inch (1.25 centimeters) hot water into pans and set timer for 30–40 minutes (time could vary depending on temperature of water in water bath).

6 Bake until control product (made with whole eggs and whole milk) is firm but still jiggles. Remove all baked custards from oven after same length of time, even though some will not have firmed up properly. If necessary, however, adjust bake times for oven variances.

7 Record bake times in Results Table, which follows.

8 Check final oven temperature. Record results here: _____.

9 If desired, check temperature of baked custard (in center point) and record in Results Table under Additional Comments. For temperatures to be meaningful, they must be taken immediately after custards are removed from oven.

10 Remove custard cups from hot pans and cool to room temperature.

Results

Evaluate the sensory characteristics of completely cooled products and record evaluations in Results Table. Be sure to compare each in turn with the control product and consider the following:

- Appearance (color, translucency, firmness, etc.)
- Texture and mouthfeel (firmness, smoothness, creaminess, brittleness, etc.)
- Flavor (sweetness, egg flavor, fullness of flavor)
- Overall acceptability, from highly unacceptable to highly acceptable, on a scale of 1 to 5
- Any additional comments, as necessary

RESULTS TABLE SENSORY CHARACTERISTICS OF BAKED CUSTARDS
MADE WITH DIFFERENT EGGS AND LIQUIDS

TYPE OF EGG	LIQUID	BAKE TIME (IN MINUTES)	APPEARANCE	TEXTURE AND MOUTHFEEL	FLAVOR	OVERALL ACCEPTABILITY	ADDITIONAL COMMENTS
Whole egg	Whole milk						
Egg white	Whole milk						
Egg yolk	Whole milk						
Whole egg	Cream						
Whole egg	Soy milk						
Whole egg	Water						

Sources of Error

List any sources of error that might make it difficult to draw the proper conclusions from your experiment. In particular, consider any differences in how long the milk was heated or held, any difficulty dispensing equal volumes of custard mix into cups, how high water was filled in water bath, whether water spilled into custard, differences in final custard temperature (if measured), and any problems with ovens.

_____

_____

_____

State what you could do differently next time to minimize or eliminate each source of error.

_____

_____

_____

Conclusions

Select one from the choices in **bold** or fill in the blanks.

1 The custard with the deepest yellow color was made with **whole eggs/egg white/egg yolk**. This is because this custard was highest in _____, the pigment that provides a yellow color to eggs. Other differences in appearance of these three custards were as follows:

_____

_____

_____

2 Baked custards appear firm if structure has formed. Which of the following are structure builders; that is, which firmed up in baked custard, as expected: **whole eggs/egg whites/ egg yolks**?

3 Eggs interact with dairy proteins and calcium salts for a **softer/firmer** set. That is why the baked custard made with milk was **softer/firmer** than the one made with water.

4 The proteins and calcium salts in soy milk interact with egg proteins **less than/more than/the same as** the proteins and salts in dairy whole milk. That is why the baked custard made with soy milk was **softer than/firmer than/the same as** the one made with whole milk and whole eggs.

5 Of the baked custards made with different liquids, the one with the smoothest, creamiest mouthfeel was made with whole egg and **whole milk/heavy cream/soy milk/water**. This is probably because this ingredient is **high/moderate/low** in tenderizing _____

_____

_____.

6 Of the baked custards made with different eggs, the one with the fullest, richest flavor was made with **whole eggs/egg whites/egg yolks**. Specific differences in flavor among these samples include:

_____

_____

_____

7 Other comments I would like to add about differences in the custards or about the experiment:

_____

_____

_____

❹ Experiment: How Different Eggs Affect the Overall Quality of Muffins

Objectives

Demonstrate how the type of egg affects

- Crust color
- Crumb color and structure
- Moistness, tenderness, and height of the muffins
- Overall flavor of the muffin
- Overall acceptability of the muffin

Products Prepared

Muffins made with

- Whole egg (control product)
- No egg (with additional water [75 percent], oil [10 percent], and milk solids [15 percent] to replace egg)
- Egg white
- Egg yolk
- Liquid whole egg substitute (for example, Egg Beaters)
- Other, if desired (one-half egg yolk and one-half water to match the amount of water in whole egg, reconstituted dried whole egg, reconstituted dried egg substitute, frozen pasteurized whole egg, etc.)

Materials and Equipment

- Scale
- Sieve
- Stainless-steel bowls
- Whisk
- Muffin batter (see Formula), enough to make 24 or more muffins of each variation
- Muffin pans (2½" or 3½"/65 or 90 mm size)
- Paper liners or pan spray
- Size #16 (2 fl. oz./30 ml) portion-control scoop or equivalent
- Half sheet pans (optional)
- Oven thermometer
- Wooden pick, for testing
- Serrated knife
- Ruler

Formula

Basic Muffin Batter

Yield: 24 muffins (you will have some excess batter)

INGREDIENT	POUND	OUNCE	GRAMS	BAKER'S PERCENTAGE
Flour, pastry	1	4	570	100
Sugar, regular granulated		8	225	40
Salt (1 tsp/5 ml)		0.2	6	1
Baking powder		1.2	35	6
Butter		7	200	35
Eggs, whole		6	170	30
Milk	1		455	80
Total	**3**	**10.4**	**1,661**	**292**

Method of Preparation

1   Preheat oven to 400°F (200°C).

2   Sift dry ingredients together into bowl.

3   Melt butter; cool slightly.

4   Whisk egg lightly; blend in milk and melted butter.

5   Pour liquids onto dry ingredients and mix just until flour is moistened. Batter will look lumpy.

Method of Preparation
(for muffins made with no egg)

Follow the Method of Preparation for the control product (above) except make the following adjustments:

1   Sift 1 ounce (28 grams) dried milk solids with dry ingredients.

2   Add ½ ounce (14 grams) oil and 4½ ounces (128 grams) water to liquid ingredients.

Procedure

1   Prepare muffin batter using the above formula or using any basic muffin formula. Prepare one batch of batter for each variation.

2   Line or lightly spray muffin pans with pan spray.

3   Label muffin pans or ovens with type of egg to be added to muffin batter.

4   Scoop batter into prepared muffins pans using level #16 scoop (or any scoop that fills cup one-half to three-quarters full). If desired, place muffin pans on half sheet pans.

5   Use an oven thermometer placed in center of oven for an initial reading of oven temperature. Record results here: _____.

6 When oven is properly preheated, place filled muffin pans in oven and set timer for 20–22 minutes.

7 Bake until control product (made with whole eggs) springs back when center top is lightly pressed and wooden pick inserted into center of muffin comes out clean. Control product should be lightly browned. Remove all muffins from oven after same length of time, even though some will be paler in color or have not risen properly. If necessary, however, adjust bake times for oven variances.

8 Record bake times in Results Table 1.

9 Check final oven temperature. Record results here: _____.

10 Remove muffins from hot pans and cool to room temperature.

Results

1 When muffins are completely cooled, evaluate height as follows:
- Slice three muffins from each batch in half, being careful not to compress.
- Measure height of each muffin by placing ruler along the flat edge at the muffin's center point. Record results for each of three muffins in 1/16" (1 mm) increments and record results in Results Table 1.
- Calculate the average muffin height for each batch by adding the heights of the muffins and dividing by 3. Record results in Results Table 1.

2 Evaluate the shape of muffins (even rounded top, peaked top, dips in center, etc.) and record results in Results Table 1.

RESULTS TABLE 1 SIZE AND SHAPE OF MUFFINS MADE WITH DIFFERENT TYPES OF EGG

TYPE OF EGG	BAKE TIME (IN MINUTES)	HEIGHTS OF EACH OF THREE MUFFINS	AVERAGE HEIGHT OF ONE MUFFIN	MUFFIN SHAPE	ADDITIONAL COMMENTS
Whole egg (control product)					
No egg (water, oil, and DMS as replacement)					
Egg white					
Egg yolk					
Liquid whole egg substitute					

RESULTS TABLE 1 (continued)

TYPE OF EGG	BAKE TIME (IN MINUTES)	HEIGHTS OF EACH OF THREE MUFFINS	AVERAGE HEIGHT OF ONE MUFFIN	MUFFIN SHAPE	ADDITIONAL COMMENTS

3 Evaluate the sensory characteristics of completely cooled products and record evaluations in Results Table 2. Be sure to compare each in turn to the control product and consider the following:

- Crust color, from very light to very dark on a scale of 1 to 5
- Crumb appearance (small/large air cells, uniform/irregular air cells, tunnels, etc); also, evaluate color
- Crumb texture (tough/tender, moist/dry, gummy, spongy, crumbly, etc.)
- Flavor (egg flavor, floury taste, saltiness, sweetness, etc.)
- Overall acceptability, from highly unacceptable to highly acceptable, on a scale of 1 to 5.
- Any additional comments, as necessary

RESULTS TABLE 2 SENSORY CHARACTERISTICS OF MUFFINS MADE WITH DIFFERENT TYPES OF EGG

TYPE OF EGG	CRUST COLOR	CRUMB APPEARANCE AND TEXTURE	FLAVOR	OVERALL ACCEPTABILITY	ADDITIONAL COMMENTS
Whole egg (control product)					
No egg (water, oil, and DMS as replacement)					
Egg white					
Egg yolk					
Liquid whole egg substitute					

Sources of Error

List any sources of error that might make it difficult to draw the proper conclusions from your experiment. In particular, consider if there were differences in how batters were mixed and handled, any difficulty in dispensing equal volumes of batter into muffin pans, and any problems with ovens.

_____

_____

_____

State what you could do differently next time to minimize or eliminate each source of error.

_____

_____

_____

Conclusions

Select one from the choices in **bold** or fill in the blanks.

1   The muffins with the least amount of browning were made with **no egg/whole egg/egg white**. This is probably because these muffins were **lowest/highest** in protein, which is necessary for **caramelization/Maillard browning**. The differences were **small/moderate/large**.

2   The muffins that were most tender were made with **no egg/whole egg/egg white**. This is probably because these muffins were **lowest/highest** in egg protein, which is classified as a structure **builder/tenderizer**. The differences were **small/moderate/large**.

3   The muffins that tasted very moist, even gummy, were made with **no egg/whole egg/egg white**. This suggests that even though they contain moisture (water), eggs also contain driers, primarily **egg proteins/sugars/oils**, that trap water. In other words, the presence of moisture (water) **does/does not** always result in the perception of moistness.

4   The muffins made without egg did not collapse because they contain other structure builders, namely the gluten and _____ in flour.

5   The muffins made with egg yolk **were/were not** as tender as the muffins made with no egg. This means that they **did/did not** have more structure than the muffins made with no egg. In other words, egg yolks can be classified as **structure builders/tenderizers**.

6   Muffins made with egg yolk **were/were not** acceptable overall. Compared with muffins made with whole egg, those made with egg yolk had the following differences in appearance, texture, and flavor:

_____

_____

_____

Overall, these differences were **small/moderate/large**.

7 Muffins made with egg white **were/were not** acceptable overall. Compared with muffins made with whole egg, those made with egg white had the following differences in appearance, texture, and flavor:

_____

_____

_____

Overall, these differences were **small/moderate/large**.

8 In my opinion, the best-tasting muffins were made with _____ because

_____

_____.

9 Other comments I would like to add about differences in the muffins or about the experiment:

_____

_____

_____

⑤ Experiment: How Different Ingredients and Treatments Affect the Quality and Stability of Meringue

Objectives

Demonstrate how various ingredients and treatments affect
- The time it takes to fully whip meringue
- Meringue volume
- Meringue stability
- The appearance, flavor, and mouthfeel of meringue
- The overall acceptability of meringue

Products Prepared

Meringue prepared the following ways
- Common soft meringue (control product, made with one part sugar to one part egg white)
- Common hard meringue (made with two parts sugar to one part egg white)
- With cream of tartar
- With no sugar
- With sugar added all at once, in beginning
- Swiss meringue method
- Italian meringue method
- Other (with small amount of egg yolk or with shortening on bowl; made with frozen pasteurized egg whites; made with dried egg whites, whites not warmed before whipping, whipped on high speed, underwhipped, added salt, etc.)

Materials and Equipment

- Scale
- Mixer with 5-quart mixing bowl
- Sieve (optional)
- Wire whip attachment
- Stopwatch or count-up timer
- Double boiler
- Instant-read thermometer
- Stainless-steel saucepans
- Candy thermometer
- Meringue (see Formula), enough to make 16 ounces (450 grams) or more of each variation
- Spoon
- Clear volumetric measuring cups (16 fl. oz./500 ml, or equivalent, one per test product)
- Straight-edge
- Pastry bag with plain tip (optional)
- Parchment paper (optional)

Formula

Common Soft Meringue

INGREDIENT	POUND	OUNCE	GRAMS	BAKER'S PERCENTAGE
Egg whites		8	225	100
Sugar, granulated		8	225	100
Total	**1**		**450**	**200**

Method of Preparation
(for control product, common soft meringue)

1 Warm egg whites to room temperature.

2 Pass sugar through sieve, if necessary, to remove lumps.

3 Using whip attachment, beat egg whites at medium speed.

4 After whites begin to foam, begin adding sugar gradually and whip until soft peaks form.

Method of Preparation
(for common hard meringue)

Follow the Method of Preparation for the control product, but double amount of sugar used.

Method of Preparation
(for meringue made with no sugar)

Follow the Method of Preparation for the control product, but omit the added sugar.

Method of Preparation
(for meringue made with cream of tartar)

Follow the Method of Preparation for the control product, but add ¼ teaspoon (1.25 ml) cream of tartar in step 3, when whites just begin to foam.

Method of Preparation
(for Swiss meringue)

1   Combine egg whites and sugar in a double boiler that contains hot (not boiling) water.

2   Whip mixture continuously until it reaches 115°F (45°C).

Method of Preparation
(for Italian meringue)

1   Begin heating sugar with 1½ ounces (45 grams) water. Stir to dissolve.

2   Boil sugar syrup, without stirring, until temperature reaches 245°F (118°C).

3   In the meantime, whip egg whites at medium speed.

4   Continue whipping egg whites while gradually adding hot sugar syrup in a slow, steady stream.

5   Continue to whip until meringue is cool.

Procedure

1   Prepare meringue using the formula above, or using any basic common soft meringue formula. Prepare one batch of meringue for each variation.

2   Measure the time it takes for soft peaks to form. Record results in Results Table 1, which follows.

Note: There is a small but real risk of the presence of salmonella bacteria in egg white. Where consumption of unpasteurized egg white is outlawed or undesired, evaluate flavor by smell only, omit evaluation of sweetness, and use fingertips or a spoon to evaluate texture in place of mouthfeel. Or conduct this experiment using pasteurized egg whites.

Results

1   Measure density of meringue as follows:
   • Carefully spoon sample of each meringue into tared clear measuring cup.
   • Visually check cup to confirm that no large air gaps are present.
   • Level the top surface of the cup with a straight-edge.
   • Weigh the amount of meringue in each cup and record results in Results Table 1.
   • If desired, convert density measurements into specific gravity by dividing the density (weight per volume) of each meringue by the weight of an equal volume of water.

2   Measure stability of meringue as follows:
   • Hold samples in clear cups at room temperature or warmer for 30 minutes or longer, if time permits. Alternatively, pipe meringues onto parchment paper using a pastry bag with a plain tip before holding.
   • Evaluate loss in volume, change in appearance, and increase in liquid at bottom of container or on parchment. Record results in Results Table 1.

RESULTS TABLE 1 WHIP TIME, MERINGUE VOLUME, AND MERINGUE STABILITY FOR DIFFERENT MERINGUES

TREATMENT	TIME TO REACH SOFT PEAK (IN MINUTES)	DENSITY OF MERINGUE	SPECIFIC GRAVITY OF MERINGUE (OPTIONAL)	MERINGUE STABILITY	ADDITIONAL COMMENTS
Common soft meringue (control product)					
Common hard meringue					
Common soft meringue with cream of tartar					
With no sugar					
Sugar added all at once, in beginning					
Swiss meringue					
Italian meringue					

3   Evaluate the sensory characteristics of freshly whipped meringue and record evaluations in Results Table 2, which follows. Be sure to compare each in turn to the control product and consider the following:
   • Appearance (air cell size, gloss, whiteness)
   • Flavor (sweetness, sourness, fresh egg flavor, off flavors)
   • Mouthfeel (density and body, softness/firmness)
   • Overall acceptability for use on a lemon meringue pie
   • Add any additional comments, as necessary

RESULTS TABLE 2 SENSORY CHARACTERISTICS OF DIFFERENT
TREATMENTS OF MERINGUE

TREATMENT	APPEARANCE	FLAVOR	MOUTHFEEL	OVERALL ACCEPTABILITY	COMMENTS
Common soft meringue (control product)					
Common hard meringue					
Common soft meringue with cream of tartar					
With no sugar					
Sugar added all at once, in beginning					
Swiss meringue					
Italian meringue					

Sources of Error

List any sources of error that might make it difficult to draw the proper conclusions from your experiment. In particular, consider any differences in how quickly sugar was added and how fully whipped the meringues were.

_____

_____

_____

State what you could do differently next time to minimize or eliminate each source of error.

_____

_____

_____

Conclusions

Select one from the choices in **bold** or fill in the blanks.

1   As the amount of sugar increases, the density of meringue **increases/decreases/stays the same**. Likewise, increasing the amount of sugar **increases/decreases/does not change** the firmness of the meringue when tasted. Other effects of sugar on the appearance, flavor, and mouthfeel of meringue are as follows:

_____

_____

_____

2   As the amount of sugar increases, meringue lasts for a **longer time/shorter time** before losing stability. Signs of an unstable meringue included the following:

_____

_____

_____

3   The egg whites that whipped up the fastest had **no sugar/double the weight of sugar to egg white (hard meringue)**. This is because sugar **slows down/speeds up** the unfolding of egg proteins, an important first step in whipping egg whites.

_____

_____

_____

4   The main purpose for adding cream of tartar to meringue is for **flavor/stability/volume**. Other **acids/alkalis** that could be used for this purpose instead of cream of tartar include

_____

_____

_____

5   Cream of tartar added a **sour/salty** taste to meringue. The difference was **small/moderate/large**. Other differences in the sensory characteristics of meringue made with cream of tartar include the following:

_____

_____

_____

6   The advantages and disadvantages, if any, of adding sugar all at once versus adding it slowly (control product) include the following:

_____

_____

_____

7 The main differences in stability, appearance, flavor, and mouthfeel among the Swiss, Italian, and common (control product) meringues were as follows:

_____

_____

_____

8 Other comments I would like to add about differences in the meringues, or about the experiment:

_____

_____

_____

9 Identify which meringue might be best for each of the following applications; justify your answers.

a   Angel food cake

_____

_____

_____

b   Lemon meringue pie, to be served immediately

_____

_____

_____

c   Lemon meringue pie, to be held for 3 days before serving

_____

_____

_____

d   Smooth, rich, and full-bodied buttercream

_____

_____

_____

e   Light and airy buttercream

_____

_____

_____

f   Piped and baked meringue shells

_____

_____

_____

11

Leavening Agents

Introduction

Leavening gases, despite their importance, often play a behind-the-scenes role in baking. For instance, air (one of three main leavening gases in baked goods) does not show up in formulas, and steam (another of the three main leavening gases) is added indirectly in the form of eggs, milk, applesauce, and other ingredients that contain water. Baking powders, which are a source of carbon dioxide, all look alike and they are added in small amounts, so it might seem that there is nothing to learn about them. In fact, baking powders have some interesting and important differences that are often overlooked. Likewise, yeast, another source of carbon dioxide, can differ in significant ways. This chapter discusses those differences. It also discusses each of the three main leavening gases in baked goods—air, steam, and carbon dioxide—and how each contributes to leavening.

The Process of Leavening

Leavening agents—leaveners—cause baked goods to rise, providing lightness and volume. Leavened baked goods are more porous and tender than unleavened, and they are also easier to digest.

Four events must happen for baked goods to rise properly:

1   Sufficient air bubbles must be added to raw batters and doughs.
2   Gases must form and expand from the heat of the oven, enlarging air bubbles.
3   Still-flexible cell walls must stretch from the pressure of expanding gases.
4   Cell walls must dry out and set, defining the final volume and shape of the baked good.

Although we think of leavening as happening in the oven, it starts in the mixing bowl as soon as air is creamed, beaten, or stirred into batters and doughs.

Before discussing the leavening process in more detail, it helps to understand that there are three forms of matter: *solid*, *liquid*, and *gas*. When temperatures change, matter can change from one physical form to another. For example, as temperatures rise, solid ice melts to liquid water, and liquid water evaporates to gaseous steam. Heat causes these changes, and in the process, molecules move faster and spread farther apart. This expansion is the basis for leavening.

As gases expand from the heat of the oven, they push on wet, flexible cell walls, causing them to stretch. As long as cell walls stretch without breaking, volume increases. Eventually, cell walls set into a semirigid structure and can no longer stretch. Pressure builds within the air bubbles, until cell walls break. At this point, leavening ceases and gases evaporate out of the baked good. When baked goods are removed from the oven, remaining gases evaporate or contract back to their original volume. Products with strong structure and a porous crumb retain their shape. Those with wet, weak structures that have not set—such as soufflés and underbaked cakes—shrink in size or collapse as the gases evaporate or contract.

Timing is important. For best volume, gas expansion must occur while the baked good's structure is still stretchy and flexible, yet intact. In the case of yeast-raised baked goods, these ideal conditions occur during bulk fermentation, proofing, and the early stages of baking. Bread dough made with rye and other flours that do not contain sufficient gluten does not rise properly because, without gluten, the dough does not stretch into a thin, flexible film, able to retain gases. Instead, gases from fermentation escape from these doughs soon after they are formed.

Leavening Gases

Recall from Chapter 3 that the three main leavening gases in baked goods are *steam, air,* and *carbon dioxide.* Actually, all liquids and gases expand when heated, so all liquids and gases leaven, at least to some degree. It is just that steam, air, and carbon dioxide are common and plentiful in baked goods. Other liquids and gases that can be important in certain baked goods include alcohol and ammonia.

It is also common to categorize leavening agents according to the way the leavening gas is added to baked goods. When categorized in this manner, the three types of leaveners are *physical, biological,* and *chemical.* Physical (mechanical) leaveners include steam and air. Yeast are biological leaveners that produce, among other things, carbon dioxide. Baking powder, which also produces carbon dioxide, is one of several chemical leaveners. Information about each of these is included throughout the chapter.

Steam

Steam (water vapor) is the gaseous form of water. It forms when water, milk, eggs, syrups, or any other moisture-containing ingredient is heated. Since the conversion of water to steam is considered a physical change, steam is called a *physical leavener.* Steam is a very effective leavening agent because it expands to occupy over 1,600 times more space than water. Imagine the power of this huge increase in volume.

All baked goods rely on steam for at least some of their leavening because all baked goods contain water or another liquid. In fact, many baked goods rely on steam for leavening more than one might imagine. Sponge cakes, for example, rely on steam as much as air. That is because sponge cake batters are high in eggs, which are high in water. For steam to be an effective leavening agent, however, the oven temperature must be high enough for water to evaporate to steam at a fast enough rate.

Certain baked goods, such as popovers and choux pastry, are leavened almost exclusively by steam. These steam-leavened baked goods not only contain large amounts of liquid, but they are baked in very hot ovens to maximize the leavening power of steam.

Steam has other uses in baked goods. For example, steam is injected into ovens during the early stages of bread baking. This keeps crusts from forming too early, allowing bread to rise to its fullest potential without the constraints of a hardened crust. Once the crust does form, it is crisp and glossy, since the added steam allows for the full gelatinization of starches. Because crust formation is delayed, however, steam injection produces a thinner crust than when no steam is used.

> **HELPFUL HINT**
>
> *If volume is low in baked goods, it could be that leavening was not properly timed with structure formation. Ask yourself the following questions, and make the appropriate changes.*
>
> - *Is batter or dough temperature off? Temperature affects leavening. Temperature also affects the thickness of batters and doughs, which influences how well expanding gases are held in. Cake batters that are too warm, for example, activate leavening too soon, and the cakes will have a coarse crumb, low volume, and tend to crumble easily. Cold cake batters activate leavening too late, and the cakes will have peaked and broken tops with low volume and a tough, tight crumb.*
> - *Is the oven working properly, and is it set to the correct temperature? For example, a low oven temperature slows the formation and expansion of gases. This is a problem especially with steam-leavened baked goods such as choux pastry, puff pastry, and certain sponge cakes. On the other hand, if oven temperature is set too high, the outside crust could form and harden on the baked good before leavening gases have a chance to expand.*
> - *Is the product properly formulated, and were ingredients measured accurately? High amounts of sugar and fats slow the coagulation of proteins and the gelatinization of starches, causing gases to be released before structure sets.*
> - *Is the baking powder too fast- or slow-acting? You will learn shortly that baking powders vary in how quickly carbon dioxide is released, with slow-acting baking powders releasing most of their gases late in the baking process.*
> - *Was unbaked batter left out too long before it was baked? Over time, small bubbles merge with larger bubbles, especially when the batter is thin, and large bubbles easily rise to the surface of batters and doughs, only to escape.*

A Brief History of Leavening

The very first breads were unleavened. They were more like flat tortillas made by moistening and baking ground nuts, cereal grains, or seeds. The Egyptians were probably the first to leaven bread. As early as 2300 BC, they used breadmash, which contained wild yeast from the air, to lighten doughs.

For many centuries after that, yeast was the only leavening agent added to baked goods. Chemical leavening agents were not introduced until the late 1700s. The first popular chemical leavening agent was pearl ash, a crude form of potassium carbonate, an alkali. Pearl ash was removed from the ashes of wood. Next came baking soda, also called sodium bicarbonate, which was used with sour milk or a cultured dairy product.

Almost a hundred years went by before cream of tartar, the acid by-product of winemaking, was commercially available. It was used in the first commercial baking powder, made by mixing cream of tartar and baking soda with cornstarch. This first baking powder was produced in San Francisco, near a winemaking region of California.

Baking powders were refined throughout the 1800s and 1900s, with newer, more versatile acids replacing cream of tartar. Today, several types of baking powders are available. They are discussed later in this chapter.

While these advancements were happening with chemical leavening agents, improvements were also made with yeast. Baker's yeast was first purified and sold in the 1800s. No longer was the baker at the mercy of the flavor and gassing properties of wild yeast starters. Few changes were made until the 1940s, when active dry yeast was developed. While active dry yeast is much less perishable than fresh yeast, it did not perform as well as fresh yeast and was not widely used by professional bakers. Not until the late 1970s, when instant yeast was developed, was there a product that combined the convenience of dry yeast with the performance of fresh.

The Magic Puff of Choux Pastry

Choux paste leavens by steam and bakes into hollow shells that can be filled with pastry cream, whipped cream, or savory fillings. Although thick and pasty from being cooked on the stovetop, choux paste contains a large amount of liquid from water or milk, and eggs. It is baked in a very hot 425°F (220°C) oven, which allows the liquid to quickly evaporate to steam during the first 10 minutes of baking. This powerful leavening potential is captured by the high amount of eggs and the gelatinized starch granules in choux paste.

Recall that raw egg proteins are twisted and coiled. As the steam expands, egg proteins uncoil and stretch, and the paste puffs. Steam continues to expand, putting pressure on the stretched egg proteins. Eventually, most of the egg protein structure breaks from the pressure, creating a characteristic cavity in the baked choux paste. However, the outside shell wall—dry from the high heat—resists breakage. Gelatinized starch and coagulated egg proteins in these walls harden and set, defining the shell's final volume and shape.

Choux pastry shells must be thoroughly baked. If side walls are even slightly moist, they will be weak. When the shells are removed from the oven, steam condenses back to water, taking up less space, and still-wet walls recoil. When this happens, shells shrink and collapse.

To keep shrinking and collapsing from happening, do not rely on color alone to determine if choux pastry shells are properly baked. Instead, remove a test shell from the oven, break it open, and check that it is dry. If it is dry and does not collapse, then it is safe to remove the entire batch from the oven.

Air

It is easy to understand the importance of air to angel food cake and to sponge cake. After all, both contain egg whites that are whipped, and this adds volumes of air to the batter. It is a little harder to understand the importance of air to other baked goods such as cookies and biscuits, because these batters and doughs do not noticeably change in volume after mixing.

But without air, baked goods would not leaven.

Before discussing the importance of air to leavening, it is important to understand how air gets into batters and doughs. Like steam, air is a physical leavener. That is, air is added to batters and doughs by physical means—by creaming, whipping, sifting, folding, kneading, and even stirring. In fact, it is nearly impossible to mix ingredients without adding some air. These physical processes also serve to break large air cells into smaller ones for a finer, more uniform crumb. For example, bread dough that has undergone bulk fermentation is punched down to subdivide enlarged gas bubbles into many smaller ones.

Air's Important Role in Leavening   Like water, air is present in all baked products. Unlike water, air is already a gas. Recall from Chapter 3 that air is composed of a mixture of gases, primarily nitrogen. While it expands a little when heated, air is already a gas and does not expand nearly as much as water. Air's role in leavening is subtler but no less important. Here's why.

When air is added to batters and doughs, it is added as small air bubbles or air cells that get uniformly distributed during mixing. These air cells present in the raw batter or dough can be thought of as seed cells. During baking, steam and carbon dioxide gas move to these seed cells, enlarging them. No matter how much water vaporizes into steam, no matter how much carbon dioxide is produced, no new air cells form during baking. Instead, steam and carbon dioxide fill and enlarge the air cells that are already present in the batter or dough. Without these air cells, there would be no place for the gases to go except out. Without these air cells, there would be no leavening.

Understand this: steam and other leavening gases may be formed during the baking process, but no new air cells form. The existing ones simply expand in size.

This leads to an explanation of air's important role in baking. The number of air cells in batters and doughs

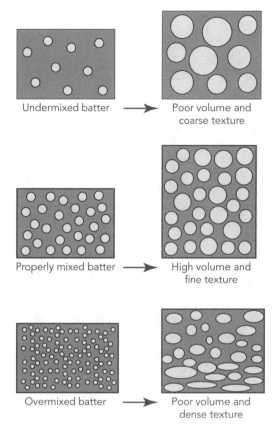

Figure 11.1   The effect of mixing on the volume and crumb structure in baked goods

helps define the baked good's crumb structure. Figure 11.1 shows the relationships among the amount of mixing, the number of seed cells, and the final texture and volume of baked goods.

For example, if cake batter is undermixed and too few air cells are whipped into it, the cake's crumb will likely be coarse and the baked cake will be low in volume. Gases that expand during baking move to the few air cells formed during mixing, making them very large. The fewer the air cells, the larger those few will grow. Large air cells in baked goods mean a coarse crumb.

> **HELPFUL HINT**
>
> *Following instructions carefully when preparing baked goods is as important as weighing ingredients properly. Be sure you understand what it means to whip, cream, knead, fold, and sift ingredients, because different mixing methods provide different levels of aeration, and therefore affect leavening. Unless these functions are executed properly, batters and doughs will not aerate properly, and crumb appearance and volume will suffer.*

Likewise, overmixed batters and doughs will contain many seed cells. Cell walls become overstretched, thin, and weak. During baking, these thin cell walls stretch further and collapse. Again, the baked good will have poor volume.

Carbon Dioxide

Of the three main leavening gases, carbon dioxide is the only one that is not present in all batters and doughs (while carbon dioxide is present in air, it is present in trace amounts only). Carbon dioxide forms from two sources: yeast fermentation, which is a biological leavener, and chemical leavening agents such as baking soda and baking powder.

When it is first generated, carbon dioxide typically dissolves in the liquids that are present in batters and doughs in much the same way that it dissolves in carbonated beverages. Only when enough carbon dioxide is generated, or when it is warmed from the heat of the oven, does carbon dioxide move into existing air bubbles, causing them to expand.

The two sources of carbon dioxide, yeast fermentation and chemical leavening agents, are discussed in the sections that follow.

Yeast Fermentation

The biological or organic production of carbon dioxide results primarily from yeast fermentation. While bacterial fermentation occurs under certain conditions (with sourdoughs, for example), yeast produce the gases needed for leavening while bacteria produce mostly acids and other flavor molecules.

Yeast cells are very small single-celled microorganisms, so small that approximately 15 trillion of them are in one pound of compressed yeast. Fermentation is a process in which yeast cells break down sugars for energy. Yeast uses the energy for survival, growth, and reproduction. Figure 11.2 shows a yeast cell reproducing by budding. Over time, the bud enlarges and eventually pinches off from the mother cell. Visible on the yeast cell in Figure 11.2 are scars from previous buddings. Although yeast breads had been produced for thousands of years, it wasn't until the mid-1800s that Louis Pasteur proved that living yeast was necessary for fermentation.

Yeast can be thought of as tiny enzyme machines, breaking sugars into smaller and simpler molecules with every step. Yeast lacks amylase and cannot break down starch into sugar, though. That is why amylase is often an important additive in bread baking, especially in lean doughs, which consist of little more than flour, water, salt, and yeast. Malted barley flour (dry malt) is the most common means of adding amylase into lean doughs.

Before it was understood that there are many steps in the breakdown of sugars to carbon dioxide, it was thought that an enzyme called *zymase* was responsible. We now know that there are many steps to this process, including a ten-step process called *glycolysis*, and separate enzymes control each step. The term *zymase* is still sometimes used to refer to the many enzymes in yeast that take part in the breakdown of sugars. The overall process is simplified as follows:

$$\text{sugar} \xrightarrow{\text{yeast}} CO_2 + \text{alcohol} + \text{energy} + \text{flavor molecules}$$

When asked, many bakers would say that the most important end product of fermentation is carbon dioxide. However, fermentation produces as much alcohol as it does carbon dioxide. Alcohol evaporates to a gas and expands during the early stages of baking. This adds significantly to oven spring, the fast rising of bread during the first few minutes of baking, making alcohol an important leavening gas in yeast-raised baked goods.

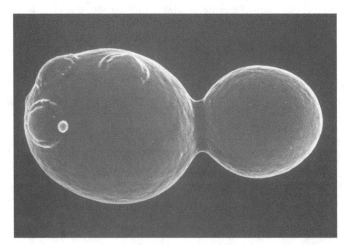

Figure 11.2 Budding yeast cell

Bread flavor comes from three main sources: flavor of the ingredients themselves, especially from the flour and the yeast; Maillard browning that occurs during baking; and flavor generated during yeast fermentation. All three of these can be controlled by the baker.

Artisan bread bakers, in particular, actively work to improve bread flavor through controlling the process of yeast fermentation. Pre-ferments, for example, are commonly used to add flavor to breads, especially those that have a short fermentation time. A pre-ferment—either a liquid batter (poolish) or stiff dough (sponge)—contains yeast along with a portion of flour and water from a bread formula. The pre-ferment is allowed to ferment for several hours or overnight, allowing for the development of a distinctive but not overpowering flavor.

Another method used by bakers is to add a portion of dough from a prior batch into a new batch. This so-called old dough, or *pâte fermentée*, usually adds a slightly stronger, more acidic flavor than a poolish or sponge, because it has already been through a full fermentation.

Bagels and certain other yeast doughs are typically retarded (refrigerated) overnight, or for up to 18 hours. To retard, divided and formed dough is held refrigerated at 35°–42°F (2°–5°C). At this temperature, lactic acid bacteria (present in flour and yeast) are still active, even as yeast are greatly slowed. As they ferment, these bacteria produce flavors that are different in character from those from yeast fermentation.

For stronger flavor still, bakers can prepare a natural starter that relies on the action of wild yeast and bacteria. Natural starters are described on page 307.

Besides carbon dioxide and alcohol, small amounts of flavor molecules, including many acids, are produced during fermentation. These molecules are sometimes overlooked because there are too many to name, and each is generated in such small amounts. But they are the source of the distinctive aroma of freshly baked yeast bread. Often long, slow fermentation is best for developing the most desirable flavor molecules.

At the same time that they are consuming sugars, yeast also use the nitrogen in amino acids to grow and reproduce. Amino acids are the building blocks of proteins, but they are available to yeast only after proteins are broken down by protease enzymes. Once the amino acids are released from proteins, they are transformed into flavorful molecules during fermentation and proofing, adding additional complexity to the flavor of well-made bread.

Factors Affecting Yeast Fermentation

The rate of yeast fermentation is affected by several important factors. Fast fermentation is desirable when time is a constraint. Slower fermentation is desirable for developing both flavor and gluten strength. Bakers often adjust one or more of the following factors to optimize the rate of fermentation.

- *Temperature of dough.* Yeast is dormant at 32°–34°F (0°–1°C) and begins to be quite active starting at about 50°F (10°C). As dough temperature rises above this, the rate of yeast fermentation increases. By about 120°F (50°C), fermentation slows, because yeast cells begin to die. Fermentation essentially stops at 140°F (60°C), when most yeast cells are dead. (These temperatures are estimates only; actual temperatures depend on the dough formula and on the strain of yeast in question.) Optimum fermentation is often given as 78°–82°F (25°–28°C). At lower temperatures (60°F/15°C or below), fermentation of bacteria, not yeast, is often favored. Since bacteria produce more acids when they ferment, dough that is retarded (refrigerated) can develop a strong sour taste. At higher temperatures than optimal (85°–100°F/30°–38°C), fermentation is fast, so bread dough rises quickly but the flavor is generally much less complex.

- *Amount of salt.* Salt retards (inhibits) yeast and bacterial fermentation, with higher levels of salt slowing fermentation. While the typical amount of salt in yeast doughs falls within the narrow range of 1.8–2.2 percent (baker's percentage), bakers can vary the amount of salt in a pre-ferment, making up the difference in the final mix. A pre-ferment contains yeast and a portion of other ingredients from the formula. It is fermented before the makeup of the final dough. For a short fermentation, the pre-ferment is made with a low amount of salt or none at all; for a longer one, it contains more. High salt levels, in particular, limit the production of acids, because salt is especially effective at limiting bacterial fermentation.

- *Amount of sugar.* Yeast typically consume about 3–5 percent (baker's percentage) sugar in dough as they ferment. This means that up to about 5 percent, the more sugar added, the more yeast fermentation. Larger amounts of sugar—especially those above 10 percent—slow fermentation. For this reason, a common method for preparing rich, sweet doughs, which often contain 20 percent or more sugar, is to use a sponge or other pre-ferment. Because large amounts of sugar are not added to the sponge, yeast can ferment without inhibition.

- *Type of sugar.* Sucrose, glucose, and fructose are all fermented rapidly; maltose is fermented slowly; lactose is not fermented at all. A mix of both fast- and slow-fermenting sugars is important with lean yeast doughs (those with low levels of added sugar). This provides for continued gassing through final proof.

- *The pH of dough.* The optimum pH for yeast fermentation is an acidic 4 to 6. Above and below that pH, yeast fermentation slows. As yeast ferments, it produces acids that lower pH to this ideal range.

- *Presence of antimicrobial agents.* Certain antimicrobial agents slow or stop yeast fermentation. For example, when calcium proprionate is added to commercial doughs to prevent mold growth in breads, it must be added properly so that it does not prevent yeast fermentation.

- *Presence of spices.* Most spices, including cinnamon, have strong antimicrobial activity and can slow yeast fermentation. Instead of mixing cinnamon directly into dough, make cinnamon breads and rolls by sprinkling cinnamon and sugar onto dough, then roll and shape the dough like a jelly roll before baking.

- *Chlorine content in water.* Chlorine is an antimicrobial agent, and high levels of chlorine in water can inhibit yeast fermentation. Most water supplies do not contain high levels of chlorine, however, so this is typically not an issue. Where chlorine content is high, though, water can be passed through a carbon filter to remove the chlorine. Or water can be allowed to sit out at room temperature overnight to allow chlorine to evaporate.

- *Addition of yeast foods.* Ammonium salts such as ammonium chloride or ammonium phosphate are a source of nitrogen for growing yeast. Likewise, calcium salts such as calcium carbonate and calcium phosphate provide calcium for optimum yeast fermentation. Ammonium and calcium salts are added to many dough conditioners.

- *Amount of yeast.* For the most part, the more yeast, the faster the fermentation. However, a large amount of yeast can add an undesirable yeasty flavor. A large amount of yeast can also exhaust dough—especially a lean dough—of sugars needed for fermentation during final proof and oven spring. That is why it is best to use a smaller amount of yeast when using a long fermentation time. A good starting point is 2 percent or less of yeast (baker's percentage), although some bread formulas call for up to 6 percent yeast.

- *Type of yeast.* Some yeast products sold to bakers contain fast-fermenting yeast, good for no-time doughs. This is particularly true of instant yeast, discussed in a following section. Quick-fermenting yeasts are not as desirable, however, when a long fermentation time is used, since there might not be enough yeast activity to survive through final proof.

Some yeast strains grow well in rich doughs—doughs that are high in sugar. Yeast that grow well in high-sugar environments are sometimes called *osmotolerant yeast.* Two brands of osmotolerant yeast are SAF Gold Label and Fermipan Brown. The name "osmotolerant" comes from the fact that sugar increases the osmotic pressure in dough by tying up water, and osmotolerant yeast can tolerate, if not thrive in, this high osmotic environment.

Although regular (non-osmotolerant) yeast can be used in sweet rich doughs, it can take an hour or more for the yeast to adapt to the high-sugar environment. Until it adapts, the regular yeast will not produce much carbon dioxide or alcohol. Even then, it can take two to three times the amount of regular yeast to get the same gas production as in lean doughs.

Lactic acid bacteria flourish in sourdough starters, and as they grow they produce acids, primarily lactic acid and acetic acid (the acid in vinegar). These acids not only provide the characteristic flavor of sourdoughs, but they also restrict the growth of less acid–tolerant microorganisms, ones that are potentially less friendly. The acids also lower pH, and this weakens gluten, so dough becomes softer and more extensible.

Lactic acid bacteria also release protease enzymes, which further soften dough by breaking down gluten proteins into their individual amino acids. The amino acids are then transformed into other acids and flavor molecules, and they are also more available to take part in Maillard browning. This provides color and additional flavor once the dough is baked in the oven. The antimicrobial effect of acids (and other molecules) extends to the baked bread, so that mold won't grow as readily on sourdough as it does on other baked products.

Types and Sources of Yeast

Bread can be made from a traditional, naturally fermented sourdough starter, called *levain* in French. Starters are prepared by mixing flour and water and allowing wild yeast and lactic acid bacteria in the flour and air to ferment the mix. Sometimes rye flour, onion, potato, or another source of food for microorganisms is added to the flour and water.

After a week or so of caring and feeding, the starter is ready to use. A portion of it is made into a preferment, then used to leaven a batch of bread. Because different microorganisms and different ways of handling a starter affect flavor, not all sourdough breads taste alike. While San Francisco sourdough bread is noticeably sour, French sourdough bread (*pain au levain*) is usually milder.

Fresh starter does not need to be made for each new day's production. Instead, a small amount of starter is mixed with fresh flour and water and saved for the next day's bread. Or as described earlier, a piece of raw dough from one day's production (called "old dough," or *pâte fermentée*) is added to the next day's sponge. In fact, some bakeshops pride themselves on the number of years they have continued to bake from their original starter.

A more consistent source of yeast is to use pure yeast cultures. While all yeast purchased for bread baking consist of baker's yeast (*Saccharomyces cerevisiae*), many different strains and several different forms of baker's yeast are available. Most strains are selected to ferment quickly, so pure yeast cultures typically ferment faster than sourdough starters. The strains selected for instant yeast, in particular, are often the fastest of all.

The three main forms of yeast available to the baker today are compressed, active dry, and instant. As you read the descriptions that follow, notice that each type of yeast works best within a specific temperature range. These temperature ranges are important for achieving optimum results with each product.

Compressed Yeast Fresh compressed yeast comes as moist cakes, blocks, or crumbles that are about 30 percent yeast, the rest moisture. It can vary in color, but it generally has a light grayish tan color, crumbles easily, and has a pleasant yeasty aroma. The most common way to use compressed yeast is to first dissolve it in twice its weight of warm (100°F/38°C) water. While compressed yeast can be crumbled directly into dough, this is not recommended, since it risks uneven distribution of yeast throughout the dough.

Active Dry Yeast Active dry yeast (ADY) comes as dry granules sold in vacuum-packed jars or pouches. Because of its convenience relative to fresh yeast, active dry yeast has been popular for years with consumers. To use, active dry yeast is dissolved in four times its weight in very warm (105°–115°F/41°–46°C) water. It is used at half the level as fresh compressed yeast.

Active dry yeast is dried to less than 10 percent moisture in a spray drier. Spray-drying is a fairly harsh treatment, and the outside layer of each granule consists of dead yeast cells. In fact, every pound of active dry yeast contains about one-quarter pound of dead yeast. Since dead and damaged yeast release glutathione, a reducing agent that is detrimental to the quality of gluten in dough, active dry yeast is not popular with professional bakers. It tends to produce slack, sticky doughs and dense loaves, especially when dissolved in cool water. It is in cool water that glutathione tends to leak more easily from dead yeast cells into dough. The tendency of active dry yeast to slacken dough can be used to advantage when it is used in pizza or tortilla production, where extensible dough is desirable.

Instant Yeast Instant yeast was developed in the 1970s. It is instant because it can—and should—be added directly to dough without first hydrating in water. The rod-shaped granules are highly porous, so they easily hydrate right in the dough.

As with active dry yeast, instant yeast is sold dried and vacuum-packed. However, the drying process (a fluidized bed) that produces instant yeast is much gentler than the one used for active dry yeast, so while there are

still some dead and damaged yeast present, there is not the same high level. In addition, some brands of instant yeast, such as SAF Red Label, contain ascorbic acid, a maturing agent that strengthens gluten. This counteracts the weakening effects of dead yeast on gluten.

Instant dry yeast is more vigorous than either compressed or active dry, so it is easy to overproof doughs leavened with it. For this reason, instant yeast is often used when fermentation time is short, as it is in conventional or no-time doughs. Use only one-quarter to one-half instant yeast for the amount of fresh compressed yeast called for in a formula, and be sure when using instant yeast that initial dough temperatures are between 70° and 95°F (21°–35°C).

Chemical Leaveners

The chemical production of gases occurs when chemical leaveners break down in the presence of moisture or heat, giving off gases. Before discussing chemical leaveners, bench tolerance should be defined. *Bench tolerance* is a measure of how well batters and doughs withstand (tolerate) being held before baking, without risking a large loss in leavening gases. Bench tolerance is an important consideration for commercial bakeshops, which need to produce consistent product, time after time, even if a batch is large and sits on the bench for a while before it is baked. Bench tolerance is affected by the thickness of the batter or dough, with heavy doughs typically having better bench tolerance than thin batters. Bench tolerance is also affected by the leavening agent used.

The most common chemical leavener is baking soda combined with one or more acids. The acids are either added separately from the baking soda, or both are added together in the form of baking powder. Baking ammonia is another chemical leavener, more common in Europe than in North America.

Baking Soda + Acid

Baking soda is another name for sodium bicarbonate or bicarbonate of soda. Like baking ammonia, baking soda decomposes and gives off gas in the presence of moisture and heat. However, baking soda by itself is not a practical leavening agent because very high amounts are needed to produce sufficient carbon dioxide for

leavening. High amounts of baking soda produce yellow or green discoloration and a strong salty, chemical bite from sodium carbonate residue left behind.

When baking soda is used for leavening, it is used with one or more acid. Acids react with baking soda in the presence of moisture, so the baking soda breaks down more quickly and easily to carbon dioxide and water. With acid, less baking soda is needed to produce carbon dioxide for leavening, so there is less discoloration and fewer chemical off flavors.

Any acid can be used with baking soda. Table 11.1 lists common acid ingredients used in baking. Each reacts differently and each produces a different salt residue, but the overall reaction is as follows:

baking soda + acid $\xrightarrow{\text{moisture}}$ carbon dioxide + water + salt residue

Both unreacted baking soda and the remaining salt residue contribute to off flavors when high levels of baking soda are added to baked goods.

There are a few disadvantages to using the ingredients from Table 11.1 as acids in baked goods. One disadvantage is that they can vary in acid content. For example, buttermilk, sour cream, and yogurt increase in acidity as they age. Another disadvantage is that these ingredients tend to react with baking soda almost immediately, especially in thin batters. Where this is true, the batter has poor bench tolerance and must be baked immediately upon mixing.

Baking Ammonia

Baking ammonia is another name for ammonium bicarbonate, used for leavening. When ammonium bicarbonate is exposed to heat in the presence of moisture, it quickly decomposes into ammonia, carbon dioxide, and water. All three are sources of leavening in baked goods.

Many European packaged cookies and crackers are leavened with baking ammonia. In fact, the best application of baking ammonia is in small dry cookies and crackers or choux paste. When properly used in these products, baking ammonia leaves no chemical residue. Be careful with baking ammonia, though; do not breathe in the powder, which has a very strong ammonia smell.

Baking ammonia has certain unique features that make it particularly suited for use in small, dry baked goods and unsuitable for use in large or moist products. Baking ammonia:

- Reacts rapidly in the presence of water and heat
- Increases uniformity and spread in cookies
- Increases browning
- Produces a crisp, porous crumb
- Adds an ammonia-like off flavor to still-moist baked goods

Unlike baking soda and certain baking powders, baking ammonia is not very reactive at room temperature, which means that batters and doughs containing baking ammonia have good bench tolerance. However, baking ammonia quickly breaks down in the presence of heat (104°F/38°C), so it is considered relatively fast-acting.

Baking ammonia should be used only in small products that bake to a low moisture content (less than 3 percent moisture), so that the ammonia gas can fully bake out. Otherwise, baked goods will have an ammonia off flavor. This means that one should never use baking ammonia in muffins, biscuits, cakes, or soft and moist cookies.

TABLE 11.1 COMMON ACID INGREDIENTS USED IN BAKING

Buttermilk
Yogurt
Sour cream
Fruits and fruit juices
Vinegar
Most syrups, including molasses and honey
Brown sugar
Unsweetened chocolate and natural cocoa

Baking Powders

There are several different types of baking powders. All contain baking soda, one or more acids (in the form of acid salts) and starch or another filler. Acid salts release acid once they dissolve in water. For example, cream of tartar, also called *potassium acid tartrate*, is an acid salt. When cream of tartar dissolves in batter or dough, tartaric acid is released. The tartaric acid reacts with baking soda to produce carbon dioxide gas for leavening. Often, for simplicity, acid salts are simply called acids.

All baking powders release the same minimum amount of carbon dioxide. By law this is 12 percent of the weight of baking powder. This means that most baking powders are more or less interchangeable—as long as they are still fresh. While they are interchangeable, they are not necessarily identical. To discuss baking powders and their differences, it is helpful to categorize them.

It was once useful to categorize baking powders as either single- or double-acting. This is no longer useful, since essentially all baking powders sold today are double-acting. Instead, a good way to categorize baking powders is by their reaction rates. Another is by the type of acid each contains. You will see shortly that these two categories are related.

What Does It Mean to Be Single-Acting or Double-Acting?

Single-acting baking powder contains an acid that dissolves quickly in room temperature water. No heat is required for the acid to dissolve. As soon as it dissolves, it is available to react with baking soda and produce carbon dioxide gas.

Single-acting baking powders have poor bench tolerance because they react so quickly, but they are great for lightening batters and doughs. Double-acting baking powders contain two (or more) acids: one that dissolves and reacts with baking soda at room temperature and another that requires heat to dissolve and react. In some cases, double-acting baking powder contains only one acid, but the acid is treated so that some of it dissolves at room temperature and the rest of it requires heat to dissolve.

Single-acting baking powders are no longer sold because they release carbon dioxide too quickly, producing batters with poor bench tolerance. When first developed in the 1800s, however, the quick release of carbon dioxide was thought to be desirable because it more closely simulated gas production by yeast, which mostly takes place before baking. But chemically leavened baked goods are very different from yeast breads. Their batters do not contain sufficient gluten to hold much gas before baking. Chemically leavened baked goods need gases timed to release when structure-building proteins coagulate and starches gelatinize.

How Is DRR Measured?

The DRR (*dough rate of reaction*) is a test for measuring the amount of carbon dioxide released from baking powder when dough is mixed and held before baking. When DRR is tested, biscuit mix is placed in an airtight mixing bowl. The bowl is attached to a device that measures the amount of gas released as water is added and as the mixture is stirred at a specified temperature for a specified length of time. Often, the DRR—the percentage of carbon dioxide that is given off—is measured at 80°F (27°C) after 2–3 minutes of mixing and also during 8 or 16 minutes of bench time. Figure 11.3 shows the dough rates of reaction for two different baking powders. Notice that the fast-acting baking powder gives off about 70 percent of its carbon dioxide very quickly. The slow-acting baking powder will not give off much carbon dioxide until exposed to heat.

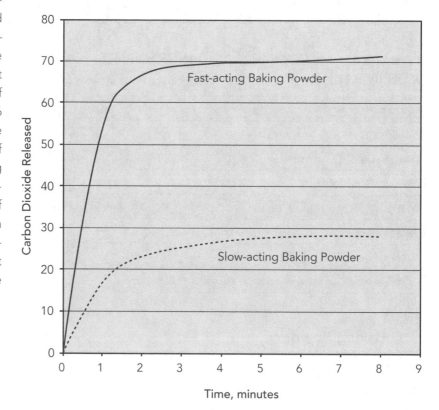

Figure 11.3 Dough Reaction Rates for baking powders made from two different acids

TABLE 11.2 A COMPARISON OF COMMON ACID SALTS IN BAKING POWDERS

ACID SALT	MAJOR FEATURES
Cream of tartar	Fast-acting: releases over 70 percent of carbon dioxide during the early stages of mixing, which is too quick for general use; very clean flavor, little aftertaste; fast action lowers pH, to give a whiter crumb than most; expensive.
MCP (monocalcium phosphate; also called calcium acid phosphate)	Fast-acting: releases almost 60 percent of carbon dioxide during mixing; often coated so it dissolves and reacts more slowly; relatively clean taste; a very common acid salt in household and commercial baking powders, when combined with slower-acting SAS or SAPP.
SAS (sodium aluminum sulfate; alum)	Slow-acting: requires heat to release acid, but releases it all during early stages of baking, by about 120°F (50°C); bitter aftertaste when used alone; combined with fast-acting MCP for the most common household baking powder.
SALP (sodium aluminum phosphate)	Slow-acting: requires heat to release acid; mild taste; combined with a coated MCP for most common baking powder added to biscuit mixes, corn muffin mixes, self-rising flours, cake mixes.
SAPP (sodium acid pyrophosphate)	Many kinds available, all slow-acting—releasing only 25–45 percent of their carbon dioxide within 16 minutes of bench time; most have strong chemical aftertaste; combined with fast-acting MCP for the most common commercial baking powder.

Dough Rates of Reaction All baking powders release about the same amount of carbon dioxide and all are essentially double-acting, releasing some gas at room temperature and the rest when heated. Baking powders differ, however, in how much carbon dioxide is released at room temperature, how much is released with heat, and how quickly all this happens. In other words, baking powders differ in their dough rates of reaction (DRR).

Bakers often speak of baking powders as being fast-acting or slow-acting. A *fast-acting baking powder* has a fast DRR and releases more of its carbon dioxide during the first few minutes of mixing and less of it in the oven. For example, a common fast-acting baking powder releases about 60–70 percent of its total carbon dioxide during mixing and another 30–40 percent during baking. By releasing a good amount of carbon dioxide during mixing, fast-acting baking powders assist in seeding batters and doughs with air bubbles, for a fine crumb. The added leavening gas also lightens heavy doughs, making them easier to shape and handle.

A *slow-acting baking powder* releases a smaller amount of carbon dioxide during mixing and a larger amount in the oven. For example, the most common slow-acting baking powders release about 30–40 percent of their total carbon dioxide during mixing and another 60–70 percent during baking. This is especially important for high-ratio cakes, which set later in the baking process than most other baked goods. By using a slow-acting baking powder with these cakes, most of the carbon dioxide is released about when the cell walls are drying and starting to set, for maximum volume.

Type of Acid A listing of acids used in baking powders reads like alphabet soup—MCP, SAS, SAPP, SALP, and more. The important point here is not to memorize names and features but to understand that differences in acids exist. A comparison of the five major acids used in baking powders is given in Table 11.2. Notice in the table that acids differ in reaction rates, flavor, and price.

Baking powders for professional bakeshops are designed to provide some carbon dioxide quickly—to lighten batters and doughs during mixing—but to generate most of it when baking is well under way, for best bench tolerance and product expansion. Baking powders for professionals are most apt to contain a mixture of SAPP and MCP, but they can also contain SAS and MCP. Eagle double-acting is a SAPP/MCP baking powder; Clabber Girl is an SAS/MCP baking powder.

Functions of Chemical Leaveners

Chemical leaveners such as baking ammonia, baking soda, and baking powders contribute a number of functions to baked goods, including the following.

Cake doughnuts and cakes both do best with slow-acting baking powders, where more carbon dioxide is released after heat is applied than before. However, cake doughnuts require faster release of carbon dioxide than cakes do. With doughnuts, which fry up in minutes, if carbon dioxide releases too slowly, the crust sets before leavening occurs. Once leavening takes place, the force of expanding gases cracks the doughnut's surface or produces pinholes on it. If this happens, the doughnut absorbs fat in its cracks and pinholes and becomes soggy and greasy.

For best volume and symmetry in cakes, generation of carbon dioxide must be timed with protein coagulation and starch gelatinization. Cakes—especially liquid shortening cakes—contain high amounts of fat and sugar that delay the coagulation of egg proteins and the gelatinization of starches. If the generation of carbon dioxide is to be timed with these processes, then the baking powder must be slower-acting than most.

Because most commercial baking powders are designed more for cakes than for doughnuts, bakers and pastry chefs often use mixes when frying doughnuts. Doughnut mixes already contain the proper type and amount of baking powder, and other ingredients, for optimum doughnut quality.

Leavening The main reason chemical leaveners are added to baked goods is for leavening (rise). With chemical leaveners, leavening occurs when the leavening agents break down, releasing gases that expand during the baking process.

Some products, such as baking powder biscuits, quick breads and muffins, and certain cakes, rely heavily on chemical leaveners for their volume. With other products, however, baking powder plays only a supporting role. Liquid shortening cakes, for example, are leavened more by steam and air than by any added baking powder.

Because most chemical leaveners begin to work right in the mixing bowl, they also lighten and thicken batters and doughs, making them easier to mix and shape.

Tenderizing As with all leavening, as gases form and expand, cell walls in baked goods stretch and thin out. This makes them easier to bite through; that is, this makes baked goods more tender, and it makes leavening agents tenderizers.

Adjusting pH Many batters and doughs have a neutral pH if no baking powder, baking soda, or other chemical leavener is added. Cream of tartar (an acid) tends to decrease pH, while baking ammonia and baking soda (both alkalis) tend to increase pH. Fast-acting baking powders, which release acidic carbon dioxide quickly, decrease pH of batters and doughs, while slow-acting baking powders do not, and can even increase pH.

Changes in pH affect many things in baked goods, including color, flavor, crumb texture, and gluten strength. For example:

- A small amount of baking soda in chocolate brownies or gingerbread provides a darker, richer-looking product. The higher pH also smoothes out the flavor in gingerbread and chocolate, so that it is mellower and less sharp (unless a very high amount of baking soda is added; high levels of baking soda give baked goods a sharp, chemical taste).

- A small amount of baking soda or baking ammonia in cookies increases pH, weakening gluten. The result is more spread, more tenderness, and a coarser, more open crumb that dries and crisps more quickly. The higher pH from baking soda also increases the rate of browning.

- A small amount of cream of tartar in baking powder biscuits decreases pH and weakens gluten. The result is more tenderness. Unlike with baking soda, the lower pH from cream of tartar also provides a whiter crumb, often one that is fine and tight.

Providing for a Finer Crumb Recall that creaming, whipping, sifting, folding, kneading, and stirring are physical processes that add small air cells (seed cells)

Cornstarch serves two main functions in baking powder. First, cornstarch absorbs moisture, so that baking soda and acid do not react in the box. Don't tempt fate, though: even with cornstarch, baking powders should be covered after each use and discarded when old.

Cornstarch also serves to standardize baking powders, so that an ounce of one brand provides the same leavening potential as an ounce of another.

to batters and doughs. Chemical leaveners—those that release carbon dioxide during mixing—contribute to the size of these air cells, which through continued mixing increase the number of seed cells in batters and doughs. Seed cells are important for defining the crumb of baked goods. The more small seed cells in raw batters and doughs, the finer the crumb of the baked good.

Adding Flavor Small amounts of baking powder and baking soda have a distinct salty-sour flavor that

> **HELPFUL HINT**
>
> *Be careful when weighing baking soda and other chemical leavening agents. While a small amount can be beneficial to flavor, texture, and color, too much often leaves a bitter chemical aftertaste and discolors baked goods.*

is characteristic of certain baked goods such as baking powder biscuits, scones, and Irish soda bread.

Storage and Handling

Yeast

Compressed yeast lasts 2 weeks, sometimes more, when stored wrapped tightly in plastic and refrigerated, and 2 to 4 months when frozen. Do not use compressed yeast if it has darkened extensively and turned gummy or if it has an off aroma. This could indicate bacterial contamination.

Active dry yeast is low in moisture and vacuum packaged, for an extended shelf life of 18–24 months at room temperature without much loss in activity. Once open, active dry yeast still lasts several months at room temperature, longer if frozen or refrigerated. Be sure to warm yeast to room temperature before use, if necessary.

Like active dry yeast, instant yeast is low in moisture and is vacuum packaged. If unopened, it will last up to 2 years at room temperature without much loss in activity. If it is opened, refrigerate for several months or more, or freeze.

Chemical Leavening Agents

All chemical leavening agents should be stored in tightly covered containers at room temperature. Even then, baking powder has a shelf life of only 6 months to 1 year. Leaving baking powder containers uncovered can significantly reduce shelf life, since it can lead to moisture absorption, caking, and a loss in potency. Chemical leaveners also pick up off odors if left uncovered.

Baking soda and baking powders can also clump and cake when wet utensils are used to dispense them. Although baking soda will not lose its potency when it absorbs moisture, it could cause "hot spots" in batter and doughs. This manifests itself as dark spots on the surface of cakes, for example. If necessary, pass baking soda through a fine chinois before use to break up clumps, or discard.

Questions for Review

1 List the four events that must happen for baked goods to rise properly.

2 What are the three main leavening gases in baked goods?

3 Name a biological leavener that is a source of carbon dioxide.

4 Name a chemical leavener that is a source of carbon dioxide.

5 From what is steam generated? Why is steam classified as a physical leavener?

6 List three ingredients that contribute to the steam leavening of baked goods.

7 Name a baked good leavened primarily by steam.

8 List three different physical means of adding air cells into batters and doughs.

9 Which of the three main leavening gases expands the most from the heat of the oven?

10 Which occurs in the oven to cause baked goods to rise: new air cells form, or existing air cells expand?

11 Why is it important not to undermix batter? Why is it important not to overmix?

12 Which—yeast or bacteria—produces more of the carbon dioxide for leavening during fermentation and which produces more of the acids for flavor?

13 Which of the following is a source of food for yeast, and which must be first broken down by enzymes: starch; sugar.

14 What are the main end products of yeast fermentation?

15 How is a sourdough starter made and what is it used for?

16 List and describe factors that affect the rate of yeast fermentation.

17 List the three main forms of baker's yeast available. Describe an advantage and a disadvantage of each.

18 At what temperature range should each of the three main forms of baker's yeast be used?

19 What is meant by "bench tolerance"?

20 What are some unique features of baking ammonia?

21 Which of the following would be better leavened with baking ammonia: crisp, dry cookies or soft, moist cookies? Explain your answer.

22 What are two other names for baking soda?

23 Why is acid usually added along with baking soda when baking soda is added for leavening?

24 Besides one or more acid, what else is needed to generate carbon dioxide from baking soda?

25 List some common acid ingredients that will react with baking soda to produce carbon dioxide.

26 What is the difference between baking soda and baking powder?

27 What is meant by an "acid salt"? Name an acid salt.

28 What are two ways of categorizing baking powders?

29 Which requires heat for the release of all of its carbon dioxide: a single-acting or a double-acting baking powder?

30 What is meant by the dough rate of reaction (DRR)?

31 Which provides better bench tolerance to batters: a fast-acting or a slow-acting baking powder?

32 What are two advantages of fast-acting baking powders? What is the main advantage of slow-acting baking powders?

33 If the amount of baking powder in a batter or dough is doubled, will the volume double? Why or why not?

34 Besides leavening, what are the other functions of chemical leaveners in baked goods?

Questions for Discussion

1 You are short on time. Why will an increase in chemical leaveners not make up for a decrease in mixing time?

2 Describe the process of yeast fermentation. Be sure to include a description of the starting material and the end products, and explain the importance of each end product to either the baker or the yeast itself.

3 What do you think will happen if the proteins in a baked good coagulate and the starches gelatinize before much carbon dioxide is generated? Explain.

4 Traditional gingerbread formulas call for baking soda and for molasses as the main sweetener. Would you expect this to be a bench-tolerant formula or not? Why do you think some formulas for gingerbread contain both baking powder and baking soda?

5 Why do cake doughnuts require a slightly faster-reacting baking powder than most cakes?

6 If a little bit of baking powder is good, will more be better? Why or why not?

7 Why do you think some choux paste formulas include a small amount of baking ammonia rather than baking powder?

8 Why do you think a formula for chocolate biscotti might contain both baking soda and baking powder?

Exercises and Experiments

① Exercise: Sensory Characteristics of Chemical Leavening Agents

Prepare the tartrate baking powder, using the formula given, then complete the Results Table, which follows. In the second column, record brand names and any descriptive information (bench-tolerant, fast-acting, double-acting, etc.) from the package labels of each of the chemical leavening agents. In the third column, copy the ingredient list from the package. Use fresh samples to evaluate the appearance and taste of each product. Because they all are white powders, it is particularly important that you taste them and describe what you taste. Use this opportunity to identify different chemical leavening agents from their sensory characteristics alone. Add any additional comments or observations that you might have to the last column in the Results Table. Use the two blank rows at the bottom of the Results Table to evaluate additional chemical leavening agents, if desired.

Formula

Baking Powder, Tartrate Type

INGREDIENT	OUNCES	GRAMS
Baking soda	1	30
Cream of tartar	2.3	70
Cornstarch	0.5	15
Total	3.8	115

Method of Preparation

Sift ingredients together three times onto parchment paper.

RESULTS TABLE A COMPARISON OF CHEMICAL LEAVENING AGENTS

CHEMICAL LEAVENER	BRAND OR DESCRIPTION	LIST OF INGREDIENTS	APPEARANCE	TASTE	ADDITIONAL COMMENTS
Cream of tartar					
Baking soda					
Baking powder, SAPP type					
Baking powder, SAS type					
Baking powder, tartrate type					

Use information from the table above and from your textbook to answer the following questions. Select one from the choices in **bold** or fill in the blanks.

1   The main taste from cream of tartar is **sweet/salty/sour/bitter**. This is because cream of tartar is the potassium salt of _____, which is released when cream of tartar dissolves in batters and doughs.

2 The taste of baking soda can best be described as _____
_____
_____.

3 When baking powder dissolves in the mouth, there is a tingling on the tongue. This tingling is from the generation of _____, one of the three main leavening gases in baked goods.

4 The different baking powders had **very similar/very different** tastes. This is because ____
_____
_____.

❷ Experiment: How the Type and Amount of Leavening Agent Affects the Overall Quality of Baking Powder Biscuits

Objectives

Demonstrate how the type and amount of leavening agent affects
- Browning on the crust of baking powder biscuits
- Crumb color and structure
- Tenderness and height
- Overall flavor
- Overall acceptability

Products Prepared

Baking powder biscuits made with
- Full amount of commercial SAPP baking powder (control product)
- No baking powder
- Twice the amount of SAPP baking powder
- Full amount of tartrate baking powder (use formula in Exercise 1)
- Baking soda instead of baking powder
- Other, if desired (half the amount of baking powder, SAS baking powder, etc.)

Materials and Equipment
- Scale
- Sieve
- Parchment paper
- Mixer with 5-quart mixing bowl
- Flat beater attachment
- Bowl scraper
- Half sheet pans
- Biscuit dough (see Formula), enough to make 6 or more biscuits of each variation
- Rolling pin
- Height guide
- Dough cutter, 2½" (65 mm) size, or equivalent
- Oven thermometer
- Serrated knife
- Ruler

Baking Powder Biscuits

Yield: *6 biscuits*

INGREDIENT	POUNDS	OUNCES	GRAMS	BAKER'S PERCENTAGE
Flour, pastry	1		500	100
Salt		0.3	10	2
Sugar, regular granulated		1	30	6
Baking powder		1	25	6
Shortening, all-purpose		6	190	38
Milk		9.5	300	60
Total	**2**	**1.8**	**1,055**	**212**

Method of Preparation

1 Preheat oven 425°F (220°C).

2 Set aside about ½ ounce (15 grams) of flour for dusting work surface.

3 Blend the rest of the dry ingredients thoroughly by sifting together three times onto parchment paper.

4 Place dry ingredients into mixer bowl and cut in shortening on low speed using flat beater for 1 minute. Stop and scrape bowl.

5 Add milk and stir on low speed for 20 seconds; dough should just barely hold together, with some dry ingredients remaining unincorporated.

6 Transfer dough to a lightly floured surface (use flour set aside in step 2) and fold lightly six times, rotating dough 90 degrees after each fold.

Procedure

1 Line sheet pans with parchment paper; label with type and amount of leavening agent to be added.

2 Prepare biscuit dough using the formula above or using any basic baking powder biscuit formula. Prepare one batch of dough per variation.

3 Roll out dough to a thickness of ½" (12.5 mm) using a height guide to keep consistency throughout.

4 Cut with a floured cutter, using a straight up-and-down motion; do not twist cutter and do not reroll dough.

5 Space biscuits evenly on parchment-lined sheet pan, placing six on one half sheet pan.

6 Use an oven thermometer placed in center of oven for an initial reading of oven temperature. Record results here: _____.

7 When oven is properly preheated, place sheet pans into oven and set timer for 20–22 minutes.

8 Bake biscuits until control product (with full amount of SAPP baking powder) is light brown. Remove *all* biscuits from oven after same length of time. If necessary, however, adjust bake times for oven variances.

9 Record bake times in Results Table 1 (below).

10 Check final oven temperature. Record results here: _____.

11 Remove biscuits from hot pans to cool to room temperature.

Results

1 When biscuits are completely cooled, evaluate height as follows:
- Slice three biscuits from each batch in half, being careful not to compress.
- Measure height of each biscuit by placing a ruler along the flat edge at the center of the biscuit. Record results for each of three biscuits in ¹⁄₁₆" (1 mm) increments in Results Table 1.
- Calculate the average biscuit height by adding the heights of the three biscuits and dividing by 3. Record results in Results Table 1.

2 Note in Biscuit Shape column of Results Table 1 whether biscuits have slumped or held their shape. Also note whether biscuits are lopsided; that is, if one side is higher than the other.

RESULTS TABLE 1 HEIGHT AND SHAPE OF BISCUITS MADE WITH DIFFERENT AMOUNTS AND TYPES OF CHEMICAL LEAVENERS

TYPE AND AMOUNT OF LEAVENER	BAKE TIME (IN MINUTES	HEIGHTS OF EACH OF THREE BISCUITS	AVERAGE HEIGHT FOR ONE BISCUIT	BISCUIT SHAPE	ADDITIONAL COMMENTS
Commercial SAPP baking powder (control product)					
No baking powder					
Twice the amount of baking powder					
Tartrate baking powder					
Baking soda instead of baking powder					

3 Evaluate the sensory characteristics of completely cooled products and record evaluations in Results Table 2. Be sure to compare each in turn with the control product and consider the following:
- Crust color, from very light to very dark, on a scale of 1 to 5
- Crumb appearance (flaky, dense, airy, etc.)
- Crumb texture (tough/tender, moist/dry, flaky, etc.)
- Overall flavor (sweet, salty, metallic/chemical, sour, etc.)
- Overall acceptability, from highly unacceptable to highly acceptable, on a scale of 1 to 5
- Add any additional comments, as necessary

RESULTS TABLE 2 SENSORY CHARACTERISTICS OF BISCUITS MADE WITH DIFFERENT TYPES AND AMOUNTS OF CHEMICAL LEAVENERS

TYPE AND AMOUNT OF LEAVENER	CRUST COLOR	CRUMB APPEARANCE AND TEXTURE	OVERALL FLAVOR	OVERALL ACCEPTABILITY	ADDITIONAL COMMENTS
Commercial SAPP baking powder (control product)					
No baking powder					
Twice the amount of baking powder					
Tartrate baking powder					
Baking soda instead of baking powder					

Sources of Error

List any sources of error that might make it difficult to draw the proper conclusions from your experiment. In particular, consider any differences in mixing, kneading, and rolling dough, and any problems with the ovens.

_____

_____

_____

State what you could do differently next time to minimize or eliminate each source of error.

_____

_____

_____

Conclusions

Select one from the choices in **bold** or fill in the blanks.

1   As the amount of baking powder increased from none to the full amount, the height **increased/decreased/stayed the same**. This means that the baking powder **is/is not** important to the rise in baking powder biscuits.

2   As the amount of baking powder increased from none to the full amount, the flavor changed as follows:

_____

_____

_____

3   As the amount of baking powder increased from none to the full amount, the color of the crust got **lighter/darker**. The difference was **small/moderate/large**. Because browning **increases/decreases** as the pH of dough increases, it is possible that the dough with the baking powder had a **higher/lower** pH.

4   As the amount of baking powder doubled from the full amount to twice the amount, the height **doubled/did not double**. One explanation for this is that all of the three main leavening gases in baked goods **were/were not** doubled. Another reason for this result is as follows:

_____

_____

_____

5   The least tender baking powder biscuit was made with **no/the full amount of/twice the amount of** baking powder. The difference in tenderness was **small/moderate/large**. This difference in tenderness can be explained as follows:

_____

_____

_____

6 The differences between the biscuits made with tartrate baking powder and those made with a regular commercial baking powder were **small/moderate/large**. The main difference was as follows:

_____

_____

_____

Which of these two biscuits, if either, did you prefer, and why?

_____

_____

_____

7 Biscuits made with baking soda were **lighter/darker** in color than the other biscuits. This is because baking soda is an **acid/alkali** that **increases/decreases** pH, and this **speeds up/ slows down** browning.

8 Biscuits made with baking soda were **taller than/shorter than/the same in height as** the biscuits made with no baking powder or baking soda. This means that baking soda by itself **leavened/did not leaven** the biscuits. The reason baking soda by itself is not used as a chemical leavener is because _____

_____

_____

9 The biscuits that had a pretzel-like flavor were made with **no baking powder/baking powder/baking soda**. Because pretzels are traditionally boiled in an alkali (lye) solution before baking, this flavor must be characteristic of the browning reactions that occur at a **low/high** pH.

10 How can you tell when baking soda is mistakenly used instead of baking powder?

_____

_____

_____

11 How can you prevent baking soda from mistakenly being used instead of baking powder, and vice versa?

_____

_____

_____

12 Other noticeable differences between the products were as follows:

_____

_____

_____

Thickening and Gelling Agents

12

1 Define various thickening and gelling agents used in bakeshops and describe their characteristics and uses.

2 Describe the process of starch gelatinization and factors that affect it.

3 Describe the functions of thickening and gelling agents.

4 Provide guidelines for selecting a thickening or gelling agent.

Introduction

The simplest way to thicken food is to add an ingredient that is itself thickened or gelled. Heavy cream, sour cream, many cheeses, jams and jellies, fruit purees, thick syrups, yogurt, and buttermilk are useful thickeners in the bakeshop. These ingredients do more than thicken, of course. They add flavor, they alter appearance, and they contribute to the nutritional value of the final product.

Other ingredients are added exclusively—or almost so—to thicken and gel. These so-called thickening and gelling agents (gelatin, vegetable gums, and starches) are added to fillings, glazes, sauces, and creams. They function by absorbing or trapping large amounts of water. The most common thickening and gelling agent in the bakeshop is not often thought of as one, however, because it is used in so many products for so many reasons. This common thickening and gelling agent is the egg. Eggs were discussed separately in Chapter 10.

There are other ways to thicken and gel food products besides adding an ingredient. For example, the formation of an emulsion or foam provides thickening and sometimes gelling. This is why heavy cream, which is an emulsion of butterfat droplets in milk, is thicker than milk. When it is whipped, the heavy cream foams, and in the process it thickens further. The more the cream is whipped, the more it foams and the stiffer it becomes—all without the use of a thickening agent.

The Process of Thickening and Gelling

Thickening and gelling agents—gelatin, vegetable gums, and starches—have one thing in common: they are all composed of very large molecules. Some, such as starches and gums, are polysaccharides. Others, such as gelatin, are proteins.

Polysaccharides are very large molecules made of many (*poly*) sugar molecules (*saccharides*) linked one to the next. Often thousands of sugar molecules are linked together in a single polysaccharide molecule. Sometimes all sugar molecules in a polysaccharide are the same, but often there is a mix of two or more different sugars. What distinguishes one polysaccharide from another is the type of sugar that makes it up, how many are linked together, and how they are linked. Recall from Chapter 8, for example, that starch molecules are made up of glucose sugars, and inulin consists primarily of fructose. Besides being different in the type of sugar, starch and inulin differ in the number of sugars. Starch, with thousands of sugar units, is a much more effective thickener and gelling agent than inulin, which has at most sixty sugars. Both, however, are classified as polysaccharides.

Proteins are very large molecules made of many amino acids linked one to the next. Often thousands of amino acids are linked together in a single protein molecule. More than twenty common amino acids make up proteins. What distinguishes one protein from another is the number and arrangement of these amino acids within the protein molecule.

Thickening occurs when water and other molecules or particles in a product move around rather slowly. For example, this will happen when large molecules, such as certain polysaccharides and proteins, bump and loosely entangle. It also happens when water is absorbed and trapped by swollen starch granules, or when air bubbles (in foams) or fat droplets (in emulsions) slow water movement.

Gelling occurs when water and other molecules in a product are prevented from moving around at all. For example, this will happen when large molecules such as certain polysaccharides and proteins bond or tightly entangle with one another, forming a large web or network that traps water and other molecules. Despite acting like solids, gels are still mostly liquid. In fact, some gelling agents (such as agar) are so effective that a gel can form even when water makes up over 99 percent of the product. Some thickening and gelling

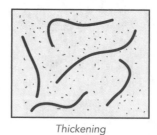
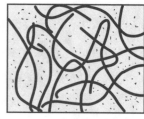

Thickening   *Gelling*

Figure 12.1 Pectin and some other polysaccharides thicken at lower concentrations and gel at higher concentrations

agents do both; that is, some thicken when used at low levels and gel when used at higher levels. Figure 12.1 shows large molecules entangling loosely to thicken, and more tightly to gel. Examples of thickening and gelling agents that both thicken and gel include gelatin, cornstarch, and pectin. Other ingredients only thicken. They will not gel, no matter how much is used. Instead, they get thicker and gummier. Examples of ingredients that only thicken include guar gum, gum arabic, and waxy maize starch.

Gelatin

Gelatin, whether in powder form or sheets, is a staple in the bakeshop. When properly prepared, it forms an appealing crystal clear gel with bounce and spring. Best of all, gelatin melts quickly and cleanly when eaten.

Gelatin has many uses. It is a necessary ingredient in Bavarian creams, fruit mousses, and cold soufflés. It is a good stabilizer for whipped cream and many cake fillings, and it provides the characteristic texture of marshmallows and gummy confections. Gelatin mixtures, when cooled to thicken, can be whipped much as egg whites can be whipped.

Gelatin is an animal protein. Most food-grade gelatin is extracted from pigskin, although small amounts are from cattle bones and hides. A specialty form of gelatin is purified from fish; fish gelatin is called *isinglass*. Gelatin is not found in any vegetable sources.

How Gelatin Is Produced

Food-grade gelatin is sometimes called *Type A gelatin* (A for the acid treatment it receives). To produce Type A gelatin, chopped clean pigskins are soaked for several hours or days in cold acid. This breaks down the pigskin's connective tissue, transforming its rigid, ropelike protein fibers (called *collagen*) into smaller invisible strands of gelatin that thicken or gel when cooled. Hot water is then used for dissolving gelatin and extracting it from the pigskins. This process is repeated up to six times, with each extraction occurring at a progressively higher temperature. By the last extraction, water is at the boiling point and the last bits of usable gelatin are removed.

The best-quality gelatin comes from the first extraction. It has the strongest gel, the clearest, lightest color, and the mildest flavor. It also solidifies fastest. Later extractions produce weaker gelatin that is darker in color and slightly meaty in flavor. With each extraction, the gelatin solution is filtered to purify it, concentrated, formed into sheets or "noodles," dried, and ground into coarse granules or a fine powder. The manufacturer then blends ground gelatin from different extractions to standardize gelatin from batch to batch. The ground gelatin is either sold as is or made into sheet gelatin. To make sheet gelatin, also called *leaf gelatin*, ground gelatin is redissolved, reheated, then cast, cooled, and dried as a gel film.

Gelatin is rated by its gel strength, also called *Bloom rating*. Gelatin with a high Bloom rating forms firm gels. Because Bloom rating is related to gelatin quality, gelatin with a high Bloom rating also has a light color and clean flavor. It sets fast and produces a shorter, less stringy gel than gelatin with a lower Bloom rating.

Most food-grade gelatins range from about 50 to 300 on the Bloom scale. Gelatin sold to pastry chefs is

A Brief History of Gelatin

Early recipes calling for gelatin describe how to first boil calves' hoofs. Not until the early 1800s was purified gelatin available for purchase, although a British patent for its manufacture was issued as early as the mid-1700s. Throughout the 1800s, gelatin was sold shredded or in sheets.

Powdered gelatin was a later invention. It came about in America in the late 1800s at the request of housewives. In response, Knox Gelatine dried gelatin sheets until brittle, then pulverized them into granules, which were easy to measure with measuring spoons. Granular gelatin also had the advantage of dissolving faster than shredded gelatin. The powdered gelatin industry was born, with Jell-O gelatin just a few years away.

The Bloom scale is a rating system that was invented in the 1800s. It was named for the French chemist who devised a standard test and an instrument—the Bloom gelometer—for measuring gel strength. The gelometer measures the force it takes for a small plunger to sink a certain distance into a gelatin gel prepared under standardized conditions. The more force required, the higher the bloom rating and the stronger the gel. Although more reliable instruments have replaced the gelometer, gel strength is still reported as Bloom rating, also called *Bloom value* or *Bloom strength*.

rarely, if ever, labeled with its Bloom rating, but manufacturers can provide that information. Most powdered or granular gelatin in bakeshops in North America is rated about 230 Bloom.

Sheet gelatin is often designated by the name of a precious metal. At about 250 Bloom, platinum-labeled gelatin sheets are closest in Bloom rating to most powdered gelatins. Table 12.1 compares the approximate Bloom ratings and weights for different grades of sheet gelatin. Notice that the weight of the sheet increases as the Bloom rating decreases. This makes it easy to switch from one quality of sheet gelatin to another, as long as sheets are counted, not weighed. If a formula calls for ten sheets, use ten sheets of gelatin, no matter the Bloom rating. The actual amount being added is automatically adjusted by a change in weight per sheet.

North America and the European Union follow strict quality control guidelines for gelatin manufacture. These guidelines have been reviewed and updated since mad cow disease spread through cattle herds in Great Britain in the late 1980s. Mad cow disease (bovine spongiform encephalopathy, or BSE) is a disease that infects the brain and spinal cord of cattle. To date, it has not been found in gelatin products, but precautions are taken to ensure that all raw materials used in gelatin

HELPFUL HINT

Inexperienced pastry cooks sometimes have difficulty adding gelatin solutions to cold preparations. If they are not careful, the gelatin lumps and the mixture must be discarded. This can happen when stabilizing whipped cream with gelatin, for example.

To avoid lumps, be sure the gelatin solution is hot—at least 140°F (60°C)—and not just warm. Temper the mixture by stirring a small amount of whipped cream into the hot solution, then add this mixture slowly to the whipped cream. Tempering serves to dilute the gelatin while it is still warm, so that as it cools, it gels more slowly and uniformly.

manufacture are from healthy animals that have been approved for human consumption.

How to Use Gelatin

The term *bloom* has another meaning besides gelatin gel strength. It also refers to the method used for hydrating gelatin; that is, for adding it to cold liquid and allowing it to swell. Gelatin is first hydrated so that it is less likely to clump later in use.

To bloom powdered gelatin, add the granules to five or ten times its weight in cold liquid. Sheets are typically added to excess cold water, then removed and gently squeezed. Use almost any liquid to bloom gelatin, as long as the liquid is cold. However, certain fruit juices, such as pineapple, kiwi, and papaya, must be heated and cooled before use. Heat inactivates the protease enzymes in these fruits. Protease enzymes break down gelatin and other large proteins into short strands, preventing them from gelling. Liquids that are high in acid, such as lemon juice, may weaken gelatin slightly, but they will not liquefy it unless the gelatin is heated in the acid. If gelatin is used with highly acidic ingredients, a slightly higher level of gelatin may be needed.

TABLE 12.1 DIFFERENT GRADES OF SHEET GELATIN

GELATIN	APPROXIMATE BLOOM RATING	AVERAGE WEIGHT PER SHEET
Platinum	250	0.06 ounces (1.7 grams)
Gold	200	0.07 ounces (2.0 grams)
Silver	160	0.09 ounces (2.5 grams)
Bronze	140	0.12 ounces (3.3 grams)

Gelatin dissolved in hot liquid can be thought of as invisible strands moving around rapidly. As the solution cools, the tiny strands begin to slow. Sections of strands coil up like telephone cords and the coiled sections double over onto themselves. Often, a section from one strand wraps itself around another strand's coil. Over time, these tangled sections stack up, forming *junctions*. Water, trapped in this three-dimensional web, is unable to move around. The mixture is now a soft solid.

These junctions are very fragile and easily broken with the smallest amount of heat. In fact, gelatin generally melts completely to a liquid at about 80°–90°F (27°–32°C), which is lower than body temperature. This provides for a pleasant mouthfeel. The actual melting temperature, however, depends on the gelatin's Bloom rating and on the level of gelatin used.

Most of the gelled junctions in a gelatin web form within the first hour or two of chilling, but the process continues over the next 18 hours or so. Mousses and creams prepared with gelatin are always firmer the second day, even when they are well covered and have not dried out.

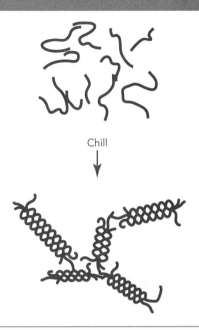

Chill

Gelatin granules and gelatin sheets typically take from 5 to 10 minutes to hydrate properly. Once bloomed, gelatin is heated gently in a saucepan to melt before adding it to cold preparations.

If a formula calls for hot liquid, there is no need to heat gelatin separately to melt. It is faster and easier to add the bloomed gelatin directly to the hot liquid. Do not allow gelatin to boil, and remove it from the heat as soon as the gelatin dissolves. Extended heat damages gelatin and lowers its Bloom rating.

Switching Between Sheets and Powders

Which is better, gelatin sheets or gelatin powder? This question has no one right answer. Some bakers and pastry chefs favor sheet gelatin, others favor powder. Sheet gelatin is more popular in Europe than in the rest of the world.

Whichever they favor, versatile chefs know how to use either sheet or powdered gelatin, and they know how to substitute one for the other. Before discussing how to do this, it is helpful to first understand the advantages and disadvantages of each form of gelatin.

Sheet gelatin cannot spill, so it is less messy than powder. Sheets can be counted, and many find this easier than weighing, at least for small-scale production. For large-scale production, however, this is no longer an advantage; it is easier to weigh large quantities of sheets than to count them. When the sheets are added to excess water, the user must be careful that they do not dissolve and disappear completely in too-warm water.

Powdered gelatin is produced worldwide and in much larger quantities than sheet gelatin. This high volume provides for economies of scale that keep prices low. And because powder is produced in the United States, there are no added import costs to drive up prices.

Convenience is as important as—sometimes more important than—cost. Convenience means different things to different people. While some find counting sheets more convenient than weighing powder, others find the opposite to be true. Probably the greatest inconvenience, however, is running out of an ingredient altogether. If this happens with sheet gelatin, it could be difficult to receive a new shipment quickly. Sheet gelatin is a specialty item imported from Europe, and

> **HELPFUL HINT**
>
> *When blooming gelatin sheets in excess water, the water should be about room temperature (70°F/21°C) or cooler. Don't forget that water from the tap is warmer in the summer than it is in the winter, and that it is warmer in Tucson, Arizona, than it is in Toronto, Ontario. Some chefs bloom sheet gelatin the same way as powdered gelatin, by adding it to five or ten times its weight in water.*

it is not available from all purveyors. Powdered gelatin, however, is readily available from most purveyors and, in a pinch, can be purchased at a supermarket.

In theory, sheet and powdered gelatin can be used interchangeably. In practice, the conversion between sheets and powder depends on Bloom rating. For powdered gelatin with a rating of 230 Bloom, the following conversion holds, in most cases:

17 gelatin sheets = 1 ounce (28 grams) gelatin powder

This does not necessarily mean that 17 gelatin sheets weigh 1 ounce (30 grams), although that is essentially true for platinum sheets. Instead, it means that 17 sheets of any grade provide about the same gelling strength as 1 ounce (30 grams) of powder. When converting from powder to sheets or vice versa, or when converting from one brand or type of gelatin to another, it is always a good idea to prepare a test batch first to confirm that the conversion works.

Also remember when converting between sheets and powder that gelatin absorbs about five times its weight in water. That is, 1 ounce (30 grams) of gelatin absorbs about 5 ounces (150 grams) of liquid. While this water is always listed in formulas using powdered gelatin, it is not listed in formulas where sheets are placed in excess water. This difference in water should be considered when converting between sheets and powder.

Vegetable Gums

Vegetable gums are polysaccharides that absorb large quantities of water, swelling to produce thick liquids and gels. Gums were discussed in earlier chapters, since pentosan and beta-glucan gums are found in cereal grains, especially rye and oats. While some gums have a gummy texture, most do not when used correctly. All are vegetable in origin, meaning that they are extracted and purified from trees, bushes, shrubs, seeds, seaweed, or microorganisms. Many are all natural. Others, such as cellulose gum, are from natural sources but are chemically modified to improve their properties.

All vegetable gums are an excellent source of soluble dietary fiber. Dietary fiber consists of polysaccharides that are not digested by the human body. Health experts recommend that consumers eat more fiber, since it offers certain health benefits.

Pectin

Pectin is present in all fruits, but fruits vary in the amount of pectin they contain. Fruits high in pectin include apples, plums, cranberries, raspberries, and citrus peel. These and other fruits high in pectin can be made into jams and jellies without any added pectin.

Pectin thickens and, in the presence of acid and high amounts of sugar, it gels. Pectin gels are clear, not cloudy, and they have an attractive sheen and clean flavor. This makes pectin a great choice with fruit products. Pectin is commonly used in mirrors, glazes, jams and jellies, bakery fillings, and fruit confections. It can be purchased as a dry powder, which is typically extracted and purified from citrus peel or apple skins.

Agar

Agar (also called *agar-agar*, or *kanten* in Japan) is derived from any of several species of red seaweed (*Gracilaria* or *Gelidium*, for example). Asian cultures have used agar for centuries. Today it is harvested worldwide and commonly sold in the United States as dry powder or as strands (Figure 12.2). While strands require soaking and several minutes of boiling in water to dissolve, agar powder dissolves in hot water in about a minute. Both strands and powder gel quickly as they cool, much more quickly than gelatin.

Agar is a polysaccharide and not a protein like gelatin, but it is sometimes nicknamed the "vegetable gelatin" because gels made from agar are similar to those made from gelatin. While they are similar, agar and gelatin gels are not identical. For one thing, much less agar is needed than gelatin, and agar gels stay firm without refrigeration. This makes agar useful for firming piping gels and in certain jellied confections. Agar is also a good warm weather stabilizer for icings and fillings, and it can be used to replace pork-based gelatin whenever dietary or religious restrictions warrant its use. However, because agar does not melt as readily as gelatin, it does not have as pleasant a mouthfeel, especially if used improperly.

Figure 12.2 Red seaweed, in back, and two forms of agar, which are purified from it

Agar cannot be whipped as gelatin can, and it does not stabilize aerated products well. This means it cannot substitute for gelatin in certain products such as Bavarian cream, fruit mousses, and marshmallow.

The often-cited conversion between gelatin and agar is 8:1, meaning that agar is eight times stronger than gelatin. However, agar and gelatin are both natural products and, like all natural products, they vary in gel strength from one manufacturer to another. While this is a good starting level, the only way to know how much agar to use in a product is to evaluate a series of products prepared with different levels of agar and see what works best.

Carrageenan

Carrageenan, like agar, is extracted from a red seaweed (*Chondrus*). Pastry chefs are generally less familiar with carrageenan than with agar, but it is used in many commercial food products for thickening and gelling. It is particularly effective when used in milk products, which is why it is added to eggnog, chocolate milk, ice cream, and instant flan mixes. In another form, carrageenan is called *Irish moss*. Irish moss is popular in the Caribbean for thickening beverages and as an aphrodisiac.

Guar and Locust Bean Gum

Guar gum and locust bean gum are from the endosperm of beans growing in pods that look much like string beans or pea pods. Guar gum is from the beans of a plant (*Cyamopsis tetragonoloba*) that grows in India and Pakistan. Locust bean gum, also called *carob gum*, is from the beans of an evergreen tree (*Ceratonia siliqua*) originally from the Mediterranean. While locust bean gum is from the bean, another food ingredient, carob powder, is from the pod that contains the locust beans (Figure 12.3). To make carob powder, also called *carob flour*, the beans are removed and the pods are roasted and ground. Carob powder is sometimes used as a cocoa powder substitute.

Both guar gum and locust bean gum are used as thickeners in a broad range of products including

Figure 12.3 Carob powder is ground from dried, roasted locust bean pods, while locust bean gum is extracted from the beans. **Clockwise from top:** carob powder, locust bean pods, locust beans, locust bean gum

A Brief History of Carrageenan

It is interesting to see how chefs make creative use of local ingredients. For example, red seaweed was once a popular gelling agent in Europe. Cooks would make a flan-type pudding by boiling seaweed with milk, then cooling. One source of the seaweed was off the coast of Ireland near a town called Carragheen. Today, the gum purified from this seaweed is called carrageenan.

cream cheese and sour cream. They also are commonly used in frozen foods, such as ice cream and frozen pasteurized egg whites, to prevent ice crystal growth and freezer damage.

Gum Arabic

Gum arabic is purified and dried from the *exudate* (gummy sap) of a tree (*Acacia*) that grows in Africa. The sap forms when a tree trunk or branch has been damaged, either through extreme climatic conditions or deliberate knife cuts. Gum arabic is good at stabilizing emulsions while maintaining a pleasing, nongummy mouthfeel. That is why it continues to be used in icings, fillings, and certain flavorings, even when its supply is scarce.

Gum Tragacanth

Gum tragacanth is obtained in a way similar to gum arabic, but it is from a shrub (*Astragalus*) that grows in the Middle East. Much thicker than gum arabic, gum tragacanth is probably best known to pastry chefs as an ingredient in gum paste, used by cake decorators to create flowers and other designs. Gum tragacanth is

extremely expensive because its main supply is in a politically unstable part of the world. For this reason, gum tragacanth is being replaced by other gums in most foods.

Xanthan Gum

Xanthan gum is a fairly new gum, in use since the 1960s. It is produced when a certain microorganism (*Xanthomonas campestris*) undergoes fermentation. Xanthan gum thickens without feeling thick and heavy, so it is commonly used in salad dressings to keep ingredients suspended.

Xanthan gum is often used along with starch—often rice starch—to replace wheat flour in gluten-free baked goods, including breads and cakes. Xanthan gum, used at about 2–3 percent, helps batters and doughs hold in gases for proper leavening, which provides an acceptable crumb to these baked goods.

Methylcellulose

Methylcellulose, also called *modified vegetable gum,* is one of several gums derived from cellulose. Cellulose makes up the cell walls of all plants and is the most plentiful polysaccharide on earth. Modified vegetable gum is made commercially by chemically modifying wood or cotton cellulose fibers. It is not considered a natural gum because of these chemical modifications.

Modified vegetable gum has a unique property, however, that makes it useful in bakery fillings. While most gels thin out at oven temperatures and thicken as they cool, modified vegetable gum gels at oven temperatures and thins out as it cools. Instead of bleeding and running as it is baked in Danish pastries, a bakery filling made with modified vegetable gum holds its shape. Methylcellulose has also been used by pastry chefs to create "hot ice cream," that is, crème anglaise that holds its shape when hot but melts as it cools.

Starches

Like gums, starch molecules are polysaccharides. This means that they are large, complex carbohydrate molecules made of many sugar units bonded one to the next. In the case of starch, the sugar units are glucose molecules.

Not all starch molecules are alike, however. Glucose units in starch can be arranged in one of two ways: either

as long, straight chains or as short but highly branched ones. Straight-chain starch molecules are called *amylose,* while the much larger, branched starch molecules are called *amylopectin* (Figure 12.4). Although amylose is a straight chain, the chain typically twists into a helical shape, while amylopectin, with its many branches, looks like a flat coral fan. Whether amylose, amylopectin, or

Starches are close to 100 percent pure and can be sold as coarse granules, flakes, and pearls (tapioca), but mostly they are sold as fine powders, sometimes called flours. This term is somewhat misleading, though. True potato flour, for example, is made from the entire potato, dried and ground. While it consists primarily of starch, it also contains small amounts of protein, fats, and vitamins, and has a distinct potato flavor. Ground potato starch, however, is essentially all starch, and has a bland flavor. To make the distinction between these two products, finely ground potato starch is sometimes more accurately called potato starch flour. Still, be careful. While "corn flour" in North America refers to the entire corn endosperm finely ground, "cornflour" in the UK refers to pure cornstarch. If you are not sure about the ingredients you are using, check the ingredient label or the nutrition information to determine if the product is 100 percent starch.

a mix of both, starch molecules are tightly packed in an orderly fashion inside starch granules.

Starch granules are small, gritty particles that are found in the endosperm of cereal grains, such as wheat and corn grains. Starch granules are also found in the

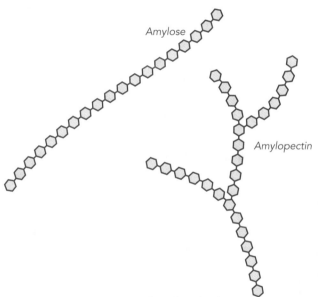

Figure 12.4 Segments of starch molecules

tubers and roots of certain plants, including potatoes, yuca (also called cassava or manioc), and arrowroot. Starch granules vary in size and shape, depending on the starch. For example, potato starch granules are relatively large and oval in shape, while cornstarch granules are much smaller and more angular. Starch granules also grow larger over time, forming rings of starch molecules, much as growth rings form on a tree as it matures.

Different types of starches—corn, potato, arrowroot, or tapioca—have properties uniquely their own. Some of the differences have to do with the distinctive size and shape of each starch's granules. Most differences, however, occur because of the amount of amylose and amylopectin in each, or the size of the molecules. Table 12.2 summarizes the major differences between starches that are relatively high in amylose, such as cornstarch (about 27 percent amylose), and those that are high in amylopectin, such as waxy maize starch (over 99 percent amylopectin). Root starches, which could be considered medium-amylose, have properties somewhere between the two.

TABLE 12.2 COMPARISON OF HIGH-AMYLOSE AND HIGH-AMYLOPECTIN STARCHES

HIGH IN AMYLOSE	HIGH IN AMYLOPECTIN
Cloudy when cooled	Relatively high clarity
Forms a firm, heavy-bodied gel when cooled	Thickens, does not gel
Gel tightens and weeps over time	Much less likely to weep over time
Not freezer stable; tends to tighten and weep	Much less likely to weep when thawed
Much thicker cold than hot	Essentially the same thickness hot or cold
Tends to mask flavors	Less likely to mask flavors

This section covers four main types of starches: cereal starches, root starches, modified food starches, and instant starches. Actually, all starches begin as either cereal or root starch. Instant starches and modified food starches are manufactured from these.

Cereal Starches

Cereal starches are extracted from the endosperm of cereal grains. Cornstarch, for example, is purified from the endosperm of corn kernels. Other cereal starches include rice starch, wheat starch, and waxy maize.

Cornstarch is the most common starch used in the bakeshop. In North America, cornstarch has the advantage of being inexpensive and readily available. Cornstarch should be your first choice for starch in the bakeshop, unless for some reason it does not meet your particular needs.

Waxy maize is a type of cornstarch, one that is extracted from a very different corn kernel and has different properties than regular cornstarch. While most cereal starches are high-amylose starches, waxy maize is a high-amylopectin starch (see Table 12.2). Waxy maize starch, sometimes called *waxy cornstarch*, will be discussed in the section on modified food starch, because it is almost always used in its modified form.

Figure 12.5 Tapioca starch develops a long stringy texture unless it is treated with moisture and heat or is chemically modified. **Left:** quick-cooking tapioca granules produce a short texture; **right:** untreated tapioca flour produces an unappealingly long, stringy texture

Root Starches

Root starches are extracted from various root or tuber plants. Root starches differ from cereal starches in many ways, partly because they are lower in smaller amylose molecules and higher in amylopectin. While they are generally more expensive than cornstarch, they do not have a cereal flavor, have better clarity, and produce a softer gel. Potato starch, arrowroot (*Maranta arundinacea*), and tapioca are examples of root starches.

Tapioca is extracted from yuca root, also called manioc or cassava. Yuca—not to be confused with the cactus yucca—is a versatile root used in South America and the Caribbean in the same way potatoes are commonly used. After cornstarch, tapioca is the most common starch used in North America.

In its finely ground form, tapioca is best used in baked goods such as biscuits, flat breads, and cookies. When sauces, pie fillings, and creams are made with this unmodified tapioca, they can develop an unappealingly long and stringy texture (Figure 12.5). For these types of products, it is better to use quick-cooking granules or tapioca pearls, which have been specially processed to reduce stringiness.

To make granules and pearls, the manufacturer moistens tapioca starch until damp, then allows it to agglomerate (clump) into granules or spherical particles called *pearls*. The granules or pearls are heated and dried, gelatinizing the outer layer of starch. Granules and pearls tend to cook into a shorter, less stringy texture than unmodified tapioca starch flour. Quick-cooking granules, such as Minute brand tapioca, dissolve quickly after a short soaking, while pearls must be soaked for several hours or overnight before use. Tapioca pearls become translucent when cooked, but they retain their size and shape in the finished product. Tapioca is imported from Southeast Asia or South America and is more expensive than cornstarch.

Notice from Table 12.2 that high-amylose starches, such as cornstarch, are cloudy when cooled, and they tend to have a heavy body and a cereal flavor. While these are not always disadvantages, they can be. When they are, root starches are a better choice.

Modified Food Starches

Modified food starches are starches that have been treated by the manufacturer with one or more chemicals approved for use by government agencies. Modified

When Is Wheat Starch Used in the Bakeshop?

Recall that regular white flour is about 68–75 percent starch. Any time flour is used in the bakeshop, wheat starch is being used. Flour also contains gluten-forming proteins, which, along with wheat starch, contribute to thickening and gelling.

Besides its use in batters and doughs, flour is sometimes used instead of cornstarch to thicken pastry cream and home-style apple pie. It adds a subtle taste of its own and a creamy off-white color.

food starches are designer starches; that is, they are designed by the manufacturer to have certain desirable features. For example, starches can be modified to increase their stability against excessive heat and acid, which thin out starch-thickened products. They can also be modified for better stability when frozen, which causes starch gels to tighten, clump, and weep.

Starches can be modified for other reasons besides improved stability. For example, starches can be modified to change their texture, as is the case with tapioca starches, or to speed up or slow down how quickly they gelatinize. However, the main reason to use a modified food starch in the bakeshop is for added stability.

While any starch—corn, potato, arrowroot, tapioca, or waxy maize—can be modified, most modified food starches are made from waxy maize starch. Waxy maize starches have many desirable features to begin with. Compared with regular cornstarch, for example, waxy maize starches are relatively clear and clean tasting. Some modified food starches (for example, Colflo 67) are *cook-up starches*, because they must be cooked just like any regular starch. Other modified food starches are instant starches.

Instant Starches

Instant starches thicken and gel without heat. They are different from modified starches, although most instant starches are also modified. Instant starches are sometimes called *pregelatinized* or *cold-water swelling*. To make a starch instant, the manufacturer either precooks (pregelatinizes) and then dries the starch, or makes some other change to the starch so that the granules absorb water without heat. While instant starches

do not require heat to thicken, most are not damaged if they are heated.

Because instant starches do not require heat to thicken, they are ideal for thickening products that are heat sensitive. For example, the bright green color and delicate flavor of a kiwi coulis is not damaged when the coulis is thickened with an instant starch.

Instant starches are also fairly quick to use. This makes them ideal for last-minute thickening of sauces for plated desserts, for example. Remember, though, that instant starches are specialty starches and, as such, cost more than regular cornstarch, often two or three times more. Instant starches also do not necessarily have the same texture as regular cook-up starches and cannot totally replace cornstarch in the bakeshop.

Instant Clearjel and Ultrasperse 2000 are the names of two common instant starches. Both are waxy maize starches that have been modified as well as precooked. This makes them both instant and stable.

Process of Starch Gelatinization

Recall from earlier in the chapter that starch molecules are tightly packed in an orderly fashion inside starch granules. When starch granules are placed in cold water, the starch molecules inside the granules attract water and the granules swell slightly. If the water is heated, the starch granules undergo an irreversible process called *gelatinization*.

Gelatinization is a disruption of the orderliness of starch granules and the swelling of these granules. It occurs when large amounts of water move into the granules, separating and surrounding starch molecules, pushing them apart. If sufficient water is not present or sufficient heat is not applied, the granules will not fully gelatinize. Large granules typically gelatinize first, with smaller granules taking more time to fully absorb water and swell.

Since water is trapped by gelatinized starch molecules, it cannot move freely. Likewise, the swollen starch granules cannot move freely, because they are pressed against each other. With nothing moving, the starch mixture is thickened. This thickening is the beginning of a process sometimes called *pasting*. As heating continues, the granules continue to swell and starch molecules, especially smaller amylose molecules, leach out of the granules and into the hot liquid. At this point, with most of the granules fully swollen and only some starch leached from the granules, the starch mixture is properly cooked. It should be removed from the heat and cooled.

If the mixture is heated beyond this point, and if enough water is present, the granules continue to spill their contents, becoming smaller and more deformed in shape, until finally they rupture completely. At this point, all that is left are small granule fragments and freed starch molecules. Mixing and stirring speeds up the rupturing of starch granules, since large, swollen granules are easily broken apart. Figure 12.6 shows the process of starch gelatinization.

As the starch solution cools, starch molecules slow down and entangle, trapping additional water and thickening. If there is a high enough concentration of entangled amylose molecules, the solution gels as it cools.

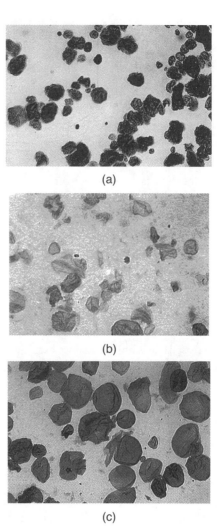

Figure 12.7 **(a)** Starch granules undercooked; **(b)** Starch granules properly cooked; **(c)** Starch granules overcooked.

Notice that there is an optimum amount of heat for proper thickening and gelling. Too little heat and too few granules swell, let alone release starch molecules. Too much heat and too many granules break down. Either way—undercooking or overcooking starch mixtures—causes too little thickening and gelling. Figure

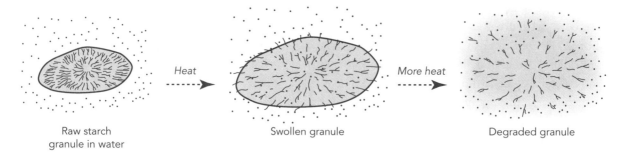

Figure 12.6 The process of starch gelatinization

12.7 compares the appearance of starch granules under the microscope, when cooked to varying degrees.

Undergelatinizing starch (undercooking it) creates other problems as well. Because raw granules are hard and dense, undercooked starch feels gritty in the mouth. Undercooked starch is more opaque and typically has a raw starch taste. If stored for a day or more, under-cooked starch mixtures tend to weep, meaning unat-tractive droplets or even pools of water form around the gel. Because undercooked starch has different char-acteristics from overcooked starch, it is easy to tell if a too-thin starch mixture has been undercooked or over-cooked. Table 12.3 summarizes the characteristics of undercooked and overcooked starches.

Many factors affect the gelatinization temperature of starches and the amount of cooking required to fully gelatinize them. The higher the gelatinization tempera-ture, the longer it takes for starch to gelatinize and the greater the tendency for the starch to be easily under-cooked. Likewise, the lower the gelatinization tempera-ture, the less time it takes for the starch to gelatinize and the greater the tendency for the starch to be easily overcooked. The most important factors that affect the gelatinization temperature of starch are itemized in the list that follows.

- *Type of starch.* Each type of starch has an optimum amount of heat required for proper gelatinization. Check with the manufacturer for guidelines on the use of a modified food starch, since some gelatinize at a higher temperature than cornstarch and others gelatinize at a lower temperature. The amount of time required to fully gelatinize root starches varies with the formula, but it is always less than the amount of time required to fully gelatinize cornstarch. Most times, unmodified root starches should not be brought to a boil. When cooked for too long, unmodified root starches become excessively stringy in texture. If this occurs, the sauce or filling should be remade and cooked for a reduced length of time, or the root starch should be replaced with a modified one.

- *Amount of tenderizers: sweeteners and fats.* Sweeteners and fats slow the rate at which starch granules absorb water and swell. The more slowly they absorb water, the longer it takes starch granules to gelatinize. In fact, if enough sugar is present, it completely pre-vents starch from gelatinizing. This is one way that sugars and fats tenderize baked goods: They reduce the amount of structure-building starch gelatiniza-tion that occurs. Sugar also increases the translu-cency of starch-thickened mixtures.

- *Amount of acid.* Acid hydrolyzes (breaks down) large starch molecules into smaller ones, reducing their thickening power. Acid also disrupts starch granules so that they gelatinize more quickly and easily. In fact, if enough acid is present, gelatinization occurs so quickly that the starch mixture appears to not thicken at all.

Selecting a Starch

The number and variety of starches available to the pastry chef can seem bewildering at first. There are many native starches—cornstarch, rice, tapioca, arrow-root, and potato starch—plus modified and instant

TABLE 12.3 UNDERCOOKED AND OVERCOOKED STARCH SOLUTIONS

UNDERCOOKED	OVERCOOKED
Too thin	Too thin; may be stringy
Gritty	Smooth
Opaque	Extremely clear
Raw starch taste	No raw starch taste
Tends to weep	Does not weep

TABLE 12.4 QUESTIONS TO CONSIDER WHEN SELECTING A THICKENING AND GELLING AGENT

Is clarity important? If yes, use a root starch or a modified food starch; better yet, don't use a starch. Use gelatin or a vegetable gum such as agar or pectin.
Are you thickening or gelling a heat-sensitive product such as kiwi or strawberry? If yes, use an instant starch, or use gelatin.
Is a sharp, clean flavor important, such as in a fruit pie filling or glaze? If yes, use a root starch; better yet, use gelatin or pectin.
Are you thickening a product that contains a high amount of acid, such as lemons or cranberries? If yes, use a root starch; better yet, use a modified food starch.
Are you planning to freeze the product? If yes, use a root starch; better yet, use a modified food starch.
What is the desired consistency? For example, would you prefer a soft gel to a firm, heavy-bodied one? If yes, use a root starch, or use cornstarch and stir the mixture as it cools.
Are there any price constraints? If yes, your best choice is cornstarch, but all starches are relatively inexpensive when compared to most other thickening and gelling agents.

starches. When confronted with as many choices as this, it is helpful to systematically think through your needs, then consider the options available.

The list of questions in Table 12.4 was designed to help narrow the choices when selecting a starch or a gum. Understand, however, that cornstarch should be the first choice in the bakeshop because it is a good all-purpose starch, low in cost and readily available.

For more details on the advantages and disadvantages of different starches and gums, refer to Table 12.5.

Functions of Thickening and Gelling Agents

Main Functions

Providing a Thickened or Gelled Texture   To say that an ingredient provides a thickened or gelled texture to sauces, fillings, glazes, and creams is to say that the ingredient provides structure. While thickening and gelling is the formation of a very soft structure, recall that starch, in particular, also contributes to structure in baked goods.

Increasing Stability   Thickening and gelling agents are sometimes called *stabilizers*, meaning that they prevent undesirable changes from occurring in foods. Actually, thickening and gelling agents typically provide stability by their ability to thicken or gel. For example, gelatin stabilizes whipped cream primarily by gelling. This solidifies the walls surrounding air bubbles in whipped cream and prevents them from breaking. Guar gum stabilizes frozen egg whites primarily by

thickening them. This prevents the formation of large, damaging ice crystals and allows the egg whites to whip fully.

Providing Gloss or Sheen to Sauces, Fillings, and Glazes   Many thickening and gelling agents form a smooth layer that clings to the surfaces of ingredients. This smooth layer reflects light in a way that provides gloss or sheen to many sauces, fillings, and glazes. Mirror glazes on cakes are a good example of this feature. Mirror glazes are commonly made with gelatin or pectin, two gelling agents that not only provide sheen but also are crystal clear.

Additional Functions

Softening and Tenderizing Baked Goods   Starch added to baked goods interferes with the formation of gluten and egg structure. This is especially true when

TABLE 12.5 A COMPARISON OF THE PROPERTIES AND USES OF STARCHES AND GUMS

STARCH	PROPERTIES	IDEAL USES
Cornstarch	Cloudy when cooled; good sheen Heavy body; gels if concentration is high Not stable to excessive heat, acid, freezing, mixing Gel tightens and weeps over time Masks many flavors High gelatinization temperature	Puddings, cream pies
Arrowroot	Moderate to high clarity; high sheen Soft gel; can be stringy Relatively stable against acid, heat, mixing, freezing Relatively low gelatinization temperature Relatively clean flavor	Fruit pies and sauces
Tapioca	Moderate to high clarity; high sheen Soft gel; can be stringy Relatively stable against acid, heat, mixing, freezing Relatively low gelatinization temperature Relatively clean flavor Available as pearls, granules, powder	Fruit pies and sauces Tapioca pudding
Waxy maize	Moderate to high clarity Thickens, does not gel Relatively stable against acid, heat, mixing, freezing Relatively clean flavor	Base for many modified starches; not typically available unmodified
Modified food starch	Highly stable against acid, heat, mixing, freezing Variable gelatinization temperature Other properties vary with brand	Frozen foods Steam table applications High-acid products
Instant starch	No heat required Properties vary with brand	Last-minute plating Heat-sensitive products
Flour	Cloudy; yellow-tinged color Heavy body Imparts a flavor; masks or mellows flavors	Pastry cream Home-style pie fillings
Gelatin	High clarity, high sheen Forms firm, bouncy gel At typical usage levels, melts in the mouth and at room temperature Clean flavor Available as sheets, powder	Gelatin desserts Stabilized whipped cream Confections (gummy bears)
Agar	Moderate to high clarity Forms very firm gel, bouncy gel Stable (does not melt) at room temperature or in mouth Usage level varies with purity Available as sheets, strands, and powder	As a gelatin substitute for: **a.** Vegetarians and people with religious dietary restrictions **b.** Use with raw pineapple, etc.
Pectin	High clarity, high sheen Thickens or gels Clean flavor Generally requires high acid and high sugar concentrations	Fruit jams, jellies, fillings Glazes High-quality jelly confections

Starch retrogradation is a process in which starch molecules in a cooked or baked and cooled product bond more and more closely over time, increasing structure. It is as if the starch molecules wish to return (*retro*) to the tightly bonded state of ungelatinized starch granules. When this happens to starch-based creams and pie fillings, products shrink and firm up, becoming tough and rubbery. The shrinking network of tightly bonded starch molecules squeezes out water, causing weeping, also known as *syneresis*. It is this process that makes high-amylose starches, such as cornstarch, inappropriate for creams and fillings that are to be frozen or refrigerated for any length of time.

When starches retrograde in baked goods, the soft crumb becomes dry, hard, and crumbly. In other words, starch retrogradation is a primary cause of staling in baked goods. As with creams and fillings, water is squeezed out of the starch, but it is not evident in baked goods because other ingredients absorb the water.

Starch retrogradation (staling) of baked goods can be delayed by covering products to prevent moisture loss; by storing products at room temperature or in the freezer—not in the refrigerator, where retrogradation is fastest; and by adding ingredients that slow down the process. Sugars, proteins, fats, and emulsifiers are all effective at delaying starch retrogradation. While bakers might not add emulsifiers directly, every time a high-ratio shortening is used, effective antistaling emulsifiers are being added. Because pastries contain large amounts of all of these ingredients, they are slower to stale than breads and rolls.

there is not enough water for starch to gelatinize, as is the case for cookies and pie dough. It is only through gelatinization that starch forms structure; otherwise it consists of hard, gritty particles that interfere with protein webs that gluten or eggs form.

Absorbing Moisture Recall that flour is a drier because it contains starch, gums, and proteins. All starches and gums, in fact, are driers, because they absorb moisture and often fats and oils.

Cornstarch in particular is added to dry powdered products to absorb moisture. This prevents caking and keeps the dry powder free flowing. For example, cornstarch is added to finely pulverized powdered confectioners' sugar. Cornstarch is also commonly added to baking powder. Besides keeping baking powder free-flowing, cornstarch serves as a bulking agent to standardize baking powders. It also prevents losses in activity. As cornstarch absorbs moisture, it prevents the reaction of acid and baking soda and the release of carbon dioxide, an important leavening gas.

Storage and Handling

All thickening and gelling agents should be stored covered. This prevents them from absorbing moisture.

The following guidelines should be followed when working with starches to ensure maximum thickening and gelling.

Separating Granules

Before heating starches, and many other thickening and gelling agents, be sure dry particles are well-separated from each other. If granules are not separated before heating, they will clump. If this happens, they must be sieved out, and this lessens the thickening ability.

Following are the three main ways of separating dry granules from one another. The first two are commonly used in bakeshops.

- Blend granules with other dry ingredients such as granulated sugar. The rule of thumb is to add at least four or five parts sugar to one part dry starch (or gelatin, or gum).
- Add granules first to *cold* water, making a paste or slurry. This technique is used with gelatin when it is bloomed, and it can be used with most starches except instant starch. Many instant starches—and other ingredients like guar gum that absorb cold

water quickly—clump when added directly to cold water. These ingredients must be blended with dry ingredients first, or blended with fat.

- Blend granules with fat such as butter or oil. Culinary chefs use this technique whenever they prepare roux, which is flour blended with and cooked in melted butter.

Cooking and Cooling Starch

Be sure to cook starch long enough without overcooking it. Cornstarch mixtures start to thicken before they come to a boil, but continue heating them to ensure that all starch granules are fully hydrated and swollen. A good rule of thumb for cornstarch is to bring it to a boil and boil gently for 2 or 3 minutes. This is a guideline that works well with most cornstarch mixtures, but it is too much heating for root starches, which should not be brought to a boil.

Be sure to stir a starch mixture evenly and constantly while cooking to prevent scorching or burning. Cool immediately upon cooking to avoid overcooking. For a creamy-smooth texture, stir while cooling; for maximum thickening and gelling, cool without stirring.

Questions for Review

1 What units make up all polysaccharides? Describe the difference between starch and inulin in the type and number of units each contains.

2 What units make up all proteins? Which common thickening and gelling agent is a protein?

3 Describe the difference between thickening and gelling.

4 Name three sources of gelatin. Which of these is the main source of gelatin used in foods?

5 Describe how most food-grade ground gelatin is produced.

6 Describe how sheet gelatin is produced.

7 What is meant by the "Bloom rating" of gelatin?

8 How is the Bloom rating of gelatin measured?

9 What does it mean to "bloom gelatin"? Why is it done?

10 How is powdered gelatin typically bloomed?

11 How is sheet gelatin typically bloomed?

12 Why must fresh pineapple juice be heated before it can be added to gelatin?

13 How do acidic ingredients, such as lemon juice, affect gel strength?

14 Name a gum extracted from each of the following vegetable products: seaweed, apple peel, sap from a tree, endosperm of a seed.

15 Which gum is particularly useful for thickening and gelling fruit products?

16 Which gum is sometimes used as a gelatin substitute and is sometimes called vegetable gelatin?

17 What thickening and gelling agent is extracted from the endosperm of cereal grains?

18 Give examples of cereal starches and root starches.

19 What two reasons could explain why starches differ from each other in properties (gel strength, clarity, flavor, stability, etc.)?

20 Describe the main differences in properties between a typical cereal starch and a root starch.

21 Why should cornstarch not be used to thicken pastry cream that will be frozen? What starch is the best choice to use instead?

22 What is the main reason for using a modified food starch?

23 What are the two main reasons for using an instant starch?

24 How should an instant starch be used so it is less likely to clump?

25 Draw the process of starch gelatinization. Label your drawings, and be sure to show the major differences in raw, swollen, and degraded granules.

26 Describe what happens to starch granules as they are heated in the presence of water, and explain how thickening and gelling changes in the process.

27 Which is more likely to require more heat to gelatinize: cornstarch or a root starch?

28 You switch from cornstarch to tapioca as a thickener in a fruit sauce. The sauce becomes unacceptably stringy when it cools. What should you do differently next time to prevent this from happening?

29 Does sugar speed up or slow down the process of starch gelatinization?

30 Does acid speed up or slow down the process of starch gelatinization?

Questions for Discussion

1 About how much water will 5 sheets of gelatin absorb when they are properly bloomed? Show your work, and assume that the sheets weigh 0.1 ounce (3 grams) each.

2 A formula calls for 5 sheets of gelatin but only powdered gelatin is available (assume Bloom rating of 230 for powdered gelatin). How much powdered gelatin should be weighed out? What adjustments should be made with water, if any? Show your work.

3 A formula calls for 5 sheets of gelatin but only powdered gelatin is available. The standard calculation to convert from sheets to powder was made, but a Bavarian cream comes out too firm. Assume ingredients were weighed properly. What went wrong?

4 Why might a butterscotch cream pie, which is high in sugar, have half the sugar added after the cornstarch-milk-egg mixture is already cooked? If all the sugar were added to the butterscotch cream pie before the mixture is cooked, what might happen to the texture, appearance, and mouthfeel of the pie?

5 A starch-thickened cherry pie filling doesn't taste tart enough, so more lemon juice is added. Why is it best to add the lemon juice after the cherry pie filling is cooked and cooled? Even better than adding the lemon juice at the end of the cook time is to use a starch that is stable to acid. What starch is the best choice for acid stability?

6 Your assistant shows you a starch-thickened sauce that is too thin. Explain how you can tell by looking at and tasting the sauce whether the starch was undercooked or overcooked.

Exercises and Experiments

❶ Exercise: Thickening Agents in Bakeshop Products

Look up formulas for the common bakeshop products listed in the left column of the following table and place a checkmark in the box indicating which of the thickening agents listed in the top row contributes to the thickening and gelling of each.

PASTRY PRODUCT	EGGS (SPECIFY WHOLE, WHITES, OR YOLKS)	GELATIN	STARCH	FRUIT PULP/ FRUIT PECTIN	CHEESE
Pastry cream					
Crème brûlée					
Banana cream pie					
Fruit pie filling					
Chiffon pie					
Bavarian cream					
Cheesecake					
Pumpkin pie					

❷ Exercise: How Different Grades of Sheet Gelatin Compare

Fill in the Results Table, summarizing differences between two grades of sheet gelatin. Use fresh gelatin for this exercise, since gelatin sheets pick up moisture during storage. Use the following steps as a guide in completing the table:

1   Use your textbook to find the average Bloom rating for each grade of gelatin. Record answers in column 1.

2   Read the net weight per box for each gelatin directly off the box and fill in the column labeled Weight per Box.

3   Weigh 10 sheets of each grade of sheet gelatin (to one number after the decimal point) and record weights of each sheet in the third column in Results Table 1.

4 Calculate the average weight per gelatin sheet by dividing the total weight of 10 sheets by ten. Record calculated weight per sheet in the fourth column.

5 Estimate the number of sheets per box by dividing the weight per box by the average weight per sheet. Record in the fifth column.

6 Estimate the number of sheets per ounce by dividing 28.35 (the number of grams per ounce) by the average weight for one sheet (in grams). Record results in sixth column.

7 Record in the Comments column the sensory characteristics of the sheets: Touch the sheets and compare how the different grades compare in feel (which feels thicker, heavier). Next, if available from the following experiment, smell warmed gelatin solutions. Record strength of meaty aroma, comparing each to the aroma of the powdered gelatin solution.

RESULTS TABLE COMPARISON OF DIFFERENT QUALITY GRADES OF SHEET GELATIN

GELATIN GRADE	AVERAGE BLOOM RATING	WEIGHT PER BOX (GRAMS)	WEIGHTS OF EACH OF TEN SHEETS (GRAMS, FROM WEIGHING)	AVERAGE WEIGHT FOR ONE SHEET	ESTIMATED NUMBER OF SHEETS PER BOX	ESTIMATED NUMBER OF SHEETS PER OUNCE	COMMENTS
Silver							
Bronze							

Conclusions

Select one from the choices in **bold** or fill in the blanks.

1 As the quality (Bloom rating) of gelatin sheets increases, the weight per sheet **increases/decreases/stays the same**. This allows different grades of gelatin sheets to be used interchangeably when they are **weighed/counted**.

2 As the quality (Bloom rating) of gelatin sheets increases, the sheets feel **thicker/thinner.**

3 As the quality (Bloom rating) of gelatin sheets increases, the number of sheets per box **increases/decreases/stays the same**. If the cost per box of bronze sheets is $53 and the cost per box of silver is $58, which is more economical to use? Show your work. (*Hint*: calculate and compare the cost per sheet.)

_____

_____

_____

4 Based on your results, if a formula calls for 30 grams of bronze sheets and you substitute 30 grams of silver sheets, your product will likely turn out **softer/firmer/about the same**. This is because _____

_____

_____.

5 How would you describe the differences between your calculated average weights of the different types of gelatin sheets and the stated values given on page 326 in the text: **no difference/small difference/moderate difference/large difference**? How can you explain these differences, if there were any?

_____

_____

_____

③ Experiment: How Different Amounts and Brands of Gelatin Compare in Stabilizing Whipped Cream

This experiment uses stabilized whipped cream as a means of understanding different forms of gelatin and how they differ in use and usage levels. Gelatin solutions will be prepared using 10 sheets of gelatin or using one ounce (30 grams) of powdered gelatin. This is a standard conversion used by some pastry chefs, and you will see whether this conversion holds true.

Objectives

- Demonstrate the effect of overstabilizing products on flavor, texture and mouthfeel, and overall quality
- Compare stabilized whipped cream made with sheet gelatin and powdered gelatin
- Compare stabilized whipped cream made with sheet gelatin of different quality levels
- Practice tempering hot mixtures into cold

Products Prepared

Whipped cream stabilized with
- No added gelatin (control product)
- Half the amount of gelatin solution made with powdered gelatin
- Full amount of gelatin solution made with powdered gelatin
- One and a half times the amount of gelatin solution made with powdered gelatin
- Sheet gelatin, bronze, 140 Bloom, full amount of gelatin solution, using 10 sheets for 1 ounce (30 grams) gelatin powder
- Sheet gelatin, silver, 160 Bloom, full amount of gelatin solution, using 10 sheets for 1 ounce (30 grams) gelatin powder
- Other, if desired (additional levels of gelatin, different brands of powdered gelatin, commercial stabilizer, agar in place of gelatin [at 8 to 1 conversion, or 12 percent the amount of gelatin])

Materials and Equipment

- Mixer with 5-quart mixing bowl
- Whip attachment
- Scale
- Stainless-steel bowls
- Stabilized Whipped Cream (see Formula), enough to make 1-2 cups (250-500 ml) of each variation
- Plates, 6" (15 cm); small bowls; or equivalent
- Plastic wrap
- Stopwatch or count-up timer
- Instant-read thermometer

Formula

Stabilized Whipped Cream

INGREDIENT	POUNDS	OUNCES	GRAMS	BAKER'S PERCENTAGE
Heavy cream		8	250	100
Vanilla extract (1 tsp/5 ml)		0.2	5	2
Sugar, regular granulated		1	30	12
Gelatin solution		variable	variable	variable
Total		**9.45–9.95**	**292.5–307.5**	**114–115**

Method of Preparation

1 Chill cream, bowl, and whip attachment thoroughly.

2 Prepare gelatin solution as follows:
- Add 1 ounce (30 grams) gelatin powder or 10 sheets gelatin (weight is variable) to 5 ounces (150 grams) cold water. (*Note:* If desired, sheets can be used the traditional way, adding sheets into excess water and squeezing gently; however, the amount of water absorbed by the gelatin tends to vary with water temperature, soak time, and amount of squeezing.)
- Allow to bloom for 5–10 minutes.
- Warm bloomed gelatin gently, just until gelatin dissolves. Keep warm.

3 Add vanilla and sugar to cream.

4 Whip cream on medium to a very soft peak only. For control product (with no added gelatin), continue with step 2 of Procedure.

5 Weigh gelatin solution into a tared warm bowl, using the following amounts:
- For half the amount of solution, use 0.25 ounce (7.5 grams).
- For full amount of solution, use 0.5 ounce (15 grams).
- For one and a half times the amount of solution, use 0.75 ounce (22.5 grams).

6 Add a small amount of whipped cream to warm gelatin solution, to temper.

7 Quickly add tempered solution into whipped cream, whipping rapidly without overwhipping.

8 Taste a small amount of stabilized whipped cream to confirm that it is smooth and that gelatin did not bead or ball up. If whipped cream is not smooth, discard and begin again.

Procedure

1 Prepare whipped cream samples, whipped to a very soft peak only, using the formula given or any basic formula for whipped cream stabilized with gelatin. Prepare one batch of whipped cream for each variation.

2 Transfer samples from each batch of cream onto plates or bowls and spread into smooth, even layers. Cover with plastic wrap to prevent drying. Label each sample with type and amount of gelatin added and time it is placed under refrigeration.

3 Refrigerate cream samples until all are cooled to 35°–40°F (2°–4°C). Record length of time that each sample is cooled in Additional Comments column of the Results Table. *Note:* Gelatin continues to firm up during the first 18 hours after preparation. If possible, allow samples to cool overnight before evaluating.

Results

Evaluate the sensory characteristics of cooled samples and record evaluations in the Results Table. Be sure to compare each in turn to the control product and consider the following:

- Appearance
- Flavor intensity, from very low in flavor to very high, on a scale of 1 to 5
- Firmness, from very soft to very firm, on a scale of 1 to 5
- Mouthfeel (lightness/heaviness on tongue, mouthcoating, how quickly it melts)
- Overall acceptability, from highly unacceptable to highly acceptable, on a scale of 1 to 5
- Add any additional comments, as necessary

RESULTS TABLE SENSORY CHARACTERISTICS OF WHIPPED CREAM STABILIZED WITH DIFFERENT TYPES AND AMOUNTS OF GELATIN

TYPE OF GELATIN	AMOUNT OF GELATIN	APPEARANCE	FLAVOR INTENSITY	FIRMNESS AND MOUTHFEEL	OVERALL ACCEPTABILITY	ADDITIONAL COMMENTS
None (control)	No added gelatin					
Powdered	Half the amount					
Powdered	Full amount					
Powdered	One and a half times the amount					
Sheet, bronze	Full amount					
Sheet, silver	Full amount					

Sources of Error

List any sources of error that might make it difficult to draw the proper conclusions from your experiment. In particular, consider differences in the extent to which the creams were whipped, how long each was cooled, whether all were cooled to the same temperature, and any difficulties tempering warm gelatin with cold whipped cream.

_____

_____

_____

State what you could do differently next time to minimize or eliminate each source of error.

_____

_____

_____

Conclusions

Select one from the choices in **bold** or fill in the blanks.

1 As the amount of gelatin increased from none to 1½ times the full amount, the flavor of the whipped cream **increased/decreased/stayed the same**. This was probably because __
_____. The difference was **small/moderate/large**.

2 As the amount of gelatin increased from none to 1½ times the full amount, the firmness of the whipped cream **increased/decreased/stayed the same**. In addition, as the amount of gelatin increased, the whipped cream melted in the mouth **more slowly/more quickly/ about the same**. The difference was **small/moderate large**.

3 Overall, the amount of gelatin that gave the most appealing flavor and mouthfeel was **no gelatin/half the amount/the full amount/one and a half times the amount.** However, the amount of gelatin that will likely stabilize whipped cream best (that is, will keep it whipped and aerated longest) is **no gelatin/half the amount/the full amount/one and a half times the amount.**

4 Overall, the creams stabilized with the two different grades (bronze and silver) of sheet gelatin were **very similar/somewhat similar/very different**. The main differences, if any, were as follows:

_____
_____
_____

5 Based on the results of this experiment, bronze and silver sheets **are/are not** interchangeable, sheet for sheet, when stabilizing whipped cream. Explain your answer.

_____
_____
_____

6 When comparing the bronze sheets to gelatin powder, the texture of the whipped cream made with the full amount of bronze sheets was **softer than/firmer than/about the same as** the texture of the whipped cream made with the full amount of gelatin powder. This means that the conversion between the bronze sheets and the gelatin powder used in this experiment (10 sheets gelatin equals 1 ounce/30 grams powdered gelatin) was approximately **correct/not correct** because the bronze sheets are **lower/higher/the same** in Bloom rating as this brand of powdered gelatin. Next time, for that amount of powdered gelatin, **fewer/more/the same number of** bronze sheets should be used.

7 Other comments I would like to add about the samples or the experiment:

_____
_____
_____

4 Experiment: How Different Starches and Cook Times Compare When Thickening a Fruit Juice Filling

Objectives

Compare the appearance, flavor, and texture of fruit juice fillings
- Made with different starches
- Cooked for different lengths of time

Products Prepared

Fruit juice fillings prepared with
- No added starch, boiled gently 2 minutes
- Cornstarch, boiled gently 2 minutes (control product)
- Cornstarch, not boiled
- Cornstarch, boiled gently 8 minutes
- Tapioca starch flour (or arrowroot or potato), boiled gently 2 minutes
- Tapioca quick-cooking granules, boiled gently 5 minutes
- Instant starch (such as National Ultrasperse 2000 or Instant Clearjel), not cooked
- Modified food starch (cook-up, such as National Frigex HV, Clearjel, or ColFlo 67), boiled gently 2 minutes (or according to manufacturer's recommendation)
- Other, if desired (tapioca quick-cooking granules at 25 percent higher level [1 ounce/28 grams], tapioca pearls, rice starch, bread flour)

Materials and Equipment

- Scale
- Stainless-steel bowls
- Whisk
- Stainless-steel saucepans
- Heat-resistant silicone spatula
- Plastic tasting spoons
- Fruit juice filling (see Formula), enough to make about 15 ounces (450 grams) or more of each variation
- Stainless-steel bowls
- Water bath
- Instant-read thermometer
- Plates, 6" (15 cm); clear cups, 1 fl. oz. (30 ml); or equivalent
- Plastic wrap or covers for cups

Fruit Juice Filling

Yield: *24 ¾-ounce servings*

INGREDIENT	OUNCES	GRAMS	BAKER'S PERCENTAGE
Fruit juice, white grape or other	14	400	100
Starch	0.8	22	6
Sugar, regular granulated	1	30	7
Total	**15.8**	**452**	**113**

Method of Preparation
(for fruit fillings with no added starch, control 2 minute boil cornstarch, 8 minute boil cornstarch, tapioca starch, and modified food starch)

1   Select any clear fruit juice such as white grape, apple, or cranberry. For low-acid juices like white grape or apple, add a small amount of acid to the entire amount of juice used throughout the experiment (3–6 grams citric acid, or juice of two or more lemons, for every 32 fl. oz./1 liter of juice). This will accentuate results on products cooked for different lengths of time.

2   Place starch and sugar in bowl. Stir to blend. For unthickened sauce, place only sugar in bowl.

3   Add 5 ounces (150 grams) of fruit juice to starch-sugar and whisk until dispersed.

4   Place remaining fruit juice in saucepan and bring to a boil.

5   Add starch-juice mixture to boiling liquid, stirring constantly with a heat-resistant silicone spatula.

6   For unboiled fillings, remove from heat immediately and proceed with step 8.

7   For boiled fillings, return mixture to a boil and boil for the stated amount of time (2 or 8 minutes), stirring constantly. For fillings boiled for 8 minutes, add a measured amount of water, if necessary, to prevent burning from excessive water evaporation.

8   Remove from heat and cool slightly.

9   Use a tasting spoon to taste a small amount of thickened filling, confirming that it is smooth and that starch did not bead or ball up. (Do not confuse grittiness of undercooked starch with beading/balling of improperly dispersed starch.) If filling is not smooth, do not strain; discard and begin again. Do not reuse tasting spoon without first washing it thoroughly; saliva contains a very potent amylase that will thin out fillings.

Method of Preparation
(for fruit filling thickened with quick-cooking tapioca granules)

In step 3, add granules and sugar into full amount of cold fruit juice. Set aside for 15 minutes to soak. Omit steps 4 through 6 and proceed as above with step 7, boiling for a full 5 minutes. Granules will be translucent but still intact.

Method of Preparation
(for fruit filling thickened with instant starch)

In step 3, slowly sprinkle starch/sugar onto full amount of cold fruit juice, while stirring gently with a whisk. (Too much whisking will trap air into filling.) Omit steps 4 through 9.

If starch begins to clump (this may occur with instant starches that are very fine powders), start by first blending starch with additional sugar, up to five parts by weight.

Procedure

1 Label plates or cups with type of starch to be used to thicken fruit juice filling.

2 Prepare fruit juice filling using the formula above, or using any basic fruit juice filling made from clear juice. Prepare at least 15 ounces (450 grams) of each variation.

3 Transfer hot filling to tared stainless-steel bowl and cool in water bath to about 120°F (50°C), gently stirring; omit this step when using instant starch.

4 After cooling samples to 120°F (50°C), weigh bowl and filling; add back water to replace any lost to evaporation (for most sauces, this means bringing back weight of sauce to 15.8 ounces (452 grams). For filling made with no added starch, it will be 15.0 ounces (430 grams). Record amount of water added back in Additional Comments column of Results Table, which follows. (*Note:* If cornstarch samples begin to gel, it will be difficult to blend in water. Either use warm water, rewarm filling slightly, or do both.)

5 Transfer finished/cooled filling to labeled plates or clear cups, filling all plates or all cups to the same level.

6 Cover samples with covers or plastic wrap and refrigerate to cool to 35°–40°F (2°–4°C).

Results

1 Before tasting products, check temperature to confirm that product is properly cooled to 35°–40°F (2°–4°C). Record product temperatures in Results Table.

2 Evaluate the sensory characteristics of completely cooled fruit fillings and record evaluations in the Results Table. Be sure to compare each filling in turn with both the unthickened filling (for flavor evaluation) and the control product (cornstarch, 2-minute boil), and consider the following:

- Appearance (shiny/dull, translucent/opaque, thick/thin/gelled, short body/long body, etc.)
- Flavor (raw starch taste, sweetness, sourness, fruit flavor, etc.)
- Mouthfeel and texture (smooth/gritty, thick/thin/gelled, heavy-bodied, mouthcoating, etc.)
- Overall acceptability, from highly unacceptable to highly acceptable, on a scale of 1 to 5
- Any additional comments, as necessary

RESULTS TABLE SENSORY CHARACTERISTICS OF THICKENED FRUIT FILLINGS MADE WITH DIFFERENT STARCHES HEATED FOR DIFFERENT LENGTHS OF TIME

TYPE OF STARCH	TEMPERATURE OF REFRIGERATED FILLING	APPEARANCE	FLAVOR	MOUTHFEEL/ TEXTURE	OVERALL ACCEPTABILITY	ADDITIONAL COMMENTS
No added starch, 2-minute boil						
Cornstarch, 2-minute boil (control product)						
Cornstarch, not boiled						
Cornstarch, 8-minute boil						
Tapioca starch (flour)						
Tapioca instant granules						
Instant starch						
Modified food starch						

Sources of Error

List any sources of error that might make it difficult to draw the proper conclusions from your experiment. In particular, be aware of difficulties in controlling the rate of cook and total cook time, the amount of stirring as samples cooled, adding water back to cooled samples, and final sample temperatures. Also note whether sample cups were filled to identical heights (especially important for evaluating clarity and firmness).

_____

_____

_____

State what you could do differently next time to minimize or eliminate each source of error.

_____

_____

_____

Conclusions

Select one from the choices in **bold** or fill in the blanks.

1   In general, the fruit fillings with the best clarity were made with properly cooked **cornstarch/tapioca (or other root starch)**.

2   In general, the fruit fillings with the firmest gel or most thickening were made with properly cooked **cornstarch/tapioca (or other root starch)**.

3   The starch with the cleanest flavor should taste the closest to the **unthickened/undercooked/overcooked** fruit filling. The fruit filling that in fact did have the truest fruit flavor was thickened with **cornstarch/tapioca (or other root starch)**.

4   Compared with the cornstarch-thickened fruit filling that was properly boiled for 2 minutes, the undercooked fruit filling thickened **more/less/the same amount**. The undercooked filling also had **greater clarity than/less clarity than/the same clarity as** the properly cooked one. Other differences between the undercooked fruit filling and the properly cooked one are as follows:

_____

_____

_____.

These differences were overall **small/moderate/large**.

5   Compared with the cornstarch-thickened fruit filling that was properly boiled for 2 minutes, the overcooked fruit filling thickened **more/less/the same amount**. The overcooked filling also had **greater clarity than/less clarity than/the same clarity as** the properly cooked filling. Other differences between the overcooked fruit filling and the properly cooked one are as follows:

_____

_____

_____.

These differences were overall **small/moderate/large**.

6 The unmodified finely ground tapioca starch had a much **shorter/longer (stringy)** body than the tapioca instant granules. Other differences between the fruit filling made with the instant granules and the filling made with the finely ground tapioca are as follows:

_____

_____

_____.

These differences were overall **small/moderate/large**.

7 A good way to tell which products received more total heat exposure is to compare the fillings for the amount of water that was added back to compensate for water lost through evaporation. The product that should have had the most water added back is the cornstarch-thickened sauce **boiled for 2 minutes/boiled for 8 minutes/not boiled at all**. The sauces that should have about the same amount of water added back include the following:

_____

_____

_____.

Based on the actual amounts of water that were added back, the following products probably received more heat exposure than they should have:

_____

_____

_____.

Likewise, the following products probably received less heat exposure than they should have:

_____

_____

_____.

8 The instant starch used in this experiment is called _____.
It differed in sensory qualities from properly cooked cornstarch in the following ways:

_____

_____

_____.

9 The modified food starch used in this experiment is called _____.
It differed in sensory qualities from properly cooked cornstarch in the following ways:

_____

_____

_____.

13

Milk and Milk Products

Introduction

Milk and milk products (dairy ingredients) sold in North America are produced mostly from domesticated cows. They are complex ingredients that contain a mix of proteins, sugar (lactose), vitamins, minerals, emulsifiers, and milk fat. While dairy ingredients are not absolutely essential to many baked goods, they do perform some valuable functions, making them important ingredients in the bakeshop.

Both the U.S. and Canadian federal governments regulate minimum milk fat amounts in milk and milk products. They also regulate processing conditions for pasteurization, maximum allowable bacterial counts, acidity levels, and additives allowed. Certain states and provinces have more stringent regulations that are enforced within their borders. Milk fat requirements and pasteurization times and temperatures provided below represent U.S. and Canadian federal standards.

For information on butter, see Chapter 9.

Common Commercial Processes to Milk and Milk Products

Pasteurization

Essentially all dairy products sold in North America are pasteurized (certain aged cheeses are the exception). *Pasteurization* is a process that eliminates pathogenic (disease-causing) microorganisms and reduces the number of many other microorganisms in food, without adversely affecting the overall quality of the food. Louis Pasteur invented the process of pasteurization in the mid-1800s.

The most common commercial means of pasteurizing milk is high-temperature, short-time (HTST) pasteurization, in which milk is heated to a high temperature, at least 161°F (72°C), for a minimum of 15 seconds. Ultra-high-temperature (UHT) pasteurization (*ultrapasteurization*) involves heating the product to an even higher temperature, often 280°F (138°C), for 2 seconds. UHT milk has a slightly different flavor from HTST milk because milk flavor is very heat sensitive. UHT milk also has a longer shelf life because the higher temperature is much more lethal to bacteria, destroying essentially all bacteria in milk. However, unless UHT products are specially packaged to prevent the entry of microorganisms, they must be treated like HTST products and refrigerated at all times.

Homogenization

If fresh milk is taken straight from the cow and allowed to sit, cream eventually rises to the top. To prevent this separation, most dairy products sold in North America are homogenized. *Homogenization* is a process in which milk is forced under high pressure through small openings in a metal plate, breaking the milk fat into tiny droplets (Figure 13.1). As soon as the droplets form, milk proteins and emulsifiers form a protective film around each one, preventing them from reuniting. The tiny droplets stay suspended indefinitely, and milk fat no longer separates and rises to the top as a cream layer. In other words, homogenized dairy products are stable emulsions of fat droplets suspended in milk.

Separation

Cream is easily separated from milk in a milk separator. A separator is a type of centrifuge that spins very quickly, causing cream in milk to separate off because of its lighter density. The process is much faster than relying on gravity for the cream to rise.

Why Drink Boxes of Milk Do Not Require Refrigeration

Milk is usually purchased in the dairy case and stored in the refrigerator. How is it, then, that milk such as Horizon or Parmalat milk can be sold in drink boxes that are not refrigerated?

Think of drink boxes of milk as the modern equivalent of canned milk. The milk in these boxes has been ultra-pasteurized, then cooled and specially packaged under sterile conditions so that the product inside is essentially bacteria free. The process is called *aseptic processing*, and no preservatives or food irradiation are involved. A similar process is used for pasteurizing and packaging coffee cream in single-use plastic containers.

Because the product is essentially bacteria free and is in containers that do not allow entry of microorganisms, milk in sealed drink boxes is as safe as canned milk. Once opened, however, milk that has been aseptically packed in drink boxes, or that has been canned, must be refrigerated.

Milk and Other Emulsions

Oil and water don't mix, but they can be made to coexist temporarily or, sometimes, for extended lengths of time. This is true of emulsions, which by definition consist of two liquids in which one liquid forms droplets that are suspended in the second liquid. When the droplets are very tiny, and when they are protected by the right emulsifier, the emulsion can last a very long time. A properly made mayonnaise, for example, is considered a permanent emulsion because it is stabilized by the very effective emulsifiers (and emulsifying proteins) in egg yolks.

There are two basic types of food emulsions: oil-in-water (O/W) emulsions and water-in-oil (W/O) emulsions. In an oil-in-water emulsion, droplets of oil are suspended in water (or milk, fruit juice, eggs, etc.). Examples of O/W emulsions include milk and cream, mayonnaise, ganache, and liquid shortening cake batter. In a water-in-oil emulsion, droplets of water are suspended in oil (or a plastic fat). There are only a few water-in-oil food emulsions, with the main one being butter.

Whether a mix of oil and water becomes an O/W or W/O emulsion depends on a few factors, including the amount of each liquid available and the type of emulsifiers present. Notice that cream is an oil-in-water emulsion while butter is an water-in-oil emulsion. To turn cream into butter requires a total inversion of the emulsion from O/W into W/O. This requires a lot of energy, which is why cream must be vigorously whipped or churned to form butter.

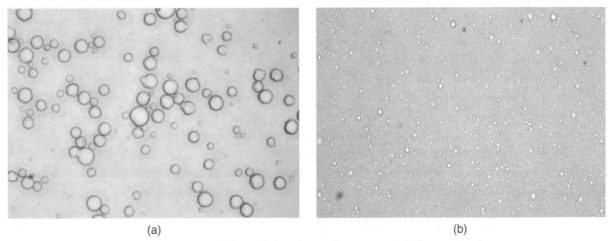

(a)   (b)

Figure 13.1   Effect of homogenization on milk fat in whole milk **(a)** unhomogenized, **(b)** homogenized

Casein proteins in milk associate with calcium and phosphorus to form small spherical structures called *micelles*. Like the tiny droplets of fat in milk, micelles are too small to see or feel. But light cannot pass through the casein micelles. Instead, it bounces off them in many directions. When light scatters like this, it appears white. Most of the whiteness of milk is from the scattering of light off casein micelles. Some of the light, however, is scattered off fat droplets, making whole milk appear whiter and more opaque than fat-free milk. As the amount of milk fat increases much higher, as it does in heavy cream and certain cheeses, the product takes on a buttery yellow appearance from the carotenoids in the milk fat.

Makeup of Milk

Milk directly from the cow contains proteins, lactose, vitamins, minerals, and milk fat. From Figure 13.2, however, it is clear that milk is composed mostly of water. Not counting milk fat, the solids in milk are appropriately called *milk solids not fat*, or MSNF. There are legal minimum requirements for the amount of milk fat and MSNF in most dairy products.

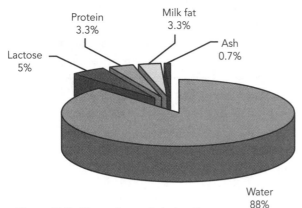

Figure 13.2 The makeup of whole milk

Protein 3.3%
Milk fat 3.3%
Lactose 5%
Ash 0.7%
Water 88%

Other than a slight sweetness, the flavor of fresh milk is relatively mild. As the amount of milk fat in milk products increases, however, the rich dairy flavor increases, because most dairy flavors are in the fat.

Small amounts of the emulsifiers lecithin and mono- and diglycerides are also in milk fat, as are carotenoid pigments. Carotenoids provide dairy products with a slight yellowish color. Mostly, however, milk fat contains triglycerides (fat molecules), especially saturated ones.

Although milk contains only about 3.3 percent protein, the proteins in milk are very important. These proteins fall into two main categories: casein proteins and whey proteins. *Casein proteins* are easily coagulated with acids or enzymes. Coagulated or clabbered casein proteins aggregate with one other in a manner somewhat similar to coagulated egg proteins. Like egg proteins, casein proteins thicken and gel as they coagulate. This is the basis for the manufacture of cheeses, yogurt, sour cream, and other cultured dairy products.

When cheese is made, a clear greenish liquid drains from the cheese curd. While coagulated casein proteins form the cheese curd, the clear liquid, known as *whey*, contains whey proteins. *Whey proteins* form a film along the bottom of pans and on the surface of milk when milk is heated. Milk must not be left unattended on the heat because a film of whey quickly burns onto the pan bottom, ruining flavor and color.

> **HELPFUL HINT**
> *If sugar is in a formula where milk or cream is heated, add some or all the sugar to the milk before heating to prevent whey proteins from coating and sticking to the bottom of the pan.*

Whey proteins are just one of the nutrients in whey. Whey is also rich in lactose, calcium salts, and riboflavin. The slight greenish tinge in whey is from riboflavin, one of the B vitamins in milk.

Lactose, also called milk sugar, makes up about 50 percent of the MSNF of milk. Its sweetness, which is about one-fifth that of sucrose, contributes to the characteristic flavor of milk. Lactose is a disaccharide consisting of a glucose molecule bonded to galactose. Unlike most sugars, lactose is not fermented by yeast.

Many people experience intestinal discomfort after consuming large quantities of milk. This *lactose intolerance* occurs because their bodies do not contain high enough levels of the enzyme lactase that breaks down lactose to glucose and galactose. Lactose intolerance causes intestinal discomfort, but it is not a life-threatening allergy. Those experiencing the discomforts of lactose intolerance should avoid dairy products or consume only those low in lactose, such as cultured dairy products and cheese.

Milk Products

All milk products are legally defined by the percent milk fat that they contain. Figure 13.3 compares the milk fat content of several common dairy products.

Fluid Milk

Fluid milk is classified by its fat content, which is standardized by the processor. Fat content in milk ranges from 3.25% or higher for whole milk to essentially 0% for fat-free (skim) milk. The minimum MSNF for milk is 8.25% in the United States and 8.0% in Canada; the rest is water.

For freshest dairy flavor, fluid milk is the product of choice. Fluid—not dry—milk is best in baked custards, cream pies, vanilla custard sauce, frozen desserts, and pastry cream. When using fluid milk in yeast doughs, scald it first by heating to about 180°F (82°C). This denatures the whey protein, glutathione, that interferes with gluten development.

Dry Milk

Dry milk solids (DMS) are made by removing most (all but about 3–5 percent) of the water from fat-free or whole milk. Most DMS is made by the spray-dry process, in which partly evaporated milk is sprayed as a fine mist into a heated chamber. The milk dries almost instantly and falls to the bottom of the chamber as a powder.

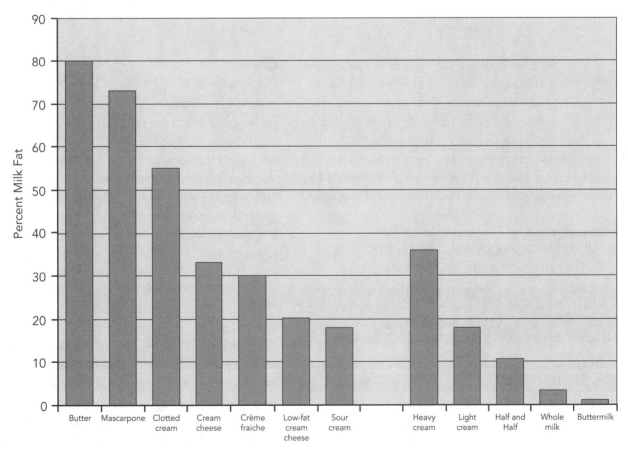

Figure 13.3 The amount of milk fat in dairy products

It is very easy to convert formulas that call for fluid milk to ones using dry milk solids. For every pound of fluid whole milk, use 2 ounces (0.12 pounds) DMS and 14 ounces (0.88 pounds) water. If your formula is in metric units, use 120 grams DMS and 880 grams water for every liter of milk. Blend the DMS with dry ingredients such as flour and sugar, or cream it with shortening. Unless it is instantized, DMS does not easily mix with water, so it is best not to reconstitute it before use.

Dry milk solids can be purchased as is or "instantized." Instant dry milk solids are less likely to clump during storage and, more important, dissolve quickly and easily when added to liquids. Instant dry milk solids consist of lighter, larger particles than regular DMS.

Dry milk takes up less space in the bakeshop than fluid milk, and it requires no refrigeration. When DMS is made from whole milk, it is sometimes called *dry whole milk* or *powdered whole milk*. Because dry whole milk contains milk fat, it oxidizes easily, producing a rancid off flavor. When DMS is made from fat-free milk, it is sometimes called *nonfat dry milk*, *powdered skim milk*, *NDM*, or *NFDM*. Nonfat dry milk has a much longer shelf life than dry whole milk and is much more common in bakeshops.

DMS does not have the same fresh dairy flavor as fluid milk, so it should not be used in custards and creams. Instead, use DMS in baked goods like breads, cakes, and cookies. Although many cake, bread, and muffin formulas call for fluid milk, dry milk solids are acceptable, even desirable, in these products.

DMS can be purchased with varying amounts of heat treatment. High-heat DMS is held at 190°F (88°C) for a minimum of 30 minutes, then dried. It is the best choice for use in yeast-raised baked goods because the heat treatment denatures the whey protein fragment (glutathione) that reduces gluten development and bread quality. The heat treatment also increases the ability of milk proteins to absorb water.

Low-heat DMS is not often used in the bakeshop, although it would be acceptable for all baked goods except yeast-raised doughs. Instant nonfat dry milk purchased in the supermarket is an example of low-heat DMS. While it has a fresher taste than high-heat DMS, low-heat DMS does not provide the added benefits to baked goods that high-heat DMS does. However, low-heat dry milk solids are better for increasing the solids of ice cream mixes, where a less-processed flavor is desirable.

Cream

Cream sold in North America is pasteurized, often under UHT conditions. The main advantage of UHT (ultrapasteurized) cream is that it has an extended shelf life. While cartons of cream used in the bakeshop are often UHT pasteurized, they are not aseptically packed and therefore must be refrigerated.

Besides being pasteurized, cream is usually homogenized. Homogenization makes whipping more difficult, but many heavy creams and whipping creams contain added emulsifiers and stabilizing gums to aid in whipping. At very high levels of fat—around 40%—homogenized cream whips easily.

Cream is classified by the amount of milk fat it contains. Milk fat contributes much of the creamy, rich flavor of cream. It forms tiny oil droplets and small solid fat particles that stay suspended when the cream is homogenized. It is the presence of these droplets and fat particles that gives cream its thick, smooth consistency. Because cream is high in fat, it is also high in carotenoid pigments that dissolve in fat, giving it a yellowish creamy tinge.

TABLE 13.1 MINIMUM MILK FAT STANDARDS FOR CREAM PRODUCTS SOLD IN THE UNITED STATES AND CANADA

NAME	U.S. MINIMUM STANDARD	CANADIAN MINIMUM STANDARD
Heavy cream	36%	—
Whipping cream	30%	32%
Cream	—	10%
Light cream	18%	—
Half-and-half	10.5%	—

England is known for the quality of its dairy products, including its cream. Two common types of cream sold in Great Britain are single cream and double cream. Single cream is equivalent to American light cream. Double cream, at over 48% milk fat, is thicker and richer than any cream commonly sold in North America. Double Devon cream, from Devonshire, England, is considered by many to be the finest in Great Britain.

How is it that the addition of sugar allows an opened can of sweetened condensed milk to sit at room temperature and not spoil? After all, sugar is a source of food for most microorganisms.

Microorganisms require more than food to survive. They require moisture and warmth, for example, and most require air (oxygen). Moisture is extremely important to microorganisms, as it is to all living things. If moisture is unavailable, microorganisms dehydrate and their cells shrivel and malfunction.

Recall that sugar is hygroscopic; that is, it attracts water and bonds to it. When water is bound to sugar, it is unavailable to microorganisms. Just as sailors at sea cannot quench their thirst with seawater, microorganisms cannot easily quench their thirst with sugar syrup. Their cells shrivel and they cannot function, as if water were not present at all. The water activity is said to be lowered and the osmotic pressure raised by the high concentration of sugar or salt. Below a certain water activity and above a certain osmotic pressure, microorganisms cannot survive.

This is what happens in sweetened condensed milk. Even though it is liquid, it has a low water activity, so it will not easily spoil.

In the United States, heavy cream contains between 36 and 40% milk fat. It is often the only cream stocked in the bakeshop. Other cream products include whipping cream, light cream, and half-and-half. Light cream from the United States can be made by mixing equal parts heavy cream and whole milk; half-and-half can be made by mixing equal parts light cream and whole milk.

Nationally, Canada has two types of cream: cream and whipping cream. Canadian provincial governments often regulate the milk fat content of other cream products such as table cream, half-and-half, cereal cream, and light cream sold regionally. Table 13.1 lists the minimum milk fat standards for cream products in both the United States and Canada.

Evaporated Milk and Sweetened Condensed Milk

Evaporated milk and sweetened condensed milk are specialty ingredients that have occasional uses in the bakeshop. They are generally purchased in cans, which can be stored at room temperature until opened. Both are made by removing water from milk. Evaporated milk is concentrated until it contains twice the milk fat and twice the MSNF of regular fluid milk. Sweetened condensed milk has had more water removed and has sugar added. Low-fat and fat-free versions of both evaporated and sweetened condensed milk are available.

Evaporated milk and sweetened condensed milk cannot be used interchangeably. The main difference between the two products is the sugar that is added to sweetened condensed milk. Because of this sugar, sweetened condensed milk is thicker, sweeter, and denser, and it has a more caramelized color and flavor than evaporated milk. The color and flavor are the result of Maillard browning that occurs from heating the products.

The added sugar in sweetened condensed milk means that it can be—but usually is not—left open at room temperature for days and it will not spoil.

Evaporated and sweetened condensed milks cost more than liquid whole milk, but there are advantages to each. They are easier to store because they take up less space, and they last indefinitely at room temperature

Fermented (cultured) dairy products have a long history of use for their health benefits. It is thought that when the friendly bacteria from these products make it to the intestinal tract, they help maintain the health of the intestinal tract by reducing the growth of undesirable bacteria. When consumed for health benefits, these live bacteria are often called *probiotics*. Recall from Chapter 3, however, that bacteria and other microorganisms die during the baking process. Whatever health benefits are provided by the probiotics in cultured dairy products are lost during baking.

until opened. This is particularly important in tropical regions where refrigeration is not readily available. More important, the low water content and caramelized flavor in these products can be used to advantage. For example, a common use of sweetened condensed milk is in making Mexican flan, which is custard with a caramelized milk flavor. Mexican flan is traditionally made with milk that has been boiled and evaporated with sugar, which is essentially sweetened condensed milk. Other common uses for sweetened condensed milk and evaporated milk are pumpkin pie, fudge, and caramel, where it provides a creamy, smooth texture. Evaporated milk substitutes for cream in certain low-fat products.

Cultured Dairy Products

Cultured dairy products are fermented by the addition of live bacteria, usually lactic acid bacteria. *Lactic acid bacteria* ferment lactose to lactic acid and other flavorful products. The lactic acid lowers the pH of cultured dairy products and provides a pleasant sour flavor. It also thickens and gels cultured dairy products because the acid causes casein proteins to coagulate. Lactic acid bacteria are considered friendly bacteria because they have positive effects on the flavor and texture of dairy products and because they help prevent the growth of undesirable spoilage bacteria in these foods. It is because of friendly bacteria that cultured dairy products have a longer shelf life than milk products that are not cultured.

Often, formulas for baked goods that contain cultured dairy products also contain baking soda. When acid from the dairy product reacts with baking soda, carbon dioxide gas is produced. This can be a significant source of leavening for some baked goods. If there is more acid in the dairy product than is needed to react with the baking soda, the excess acid will lower the pH of the mix, tenderizing and whitening the baked product.

Cultured Buttermilk   Originally, buttermilk was the fluid remaining after cream was churned into butter. Today, cultured buttermilk is made by adding lactic acid bacteria to milk, usually low-fat (1% milk fat) or fat-free milk. It is thicker than regular milk because of the effect of acid on the casein proteins.

Cultured buttermilk is used in buttermilk biscuits and certain other baked goods primarily for flavor, although it can whiten, tenderize, and leaven in some cases. Traditional Irish soda bread is leavened entirely with buttermilk and baking soda. Cultured buttermilk can also be purchased as a dry powder.

A reasonable substitute for cultured buttermilk is *sour milk*, prepared by adding 1 tablespoon (15 milliliters) vinegar to 8 ounces (225 grams) fluid milk. Sour milk does not have the thick consistency of cultured buttermilk and it has a sharper sourness, but it does provide the same acidity for tenderizing, whitening, and leavening. Notice that sour milk is not the same as soured milk, which is milk that has spoiled. Soured, spoiled milk has an unpleasant flavor and should never be used in baked goods.

Other cultured milk products include kefir cultured milk and acidophilus cultured milk. These products are similar to buttermilk but are cultured with different bacteria, giving them distinctive flavors.

Yogurt   Yogurt is similar to cultured buttermilk in that it is a cultured dairy product made by adding bacteria to fluid milk and allowing the bacteria to ferment, producing acids. Yogurt is made with a mix of different bacteria (*Lactobacillus bulgaricus* and *Streptococcus thermophilus*). This typically gives it a stronger, more acidic flavor than buttermilk and a firmer gel-like consistency. Yogurt can be used as a low-fat substitute for sour cream.

Greek-style yogurt is made by draining much of the liquid whey from yogurt. The resulting yogurt,

Start with any yogurt, including low-fat or fat-free yogurt, to make Greek-style yogurt. Avoid brands that contain added starches or gums, since the starches and gums prevent whey from draining freely.

To drain, place yogurt on several layers of cheesecloth and hang over a bowl to catch the whey. Keep it loosely covered and refrigerate. The process takes as little as several hours, but continue to drain for a day or more, if drier cheese is preferred.

---

sometimes called "yogurt cheese," is similar to cream cheese in texture, but it has a stronger acid bite. Greek-style yogurt can be used as a substitute for cream cheese in cheesecakes, icings, and fillings.

Sour Cream   In the United States, sour cream is made by adding lactic acid bacteria to light cream (18–20% milk fat). In Canada, sour cream can be slightly lower in milk fat (14% minimum). The lactic acid causes the proteins in sour cream to coagulate to a gelled consistency; gums and starches may be added to further thicken the product. The added gums and starches will also keep the liquid whey in sour cream from separating out. If the whey does separate, stir it into the sour cream before use.

Use sour cream in cheesecakes, coffee cakes, and certain pastry doughs. Low-fat and fat-free sour cream products are available. These products are higher in moisture and less rich in flavor than regular sour cream. Low-fat sour cream, which is essentially cultured half-and-half (minimum 10.5% milk fat), is often satisfactory as a substitute for regular sour cream in baking.

Crème Fraîche   Crème fraîche is a cultured cream product used throughout France. The traditional way of making crème fraîche is to set unpasteurized milk in a pan at room temperature, allowing cream to rise to the top. After about 12 hours, the cream is skimmed off. During that time, natural bacteria in the unpasteurized milk ripen the cream, turning it into a mildly sour, thickened product. Because crème fraîche is high in fat (minimum 30% in France), it is much smoother, richer, and more velvety than sour cream. In Mexico, a similar product is called *crema fresca*.

Pastry chefs sometimes make a substitute crème fraîche by adding a small amount of cultured buttermilk or sour cream to heavy cream and allowing it to stand in a warm spot for 8 hours or more before refrigerating. As the cream ripens from the growth of the lactic acid bacteria, it thickens and develops a sour flavor. This product is similar to sour cream, except it has a higher milk fat content.

Clotted Cream   Clotted cream is a thick, spreadable dairy product with a minimum fat content of 55% and a nutty, cooked milk flavor. The most prized clotted cream is arguably from Devon, the county in England where it has been made for centuries. The traditional way of making Devonshire clotted cream starts like crème fraîche, with ripened cream rising from milk set out in shallow pans. The milk is slowly heated to about 180°F (82°C) and held for about an hour until it starts to form a golden colored crust. The scalded mix is slowly cooled, and the thick crust of buttery clotted cream is skimmed off the top. Clotted cream is traditionally paired with jam and served on scones at teatime in England.

Small quantities of clotted cream are still made the traditional way at dairy farms in southwestern England, but clotted cream today is more likely to be made by cooking and slowly cooling fresh (not cultured) cream, already separated from the milk.

Cheeses

Cheese is made when coagulated casein milk proteins (curds) are separated from whey. Most, but not all, cheeses are classified as cultured dairy products, meaning that live bacteria produce acid that forms cheese curd.

Cheese can be unripened or ripened (aged). Soft, unripened cheeses, like cream cheese, Neufchâtel, baker's cheese, ricotta, and mascarpone, are the most common cheeses used in the bakeshop. Ripened cheeses typically have stronger, more distinct flavors. Examples of ripened cheeses include Parmesan cheese, blue cheese, cheddar cheese, and Brie.

Cream Cheese, Neufchâtel, and Baker's Cheese

Cream cheese, Neufchâtel, and baker's cheese are similar. Their curds form from the addition of lactic acid bacteria and often enzymes to milk or cream. Once liquid whey is drained off, the curds are processed until they have the right consistency. All three cheeses have a mild, slightly acidic flavor and a soft, smooth texture. All are used in pastry fillings and cheesecakes. Often, gums are added to increase creaminess and firmness, especially in the lower fat cheeses. Usually a combination of xanthan gum, locust bean, and guar gums are added.

Of the three, cream cheese is the highest in fat. It must contain a minimum of 33% milk fat (30% in Canada), the same as whipping cream. Neufchâtel is lower in fat (20% minimum) than cream cheese; in fact, Neufchâtel is often labeled "low-fat cream cheese." Baker's cheese is essentially fat-free and is sometimes labeled "fat-free cream cheese." Baker's cheese is less expensive than cream cheese but it is also noticeably less rich.

Because low-fat and fat-free versions of cream cheese often contain high levels of gums, these products can be successfully used in products like low-fat cheesecake without sacrificing texture. The flavor of low-fat cheesecake, however, is usually not as rich, full, and satisfying unless some adjustments are made. Many flavors dissolve in fat, and when fat is removed, flavors are released differently, often more quickly. With a little bit of experimenting, however, full-flavored lower-fat versions of cheesecake and many other dairy-based desserts can be created. Chapter 17 provides suggestions for improving the flavor of food products, including low-fat foods.

Ricotta Cheese

Ricotta cheese has a slightly grainy consistency and a mildly sweet dairy flavor. Originally, thrifty Italian housewives made ricotta cheese by adding acid to liquid whey that was left over from cheese making. Today, ricotta is often made by adding acid or bacteria and enzymes to whole milk or part-skim milk. This soft, moist cheese is used in cannoli, ricotta cheesecake, and other Italian specialties.

Mascarpone

Mascarpone is an Italian cheese best known as an ingredient in tiramisu. At 70–75% milk fat, mascarpone is almost as high in fat as butter. Its flavor and texture are a cross between cream cheese and butter, or similar to a very rich clotted cream. Mascarpone is commonly made by adding acid to heated heavy cream. The combination of acid and heat coagulates the casein, forming a fine, smooth curd that drains slowly from liquid whey. Since mascarpone is a relatively easy cheese to make, some specialty pastry shops prepare their own.

Quark

Quark originates from Germany. Different versions of this mild, unripened soft-curd cheese are available with different amounts of fat. Quark has a texture that is slightly smoother than ricotta. If quark is unavailable, ricotta cheese can be substituted by blending it in a food processor; for higher-fat quark, mix ricotta cheese with cream cheese. Quark is used in German cheesecake and in other pastries.

Whey Products

Recall that liquid whey, the greenish by-product of cheese manufacturing, is high in proteins (whey proteins) and lactose. It is also high in many vitamins and minerals such as riboflavin, calcium, and phosphorus.

Liquid whey was once discarded or used as animal feed. Today it is converted into many valuable products. One such product is dry whey powder, made by pasteurizing and drying liquid whey. Dry whey is similar in many ways to DMS and can be used in baked goods at a lower cost.

Functions of Milk and Milk Products

The following functions apply primarily to fluid milk and to dry milk solids (DMS). Where a function applies to one dairy product and not to others, it is specified.

Main Functions

Increasing Crust Color The combination of proteins and lactose, a fast-browning sugar, in dairy products provides the right mix for Maillard browning. Recall that Maillard browning is the breakdown of sugars and protein, and that it contributes color and fresh-baked flavor to baked goods. When baked goods are prepared with milk instead of water, baking times and temperatures may need to be lowered to reduce excessive browning.

Delaying Staling Several components in dairy products, including proteins, lactose, and milk fat, delay staling caused by starch retrogradation in the crumb of baked goods. This is particularly noticeable in lean yeast breads, which are typically low in stale-retarding ingredients like sugar and fat. By preventing staling, dairy products extend shelf life in baked goods.

Increasing Crust Softness Products like bread and cream puffs that are made with milk instead of water have softer crusts than those made with water. For example, crusty French baguettes contain water. Soft-crusted pullman or pan bread contains milk. Softening likely occurs because milk proteins and sugar bond to water, delaying its evaporation from the crust.

Blending Flavors and Providing Richness in Flavor Milk modifies the flavor of baked goods. In cakes and breads, for example, milk blends flavors and reduces saltiness. In baked custards, vanilla custard sauces, and pastry cream, milk products are essential in providing a rich, full flavor, especially when they are high in milk fat.

Providing a Fine, Even Crumb to Baked Goods Some baked goods—yeast breads, in particular—have a finer, more even crumb when prepared with milk or dry milk solids. It is likely a combination of milk proteins, emulsifiers, and calcium salts in milk that help stabilize small air bubbles. The smaller the air bubbles, the finer the crumb.

Forming a Stable Foam Cream whips into foam if it has a minimum milk fat content of about 28%. Both whipping cream and heavy cream can be whipped satisfactorily, but heavy cream, because of its higher fat content, produces a more stable (but denser) foam.

Besides using cream with a higher fat content, you can stabilize whipped cream by first chilling the cream to solidify some of the milk fat; by slowly adding sugar while whipping; or by folding in a gelatin solution or other stabilizer. Many brands of heavy cream contain added emulsifiers, such as mono- and diglycerides, to aid whipping.

Milk proteins also form stable foams. For example, the froth on cappuccino is from milk proteins trapping air. Evaporated milk, which is high in milk proteins, can be whipped to a stable foam when chilled, producing a whipped cream substitute.

> **HELPFUL HINT**
>
> *Be sure heavy cream is well chilled before whipping, and if the bakeshop is warm, chill the bowl and whisk as well. This way, milk fat in the cream hardens into solid fat crystals that effectively trap and hold air as the cream is whipped.*

Other Functions

Aiding in the Creaming of Shortening The addition of dry milk solids to creamed shortenings aids air incorporation and stabilization. The emulsifiers and proteins in dry milk seem to provide these benefits.

Absorbing Moisture Proteins in milk act as driers, absorbing moisture and increasing the water absorption rate of yeast doughs. The amount of extra water needed in yeast doughs is ounce for ounce about the same as the amount of DMS added. This means yeast doughs made with milk require more liquid than doughs made with water. This ability to absorb water contributes to the ability of milk proteins to delay bread staling.

Aiding in the Coagulation of Egg Proteins Custards made with water instead of milk do not firm up properly, because milk aids egg coagulation. Milk also has been shown to firm up the crumb in cakes, making them spongier and more resilient. It appears that both

Both whipped cream and whipped egg white are foams, meaning that they contain air bubbles trapped in liquid. Both are more stable but take longer to whip when sugar is added. Both, when overwhipped, collapse into clumps floating in a pool of liquid. Beyond that, whipped cream and whipped egg white are quite different. While proteins stabilize whipped egg white, it is milk fat that stabilizes whipped cream. Here is how it works.

Whipping disrupts a protective film that surrounds fat droplets, also called *fat globules*, suspended in cream. The unprotected fat globules form tiny clumps, solidified and reinforced with tiny fat crystals. These globules and clumps of milk fat surround each air bubble, separating and suspending them in cream. Continued whipping causes more fat globules to clump, forming an extensive three-dimensional network that stiffens the cream as it whips. Because the 3-D network that stiffens cream consists of solid crystals of milk fat, cream whips up best when it is well-chilled, unlike egg white, which whips up best when egg proteins are warm.

Fat clumps are not as effective as egg proteins in stabilizing foams, so while egg white increases up to eight times in volume, cream barely doubles. If whipped cream is aerated beyond where it has doubled, fat clumps grow into large grains of butter, the foam collapses, and liquid buttermilk separates out.

---

milk proteins and the calcium salts in milk strengthen egg structure, much as the calcium salts in hard water strengthen gluten structure.

Providing Moisture Because fluid milk is about 88 percent water, anytime it is used in baked goods, it contributes moisture for dissolving sugars and salts, for developing gluten, and for gelatinizing starch granules. Even heavy cream is over 50 percent water.

Adding Nutritional Value Milk contains high-quality protein, vitamins (riboflavin, vitamin A, and vitamin D) and minerals, especially calcium. This reflects the fact that milk is the sole source of food for the newborn calf. However, dairy products such as heavy cream that contain milk fat are high in saturated fat, which increases blood cholesterol and contributes to coronary heart disease.

Milk is a significant source of calcium in North America. Calcium is needed for bone growth, and a lack of calcium in the diet has been associated with osteoporosis, a serious loss of bone structure. Milk is fortified with vitamin D because vitamin D aids in the absorption of calcium in the body.

Storage and Handling

Fluid milk and reconstituted dry milk products spoil easily. Bacteria multiply and produce acids and off flavors, souring the milk. While it is usually not harmful, soured milk has an unpleasant flavor and should be discarded.

Beyond bacterial spoilage, the flavor of milk is highly susceptible to other changes, either from absorbing aromas or from chemical reactions that occur from exposure to excessive heat or light.

Pasteurized whole milk has a shelf life of about 2 weeks. It and all other dairy products are marked with a shelf life or use-by code. These codes are meant as a guide. Actual shelf life depends on many factors, the main one being how well the product has been stored.

Always smell and taste dairy products before use, and use your judgment in deciding whether an ingredient is appropriate or not. Do not mistake the formation of a layer of fat in heavy cream for a sure sign of spoilage. If a layer of fat forms, shake the container before use.

The following guidelines should be followed when handling fluid milk, to ensure microbiological safety and freedom from the development of off flavors.

- Check the temperature when it is delivered; it should be 45°F (7°C) or less. If it is warmer, reject the shipment.
- Always refrigerate milk when not in use, ideally at 34°–38°F (1°–3°C).

Ultraviolet light from the sun or from fluorescent lighting is high in energy and causes chemical changes to occur in foods. Some of these changes produce off flavors in milk stored in transparent containers. These changes can occur quickly, within an hour of exposure. They significantly reduce the acceptability of milk with consumers, and they can reduce the nutritional quality of milk.

One light-induced chemical change involves the breakdown of an amino acid in milk protein. This reaction takes place in the presence of the vitamin riboflavin. The result is the production of an off flavor in milk and a loss of riboflavin. The light-induced off flavor is sometimes described as the smell of burnt feathers or burnt potatoes, and it can happen within minutes of exposure to bright sunlight, longer under fluorescent lighting.

Another light-induced flavor change in milk is the breakdown of vitamin A, which is most likely to occur in low-fat and fat-free milk products. When vitamin A breaks down, it produces an oxidized off flavor that is sometimes described as the smell of wet cardboard or old oil. Again, the nutritional quality of the milk is reduced from exposure to light, this time with the destruction of vitamin A. Ironically, this cardboard flavor is more likely to occur in milk stored in clear plastic containers, not those stored in cardboard cartons.

- Close containers immediately after use. Stray microorganisms from the air can land in open cartons and shorten shelf life.
- Maintain a clean refrigerator. Odors from other foods or from unclean conditions can pass through containers and be absorbed. If necessary, use separate refrigerators for foods that have strong odors.
- Protect from light. Fluid milk is susceptible to ultraviolet (UV) light damage.

While cultured dairy products like yogurt, buttermilk, and sour cream have an extended shelf life, their acid content continues to increase over time. Their flavor gradually becomes stronger, sharper, and more pronounced. Mold can grow on cultured products that have been improperly stored or stored too long. Any cultured dairy product containing mold should be discarded.

Soft, unripened cheeses used in the bakeshop are highly perishable. Those high in moisture, such as ricotta cheese, are especially perishable. Once opened, ricotta cheese should be used within two to five days. Cream cheese, Neufchâtel, and baker's cheese last a little longer. Once opened, they should be tightly wrapped or covered to prevent drying, and they should be stored in the refrigerator for no more than two weeks.

Nonfat dry milk is easy to store. It needs no refrigeration unless reconstituted, but it should be covered and kept in a cool, dry place. This keeps dry milk from absorbing strong odors and from clumping and caking with changes in moisture. If nonfat dry milk absorbs water and hardens or clumps, pulverize and sift it before use. While it has a long shelf life—at least a year and possibly up to three, if properly stored—nonfat dry milk eventually develops off flavors, and darkens and browns. Whole dry milk contains milk fat that oxidizes to a rancid, off flavor. Whole dry milk has a maximum shelf life of only 6 months, even when stored under ideal conditions.

Canned evaporated and sweetened condensed milk do not spoil even after several years, if unopened. Over time, however, they darken, develop stronger flavors, and change in consistency. Once opened, evaporated milk requires refrigeration, and it is best to do so with sweetened condensed milk as well.

Questions for Review

1 Why is milk pasteurized? Why is it homogenized?

2 What is UHT milk? How does it differ from regular pasteurized milk?

3 What are MSNF?

4 What is in milk fat?

5 Name the two main categories of proteins in milk.

6 What does whey consist of?

7 What is DMS? Why is DMS not recommended for use in custard cream pie?

8 What is the difference between low-heat and high-heat DMS? Which is more commonly used in the bakeshop? In what products is it commonly used?

9 A formula calls for light cream but all that is available is whole milk and heavy cream. What should you do?

10 A formula calls for evaporated milk, but all that is available is sweetened condensed milk. Can sweetened condensed milk be used instead of evaporated milk? Why or why not?

11 What is meant by a "cultured dairy product"? Provide examples of cultured dairy products.

12 What is a probiotic? How does heat from the oven affect probiotics?

13 How might cultured dairy products contribute to leavening in baked goods?

14 How might cultured dairy products contribute to a whiter crumb in baked goods?

15 What is the difference between cream cheese, Neufchâtel, and baker's cheese?

16 Which types of dairy products can be successfully whipped into a stable foam?

17 List four factors important in producing stable whipped cream.

18 Why might it be better to add DMS with sugar when creaming fat than to add it later with flour and other dry ingredients?

19 How do dairy products, such as milk, extend the shelf life of baked goods?

20 Why should dry milk solids be stored covered in a cool dry place?

Questions for Discussion

1 A formula calls for 32 ounces (1 liter) of milk, but you would like to use dry milk instead. How much dry milk and water should be substituted for liquid milk?

2 You want to produce a baked custard dessert for people with lactose intolerance. You try using soy milk instead of whole milk, but find that the baked custard doesn't set up properly. Why might this be?

Exercises and Experiments

① Exercise: Sensory Characteristics of Dairy Products

In the Results Table, fill in the Description column with the brand name of each dairy product. Include additional information from the label that describes and differentiates the product from others of the same kind (dry milk solids could be instant or noninstant, and high-heat-treated or low; heavy cream could have a stated percent milk fat and could be ultrapasteurized or not). Next, record the list of ingredients for each dairy product, if applicable. Then, compare and describe the products in appearance, consistency, and flavor. Use this opportunity to identify different dairy products from their sensory characteristics alone. Add any additional comments or observations that you might have to the last column in the table. Three rows are left blank for the evaluation of additional dairy products, if desired.

RESULTS TABLE DAIRY PRODUCTS

DAIRY PRODUCT	DESCRIPTION	LIST OF INGREDIENTS	APPEARANCE	TEXTURE/ MOUTHFEEL	FLAVOR	ADDITIONAL COMMENTS
Nonfat (skim) milk						
Whole milk						
Heavy cream						
Evaporated milk						
Sweetened condensed milk						
Cultured buttermilk						
Sour cream						
Low-fat sour cream						
Dry milk solids, low-heat treated (reconstituted with water)						

(continues)

RESULTS TABLE DAIRY PRODUCTS *(continued)*

DAIRY PRODUCT	DESCRIPTION	LIST OF INGREDIENTS	APPEARANCE	TEXTURE/ MOUTHFEEL	FLAVOR	ADDITIONAL COMMENTS
Dry milk solids, high-heat treated (reconstituted with water)						

Use information from the table above and from your textbook to answer the following questions.

1   Describe in one sentence the difference in flavor and mouthfeel between nonfat milk and whole milk.

_____

_____

_____.

2   Evaporated milk is sometimes used as a low-fat substitute for heavy cream in baked goods and desserts. Which of the following products do you feel this would be most successful in: pastry cream, whipped cream, pumpkin pie?_____ Explain your answer.

_____

_____

_____.

3   Besides being sweeter, what else is different between the flavor of sweetened condensed milk and evaporated milk? _____.
Based on your evaluations of the two products, if a formula calls for one, do you think you could substitute it with the other? _____ Explain your answer.

_____

_____

_____.

4   What makes buttermilk and sour cream both taste sour? _____.
What is the main reason why they are thick? _____.
Sour cream sometimes has added starches and vegetable gums to further thicken it and to keep it from separating. Which, if any, of these was added to your sour cream?_____
_____.

5 How would you describe in one sentence the difference in flavor and mouthfeel between sour cream and low-fat sour cream?

_____
_____
_____.

What ingredients are added to low-fat sour cream that might give it a creamy mouthfeel?

_____
_____
_____.

6 Which reconstituted DMS (low-heat or high-heat) has flavor and color that best matches that of nonfat milk?

_____
_____
_____

7 If you usually add low-heat DMS to ice cream for a heavier body, do you think it would be acceptable to substitute high-heat DMS instead? Explain your answer.

_____
_____
_____

If you usually add high-heat DMS to cake batter, do you think it would be acceptable to substitute low-heat DMS instead? Explain your answer.

_____
_____
_____

❷ Experiment: Comparing the Quality of Éclair Shells Prepared with Milk and Water

Choux paste is the name of the dough used in making cream puffs, profiteroles, and éclairs. It is just as often made with milk as it is made with water. While either liquid can be used, the results are somewhat different. In this experiment, you will prepare choux paste (also called pâte à choux or éclair paste), bake up éclair shells using both liquids, and evaluate the results for yourself.

Objectives

Demonstrate how the type of liquid used in choux paste affects
- The crispness and the extent of Maillard browning on the crust of éclair shells
- The moistness, tenderness, and height of the éclair shells
- The overall flavor of the éclair shells
- The overall acceptability of the éclair shells

Products Prepared

Éclair shells made with

- Water (control product)
- Milk
- Other, if desired (50/50 blend of water and milk, soy milk, milk with butter instead of shortening, etc.)

Materials and Equipment

- Scale
- Heavy-bottom saucepan
- Wooden spoon
- Mixer with 5-quart mixing bowl
- Flat beater attachment
- Large plain tip
- Large pastry bag
- Pâte à choux dough (see Formula), enough to make 12 or more éclairs of each variation
- Half sheet pans
- Parchment paper
- Oven thermometer
- Serrated knife
- Ruler

Formula

Pâte à Choux (Choux Paste)

Yield: *12 éclair shells*

INGREDIENT	POUNDS	OUNCES	GRAMS	BAKER'S PERCENTAGE
Eggs, whole		8	225	181
Water		8	225	181
Shortening, all-purpose		3	85	68
Salt		0.1	3	2.4
Bread flour		4.4	125	100
Total	**1**	**7.5**	**663**	**532.4**

Method of Preparation

1 Preheat oven to 425°F (220°C).

2 Have eggs at room temperature.

3 Combine water, shortening, and salt in a heavy saucepan. Bring to a full boil, melting shortening completely.

4 Remove pan from heat and add flour all at once. Stir quickly and vigorously with a wooden spoon.

5   Return to heat and continue stirring vigorously until dough forms a smooth, dry ball that does not cling to the spoon or to the sides of the pan. Do not overcook or dough will not puff properly.

6   Transfer dough to bowl of mixer with flat beater and add eggs slowly (about 2 ounces/60 grams at a time), beating on medium speed after each addition. Eggs should be completely mixed in before the next portion is added. If desired, eggs can be beaten in by hand.

7   Continue beating mixture until all egg is absorbed. Dough should hold its shape when lifted on the end of a spoon, but it should still be smooth, moist, and workable.

8   Place a plain tip in pastry bag and fill bag with choux paste.

Procedure

1   Preheat oven to 425°F (220°C).

2   Prepare choux paste using formula above or using any basic choux paste formula (use all-purpose shortening instead of butter to eliminate milk solids coming from fat). Prepare one batch of dough for each variation.

3   Line sheet pans with parchment paper; label with the type of liquid to be used in choux paste.

4   Pipe dough onto lined sheet pans into strips about ¾" (2 cm) wide and 3" (8 cm) long, or into any standardized shape.

5   Use an oven thermometer placed in center of oven to read initial oven temperature. Record results here: _____.

6   When oven is properly preheated, place filled sheet pans in oven and set timer for 10 minutes, or according to formula. Bake at 425°F (220°C) for 10 minutes.

7   Reduce heat to 375°F (190°C) and finish baking at that temperature for another 10–15 minutes, or according to formula.

8   Bake until control éclairs are brown and firm to touch. To confirm doneness, remove one éclair from oven and allow to cool; if éclair holds its shape and does not collapse, remove remaining éclairs from oven.

9   Record bake times in Results Table 1, which follows.

10 Check final oven temperature. Record results here: _____.

11 Allow éclairs to cool slowly to room temperature on sheet pans in a warm place.

Results

1   When éclairs are completely cooled, evaluate average height as follows:
   • Slice three éclair shells from each batch in half lengthwise, being careful not to compress.
   • Measure height of each éclair shell by placing a ruler along the flat edge at its center. Record results for each of three éclair shells from each batch in ¹⁄₁₆" (1 mm) increments in Results Table 1.
   • Calculate the average éclair shell height by adding the heights of the éclairs and dividing this by 3. Record results in Results Table 1.

RESULTS TABLE 1 EVALUATION OF BAKE TIMES AND HEIGHT OF ÉCLAIR SHELLS MADE WITH DIFFERENT LIQUIDS

TYPE OF LIQUID	BAKE TIME (IN MINUTES)	HEIGHTS OF EACH OF THREE ÉCLAIR SHELLS	AVERAGE HEIGHT FOR ONE ÉCLAIR SHELL	ADDITIONAL COMMENTS
Water (control product)				
Milk				

2 Evaluate the sensory characteristics of completely cooled products and record evaluations in Results Table 2. Be sure to compare each in turn to the control product and consider the following:

- Crust color, from very light to very dark, on a scale of 1 to 5
- Crust texture (soft/crisp, moist/dry, etc.)
- Inside appearance (color, amount of webbing, etc.)
- Inside texture (tough/tender, moist/dry, etc.)
- Flavor (egg flavor, floury taste, saltiness, etc.)
- Overall acceptability, from highly unacceptable to highly acceptable, on a scale of 1 to 5
- Add any additional comments, as necessary.

RESULTS TABLE 2 SENSORY CHARACTERISTICS OF ÉCLAIR SHELLS MADE WITH DIFFERENT LIQUIDS

TYPE OF LIQUID	CRUST COLOR AND TEXTURE	INSIDE APPEARANCE AND TEXTURE	FLAVOR	OVERALL ACCEPTABILITY	ADDITIONAL COMMENTS
Water (control product)					
Milk					

Sources of Error

List any sources of error that might make it difficult to draw the proper conclusions from your experiment. In particular, consider any difficulties in mixing and handling dough, how long dough was heated in saucepan, and any problems with ovens or with bake times.

_____

_____

_____

State what you could do differently next time to minimize or eliminate each source of error.

_____

_____

_____

Conclusions

Select one from the choices in **bold** or fill in the blanks.

1   The extent of browning tended to **increase/decrease** when éclair shells were made with milk instead of water. The difference in color was **small/moderate/large**. The reason for the difference is _____

_____

_____.

2   The crust tended to get **crisper/softer** when éclair shells were made with milk instead of water. The difference was **small/moderate/large**. The reason for the difference is_____

_____

_____.

3   The difference in flavor between the éclair shells made with milk and the ones made with water was **small/moderate/large.** The flavor difference can be described as follows:

_____

_____

_____.

4   Other differences between the éclair shells made with milk and those made with water were as follows (consider differences in bake times, height, moistness, etc.):

_____

_____

_____.

5   Of the two different éclair shells, the one I prefer is _____. The reasons for my preference are:

_____

_____

_____.

Nuts and Seeds

Chapter Objectives

1. Describe the makeup of nuts and relate this to their nutrition.

2. Explain factors that affect the cost of nuts.

3. List common nuts and describe their characteristics and uses.

4. Describe how to best store and handle nuts.

Introduction

Some formulas that call for nuts list them as optional ingredients. While it is true that leaving nuts out of many formulas will not result in a failed product, nuts add important value to many baked goods. They provide flavor, textural contrast, and visual appeal. They can be used almost interchangeably, without making adjustments to a formula. Taste, of course, will change, since nuts differ markedly in flavor. But for the most part, nuts function similarly in baking. Chestnuts are the exception. Chestnuts are very different from other nuts and generally cannot be used in place of others.

Most nuts grow on trees. Tree nuts include almonds, cashews, hazelnuts, macadamias, pine nuts, pecans, pistachios, and walnuts. Not included in this category are peanuts, which are legumes that grow underground on peanut plants. Sesame and other seeds typically grow on herbaceous (nonwoody) plants.

Composition of Nuts, Kernels, and Seeds

Nuts are a good source of protein, fiber, vitamins, and minerals. While nuts are high in fat, the fatty acids in nuts (except coconut) are mostly unsaturated. From a health standpoint, unsaturated fatty acids are considered desirable. Nuts also contain a significant amount of polyphenolic compounds, beneficial to good health. In fact, nuts are a part of a traditional Mediterranean diet, considered a model diet for good health.

Nuts vary in composition, but most contain more fat or oil than anything else. Figure 14.1 compares the fat content of nuts to butter. Notice that nuts vary widely in their fat content, but most range from 50 to 65 percent oil. Chestnuts and coconuts fall below this range, and macadamia nuts, at 75 percent oil, approach the amount of fat in butter. Because of their high oil content, most nuts should be used sparingly in low-fat baked goods.

Customers should be specifically told when nuts are present in a product, because some people have severe allergic reactions to nuts. One easy and attractive way to remind customers of the presence of nuts in a product is to garnish the top with the type of nut it contains.

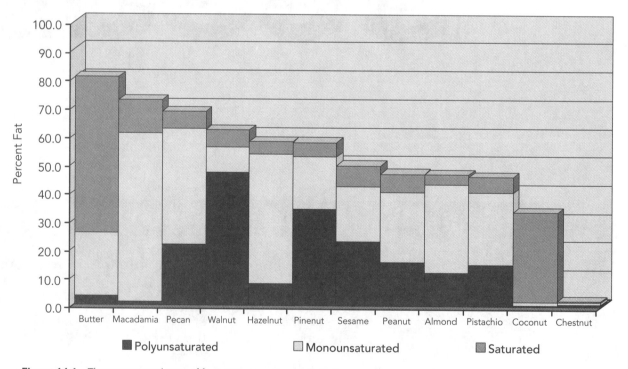

Figure 14.1 The amount and type of fat in nuts compared with butter

When Is a Nut Not a Nut?

Botanists differentiate nuts from seeds, legumes, and kernels. To a botanist, a nut is a dry one-seeded fruit that does not split open at a seam when mature. While botanists classify chestnuts, hazelnuts, and sometimes walnuts and pecans as true nuts, other "nuts" are not. Almonds, coconuts, and macadamias are the seeds within the fruit's pit (stone). Peanuts are seeds of a legume (bean), and pine nuts are seeds of a pinecone. In most bakeshops, and for our purposes, all are considered nuts, while seeds are typically smaller than nuts and are not contained in hard shells. Examples of seeds are sesame, poppy, sunflower, and pumpkin.

Actually, all nuts are, or contain, the seed of a plant. Seeds consist of three main parts: an embryo that sprouts into a seedling, an endosperm that provides adequate food for the young seedling, and a seed coat that protects the seed. When planted, seeds grow into new plants.

Cost

Nuts are an expensive ingredient. They can range in price from several dollars to ten or more dollars per pound. Many factors contribute to the price of nuts. The main factors are as follows.

- *Type of nut:* Certain nuts, like pine nuts and macadamia nuts, are significantly more expensive than peanuts or almonds, mainly because of difficulties in handling.
- *Added processing or difficulty in processing:* Walnuts, for example, are fragile and difficult to remove from their shells intact. This makes walnut halves more expensive than broken pieces.
- *Crop year:* Nuts are a natural agricultural product. If Georgia, which is a major producer of pecans, has heavy rains one year, this could wipe out its entire pecan crop, leading to an increase in price.
- *Packaging:* Some nuts, such as walnuts, can be purchased in vacuum-packed cans to prevent oxidative rancidity. Expect this type of packaging to add to the cost of the nuts.
- *Amount purchased at one time:* As with any ingredient, purchasing in bulk can lower costs.

When cost is an issue—or when calories are—consider creative ways to stretch the use of nuts. For example, changing the size and shape of a nut changes its perception. Figure 14.2 shows how sliced almonds (bottom left) can provide a greater visual impact and better coverage on baked goods than slivered almonds (bottom right). Sesame seeds (top), being less dense than almonds, provide the most complete coverage of all.

Figure 14.2 Visual impact changes with the size, shape, and density of nuts and seeds. **Top:** sesame seeds are light in weight, and a given weight of seeds covers a large area; **bottom left to right:** the same weight of thinly sliced almonds provides less coverage and slivered almonds cover least of all

Anaphylactic shock is a severe and sometimes fatal allergic reaction that some individuals have to certain proteins, including those in tree nuts, peanuts, and sesame seeds. The body reacts to the presence of these proteins by releasing massive doses of chemicals that causes shock, the swelling of air passages, and sometimes death. Often, only very small amounts of these foods are needed to trigger anaphylactic shock in hypersensitive individuals. The best way to prevent anaphylactic shock is to avoid those foods known to cause the reaction. Because death can occur within minutes, hypersensitive individuals often carry medication (an adrenaline kit) to take if they accidentally consume the wrong foods.

Common Nuts, Kernels, and Seeds

Almonds

The two main types of almonds are bitter and sweet. Bitter almonds are used for flavoring. Almond extract and amaretto liqueur, for example, can be made from the oil of bitter almonds.

Sweet almonds are used in baking. California is the largest producer of these almonds in the world, and almonds are the number one nut in America, at least in the bakeshop. Almonds have a long tradition of use throughout Europe and appear in many formulas, including meringues, marzipan, biscotti, macaroons, and pastry doughs.

Almonds are mild flavored, so they are best when toasted before use to develop flavor. They come either natural (with the brown skin still intact) or blanched.

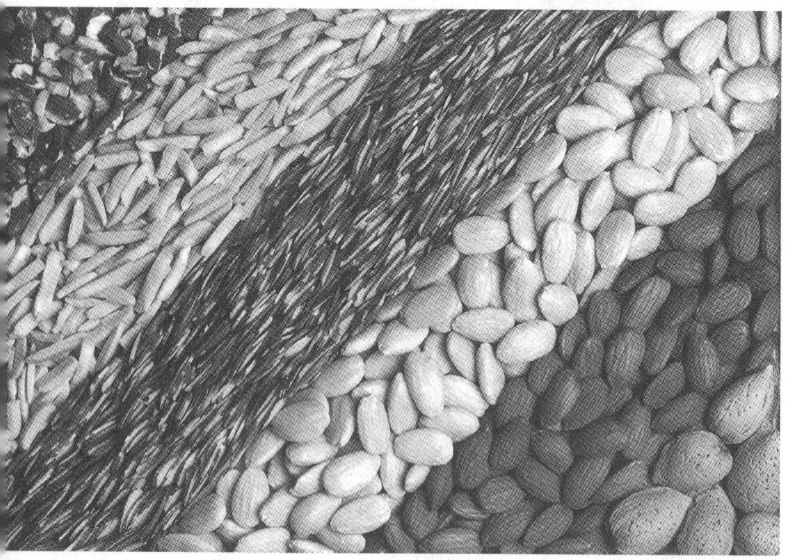

Figure 14.3 Almonds. **Top left to bottom right:** chopped natural, slivered blanched, sliced natural, whole blanched, whole natural, in shell

The brown skin (seed coat) of natural almonds provides a contrast in color that is desirable for visual appeal. For example, the brown skin of natural almonds highlights the presence of the nuts in almond biscotti. The skin also provides a slight astringency that contributes to overall flavor. Recall from Chapter 4 that astringency is a taste characteristic that results in a drying sensation in the mouth from the presence of tannins.

Blanched almonds have the brown skin removed. They have a sweeter, milder flavor than natural almonds and are more common than natural nuts in the bakeshop. With their polished white appearance, blanched almonds have a more refined, premium-quality image. To blanch almonds, pour boiling water over the nuts, let them sit for several minutes, then slide off the skins.

Almonds can be purchased in many forms, including whole, sliced, slivered, chopped, or ground into butter, flour, or paste (Figure 14.3). Because of this variety in form, and because of the mild, pleasant flavor, almonds have a reputation as a highly versatile nut.

Almond paste consists of blanched almonds finely ground to a paste with sugar. Almond paste often contains binding and flavoring agents, in particular bitter almond extract. Marzipan is almond paste and sugar mixed into pliable dough. Think of marzipan as edible modeling clay. Marzipan is traditionally colored and shaped into small fruits and whimsical animals. It can be rolled and used for covering cakes.

Cashews

Kidney-shaped cashew nuts are native to Brazil, but the top producer of cashews today is Vietnam. Cashews have a sweet, mild flavor and an ivory white appearance.

How to Make Nut Butters and Nut Flours

Nut butters do not contain butter; rather, they are pastes made by finely grinding nuts. Any nut can be used, but peanut, almond, and hazelnut are probably the most common nut butters.

To make nut butter, grind roasted nuts in a food processor. The roasting and grinding help to release the nuts' natural oils, for a smooth, creamy consistency. If necessary, add a small amount of oil for extra smoothness. Salt, honey, or syrup can be added for flavor.

Nut flours are also made in the food processor. When making nut flours, be careful not to overprocess, or you will release too much oil and end up with a paste. To prevent overprocessing, combine nuts with granulated sugar in the bowl of the food processor and pulse repeatedly. The pulsing and the presence of sugar prevents the release of oils. Nut flours are used in pastry doughs and cake batters.

What's the Difference Between Coconut Cream and Cream of Coconut?

Although coconut cream and cream of coconut sound like the same product, they are not. Coconut cream is the oil-rich layer that rises to the top of coconut milk. Like coconut milk, coconut cream is unsweetened. Cream of coconut is a thick, sweet liquid made from coconut milk and sugar. Cream of coconut is used primarily in mixed drinks such as piña coladas. The two are not interchangeable.

While the bulk of cashews are eaten directly as a snack, cashews are used in brittles and other confectionery, as well as in cookies and other baked goods. Because of their bland flavor and pale color, cashews are sometimes soaked in water and blended into a smooth cream, which can be used in vegan products to replace dairy cream in frozen desserts and cheese in cheesecakes.

Cashews can be expensive because they are difficult to remove from their shells. Part of the difficulty is the presence of a skin irritant in the shell that is similar to the irritant in poison ivy and poison oak. To remove the shell without contaminating the cashew meat with this irritant, the nuts are steamed, roasted, or cooked in oil. This opens the shell so the nutmeat can more easily be removed, which is often done manually by skilled workers. These nuts are generally labeled as raw, because while the shells were exposed to high heat, the nuts themselves were not roasted. Besides Vietnam, other large producers of cashews today are Brazil and India, countries with the tropical climate required for their growth.

Chestnuts

Chestnuts are very high in moisture and in carbohydrates, and very low (less than 5 percent) in oil. Chestnuts are cooked before use, giving them a characteristic soft, mealy texture. They are not interchangeable with other nuts.

Chestnuts are available fresh only in the fall and early winter months. During the rest of the year, they can be purchased already cooked, either frozen or canned, whole or pureed. Once opened, canned chestnuts should be refrigerated or frozen, to prevent mold growth. Chestnuts are also available dried and ground to a flour, or candied (*marrons glacés*).

Coconuts

Coconuts are a tropical nut, which sets them apart from most nuts used in the bakeshop. Like other tropical nuts such as the palm kernel, cacao (source of chocolate), and shea nut, coconut meat is very high in saturated fat (see Figure 14.1).

Several products are derived from coconut meat, including coconut milk and desiccated, sweetened, or toasted coconut. Desiccated, sweetened, and toasted coconut products are cut to various sizes, from large shreds to fine flakes. *Macaroon coconut* is desiccated, sweetened, or toasted coconut that consists of fairly fine flakes.

Desiccated coconut is made by drying coconut from about 50 percent water down to less than 5 percent.

Desiccated coconut, also called dried coconut, is a concentrated source of coconut oil and coconut flavor.

Sweetened coconut is made by cooking coconut with sugar before drying. Often, sweetened coconut contains additives to keep it soft and flexible (glycerine, for example) and to keep it white (a sulfiting agent). Sweetened coconut is the form of coconut most familiar to North American consumers. It can be toasted to a golden brown color and sold as *toasted coconut.* Toasted coconut is used primarily as a garnish on cakes and doughnuts.

Coconut water is the clear liquid in the center of a mature coconut, sometimes consumed as a refreshing beverage. Coconut water is often mistaken for coconut milk. *Coconut milk* is made by combining grated coconut meat with hot water and squeezing the liquid through a filter. Coconut milk is unsweetened and can be purchased canned or frozen. If a can of coconut milk is opened and the top layer, which is rich in coconut oil, is skimmed off, the skimmed-off layer is called *coconut cream.*

Hazelnuts

Hazelnuts are also called filberts. They are grown primarily in the Mediterranean region, but in the United States, small amounts are grown in Oregon. Hazelnuts have only recently become popular in North America. In Europe, they have been popular for many years, especially when paired with chocolate in desserts and confections. The combination of hazelnuts and chocolate ground smooth is called *gianduja.*

Hazelnuts can be purchased whole, diced, or sliced. As with almonds, they come with or without their skins. Toasting greatly enhances the distinctive flavor of hazelnuts, as it does with almonds. In fact, of all the nuts, hazelnuts probably benefit the most from toasting.

Macadamia Nuts

Macadamia nuts are native to Australia, but today they are more widely grown in Hawaii. Macadamia nuts are highest in oil of all the common nuts, which gives them a rich, creamy flavor and texture. Because the shell of the macadamia nut is hard to crack, shelled macadamia nuts are expensive and should be used only in baked goods with an upscale image and a price to match.

Peanuts

Peanuts, being a legume, are higher in protein than tree nuts. They are native to South America and, while very popular in North America, are rarely used in Europe. The two most common varieties of peanuts are the Virginia peanut and the smaller Spanish peanut.

Peanuts are plentiful and inexpensive. Raw, untoasted peanuts have a beany flavor, so peanuts are typically toasted before use. Peanuts come whole, halved, diced, and ground into peanut butter. As with most nuts, peanuts pair nicely with chocolate.

Pecans

Pecans are native to North America and in the United States, they are grown in the South and Southwest. As with walnuts, fancy pecan halves are expensive compared with the cost of pieces. Use the halves where appearance is important. Specialty items such as pecan pie, Southern pralines, and butter pecan ice cream are three traditional uses of pecans.

Pine Nuts

Pine nuts are also called *pignoli* or *piñon nuts.* They are the seeds on the cone of a piñon tree, a type of low-growing pine. Fresh pine nuts have a mild, sweet flavor that is characteristic of certain Mediterranean, Middle Eastern, and Mexican specialties. Because they are difficult to remove from the pine cone, pine nuts are expensive and should be used with care.

Pistachios

Pistachio nuts have a unique green color that adds a different look to baked goods. While they are native to the Middle East, in recent years a large amount of pistachio nuts have been cultivated in California. Although pistachio nuts have traditionally been a snack nut, expect to see greater use of pistachios in the bakeshop, as the availability of shelled pistachio nuts increases.

Pistachio nuts are best used untoasted or lightly toasted, to preserve their bright green color and distinctive flavor. Pistachios are a traditional garnish on cannoli. They are also used in ice creams, biscotti, and baklava.

Sesame Seeds

Sesame seeds were first cultivated in India but were traded throughout Asia literally thousands of years ago. This makes sesame one of the oldest food flavors, and it is why the seeds are deeply entrenched in cuisines throughout Asia, the Middle East, and the Mediterranean.

Sesame seeds grow in pods on a tall herbaceous plant, with each tiny tear-shaped seed protected in a thin, edible hull. Natural sesame seeds are sold in the hull. When the hull is removed, the seeds are called either *hulled* or *dehulled*. Hulled seeds are more typically used in the bakeshop than unhulled seeds, but either can be used. Mild, creamy white sesame seeds are the most common, but black and other colored seeds are available.

Sesame seeds are commonly sprinkled on top of breads, buns, bagels, and crackers. This allows the seeds to toast in the oven during baking. Toasting develops a deep, rich toasted aroma and a light crunch. Benne wafers (thin crisp sesame seed cookies) are a Southern specialty. Benne is the African name for sesame seeds, which slaves brought to the United States and Caribbean islands.

Sesame seeds are not listed as a major allergen in the United States, although they are in Canada. In any case, sesame seeds can cause anaphylactic shock in a small number of individuals, so be sure your customers know when sesame seeds are in any of your products.

Walnuts

The English walnut is by far the most popular variety of walnut used in the bakeshop. A second variety, the black walnut, has a very strong flavor and a hard shell that is difficult to crack cleanly. Black walnuts are native to North America and can be purchased as a specialty item, but they are high priced and their strong flavor is not appreciated by all. Because they are difficult to remove from the shell, black walnuts are purchased as irregular-shaped pieces; they do not come whole or in halves. A classic use of black walnuts is in black walnut ice cream.

Shelled English walnuts—walnuts sold out of their shell—come as fancy halves and in various size pieces. They come in a variety of colors, from extra light to amber. The outside color of the walnut is an indication of how much sunlight the walnut received. The more sunlight, the darker the color and the stronger the flavor. The characteristic flavor of a walnut is somewhat astringent. Its flavor is more pronounced than almonds, and for this reason it is not toasted as often before use.

About two-thirds of the world's supply of walnuts comes from California. Walnuts are very common in North American baked goods such as brownies, quick breads, muffins, cookies, and coffee cakes. They are also used in pastries throughout Europe as well as the Middle East, where they originated.

Toasting Nuts

Nuts are toasted to develop flavor by allowing chemical reactions, including Maillard browning (the reaction of sugars and proteins), to occur. Toasting also improves the flavor of slightly stale nuts. Besides improving flavor, toasting darkens the color and crisps the texture of nuts.

To toast, spread nuts in a single layer on a sheet pan. Place in an oven at 325°–350°F (160°–175°C) for 5–10 minutes or longer. Watch carefully; different nut varieties require different toasting times, because of differences in size and oil content. Properly toasted nuts have a uniform, light brown color and sweet nutty taste.

Do not try to toast nuts at too high an oven temperature or by cooking them on top of the stove. Stovetop heat, especially, is hard to control, and it is too easy to burn the outside of the nut while the inside stays raw and flavorless.

Once nuts are toasted, remove them immediately from the hot sheet pan to prevent burning from carry-over cooking. Allow nuts to cool before use. Store leftover toasted nuts in an airtight container and refrigerate. Toasted nuts oxidize more quickly, so they should be used within a few days.

Storage and Handling

Nuts undergo oxidative rancidity when they are not handled properly or when they are stored for too long. At first, the change is subtle, and the nuts will still be acceptable although less "special." Eventually, the flavor is unpleasant and the nuts should be discarded. It is the oil in nuts that oxidizes, developing stale or rancid off flavors as it breaks down. Aged nuts are also more bitter and less sweet than fresh nuts.

Some nuts are more easily oxidized than others are. How fast a nut oxidizes has more to do with the type of oil it contains than how much oil is in it. For example, walnuts oxidize faster than hazelnuts even though hazelnuts contain the same or slightly more oil than walnuts. This is because walnuts are highest in ALA, an omega-3 polyunsaturated fatty acid (Figure 14.1). Like all polyunsaturated fatty acids, ALA oxidizes at an extremely fast rate.

Recall from Chapter 9 that oxygen, heat, light, and metal catalysts all contribute to oxidative rancidity in fats. If these can be controlled, oxidative rancidity can be minimized. While the following suggestions are not always practical or necessary, they are worth considering.

- Purchase only the amount of nuts you will use in two to three months. Practice FIFO inventory control: first in, first out.
- Keep nuts whole until ready to use. Chopped nuts have more surface area exposed to air and therefore oxidize faster.
- Do not toast nuts until ready to use; toasting initiates the oxidation of the nut oils.

HELPFUL HINT

The following is a list of common nuts and the average amount of polyunsaturated fatty acids present in 1 ounce (30 grams) of each. Because the rate of oxidative rancidity is mostly related to the amount of polyunsaturated fatty acids, this chart is helpful in understanding which nuts will likely undergo rancidity rapidly. This, in turn, can help you decide on quantities to purchase at one time or how to best store certain nuts.

Walnuts	13 grams
Pine nuts	9 grams
Pecans	6 grams
Peanuts	4 grams
Pistachios	4 grams
Almonds	3 grams
Hazelnuts	2 grams
Cashews	2 grams
Macadamias	1 gram

- Store nuts at low temperatures, especially if toasted, since heat accelerates rancidity; refrigerate at 35°–40°F (2°–4°C), or freeze.
- Keep nuts away from sunlight; sunlight, like heat, is a form of energy that speeds up oxidative rancidity.
- Purchase nuts in vacuum packaging, to exclude oxygen. Likewise, nuts are ideally stored in vacuum-packaged bags, or at least in tightly covered containers.

Food scientists have a rule of thumb that they use to predict how much longer food will stay fresh when it is stored at low temperatures. The rule of thumb, which works reasonably well with nuts, is for every 15°F (10°C) decrease in temperature, product will last about twice as long.

Twice as long is huge. Let's assume, for example, that a bakeshop keeps their walnuts handy, near the ovens where it is quite warm (90°F/35°C). Let's also assume that the walnuts start tasting stale and rancid after about 1 month. If the walnuts are moved instead to a cooler spot, where the temperature is at 75°F/25°C, the nuts should now last about 2 months. And, if an even cooler spot is found (60°F/15°C), the walnuts should stay fresh about 4 months, which is twice as long again. Imagine how much more effective refrigeration and freezing are at extending shelf life of nuts.

Of course, the reverse is true as well, so that for every 15°F (10°C) increase in temperature, product will last about half as long.

- Purchase nuts with added antioxidants, like BHA, BHT, or vitamin E. Antioxidants interfere with the process of oxidative rancidity, greatly slowing it down. If antioxidants have been added to nuts, they will be listed on the label.

- One last consideration when dealing with nuts: always cover them when not in use. This keeps out odors from strong-smelling foods such as onions, and keeps out insects and rodents. It will also keep away moisture, which makes nuts soggy, moldy, and likely to oxidize.

Questions for Review

1 What is anaphylactic shock?

2 What is an easy yet attractive way to remind customers of the presence of nuts in a baked product?

3 Which common nut is highest in oil? Which is lowest? What is the approximate oil content of each?

4 List and explain five factors that contribute to the cost of nuts.

5 What is the difference between natural and blanched almonds? Why might one be used over the other?

6 What is astringency? What part of the nut is most apt to be astringent?

7 What is the difference between almond paste and marzipan?

8 What is coconut milk?

9 What is the difference between coconut cream and cream of coconut?

10 What is gianduja?

11 What is ALA and its benefits? Which nut is it found in at high levels?

12 How does sunlight exposure affect the qualities of walnuts?

13 What is the main reason that walnuts oxidize at a much faster rate than most other nuts?

14 Name a nut that is relatively expensive; name one that is relatively inexpensive.

15 In what two ways does toasting nuts improve their flavor?

16 Name a nut that benefits greatly from toasting; name one that is probably best untoasted or only lightly toasted.

17 Although macadamia nuts are extremely high in fat, they oxidize and turn rancid only slowly. Why is that?

Questions for Discussion

1 Why might it be better to purchase peanuts raw and toast them as needed, instead of purchasing them already toasted?

2 Assume that pine nuts you have just purchased are expected to remain fresh for only two months when stored at room temperature (70°F/21°C). Use the rule-of-thumb relationship between temperature of storage and shelf life to calculate how long these pine nuts should remain fresh if refrigerated (40°F/5°C).

Exercises and Experiments

❶ Exercise: How to Decrease Oxidative Rancidity in Nuts

Explain the reason that each of the following techniques works to decrease oxidative rancidity in nuts (for the purposes of this exercise, focus on decreasing oxidative rancidity only, even though some of the following might not be practical or desirable in all bakeshops). The first is completed for you.

1 Chop nuts immediately before use, rather than ahead of time.

Reason: Chopping exposes more surface area to air (oxygen), which initiates oxidative rancidity.

2 Store nuts under refrigeration until ready to use.

Reason: _____
_____
_____

3 Practice FIFO (first in, first out).

Reason: _____
_____
_____

4 Purchase and hold nuts in vacuum packaging.

Reason: _____
_____
_____

5 Store nuts in opaque, rather than clear, containers.

Reason: _____
_____
_____

6 Use hazelnuts or almonds rather than walnuts or pine nuts.

Reason: _____
_____
_____

7 If toasting nuts, toast just before use.

Reason: _____
_____
_____

② Exercise: Sensory Characteristics of Nuts and Seeds

In the Results Table, fill in alternative names, if any, for each nut. Next, compare and describe the nuts in appearance, texture, and flavor. Use this opportunity to identify different nuts from their sensory characteristics alone. Add any additional comments or observations that you might have to the last column in the table. For example, are almonds blanched or not? Are they whole or slivered? Are they toasted or not? Two rows are left blank, for the evaluation of additional products, if desired.

RESULTS TABLE   NUTS AND SEEDS

NUT OR SEED	ALTERNATIVE NAMES	APPEARANCE	TEXTURE	FLAVOR	ADDITIONAL COMMENTS
Almonds					
Cashews					
Chestnuts					
Coconuts					
Hazelnuts					
Macadamia nuts					
Peanuts					
Pecans					
Pine nuts					
Pistachios					
Sesame seeds					
Walnuts					

Use information from the table above and from your textbook to answer the following questions. Select one from the choices in **bold** or fill in the blanks.

1   While most nuts are very high in fat (most are greater than 50 percent fat), **hazelnuts/chestnuts/pine nuts** are quite low in fat. Instead, these nuts are high in water and

protein/carbohydrates, giving them a different texture than the other nuts. The best way to describe the texture of these nuts is_____

_____

_____.

2 While all nuts can oxidize and become rancid, those with the **highest/lowest** amount of polyunsaturated fatty acids oxidize the fastest. From this, the three nuts from above that are most likely to oxidize and become rancid are _____, _____, and _____. Based on your evaluation of these nuts, did any of them appear oxidized? If so, list the nuts that appeared oxidized, and state if the extent of oxidation seemed slight, moderate, or great.

_____

_____

_____

3 Select any two nuts of your choice that you feel are quite different from each other.

_____

_____

_____

Describe in one sentence how they differ.

_____

_____

_____

4 Select any two nuts of your choice that you feel could be easily substituted for one another because they are most similar in appearance, texture, and flavor.

_____

_____

_____

Describe in what specific ways they are similar, and describe any differences.

_____

_____

_____

❸ Experiment: How the Type of Nut Affects the Overall Quality of Cookies

Objective

Demonstrate how the type of nut and toasting affect the appearance, flavor, texture, and overall acceptability of cookies

Products Prepared

Cookies made with

- No added nut (control product)
- Almonds, natural, sliced, toasted
- Almonds, blanched, sliced, toasted
- Almonds, blanched, sliced, untoasted
- Almonds, blanched, slivered or diced, toasted
- Walnuts, diced, toasted
- Sesame seeds, whole, toasted
- Other, if desired (hazelnuts, pine nuts, macadamia nuts, peanuts, etc.)

Materials and Equipment

- Scale
- Sieve
- Parchment paper
- Mixer with 5-quart mixing bowl
- Flat beater attachment
- Bowl scraper
- Nut Bar Cookies dough (see Formula), enough for one half sheet pan of each variation
- Half sheet pans
- Silicone pads (optional)
- Rolling pin (optional)
- Dough cutters, 2½" (65 mm) or equivalent (optional)
- Pastry brush
- Oven thermometer
- Serrated knife

Formula

Short Dough

Yield: One half sheet pan

INGREDIENT	POUNDS	OUNCES	GRAMS	BAKER'S PERCENTAGE
Flour, pastry		12	350	100
Salt (1 tsp./5 ml)		0.2	6	1.7
Butter, unsalted		4	115	33
Shortening, all-purpose		4	115	33
Sugar, regular granulated		4	115	33
Eggs		1.5	45	13
Zest of 1 orange (optional)		0.1	4	1.1
Total	**1**	**10**	**750**	**214.8**

Method of Preparation

1 Have ingredients at room temperature.

2 Blend flour and salt thoroughly by sifting together three times onto parchment paper.

3 Combine shortening, butter, and sugar in mixing bowl and mix on low speed using flat beater for 1 minute. Stop and scrape bowl, as needed.

4 Cream mixture on medium for 3 minutes. Stop and scrape bowl.

5 Add eggs (and zest, if using) slowly while mixing on low for 30 seconds. Stop and scrape bowl.

6 Add flour to creamed mixture and blend on low for 1 minute. Stop and scrape bowl.

7 Set aside until ready to use.

Formula

Nut Bar Cookies

Yield: *One half sheet pan*

INGREDIENT	POUNDS	OUNCES	GRAMS	BAKER'S PERCENTAGE
Short Dough (above)	1	10	750	100
Nuts		4.5	125	17
Egg wash (egg white diluted with water)		as needed	as needed	as needed
Total	1	14.5	875	117

Method of Preparation

1 Preheat oven to 375°F (190°C). Line half sheet pan with parchment paper or silicone pad.

2 Chop and toast nuts, as required.

3 Pat dough evenly into lined half sheet pan. Alternatively, chill dough, then roll out to ⅛" (3 mm) thick. Cut into shape with cookie cutter and place on lined half sheet pan.

4 Brush with egg wash.

5 Distribute nuts evenly onto dough. Press lightly into dough.

Procedure

1 Prepare nut bar cookies using the formulas above, or using any short dough formula with nuts. Prepare one batch for each variation.

2 Label each batch with type of nut added.

3 Use an oven thermometer placed in center of oven to read initial oven temperature. Record results here: _____.

4 When oven is properly preheated, place filled sheet pans in oven and set timer for 30–35 minutes.

5 Bake cookies until control product (with no added nuts) is golden brown. Remove *all* cookies from oven after same length of time. If necessary, however, adjust bake times for oven variances.

6 Record bake times in the Results Table, which follows.

7 Check final oven temperature. Record results here: _____.

8 Remove sheet pan from oven and let stand 1 minute, to firm slightly.

9 If not cut with cookie cutter, use knife to score bars into rectangles while still warm.

10 Remove cookies from pan and cool to room temperature.

Results

Evaluate the sensory characteristics of completely cooled products and record evaluations in the Results Table. Be sure to compare each in turn with the control product and consider the following:

- Appearance (visibility of nuts/contrast in color with cookie; coverage of cookie dough with nut)
- Texture of nuts (softness, crunchiness, etc.)
- Flavor (nut aroma, sweetness, astringency, etc.)
- Overall acceptability, from highly unacceptable to highly acceptable, on a scale of 1 to 5
- Add any additional comments, as necessary

RESULTS TABLE SENSORY CHARACTERISTICS OF COOKIES MADE WITH DIFFERENT NUTS

TYPE OF NUT	BAKE TIME, MINUTES	APPEARANCE	TEXTURE OF NUTS	FLAVOR	OVERALL ACCEPTABILITY	ADDITIONAL COMMENTS
None						
Almonds, natural, sliced, untoasted						
Almonds, blanched, sliced, untoasted						
Almonds, blanched, sliced, toasted						

(continues)

TYPE OF NUT	BAKE TIME, MINUTES	APPEARANCE	TEXTURE OF NUTS	FLAVOR	OVERALL ACCEPTABILITY	ADDITIONAL COMMENTS
Walnuts, diced, toasted						
Sesame seeds, whole, toasted						

Sources of Error

List any sources of error that might make it difficult to draw the proper conclusions from your experiment. In particular, consider any problems properly creaming, toasting nuts, or any problems with the ovens.

_____

_____

_____

State what you could do differently next time to minimize or eliminate each source of error.

_____

_____

_____

Conclusions

Select one from the choices in **bold** or fill in the blanks.

1   Using blanched almonds instead of natural (unblanched) almonds made a **small/moderate/large** difference in how the cookies looked and tasted after they were baked. The differences were as follows:

_____

_____

_____

2   Toasting the almonds before baking made a **small/moderate/large** difference in how the cookies looked and tasted after they were baked. The differences were as follows:

_____

_____

_____

3 One function of nuts is to add a crunchy texture to baked goods. In this experiment, the nut that added the crunchiest texture was the _____

_____

_____.

4 Differences in how well each type of nut covered the surface of the short dough were **small/ moderate/large**. The nut that covered the dough most completely was **sliced almonds/ diced walnuts/whole sesame seeds**. The difference in coverage was primarily due to differences in _____

_____

_____.

5 Which cookies do you feel were the best-tasting, and why?

_____

_____

_____

6 Other comments I would like to add about the cookies or about the experiment:

_____

_____

_____

15

Cocoa and Chocolate Products

Introduction

Chocolate is one of the most popular food flavors in the Western world, second only to vanilla. Unlike vanilla, however, which is essentially a flavoring, chocolate has been used over the centuries as food, medicine, aphrodisiac, and money. It was part of ancient religious rituals in Mayan culture, and became a ritual in daily life for seventeenth- and eighteenth-century Europeans who could afford their daily hot chocolate.

The cacao tree, the source of cocoa and chocolate, is a finicky plant that grows in relatively few regions of the world. Climatic conditions, rainfall in particular, affect the size of the annual harvest, as does the spread of fungus infections. Fungus infections have been a problem particularly in Brazil and other parts of South America in recent years. Political instability is also a threat to the size of the harvest in places like Côte d'Ivoire (Ivory Coast) in western Africa, the largest cocoa bean supplier in the world.

Yet today more than ever, bakers and pastry chefs have a wide selection of cocoa and chocolate products from which to choose. Such a selection can seem bewildering, especially since cocoas and chocolates vary substantially in cost and quality. The first step in selecting cocoa and chocolate products for the bakeshop is to understand the makeup and functionality of each. Next, develop an educated palate by tasting and evaluating a wide range of products. Finally, include other important criteria—price, for example—in the selection process.

Cocoa Beans

Cacao (or cocoa) beans are the seeds or kernels from the fruit pods of the cacao tree (Figure 15.1). They are similar in many ways to other nuts and seeds, like almonds and sunflower seeds. Just as almonds and sunflower seeds are encased in a protective shell, so too are cocoa nibs. Cocoa nibs—the edible part of the cocoa bean—are what are processed into cocoa and chocolate.

Types of Cocoa Beans

While there are many types of cocoa beans, most fall into three main categories: forastero, criollo, and trinitario.

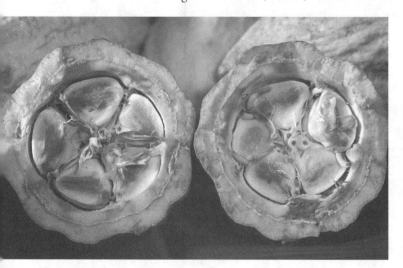

Figure 15.1 In this cross-section of a whole cocoa pod, you can see the cocoa beans surrounded by the fruit.

The majority (90 percent or more) of cocoa beans are forasteros, which are, for the most part, considered basic or bulk beans. Forasteros are the workhorses of the cocoa industry. They originated in South American rain forests but today are grown throughout the cocoa-growing world, especially in western Africa. They are relatively easy to grow because they withstand changes in climate and are resistant to fungus and disease. The beans are dark and have a full chocolate flavor with plenty of middle and base notes. While they provide a chocolate earthiness, forasteros lack the subtle aroma of criollo beans.

Light-colored criollo beans are considered fine or flavor beans by the cacao industry because of their complex fruity aromatic top notes. The term "noble" is often used to market chocolate products made with fine flavor beans like criollos. Criollos are also typically low in bitterness and astringency, but they are generally lightly roasted, so they often retain more of the natural acid taste of the raw bean. Criollo beans are expensive because yields are low and the trees are susceptible to disease, making them difficult to grow. Criollo beans were the beans prized by the ancient Mayans. Today less than 2 percent of the world supply of cocoa beans is criollo, and the size of the crop is shrinking as criollo trees are replaced with hardier varieties. Central and South America, the Caribbean, and Indonesia are known for their criollo and other flavor beans.

The Growing and Handling of Cocoa Beans

Cacao trees (*Theobroma cacao*) grow near the equator on small cocoa plantations or in tropical rain forests. Most commercial cacao trees grow in Africa, but other major growing regions include South and Central America and the islands of Indonesia and Malaysia in Southeast Asia. A limited number of trees are cultivated in other locales, such as Hawaii.

Cocoa pods grow off the limbs and trunks of cacao trees. Because the trees are fragile, the pods must be harvested by hand. Skilled workers cut down the pods with machetes, selecting only fully ripe ones for best flavor. Each pod holds about twenty to forty cocoa beans surrounded by a thin layer of white fruit pulp. The beans are removed from the pods, white fruit pulp intact, and are piled, covered, and allowed to ferment. Fermentation is the first step in the conversion of raw bean to flavorful chocolate, requiring two days to one week, depending on the type of bean. Fermentation involves a complex series of reactions that occur as microorganisms ferment sugars in the pulp and as enzymes break down various components in the bean. Fermentation darkens the bean's color and changes its flavor. It increases the bean's acidity, decreases its astringency and bitterness, and generates flavor precursors that are important to flavor development later during roasting and conching.

Once the fruit pulp warms and liquefies, it drains from the beans. The beans are then dried (cured), often directly in the sun but sometimes over an open fire or with hot air. During drying, beans lose nearly half their weight and some acidity to evaporation. If dried improperly or incompletely, they pick up off flavors, including smoky or moldy flavors. Once dried, the beans are packed in burlap bags and shipped around the world to processing plants where they are cleaned, roasted, removed from their shells, and further processed.

Varietal and Single-Origin Chocolates

Varietal chocolates, like varietal wines, are made from one type of bean. Single-origin chocolates—also called *grand crus*, in the tradition of wines—are made from beans grown entirely in a specific region or a single plantation. Many specialty chocolate manufacturers sell varietal and single-origin chocolates, at premium prices. Tasting single-origin chocolates is a way to broaden your knowledge of chocolate, although some of them are an acquired taste.

Look for chocolates made from the following varietal and single-origin flavor beans: Chuao, Maracaibo, and Porcelana criollos from Venezuela; Arriba, a criollo from Trinidad; Nacional, from Ecuador, a flavor bean related to the forastero; Carenero Superior and Rio Caribe, two trinitario beans from Venezuela, and many more.

Trinitario beans are believed to be a cross between the forastero and the criollo, and they have characteristics of each. Like criollos, most trinitarios are considered flavor beans, although their flavor is less fruity and more earthy. Like forasteros, trinitario trees are hardy. They were first hybridized on the island of Trinidad in the 1700s, when forastero trees were imported to replace criollos destroyed by a major blight. Less than 5 percent of the world crop of cocoa beans is trinitario.

Most cocoa and chocolate products are produced from a blend of beans, with forasteros providing the base notes and the finish, and small amounts of flavor beans providing aromatic, often fruity, top notes.

Makeup of Cocoa Beans

Like most nuts and seeds, cocoa nibs contain valuable nutrients. Figure 15.2 compares the makeup of roasted cocoa nibs to roasted almonds and sunflower seeds. Although there are some differences (most notably, almonds are highest in protein), there are many similarities. All are very high in fat and low in water, and all are a good source of dietary fiber and minerals (ash).

As with other sources of tropical fats like coconuts and palm kernels, cocoa nibs contain fat that is naturally saturated and is solid at room temperature. Although saturated, cocoa butter does not appear to raise blood cholesterol levels the way most saturated

Scientists have conducted numerous studies in recent years to determine if there is a chemical basis for the cravings many people report having for chocolate. Most studies have focused on determining if specific chemicals in chocolate have calming or euphoric effects or act as mild antidepressants. In fact, chocolate does contain a mix of substances (theobromine, magnesium, tyrosine, phenylethylamine, anandamide, and N-acylethanolamine) that affect brain chemistry. However, many other everyday foods contain these same substances, often at higher levels. But it is possible that chocolate contains a special combination of substances that provides an effect unique to chocolate. Or it might simply be that the pleasurable sensory characteristics of chocolate—its taste, smell, and mouthfeel—are what we crave.

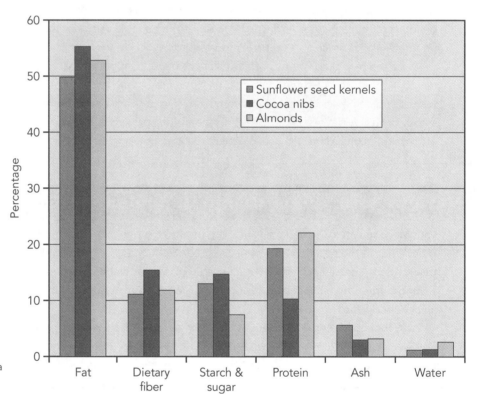

Figure 15.2 The makeup of cocoa nibs, sunflower seeds, and almonds

fats do. Besides containing fat high in saturated fatty acids, cocoa butter contains small amounts of lecithin and other natural emulsifiers.

Everything in cocoa beans that is solid but is not cocoa butter is collectively referred to as *cocoa solids nonfat*. Cocoa solids nonfat includes large amounts of proteins and carbohydrates. The carbohydrates in cocoa beans consist of starch, dietary fiber (cellulose and pentosan gums), and dextrins. *Dextrins* are starch fragments produced when starches are broken down by high heat, as when cocoa beans are roasted. Like starch, dextrins absorb water, but to a lesser degree.

Cocoa solids nonfat also includes small amounts of acids, color and flavor, vitamins and minerals, and polyphenolic compounds. Besides providing health benefits, polyphenolic compounds contribute to the color and flavor of cocoa beans. Finally, cocoa solids nonfat contains caffeine and theobromine, a mild caffeine-like stimulant. Theobromine, like caffeine, has a bitter taste, characteristic of chocolate.

For thousands of years, chocolate was used by the Mayans in Central America as a drink in religious ceremonies, earning its reputation as food of the gods. It was also ground with maize and other seeds and grains, seasoned, and consumed as food. In its most refined form, chocolate beverages were poured from one vessel to another at great heights, creating quantities of foam. One reason beans were roasted was to intensify this foam.

When Christopher Columbus first met Mayan traders in 1502, he sensed that cocoa beans were held in esteem, but he did not fully comprehend their significance. Hernando Cortés, the Spanish conquistador, invaded Mexico in 1519. By then, the Spanish were aware of the importance of the cocoa bean to the New World, at least in its role as money. More than a means of monetary exchange, however, *cacahuatl* was symbolic to the Aztecs of blood and the human heart. It was their most valued beverage, savored almost exclusively by nobility, warriors, and elite merchants. Spanish accounts report Montezuma, emperor of the Aztecs, sipping from fifty golden goblets of chocolate at a banquet feast.

As consumed by the Aztecs—cold, colored with red annatto, and flavored with dry chile—chocolate was rejected by the Spanish invaders. Eventually, however, chocolate made its way to the Spanish court (some say brought by Cortés himself). The Spanish heated chocolate, sweetened it with cane sugar, and flavored it with vanilla and cinnamon. Part medicine, part invigorating beverage, chocolate spread through western Europe even as the Spanish kept its process a secret for years. As the 1600s progressed, hot chocolate became a trendy, healthful drink throughout Europe, enjoyed by those who could afford it.

Common Cocoa and Chocolate Products

Cocoa beans are grown in the tropics, but they are processed into cocoa and chocolate products where they are consumed, throughout Europe, North America, and other regions of the world. Cocoa and chocolate products can be categorized as cocoa products, chocolate products, and confectionery coatings. *Cocoa products* are unsweetened. They include cocoa nibs, chocolate (cocoa) liquor, cocoa powder, and cocoa butter. *Chocolate products* are sweetened. They are highly processed and more refined than cocoa products, and while they vary in price, expect to pay a premium for them. Chocolate products include bittersweet dark chocolate, sweet chocolate, milk chocolate, white chocolate, and couvertures. *Confectionery coatings* are low-cost products made from cocoa, vegetable fats other than cocoa butter, and sugar. Both chocolate products and confectionery coatings can be purchased as blocks (often 10 or 11 pounds/4.5 or 5 kilograms) or drops, also called coins or chips. Because they are small in size, drops are convenient to melt and use.

Cocoa and chocolate products must meet minimum standards set by law. These standards clarify differences among products, but they do not eliminate the large variation in makeup and quality that exists between brands. Standards vary from one country to the next. The definition of milk chocolate, in particular, changes from North America to Switzerland to the United Kingdom.

In the descriptions that follow, U.S. and Canadian regulations are provided throughout, while Tables 15.1 through 15.3 and Table 15.5 summarize and compare product regulations for the United States, Canada, and the European Union (EU). The EU includes France, Belgium, Great Britain, Germany, and twenty-three other countries. Switzerland, an important chocolate producer, is not an EU member; it sets its own regulations.

The chocolate industry has changed over the years. At one time, the industry consisted of skilled craftsmen running small operations. Today, large manufacturers transform the bulk of the world's cocoa beans into cocoa and chocolate products. These manufacturers have the ability to produce consistent product at a moderate cost. One way they maintain consistency is by blending beans from around the world. Another way is through large-scale computer-controlled manufacturing processes.

The Role of Technology in Chocolate Manufacturing

Chocolate has a rich and romantic history, and it is fun to learn about the role of kings, queens, and conquistadors in the story of chocolate. But a closer look at chocolate's history reveals the importance of technology. Without technology, chocolate would never have risen in quality and popularity in quite the same way. The steam engine, a product of the Industrial Revolution, made chocolate affordable and appealing to the common man, for example. The invention of the cocoa press in 1828 reduced prices and increased appeal even more. Later in the 1800s, Rodolphe Lindt, a Swiss manufacturer, developed a means of refining the flavor and mouthfeel of chocolate through conching. Around the same time another Swiss, Daniel Peter, created the first milk chocolate by incorporating Henri Nestlé's newly invented condensed milk into chocolate.

Advances in technology continue today, increasing the quality and maintaining the cost of cocoa and chocolate products. Look for references to these and other technology improvements throughout this chapter.

At the same time that most of the chocolate industry has consolidated into a few large-scale mass producers, artisan chocolate manufacturers have begun producing small quantities of specialty products. Artisan chocolate manufacturers tend to use more traditional methods of processing beans, and they are likely to create specialty chocolates made from varietal or single-origin beans.

The first step in converting cocoa beans (single-origin or otherwise) into cocoa and chocolate products is to clean and roast the bean.

Cocoa Products

Cocoa Nibs Small bits of roasted cocoa nib can be purchased as a specialty ingredient. Just as cocoa beans can be thought of as nuts, cocoa nibs (also called *cacao nibs*) can be thought of as chopped nuts. Nibs contain everything that is found in the cocoa bean including a large amount of cocoa butter and an almost equal amount of cocoa solids nonfat. Because they are unsweetened, cocoa nibs have a strong bitter chocolate taste.

Figure 15.3 Cocoa nibs can be thought of as chopped nuts. **Clockwise from top:** cocoa pod, whole roasted cacao beans, chopped cocoa nibs

TABLE 15.1 U.S., CANADIAN, AND EU STANDARDS FOR COCOA POWDER

REGULATING BODY	NAME	COCOA BUTTER	OTHER REGULATIONS
United States	High-fat cocoa	22% (min)	
European Union	Cocoa	20% (min)	Calculated on a dry weight basis
United States and Canada	Cocoa	10% (min)	In United States, 22% maximum
United States and Canada	Low-fat cocoa	10% (max)	
European Union	Fat-reduced cocoa	8–20%	Calculated on a dry weight basis
United States and Canada	Fat-free cocoa	0.5% (max)	

Data from U.S. 21CFR163 2002; Canada CRC, c.870, B.04 Dec 31. 2001; EU Directive 73/241/EEC

The roasting process is an important step in the transformation of bean to cocoa and chocolate. Roasting takes several minutes to an hour or more, at temperatures that range from 200° to 400°F (95°–200°C). Roasting conditions depend on the size and variety of bean and on the end result desired. For example, criollo flavor beans are typically roasted for a shorter time or at lower temperatures than forasteros so that valuable aromas are not lost to evaporation.

Roasting loosens the shell for easy removal, reduces the amount of moisture, and destroys microorganisms and other undesirable pests so that the bean is suitable for consumption. Roasting also darkens the color and changes the flavor of cocoa beans. The flavor changes as heat evaporates acids and other volatile flavor molecules. Heat also initiates many complex chemical reactions, including Maillard reactions, which involve the breakdown of sugars and other carbohydrates in the presence of proteins. As roasting progresses, Maillard reactions produce deep, earthy middle and base notes and darkly colored compounds.

While the traditional means of roasting is to dry-roast whole beans, newer roasting methods involve pretreating beans with steam or infrared heat. Pretreatment allows shells to be removed before roasting. Once shells are removed, nibs are broken into particles of uniform size. Alternatively, the nibs are reduced to a paste, which is roasted as a thin film. Either method provides the manufacturer with better control over the roasting process so that beans are more evenly roasted.

As with coffee, people have personal preferences for the degree of roast that they prefer in their chocolate.

Like coffee beans, cocoa nibs provide instant impact in baked goods and confections, but they should be used sparingly because of their strong bitter bite. Figure 15.3 shows chopped cocoa nibs, along with whole roasted cacao beans and a cocoa pod that contains the beans.

Chocolate Liquor and Unsweetened Chocolate

Chocolate liquor is produced by finely grinding chocolate nibs through a series of rollers. The word *liquor* refers to the liquid state of chocolate when it is warm; it does not indicate the presence of alcohol. If chocolate nibs are thought of as chopped nuts, chocolate liquor can be thought of as nut butter; that is, nuts ground to a smooth paste. Unlike almond butter or peanut butter, however, chocolate liquor (also called cocoa liquor) hardens into solid blocks when cooled, because cocoa butter is solid at room temperature. When sold as solid blocks, chocolate liquor is called *unsweetened chocolate*, *cocoa mass* or *cacaomasse*, *bitter chocolate*, or *baking chocolate*.

Like nibs, unsweetened chocolate is high in cocoa butter. By law, unsweetened chocolate must contain a minimum of 50 percent cocoa butter (and in the United States, a maximum of 60 percent). Because it is high in valuable cocoa butter, unsweetened chocolate is an expensive ingredient. It is often worth the price, however, because cocoa butter contributes to the full flavor of unsweetened chocolate. Unsweetened chocolate is the ingredient of choice for the richest chocolate flavor in baked goods.

Besides containing cocoa butter and very small amounts of moisture, unsweetened chocolate contains cocoa solids nonfat. Since it is made from pure nib, this is generally all that is in unsweetened chocolate (by law, however, it can contain small amounts of added milk fat, ground nuts, flavorings, and alkali). Recall that cocoa solids nonfat includes acid. The acid in unsweetened

---

HELPFUL HINT

Here are some guidelines when deciding which cocoa or chocolate product to use in the bakeshop.

- *Use unsweetened chocolate for the richest chocolate flavor in baking, and where convenience and cost are not important.*
- *Use higher-fat 22/24 cocoa powder for general baking needs; that is, for ease in use with a small compromise in flavor.*
- *Use regular 10/12 cocoa powder for lower-fat products and where ease in use and a lower cost are important.*
- *Use couvertures and other sweetened chocolates for mousses, ganaches, garnishes, and confections.*

At the start of the 1700s, hot chocolate was too expensive for the common man. Joseph Fry, an English physician who counseled his patients on the medicinal qualities of chocolate, was the first to mechanize and mass-produce the grinding of cocoa beans. Before then, chocolate was manually ground as it had been for thousands of years, between a stone rolling pin and a stone surface (mano and metate). Mass production reduced the price of chocolate and improved its fineness, which increased its appeal.

Still, an unattractive slick of melted cocoa butter formed on the surface of hot chocolate. When C. J. Van Houten from the Netherlands developed a process in 1828 for pressing excess cocoa butter from chocolate, cocoa powder was produced and the problem was solved.

For a few years after cocoa powder was invented, nobody knew what to do with the leftover cocoa butter. Finally, in the mid-1800s, Fry and Sons combined cocoa butter and sugar with chocolate, creating the first popular chocolate candy bar. Because there was now a market for cocoa butter, the price of cocoa dropped, making hot cocoa available to the masses.

chocolate is available to react with baking soda in baked goods, producing small amounts of carbon dioxide gas for leavening.

While unsweetened chocolate provides a wonderful rich chocolate flavor to baked goods, it must be carefully melted before use. A much easier, less messy, and less expensive ingredient used in baked goods is cocoa powder. When using cocoa powder, additional shortening or butter is added as well (Figure 15.4).

Figure 15.4 Shortening and cocoa **(top)** can be used in place of unsweetened chocolate **(bottom)** in baked goods

Natural Cocoa Powder When chocolate liquor is squeezed and pressed under high pressure, heat builds and melts cocoa butter, some of which drains from the chocolate. The remaining presscake is finely ground and sold as natural cocoa powder. The color of natural cocoa ranges from light yellowish brown (tan) to dark yellowish brown, depending on the source of bean and amount of roasting. Because valuable cocoa butter is removed and sold separately, cocoa powder is less expensive than unsweetened chocolate.

Like chocolate liquor, natural cocoa powder is acidic, having a pH typically between 5 and 6. The acids in natural cocoa react with baking soda to produce a small amount of carbon dioxide gas for leavening.

Cocoa powder does not contain added sugar. There are sweetened cocoas on the market, convenient for preparing hot cocoa and other beverages. These sweetened cocoas, which are also called *hot cocoa mixes*, are not used in baking.

One way to classify cocoa powder is by the amount of cocoa butter it contains. Regular cocoa powder, often simply called *cocoa*, is commonly used for baking in North America. Cocoa has a minimum of 10 percent cocoa butter by law, and it generally ranges around 10–12 percent. In fact, manufacturers often designate regular cocoa as 10/12 cocoa. Figure 15.5 shows what else, besides 10–12 percent cocoa butter, is in regular cocoa powder.

Low-fat cocoa in North America has less than 10 percent cocoa butter, but some cocoas, labeled "fat-free," contain 0.5 percent cocoa butter or less. Removing this

Substituting Cocoa Powder for Unsweetened Chocolate

Cocoa should not be substituted directly for unsweetened chocolate in baked goods because it is higher in nonfat solids and lower in fat. Less cocoa is needed compared with the amount of unsweetened chocolate, and fat—usually shortening—must be added along with the cocoa.

To calculate the amount of 22/24 cocoa powder used in place of unsweetened chocolate, multiply the amount of chocolate by ⅝ or 0.63. To calculate the amount of shortening to add, multiply the amount of chocolate by ⅜ or 0.37. For 10/12 cocoa, the multiplying factors are 9⁄16 or 0.56 for the amount of cocoa powder and 7⁄16 or 0.44 for the amount of shortening.

This gives the following approximate conversions for unsweetened chocolate:

$$1 \text{ pound unsweetened chocolate} = 10 \text{ ounces } 22/24 \text{ cocoa powder} + 6 \text{ ounces shortening}$$
$$= 9 \text{ ounces } 10/12 \text{ cocoa powder} + 7 \text{ ounces shortening}$$

$$1 \text{ kilogram unsweetened chocolate} = 630 \text{ grams } 22/24 \text{ cocoa powder} + 370 \text{ grams shortening}$$
$$= 560 \text{ grams } 10/12 \text{ cocoa powder} + 440 \text{ grams shortening}$$

Since shortening has twice the shortening power of cocoa butter, bakers and pastry chefs often reduce the amount of shortening by one-half (for example, from 6 ounces to 3 ounces per pound of chocolate; from 370 grams to 185 grams per kilogram of chocolate).

To use cocoa powder, sift it with dry ingredients, cream it with shortening and sugar, or dissolve it in hot liquid. Some chefs find that dissolving cocoa in hot liquid before use releases flavor.

While the results are not identical when cocoa is used in place of chocolate, the product will be lower in cost, easier to make, and perfectly acceptable.

---

much cocoa butter requires a special process (supercritical gas extraction, for one), so fat-free cocoas are expensive and not commonly used in the bakeshop.

A fourth category of cocoa powder sold in the United States is *high fat* or *breakfast cocoa*, which has a minimum of 22 percent cocoa butter. Manufacturers

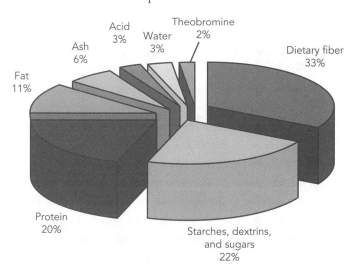

Figure 15.5 Makeup of 10/12 cocoa powder

often designate it as 22/24 cocoa, because of its typical fat content. Either 10/12 or 22/24 cocoa can be used in baking, and while they can be substituted one for the other, higher-fat cocoas provide a richer flavor at a higher cost.

Regular cocoa powder from the European Union is equivalent to American 22/24 cocoa in makeup. It is sometimes designated as 20/22 cocoa because, when measured according to the EU method (on a dry weight basis), it analyzes at 20–22 percent cocoa butter. Table 15.1 summarizes government regulations in the United States, Canada, and the European Union for cocoa. Notice that cocoa considered fat-reduced in the European Union is not necessarily the same as North American low-fat cocoa.

Dutched Cocoa Powder Dutch process (dutched) cocoa is more common than natural cocoa in bakeshops. Like natural cocoas, dutched cocoas are typically sold as 10/12 or 22/24 cocoas. Low-fat and fat-free versions are also available.

Natural cocoa powder does not disperse easily in water. In 1828, the same year that he developed a method for producing cocoa powder, C. J. Van Houten discovered that by treating cocoa with alkali, cocoa powder dispersed easily. Because Van Houten was Dutch, the cocoa was called dutched cocoa. Dutched cocoa spread in popularity throughout Europe because it dispersed easily, but also because the alkali treatment gave the cocoa a darker, richer color and a mellower flavor.

What Is Carob Powder?

Carob powder or flour is sometimes used in place of cocoa powder in confections, baked goods, and beverages. Although it looks like cocoa powder, carob powder is not a cacao product. It is made from locust bean (carob) pods that are roasted, then ground. Recall from Chapter 12 that another food ingredient, locust bean (carob) gum, is extracted from the bean contained in this same pod.

Carob powder is considered by some to be a healthful alternative to cocoa powder because it is low in fat and does not contain caffeine-like stimulants. However, some carob products, such as carob chips, can be high in added fat. Carob has also been used as a low-cost cocoa substitute when prices of cacao products were high.

While natural cocoa has not been chemically treated, dutched cocoa has been treated with a mild alkali to neutralize the natural acidity of cocoa and to increase pH to 7 or above. An example of an alkali is sodium bicarbonate (baking soda), but this is not commonly used for dutching cocoa. Instead, potassium carbonate is often used. If cocoa has been dutched, its ingredient label will read: cocoa processed with alkali. The cocoa may be called alkalized, dutched, or European-style. In contrast, natural cocoa is sometimes called nonalkalized or regular cocoa.

The dutching process darkens the color of cocoa, making it look richer and often redder than natural cocoa. Dutched cocoas vary in color from light reddish brown to dark brown or dark reddish brown. The final color depends on the amount of dutching the cocoa has undergone. Because the alkali treatment is applied to nibs before they are ground and pressed, unsweetened chocolate is also available dutched.

Besides affecting color, dutching changes the flavor of cocoa. Dutched cocoa has a smoother, mellower flavor than natural cocoa. It is less sharply astringent and acidic, is more full-bodied, and disperses more easily in water.

Dutched and natural cocoas can be substituted for each other, despite differences between them. Deciding which to use is mostly based on personal preference.

North American consumers tend to use natural cocoa in home-baked goods, while European consumers tend to use dutched cocoa. However, professional pastry chefs on both sides of the Atlantic typically prefer dutched cocoas for all applications because of its richer color and smoother flavor. Because natural cocoas are slightly acidic while dutched cocoas are alkaline, some chefs adjust the amount of baking soda and acid in formulas accordingly.

Cocoa Butter Cocoa butter, the fat naturally present in cocoa beans, is sold as pale yellow bars or flakes. When it is pressed from chocolate liquor during the production of cocoa powder, it has a deep tan color and a distinctively chocolate flavor. It is filtered to remove cocoa particles and partly or wholly deodorized to remove most, if not all, of its chocolate flavor.

Cocoa butter is an expensive fat, valued in the confectionery and cosmetics industries for its unique and pleasant melting characteristics.

Bakers and pastry chefs use cocoa butter to thin melted chocolate and couvertures for more even coating and dipping. While this is its main use, cocoa butter is also brushed onto pastry shells so they won't get soggy from moist fillings. Because it is highly saturated, cocoa butter resists oxidative rancidity, but it will eventually develop a rancid off flavor.

Why Are Color and Flavor Removed from Cocoa Butter?

When purchased for the bakeshop, cocoa butter is highly refined; that is, it is pale in color and mild in flavor. Why would pastry chefs want this bland product instead of a richly colored and flavorful cocoa butter, straight from chocolate liquor?

As described earlier, cocoa butter is often added to sweetened chocolate products to alter their consistency. Because pastry chefs often pay premium prices for carefully selected and processed chocolate, they typically do not want anything—not even another cocoa product—altering the flavor and appearance of their premium chocolate.

Another use for cocoa butter is as a protective water-resistant coating on pastry. Once again, neutral flavor is desirable in this application as well.

What Gives Cocoa Butter Its Unique Melting Characteristics?

Cocoa butter is extremely hard and brittle at room temperature because it is high in saturated fatty acids. But compared with other saturated fats such as all-purpose shortening and lard, cocoa butter has a very sharp melting curve and a low final melting point, giving it a unique and pleasant melt-away mouthfeel. The figure below compares the melting curves of cocoa butter with all-purpose shortening. Notice that cocoa butter starts with a very high (85 percent) solid fat content at room temperature (70°F/ 21°C), but that by 95°F (35°C), it has melted completely.

What makes cocoa butter so unique? Recall from Chapter 9 that most food fats contain a broad mix of fatty acids. Each fatty acid has its own distinct melting point, so most food fats melt slowly over a wide temperature range. Cocoa butter, in contrast, consists of relatively few types of fatty acids, which all melt just below body temperature. It is this uniquely homogeneous mix of fatty acids that gives cocoa butter its fast-melting, pleasant mouthfeel.

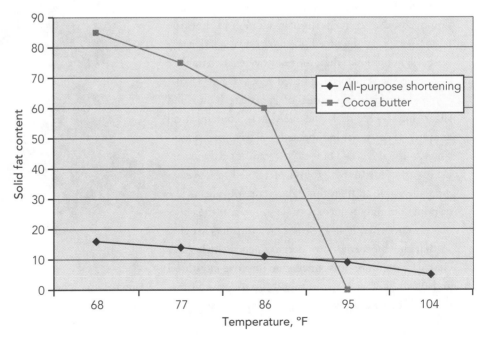

Melting curves of cocoa butter and all-purpose shortening

Conching is a process in which ingredients are mixed, kneaded, and gently heated for several hours or days, depending on the type of equipment and on the desired end results. During conching, sugar and cocoa particles are ground smooth and coated with a film of cocoa butter. In a process that is the reverse of seizing, water evaporates through gentle heating, so the chocolate becomes smoother and shinier. Heat also drives off acids and other volatile ingredients, further refining flavor. Finally, heat continues the development of flavor from chemical reactions begun in the roaster. It is as if conching reduces the coarseness of both flavor and texture, and the chocolate changes from a dull, lumpy paste to a smooth, mellow-tasting liquid, ready for molding and cooling.

Rodolphe Lindt, a Swiss chocolate manufacturer, designed the first conch in 1879, creating the smoothest of eating chocolates, so smooth he called it *fondant chocolate*. The conch received its name from its shape, which followed the curve of a conch shell. The original conch had heavy rollers that plowed back and forth through waves of chocolate. Similar horizontal conches are still in use today in traditional chocolate factories. These conches often require seventy-two or more hours to complete the process and are said to produce the finest flavored chocolates.

Today, there are newer designs for conches that more efficiently complete the flavor and particle size refinement processes. For example, rotary vertical conches are equipped with blades that vigorously scrape chocolate against ribbed walls and keep it in constant motion while strong air currents blow through.

There is no one best process for conching, and manufacturers control the time, temperature, and speed of conching to achieve the results that they desire. This is one step among many by which manufacturers distinguish their brand of chocolate from others.

Chocolate Products

Bittersweet Dark Chocolate Bittersweet dark chocolate is not the same as bitter, unsweetened chocolate. Like all chocolate products, bittersweet dark chocolate (also called *bittersweet*, *dark*, or *semisweet chocolate*, or simply *chocolate*) contains sugar in addition to chocolate liquor. Because of the added sugar, bittersweet dark chocolate will not produce the same results when used in place of unsweetened chocolate in baked goods (Figure 15.6).

Besides containing a mix of chocolate liquor and sugar, bittersweet dark chocolate may contain small amounts of dairy, natural and artificial flavorings, emulsifiers, nuts, and cocoa butter. In a traditional chocolate factory, this mixture is ground or refined in a *melangeur*, then ground finer through a series of rollers. The grinding not only reduces particle size so that the chocolate is not gritty, it also releases fat from the particles, so that the chocolate flows better when melted. After chocolate is ground it is conched to improve mouthfeel and flavor. The result is a smooth, homogenized mix of fine chocolate, milk, and sugar particles evenly suspended in cocoa butter.

After chocolate is conched, it is tempered, molded, and cooled. *Tempering* is a process of carefully melting,

Figure 15.6 Brownies made with bittersweet dark chocolate instead of unsweetened chocolate **(top)** have a shiny cracked surface, characteristic of high-sugar formulas. They are soft and gooey on the inside, making them more difficult to cut than brownies made with unsweetened chocolate **(bottom)**

cooling, and holding chocolate products at the proper temperatures to ensure that cocoa butter crystallizes properly. Tempering is the final step in assuring that chocolate has the proper mouthfeel and appearance. Since bakers and pastry chefs must temper chocolate products before use, tempering is discussed in more detail in a later section.

Bittersweet dark chocolate (often in the form of couverture) is used in creams, mousses, ganache fillings and glazes, coatings, icings, sauces, and chocolate chip cookies (in the form of chocolate chips). It is these products, not baked goods, that benefit most from the refined flavor and smooth mouthfeel of fine chocolate. While different brands of bittersweet dark chocolate can be used interchangeably, results vary because brands vary in color, flavor, and amount of sugar and cocoa solids.

Unlike unsweetened chocolate and cocoa powder, bittersweet dark chocolate is rarely used in batters and doughs. The use of bittersweet dark chocolate adds an unnecessary expense to baked goods because of the added cost of conching and refining. The contributions of conching and refining are clear when chocolate is eaten as is or in products such as creams, mousses, ganaches, and so on. Once highly refined and conched chocolate is added to batters and doughs, the benefits of these processes are minimal. But when a formula does call for bittersweet dark chocolate, unsweetened chocolate should not be used in its place without adjusting the formula.

In North America, bittersweet chocolate must contain a minimum of 35% cocoa solids (in the United States, the 35% minimum must be chocolate liquor), meaning that it can contain up to 65 percent sugar. Table 15.2 compares the U.S. standard for bittersweet chocolate with that for other chocolates. Table 15.3 compares Canadian standards for chocolates.

TABLE 15.2 U.S. STANDARDS FOR CHOCOLATE

CHOCOLATE	CHOCOLATE LIQUOR (MINIMUM)	DAIRY SOLIDS	OTHER STANDARDS
Bittersweet	35%	12% (max)	
Milk	10%	12% (min)	
White	0%	14% (min)	20% (min) cocoa butter; 3.5% (min) milk fat; 5% (max) whey; 55% (max) sugar

From U.S. 21CFR163 2002

TABLE 15.3 CANADIAN STANDARDS FOR CHOCOLATE

CHOCOLATE	TOTAL COCOA SOLIDS* (MINIMUM)	DAIRY SOLIDS	COCOA BUTTER (MINIMUM)	COCOA SOLIDS NONFAT (MINIMUM)	OTHER STANDARDS
Bittersweet	35%	5% (max)	18%	14%	
Milk	25%	12% (min)	15%	2.5%	
White	0%	14% (min)	20%	—	3.5% (min) milk fat; 5% (max) whey

*From chocolate liquor, cocoa powder, and cocoa butter

From Canada CRC, c.870, B.04 Dec 31, 2001

What If Chocolate Brownies Were Made with Bittersweet Chocolate?

Chocolate brownies are typically made with unsweetened chocolate or with cocoa. If bittersweet dark chocolate was used instead without adjusting the formula, the brownies would turn out different. They would be lighter in color, have a milder chocolate flavor, and be sweeter. They would also be moister and more tender. In fact, depending on the brand used, they could look and taste more like blond brownies than chocolate brownies, because bittersweet dark chocolate is lower in cocoa solids than unsweetened chocolate. In place of cocoa solids, bittersweet dark chocolate contains sugar—sometimes up to 65 percent sugar.

Because of the added processing that bittersweet chocolate undergoes, these brownies would likely be more expensive, too. In a pinch, however, 2 pounds (or 1,000 grams) of most brands of bittersweet dark chocolate can be used in place of 1 pound (or 500 grams) unsweetened chocolate. Because bittersweet chocolate contains sugar, the amount of sugar in the formula should be reduced by 1 pound (or 500 grams).

What Is Meant by "Percent Cacao"?

Because many chocolate products contain sugar and other ingredients, they are often labeled with a declaration of a minimum amount of cacao or cocoa solids, sometimes simply called *percent cacao* or *percent cocoa*. The European Union requires this by law of all its member countries. Cocoa solids, in this case, are not the same as cocoa solids nonfat. Instead, it represents the combined total of all ingredients from the cocoa bean, including chocolate liquor, ground cocoa nib, cocoa powder, and cocoa butter. In other words, it represents the combined total of cocoa solids nonfat and cocoa butter. The label declarations do not state how much of the cocoa solids are nonfat and how much are from added cocoa butter, but manufacturers are usually willing to provide this information when asked. All else being equal, a higher level of cocoa solids nonfat provides a stronger chocolate flavor. A higher level of cocoa butter means the product will be thinner when melted, which is important when chocolate is used as a coating.

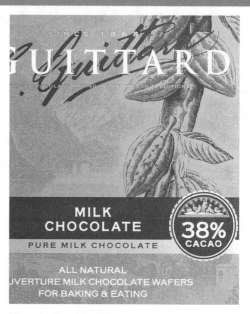

Photo by Ron Manville

Many bittersweet chocolates exceed these minimum standards, some containing 50 percent cocoa solids or more. Often manufacturers use the term *bittersweet* when a chocolate contains more than 50 percent cocoa solids and *semisweet* when it contains between 35 percent and 50 percent, but there is no law that says they must. While price does not necessarily reflect quality, cocoa solids are more expensive than sugar, so the more cocoa solids in chocolate, often the higher the cost.

In the European Union, the equivalent to bittersweet dark chocolate is more often simply called *chocolate*.

While European chocolate couverture does not meet minimum standards for bittersweet chocolate in North America, most European dark couverture chocolates exceed them. Dark couverture chocolate will be discussed in more detail.

Milk Chocolate

Milk chocolate is a sweetened chocolate product typically low in cocoa solids but containing a good amount of milk solids instead (see Tables 15.2 and 15.3). As with bittersweet dark chocolate, milk chocolate often

Chocolate mousse is typically made with bittersweet dark chocolate. If milk chocolate was used instead, the mousse would likely come out quite different. It would be lighter in color; in fact, it might look more like butterscotch mousse than chocolate mousse, because milk chocolates are low in cocoa solids nonfat.

The low amount of cocoa solids also means that milk chocolate mousse would likely be softer and less firm than one made with bittersweet dark chocolate. In fact, some milk chocolate mousses fail to set up.

Finally, milk chocolate mousse would be sweeter than one made with bittersweet dark chocolate, maybe too sweet and too weak in flavor. The flavor often is more buttery, creamy, caramel, or vanilla than chocolate. These flavors come through aerated products more strongly than does chocolate.

Does this mean that milk chocolate should never be used in chocolate mousse? No, but it is often difficult to predict how well any particular milk chocolate will work without first trying it. To increase your chances of success, select a milk chocolate with a strong flavor and one that is relatively high in cocoa solids and low in sugar; use a combination of milk and bittersweet chocolates; or use a formula designed specifically for milk chocolate.

---

contains natural or artificial vanilla flavoring, emulsifiers, and cocoa butter. The rest is sugar. Milk chocolate undergoes refining, conching, tempering, and molding processes similar to those of bittersweet dark chocolate.

Most milk chocolates are sweet and mellow in flavor. While they lack chocolate bitterness, many do have interesting flavors from dairy solids. American milk chocolate, for example, often has a sour or ripened milk flavor, while Swiss chocolate has a mildly cooked milk flavor. British milk chocolate often is strongly caramelized from the addition of milk crumb. *Milk crumb* is a dry, crumbly powder made by heating condensed milk with sugar, with or without the addition of chocolate liquor. The caramelized flavors come from Maillard reactions that occur when milk and sugar are heated together.

Milk chocolate cannot generally be used in formulas designed for bittersweet dark chocolate because it is too low in cocoa solids and too mild in flavor to really work well. It is softer than bittersweet dark chocolate because it is lower in cocoa solids, but also because of milk fat from the added dairy ingredients. Milk fat is soft and oily at room temperature, and solid cocoa butter crystals tend to dissolve in the milk fat. The primary use of milk chocolate (often in the form of couverture) in the bakeshop is for dipping and coating, and for chocolate garnishes and decorations.

White Chocolate White chocolate is made from sugar, cocoa butter, milk solids, and natural or artificial vanilla flavoring; emulsifiers are optional. In other words, white chocolate is essentially milk chocolate without the cocoa solids nonfat. For many years, there was no permanent legal definition for white chocolate in the United States; this changed in 2002 when the FDA created a standard of identity for white chocolate. This standard is defined in Table 15.2 and is the same as that for white chocolate in the European Union.

The flavor of white chocolate is predominantly vanilla. White chocolate has essentially no chocolate flavor because the cocoa butter is typically deodorized before use. Because white chocolate is totally lacking in cocoa solids nonfat, it cannot be substituted directly for bittersweet or milk chocolate in most formulas. When it is, expect a softer set even though white chocolate sets up faster than other chocolates. White chocolate is used in creams, mousses, ganache fillings and glazes, coatings, cheesecake, icings, various confectionery, and cookies (as white chocolate chunks).

Couverture Chocolates *Couverture* is French for "coating." Couverture chocolate is chocolate with a minimum of 31 percent cocoa butter (in the case of milk chocolate couverture, the minimum 31 percent includes milk fat). Think of couvertures as higher-quality chocolate products, with higher levels of cocoa butter and often additional conching and refining adding to their cost.

Many bakeshops stock both milk chocolate and dark chocolate couvertures. Couvertures are used primarily for chocolate garnishes and decorations, or for dipping and coating cakes, cookies, candies, and confections.

Ganache is a simple mixture of heavy cream and melted chocolate. To make ganache, bring fresh cream just to a boil, add chopped chocolate, and stir until the chocolate melts completely. Ganache has many uses including as a glaze or icing for cakes, in chocolate truffles, and, when whipped, as a light filling.

The proportion of chocolate to cream in ganache can vary, with higher amounts of chocolate providing a firm consistency, and higher amounts of heavy cream producing a softer one. For further variety, other liquids such as milk, juice, or coffee can be substituted for heavy cream, and butter or egg yolks can be added for richness. Since chocolate products vary in the amount of chocolate liquor each contains, ganache consistency also varies with the type and brand of chocolate.

Scientifically, ganache is an oil-in-water emulsion of milk fat droplets and cocoa butter crystals suspended in liquid, stabilized by natural emulsifiers and proteins in milk and in chocolate. Too much bittersweet chocolate or too much added butter sometimes causes the emulsion to break and fats to separate from the liquid. When this happens, whisk ganache slowly into a small amount of heavy cream to reemulsify.

Couvertures can also be used interchangeably with regular chocolate products in creams, mousses, ganache, and icings. Couvertures are not typically added to batters and doughs for the same reason that chocolate is not.

Couverture has several advantages over chocolate. The added cocoa butter better coats sugar and cocoa particles, allowing them to flow more easily. With particles flowing easily past each other, couvertures are thin, so they fill molds and coat products more evenly (Figure 15.7). In contrast, when semisweet chocolate chips are melted, the melted chocolate is thick. The sugar and cocoa particles tend to clump, thickening the chocolate. This thickness is necessary for the manufacturer to properly deposit chocolate into drops, but it means that chips designed for chocolate chip cookies are too thick to use for coating and dipping (unless the pastry chef adds cocoa butter or another fat before use). On the other hand, chocolate chips maintain their shape when baked into cookies, while some couverture chocolates—those that are particularly thin-melting—do not.

The added cocoa butter in couverture also provides an attractive glossy finish—as long as the couverture is properly tempered. Because cocoa butter is extremely

Figure 15.7 Couverture chocolates are designed to be thin when melted, so they can coat evenly

solid at room temperature, high-quality couvertures exhibit a characteristic snap that is absent from products with lower amounts of cocoa butter. Higher amounts of cocoa butter also mean a smoother, more melt-away mouthfeel. Notice that these advantages are important when couvertures are used for coating, dipping, and molding, or for creating chocolate garnishes

> **HELPFUL HINT**
>
> *Manufacturers often provide information on the consistency and best uses of a couverture right on its label. Check there first, or go to the manufacturer's Web site for this and more information.*

Melted chocolate and couvertures are complex mixtures of finely pulverized sugar, cocoa, and milk particles floating in a pool of cocoa butter. Because there is often more cocoa and milk than cocoa butter, and sometimes more sugar than everything else, the pool can get crowded. When this happens, the melted mix can be very thick as particles bump, tangle, and clump. Emulsifiers like lecithin can help thin out melted chocolate, so it flows smoothly and evenly.

Small amounts of lecithin are naturally present in chocolate liquor, but additional amounts are commonly added to chocolate products. Like all emulsifiers, part of the lecithin molecule is attracted to fat and part of it is attracted to water (and all things that dissolve in water). The fat-loving (lipophilic) part of a lecithin molecule extends into the pool of cocoa butter. The water-loving (hydrophilic) part of the molecule interacts with and surrounds sugar, which is also water-loving. This keeps the sugar particles from clumping and the melted chocolate thin.

Lecithin is approved for use in chocolates and couvertures in North America and in Europe. Because it is less expensive and about ten times more efficient than cocoa butter at thinning chocolate, lecithin is often used for lowering the cost of chocolates. Lecithin is also added to expensive couvertures as a final adjustment of consistency.

Chocolates thinned with lecithin do have some different characteristics, however. For example, they do not shrink as much on cooling as do couvertures with higher levels of cocoa butter. This makes it more difficult to remove them from chocolate molds. Since only a very small amount (usually 0.1–0.3 percent) of lecithin is needed, however, the flavor of the chocolate is not diluted as it can be when higher amounts of refined cocoa butter are used.

and decorations; they are lost when couvertures are used in baked goods. Table 15.4 summarizes the important functions of cocoa butter in couvertures and other chocolate products.

TABLE 15.4 FUNCTIONS OF COCOA BUTTER IN COUVERTURES

Thins viscosity of melted chocolate
Shrinks on cooling for easy removal of chocolate from molds
Provides sheen
Provides firmness with snap
Provides a smooth, melt-away mouthfeel

European law defines couvertures; Canadian and U.S. laws do not. This does not mean that North American chocolate products never meet the standards of couvertures; it simply means that they are not labeled as such. If it is important to know the amount of cocoa butter present in a chocolate product, ask the manufacturer. Table 15.5 summarizes European Union regulations for couverture chocolates.

Confectionery Coatings

Confectionery coatings go by many names, including *compound coatings*, *glazes* (pâte à glacer), *summer coatings*, *nontempering coatings*, or simply *coatings*. Sometimes confectionery coatings are called *chocolate coatings*, but

TABLE 15.5 EUROPEAN UNION REGULATIONS FOR COUVERTURE CHOCOLATES

COUVERTURE PRODUCT	MINIMUM COCOA BUTTER	OTHER REGULATIONS
Couverture chocolate	31%	> 2.5% cocoa solids nonfat
Dark couverture chocolate	31%	> 16% cocoa solids nonfat
Couverture milk chocolate	31% (includes milk fat)	> 2.5% cocoa solids nonfat; > 14% milk solids; < 55% sucrose

Member countries of the European Union are allowed by law to add up to 5 percent tropical oils, such as palm oil or shea oil, into their chocolate products. However, these products cannot be legally sold as chocolate in North America.

this is not legally correct. In North America, the word *chocolate* is reserved for products that contain cocoa butter as the only fat (small amounts of milk fat are allowed). Confectionery coatings contain vegetable fats such as partially hydrogenated soybean, palm kernel, or coconut oil. While some coatings are quite good in quality, coating fat is still imitation cocoa butter, just as margarine is imitation butter. Because they can be made from partially hydrogenated fats, confectionery coatings can be a source of trans fats, thought to increase coronary heart disease.

Since confectionery coatings do not contain cocoa butter, many are less expensive than real chocolate couvertures. As with any ingredient, however, product quality varies from one brand to the next. For example, the oils in some confectionery coatings are specially processed—*fractionated*—so that they have melting properties very similar to those of cocoa butter. Some of these coatings can be as pricey as some real chocolate couvertures, but they will have a melting mouthfeel and glossy shine without the need to temper. Certain other confectionery coatings have a higher melting point than cocoa butter. While too high a melting point gives the coating an unappealing waxiness, high-melting coatings hold up in warm weather.

Confectionery coatings are available as dark, milk, and white versions. Coatings are also available in a rainbow of colors.

Handling Chocolate Products

Unsweetened chocolate and chocolate products are usually melted before use. They must be melted carefully, because they contain a mix of proteins and carbohydrates that are easily overheated. When chocolate overheats, it becomes thick, lumpy, and dull. If this occurs, throw out the chocolate and begin again. It is especially easy to overheat milk and white chocolates because they contain dairy ingredients that burn and scorch easily.

Chocolate can be melted in a microwave or in a double boiler. In either case, never leave melting chocolate unattended, and be sure to stir often so hot spots do not develop and overheat the chocolate.

Keep water and steam away from melted chocolate. Be sure, for example, to dry off the surfaces of strawberries and other fresh fruits that are dipped in chocolate. Water causes chocolate to seize up and thicken as hygroscopic sugar particles absorb water and become sticky. Sticky particles cannot flow easily past each other, greatly increasing viscosity or thickness. Once thickened in this manner, chocolate products are no longer useful for dipping and coating.

> **HELPFUL HINT**
>
> *Although not useful for dipping and coating, seized chocolate has its uses. By intentionally adding a small amount of water to chocolate, for example, chocolate is easily piped. Unintentionally seized chocolate can be used in ganaches, fillings, and other products that combine chocolate with liquid ingredients.*

Tempering Chocolate

When chocolate is melted and allowed to cool on its own, it takes a while for it to set. When it does finally set, it will have a dull appearance and an unappealing texture. Over time, unattractive gray-white streaks called *fat bloom* appear on the surface, and the chocolate could become gritty, even crumbly. All this happens because of the way cocoa butter in chocolate solidifies when it cools on its own. This is why chocolate products must first be tempered before they are allowed to set.

Tempering is the process of controlling the melting and cooling of chocolate before it sets. The goal of tempering is to solidify the cocoa butter in chocolate into a form that provides the most appealing appearance, texture, and flavor. Tempering is a skill that anyone who works with chocolate must learn.

There are several different methods for tempering chocolate. Each method uses a different combination of temperature, time, and amount of agitation. One method is to place chopped chocolate in a bowl set over hot water and to melt, cool, and rewarm the chocolate in bulk. Another method is to add shaved bits of tempered chocolate to melted chocolate, to seed and cool it simultaneously. No matter the method used, the goal is the same: to form cocoa butter into the proper fat structure for the most appealing appearance, texture, and flavor.

Tempering and Fat Crystals Cocoa butter, like all fats, is *polymorphic*, which means that it can solidify

When liquid fat solidifies into solid fat crystals, it solidifies in one of two ways. Either new seed crystals form from the liquid fat in a process called *crystal nucleation*, or existing crystals grow larger in a process logically called *crystal growth*.

Tempering is a means of favoring seed crystal nucleation of beta (type V) crystals. Tempering is sometimes appropriately called *precrystallization*, since it sets the stage for proper crystallization; that is, crystal growth of stable beta crystals, as chocolate cools and sets.

As with most practices in the bakeshop, the proper tempering of chocolate is a balancing act. In this case, temperature, time, and the amount of agitation of the melted chocolate must all be balanced. The wrong amount of any one of these three factors will result in the formation of the wrong amount of seed crystals. If too many seed crystals form, the chocolate is said to be overtempered or overseeded. If too few seed crystals form, the chocolate is undertempered or underseeded.

One way that chocolate becomes overtempered is by cooling it too much before use. Overtempered chocolate contains too many seed crystals. It is thick because so much of it has already solidified; this keeps it from coating evenly. Overtempered chocolate is also difficult to remove from chocolate molds because it doesn't shrink. Chocolate shrinks as it cools because solid beta fat crystals pack together tightly. Overtempered chocolate already contains a lot of solid fat crystals, however, so it shrinks less as it cools in the mold.

One way that chocolate becomes undertempered is by not cooling it enough before use. Undertempered chocolate has too few seed crystals. Because too little of the fat has solidified, it will take longer for the chocolate to set as it cools. More important, there are not enough beta seed crystals present, so the chocolate solidifies into a mix that includes unstable crystals. These unstable crystals bloom shortly after the chocolate sets.

into crystals of different shapes. Each crystal shape (form) also has different properties. The three most common crystal forms for cocoa butter, listed in order of increasing melting point, density, and stability, are alpha (α; also called form II), beta prime (β'; form IV), and beta (β; form V). The beta form (form V) is the most desirable of the three because it provides chocolate with snap, gloss, and a smooth mouthfeel. Beta crystals also have the highest melting point of the three, making them the most stable and the least likely to melt and bloom during storage. Beta crystals have these features because the fat molecules are more tightly packed than they are in other crystal formations.

When melted chocolate is allowed to cool without proper tempering, unstable alpha and beta prime crystals form. These unstable crystals set into chocolate that is soft, dull, and does not snap when broken. Because these crystals do not pack as tightly as beta crystals, untempered chocolate placed in molds will be difficult to remove, since the chocolate will not shrink as it cools.

Untempered chocolate might look somewhat acceptable when first hardened, but the unstable crystals transform in an uncontrolled manner to large, coarse beta crystals during storage. These large, coarse beta crystals are sometimes called form VI crystals, to differentiate them from the more desirable form V beta crystals that form from properly tempered chocolate. Eventually the coarse form VI crystals migrate to the chocolate's surface, where they appear as fat bloom. With this change, chocolate becomes gritty, sometimes crumbly, in texture. Because texture affects flavor perception, bloomed chocolate does not have the right flavor, either. Refer back to Table 15.4. All of these desirable features of cocoa butter in chocolate are lost when chocolate is not properly tempered.

To ensure that large numbers of small, stable beta crystals form, chocolate products are tempered. Tempering involves gently heating chocolate (115°–120°F/46°–49°C) to dissolve all crystals; cooling and agitating it at a temperature (78°–81°F/26–27°C) that encourages the formation of desirable beta seed crystals; warming it slightly (86°–90°F/30°–32°C) to melt any undesirable low-melting crystals that also formed, then cooling gently to room temperature to set (Figure 15.8). As the chocolate cools and sets, the presence of beta seed crystals from tempering encourages the growth of these

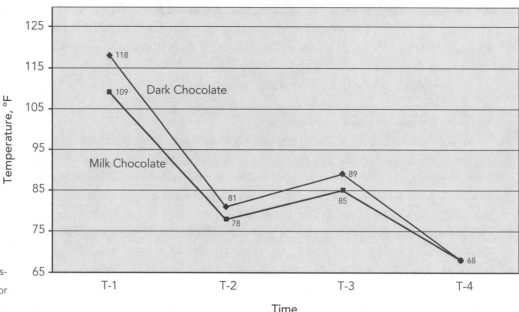

Crystalization Cooling Curves for Chocolate

Figure 15.8 Typical crystallization cooling curves for dark and milk chocolates

crystals. Because beta crystals take time to grow properly, chocolate must be cooled and allowed to set slowly. That is, tempered chocolate should not be placed in the cooler or freezer to speed the process.

The temperature ranges provided above are broad guidelines. Milk fat, emulsifiers, and other ingredients affect the crystallizing behavior of cocoa butter, which is why milk chocolates must be tempered at lower temperatures than bittersweet dark chocolates. Milk chocolate is also more easily damaged by excessive heating. Each brand of chocolate has its own ideal tempering pattern, and it is best to ask the manufacturer for specific tempering guidelines. Tempering guidelines are often provided as crystallization cooling curves like those shown in Figure 15.8. While crystallization cooling curves can be helpful, they do not tell you how long the chocolate is best held at each temperature. Figure 15.8 arbitrarily labels the different times as T-1 through T-4.

Functions of Cocoa and Chocolate Products

Providing Color

Cocoa and chocolate products have colors that range from light tan to dark mahogany, even black. They vary in color for many reasons; the eight main ones are listed in Table 15.6. Of these reasons, the cocoa grower controls the first three while the manufacturer controls the next four. The last, the amount of baking soda and final pH of a baked good, is under the control of the baker or pastry chef.

Providing Flavor

Flavor is a primary reason for using cocoa and chocolate products in the bakeshop. There are regional preferences for chocolate flavors and styles of chocolate. For example, many French, Belgians, and Germans prefer dark chocolate, but most of the world prefers milk chocolate by a wide margin. A recent trend on both sides of the Atlantic, however, is the consumption of so-called extreme dark chocolates. Extreme dark chocolates are very dark and bitter because they are high in cocoa solids.

Cocoa and chocolate products vary in flavor for the same reasons that they vary in color (Table 15.6), but the two do not necessarily coincide. That is, a dark-colored chocolate does not necessarily have the strongest chocolate flavor. Recall that flavor-rich criollo beans are light in color, and that dutching darkens color while it mellows flavor.

Why You Can't Always Judge Cocoa by Its Color

Fat content is one of the eight major factors affecting color of cocoas and chocolates. The more cocoa butter in cocoa, for example, the darker and richer it appears. This makes 22/24 cocoa a good choice for dusting truffles and plated desserts.

You might think that 22/24 cocoa would also provide a darker, richer color in baked goods such as cakes and cookies. But the rich look of high-fat cocoa is an illusion. The more fat in cocoa, the fewer coloring agents it actually contains (the coloring agents are in the nonfat portion of cocoa). The rich look of high-fat cocoa is from the perception of light as it reflects off fat-coated cocoa particles. Once mixed into batters and doughs, cocoa powder takes on a different look. The color no longer depends on the amount of fat in the cocoa powder; it depends on the amount of coloring agents present in the cocoa solids nonfat. All else being equal, if there is any difference in appearance between a cake baked with a 22/24 cocoa and one baked with a 10/12 cocoa, it is the lower-fat cocoa that will provide a darker color.

What Puts the Devil in Devil's Food Cake?

Recipes abound for devil's food cake, an American classic. Devil's food cake is mild tasting yet it has a rich, dark, reddish brown color. It is typically made with cocoa, not chocolate, and the cocoa of choice is natural cocoa.

What makes devil's food cake dark and rich looking? Baking soda. Small amounts of baking soda react with acids in natural cocoa. This provides some carbon dioxide for leavening, but any excess baking soda increases the pH of the batter. This slightly higher pH darkens the cocoa and provides it with a smoother cocoa flavor. It is as if the cocoa were dutched right in the batter.

Care must be taken that excessive amounts of baking soda are not added to devil's food cake. Too much baking soda is detrimental to flavor, adding a chemical off taste. Too much baking soda also overtenderizes cell walls. When this happens, the cell walls break, forming a coarse crumb and a cake that flattens unattractively.

The perception of chocolate flavor changes with context. That is, milk chocolate that seems well balanced on its own might taste weak when paired with other flavors. On the other hand, a bittersweet that seems strong and bitter when tasted alone could provide the right balance of flavor to a finished product. When selecting chocolate or couverture to use in products, be sure to taste a sample of the finished product before preparing large quantities.

Here are a few additional points to consider when working with chocolate for flavor.

- Cocoa and chocolate products with a higher amount of cocoa butter typically provide a richer, fuller chocolate flavor because cocoa butter itself, when not deodorized, has flavor. That is why unsweetened chocolate, not cocoa powder, is preferred for the richest, most decadent chocolate desserts.
- Vanilla flavor is so commonly used in chocolate products in North America that sometimes the way to increase "chocolate" flavor in a product is to add a small amount of vanilla.

TABLE 15.6 MAJOR CAUSES OF COLOR AND FLAVOR VARIATION IN CHOCOLATE AND COCOA PRODUCTS

Bean variety and country of origin
Bean maturity and ripeness
Handling of beans: fermentation, drying, and storage
Roasting conditions
Conching conditions
Amount of fat
Amount of dutching and final pH of cocoa or chocolate
Amount of baking soda and final pH of finished product (in baked goods)

ORAC stands for Oxygen Radical Absorbance Capacity. It is a sophisticated test that measures the antioxidant activity of food products in the laboratory. While it seems reasonable to assume that products with high antioxidant activity in the lab will also have high antioxidant activity in the human body, this remains unproven. Clinical studies are needed to relate ORAC units to actual health benefits in humans. The high level of ORAC units in chocolate products, however, is impressive. It is derived partly from the high level of polyphenolic compounds (specifically, the flavonoids) in cocoa beans.

According to the USDA's 2007 list of ORAC values for selected foods, the ORAC units for 100 grams of various food products are as follows:

49,926	Unsweetened chocolate
20,823	Dark chocolate
13,541	Walnuts
7,528	Milk chocolate
7,581	Plums, black
6,552	Blueberries
4,882	Raspberries
3,577	Strawberries
2,341	Pomegranate juice
1,034	Onions
728	Corn

- Natural cocoas tend to have pronounced sharp, fruity, acidic flavors. Dutched cocoas have smoother, fuller flavors.
- Adding baking soda to baked goods is almost like dutching cocoa or chocolate right in the baked good.

Absorbing Liquids

Cocoa solids nonfat is an extremely effective drying agent. In fact, cocoa powder absorbs more liquid than an equal weight of flour. It is proteins and carbohydrates (starches, dextrins, and gums) in cocoa solids nonfat that absorb liquids (water and oil) from cake batters, icings, fillings, mousses, and ganache. When extra cocoa is added to cake batter, for example, less flour or more liquids are needed for the right batter consistency. This is especially true if the cocoa powder has been alkalized or if it is a 10/12 cocoa; that is, one with only 10–12 percent cocoa butter and 88–90 percent cocoa solids nonfat.

Providing Structure

Cocoa solids nonfat provide structure. The starches, in particular, provide structure when they gelatinize. Just as cake with extra cocoa requires less flour for the right batter consistency, it also requires less flour for structure. Likewise, chocolate mousse made with bittersweet chocolate has more structure and substance than one made from milk chocolate—which has much less cocoa solids nonfat—or from white chocolate, which has none.

Cocoa and chocolate products—even unsweetened chocolate, which is over 50 percent fat—are not considered tenderizers. Their structure builders are so powerful that they more than compensate for the mild tenderizing effect of cocoa butter. Cocoa butter is considered to have about half the shortening or tenderizing power of all-purpose shortening, partly because it is so solid at room temperature. In fact, cocoa butter itself

> **HELPFUL HINT**
>
> *To convert a yellow cake or plain sugar cookies into chocolate cake and cookies, start by replacing 10–20 percent of the flour with cocoa powder. Depending on the type of flour and the cocoa powder, you may need to remove additional flour, or add additional water, sometimes up to 8 ounces of additional water for every pound of cocoa powder added (or 500 grams for every kilogram).*

provides firmness and structure through the formation of solid fat crystals.

Providing a Pleasing Mouthfeel

High-fat cocoa and chocolate products, especially those that are highly refined and conched, have a pleasing mouthfeel that contributes to the overall sensory effects of coatings, creams, mousses, ganache fillings and glazes, and icings. The pleasing mouthfeel is primarily from the unique melting characteristics of cocoa butter and from the lack of grittiness in these products.

It might seem that if some smoothness is good, more must be better. But if chocolate is ground too finely, it feels waxy. There are regional preferences for the mouthfeel of chocolate, just as there are preferences for flavor, with Europeans tending to prefer smoother chocolates than North Americans.

Adding Nutritional Value

While cocoa powder contains cocoa butter and small amounts of moisture (about 3 percent), it consists mostly of cocoa solids nonfat (from 76-90 percent). It is especially rich in dietary fiber and other carbohydrates (Figure 15.5), as well as protein. Cocoa is also an important source of vitamins, minerals, and polyphenolic compounds. The level of polyphenols and antioxidant activity of cocoa and chocolate products rivals that of many fruits and vegetables.

Storage

Chocolate products are a favorite food of rodents. For this reason, all chocolate should be well-wrapped and stored in covered containers.

Milk and white chocolates have the shortest shelf life of all cocoa and chocolate products because their milk solids undergo Maillard browning (the browning of sugars and proteins) even at room temperature. Stored properly, milk and white chocolates have a shelf life of six months to one year. Eventually, though, Maillard browning causes colors to darken and off flavors to develop. While cocoa butter is relatively stable to oxidative rancidity, milk fat is not. The milk fat in milk and white chocolates also contributes to off flavor development in these products as it undergoes oxidative rancidity.

Other cocoa and chocolate products, including cocoa butter, have a shelf life longer than one year, but that is true only if they are stored properly. Ideally, cocoa and chocolate products should be stored well wrapped and at a cool, consistent 55°–65°F (13°–18°C), otherwise fat bloom forms on chocolate surfaces. Do not discard chocolate that has bloomed. Its baking qualities remain unaffected, and fat bloom disappears when chocolate is tempered before use, as long as it is not severe.

Sugar bloom occurs when chocolate picks up moisture. Sugar crystals melt in the moisture, only to recrystallize on the surface as larger crystals. The gritty white crystals affect both texture and appearance. Sugar bloom remains even after chocolate is tempered. To prevent sugar bloom, store chocolate where the humidity is below 50 percent; use gloves when handling chocolate, to avoid transfer of moisture from hands; and do not warm cold chocolate unless it is very tightly wrapped. This is critical with chocolate that has been refrigerated. As refrigerated chocolate warms to room temperature, water droplets easily condense onto its surface, solubilizing sugar crystals and forming sugar bloom.

Cocoa powder is hygroscopic. If it picks up excess moisture, it clumps, develops off flavors, and could be a source of food for microorganisms. Store cocoa in a tightly covered container and away from hot, steamy areas.

All chocolate products, but especially white chocolate, should be well wrapped and kept away from strong odors. Cocoa butter, like all fats, readily picks up odors.

Questions for Review

1 How does the amount and type of fat in cocoa beans compare to that in almonds?

2 What is meant by "cocoa nib"?

3 What is the name of the caffeine-like stimulant found in cocoa nibs?

4 What changes occur in cocoa beans as they are roasted?

5 What is chocolate liquor called when it is sold as solid blocks?

6 What is the main difference in makeup between unsweetened chocolate and natural cocoa?

7 Which is more expensive to use, unsweetened chocolate or cocoa powder? Why?

8 Which should be used—unsweetened chocolate or cocoa—for the richest, most chocolate flavor in baked goods? Which should be used in low-fat products?

9 What is the main difference between 10/12 and 22/24 cocoa powders? Which is considered regular cocoa in North America, and which is considered regular cocoa in the European Union?

10 How is dutched cocoa made? How does it differ from natural cocoa in color, flavor, and acidity?

11 Why does cocoa butter provide a more pleasant mouthfeel than all-purpose shortening?

12 What is another name for semisweet chocolate?

13 A product is labeled 72% cocoa. What does this refer to? How does this percent differ from the percent cocoa butter or cocoa solids nonfat in a product?

14 How does milk chocolate compare with bittersweet chocolate in minimum percentage of cocoa solids in the U.S.? In Canada?

15 What is meant by conching? Why is conching important for chocolate products used for coating and dipping? Why is conching not as important for unsweetened chocolate used in baked goods?

16 How does the amount of cocoa butter in chocolates and couvertures affect their properties?

17 You add a small amount of vanilla extract to melted chocolate and, as you stir it in, the chocolate thickens. Why? What has happened to the sugars and proteins in the mixture?

18 Why must chocolate be tempered before it cools?

19 What does it mean when we say that cocoa butter is "polymorphic"?

20 What are the main differences between alpha, beta prime, and beta crystals?

21 Describe the process of tempering chocolate.

22 Why is the goal of tempering to form the largest number of beta crystals?

23 Which components in cocoa and chocolate make them drying or absorbing agents? Which make them structure builders?

24 How does cocoa butter compare to all-purpose shortening in its ability to shorten and tenderize?

25 What is meant by "ORAC"? How does chocolate compare to other food products in ORAC units?

26 What changes occur in white chocolate when it is stored for too long?

27 How should cocoa powder be stored? What changes happen to cocoa powder when it is stored improperly?

28 What is fat bloom? How can it be prevented?

29 What is sugar bloom? How can it be prevented?

Questions for Discussion

1 From what you know of the minimum amount of cocoa butter that is in chocolate liquor and the minimum amount of chocolate liquor required in bittersweet dark chocolate in the United States, calculate the minimum amount of cocoa butter that can legally be in bittersweet dark chocolate (show your work). How does this compare to the minimum amount of cocoa butter that must be in European dark couverture chocolate?

2 What is the percent cocoa solids in each of the following ingredients: unsweetened chocolate, cocoa powder (natural or dutched), cocoa butter?

3 A formula for chocolate cookies calls for unsweetened chocolate. If bittersweet dark chocolate is used instead, how might the cookies come out different, and why?

4 A formula for ganache calls for bittersweet dark chocolate. If milk chocolate is used instead, how might the ganache come out different, and why?

5 According to European law, what is the difference between milk chocolate and milk chocolate couverture? Which will be more expensive? Which is more likely to be used in the bakeshop for coating, dipping, and garnishing cakes, cookies, and confections?

6 For a stronger chocolate flavor in fudge cake, you add more cocoa to the basic formula. The result is a tough, dry, dense cake. Why?

7 To make a premium chocolate cake, you switch from unsweetened chocolate to an equal amount of expensive, super premium dark couverture. The result is a pale, collapsed mess that is too sweet and has little chocolate flavor. Why?

8 You are out of unsweetened chocolate for brownies and are substituting bittersweet dark chocolate (labeled 50% cacao) instead. How much bittersweet chocolate should be used for each pound (or kilogram) of unsweetened chocolate, and how should the amount of sugar be adjusted in the formula?

9 Why might chocolate cake contain baking soda? List three reasons.

10 Two fudge cakes are prepared in an identical manner using all the same ingredients in equal amounts, but different cocoas are used. List four reasons that could explain why one of the cakes looks darker than the other. Be specific.

11 Why might a darker cocoa produce a lighter cake?

Exercises and Experiments

❶ Exercise: Replacing Chocolate with Cocoa and Shortening

Using the formula provided earlier in this chapter, how much cocoa and how much shortening should be used to replace 2 pounds (or 2 kilograms) of chocolate in a cake formula? Show your work.

_____

_____

_____

❷ Exercise: Evaluating Chocolate

The best way to learn about chocolate flavor is to evaluate a range of chocolates. The chocolates should be at room temperature and, if possible, should be tempered and molded so that each chocolate is of the same size and shape for tasting. Use the Results Tables to record your evaluations of the appearance, flavor, and mouthfeel of different brands of chocolate products. Compare white chocolates with each other, then repeat with milk chocolates, and finally bittersweet dark chocolates. Include one or more confectionery coatings in your tastings, and be sure to include products that range in price. Use only those terms you feel comfortable with. After some experience, add any other terms that you feel are important. Consider the following:

- Appearance (gloss, lightness/darkness in color, redness in color, etc.)
- Snap upon breaking
- Flavor (vanilla, chocolate, fresh dairy, caramelized dairy, sweetness, sourness, bitterness, etc.)
- Texture/mouthfeel (softness/firmness, grittiness/smoothness, fast/slow melt, creaminess, etc.)
- Add any additional comments, as necessary

RESULTS TABLE   WHITE CHOCOLATE PRODUCTS

CHOCOLATE PRODUCT	BRAND NAME	PERCENT COCOA SOLIDS	APPEARANCE	SNAP	FLAVOR	TEXTURE/ MOUTHFEEL	ADDITIONAL COMMENTS
White Chocolate							
White Couverture Chocolate							
White Coating							

RESULTS TABLE MILK CHOCOLATE PRODUCTS

CHOCOLATE PRODUCT	BRAND NAME	PERCENT COCOA SOLIDS	APPEARANCE	SNAP	FLAVOR	TEXTURE/ MOUTHFEEL	ADDITIONAL COMMENTS
Milk Chocolate							
Milk Couverture Chocolate							
Milk Coating							

RESULTS TABLE BITTERSWEET DARK CHOCOLATE PRODUCTS

CHOCOLATE PRODUCT	BRAND NAME	PERCENT COCOA SOLIDS	APPEARANCE	SNAP	FLAVOR	TEXTURE/ MOUTHFEEL	ADDITIONAL COMMENTS
Bittersweet Dark Chocolate							
Dark Couverture Chocolate							
Dark Coating							

Summarize major findings from your chocolate tastings:

White chocolates

_____

_____

_____

Milk chocolates

_____

_____

_____

Bittersweet dark chocolates

_____

_____

_____

❸ Experiment: How Different Chocolates Affect the Quality of Ganache

Objectives

Demonstrate how the brand and type of chocolate affects
- Ganache appearance, flavor, and consistency
- Overall acceptability of ganache

Products Prepared

Ganache made with
- Bittersweet dark chocolate or couverture (control product, 50–55% cocoa)
- Bittersweet dark chocolate or couverture (different brand, 70–75% cocoa, higher price)
- Dark confectionery coating
- Milk chocolate or couverture
- White chocolate or couverture
- Other, if desired (milk coating, white coating, etc.)

Material and Equipment

- Scale
- Heavy-bottom stainless-steel saucepans
- Ganache (see Formula), enough to fill one half sheet pan of each variation
- Half sheet pans
- Parchment paper
- Rubber spatula
- Plain tips (optional)
- Pastry bags (optional)

Formula

Ganache

Yield: 1 pound, 5 ounces (600 grams)

INGREDIENT	POUNDS	OUNCES	GRAMS	BAKER'S PERCENTAGE
Cream, heavy		7	200	50
Chocolate, finely chopped		14	400	100
Total	1	5	600	150

Method of Preparation

1 Place cream in heavy saucepan and bring just to a boil while stirring.

2 Remove from heat.

3 Stir in chopped chocolate and set aside for a few minutes to allow the heat from the cream to melt the chocolate.

4 Stir until smooth and chocolate is completely melted.

Procedure

1 Line half sheet pans with parchment paper and label with type of chocolate to be used in each ganache.

2 Prepare ganache using the formula above or using any basic hard ganache formula. Prepare one batch of ganache for each variation.

3 Pour hot ganache onto parchment-lined sheet pans and spread into an even, thin layer using a rubber spatula. Alternatively, pipe ganache into simple rounds for bite-size servings.

4 Refrigerate to cool.

5 Determine the cost per batch for the dark chocolates and the dark confectionery coating used in preparing each batch of ganache. Record values in Results Table, which follows. If you do not have costing information, use the following prices:
   • Dark chocolate, 50–55% cocoa: $7.25 per lb ($16 per kg)
   • Dark couverture chocolate, 70–75% cocoa: $9.10 per lb ($20 per kg)
   • Dark confectionery coating, premium quality: $5.25 per lb ($11.55/kg)

Results

1 Use Brand Name column in Results Table to record any identifying information for each chocolate product used.

2 Evaluate the sensory characteristics of completely cooled products and record evaluations in Results Table. Be sure to compare each in turn to the control product and consider the following:

- Appearance (color, sheen, and consistency or thickness)
- Flavor (sweetness, bitterness, vanilla, caramel, cooked dairy aroma, etc.)
- Texture and Mouthfeel (soft/firm, thick/thin, heavy, waxy, oily, etc.)
- Overall acceptability, from highly unacceptable to highly acceptable, on a scale of 1 to 5
- Any additional comments, as necessary

RESULTS TABLE SENSORY CHARACTERISTICS OF GANACHE MADE WITH DIFFERENT BRANDS AND TYPES OF CHOCOLATE

TYPE OF CHOCOLATE	BRAND NAME	COST/BATCH	APPEARANCE	FLAVOR	TEXTURE AND MOUTHFEEL	OVERALL ACCEPTABILITY	ADDITIONAL COMMENTS
Bittersweet dark chocolate or couverture (control product)							
Bittersweet dark chocolate or couverture (different brand)							
Dark coating							
Milk chocolate							
White chocolate							

Sources of Error

List any sources of error that might make it difficult to draw the proper conclusions from your experiment. In particular, consider any differences in time it took to boil the cream, in cooling and handling the ganaches, and in the temperature of products when they are evaluated.

_____

_____

_____

State what you could do differently next time to minimize or eliminate each source of error.

_____

_____

_____

Conclusions

Select one from the choices in **bold** or fill in the blanks.

1   The difference in appearance between the dark chocolate ganaches was **small/moderate/large**. These differences can be described as follows:

_____

_____

_____.

2   The difference in firmness between the dark chocolate lower in cocoa solids (control product; 50–55% cocoa) and the one higher in cocoa solids (70–75% cocoa) was **small/moderate/large**. The control product was **softer/firmer**, probably because it was **lower/higher** in cocoa solids nonfat, which contains important driers and structure builders, namely

_____

_____

_____.

3   The difference in flavor and mouthfeel between the dark chocolate ganaches was **small/moderate/large**. These differences can be described as follows:

_____

_____

_____.

4   The difference in flavor and mouthfeel between the dark chocolate lower in cocoa solids (control product; 50–55% cocoa) and the dark confectionery coating was **small/moderate/large**. These differences can be described as follows:

_____

_____

_____.

5 The difference in cost per batch between using a dark chocolate with 50–55% cocoa (control product) and one higher in cocoa was **small/moderate/large**. In my opinion, the quality difference between the two ganaches **justifies/does not justify** the use of the more expensive chocolate in this product because _____

_____

_____.

6 The difference in cost per batch between the dark chocolate lower in cocoa solids (control product; 50–55% cocoa) and the dark confectionery coating was **small/moderate/large**. In my opinion, the quality difference between the two ganaches **does justify/does not justify** the use of the more expensive chocolate in this product because _____

_____

_____.

This same conclusion probably holds for other products that are similar to ganache, such as (*list two or three similar products*) _____

_____

_____.

This same conclusion might not hold for products that are much different from ganache, such as _____

_____

_____.

7 Other differences between the ganaches made with different chocolates were as follows (consider, for example, how quickly they cooled and solidified):

_____

_____

_____.

16

Fruit and Fruit Products

Chapter Objectives

1. List and explain different forms of fruit that can be purchased for the bakeshop.

2. Using apples and blueberries as examples, present factors to consider when selecting from different fruit varieties.

3. Describe the ripening process.

4. Describe how to best store and handle fruits.

Introduction

Fruit is nature's sweet. It is the centerpiece of many traditional desserts such as fruit tarts and pies, poached pears, and apple strudel, and it complements many plated desserts. Fruit is an important source of flavor, color, and texture in the bakeshop.

Fruit and fruit products today are different from those found in bakeshops as little as thirty years ago. Today, there is widespread use of frozen fruit purees, and flavors once considered exotic, such as mango and kiwi, are almost as common as strawberry and apple.

New fruit varieties are continually being bred, such as the boysenberry and the Marion blackberry, and new ones imported and popularized, such as the sweet Meyer lemon and the nashi or Asian pear.

This chapter is not meant to be all-inclusive and it will not discuss each and every fruit. Instead, it focuses on a few common fruits and fruit forms, with the understanding that the principles of proper selection, storage, and use of fruit in general will provide the foundation for adapting to a changing industry.

How Fruit Is Purchased

Fruits can be purchased fresh, frozen, canned, or dried. They can be whole, sliced, or pureed, packed in water or sugar, and sold as jam or as a prepared pie or bakery filling.

More fresh fruit is available year-round today than ever before, as early- and late-ripening cultivars of fruits are developed, and as more fruit from the Southern Hemisphere is exported to North America during the winter. Ideally, fruit used in the bakeshop is fresh and fully ripe, but this is not always possible. For example, fresh blueberries purchased in the middle of winter might have poor color or flavor—or be prohibitively expensive. While some bakers and pastry chefs, for practical or philosophical reasons, use fruit only when it is in season locally, others like to use all types year-round, in season or not. Most common fruits such as apples and strawberries are available fresh year-round, but certain specialty fruits, such as pomegranate and lychee, are available only certain months of the year.

Purchasing fresh fruit in season is no guarantee of quality. Fruit is highly perishable, and poorly stored fruit will lose its value relatively quickly. Fruit is a natural agricultural product, and its quality varies throughout the season and from one growing region to the next. It also varies from one year to the next, partly because climatic conditions change from year to year. Depending on the amount of sun and rainfall and the length of the growing season, fruit can be weak-tasting and poor in color, or it can be sweet, vibrant, and bursting with flavor. Finally, different varieties of the same fruit can vary widely in quality.

Processed fruit—frozen and canned—provides certain benefits over fresh. Besides being available year-round, processed fruit is less perishable than fresh, and its quality is generally more consistent. When fruit is out of season, processed fruit often has better quality than fresh and can be less expensive. Out-of-season fruit must be shipped long distances, often from South and Central America, Australia, or New Zealand. The cost of shipping is high and the toll on quality even greater.

Even when fresh fruit is in season, reasonably priced, and high in quality, processed fruit products have a place in many bakeshops. Frozen puree, for example, need only be thawed and canned apples opened before use, with little manpower and no waste.

Frozen Fruit

Frozen fruit comes whole, sliced, diced, and pureed. *Straight-pack* frozen fruit is sold with the fruit placed directly into a pail or box, then frozen solid. Because freezing takes place slowly, straight-pack fruit often loses its piece integrity. Where this is not important, straight-pack fruit quality can be quite acceptable. A disadvantage of straight-pack fruit is that the whole pail or box must be thawed before use.

Individually quick frozen (IQF) fruit consists of whole fruit or fruit pieces that are quickly frozen and then packed into pails, boxes, or bags. As long as IQF fruit is not thawed and refrozen, the fruit pieces remain separate. It is a good choice when fruit is added to muffins, as with blueberry or cranberry muffins. IQF fruit is more expensive than straight-pack fruit, but it

How Are New Fruit Varieties Developed?

New and improved varieties of fruits are constantly entering the marketplace. New fruits often have improvements over older ones in flavor, texture, appearance, and size, providing a benefit to the consumer. Other times, the improvements are in disease resistance, yield per acre, and other benefits to the farmer.

How are new varieties developed, and who does the work? One technique that has been used for years is plant breeding. The first step in breeding plants is to select two plants with different desirable traits. For example, one strawberry might have great flavor and a firm texture but require large amounts of water to grow. A second plant might require little water, but it may have poorer flavor and texture. By transferring the pollen from one plant to another, the plant breeder hopes to generate seeds for plants with features that are the best of both. The only way to find out if this has happened is to plant seeds from the cross-pollination and determine if any grow into plants with the right combination of flavor, texture, and water requirements. It is a time-consuming, expensive, hit-or-miss process, but most fruits are bred in this manner.

To get an idea of the size of such an undertaking, consider the following. Researchers at the University of California Strawberry Breeding Program grow around 10,000 seedlings in a nursery by crossbreeding parent plants. Each plant is evaluated for vigor, fruit quality, and yield, and about 200–300 are chosen and allowed to propagate and be planted in outdoor fields. Each outdoor-grown plant is further evaluated before one or more is selected for widespread planting.

The State of California relies on these traditional plant-breeding techniques, not on genetic engineering, to develop new strawberry cultivars. Why would the state spend so much time and money breeding a better strawberry? Over 80 percent of the strawberries consumed in North America are grown in California, making strawberries a multibillion-dollar business for the state.

Grading of Fruit

Fruits are natural products that vary greatly in quality. Both Canada and the United States have national programs for grading the quality of fruit grown and sold in their countries. The program run by the U.S. Department of Agriculture (USDA) is voluntary. Fruit in the United States that is not graded is not necessarily lower in quality; it could simply mean that the processor chose not to take part in the USDA grading program.

Each fruit has a different set of standards to meet, but the standards for all fruits are based on several common characteristics, including size, shape, color, and the amount of damage and decay allowed.

has one large advantage: With IQF fruit, as much or as little fruit as needed can be used without thawing a whole container.

HELPFUL HINT

Before adding IQF fruit such as blueberries to muffin or coffee cake batter, coat the fruit with a light dusting of flour. This will make the juice from the thawing fruit less likely to mix with the batter and discolor it. Or layer the fruit on top of the batter instead of mixing it in. During baking, as the fruit sinks, it will do so with a minimum amount of bleeding.

The faster freezing of IQF fruit means that smaller ice crystals form, and this often means less damage to fruit integrity than with straight-pack fruit. However, do not expect the same quality from IQF fruit as you would from peak-quality fresh fruit. Even when frozen quickly, most fruits shrivel and exude some liquid as they thaw. Certain fruits, such as cranberries and apple slices, hold up well while others—for example, strawberries and raspberries—become soft and mushy. IQF fruit often loses flavor as well after extended freezing. For the best color and flavor in frozen fruits, consider using sugar- or syrup-packed fruit.

Sugar- or *syrup-packed* frozen fruit has a certain amount of granulated sugar or glucose corn syrup added before freezing. This protects the fruit from air exposure, which can damage color and flavor. Sugar-packed frozen fruit also retains its vitamin C (ascorbic acid) better than IQF fruit, and the sugar firms up the pectin in fruit cell walls. In other words, sugar-packed frozen fruit often has better quality than straight-pack or IQF fruit, at a moderate price.

Because most bakeshop items have sugar added to them, sugar-packed frozen fruits fit well with bakeshop practices. One disadvantage is that the whole container must be thawed before use, making it less convenient than IQF fruit.

With sugar-packed frozen fruit, be sure to adjust your formula for the amount of sugar added. Sugar-packed fruit typically comes as a 4 + 1, 5 + 1, or 7 + 1 pack. The numbers refer to the ratio of fruit to sugar. For example, 4 + 1 strawberries consist of 4 parts strawberries to 1 part sugar, or ⅘ = 80 percent fruit and ⅕ = 20 percent sugar. It is very common for strawberries to be sold as a 4 + 1, just as it is common for cherries to be sold as a 5 + 1 pack (16.7 percent sugar) and apples to be sold as a 7 + 1 (12.5 percent sugar).

Frozen Fruit Purees Frozen fruit purees are a convenient but expensive form of fruit, most commonly used in sauces, sorbets, Bavarian creams, mousses, and ice creams. Frozen fruit purees are a staple in many bakeshops, as important as prepared fondant, extracts, and liqueurs.

Fruit purees are made by straining and pureeing cleaned fruit, then heating to pasteurize and to deactivate enzymes. Some purees have sugar added, and pectin or other thickeners may be added to control consistency. Even single-strength purees are concentrated sources of fruit flavor, but some brands have water removed so that 1 measure of puree equals 2 or more measures of fresh fruit.

Purees come in a wide variety of flavors, with or without seeds. Some fruit purees, such as raspberry and cherry, can be of excellent quality. Others, such as kiwi, are more difficult for the manufacturer to heat-process without a loss in flavor and color. Use fresh puree as your guide before deciding if the quality of a frozen fruit puree is up to your standards and is worth the added cost.

Canned Fruit, Fruit Fillings, and Jams

Expect canned fruit, fruit fillings, and jams to have less fresh flavor and sometimes a softer texture than fresh fruit. However, sometimes fresh fruit flavor, color, and texture are not the goal. Consider caramelized peach sauce, for example, slowly simmered with spices. Canned peaches have a more consistent flavor, color, and texture, will be easier to use, and will be lower in cost than fresh. Because the sauce is simmered and spiced, the flavor of the freshest peaches is not needed. Or consider a reduced orange glaze or strawberry jam,

To preserve the texture and often the flavor and color of cooked fruits, it is better to poach them in sugar syrup than in water. Some poaching syrups are very dilute; that is, some are as low as one part sugar to five or more parts water (or wine). Others are much more concentrated, having more than one part sugar to one part water. Before determining the amount of sugar to add to poaching liquid, consider the following.

When fruit is gently poached in sugar syrup, sugar and water freely diffuse (move) in and out of the fruit. This diffusion continues until the concentration of sugar and water in the syrup is the same as that in the fruit.

If the sugar syrup has more sugar than does the fruit, water diffuses out of the fruit to dilute the syrup (Figure 16.1). As this happens, fruit shrinks in size and often appears to have a vibrant, more appealing color (even as color diffuses out of the fruit). At the same time, sugar diffuses from the syrup into the fruit, sweetening the fruit and firming the pectin that holds it together. The more sugar in the syrup, the sweeter and firmer the fruit becomes, but also the more it shrinks.

If the sugar syrup contains less sugar than the fruit, the opposite happens. Water diffuses into the fruit and sugar diffuses out. Often, enough water moves in so that the fruit gains weight and plumps appealingly. If the fruit is poached in water, though, large amounts of water move in. The force of the water disintegrates the fruit, reducing it to mush. While this makes water a poor cooking medium for whole or sliced fruit, it is an effective means of hastening the preparation of fruit purees and applesauce.

Each fruit is different, but often a good poaching liquid for sweetening and firming fruit contains two parts liquid to one part sugar. This allows some sweetening and firming of fruit without excessive shrinkage. To further assure firm poached fruit, poach gently without boiling, and add a small amount of lemon juice to the poaching liquid. Acid from the lemon juice firms the pectin that holds fruit cells together. Lemon juice also prevents browning and adds an appealing flavor.

both with a fuller, deeper fruitiness than the fresh fruit. These are products in which fresh fruit flavor, color, and texture may be a liability.

Canned fruits are purchased several ways, varying primarily in the amount of sugar and water added. *Solid pack* canned fruit has no water added, *heavy pack* has a small amount of water or juice, and *water pack* has water added. Besides these versions, canned fruit comes with added sugar or another sweetener. If one of these sweeteners is added, it is called a *syrup pack*. Depending on the amount of sweetener, the syrup is considered light, medium, heavy, or extra heavy. Do not confuse a heavy pack with a heavy syrup pack. One is heavy in fruit, the other heavy in sweetener.

Generally, the more sweetener added, the firmer the fruit and often the better the color and flavor. This is also true when fresh fruit is cooked in the bakeshop, as when preparing poached pears.

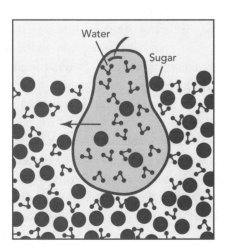
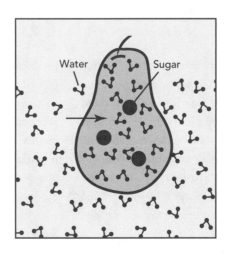

Figure 16.1 The movement of water between poaching liquid and fruit depends on the concentration of sugar in each.

Canned fruit fillings are ready-to-use products, convenient for fruit pies, Danish, and other baked goods. They vary widely in quality, so try different brands before deciding which suits your needs and your budget. While not all canned fruit fillings contain additives, some might to improve color, flavor, and consistency, and to minimize microbial growth. For example, calcium salts such as calcium chloride or calcium lactate are sometimes added to firm up the fruit. The calcium keeps pectin, which holds cells together in the flesh of fruits, from breaking down and softening. Thickeners such as starches and pectin are commonly added for thickness and to improve performance during baking; that is, so-called oven-stable fillings contain thickeners that reduce the tendency of fillings to thin out and run into pastry dough. This prevents the dough from becoming soggy and discolored.

Artificial color might be added to canned fruits that discolor easily, like cherries. Other common additives include mold inhibitors like sodium benzoate, and inhibitors to browning like citric acid, ascorbic acid (vitamin C), and sulfites. The mold inhibitors are not necessary to the canning process, because mold will not grow in properly processed canned foods. Instead, the mold inhibitor delays microbial growth once cans are opened.

Some fruit products are packed into flexible pouches instead of cans. This usually indicates that the product has been aseptically processed. *Aseptic processing* is a means of heating, cooling, and packaging foods in a sterile environment. Like canned foods, unopened packages of aseptically processed foods can be stored at room temperature without the risk of microbial growth. Once opened, they must be refrigerated. For our purposes, there is little difference between canned foods and aseptically processed ones.

Dried Fruit

Fruit was originally dried to preserve it, but today dried fruits are used for their distinctive color, flavor, and texture. The most common dried fruit is raisins, but dried figs, dates, apricots, apples, and plums are also popular. In recent years, dried cherries, blueberries, strawberries, and cranberries have also become available for use.

Some dried fruit is sold as a paste. Fig paste, for use in products like fig bars, is the most popular. Dried plum paste is sold as a fat replacer. This will be discussed shortly.

Raisins Any grape can be dried into raisins (Figure 16.2), but most raisins are dried from naturally sweet Thompson Seedless grapes, known outside North America as the sultana grape. Thompson grapes are grown primarily in the hot Central Valley of California. After they are harvested in late August, the grapes are laid out in rows in the sun for several weeks, to darken and dry before being cleaned and packed.

Figure 16.2 Grapes can dry to become raisins.

Raisins and raisin products (raisin paste, for example) contribute flavor, color, and sweetness to baked goods. They also extend shelf life of baked goods because they are hygroscopic and keep baked goods moist. Raisin products also contain small amounts of natural antimicrobial agents that help prevent mold growth.

Golden raisins are Thompson Seedless grapes that are tunnel-dried, rather than sun-dried, under carefully controlled conditions. Sulfur dioxide (or another source of sulfur, such as sulfites) is applied to the grapes to bleach their natural pigments and to prevent darkening during drying. Golden raisins have a milder raisin flavor with a slight bitter aftertaste from the sulfur dioxide. Sulfur dioxide can be used to keep other light-colored

What's the Difference Between Prunes and Dried Plums?

There is no difference between prunes and dried plums; the terms are used interchangeably, but the preferred term today is "dried plums." According to the California Dried Plum Board, however, not all plums dry well. The plum must dry in the sun without fermenting to be acceptable, and this is best done with plums that naturally contain high levels of sugar. Dried plums are not always sun-dried, though. As with raisins, plums can be dried in tunnel driers under carefully controlled conditions. Tunnel-drying is beneficial when a milder-tasting, lighter-colored dried plum is desired.

The California plum for drying is a descendant of the La Petite d'Agen plum from southwest France. This is a deep purple–skinned oval plum with amber-colored flesh. Over 99 percent of the dried plums—or prunes—from California are of this one variety, and California supplies well over 70 percent of the world's supply of dried plums.

---

dried fruits from darkening, including dried apricots, papayas, peaches, and pears. When products are treated with sulfur dioxide or another source of sulfur, they must have this information on the label.

Zante currant raisins are not related to the European red currant; Zante currants are raisins dried from Black Corinth grapes, a small dark purple grape sometimes marketed as the "champagne grape." Zante currants are about one-quarter the size of regular raisins. Regular-size raisins are also called *select raisins*. Figure 16.3 compares the size of currants with that of select raisins. While there are about 1,000 select raisins per pound (450 grams), currants can have up to 4,000 or more per pound (450 grams). Currants are popular in scones, but they can be used anywhere their smaller size is an advantage.

Baking raisins are Thompson Seedless raisins that are soft and moist because they have a higher moisture content than regular raisins. This makes them messy for out-of-hand eating, but it means that they are ready to add to baked goods and do not need to be conditioned first. Conditioning is discussed later in this chapter.

Sweetened Dried Cranberries, Cherries, Strawberries, and Blueberries Most fruits do not have the high sugar content of the Thompson grape. If dried without added sugar, these fruits tend to be tough, dry, and sour. For softness and sweetness, cranberries, cherries, strawberries, and blueberries are first infused with sugar before they are dried in a tunnel drier under controlled conditions.

Sweetened dried fruits are expensive, so be selective about how they are used. For example, sweetened dried fruit works better than fresh or frozen fruit in applications where doughs are heavy or where products are low in moisture. They are good, for example, in cookies and scones. For one, the high moisture in fresh fruit is undesirable in these doughs, especially if cookies are crisp and dry. Besides, it is difficult to mix fresh fruit into heavy dough without tearing and breaking the fruit. Dried fruit, on the other hand, mixes into heavy doughs without tearing and breaking.

In most other applications, however, consider using other forms of fruit. For example, fresh, frozen, or canned blueberries have advantages over dried blueberries in muffins. They provide a fresher, brighter fruit flavor that contrasts well with the bland taste of a muffin, and they cost less, too.

Dried Plum Paste Dried plum (prune) paste is sold as a fat replacer for baked goods. Because of its color and flavor, dried plum paste is best used in dark-colored products such as brownies and gingerbread.

Dried plum paste does not replace all the functions of fat, but it is effective at moistening and tenderizing baked goods. It contains several components, including

(a)	(b)

Figure 16.3 **(a)** Select raisins **(b)** Zante currants

fructose, glucose, pectin, and sorbitol, that provide these functions. Recall from Chapter 8 that sorbitol is a type of sweetener called a polyol, one that is very hygroscopic.

For more on using dried plum paste, see pages 480-481.

Common Fruits

Many fruits are available to the baker and pastry chef, too many to discuss here. Whether peaches or pears, plums or cherries, the same general rules hold for selecting one variety over another. The following discussion focuses on selecting from among different varieties of apples and blueberries, but these same guidelines can be applied to all fruits.

Apples

There are many varieties of apples to choose from, and the apple industry continually comes out with new ones. Some new apple varieties are chance seedlings that are accidentally discovered, while others are intentionally bred from parent apples that have desirable characteristics.

In Canada and the northeastern United States, McIntosh is the number one apple. In the United States, Red Delicious, Golden Delicious, and Granny Smiths have been the three top varieties for the past decade or so. That is changing as new tree varieties (such as Braeburn, Fuji, Gala, Jonagold, and Honeycrisp) planted in the United States in the 1990s begin to bear larger harvests. Fuji is the most popular apple in Japan, while Jonagold is already well-known in Europe.

Each variety has its own characteristic color, flavor, and texture. As with all fruits, the balance of sweetness to sourness in an apple is important, especially when they are consumed fresh. Understand, however, that no one apple is ideal for all applications. For example, many consider Rome Beauty best for whole baked apples, Golden Delicious or Cortland for fresh fruit applications, and Granny Smiths for apple pies. Opinions vary, though, and that is why it is helpful to have some knowledge and personal experience with different apple varieties, so you can form your own opinions. The same is true for other fruits as well.

When evaluating different varieties of any fruit, including apples, be aware that fruits are natural agricultural products that vary in quality over the course of the year and from year to year. Any conclusions reached about the quality of Granny Smith apples relative to McIntosh, for example, will be different when the evaluation is completed in the fall, when most apples are harvested, from one completed in the spring. Apples are harvested year-round, but each variety has its own peak harvest time. If it is not peak harvest time for a particular apple variety, the apple may have been stored in controlled atmosphere (CA) storage.

Apples for Pie or Strudel Much of selecting the appropriate apple for a pie or strudel is personal preference or the preference of your customers. The important point to understand is that differences in apples do exist, and which apple you select will affect the quality of your pie. Here are some points to consider when selecting an apple variety for pie or strudel.

What Is CA Storage?

Controlled atmosphere (CA) storage is a method of storing fruits, such as apples, so they remain fresh for a long time, as much as six months or more. CA stored apples are placed in large rooms that are kept at temperatures just above freezing, with the amount of moisture, oxygen, and other gases tightly controlled. CA apples may appear fresh, but noticeable changes can occur to both flavor and texture.

CA stored apples lose some of their sourness and aroma, but they often get sweeter. Their texture often becomes undesirably mealy, and they brown more quickly once sliced. If you find that the apples you receive are not up to par, change to a different variety, use frozen or canned, or offer an item only in season.

Does an Apple a Day Keep the Doctor Away?

Modern science often rediscovers the truths of old wives' tales. Apples, for example, are a good source of dietary fiber and of polyphenolic compounds. Dietary fiber performs many functions in the body, including prevention of cancers and cardiovascular diseases.

Polyphenolic compounds (polyphenols) are a large class of compounds found in plant products, including fruits. Sometimes called *flavonoids*, polyphenols are powerful antioxidants that reportedly guard against cancer and cardiovascular diseases. Foods that contain polyphenols and other beneficial compounds are sometimes called *functional foods*, because they function beyond providing the common nutrients important for basic health.

Apples are not the only fruit beneficial to good health. Most fruits are good sources of dietary fiber, and many contain plant pigments that do more than provide color. Anthocyanins, the reds and purples in the plant world, are polyphenolic compounds, and like other polyphenolic compounds, they have antioxidant activity and many health benefits. Blackberries, blueberries, cherries, cranberries, pomegranates, raspberries, red grapes, and strawberries are all rich in anthocyanins that together contribute to good health.

Carotenoids are another class of plant pigments that are powerful antioxidants and contribute to good health. Carotenoids are yellow, orange, and orange-red pigments. Peaches, pears, melons, citrus, papayas, and mangoes are but a few fruits naturally high in carotenoids.

Health guidelines for North Americans include the recommendation to increase consumption of fruits and vegetables. In the United States, a program called "5 A Day for Better Health" is sponsored by several health organizations to encourage Americans to eat five or more servings of fruits and vegetables a day.

What Makes Apples Crisp and Juicy?

Everyone loves crisp and juicy apples, and consumers often reject ones that are soft and mealy. Crisp, juicy apples are typically hard, too. Apples are hard because the cells that make up the flesh of these apples are close and well-cemented with a strong pectin network. Usually, too, the cells in firm apples are full of water. This water presses on cell walls, giving each cell rigidity and shape, much like water balloons. Biologists call this *turgor pressure*. When you bite into a firm, crisp apple, the pectin cement holds tight, so you bite harder until your teeth slash through cell walls. This releases the watery contents of the cells into your mouth, for a juicy sensation. The fast release of the cell contents also creates vibrations in the air that produce a crisp sound.

Cells in soft and mealy apples are weakly cemented because the pectin network has broken down. When you bite into a soft, mealy apple, the pectin cement between cells gives under your bite and the cells separate from each other without breaking. The mealy sensation is from a mouthful of dry, grainy cells, still holding their contents. The mealy apple might contain just as much moisture as a juicy one, but with the cells intact, you will not perceive it.

All apples soften and develop mealiness as they age, because enzymes naturally present in the fruit break down pectin during ripening. If the apple is not refrigerated, or if it is refrigerated under low humidity, however, it softens and develops mealiness even faster. That is why it is important to store apples refrigerated and under high humidity. This is especially true for certain apple varieties, like Red Delicious, that easily soften and turn mealy.

- *Aroma:* If the apple doesn't have the aroma of an apple, you'll end up with a sugar pie or a spice pie. Varieties that have a distinct, strong apple aroma include McIntosh, Empire, and Jonathan; apples with little aroma include Rome Beauty, Red Delicious, and Granny Smith. Some apples, including Golden Delicious, have a pear-like aroma.
- *Texture:* Crisp, firm rather than soft, mealy apples are generally preferred in pies. Examples of firm apples include Cortland, Granny Smith, Northern

Many fresh fruits—and vegetables—begin to brown within minutes of being cut. These same fruits and vegetables also brown when frozen and thawed. This fast browning happens at room temperature. Interestingly, heat can actually prevent it. Here's how.

The browning of fresh fruits and vegetables at room temperature is caused by an enzyme called phenolase, or polyphenoloxidase (PPO). Phenolase causes polyphenolic compounds in fruits and vegetables to combine, forming large molecules that absorb light across a broad spectrum of colors. This is what makes them appear brown.

All enzymes, including phenolase, are proteins that are inactivated by heat. The amount of heat needed to inactivate phenolase varies, but typically blanching (180°F/80°C or above) for 60 seconds or less is sufficient, as long as the piece size is small enough for the heat to penetrate throughout quickly.

Blanching is more typically used for vegetables than for fruits, which are too easily cooked by the heat. Instead, enzymatic browning in fresh fruits is usually delayed by lowering the pH below 3.5 by adding acid; excluding oxygen by soaking in liquid or coating with sugar or glaze; or by selecting a variety that browns slowly.

Fruits that brown through the action of phenolase include certain varieties of apples, bananas, cherries, peaches, and pears. Phenolase activity is sometimes desirable. The brown color and distinct flavors of coffee, tea, and cocoa are partly due to enzymatic browning.

Spy, and York Imperial. A soft apple is the McIntosh. However, all apples become soft and mealy over time, especially if stored for too long in warm, dry locations. Apples that are crisp fresh are not necessarily firm enough for baking. The crisp texture of properly stored Red Delicious apples, for example, make them good for fresh fruit applications but not necessarily so for baking.

- *Sourness:* Generally, a sour apple is preferred in baking over one with little natural acidity. Acidity can be added, however, by adding lemon juice, but lemon juice adds a lemony taste and may not be the flavor you are after. An apple that is high in acidity is the Granny Smith. Those that are low in acidity include Golden Delicious and Red Delicious.

- *Sweetness:* Sweetness can easily be adjusted in an apple pie by adjusting the amount of sugar added. Apples that are low in sugar include the Granny Smith and York Imperial. Golden Delicious and Red Delicious are sweet apples.

Overall, the best apple for apple pie is one that has a strong apple aroma, firm texture, and is more sour than sweet. To achieve this, some bakers and pastry chefs combine apple varieties. For example, using Granny Smiths and McIntosh apples together in an apple pie provides the aroma of the McIntosh and the firm texture and sourness of the Granny Smith.

Apples for Whole Baking Apples selected for baking whole or sautéing slices must hold their shape when heated. Rome Beauty apples are probably the best choice, because they hold their shape and do not explode or collapse when baked or sautéed. McIntosh apples, on the other hand, tend to break open and collapse when baked, literally bursting at the seams. As you might imagine, McIntosh apples are great for making applesauce.

Apples for Fresh Fruit Applications Apples selected for fresh applications should generally be more sweet than sour. Ideally, they will be firm and crisp, and more important, they should not brown quickly. Traditional choices for fresh presentations include Cortland and Golden Delicious. Newer varieties that work well include Cameo and Fuji.

If apples are old or have been stored improperly, they will brown more quickly than if freshly harvested. To further preserve whiteness, dip apples first in water enhanced with a small amount of lemon juice. The lemon juice slows the activity of enzymes that cause browning. Ascorbic acid (vitamin C) is sometimes used for this purpose, as well.

Sometimes an unattractive green ring forms around blueberries in baked goods. In extreme cases, the green discoloration runs throughout the crumb. The discoloration forms when the anthocyanin pigments coloring the blueberries are exposed to a high pH, above 6 or so. This occurs because anthocyanin pigments are very pH dependent, changing from red at a low pH to blue or purple at a medium pH, and to green at a high pH. In fact, anthocyanins are sometimes called "nature's pH meter," because the pH of a substance can be predicted by how it alters the color of the pigment.

Discoloration can occur with any fruit or other ingredient that contains a high level of anthocyanins. Besides blueberries, cranberries, cherries, and walnuts are among the most common ingredients involved in this reaction.

The most likely causes of a high pH in baked goods are as follows:

- Too much baking soda or other alkali
- Too little cream of tartar or other acid
- A decrease in the amount of an acidic fruit or fruit juice, or its substitution with a less acidic fruit; for example, substituting half the cranberries in cranberry nut bread with apples
- A change from fast-acting to slow-acting baking powder
- Excessive bleeding of fruit into batter or dough

Blueberries

Blueberries come as two main types: wild and cultivated. Wild blueberries, also known as *low-bush blueberries*, grow on ground-hugging vines in the rocky soil of Maine and the Atlantic provinces of Canada. Cultivated blueberries, also called *high-bush blueberries*, grow on shrubs in several regions throughout the United States and Canada. Blueberries, depending on the species, sometimes go by other names, including *bilberries*, *rabbiteyes*, and *huckleberries*.

Cultivated blueberries, being relatively large, tend to provide a mouthful of juicy flavor when bitten into. They are typically preferred for fresh fruit presentations and for pies and tarts. Wild blueberries are generally more expensive per pound and less available than cultivated blueberries, yet they are often used in muffins and other baked goods. Their smaller size means that there are more wild blueberries per pound (or kilogram). Add a pound of wild blueberries to batter and there will be more points of color and flavor in your product, so less fruit can be used. The smaller size also means that there will be better uniformity of fruit throughout the batter. That is, it is less likely that there will be bites of muffin with no fruit while other bites are loaded with fruit.

Smaller fruit typically is less fragile than larger fruit, so a third advantage of using wild blueberries is that they can better withstand the abuses of mixing and heating. Finally, consumer perception is important. Wild blueberries, being less available and more expensive, are perceived as better and as having more intense flavor. Because they are perceived as being worth more, the higher cost of wild blueberries can be passed on to the consumer.

Fruit Ripening

Ripening involves a series of changes that all fruits undergo as they age. Each type of fruit undergoes changes that are characteristic of that particular fruit. In general, however, fruits soften and become juicier, develop more color and flavor, and become sweeter and less sour as they ripen.

Some fruits can ripen after they are picked, or harvested. Table 16.1 is a partial list of fruits that are successfully ripened after harvest. While this list seems clear cut, in fact, not all fruits ripen equally well. For example, bananas ripen better after harvest than probably any other fruit. They improve in all attributes,

More on the Ripening Process

When fruits ripen, enzymes in the fruit break down large molecules to smaller ones. For example, starches break down to sugars, sweetening the fruit. Acids break down, so the fruit becomes less sour. Proteins and fats break down to molecules that have a pleasing, fruity aroma. Pectin, which holds fruits together, breaks down, making fruit softer and juicier.

TABLE 16.1 FRUITS THAT RIPEN AFTER HARVEST

Apples
Apricots
Bananas
Cactus (prickly) pear
Cantaloupe
Carambola (star fruit)
Cherimoya
Guava
Honeydew melons
Kiwifruit
Mangoes
Nectarines
Papayas
Passion fruit
Peaches
Pears
Persimmons
Plums

including color, flavor, sweetness, and texture. Cantaloupes and papayas, on the other hand, soften and develop color, but they will not sweeten or improve in flavor once they are harvested.

The ability of any fruit to ripen to its fullest depends on two factors. First, fruit must be fully mature. That is, it must have reached its full size before harvest, even though it might still be hard and green. Second, the fruit must have been stored properly before ripening.

TABLE 16.2 FRUITS THAT DO NOT RIPEN AFTER HARVEST

Berry fruits
Cherries
Citrus fruits
Figs
Grapes
Pineapples
Watermelons

Many fruits, for example, will not ripen if first exposed to cold temperatures. Peaches, for example, do not ripen properly if they are stored below 46°F (8°C) for even a few hours prior to ripening. Other fruits that do not ripen properly, once refrigerated, include bananas, mangoes, and papayas. Some fruits will not ripen at all after they are harvested, even if stored properly. Table 16.2 is a partial list of fruits that cannot be successfully ripened after they are harvested. Notice that none of the berry fruits, including blackberries, blueberries, raspberries, and strawberries ripen once harvested. The same is true of citrus fruits, including lemons, limes, oranges, and tangerines. When purchasing these fruits, accept only those that are already fully ripe.

> **HELPFUL HINT**
>
> *Many fruits, when they ripen, develop color sooner than they develop flavor. For example, blueberries become dark blue days before they sweeten and become flavorful. Since blueberries are among the fruits that do not ripen after harvest, be sure to taste blueberries and other fruits before accepting a shipment or using in products.*

Do Plants Really Breathe?

Fresh, raw fruit is still living and breathing—respiring—after it is harvested. As with human respiration, plant respiration involves taking in oxygen from the air, using it to continue life-sustaining processes, and giving off carbon dioxide. In the process, starches, sugars, and other molecules are broken down and used. As with humans, if respiration stops in plants, cells stop functioning and the plant dies.

While plants do respire, unlike humans, they also undergo photosynthesis. Photosynthesis is the opposite of respiration. That is, instead of taking in oxygen and giving off carbon dioxide, during photosynthesis plants take in carbon dioxide and give off oxygen. In the process, the plant forms sugar from carbon dioxide, using water from the soil and energy from sunlight. While mammals eat to take in sugars, plants undergo photosynthesis to create them.

Does One Bad Apple Spoil the Whole Bunch?

Have you ever heard the expression that one bad apple spoils the whole bunch? It's true. Bruised and rotting fruit from Table 16.1, including apples, give off very large amounts of ethylene gas, which speeds up respiration in all fruits. If fruit is already ripe, exposure to ethylene gas causes it to rot.

Storage and Handling

Fresh Fruits

Fresh fruit can be expensive, so it is important that it be selected, stored, and handled properly. When a shipment of fruit arrives, for example, be sure to inspect it for quality and to always taste a sample before accepting the shipment. Remember that fruit is a natural agricultural product and quality can vary from one shipment to the next.

Fresh fruit that is consumed uncooked should be handled especially carefully for sanitation reasons. Fresh fruit should always be washed before use to remove dirt and microorganisms. Strawberries, in particular, grow close to the ground and pick up mold spores, while raspberries conceal insects in their caps. While fruit should be washed before use, it should *not* be washed before storage. Water left on the fruit encourages mold growth, and washed fruit absorbs water into its cells. When this happens, the fruit swells and softens in an unappealing manner.

Melons, especially cantaloupe, must be washed before cutting. Melons grow on the ground, and cantaloupe, with its rough surface, tends to harbor microorganisms. When a knife passes through the melon, microorganisms on the melon's surface can be transferred to the fruit by the knife blade.

Several important tips for storing fresh fruit are listed below. While busy bakeshops with space constraints may not be able to follow all these tips, they should be followed whenever possible.

- Store fresh fruits under high humidity, so they don't shrivel and dry. Often this means keeping them in their original packaging.
- Do not store fresh fruit in closed plastic bags or plastic wrap for extended periods, unless it is designed specifically for that use. Plastic cuts off oxygen, preventing plants, including fruits, from breathing (respiring). If the fruit comes in plastic, however, it can be stored in this original packaging. Plastic packaging used for shipping and distributing fresh fruits and vegetables is not the same as plastic bags and plastic wrap used in the bakeshop.
- Store ripe fruits at low temperatures so they will respire more slowly and last longer. For most fruits, this means refrigerating them as close to 32°F (0°C) as possible. Avoid refrigerating unripened fruits, however. Recall that many fruits, such as peaches, mangoes, and papayas, will not ripen properly if exposed to cold temperatures.

While lower storage temperatures slow respiration, not all fruits, even when ripe, should be refrigerated. Cold temperatures cause *chilling injury* to certain fruits, and this can damage their color, flavor, and texture. However, damage from chilling injury is often not evident until after the fruit is returned to warmer temperatures. Chilling injury is most likely to occur in fruits grown in tropical or semitropical regions, such as bananas, most citrus, mangoes, melons, papayas, and pineapples. Store these fruits at temperatures slightly above refrigeration, generally from 50°–60°F (10°–16°C).

Of course, it is not always possible to find a spot in the bakeshop that is warmer than the refrigerator yet colder than room temperature. If it is winter and there is a cool spot in the bakeshop, store tropical fruits there. If it is summer and it is extremely hot, refrigerate the fruit, but use it as quickly as possible.

- Store fruits from Table 16.2 away from ripe fruits listed in Table 16.1, which naturally give off a gas called ethylene. *Ethylene gas* acts as a hormone, signaling fruits to speed up respiration and to ripen. Since fruits from Table 16.2 cannot ripen any further, if these fruits are exposed to ethylene gas, they will rot. That is why, for example, lemons should not be stored near ripe apples.

- Before storing fruit, remove and discard any spoiled or rotten fruit, which gives off ethylene.

- To ripen fruit as fast as possible, store it at warm temperatures, and expose it to ethylene gas and oxygen. Closed paper bags and cardboard cartons allow oxygen in and out but trap ethylene. This means that paper bags and cardboard cartons are ideal for holding fruit for ripening. Place the paper bags or cardboard cartons in a warm spot and add a ripe apple or banana, for example, to give off ethylene.

Dried Fruits

Dried fruits are relatively safe from microbial damage, but it is still best to store dried fruits below 45°F (7°C). This prevents flavor changes and flavor loss, and it also prevents insect and rodent infestation. Since refrigeration space is often at a premium in the bakeshop, if dried fruits are held for one month or less, it is acceptable to store them in a cool spot in the bakeshop. Be sure they are well covered, to prevent moisture loss and infestation.

The glucose in dried fruit often crystallizes during extended refrigerator storage. This is sometimes called *sugaring*, and when it happens, the dried fruit becomes dry, hard, and gritty. These fruits should not be discarded; proper conditioning revives the flavor and texture of dried fruit that has sugared.

Conditioning Raisins and Other Dried Fruits Conditioning is a process of soaking raisins and other dried fruits in water or another liquid before use. Conditioning plumps the fruit so it is not dry, hard, and flavorless in the final product. Conditioning also prevents dried fruit from absorbing moisture from batters and doughs. If too much moisture is pulled from batters and doughs, the product bakes up dry.

The raisin industry recommends that raisins not be soaked in hot or boiling water, because this easily overconditions them. Overconditioned dried fruits lose valuable flavor and sweetness to the soaking solution. They tend to tear during mixing and to stain batters and doughs.

Two methods are recommended for conditioning raisins and other dried fruits. Both require planning ahead by several hours. The first method involves spraying or submerging the dried fruit with slightly warm water (80°F; 27°C), draining immediately, and covering the fruit until surface water is absorbed. This takes about 4 hours. The second method involves adding 1–2 ounces of 80°F (27°C) water per pound of dried fruit (or 80–120 grams per kilogram), covering, and soaking for about 4 hours, or until all water is absorbed. Stir or turn occasionally for even conditioning. Other liquids, such as rum or fruit juice, can be used in place of water.

Cut dried fruits such as diced dates and sweetened dried cranberries are probably best not conditioned. The cut surfaces readily pick up moisture, so there is little risk that they will stay hard in a batter or dough. The risk instead is that they will be easily overconditioned, resulting in fruits that bleed color and solids into the batter and that tear easily.

> **HELPFUL HINT**
>
> *Even when properly conditioned, raisins and other dried fruits can tear during mixing. To minimize tearing, add dried fruits during the last minute or two of mixing, and set the mixer on low speed.*

Questions for Review

1 What are the advantages of fresh fruit over frozen or canned? What are the disadvantages?

2 What is meant by straight-pack fruit? What is meant by IQF fruit? What is a 4 + 1 pack?

3 What is the main advantage of IQF fruit over straight-pack, sugar-packed, or syrup-packed fruit?

4 How does the amount of sugar in poaching liquid affect the color, flavor, and texture of poached fruit?

5 What is the difference between a heavy pack and a heavy syrup pack in canned fruit?

6 Why might a canned fruit product such as canned apple filling contain calcium chloride?

7 Name some dried fruits that are most likely to contain sulfur dioxide (or another form of sulfur). Why is it added?

8 How are golden raisins similar to regular raisins? How are they different?

9 Why might sweetened dried blueberries be a better choice in cookie dough while fresh, IQF frozen, or canned whole blueberries are better for muffins?

10 What is CA storage? How might it affect the quality of apples?

11 A shipment of underripe fresh mangoes arrives that is not needed just yet. Which of the following is better, and why: Ripen the fruit and then refrigerate it until needed, or refrigerate first, then ripen?

12 Name four fruits that are best stored above 40°F (4°C); name four that are best stored below 40°F (4°C).

13 Where is ethylene gas found and how does it affect fruit?

14 Why should ripe bananas not be stored next to grapes?

15 A bin of ripe bananas contains one that is badly bruised. Why should the bruised banana be removed from the bin?

16 A carton of unripe pears that will be needed in just a few days arrives. How should the pears be stored so that they will ripen quickly?

17 Why is it recommended that dried fruits be refrigerated for the long term?

18 Raisins that were refrigerated for one month are dry, hard, and gritty. What has happened? Should the raisins be discarded?

19 What does it mean to condition raisins? Describe two methods recommended for conditioning raisins.

20 What might happen if raisins are underconditioned?

21 What might happen if raisins are overconditioned?

Questions for Discussion

1 List and explain five reasons why fresh fruit quality can vary.

2 You are preparing strawberry ice cream using frozen strawberries. What might be the advantages of using IQF strawberries over 4 + 1 frozen ones? What might be the advantages of using 4 + 1 strawberries over IQF?

3 Using the comparison of wild and cultivated blueberries as a guide, explain some advantages of Zante currants over raisins.

4 Why is it faster to prepare a cooked fruit coulis (sweetened fruit puree) by cooking the fruit in a small amount of water and withholding sugar until after the fruit disintegrates?

Exercises and Experiments

❶ Exercise: Strawberries and Sugar

A formula calls for 8 pounds (3.6 kilograms) of strawberries and 4 pounds (1.8 kilograms) of sugar. How much of a 4 + 1 pack and how much sugar should be used instead? Show your work.

_____

_____

_____

❷ Experiment: How Different Apples Compare in Quality When Consumed Fresh

Objectives

Demonstrate how apple variety and treatment of apples affects
- The appearance, flavor, and texture of fresh apples
- The tendency of sliced fresh apples to brown
- The overall acceptability of different apple varieties in fresh fruit applications

Products Prepared

Apple slices from
- Granny Smith apples, untreated (control product)
- Red Delicious, untreated
- Golden Delicious, untreated
- McIntosh (or other fast-browning apple), untreated
- McIntosh, dipped in acidulated water for 30 seconds
- McIntosh, soaked in acidulated water for 15 minutes
- Other apple varieties, if desired (Braeburn, Cortland, Fuji, Gala, Honeycrisp, Jonagold, Macoun, Northern Spy, Rome, etc.)
- Other treatments, if desired (different amounts of lemon juice in water, different soak times, two crushed 200 mg vitamin C tablets dissolved in 14 fl. oz./400 ml water [0.1 percent ascorbic acid], commercial preps such as NatureSeal, etc.)

Materials and Equipment

- Apples, three or more for each variety and treatment
- Acidulated water: 1 tablespoon (15 milliliters) lemon juice into 16 fluid ounces (500 milliliters) water
- Parchment paper

Procedure

1   For the effects of treatments on the quality of fresh apple slices:

- Pare and slice one McIntosh apple into six or eight slices of equal size. Discard any bruised or otherwise damaged slices.
- Immediately place slices into acidulated water and soak for 15 minutes (longer, if time permits).
- After 15 minutes, remove slices from acidulated water and lay in a row on parchment paper. Label row "15-minute soak."
- Immediately slice another McIntosh apple and dip into acidulated water. Remove after 30 seconds and lay slices in a second row on parchment paper; label row as "dip."
- Immediately slice a third McIntosh apple and lay slices in a third row on parchment paper. Label row "untreated."
- Set aside at room temperature for 30 minutes or more.

2   For different apple varieties:

- Pare and slice two or more apples of each variety into six or eight slices of equal size. Discard any bruised or otherwise damaged slices.
- Lay slices from one apple of each variety in a row onto parchment paper. Label each row with the name of the apple variety and record the time that samples were laid out.

Results

1   After 30 minutes or more, evaluate McIntosh apple slices and record results in Results Table 1, which follows. Be sure to compare each in turn with the untreated McIntosh apple and evaluate the following:

- Amount of browning, from very little browning to extensive browning, on a scale of 1 to 5.
- Flavor (apple aroma, sweetness, sourness, astringency, etc.)
- Texture (hard/soft, crispy/mealy, juicy/dry)
- Overall acceptability, from highly unacceptable to highly acceptable, on a scale of 1 to 5
- Any additional comments, as necessary

2   Time permitting, repeat appearance evaluation after an additional period of time and record results in Additional Comments column of Results Table 1.

RESULTS TABLE 1 SENSORY CHARACTERISTICS OF MCINTOSH APPLES
TREATED TO PREVENT BROWNING

APPLE TREATMENT	AMOUNT OF BROWNING	FLAVOR	TEXTURE	OVERALL ACCEPTABILITY	ADDITIONAL COMMENTS
Untreated					
Dipped in acidulated water					
Soaked in acidulated water					

3   Evaluate whole and freshly cut slices of each apple variety. Record evaluations in Results
Table 2. Be sure to compare each apple in turn to the control product (Granny Smith,
untreated) and consider the following:
  • Appearance of whole apple (skin color, shape of whole apple); also note appearance of
    blossom end (opposite the stem) of apples.
  • Appearance of freshly cut flesh (color, moistness/dryness)
  • Flavor (apple aroma, sweetness, sourness, etc.)
  • Texture (hard/soft, crispy, mealy, juicy/dry)
  • Overall acceptability for fresh fruit consumption, from highly unacceptable to highly
    acceptable, on a scale of 1 to 5
  • Add any additional comments, as necessary.

4   After 30 minutes or more, evaluate appearance of cut apple slices. Be sure to compare each
apple in turn to the control product and focus on the extent of browning of each apple,
from very little browning to extensive browning, on a scale of 1 to 5.

RESULTS TABLE 2 SENSORY CHARACTERISTICS OF DIFFERENT VARIETIES OF FRESH APPLE SLICES

APPLE VARIETY	APPEARANCE OF WHOLE APPLE: SHAPE AND COLOR	APPEARANCE OF FLESH, FRESHLY CUT	FLAVOR	TEXTURE	AMOUNT OF BROWNING AFTER 30 MINUTES	OVERALL ACCEPTABILITY	ADDITIONAL COMMENTS
Granny Smith (control product)							
Red Delicious							
Golden Delicious							
McIntosh							

Sources of Error

List any sources of error that might make it difficult to draw the proper conclusions from your experiment. In particular, consider any variability that can occur from one apple of the same variety to another; also, note the seasonality of each apple variety and whether it is likely fresh-harvested or CA-stored.

_____

_____

_____

State what you could do differently next time to minimize or eliminate each source of error.

_____

_____

_____

Conclusions

Select one from the choices in **bold** or fill in the blanks.

1   Apples brown when the enzyme called _____ is active. Treating apples with acid should delay browning because acids **lower pH/raise pH** to where the enzyme is less active. The McIntosh apples used in this experiment browned **a lot/a little/not at all** when left untreated and therefore probably have **a lot of/very little/no** enzyme activity. When dipped in acidulated water, the apples browned **more than/less than/about the same as** untreated apples. The extended soak worked **better than/worse than/the same as** the acidulated water dip in preventing browning of these apples.

2 Did either treatment (dip or soak in acidulated water) affect flavor or texture of McIntosh apples? If so, describe:

_____
_____
_____.

3 Based on the results of this experiment, when apples tend to brown, it is better to **dip, then set them aside/soak them until needed** because:

_____
_____
_____.

Other fruits that might benefit from being treated with acidulated water include:

_____
_____
_____.

4 Differences in skin color among the apples varieties were **small/moderate/large**. Differences included the following:

_____
_____
_____.

5 Differences in the shape of whole apples were **small/moderate/large**. For example, the apple variety that was tall and angular, with a clear star-shaped blossom end was the **Granny Smith/Red Delicious/Golden Delicious/McIntosh**. Other differences in shape included the following:

_____
_____
_____.

6 Differences in texture among the apple varieties were **small/moderate/large**. The firmest and crispest of the apple varieties was **Granny Smith/Red Delicious/Golden Delicious/ McIntosh.** The softest, driest, mealiest apple was the _____

_____
_____
_____.

7 Differences in aroma among the apple varieties were **small/moderate/large**. In your opinion, which apple variety had the best apple aroma? _____. Survey your class to determine, for each apple variety, the number of students who rated each as having the best apple aroma. How well did members of your class agree on this?

_____
_____
_____.

8 Differences in sweetness among the apple varieties were **small/moderate/large**. From sweetest to least sweet, the apple varieties can be ranked as follows:

_____

_____

_____.

9 Differences in sourness among the apple varieties were **small/moderate/large**. From most sour to least sour, the apple varieties can be ranked as follows:

_____

_____

_____.

10 Often, but not always, the sweetest apples are the least sour, and vice versa. This **was/was not** true for the apples evaluated in this experiment. How do you explain these results?

_____

_____

_____.

Which apple, in your opinion, had the most pleasant sweet/sour balance; that is, which was neither too sweet nor too sour for your taste?_____.

11 Several factors affect how likely fruits will brown. For example, apples that are very sour will probably brown **less/more** than other apples, even when they all contain the same amount of enzyme. Which apple variety browned the fastest?_____
Which apple browned the slowest? _____ Did the sourness of the apple appear to be a factor in the amount of browning? **Yes/No** What other differences in apples do you think could explain differences in how quickly they brown?

_____

_____

_____.

12 Other comments I would like to add about differences in the apples or about the experiment :

_____

_____

_____.

13 Research the seasonality of each apple variety that you used in this experiment (www. bestapples.com; www.michiganapples.com; www.nyapplecountry.com). How might the results of this experiment be affected by the time of year (spring, summer, winter, fall) that this evaluation was completed?

_____

_____

_____

❸ Experiment: How Different Apples Compare When Baked in an Apple Crisp

Objectives

Demonstrate how apple variety affects

- The appearance of apple crisp
- The firmness and juiciness of the apples in the crisp
- The overall flavor of the apple crisp
- The overall acceptability of the apple crisp

Products Prepared

Apple crisp made with

- Granny smith apples (control product)
- Red Delicious apples
- Golden Delicious apples
- McIntosh apples
- Other apple varieties, if desired (Braeburn, Cortland, Gala, Jonagold, Northern Spy, Pippin, Rome, York Imperial, etc.)

Materials and Equipment

- Scale
- Mixer with 5-quart mixing bowl
- Flat beater attachment
- Parchment paper (optional)
- Half sheet pans
- Streusel Topping (see Formula), enough to make one half sheet pan for each apple variety
- Apple Crisp (see Formula), enough to make one half sheet pan for each apple variety
- Oven thermometer

Formula

Streusel Topping

Yield: *Topping for 5 apple crisps*

INGREDIENT	POUNDS	OUNCES	GRAMS	BAKER'S PERCENTAGE
Flour, pastry	1	5	600	100
Sugar, light brown	1		450	75
Salt (1 tsp./5ml)		0.2	6	1
Butter, unsalted		13	375	62
Total	3	2.2	1,431	238

Method of Preparation

1 Combine flour, brown sugar, and salt on low speed of mixer using flat beater. If necessary, hold parchment paper over bowl opening during mixing, to prevent loss of streusel from bowl.

2 Cut butter into chunks and add to flour mixture. Stir on low speed for 2 minutes or until well-blended and crumbly.

3 Set aside until ready to use.

Formula

Apple Crisp

Yield: *One half sheet pan*

INGREDIENT	POUNDS	OUNCES	GRAMS	BAKER'S PERCENTAGE
Apples, peeled and cored	1	8	680	100
Sugar, regular granulated		1.25	40	6
Streusel Topping (above)		10	280	42
Total	**2**	**2–3**	**960–1,000**	**144–148**

Method of Preparation

1 Preheat oven to 400°F (200°C).

2 Weigh out apples and slice each into equal-size pieces (about 16 slices for large apples).

3 Add granulated sugar, if used, to apple slices and gently combine.

4 Lay apple slices into half sheet pan in a single layer.

5 Top with an even layer of streusel topping.

Procedure

1 Prepare apple crisp using the formula above, or using any basic apple crisp formula. Prepare one batch of apple crisp for each apple variety.

2 Use an oven thermometer placed in center of oven for an initial oven temperature. Record results here: _____.

3 When oven is properly preheated, place filled pans in oven and set timer for 14–18 minutes.

4 Bake until apples in control product (made with Granny Smith apples) have softened slightly and topping is lightly brown. Remove *all* apple crisps from oven after same length of time. If necessary, however, adjust bake times for oven variances. Record bake times in Results Table 1, which follows.

5 Check final oven temperature. Record results here: _____.

6 Cool slightly or to room temperature.

Results

When apple crisps have cooled, evaluate their sensory characteristics and record evaluations in Results Table 1. Be sure to compare each in turn to the control product and consider the following:

- Appearance overall (light/dark, wet/dry, firm/crumbly)
- Texture of apples (firm/soft, crisp, mealy, juicy)
- Flavor (sweetness, sourness, apple aroma, brown sugar, butter, etc.)
- Overall acceptability, from highly unacceptable to highly acceptable, on a scale of 1 to 5
- Add any additional comments, as necessary

RESULTS TABLE 1 SENSORY CHARACTERISTICS OF APPLE CRISP MADE WITH DIFFERENT APPLE VARIETIES

APPLE VARIETY	BAKE TIME, MINUTES	APPEARANCE OVERALL	APPLE TEXTURE	FLAVOR	OVERALL ACCEPTABILITY	ADDITIONAL COMMENTS
Granny Smith (control product)						
Red Delicious						
Golden Delicious						
McIntosh						

Sources of Error

List any sources of error that might make it difficult to draw the proper conclusions from your experiment. In particular, consider if apples were evenly sliced; how evenly apples and streusel were spread in pan; and any problems with ovens.

_____

_____

_____

State what you could do differently next time to minimize or eliminate each source of error.

_____

_____

_____

Conclusions

Select one from the choices in **bold** or fill in the blanks.

1   Rank the different apple varieties used in the apple crisps from least firm to most firm.

_____

_____

_____

The differences in firmness were **small/moderate/large**.

2   Rank the different apple varieties used in the apple crisps from least sweet to sweetest.

_____

_____

_____

The differences in sweetness were **small/moderate/large**.

3   Based on this experiment, the apple crisp with the best flavor was made with **Granny Smiths/Red Delicious/Golden Delicious/McIntosh/other apple variety**. Explain why this apple crisp had the best flavor.

_____

_____

_____

4   Based on this experiment, the apple variety _most_ acceptable overall for use in an apple crisp was made with **Granny Smiths/Red Delicious/Golden Delicious/McIntosh/other apple variety**. Explain why this apple crisp was most acceptable.

_____

_____

_____

In what other baked goods do you think this apple variety would also be good?

_____

_____

_____

5   Based on this experiment, the apple variety *least* acceptable overall for use in an apple crisp was made with **Granny Smiths/Red Delicious/Golden Delicious/McIntosh/other apple variety**. Explain why this apple crisp was least acceptable.

_____

_____

_____

How might the formula be adjusted (more or less sugar, add lemon juice and/or spice, shorter bake time, etc.) to make the crisp more acceptable with these apples?

_____

_____

_____

6   Why might the results of this experiment be different from one year to the next, or even from one season or one shipment to the next?

_____

_____

_____

7   Other comments I would like to add about differences in the apples used in the apple crisps, or about the experiment:

_____

_____

_____

Natural and Artificial Flavorings

Chapter Objectives

1. Explain what is meant by a flavor profile.

2. Define different types of natural and artificial flavorings used in bakeshops.

3. Describe the characteristics and uses of the different natural and artificial flavorings used in bakeshops.

4. Describe how to best store and handle flavorings.

5. Provide methods for improving the flavor of food products.

Introduction

When asked why a particular food is liked, most people comment on its flavor, or taste. It is not that appearance and texture are unimportant. It is just that flavor is often most important of all. Flavor should likewise be uppermost on the chef's mind when preparing food. A chef should taste every batch of product made each and every day. This is one way to develop a sense of taste. More important, it is a good way to catch mistakes before they reach the customer.

Developing a sense of taste is a skill that is as important as piping chocolate or folding gelatin into whipped cream. As with any skill, it is developed through practice and experience. This idea was first introduced in Chapter 4. Because of the importance of flavor to food, it is worthwhile exploring this in more detail.

To best develop a sense of taste, practice describing flavors in a broad range of ingredients and products. Retreat to a quiet spot, smell and taste the ingredients and products, and record your comments. Compare one ingredient directly with another, one product directly with another. For example, compare the taste of molasses with dark corn syrup; compare toasted with untoasted hazelnuts; compare vanilla custard sauce made using vanilla extract with one made using vanilla bean. You will learn much more by these close comparisons than by tasting any number of items individually. If possible, discuss your evaluations with others. Try to describe the flavor of each product as completely as possible. Recall from Chapter 4 that smell and memory are connected. Take advantage of this connection to help in identifying and remembering smells. That is, if you cannot identify a smell in words, record what it reminds you of or where else you remember experiencing it.

For example, maybe you are not sure of the name of a spice, but its smell reminds you of your grandmother. Record that information, then think of why you make that memory connection. Maybe your grandmother used that particular spice in cookies she baked for you when you were young. Or maybe she had potpourri that contained that spice. Once you connect that memory with the smell and with the name of the spice, it will be easier to identify and name it in the future.

To develop a sense of taste, it helps to understand flavor profiles and food flavorings.

A Brief Review of Flavor

Recall from Chapter 4 that flavor consists of three main parts: basic tastes, trigeminal effects, and smell. Basic tastes include sweet, salty, sour, bitter, and umami sensations perceived throughout the mouth. *Trigeminal effects*, or *chemical feeling factors*, include the pungency of ginger, the burn of cinnamon, the cooling of mint, and the sting of alcohol. Smell, also called *aroma*, is often considered the most important of the three components of flavor. It is certainly the most complex. Butter aroma, for instance, is actually composed of hundreds of different chemical compounds.

Flavor Profiles

A *flavor profile* is a description of a product's flavor from when it is first smelled until after it is swallowed. For example, the flavor profile of a particular milk chocolate might start with the aromas of vanilla and roasted cocoa, continue with a sweet taste and a milky caramelized flavor, and end with lingering bitterness. The term *flavor profile* is also used to describe the distinctive flavor combinations that characterize the food of a particular culture. For example, the flavor profile of American apple pie generally includes cinnamon and lard, or the blander shortening, but not butter. In contrast, many European apple tarts and desserts, such as apple charlotte, feature butter as a predominant flavor, often supplemented with lemon, apricot, or vanilla.

Whatever the culture, a flavor is most satisfying when it contains a full flavor profile. A full flavor profile has top notes, middle notes, background or base notes, and an aftertaste or finish. Top notes are the smells that provide instant impact, the ones that first fill the bakeshop when pastries bake. Because they provide the first impression of a product's flavor, when a product is described as low in flavor, it is often low in top notes. Volatile flavors are the main sources of top notes in foods. *Volatile flavors* are flavors that evaporate easily, usually because they consist of molecules that are small and light. The smells of freshly cut lemons and ripe strawberries and peaches are classified as top notes. Because these are highly volatile, they are perceived almost immediately, but they are also easily lost once the fruit is cut and when it is cooked.

Middle notes follow top notes in a flavor profile. They come from flavor molecules that evaporate more slowly, usually because they are larger and heavier than top notes. Middle notes provide a satisfying staying power to flavor. Many caramelized, cooked fruit, egg, cream, and coconut flavors are classified as middle notes. Roasted nuts, cocoa and chocolate, and coffee also are rich in middle notes, because of Maillard browning, which occurs during the roasting process. Cultured, fermented, and aged food products such as buttermilk,

HELPFUL HINT

Because most flavor molecules dissolve in fats and are slowly released to our sensory receptors when we eat, low-fat foods often lack staying power. Adding more ingredients that are rich in middle and base notes will help improve the flavor of these products.

aged cheeses, soy sauce can also provide valuable middle notes in some products.

Background or *base notes* consist mostly of the largest, heaviest molecules that are nonvolatile. Non-volatile flavors evaporate slowly or not at all. Basic tastes and trigeminal effects are part of a flavor's background notes. If a product seems thin or weak and seems to need "something," it probably lacks middle and background notes.

Aftertaste (or *finish*) is the final flavor that remains in the mouth after food is swallowed. It is a final chance for food to leave a lasting positive impression. Again, basic tastes, especially bitterness, and trigeminal effects, often from cloves, ginger, and other spices, are important to aftertaste.

Types of Flavorings

Most, if not all, ingredients added to foods provide flavor. By *flavorings*, however, we are referring to ingredients added to foods primarily for their flavor, especially their aroma. This eliminates honey, almonds, and cocoa from being classified as flavorings, because they are equally important for the appearance, texture, and nutrition that they contribute to foods. Sugar and salt also do not fall into this category, because they provide basic tastes rather than aroma (and alter foods in many other ways).

While food flavorings contribute to a total flavor profile, they are especially good at providing aroma top notes and often trigeminal effects. Flavorings used by bakers and pastry chefs can be categorized as *herbs and spices* and as *processed flavorings*.

Herbs and Spices

Most, but not all, spices come from hot, tropical climates. The American Spice Trade Association defines a spice as any dried plant product used primarily for seasoning. Spices come from the bark of a tree (cinnamon), dried fruit (allspice and star anise), seeds (cardamom,

nutmeg, anise, and sesame), flower buds (clove, lavender, and rose), roots (ginger), and green leaves, or herbs (mint, oregano, parsley) (Figure 17.1). Notice that this definition includes herbs as a type of spice. While not commonly thought of as spices, citrus peel, coffee beans, and vanilla beans also fall into this definition.

Figure 17.1 Spices come from **(clockwise from top left)** roots (ginger), the bark of a tree (cinnamon), green leaves (mint), flower buds (clove), dried fruit (allspice), and seeds (cardamom)

High-quality cinnamon is high in cinnamon oil, but this might not be what you need. For example, when cinnamon is sprinkled generously on pastries as a garnish, a so-called high-quality cinnamon such as Vietnamese cinnamon might be too intense. Instead, the mildest, least expensive cinnamon is likely the ideal choice.

The Making of Vanilla Beans

Vanilla beans are the seed pods of a particular orchid. They are classified primarily by region of origin. For example, vanilla beans can be Mexican, Tahitian, Indonesian (Java), or from Madagascar. Madagascar vanilla is often called *bourbon vanilla* because cultivation of vanilla beans by the French first started on nearby Bourbon (Reunion) Island.

Cultivation of vanilla beans takes about a year of intense labor. Plants are hand-pollinated to produce flowers, which bloom for just a few hours before forming pods. The pods, or beans, remain on the vine for up to nine months to ripen. At this point, they are mostly green in color and still flavorless. The pods are hand-picked by workers who, through experience, identify the ripe (but still flavorless) vanilla pods that will develop top-quality flavor. Once harvested, vanilla beans are cured to develop their characteristic aroma and chocolate brown color.

The curing process varies with region. In all cases, though, it starts with heating the pods to stop the ripening process. Some producers dip the beans in boiling water; others lay them in the sun to bake or on mats over an open fire. The beans are next alternately exposed to heat by day, then covered by night, to sweat. This process is repeated for several weeks before the beans are slowly dried, then covered and aged. If properly cultivated and cured, vanilla beans can develop up to 2 percent natural vanillin. Vanillin is the main flavor molecule in vanilla.

Each type of vanilla has its own characteristic flavor because the climate and local curing practices are different. The most popular vanilla in the United States is bourbon (Madagascar) vanilla. It has a deep, rich flavor, reminiscent of wood and rum. Tahitian vanilla is distinctly different in flavor because it is from a different orchid plant. It has a sweeter, more floral aroma with hints of cherry. Very little (less than 1 percent) of all vanilla imported into the United States is Tahitian. The bulk of Tahitian vanilla is imported into Europe.

All spices contain high amounts of volatile oils. *Volatile oils* (also called *essential oils*) are oils that evaporate easily and provide strong, pleasing top notes. This makes them different from cooking oils.

The quality of a spice is related to the amount of volatile oil it contains. For example, Vietnamese (Saigon) cinnamon is considered the highest-quality cinnamon because it is very high in cinnamon oil. Often it contains twice the amount of volatile oil as Indonesian cinnamon. Its price is often twice as high, too.

Besides top notes from volatile oils, spices provide trigeminal effects. Cinnamon, allspice, cloves, ginger, anise, and many other spices provide valuable pungency to foods.

Spices are desirable because they are the real thing, but they do have certain disadvantages. Because they are agricultural products, they can vary greatly in quality, strength, and price, and insect infestation can occur. A few of the many factors that affect quality include plant variety, country of origin, method of harvesting and handling, annual climatic conditions, manufacturer's processing, and the age and storage conditions of the flavoring.

To minimize problems, purchase spices from a reputable dealer and treat them as the raw agricultural products that they are. Or instead consider using a processed flavoring.

Processed Flavorings

Processed flavorings include extracts, liqueurs, compounds, oils, emulsions, and powders. Other processed flavorings are available but are not common in bakeshops. Processed flavorings can be natural or artificial.

Processed flavorings have several advantages over spices. They are generally more consistent in flavor

Make Your Own Vanilla Extract

If you like the flavor of certain vanilla beans but want the convenience of an extract, consider making your own vanilla extract. Slice vanilla beans lengthwise, scrape them with a knife, and chop them into small pieces. Place the scrapings and finely chopped beans in a tightly closed jar with 1 fluid ounce (30 milliliters) of 80 proof vodka for each whole bean (about 0.1 ounce or 3 grams). Shake occasionally. After two or more weeks, you will have the equivalent of one-fold vanilla extract.

If your extract is not as intense as purchased vanilla extract, realize that commercial operations have the means of efficiently extracting the full flavor from the bean. To make your extract more flavorful, double the number of vanilla beans for each fluid ounce (30 milliliters) of vodka, for a two-fold extract.

---

quality and strength. There is little or no concern over insect infestation, and they can be faster and easier to use than spices. For example, it is easier to measure an ounce of lemon extract or dried lemon peel than it is to zest a lemon.

The one main disadvantage of processed flavorings sometimes cancels out all these advantages. That is, the flavor of certain processed flavorings—even natural ones—can be less true, rich, or full than the original spice. For example, lemon extract, even if natural, rarely has the same true flavor as lemon zest, and almond extract does not taste much like almonds.

Extracts   The most common processed flavorings in the bakeshop are extracts. All extracts contain alcohol. Alcohol dilutes and dissolves the flavor ingredients and preserves them by preventing microbial growth. Common flavors sold as extracts include vanilla, peppermint, orange, lemon, ginger, anise, and almond. Extracts can be natural or artificial, depending on whether the added flavor is natural or artificial. Because vanilla is, by far, the most popular flavor used in baked goods in North America, this section focuses on vanilla beans and vanilla extract, which is also the most complex of extracts.

Most extracts are made by dissolving flavoring agents in alcohol. For example, lemon extract consists of a certain amount of lemon oil added to an alcohol solution. With other extracts, however, alcohol solutions are used for extracting (removing) flavor from the plant product. Alcohol is used because it is better than water at dissolving and extracting many flavor molecules.

Pure vanilla extract, for example, is made commercially by infusing an alcohol solution with vanilla bean. The diluted alcohol gently percolates through mashed vanilla beans, often for several weeks, before aging. In the United States, a minimum of 13.35 ounces of vanilla bean is required to make one gallon (128 fluid ounces) of extract; in Canada, the minimum is 10 grams of vanilla bean for 100 milliliters of vanilla extract. This is equivalent to about one vanilla bean for each fluid ounce (2 tablespoons or 30 milliliters) of extract. Vanilla extract must also contain a minimum amount of alcohol (35 percent) and vanillin extracted from the bean. *Vanillin* is an important flavor chemical naturally present in pure vanilla. While it is only one of many flavor chemicals present, it is one convenient gauge of quality. Because the quality of vanilla beans varies greatly, the overall quality and strength of different vanilla extracts varies as well.

Vanilla bean can be used in place of vanilla extract and vice versa. About one vanilla bean goes into making each fluid ounce (30 milliliters) of vanilla extract, but do not expect one vanilla bean to provide the same flavor intensity as 1 fluid ounce of extract. The extraction process used in the commercial production of vanilla extract is extremely efficient, so that in general, one vanilla bean rarely provides the same flavor as one ounce (30 milliliters) of extract.

Vanilla beans provide a somewhat different flavor than vanilla extract. To use, a vanilla bean is first split

> **HELPFUL HINT**
>
> If a formula calls for pure vanilla extract and you wish to use vanilla beans, or vice versa, try the following conversions as a starting point.
>
> 1 fluid ounce (30 milliliters) pure vanilla extract = 3–6 vanilla beans
>
> 1 vanilla bean = 1–2 teaspoons (5–10 milliliters) extract

Vanilla beans vary greatly in price, often for good reason. First, different regions develop different quality standards for cultivating and curing the beans, with Madagascar arguably setting the standards and commanding the highest price. Second, vanilla bean production is highly labor-intensive, and labor costs vary throughout the world. Third, beans vary in length, with the longest beans prized for their ease in use and higher seed content (although not necessarily better flavor). Fourth, beans vary in their aesthetic appearance. Grade A ("gourmet" or "prime") beans have an attractive, uniformly brown color with no surface defects. They are more expensive, although not necessarily more flavorful, than Grade B ("extract") beans, which often are discolored, malformed, or split. Fifth, moist, oily beans are graded higher and cost more than dry beans. While moist beans are easier to split and scrape and are more attractive, they do not necessarily have better flavor. In fact, pound for pound, you will get more flavor from shrunken dry Grade B beans than from plump, moist Grade A ones. Grade B beans are typically used in the production of vanilla extract.

and scraped, then allowed to infuse into hot liquid, often milk. After a time, often ten to twenty minutes, the liquid becomes infused with vanilla flavor and the bean is removed. Because the infusion time is minutes instead of hours, and because the infusing liquid often does not contain alcohol and is not aged, vanilla beans provide a different flavor from the equivalent amount of vanilla extract.

Besides flavor quality, there are other points to consider when deciding between vanilla bean and vanilla extract. Table 17.1 lists some of the advantages of each.

Concentrated vanilla extracts that contain a higher amount of vanilla "extractives" for the amount of alcohol are available. The usual ratio of vanilla bean to alcohol produces a so-called 1X or *one-fold vanilla extract*. Higher folds are available. For example, a 2X vanilla extract is made by doubling the amount of vanilla bean for every gallon or liter of extract. While

> **HELPFUL HINT**
>
> *To make top-quality product consistently time after time, do not reuse vanilla beans. Spent vanilla beans have lost much of their flavor, especially their top notes.*
>
> *Instead of discarding spent vanilla beans, however, add them to dry sugar. Vanilla flavor will infuse into the sugar, which can be used in baked goods. Or add the used vanilla beans to vanilla extract, to reinforce its flavor. Beans can also be dried, ground in a spice grinder, sieved, and used for their visual appeal.*

the price per ounce or gram is higher for a two-fold extract, the price per use is lower, and the quality is just as good. If you use a two-fold extract, remember to use half as much as you would when using a one-fold. Good-quality vanilla extract can be purchased in up to a four-fold concentration.

Liqueurs In terms of using them in the bakeshop, think of liqueurs as extracts with sugar added. As with extracts, liqueurs can contain natural or artificial ingredients. They can be made from fruits, nuts, seed, berries, flowers, and more. Those that are made from neutral grain spirits (like vodka) and are clear and syrupy-sweet are called *crèmes*. Some start with Cognac, brandy, or whiskey, and provide the complex flavors of these spirits.

Liqueurs are very useful for flavoring pastries, but they can be expensive because of the taxes on alcohol. The more popular ones can be purchased as concentrated flavorings, without the alcohol, for a lower cost. Concentrated flavorings are ideal for use in creams,

TABLE 17.1 ADVANTAGES OF VANILLA BEAN AND VANILLA EXTRACT

Vanilla bean	Can select a specific type of bean for a signature flavor
	No alcohol taste
	Can include natural flecks for visual appeal
	Less likely to darken or discolor background color of light sauces
Vanilla extract	Consistent flavor from one use to the next
	Faster and easier to use
	Longer shelf life (often several years)

TABLE 17.2 LIST OF LIQUEURS

LIQUEUR	DESCRIPTION
Amaretto	Bitter almond/apricot kernel
Anisette	Anise with other herbs and spices
Baileys Irish Cream	Irish whiskey with dairy cream and caramel, chocolate, coffee, and vanilla flavors
Benedictine	Cognac with a blend of 27 plants and spices, aged in oak casks
Chambord	Cognac with black raspberry, blackberry, vanilla, citrus, and honey
Chartreuse	Bright yellow-green blend of 130 herbs
Cointreau	Dried sweet and bitter orange peel
Crème de cacao	Chocolate
Crème de cassis	Black currant
Crème de menthe	Mint
Curaçao	Dried laraha (bitter orange) peel
Drambuie	Scotch whisky with honey and a blend of herbs and spices
Framboise	Raspberry
Frangelico	Hazelnut with cocoa, vanilla, and a blend of herbs
Galliano	Bright yellow blend of herbs and spices
Grand Marnier	Cognac with bitter orange essence
Kahlúa	Coffee, with vanilla and a blend of herbs and fruit essences
Kirsch	Wild cherry
Jägermeister	Blend of herbs and spices
Limoncello	Lemon rind
Midori	Melon
Ouzo	Anise with other herbs and spices
Sambuca	Star anise and white elder flowers
Southern Comfort	Bourbon whiskey with vanilla, fruit, and spices
Strega	Blend of 70 herbs, including mint, fennel, and saffron
Tia Maria	Jamaican coffee and vanilla

where large amounts of alcohol could curdle the dairy ingredients. They can also be useful for frozen desserts, where alcohol lowers the freezing point and at high levels can prevent freezing from happening at all. Finally, concentrated liqueur flavorings can be used in products for customers who, for religious or personal reasons, choose not to consume alcohol. While concentrated flavorings have advantages over liqueurs, remember that alcohol has a taste, too. Without the burn from a liqueur's alcohol, a product might lack flavor, even when the flavor concentrate is of high quality.

Liqueurs come in all flavors and all prices. With some, such as amaretto (bitter almond) or peppermint schnapps, a single flavor predominates. With others, such as Benedictine or Drambuie, the flavor is more complex and less easily defined (see Table 17.2).

As with all flavorings, expect different brands of the same liqueur to taste different. For example, Kahlúa and Tia Maria are both coffee-flavored liqueurs, but they differ in flavor quality and sweetness. Do not assume that price is an indication of quality. The only way to know which best meets your needs is to taste and compare.

Flavor Compounds and Bases Compounds and bases contain flavorings and sugar added to ingredients such as pureed fruit, chocolate, ground nuts, or ground vanilla beans. Think of compounds as highly flavored food ingredients. They are easy to use, and their ingredients contribute to a full flavor profile. Still, the quality of a compound depends on the quality of its ingredients, and brands vary widely. Compounds come in a variety of flavors, including strawberry, raspberry, lemon, and vanilla. Marzipan, which is made from ground almonds, sugar, and almond oil, is essentially an almond compound.

Flavor Oils Recall that the volatile or essential oils in spices are major sources of aroma. These oils can be purified—distilled or pressed—from the plant and sold separately. Examples of available oils include peppermint, lemon, orange, bitter almond, cinnamon, and clove.

Flavor oils are highly concentrated and must be used with care. They are most commonly used in products where high levels of moisture are undesirable, such as chocolate products and confections. While flavor oils have their advantages, they are not for everyday use.

Instead, extracts are better for everyday use because they are less concentrated, easier to measure, and dissolve more easily in liquid batters and doughs. Read labels and you will see that many flavor extracts are oils diluted with alcohol. For example, peppermint extract contains peppermint oil, lemon extract contains lemon oil, and almond extract contains almond oil, each diluted with alcohol.

A disadvantage of flavor oils is that they provide little more than top notes. They lack a full flavor profile and are best used as a flavor supplement. For example, lemon oil or lemon extract used alone provides the flat flavor of a lemon lollipop. Combined with lemon juice and zest, the flavor becomes rich and full.

Flavor Emulsions Flavor emulsions are flavor oils dissolved in water with the aid of a starch or gum. The starch or gum (often gum arabic or xanthan gum) acts as an emulsifier, allowing the oil to blend more easily with other ingredients. This makes flavor emulsions easier to add to batters and doughs. The most common flavor emulsions are lemon and orange.

Dried and Encapsulated Flavorings Dried flavorings are not for everyday use. They are common in dry mixes, like cake or muffin mixes, though. Dried flavorings can be natural or artificial.

Encapsulated flavorings are dry spices or flavorings, specially coated to protect the flavor from moisture, light, heat, and air. Encapsulated flavorings have a longer shelf life than spices and generally survive the heat of the oven better than other flavorings.

Pure vanilla comes in two dry forms: dried vanilla bean and dry vanilla powder. *Dried vanilla bean* is 100 percent pure ground bean, with nothing added. *Pure vanilla powder* is vanilla extract that has been dried with sugar (often dextrose) or maltodextrin. Because it is more highly processed, expect to pay a premium price for pure vanilla powder.

Because they do not contain alcohol, these products tend to evaporate less readily during baking. Products that do not contain alcohol can also be used in halal products; that is, products that are permissible under Islamic food laws. Vanilla extract is not halal because it contains alcohol.

Vanilla sugar is the name generally given to sugar flavored with a touch of vanilla. Use vanilla sugar as a dusting on desserts, or to supplement the vanilla added into a formula.

Artificial Flavorings

Artificial flavorings are created from sources that sometimes have no relation to the natural flavor. By law, artificial flavorings must be labeled as either *artificial* or *imitation*. Likewise, natural flavorings must be labeled as either *natural* or *pure*. Liqueurs are the exception to this rule. In the United States, liqueurs are regulated by the Bureau of Alcohol, Tobacco, and Firearms (BATF). The BATF does not require the labeling of flavorings in liqueurs. All processed flavorings, including extracts, liqueurs, compounds, oils, emulsions, and powders, can be natural or artificial, or a combination of both.

All artificial flavorings are not created equal. Many have improved over the years, and some are quite good. The comments that follow are general comments that apply to some and not others. Before deciding which to use, determine your needs and those of your customer, then purchase accordingly.

The most common reason for using artificial flavorings is to reduce cost. While cost is not an issue for some operations, for many it is. And, because of advances in flavor chemistry, low cost no longer necessarily means low quality.

Imitation almond extract, for example, is an excellent substitute for natural almond extract. Natural almond oil is a very simple flavor, consisting of little more than a single flavor chemical, and it is easily imitated with an artificial flavoring.

Pure vanilla, however, is more difficult to reproduce because it consists of hundreds of flavor chemicals that provide deep, rich middle notes in addition to top notes. Some artificial vanilla flavorings consist of only one or two flavor top notes—primarily vanillin. Often, these simple mixtures are best at supplementing pure vanilla rather than replacing it. This is especially true

---

HELPFUL HINTS

If cost is an issue, consider using less expensive artificial vanilla flavorings in baked products, where much of the flavor of pure vanilla evaporates off. Use this saved money to purchase a high-quality vanilla extract or vanilla beans for use in unbaked products like pastry cream or vanilla ice cream, where differences in flavor quality are more evident.

Sometimes reaching for the bottle of extract or the jar of compound is not the best way to improve the flavor of a product. Here are some suggestions for other ways to improve flavor in problem products.

If flavor is weak in a mousse or cream, back off on the amount of thickener, whether it's gelatin, starch, or flour. Thick and heavy products prevent flavor molecules from escaping for taste.

Often a combination of two basic tastes provides an interesting flavor contrast in foods. For example, a sour fruit sauce is an interesting contrast to a sweet cream.

To provide richness and a full-bodied flavor to pastries, add ingredients that supply middle notes. Eggs, milk, and cream are probably the most common ingredients pastry chefs use for richness. But consider, too, coconut milk, banana puree, caramelized sugar, and maple syrup for this purpose. Small amounts of aged rum, brandy, wine, and vanilla provide depth to fruit flavors, as does the slightly "jammy" character from cooked berries such as raspberries.

If flavor in a product disappears too quickly, remember that a full flavor profile includes an appropriate finish or aftertaste. The pungency and burn of ginger, cinnamon, and other spices might provide just the lingering flavor note that the product is lacking.

While a strongly bitter aftertaste is unpleasant, a small amount from coffee, cranberries, citrus peel, or unsweetened chocolate adds interest to the aftertaste, as long as it is properly balanced with sweetness.

If a fruit sauce isn't fruity enough, consider adjusting the amount of sugar and acid. Each fruit has a characteristic sweet-sour balance that is important to its overall flavor, and sometimes the best way to increase fruitiness is to add a small amount of sugar or acid—or both.

If ginger molasses cookies lack a snappy flavor, back off on the baking soda. The color will lighten and the cookies will spread less, but the flavor will be improved.

For chocolate cheesecake, try layering chocolate with cheese instead of mixing them together. Cheesecake has a low pH, but chocolate tastes best when its pH is neutral. When chocolate is separated from the cheese, the chocolate is at its proper pH. And there is the added bonus of a flavor contrast between bitter-sweet chocolate and salty-sour cheesecake.

To balance cost and quality, consider layering two or more flavorings. For example, use an inexpensive liqueur flavor concentrate to boost the flavor provided by a liqueur, or use fresh lemon peel, a small amount of fresh lemon juice, or lemon extract to boost the flavor of bottled lemon juice.

For the look of real vanilla beans without splitting and scraping vanilla beans, consider purchasing vanilla bean paste (Figure 17.2), a compound of vanilla extract mixed with spent vanilla bean seeds and sugar. Spent seeds are left over from the making of vanilla extract.

If a formula calls for a pinch of salt, do not omit it. Salt is a flavor enhancer, which means it blends and improves flavors even when the salt itself cannot be tasted. A pinch of salt is less than ¹⁄₁₆ teaspoon (just under ⅓ milliliter).

Figure 17.2 Vanilla bean paste is a compound of vanilla extract, sugar, and seeds from vanilla beans.

Most imitation vanilla flavorings contain caramel coloring to give them the look of pure vanilla extract. When the caramel coloring is left out, these imitation vanillas are clear and colorless. Clear vanilla flavorings are sometimes used in sauces, icings, and cakes, when the whitest white is desired.

where vanilla is the predominant flavor, as in vanilla ice cream, vanilla sauce, or Chantilly cream.

What many artificial flavorings lack in complexity, however, they often make up in strength. If they appear weak, it is because they lack a full flavor profile. Whenever a flavoring lacks a full flavor, it is unlikely that doubling or tripling it will make up for this lack. Instead, the result will likely be flavor burn. *Flavor burn* is a sharp flavor or an unpleasant sting on the tongue that occurs when flavorings—either natural or artificial—are used at too high a level. It is a common problem with certain artificial flavorings, since they can be abruptly sharp. While this can be a problem in some situations, it is an advantage in others. For example, the strong taste of artificial vanillin is often needed to balance the equally strong flavors of chocolate. In fact, a large number of quality chocolate products contain vanillin in place of pure vanilla.

Their robust composition makes many artificial flavorings ideal for baked goods exposed to intense heat. That is why cookies and biscuits, in particular, benefit from the use of artificial flavorings that have good heat stability.

While many good artificial flavorings are on the market, no single flavoring works equally well in all products, and some bakery products are particularly sensitive to the quality of flavoring used.

Evaluating New Flavorings

Resist the temptation to judge the quality of flavorings by price alone or by smelling them straight from the bottle. Instead, evaluate flavorings in the actual products in which they will be used. For quick screenings, however, it is acceptable to use simple products. For example, evaluate vanilla flavorings in sweetened milk or whipped cream. Be aware, however, that flavor perception is complex, so don't expect a single flavoring to work equally well in all products. Vanilla that is wonderful in pastry cream may be weak and dull in sponge cake.

Many formulas call for flavorings to be added "to taste." This is necessary because different brands of the same flavoring often vary in strength. The first time a formula is used, determine the correct amount of flavoring to use. For example, to flavor a buttercream with vanilla extract, weigh out an amount of vanilla extract that is more than you will need. Next, add vanilla extract to the buttercream to taste. Weigh the amount of extract remaining, and subtract this amount from the original amount weighed out. The difference is the amount of extract that was added to the buttercream. Be sure to record this amount on your formula so you can refer to it time and again.

> **HELPFUL HINTS**
>
> *The high heat from cooking and baking presents special challenges with flavorings prized for their volatile top notes. While it is difficult to eliminate flavor loss completely during cooking and baking, there are several ways to reduce it to manageable levels. First, consider supplementing natural flavorings with an artificial one specially designed for baking. With artificial vanilla flavorings, select one that contains ethyl vanillin, which is especially heat stable. Also consider encapsulated flavorings, for the same reason.*
>
> *Avoid using flavorings that contain alcohol, such as extracts and liqueurs. Alcohol evaporates easily, and it can strip valuable top notes along with it. Instead, where flavor loss is a problem, try flavorings that contain nonalcohol solvents such as glycerine and water. Or try using a dry flavor such as pure vanilla powder.*
>
> *Add flavorings directly to fat. For example, cream vanilla extract into butter instead of adding it to liquids. Since many flavors dissolve in fat, they are less likely to evaporate when captured by the fat.*
>
> *Add flavorings as late in the cooking process as possible. For example, add vanilla extract to pastry cream after it is removed from the heat. Extract added too early evaporates, but if added too late, the alcohol will not evaporate and may detract from the flavor of the cream.*

Flavorings often transform pastry from ordinary to distinctly different, even memorable. For new ideas on flavors, consider studying the foods of foreign cultures, including the Middle East, South America, Southeast Asia, and the Mediterranean. You'll find, for example, that a blend of orange, coffee, honey, and spices is a classic flavoring for chocolate in Sicily.

Read about food trends and popular flavors throughout history. There you will learn of flavorings such as rosewater that were popular with Europeans before the Spanish brought vanilla from the Americas.

Bring spices from the kitchen into the bakeshop. A small amount of black pepper, for example, provides a subtle yet important finish to pumpkin pie spice. This idea is borrowed from a nineteenth-century American cookbook.

In your travels, do not stray too far away from the familiar. Customers want variety, but they are more comfortable with variations on what they know, and they will always appreciate a well-made classic more than an ill-conceived new creation.

Storage and Handling

Fresh herbs last from a few days to two weeks, as long as they are stored properly and of good quality when received. To keep from wilting and yellowing, bunch the herbs into a bouquet and place in a cup of water, stem side down. Cover leaves loosely with plastic wrap. Or wrap leaves in damp paper towels and place in plastic bags in refrigerator.

Dried spices and most other flavorings don't spoil so much as lose or change flavor and color. Certain ground spices also cake and clump. While spices retain some degree of flavor for years, they slowly degrade. Moisture, light, heat, and oxygen in air accelerate this degradation. This means that spices are best kept covered in a cool, dark spot. Whole spices last longer than ground spices because the flavors are protected by the spice's natural intact cell structure.

Vanilla and other extracts typically last indefinitely, but are best stored in a cool dry place. Vanilla beans should be in a covered container so they don't dry out.

Dried powdery specks or needles of vanillin often crystallize on the surface of beans during storage. This is natural and is not a sign of spoilage. If vanilla beans dry out, they are difficult to slice and scrape; however, do not discard. Instead, add to vanilla extract.

When handling spices and other flavorings, practice good inventory control. Ideally, purchase only enough for three to six months' use, and follow the FIFO rule—first in, first out. Do not open new containers until ready to use, because the containers are usually vacuum-sealed to exclude oxygen.

The American Spice Trade Association makes these additional recommendations for keeping ground spices as long as six months to one year.

- Close containers quickly and tightly after each use.
- Measure with dry utensils.
- Store at or below 68°F (20°C); if possible, refrigerate.
- Keep away from wet or humid locations such as washdown areas and dishwashers.

Questions for Review

1   Provide examples of where each of the following plant parts is used for flavoring food: leaf, seed, fruit, flower bud, root, and bark.

2   What is a flavor extract?

3   How is vanilla extract made?

4   How is peppermint extract made?

5   What are the advantages of vanilla extract and of vanilla bean?

6   What is meant by the "fold" of an extract?

7   When mixing batters and doughs, why is it better to cream an extract into the fat rather than add it with liquids?

8   Describe a product application in which a concentrated liqueur flavor might be more desirable than using the liqueur itself.

9   In what type of product are flavor oils most likely used?

10   What is meant by a "flavor compound"?

11   List the advantages and disadvantages of imitation vanilla flavoring.

12   Of the following products, which might benefit the most from the use of artificial vanilla flavoring, which from pure vanilla extract or vanilla bean, and why: vanilla cookies, vanilla ice cream, buttercream?

13   Explain what flavor burn is and how to prevent it.

14   What should you do if a formula calls for a flavoring to be added to taste?

15   Describe two ways of storing fresh herbs.

16   List six points to consider for maintaining the flavor of dry spices.

Questions for Discussion

1   Explain how the flavor profile of a raspberry sauce reduction (made by simmering and reducing the amount of liquid in raspberry juice) might compare to that of fresh raspberries.

2   You have created a low-fat custard cream pie by replacing cream with milk. Besides having a whiter appearance, the flavor of the pie seems weak and lacks "staying power." Review information on flavor profiles, and suggest some changes that you could make to the cream pie to improve its flavor. Alternatively, suggest flavors that could be used in an accompanying sauce that is also low-fat but could compensate for what is missing in the flavor profile of the pie.

Exercises and Experiments

① Exercise: Sensory Characteristics of Spices

Place a sample of each of the spices listed in the Results Table on a separate small white plate or shallow cup and label with name or number. Prepare a diluted sugar syrup by blending two parts water with one part sugar and stirring to dissolve, then add 2 percent (baker's percentage) of each ground spice to the sugar syrup and stir until dispersed. Use 2 grams spice (approximately 1 tsp/5 ml) for every 100 grams of syrup.

Evaluate the appearance and aroma of each dry spice and record your notes in the Results Table. Evaluate the taste and trigeminal effects of each spice by tasting the spices dispersed in syrups. Cleanse your palate between samples with unsalted crackers and water. Evaluate all attributes for seeds using dry whole seeds. In Additional Comments column of Results Table, list any memories or food products that the spice brings to mind (your mom's apple pie, your favorite cookies, baked ham, Italian sausage, etc.).

After you have completed the Results Table, review it to see if you have adequately described each spice. In particular, be sure you have adequately differentiated the following spices, which are easily confused: nutmeg and mace; allspice and cloves; anise and fennel.

Two rows are left blank, for the evaluation of additional spice samples, if desired.

RESULTS TABLE   SENSORY CHARACTERISTICS OF DRY SPICES

	SPICE	APPEARANCE	AROMA (DRY SPICE)	FLAVOR (SPICE IN SYRUP)	ADDITIONAL COMMENTS
1	Cinnamon				
2	Nutmeg				
3	Mace				
4	Ginger				
5	Cardamom				
6	Allspice				
7	Cloves				
8	Anise seed				
9	Fennel seed				
10	Caraway seed				
11					
12					

Use information from the preceding table and from your textbook to answer the following questions. Select one from the choices in **bold** or fill in the blanks.

1 The spice with the sweetest aroma was **cinnamon/cardamom/cloves**.

2 The spice with a trigeminal effect that numbed the tongue was **allspice/cloves**.

3 The trigeminal effect of ginger can be described as _____
_____
_____.

4 Select any two spices of your choice that are quite different from each other._____
_____

Describe in one sentence how they differ.

_____
_____
_____

5 Select any two spices of your choice that you feel could be easily substituted for one another because they are most similar in flavor. _____
_____

Describe in what specific ways they are similar, and describe any differences.

_____
_____
_____

6 Were there any spices that you were able to identify *only* by association with food products? If so, list the spices below and list the food product that you associate each with.

_____
_____
_____

❷ Exercise: Identifying Spices by Smell Alone

Fill small wide-mouth dark bottles with a layer of ground spices, some with one spice per bottle, others with a blend of spices. Top with a cotton ball, to hide the spice from view, and label each bottle on the bottom with its contents. Cover each bottle and shake gently, to stir up volatile molecules. Uncap and sniff, and see if you can identify the spice from smell alone. Repeat until you are able to identify all spices and all spice combinations.

❸ Experiment: How Different Vanillas Affect the Quality of Custard Sauce

Objectives

Demonstrate how different brands and types of vanilla affect the
- Appearance of vanilla custard sauce
- Flavor strength and quality of vanilla custard sauce
- Overall acceptability of vanilla custard sauce

Products Prepared

Vanilla custard sauce made with:

- Pure vanilla extract (Madagascar; control product)
- Imitation vanilla flavoring
- Vanilla bean (Madagascar)
- Other, if desired (Tahitian vanilla bean, blend of pure extract and imitation flavoring, double the amount of pure vanilla extract, double the amount of vanilla bean, double the amount of imitation vanilla flavoring, additional brands of pure extract, additional brands of imitation flavorings, etc.)

Materials and Equipment

- Scale
- Stainless-steel saucepans, 2-quart or equivalent
- Whisk
- Watch or clock
- Instant-read thermometer
- Heat-resistant spatulas
- Stainless-steel bowls
- Ice water bath
- Vanilla custard sauce (see Formula), enough to make 16 fl. oz. (500 ml) of each variation

Formula

Vanilla Custard Sauce

Yield: 2 cups (½ liter)

INGREDIENT	POUNDS	OUNCES	GRAMS	BAKER'S PERCENTAGE
Milk, whole		8	240	50
Heavy cream		8	240	50
Sugar, regular granulated		4	115	25
Egg yolks (6 yolks)		4	115	25
Vanilla extract or flavoring (1½ tsp/7.5 ml)		0.25	7	1.5
Total	**1**	**8.25**	**717**	**151.5**

Method of Preparation
(with vanilla extract)

1 Place milk, heavy cream, and sugar into 2-quart stainless-steel saucepan and bring just to a boil.

2 Using a wire whisk, gently stir egg yolks. Temper scalded milk mixture into yolks by slowly adding approximately ½ cup (125 milliliters) of it into yolks.

3 Add yolk/milk mixture back into scalded milk. Record start cook time here: _____.

4 Cook mixture over low heat until it coats back of spoon (nappe) or until it reaches 180°F (82°C), stirring constantly with a heat-resistant spatula.

5 Immediately remove from heat and transfer to a stainless steel bowl. Record end cook time here: _____.

6 Place bowl in ice water bath.

7 Add vanilla extract/flavoring and continue to cool, stirring gently.

Method of Preparation
(with vanilla bean)

1 In step 1, add 1 vanilla bean, split and scraped, to milk-cream mixture.

2 In step 5, after removing sauce from heat, remove split vanilla bean.

3 In step 7, omit vanilla extract.

Procedure

1 Prepare vanilla custard sauce using the formula given or using any basic vanilla custard sauce formula. Prepare one batch of sauce for each variation.

2 Calculate total cook time, in minutes, and record in Results Table.

3 Cool samples in ice water bath, all to same temperature (about 40°F/5°C).

4 Use cost information to determine the cost per batch for the vanilla used in each product and record in Results Table. If you do not have costing information available, use the following values:
  • Pure vanilla extract, one-fold: $1.00 per ounce (30 grams)
  • Pure vanilla extract, two-fold: $1.75 per ounce (30 grams)
  • Imitation vanilla extract: $0.25 per ounce (30 grams)
  • Vanilla bean (Madagascar): $1.00 each

Results

Evaluate the sensory characteristics of completely cooled products and record evaluations in the Results Table, which follows. Be sure to compare each in turn to the control product, evaluating each of the attributes listed in the Results Table. For your evaluation of flavor strength and quality, consider the following:
  • Immediate vanilla impact
  • Lingering vanilla middle notes
  • Sweetness
  • Alcohol taste

Enter overall acceptability, from highly unacceptable to highly acceptable, on a scale of 1 to 5. Add any additional comments, as necessary.

RESULTS TABLE   VANILLA CUSTARD SAUCES MADE WITH DIFFERENT TYPES AND AMOUNTS OF VANILLA FLAVORING

TYPE AND AMOUNT OF VANILLA	TOTAL COOK TIME (IN MINUTES)	APPEARANCE	FLAVOR STRENGTH AND QUALITY	OVERALL ACCEPTABILITY	COST OF VANILLA PER BATCH	ADDITIONAL COMMENTS
Pure vanilla extract (control product)						
Imitation vanilla flavoring						
Vanilla bean						

Sources of Error

List any sources of error that might make it difficult to draw the proper conclusions from your experiment. In particular, consider any differences in how long sauces were cooked, how vigorously they were stirred when cooled, and what temperature they were cooled to.

_____

_____

_____

State what you could do differently next time to minimize or eliminate each source of error.

_____

_____

_____

Conclusions

Select one from the choices in **bold** or fill in the blanks.

1   The difference in appearance between the sauce made with pure vanilla extract (control product) and vanilla bean was **small/moderate/large**. One difference was that the sauce made with vanilla bean was **lighter/darker** in color. Other differences include the following:

_____

_____

_____

2   The difference in the flavor profile and flavor strength between the sauce made with pure vanilla extract and vanilla bean was **small/moderate/large**. For example, the sauce made with vanilla bean was **lower/higher/the same** in flavor strength. Based on these results, when making custard sauce, 1 vanilla bean of the quality and size used in this experiment is **equal to/less than/more than equal to** ¼ ounce (7 grams) or 1½ teaspoons (7.5 milliliters) of the vanilla extract used in this experiment. These results **will/will not** likely hold if a different grade or size vanilla bean, or a different vanilla extract, is used.

3   The difference in flavor quality between imitation flavoring and pure vanilla extract was **small/moderate/large**. I would describe these differences as follows:

_____

_____

_____

4   The difference in cost per batch between vanilla beans and pure vanilla extract was **small/moderate/large**. In my opinion, the quality difference between vanilla bean and pure vanilla extract **justifies/does not justify** the use of more expensive vanilla bean in this product because _____

_____.

5   The difference in cost per batch between imitation flavoring and pure vanilla extract was **small/moderate/large**. In my opinion, this price difference **justifies/does not justify** the use of less-expensive imitation vanilla flavoring in this product because _____

_____.

This same conclusion probably holds for other products that are similar to custard sauce, such as (*list two or three products similar to custard sauce*) _____

_____.

This same conclusion probably does not hold for products that are much different from custard sauce, such as _____

_____.

6   Other noticeable differences between sauces were as follows:

_____

_____

_____

18

Baking for Health and Wellness

Introduction

Until recently, most bakers and pastry chefs did not see themselves in the business of health. Baked goods and pastries were meant to be decadent, and most were made of white flour, fat, and sugar, with smaller amounts of flavorings and other ingredients.

Go back in history, though, and man's first dessert was fruit. Even today, many cultures still use unadorned fruit to top a meal. Keep this in mind as you consider the role bakers and pastry chefs can play in advancing their customers' health.

Today in the United States, two-thirds of Americans are classified as either overweight or obese, and this is having far-reaching effects on their health and well-being. Many diseases, including heart disease, stroke, some cancers, and diabetes, can be prevented or controlled through diet. This chapter is about how bakers and pastry chefs can provide good-tasting pastries and baked goods that meet the health needs of their customers.

Healthful Baking with the Customer in Mind

Customers can't make better choices about eating if better choices aren't available to them. Bakers and pastry chefs can help by providing healthful products alongside regular ones, letting the customer choose which to eat. Providing free samples, whenever possible, lets your customer know that good health can taste good.

If at first your products are rejected, reevaluate, make changes, and try again. There is no need to lower your standards or expect that the customer will lower theirs. Healthful baked items might look and taste different, but if done right, they can be—they must be—attractive and tasty. Here are some commonsense guidelines for baking with health in mind.

- Review your current formulas and determine which are already good for health or might be especially easy to modify. For example, banana nut bread already contains healthful ingredients, and it can easily be made with oil instead of the melted butter or shortening you might currently be using.

- Before making changes to an important ingredient, make sure you understand the functions of that ingredient in your product. This will help you predict the consequences of reducing or eliminating it, and it will also help you find a suitable replacement. Remember, too, the importance of balancing tougheners and tenderizers, moisteners and driers.

- Begin with products that are highly flavored, since it is often easier to make substitutions in these products than in simpler ones. For example, it is easier to remove butter from chocolate cookies than it is from plain sugar cookies because the butter flavor is not as important to the overall flavor of the cookie.

- Keep it simple. Stay away from formulas that have many expensive and exotic specialty ingredients that you do not currently inventory. If your goal is to make a lower-fat brownie, do you need one that also contains agave syrup instead of sugar and is made with spelt instead of regular wheat? But do plan on making some changes to your current inventory of ingredients.

- Begin with step-wise changes to your products. For example, if your bread currently is made with 40 percent whole wheat, can you make a tasty one using 50 percent? Can you go higher still?

- Approach healthful baking holistically. For example, pastries made without trans fats aren't necessarily better for you if you've switched to a fat that is higher in saturated fats. Still, it isn't necessary for one product to satisfy all needs. For example, a product probably doesn't need to be fat free, gluten free, and also low in sugar.

- Try different brands of important ingredients, since they can vary in surprising ways. Plastic shortenings, in particular, vary from one brand to the next, as do soy milks. Often the only the way to know which works best is to try several.

- Think in terms of what can be added to make baked goods more healthful rather than focusing on what should be removed. For example, can you add more fruit, nuts, seeds, whole grains, or spices? These changes not only make a product more healthful, but they add value. Each also adds flavor. If done right, most customers are willing to pay more for this.

- Fruit is an easy choice for improving the nutrition of plated desserts. If a plated dessert has one mango slice, is there a way for you to add three or more without compromising your artistic integrity?
- Watch portion size. If your offerings are really flavorful and priced right, customers will appreciate smaller sizes.
- Know the difference between ingredients that provide real health benefits and those that are marketing ploys. For example, which sweeteners are really good for us, and which only make us feel better about eating sugar?
- Keep in mind that organic ingredients are not necessarily healthier, and when they are, the difference is often incremental and inconsistent. Committing to organic is primarily a lifestyle choice, a means of choosing products that inflict less damage on the environment.

- When developing a new formula, always make the original and compare products side by side. It will keep you on track and provide you with clues about what is missing or what has changed. It will help you make informed decisions as you adjust formulas.
- If you sell a product as "low-fat," "sugar-free," "high in fiber," etc., have nutrition information available to the customer to substantiate your claim. This is required by law.
- Finally, know what good nutrition really is. Refer to dietary guidelines for North Americans when creating products for your customers. See how often you can apply these guidelines in the bakeshop as you change existing products and create new ones. It might not be as difficult as you think.

Healthful eating is not a fad, but guidelines for healthful eating will change as new information on the effects of diet on health becomes available. The next section discusses current guidelines for a healthful diet.

Guidelines for a Healthful Diet

Both the U.S. and Canadian governments issue comprehensive, no-nonsense guidelines for eating a healthful diet. These guidelines translate the latest science and nutrition research into clearly written dietary recommendations for preventing disease. For example, *Dietary Guidelines for Americans* is issued every five years jointly by the U.S. Department of Health and Human Services and the U.S. Department of Agriculture. It is the basis for the USDA's MyPyramid guide to promoting overall

well-being and improving overall health. Likewise, Health Canada publishes *Canada's Food Guide*.

Based on these guidelines, most North Americans are encouraged to do the following.

- Choose fiber-rich fruits, vegetables, and whole grains often. At least half of grain products should come from whole grains, for a minimum of three whole grain servings a day. The following represent one serving of a whole grain product: one slice of

More on Nutrition Information

The U.S. Food and Drug Administration (FDA) requires that restaurants and bakeshops provide nutrition information to customers on request when a nutrient content claim or health claim is made. This means that if you claim that a product is high in fiber, for example, you must provide nutrition information to show that it is. This could be as simple as telling the customer that a high-fiber product contains 6 grams of dietary fiber per serving. When information is provided orally, also have it in writing as a backup to ensure that your staff members communicate the facts properly.

Nutrient levels may be determined using nutrition software, but the FDA considers information provided by cookbooks to be equally valid. If you decide to invest in nutrition software, realize that different versions vary in their reliability, database size, special features, and ease of use. Prices range from free to thousands of dollars.

The rate of new cases of type 2 diabetes in the United States doubled from 1997 to 2007. This mirrors the increase in obesity in this country, which is one of the two main risk factors for the disease. The other main risk factor is inactivity.

Type 2 diabetes is caused by the body's inefficient use of the hormone insulin, which signals the transport of sugar out of the bloodstream and into cells. Type 2 diabetes is now being diagnosed in children, which was unheard of twenty years ago.

Type 1 diabetes is different from type 2; it is an autoimmune disease in which the body does not produce insulin at all. Besides managing their diet and exercise, type 1 diabetics are required to take insulin shots to control blood sugar levels.

---

whole grain bread, one-half of a whole grain bagel, ½ cup cooked brown rice.

- Consume a variety of fruits and vegetables each day. In particular, select from all five vegetable groups, including dark green and orange vegetables and legumes (dry beans).
- Consume 3 cups of fat-free or low-fat milk or equivalent milk products per day.
- Select meat, poultry, dry beans and dairy products that are lean, low fat, or fat free.
- Keep fat intake between 20 and 35 percent of total calories, with most fats coming from sources of polyunsaturated and monounsaturated fatty acids such as fish, nuts, and vegetable oils.
- Limit intake of fats and oils high in saturated and/or trans fatty acids to less than 10 percent of calories, with trans fatty acid consumption as low as possible.
- Limit cholesterol to less than 300 mg per day.
- Limit intake of added sugars or caloric sweeteners.
- Limit intake of added salt. At the same time, consume potassium-rich foods such as fruits and vegetables.

These guidelines are consistent with the DASH diet for reducing hypertension (high blood pressure) promoted by the U.S. National Institutes of Health (NIH). They are also consistent with recommendations by the American Diabetes Association, which state that eating healthfully is one of the most important things that can be done to lower the risk of developing diabetes. Additional information on diabetes follows.

Diabetes and Baked Goods

Many people believe that sugar causes diabetes and that diabetics should avoid sugar at all times. In fact, eating sugar has nothing to do with developing diabetes, unless sugar consumption leads to a poor diet or to weight gain.

Diabetics do need to control their blood sugar levels, though, and they can do this through diet and exercise. First and foremost, diabetics need to control their total carbohydrate level, and sugar is a carbohydrate. Diabetics must also control other carbohydrates found in baked goods, such as starches found in breads and crackers. By focusing on total carbohydrates rather than just on sugars, diabetics can better control their blood sugar. With this in mind, they can occasionally have a small serving of dessert, as long as the total amount of

> **HELPFUL HINT**
>
> *Offer your customers—whether diabetic or not—mini versions of popular cookies and muffins as well as oversized ones. This is a good idea even with healthful items like whole grain rolls or high-fiber muffins.*
>
> *If you have access to nutrition software, calculate the nutrient contents, including total carbohydrate content, for these smaller items, and have the information available for your customers.*
>
> *According to the American Diabetes Association (ADA), for most diabetics, 15 to 30 grams of total carbohydrates is appropriate for a snack. The ADA provides the following information on the typical amount of total carbohydrates in various foods:*
>
> | | |
> |---|---|
> | *White bread, 1 slice* | *15 grams* |
> | *Brownie, 2-inch square* | *15 grams* |
> | *Cookies, 2 small (⅔ oz.)* | *15 grams* |
> | *Frosted cake, 2-inch square* | *30 grams* |
> | *Pumpkin pie, ⅛ of an 8-inch pie* | *30 grams* |
> | *Fruit pie, ⅙ of an 8-inch pie* | *45 grams* |
> | *Rice pudding, ½ cup* | *45 grams* |

Glycemic index is the most common numerical measure of the glycemic response of foods—the rate at which foods provide energy. Glucose is arbitrarily given a glycemic index (GI) of 100; in relation, sucrose has a GI of 60, fructose, 20, whole milk, 35, and white flour, 70.

"Glycemic response" refers to how fast sugars—and foods that contain sugars and other carbohydrates—break down during digestion and provide energy to the body. The faster the carbohydrates in a food product are digested, the faster they raise blood sugar levels and the higher the glycemic response. Proteins and fats do not raise blood sugar levels; only digested carbohydrates do. Dietary fiber, although made of carbohydrates, passes through the body undigested, so it also does not raise blood sugar levels.

The usefulness of the glycemic index is in dispute by nutritionists and health professionals, although in general, low-glycemic foods are considered better for health. Some weight-loss diets promote low GI foods as a means of reducing hunger, aiding in weight loss, and assisting diabetics in controlling their insulin levels. The U.S. 2005 Dietary Guidelines Advisory Committee, Health Canada, and other groups responsible for public health in North America do not make diet recommendations based on the glycemic response of food products.

carbohydrates consumed at that time is kept at a reasonable level.

When preparing baked goods for diabetics, follow the general guidelines for a healthful diet, but be especially mindful of portion size. Controlling portion size is important for everyone, but it is critical for diabetics so they can best manage the amount of carbohydrates consumed at any one time.

Many diabetics monitor and control the amount of carbohydrates they consume by using a technique called "carbohydrate counting." By using information in nutrition labels and from lists that provide average carbohydrate values for common foods, they are able to estimate the amount of carbs they consume at any given time.

Besides recommending managing diabetes through counting carbohydrates, the American Diabetes Association (ADA) supports several other useful techniques for diabetics. For example, the glycemic index (GI) of foods is an indication of how different carbohydrate-containing foods raise blood sugar. Foods with low or medium GIs include many whole grains, most fruit, nonstarchy vegetables, and dried beans. These foods have less of an effect on raising blood sugar than foods with high GIs like white bread and refined sugars. But the ADA stresses that eating foods with low or medium GIs will do no good if the total amount of carbohydrates consumed is high.

Strategies for Healthful Baking

Preparing healthful baked goods can be a challenge. It requires making intelligent decisions when substituting more healthful ingredients for standard ingredients in a favorite formula. While experience goes a long way in helping to make the right decisions in the bakeshop, understanding ingredients is invaluable.

In many ways, the ultimate goal of this book has been to put you in control of the bakeshop by presenting information about ingredients. The following sections apply the information provided throughout the book to creating more healthful baked goods.

Increasing Whole Grains

Recall that whole grains consist of the entire grain or kernel of a plant. Whether the kernel is cracked, crushed, flaked, or ground, to be considered a whole grain it must have the same proportions of the bran, germ, and endosperm as the original grain.

Recent surveys show that consumers are looking for products made with whole grains because they are aware of their healthful goodness. While some appreciate the nutty flavor of whole grains, others still prefer the blander taste of white flour. For those customers,

Here is a summary of the functions of flour in baked goods:

- Providing structure/Is a toughener
- Absorbing liquids/Is a drier
- Contributing flavor
- Contributing color
- Adding nutritional value

begin with blends of white flour and whole wheat, and consider using whole white wheat flour instead of regular (red wheat) whole wheat flour.

Whole white wheat flour is lighter in color and milder in flavor than whole red wheat flour. While it is likely that whole white wheat flour is lower in some phytonutrients, it is still an excellent way to increase whole grains in your products.

When switching from white flour to whole wheat, it's especially important to try different brands and types of flours. Whole wheat flours from both red and white wheat can be made from either hard or soft wheat. Additionally, millers can specify certain breeds of wheat, mill the grains to different degrees of fineness, and change the treatments (for example, bleaching) and additives (ascorbic acid, malted barley flour). All of these will affect the baking characteristics of the flour in important ways.

Here are some general guidelines to follow when increasing whole wheat flour in baked goods.

- In general, use coarse-grained whole wheat flours made from hard wheat for breads and other yeast-raised products. Use finer-grained whole wheat flours made from soft wheat for cakes, cookies, pie crusts, muffins, and biscuits.
- Begin by making small incremental changes in the amount of whole wheat flour that you use. Start by substituting regular (red) whole wheat for about 10 percent of the white flour, or whole white wheat flour for about 30 percent of the white flour. Try higher amounts in highly-flavored products such as gingersnaps, carrot cake, or brownies, as long as the texture does not become too heavy. Then see if your baked good can handle more.
- For yeast-raised doughs, increase the protein level of your flour by adding 2–5 percent (baker's percentage)

vital wheat gluten for strengthening. Or use white flour with a higher gluten content to compensate for the poor gluten that develops from your whole wheat flour.

- For yeast-raised doughs, reduce mix times to minimize weakening the gluten.
- Increase the amount of moisture added, since whole wheat flour is a better drier than white flour. As a rule of thumb, increase the amount of water by 1 percent for every 10 percent increase in whole wheat flour.
- For whole wheat pie crusts, add a small amount (1 percent baker's percentage) of baking powder to lighten and tenderize.

Don't forget that there are other whole grains besides whole wheat. Any time you use oatmeal, for example, whether regular rolled oats, quick-cooking, or steel-cut, you are using a whole grain. Corn flour and cornmeal are both available as whole grains. Look for corn products that are not degerminated, and be sure to store them properly, since they are high in fats that oxidize easily.

While not a grain, flaxseed is a popular addition to healthful whole grain baked goods. Whole flaxseeds should be finely ground in a blender or food processor before use to maximize the availability of their nutrients. Low levels of flaxseed (10 percent, baker's percentage) can be added to many breads and other baked goods without notice. If higher amounts are used, the amount of oil in the formula can be reduced and the amount of water typically needs to be increased because ground flaxseed is high in gums (mucilage), making it an excellent drier.

Variety is important to the consumer, and it is important for good health. However, don't assume that a more exotic grain is automatically a more healthful choice. Spelt, kamut, and emmer all have their advantages (see Chapter 6), but they are not nutritiously superior to regular whole wheat.

Reducing Salt and Sodium

Sodium is essential to good health, but in general, Americans take in more sodium than they need. Much of the sodium consumed in the American diet comes from table salt (sodium chloride) added to food.

Most salt is not added by the consumer. Instead, it comes from prepared foods, including pastries and other baked goods. Besides salt, other significant

The Benefits of Whole Grains

Whole grains appear to reduce the risk of heart disease, certain cancers, and diabetes. They contribute to intestinal health and weight control, and to control of blood sugar in diabetics. Whole grains provide these health benefits partly because they are high in fiber, both soluble and insoluble. They also contain essential fatty acids, vitamins, minerals, and numerous phytonutrients that are missing in white flour. Phytonutrients are substances in plant-based (*phyto*) foods that have special health-promoting or disease-preventing properties. The health-promoting phytonutrients in whole grains include polyphenolic antioxidants, which are also present in chocolate, fruits, and nuts.

Why Lower Salt and Increase Potassium?

Eating less salt is an important way for many to reduce the risk of high blood pressure, which may in turn reduce the risk of heart disease, stroke, congestive heart failure, and kidney damage. Diets rich in potassium help counterbalance some of sodium's harmful effects, so most Americans would benefit from more potassium in their diet.

Going by the Numbers

Sodium consumption should not be above 2,300 mg (2.3 grams) sodium each day, and the less consumed, the better. That is about the amount present in 1 teaspoon (5 milliliters) of salt. People with high blood pressure, African Americans, and those who are middle aged or older should take in even less sodium, as little as 1,500 mg per day. The recommended level of potassium in the diet is 4,700 mg, and the more consumed the better.

sources of sodium in the bakeshop include baking soda (sodium bicarbonate), baking powder, margarine, and peanut butter. Even water can be a source of sodium if it has been treated with a water softener to lower its mineral content.

Salt's primary function in baked goods is to provide flavor. Salt, of course, contributes a salty taste, but it also enhances other flavors. Baked goods in particular have more depth of flavor when properly salted, tasting less floury and flat and more balanced. Salt also minimizes metallic and chemical aftertastes.

The good news is that a small reduction in salt (10 percent or more) can be made in most baked goods with little effect on flavor. Higher reductions can be made in certain products, especially if they contain highly flavored ingredients such as spices, caramel, coffee, or toasted nuts. It is important to start slowly, though. Americans are accustomed to the taste of salt, and if the amount is lowered too much too soon, they will reject the product. As Americans begin collectively to lower their consumption of salt, their taste for it will also gradually decrease.

Here are some suggestions for reducing the amount of sodium and increasing the amount of potassium in baked goods.

- Consider the sodium content of your ingredients before selecting which to use. For example, regular SAPP (sodium acid pyrophosphate) baking powder adds about 190 mg to the sodium content of a 2-inch (5 cm) baking powder biscuit. Switch to SAS (sodium aluminum sulfate) baking powder, and the sodium content drops to 120 mg. Use a sodium-free baking powder and it drops to zero.
- The best way to increase potassium in baked goods is by adding fruits, and if possible, vegetables. The fruits can be fresh, frozen, dried, canned, or in juice form. Those especially rich in potassium include apricots, bananas, cantaloupes, oranges, peaches, and plums.

Besides improving flavor, salt has the following effects on yeast-raised baked goods:

- Controlling (slowing) yeast fermentation
- Strengthening gluten and making it harder to stretch
- Extending mix time (by strengthening gluten)
- Improving volume and crumb structure (by strengthening gluten)
- Increasing browning (by slowing fermentation)

Luckily, only small amounts of salt are needed to perform these functions. This means that the primary consideration in limiting the reduction of salt in yeast-raised baked goods is flavor.

- Sweet potato is one of the best sources of potassium of all fruits and vegetables. Try using sweet potato instead of pumpkin in pie fillings, breads, and muffins, and let your customers know why.
- Use dairy ingredients such as milk and yogurt to increase potassium, but use low-fat ones, if possible.
- Molasses is a significant source of potassium (also of calcium and iron), and the darker it is, the higher it is in potassium and other nutrients. Because of its strong flavor and dark color, molasses cannot be used in all baked goods. For those baked goods such as gingerbread that do contain molasses, consider using a darker molasses. If you do, though, back off on the amount of baking soda added. While some baking soda is necessary to react with molasses and provide leavening, an excess amount of baking soda raises pH and darkens color. If this excess baking soda is not removed, your baked goods could become too dark. While molasses won't always fit the flavor profile you are after, knowing that it has one of the best nutrient profiles of all common sweeteners might encourage you to offer molasses cookies and gingerbread more often.

Reducing Sugar

The recommendations for all North Americans, not only diabetics, are that sugars and caloric sweeteners should be limited. Brown sugars, honey, brown rice syrup, agave syrup, maple syrup, glucose corn syrup, and molasses all fit into this category and all should be consumed in moderation. This is because sugars and other caloric sweeteners provide calories but few or no vitamins and minerals (although molasses and other unrefined syrups do provide some vitamins and minerals). This makes it difficult to get needed nutrients without exceeding caloric needs, and could easily lead to weight gain.

From a nutritional standpoint, the best option for sweetening baked goods is to use fruits whenever possible. By adding raisins, dates, applesauce, bananas, and other sweet fruits to baked goods and desserts, the amount of added sugar and sweeteners can be reduced. Of course, fruits contribute flavor of their own. While this is fine for an applesauce cake or banana muffins, sometimes a more neutral taste is desired. When this is the case, consider using high-intensity sweeteners or polyols.

Low-calorie, high-intensity sweeteners can be acceptable for lowering the sugar in baked goods. They do not function well as the only sweetener in baked goods, though, because baked goods rely on sugars for more than just sweetness. Additionally, high-intensity sweeteners have a delayed sweetness and, to many people, a bitter aftertaste. But depending on the baked good, up to half the sugar may sometimes be replaced, with little ill effect.

Polyols (sugar alcohols) such as sorbitol, isomalt, and maltitol can be thought of as medium-calorie sweeteners because they are somewhat lower in calories than sugar. Although each has a different caloric content, on average polyols have half the calories of regular sugar. At the same time, they provide bulk and many other functions of sugars in baked goods, such as moistness and tenderness. Likewise, polyols are useful in confections. Glycerine and sorbitol, which are both hygroscopic, have been used for years by confectioners and pastry chefs to provide softness and moistness to confections. For hard candies, isomalt is the polyol of choice.

Polyols are carbohydrates, but because they are not fully absorbed and metabolized by the body, they do not have the same effect on blood sugar as do sugars. In fact, each gram of polyol counts as one-half gram of carbohydrates for diabetics. Polyols are generally used as a one-to-one replacement for sugar in confections and baked goods.

Products sweetened exclusively with polyols can be labeled "sugar-free." However, most polyols have a laxative effect and can cause diarrhea when consumed in large quantities. It is therefore best to use polyols to reduce the total amount of sugar and calories in baked goods and not to eliminate sugar completely.

Using Fats in Healthful Baked Goods

Americans do need to limit the total number of calories they consume, so the amount of fat in many baked goods is a problem. Croissants, puff pastry, Danish, and pie crusts in particular are high in fat. But many baked goods contain more moderate amounts of fat, and with some small adjustments, the amount can be further lowered.

Fats and oils have too many important functions in baked goods to eliminate them completely, and often a moderate amount of fat is all that is needed to make an acceptable product. The best approach is to produce lower-fat products made with "good" fats and oils.

Specific fats to reduce or eliminate include saturated fats, trans fats, and cholesterol. Cholesterol is present only in animal fats, including butter and lard. Butter is difficult to eliminate completely from the bakeshop, but it should be used judiciously since it is higher in saturated fats than any other fat used in the bakeshop. Sources of trans fats include margarines and chocolate (confectionery) coatings, as well as shortenings.

The best way to reduce saturated fats, trans fats, and cholesterol in baked goods is to use liquid vegetable oils whenever possible. Some formulas for cakes (chiffon), muffins, mealy pie crusts, brownies, and cookies are already designed to be made with oil, and these baked goods can be more healthful because of it. For example,

mealy pie crusts made with oil are always lower in fat than flaky pie crusts, because oil is more efficient than chunks of solid fat at coating flour particles and reducing the toughening of gluten. Unlike flaky crusts, mealy ones do not become unpleasantly rubbery when used with a moist filling, so they are commonly used for the bottom crust of cream pies. Since most oils are healthier fats than shortening, lard, or butter, this is an easy way to create a more healthful pie crust, with little effort.

Here are some additional guidelines to consider when using fats in healthful baked goods.

- When switching from solid fat to liquid oil, realize that essentially all oils except tropical oils are low in saturated fat, but some are lower than others. Canola oil, for example, is a good all-purpose oil to use in the bakeshop. It is particularly low in saturated fatty acids, it is available from many purveyors, and it is reasonably priced. Because it is also lower than many oils in total polyunsaturated fatty acids, it is slower to develop rancid off flavors. While Figure 9.6 on page 216 favorably compares the fatty acid profile of canola oil with that of other fats and oils, remember that any oil can be bred or genetically modified to have a fatty acid profile similar to canola oil.

- Consider blending butter with other fats in cookies, cakes, icings, etc. for a butter flavor but less saturated fat. Some all-purpose shortenings are as low as 25 percent saturated fat, compared with butter at close to 70 percent saturated fat. When substituting shortening or oil for butter, remember that both are higher in fat than butter, so adjust your formula accordingly (see page 230 for details).

- While cookies can be made with all oil instead of butter or shortening, they will likely spread more. To counteract this effect, replace some or all of the flour with cake flour.

- To lower the amount of fat in cakes, use a high-ratio shortening that contains highly effective emulsifiers that moisten, tenderize, and aerate better than fats and oils. A typical cake formula can be made with 20–40 percent less fat by switching from all-purpose shortening, butter, or margarine to a high-ratio liquid shortening, for example. Remember that liquid shortenings cannot be creamed, so the method of preparation also needs to be changed if this fat is used.

- Use low-fat dairy ingredients instead of regular cream cheese, sour cream, half-and-half, and yogurt

Functions of Fats

As is true of all important ingredients in the bake-shop, fats, oils, and emulsifiers are multifunctional. The most important functions are:

- Tenderizing
- Providing flakiness
- Assisting in leavening
- Contributing moistness
- Preventing staling
- Adding a rich, longer-lasting flavor

> **HELPFUL HINT**
>
> *Remember that ingredients such as walnuts, flaxseed, and flaxseed oil, which are high in ALA omega-3 and other polyunsaturated fatty acids, oxidize and produce rancid off flavors quickly. Be sure to order only what is needed for a three-month period, practice FIFO, and store these ingredients away from heat and light. Whenever possible, consider refrigerating them.*

in the bakeshop. These ingredients have a creamy mouthfeel from added vegetable gums. Use them in low-fat cheesecakes, baked custards, and icings.

- Replace some or all of the whole eggs in a recipe with egg whites. Because egg yolks are about one-third fat, and each yolk contains over two-thirds the recommended 300 milligram daily limit on cholesterol, eliminating them could significantly lower the cholesterol (if not the fat) in baked goods. If necessary, replace a small amount of white flour—about 5 or 10 percent—with corn flour, for a yellow color.

- Nuts are a great source of healthful fats, and they add wonderful flavor and textural contrast to baked goods. To maximize flavor, toast nuts before use. Nuts are high in fat (most are 50–75 percent fat), so when they are finely ground and added to batters and doughs, other fats can be reduced. But because they are high in fat and tend to be expensive, nuts should not be used indiscriminately. Additionally, some of your customers may be allergic to certain nuts, so be sure that products made with them are clearly labeled.

- Walnuts are high in ALA omega-3 fatty acids, a healthful fat. Other bakeshop ingredients that are high in ALA omega-3 fatty acids include ground flaxseeds, flaxseed oil, and canola oil, although flaxseed

oil is expensive and not readily available. However, flaxseed might be useful in specialty baked goods, because over half its fatty acids are ALA omega-3.

Fat Replacers Sometimes fats and oils can be reduced incrementally without replacing the fat with anything else. This is especially true if eggs or another structure builder are reduced at the same time. Most times, though, a fat replacer must be used if the fat is to be reduced by any significant amount.

Because fats perform many functions in baked goods, it is difficult for any single fat replacer to complete the job. For example, one fat replacer might provide a buttery flavor but not increase tenderness. Another might increase tenderness and moistness but not provide any flavor. Few, if any, provide flakiness, and only one, olestra, can be used in frying. Even when a combination of fat replacers is used, it is difficult to eliminate fat completely without trial and error.

To decide which of the many fat replacers to use in a particular product, first decide which functions the fat provides in that product. Next, select one or more fat replacers that perform those same functions. Table 18.1 lists the functions of specific fat replacers in baked goods, but different fat replacers do not necessarily work equally well in all products. Once again, trial and error is usually warranted.

Notice that sugars and sweeteners are listed as fat replacers. Sugars and sweeteners provide two important functions of fats: moistening and tenderizing. Be careful, however, about replacing fats with sugar, since health guidelines recommend lowering both fats and sugars. A few common fat replacers are discussed in more detail below.

- *Dried Plum Paste.* Dried plum (prune) paste is best when used in highly flavored, chewy products such as fudge brownies or soft molasses cookies. As with all dried fruits, including raisins and dates, dried plums naturally contain sugars, pectin, and fruit pulp that moisten and tenderize and provide a gummy

> **HELPFUL HINT**
>
> *So that low-fat foods have a satisfying flavor, make use of ingredients that are rich in so-called middle and base notes. Ingredients rich in middle and base notes include spices, caramelized sugar, toasted nuts, cocoa, and maple syrup.*

TABLE 18.1 FAT REPLACERS IN BAKED GOODS

TYPE	EXAMPLE	FAT FUNCTION
Butter flavor	Natural and artificial butter flavorings	Adding flavor
Emulsifiers	Mono- and diglycerides	Adding moistness, tenderness, aeration; delaying staling
Certain fruits	Prune paste, applesauce, mashed bananas	Adding aeration (from steam, if high in moisture), moistness, tenderness; delaying staling
Pureed beans	Black or cannellini (white) beans	Adding moistness, tenderness, aeration (from steam); delaying staling
Gums	Pectin, cellulose gum, xanthan gum	Adding tenderness, aeration, creamy mouthfeel
Nondigestible lipids	Olestra	Assisting in heat transfer (frying); adding moistness, fatty mouthfeel
Oat-based ingredients	Oatmeal, oat flour	Tenderizing low-moisture products; delaying staling
Starches and starch by-products	Potato starch, maltodextrins	Tenderizing low-moisture products
Sugars and sweeteners	Dextrose, granulated sugar	Adding moistness and tenderness

chewiness. In addition, dried plums are high in sorbitol, a polyol that further moistens and tenderizes.

Dried plum paste can be purchased or can be prepared by blending dried plums with water in a food processor until smooth. Add about 12 ounces of hot water for every pound of dried plums. To use in baked goods, replace each pound of fat with 8 ounces of dried plum paste. (Thinking metrically, combine about 750 grams hot water with 1 kilogram dried plums, and replace each kilogram of fat with 500 grams of the dried plum paste.) This is a starting point only; make adjustments as needed.

- *Applesauce.* Unsweetened applesauce works well as a fat replacer in muffins, quick breads, cakes, and cake-like brownies. Its high moisture content (about 88 percent) allows for good aeration in these products. This same high moisture, however, makes applesauce less acceptable for use in crisp cookies or dense, fudge-like brownies. Because applesauce is relatively bland, it does not affect flavor as much as other fruit purees.

When using applesauce instead of fat or oil, start with a one-for-one replacement, then adjust as needed. It is generally necessary to reduce the liquid in the formula to compensate for the water in applesauce. This is best done by reducing the amount of egg to rebalance tougheners with tenderizers. Rebalancing is necessary because applesauce is not as effective a tenderizer as fat and sometimes actually increases structure, since its high moisture content can increase starch gelatinization.

- *Beans.* Canned black beans are popular as a fat replacer in brownies. Although not as high as applesauce in moisture, at about 70 percent moisture black beans do require that the liquid in a formula—and sometimes the amount of egg—be reduced. Beans, including black beans, are surprisingly neutral-tasting, and they contribute to good nutrition because they are high in protein, fiber, vitamins, and minerals. Because canned beans contain salt, reduce or omit any added salt from the formula.

Food Allergies

Each year, millions of Americans have allergic reactions to food, and thousands of these reactions are serious enough for visits to the emergency room. Although most food allergies cause relatively mild symptoms (Table 18.2), severe food allergies can result in a life-threatening allergic reaction called *anaphylaxis*. This severe reaction can prevent the victim from breathing because of swelling of the mouth, throat, and airways

TABLE 18.2 COMMON SYMPTOMS OF ALLERGIC REACTIONS TO FOODS

Red bumpy rash on the skin
Redness and swelling around the mouth
Cramps, diarrhea, nausea, vomiting
Runny nose, itchy watery eyes, sneezing
Weakness and fainting

leading to the lungs. In addition, there can be a dangerous drop in blood pressure, which can lead to anaphylactic shock and death.

Allergic reactions occur when certain proteins (allergens) in food trigger a response in the body's immune system. There is currently no cure for a food allergy. The only way to prevent a reaction is to totally avoid the food. More than 160 foods can cause allergic reactions; the most common food products that trigger

HELPFUL HINT

Traces of nuts and particles of flour can be life-threatening to those who are highly allergic. Ideally, separate work surfaces, equipment, and utensils would be used when preparing foods for those with allergies. When this is not possible, review all bakeshop practices, and eliminate those, like the reuse of parchment paper, which could unintentionally pass an allergen from one product to the next. Always be scrupulous about cleaning work areas to prevent inadvertent cross-contamination and the transfer of food allergens from one product to another.

anaphylactic reactions are listed in Table 18.3. Taken together, these eight foods trigger 90 percent of food allergy cases in the United States. Notice that of these eight allergens, six are commonly used in baked goods.

In Canada, two additional foods are considered top priority food allergens: sesame seeds and sulfites (a food additive in many dried fruits). Unlike in the United States, Canadian law does not currently require manufacturers to identify allergens on food labels. This will likely change soon.

Wheat-Free and Gluten-Free Products

There is a difference between wheat allergies and celiac disease. Wheat allergies occur when the body's immune system reacts to the presence of one or more wheat proteins. It can result in anaphylaxis and death. Celiac disease is an inherited intolerance to gluten that results in an inflammation of the intestines. Because awareness has increased in the past few years about celiac disease and more people are diagnosed with it, consumers are requesting that more gluten-free products become available.

Since all gluten-free products are also wheat-free, from this point on, references will be made to gluten-free products, with the understanding that this includes wheat-free products as well.

Preparing gluten-free baked goods can be a challenge, but it is not impossible. Some traditional baked goods are already gluten-free. For example, flourless cakes are made with ground nuts instead of flour as the bulking agent, and some sponge cakes contain potato or rice starch instead of flour.

TABLE 18.3 EIGHT MAJOR SOURCES OF FOOD ALLERGENS

ALLERGEN	EXAMPLES
Wheat	All wheat flours, including durum semolina, spelt, kamut, triticale, einkorn, and emmer
Soy	Soy flour, tofu, soy lecithin, but not soybean oil
Milk	All milk and dairy products, including cream, yogurt, cheese, whey proteins, whey solids, and butter
Eggs	Includes all parts of the egg
Peanuts	Includes peanut butter
Tree nuts	Almonds, cashews, hazelnuts, macadamia nuts, pecans, pine nuts, pistachios, and walnuts
Fish	Salmon, cod, haddock, tilapia
Crustaceans	Shrimp, lobster, crab

Celiac disease is a disease of the intestinal tract brought about by the consumption of gluten (more specifically, the gliadin in gluten). When people with celiac disease consume gluten—even very small amounts of it—their bodies react by damaging the small intestine, where nutrients are absorbed by the body. Without proper absorption of nutrients, people with celiac disease (also called celiac sprue or gluten intolerance) become malnourished. They may develop a range of symptoms related to intestinal distress or to poor nutrition.

Because people with celiac disease cannot tolerate any amount of gluten, they must adhere to a strict gluten-free diet for their entire lives. This means that they cannot consume any products that contain wheat. They also cannot consume any rye or barley, and oats may be a problem for many. Those with celiac disease often are also lactose intolerant.

Celiac disease is genetic, passed down from one generation to the next. Since it is the most common genetic disease in Europe (affecting one out of every 250 Italians, for example), it is likely that many Americans have celiac disease. While celiac disease remains largely undiagnosed in this country, diagnosis is available through a blood test or through biopsy of tissue from the small intestine.

In place of wheat flour, gluten-free products usually contain some combination of rice, potato, and tapioca starches. Often soy or garbanzo bean flour is included, for added protein. Xanthan or another gum is generally added at 1–3 percent for its ability to trap air. It is this ability to trap air that allows gluten-free cakes, muffins, and breads to rise properly and have a light, airy crumb. Xanthan gum also improves the cohesiveness and flexibility of gluten-free doughs so that they can be rolled and handled without breaking (Figure 18.1). After some experimentation, it is possible to develop acceptable products for sufferers of celiac disease.

Figure 18.1 Foreground: gluten-free pie dough without added xanthan gum falls apart. **Background:** gluten-free dough with added xanthan gum holds together and can be rolled

Because gluten-free baking mixes are high in water-grabbing gums and starches, be sure that there is enough water present to both hydrate the gums and gelatinize the starches. If not, the baked product will be gritty, from starch granules that have not fully gelatinized. This is especially true of cornstarch. When this occurs, add more water if possible, bake for longer, or replace the cornstarch with another starch, such as rice starch, that gelatinizes at a lower temperature. Instant starches and precooked cornmeal, which do not need heat to gelatinize, are particularly useful in gluten-free cakes and breads that rely on the soft structure of gelatinized starch for proper texture.

Milk-Free Products

Milk is one of the most common food allergens for babies and toddlers. While most will outgrow milk allergies, not all do. Many more people have lactose intolerance. Lactose intolerance is a food sensitivity that originates in the gastrointestinal tract and is caused by the inability to digest the lactose in milk. Unlike a milk allergy, lactose intolerance is a sensitivity that does not involve the immune system. Symptoms of lactose intolerance include abdominal pain, bloating, diarrhea, and flatulence. Since these can also be symptoms of a milk allergy, it might appear that there is little distinction between the two. However, a milk allergy is more serious, and those with it must avoid milk products altogether. Those with lactose intolerance can often tolerate small or moderate amounts of milk.

Here is a summary of a few of the functions of milk in baked goods:

- Increasing crust color
- Increasing crust softness
- Delaying staling
- Improving flavor
- Adding nutritional value

Milk ingredients provide several functions in pastries and baked goods, but luckily the effects are usually small. This means that unlike eggs, fat, or flour, milk is relatively easy to leave out of many baked goods. Often simply substituting milk with water is all that is needed. For some products, however, milk is important to the balance of flavor. Without it, baked goods can taste flat.

Here are some recommendations for producing milk-free products and products for lactose intolerant individuals.

- Review formulas carefully. You might find that you already produce many milk-free products. For example, many brownies, cookies, soufflés, pies, sponge cakes, pound cakes, and breads are naturally milk free.
- Use margarine instead of butter, but check the label first. Some margarines contain milk or whey ingredients. These are not acceptable for anyone with a milk allergy, although they might be tolerated by those unable to digest lactose.
- Some dark chocolates, as well as all milk and white chocolates, contain dairy ingredients. Remember that even tiny amounts of milk proteins can be life-threatening for those with milk allergies.
- Most cakes, muffins, biscuits, and scones contain milk but can be made with water. However, milk blends flavors and reduces the raw flour taste of baked goods, so its absence will be missed in plain-tasting products.
- Kefir, yogurt, buttermilk, and other cultured dairy products are unacceptable for those with milk allergies, but they are tolerated by many with lactose intolerance. This is because lactic acid bacteria convert lactose into lactic acid. The actual amount of conversion varies with the extent of fermentation, but kefir typically is the lowest of all in lactose, sometimes having half the amount in milk.
- Because of their bland flavor and pale color, cashews are sometimes soaked in water and blended into a smooth cream that can be used to replace cream in frozen desserts and cheese in cheesecakes.

If desired, milk substitutes can be used in place of milk and other dairy ingredients. The most common milk substitute is soymilk. Other milk substitutes include rice milk, almond milk, and cashew milk. These milky substances are made by soaking and blending rice, almonds, or cashews in hot water and filtering out the solids.

Soy-Based Milk Substitutes Soymilk is typically made by blanching soybeans in hot water, then grinding them and filtering out the solids. The process actually has many complicated steps, with the result that different brands vary greatly in appearance, flavor, and mouthfeel. Most brands contain flavorings and sweeteners to mask the "beany" taste of soymilk, and are thickened with carrageenan or other gums. Because soymilk is such a common milk substitute, it is often fortified with calcium, vitamin D, and B vitamins, to mimic the nutritional profile of whole milk.

While soymilk and other milk substitutes do not necessarily function better than water in baked goods, soymilk in particular, with its high-quality protein, is most similar to regular milk in nutrients. This might be reason enough to use it instead of water in place of milk. However, soymilk can contribute a flavor of its own, and it is a food allergen in its own right.

Soymilk does not interact with egg proteins as strongly as does regular milk, so custard-based desserts will require longer cook or bake times. Additionally, some instant pudding and flan mixes—those that contain carrageenan—will not thicken or gel when made with soy or other milk replacers. Carrageenan is a vegetable gum extracted from seaweed, and it thickens and gels best in the presence of milk proteins.

Instead of soymilk, which is thin, many custard and cream desserts are better when made with soy creamer or silken tofu. Silken tofu has a custard-like texture, so it is sometimes used to replace both eggs and milk. It is the best choice for use in puddings, creams, and custard-based products including pumpkin pie, chocolate cream pie, cheesecake, crème caramel, pastry cream, and vanilla custard sauce. Just remember that soy products are highly processed, so they vary greatly from

Tofu is another name for soybean curd. The traditional way of making tofu is to coagulate soymilk using calcium or magnesium salts (*nigari*), forming a cheese-like curd. The curd is pressed, squeezing out excess liquid, much as cheese is made by separating curds from liquid whey. The more liquid is pressed out, the firmer the tofu. Tofu holds its shape when heated, and its bland flavor picks up the flavor of any liquid that it is cooked in.

If regular tofu is similar to cheese in its manufacture, silken tofu, also called *Japanese tofu*, is in some ways similar to sour cream production. The process for silken tofu starts with soymilk made with less water, heated to pasteurize, then cooled. A slow-dissolving acid (glucono-delta-lactone or GDL) is added, the soymilk is packaged, and the sealed containers are placed in a hot water bath for about an hour. GDL releases acid as it is heated in this manner, and the acid coagulates the soy proteins, forming a homogeneous gel that traps the liquid. Since none of the liquid is squeezed out, silken tofu is smooth and creamy. Silken tofu comes with different consistencies, from soft to extra firm.

When placed in the blender, silken tofu forms a thick, creamy homogeneous mass, while regular tofu breaks into small crumbles. Silken tofu is the tofu of choice when used in place of cream and other dairy products in the bakeshop.

---

one brand to the next. Try different brands to determine which works best for you.

Egg-Free Products

Eggs are important in many baked goods, but they are more important in some than in others. As when making substitutions of any important ingredient, determine the functions of egg in your baked good before selecting an egg replacer. If they serve primarily as a structure builder, they can often be replaced with another structure builder, such as starch. Often, when eggs are eliminated from a formula, the fat must be reduced to rebalance the tenderizers with the tougheners. If eggs are needed for aeration, it is possible that adding more moisture along with an ingredient that holds in expanding steam will work.

Functions of Eggs

Here is a summary of a few of the functions of eggs in baked goods:

- Providing structure/Is a toughener
- Contributing to leavening through aeration and added moisture
- Emulsifying and binding ingredients together
- Contributing flavor
- Contributing color
- Adding nutritional value

> **HELPFUL HINT**
>
> *When eliminating eggs from baked goods such as cookies, muffins, and cakes, add between 5 and 7 ounces of water or milk for every 10 ounces of egg removed (or 50–70 grams water or milk for every 100 grams egg). If desired, also add about 1.5 ounces dried milk solids (or 15 grams). The batter or dough will be stiffer than usual, but the product is less likely to bake up wet, gummy, or overly soft.*

Here are some suggestions for eliminating eggs in baked goods.

- Start with formulas that are already low in eggs. The fewer eggs called for, the easier it will be to eliminate them. For example, cookies and muffins are usually relatively easy to reformulate without eggs. In fact, some cookies, such as shortbread cookies, contain no eggs. Cakes and breads that are already low in eggs are also good choices for converting. Stay away from sponge cakes, angel food cakes, and choux paste.
- For cookies, muffins, and cakes, first try substituting water, milk, or water and dried milk solids for egg. Often, this is all that is needed. Although eggs are about 75 percent water, you will need less water than the amount in eggs, since egg proteins act as driers and structure builders.
- Fruit and bean purees work as egg replacers because they are high in moisture and contribute to leavening. These purees naturally contain vegetable gums

TABLE 18.4 EGG REPLACERS IN BAKED GOODS

EGG REPLACER	EGG FUNCTION
Water alone	Moistening/hydrating driers; providing steam for leavening
Water plus dried milk solids	Moistening hydrating driers; providing steam for leavening; adding nutrition; improving flavor and browning
Starches such as potato, rice, tapioca, precooked corn Flours and grains such as cake flour, oatmeal Starch-based egg replacer powder, with added vegetable gums	Providing structure; binding batters and doughs; thickening, to hold in air for leavening
Yellow corn flour	Adding yellow egg color to baked goods; providing structure
Silken tofu	Moistening; thickens; providing steam for leavening; adding nutrition; adding emulsifiers (lecithin); also functions as milk substitute
Flaxseed, ground and beaten into water	Moistening; providing steam for leavening; adding nutrition; binding batters and doughs; thickening, to hold in air for leavening
Fruit (banana, applesauce) and bean (black or cannellini) purees	Moistening; providing steam for leavening; adding nutrition; binding batters and doughs; also functions as partial fat substitute

and pulpy matter, so they also thicken and help hold in air.

- Oatmeal cookies are especially easy to make with water instead of eggs, since moistened oatmeal binds ingredients as it bakes. Use quick oats rather than old-fashioned or steel-cut ones, and use less water than the amount of eggs replaced, or the cookies will bake up too tender. The smaller cut of quick-cooking oats allows this form of oatmeal to thicken and bind quickly.

- For a rich, yellow color in baked goods where eggs are replaced with water or milk, substitute finely ground yellow corn flour for 10–20 percent of white flour. If available, use instant (precooked) corn flour to eliminate grittiness. Or heat the liquid from the formula to a boil, stir into corn flour, and set aside to cool before use.

- Use silken (not regular) tofu in egg-free creams and custards, including pastry cream, cream pie fillings, bread pudding, rice pudding, and cheesecake. Blend to a smooth consistency in a blender or food processor. The silken tofu can substitute for both eggs and milk. It and other soy products are best used in products with strong flavors like chocolate, coffee, caramel, and spices.

- Serve panna cotta in place of custards and flans. Panna cotta is a milk-based dessert gelled with gelatin rather than eggs. Agar could also be used to prepare milk-based gelled desserts.

- Finely ground flaxseeds are sometimes used as an egg replacer in cookies, cakes, and other baked goods. When blended at high speed with water (1 part by weight flaxseed with 4 parts water), the gummy mucilage in flaxseed thickens the mix and thickens batters and doughs. Flaxseed has a slightly nutty flavor, but when used at low levels, it is hardly noticeable.

Questions for Review

1 What are the guidelines for North Americans for whole grain consumption?

2 What are the health advantages of increasing whole grain consumption?

3 What are the guidelines for North Americans for sodium and potassium consumption?

4 Name three bakeshop ingredients that are significant sources of sodium.

5 Name three bakeshop ingredients that are significant sources of potassium.

6 What are the guidelines for North Americans for fat, oil, and cholesterol consumption?

7 Which common bakeshop ingredients are high in saturated fats? Which contain cholesterol?

8 What are the guidelines for North Americans for sugar consumption?

9 What are the eight major sources of food allergens?

10 Besides common (regular) wheat, what other grains must be labeled as wheat allergens (because they are different varieties of wheat)?

11 What is the difference between a wheat allergy and celiac disease/gluten intolerance?

12 Besides wheat, what other grains contain gluten and are not appropriate for those with celiac disease?

13 What is the difference between a milk allergy and lactose intolerance?

Exercises and Experiments

❶ Experiment: How Different Whole Wheat Flours and a Gluten-Free Mix Affect the Overall Quality of Muffins

Objectives

Demonstrate how the type of flour affects
- Crispness and the extent of Maillard browning on the crust of muffins
- Crumb color and structure
- Moistness, tenderness, and height of the muffins
- Overall flavor of muffins
- Overall acceptability of muffins

Products Prepared

Muffins made with
- Pastry flour (control product)
- Whole wheat flour (hard wheat)
- Whole wheat pastry flour (soft wheat)
- Whole white wheat flour (soft wheat)
- Gluten-free baking mix (see Formula on page 488, or purchase a pre-blended mix)
- Other, if desired (70/30 blend of pastry/whole wheat; 50/50 blend of pastry/whole wheat; 30/70 blend of pastry/whole wheat.)

Materials and Equipment

- Scale
- Sieve
- Parchment paper
- Muffin pans (2½" or 3½"/65 or 90 mm size)
- Paper liners, pan spray, or pan coating
- Mixer with 5-quart mixing bowl
- Whisk
- Flat beater attachment
- Basic Muffin Batter (see Formula), enough to make 24 or more muffins of each variation
- Size #16 (2 fl. oz./30 ml) portion-control scoop or equivalent
- Half sheet pans (optional)
- Oven thermometer
- Wooden pick, for testing
- Serrated knife
- Ruler

Formula

Gluten-Free Baking Mix

Yield: *Enough for 1 batch of Basic Muffin Batter*

INGREDIENT	POUND	OUNCE	GRAMS	BAKER'S PERCENTAGE
Rice flour, white		13.2	375	67
Potato starch		4.5	125	23
Tapioca starch		2	60	10
Xanthan gum		0.3	10	1.8
Total	1	4	570	101.8

Method of Preparation

1. Combine ingredients and sift three times through sieve.

2. Set aside until ready to use.

Formula

Basic Muffin Batter

Yield: *24 muffins (you will have some excess batter)*

INGREDIENT	POUND	OUNCE	GRAMS	BAKER'S PERCENTAGE
Flour	1	4	570	100
Sugar, regular granulated		8	225	40
Salt (1 tsp/5 ml)		0.2	6	1
Baking powder		1.2	35	6
Oil, vegetable		7	200	35
Eggs, whole		6	170	30
Milk, whole	1		455	80
Total	**3**	**10.4**	**1,661**	**292**

Method of Preparation

1 Preheat oven to 400°F (200°C).

2 Line muffin pans with paper liners, lightly spray with pan spray, or lightly grease with pan coating.

3 Sift dry ingredients together into mixer bowl. Note: if all particles (for example, bran particles) do not fit through sieve, stir them back into mixture.

4 Whisk egg lightly; blend in milk and oil.

5 Pour liquids onto dry ingredients and mix with flat beater just until flour is moistened. Batter will look lumpy.

6 Scoop batter into prepared muffins pans using level #16 scoop, about 2 ounces (57 grams) by weight each (or any scoop that fills cup one-half to three-quarters full).

7 If desired, place muffin pans on half sheet pans.

Procedure

1 Prepare muffin batter using the Basic Muffin Batter formula or using any basic muffin formula. Prepare one batch of batter for each variation.

2 Label muffin pans or ovens with type of flour to be added to muffin batter.

3 Use an oven thermometer placed in center of oven for an initial reading of oven temperature; record results here: _____.

4 When oven is properly preheated, place filled muffin pans in oven and set timer for 20–22 minutes.

5 Bake until control product (made with pastry flour) springs back when center top is lightly pressed, and wooden pick inserted into center of cake comes out clean. Control product should be lightly browned. Remove all muffins from oven after same length of time, even though some will be paler in color or have not risen properly. If necessary, however, adjust bake times for oven variances.

6 Record bake times in Results Table 1.

7 Check final oven temperature. Record results here: _____.

8 Remove muffins from hot pans and cool to room temperature.

Results

1 When muffins are completely cooled, evaluate height as follows:
  • Slice three muffins from each batch in half, being careful not to compress.
  • Measure height of each cupcake by placing ruler along the flat edge at the cupcake's center point. Record results for each of three muffins in ¹⁄₁₆" (1 mm) increments and record results in Results Table 1.
  • Calculate the average muffin height for each batch by adding the heights of the muffins and dividing by 3. Record results in Results Table 1.
  • Evaluate the shape of muffins (even rounded top, peaked top, dips in center, etc.) and record results in Results Table 1.

RESULTS TABLE 1 EVALUATION OF SIZE AND SHAPE OF MUFFINS MADE WITH DIFFERENT TYPES OF FLOUR

TYPE OF FLOUR	BAKE TIME (IN MINUTES)	HEIGHT OF EACH OF THREE MUFFINS	AVERAGE HEIGHT OF ONE MUFFIN	MUFFIN SHAPE	ADDITIONAL COMMENTS
Pastry flour (control product)					
Whole wheat flour					
Whole wheat pastry flour					
Whole white wheat flour					
Gluten-free baking mix					

2 Evaluate the sensory characteristics of completely cooled products and record evaluations in Results Table 2. Be sure to compare each in turn to the control product and consider the following:

- Crust color, from very light to very dark on a scale of 1 to 5
- Crumb appearance (small/large air cells, uniform/irregular air cells, tunnels, etc); also, evaluate color
- Crumb texture (tough/tender, moist/dry, crumbly, gritty, gummy, spongy, etc.)
- Flavor (grain flavor, floury taste, saltiness, sweetness, bitterness, etc.)
- Overall acceptability, from highly unacceptable to highly acceptable, on a scale of 1 to 5.
- Any additional comments, as necessary

RESULTS TABLE 2 SENSORY CHARACTERISTICS OF MUFFINS MADE WITH DIFFERENT TYPES OF FLOUR

TYPE OF FLOUR	CRUST COLOR	CRUMB APPEARANCE AND TEXTURE	FLAVOR	OVERALL ACCEPTABILITY	ADDITIONAL COMMENTS
Pastry flour (control product)					
Whole wheat flour					
Whole wheat pastry flour					
Whole white wheat flour					
Gluten-free baking mix					

Sources of Error

List any sources of error that might make it difficult to draw the proper conclusions from your experiment. In particular, consider if there were differences in how batters were mixed and handled, any difficulty in dispensing equal weights of batter into muffin pans, and any problems with ovens.

_____

_____

_____

State what you could do differently next time to minimize or eliminate each source of error.

_____

_____

_____

Conclusions

Select one from the choices in **bold** or fill in the blanks.

1 Muffins made with regular whole wheat flour were **shorter than/taller than/the same height as** those made with pastry flour. The difference in height was **small/moderate/large**.

2 The difference in texture between muffins made with regular whole wheat flour and those made with white pastry flour was **small/moderate/large**. The difference can be described as follows:

_____

_____

_____

3 Compare muffins that were made with whole wheat pastry flour with those made with regular whole wheat flour. What were the main differences in appearance, flavor, and texture?

_____

_____

_____

These differences were **small/moderate/large**. How do you explain these results?

_____

_____

_____

4 Compare muffins that were made with gluten-free baking mix with those made with pastry flour (control product). What were the main differences in appearance, flavor, and texture?

_____

_____

_____

These differences were **small/moderate/large**. How do you explain these results?

_____

_____

_____

5 Which muffins did you feel were unacceptable overall, and why?

_____

_____

_____

What could you do differently next time so that these muffins are more acceptable?

_____

_____

_____

6 Did you notice any other differences in the muffins, or do you have any other comments about the experiment?

_____

_____

_____

❷ Experiment: Fat Replacers in Brownies

Modifying standards formulas is often a trial and error process. The best approach is usually to make step-wise adjustments, changing only one ingredient at a time, evaluating each product along the way before deciding the next step.

This experiment is as much about the process of modifying a formula as it is about making a low-fat brownie. By first replacing the full amount of oil in brownies with black beans, then making step-wise adjustments to produce a low-fat brownie closer in quality to the full-fat product, you can learn how black beans function as a fat replacer, and how to compensate for undesirable changes when using black beans in place of fat.

Objectives

- Demonstrate the step-wise process of modifying a formula
- Demonstrate how a fat replacer affects
  - Appearance of brownies
  - Moistness, tenderness, and height of brownies
  - Flavor of brownies
  - Overall acceptability of brownies

Products Prepared

Brownies made with
- Oil (control product)
- Black bean puree
- Black bean puree with half the amount of egg
- Half oil, half black bean puree with half the amount of egg
- Other, if desired (unsweetened applesauce, unsweetened applesauce with half the amount of egg, half oil/half applesauce with half the amount of egg)

Materials and Equipment

- Scale
- Half sheet pans
- Parchment paper, silicone pad, pan spray, or pan coating
- Mixer with 5-quart mixing bowl
- Flat beater attachment

- Sieve
- Food processor
- Brownies (see Formula), enough to make one half sheet pan of each variation
- Spatula
- Oven thermometer
- Wooden pick, for testing
- Serrated knife
- Ruler

Formula

Brownies

Yield: *One half sheet pan*

INGREDIENT	POUNDS	OUNCES	GRAMS	BAKER'S PERCENTAGE
Oil, canola		12	340	150
Sugar, regular granulated	1	9	700	311
Vanilla extract		0.5	15	6.5
Eggs, whole		12	340	150
Flour, pastry		8	225	100
Cocoa powder, dutched		4.5	125	56
Baking powder		0.25	7	3
Salt		0.25	7	4.5
Total	**3**	**14.6**	**1,762**	**781**

Method of Preparation
(for control product)

1 Preheat oven to 350°F (175°C).

2 Line half sheet pans with parchment or silicone pad, lightly spray with pan spray, or lightly grease with pan coating.

3 Using flat beater, stir oil and sugar in mixer bowl on low speed for 1 minute.

4 Add vanilla extract and eggs. Mix on low speed for 30 seconds.

5 Sift flour, cocoa powder, baking powder, and salt together three times.

6 Add dry ingredients to wet ingredients and mix on low speed 30 seconds or until well blended.

7 Spread 3 pounds 8 ounces (1550 grams) batter evenly in prepared pan.

Method of Preparation
(for brownies with varying amounts of black bean puree and eggs)

Follow the Method of Preparation for the control product, except for the following changes:

1   Rinse and drain three 16 ounce (454 gram) cans of black beans in strainer.

2   Puree beans in food processor until smooth and homogeneous.

3   For brownies made with black bean puree, substitute 12 ounces (340 grams) black bean puree for the full amount of oil in step 3.

4   For brownies made with black bean puree and a lower amount of egg, substitute 12 ounces (340 grams) black bean puree for the full amount of oil in step 3. Reduce the amount of egg from 12 ounces (340 grams) to 6 ounces (170 grams) in step 4.

5   For brownies made with half oil, half black bean puree, and a lower amount of egg, use 6 ounces (170 grams) oil, 6 ounces (170 grams) black bean puree in step 3. Use 6 ounces (170 grams) eggs in step 4.

Procedure

1   Prepare brownies using the above formula or using any basic brownie formula. Prepare one batch of brownies for each variation.

2   Label sheet pans or ovens with type of fat replacer used in brownies.

3   Use an oven thermometer placed in center of oven for an initial reading of oven temperature. Record results here: _____.

4   When oven is properly preheated, place filled sheet pans in oven and set timer for 30–35 minutes.

5   Bake until brownies firm up and a wooden pick comes out clean.

6   Record bake times in Results Table, which follows.

7   Check final oven temperature. Record results here: _____.

8   Cool to room temperature and remove from pan.

Results

1   When brownies are completely cooled, evaluate height as follows:
   - Slice batch in half, being careful not to compress.
   - Measure height of brownies by placing ruler along the flat edge of the brownies at the center of the pan. Record results in $\frac{1}{16}$" (1 mm) increments and record in Results Table.

2   Evaluate the sensory characteristics of completely cooled products and record evaluations in Results Table. Be sure to compare each in turn to the control product and consider the following:
   - Crust color and appearance (light/dark, shiny/dull, smooth/rough/pocked)
   - Crumb appearance (light/dark in color, airy/dense, cake-like/gummy, etc.)

- Texture (tough/tender, moist/dry, gummy, spongy, etc.)
- Flavor (sweet, salty, bitter, chocolate, vanilla, other, etc.)
- Overall acceptability, from highly unacceptable to highly acceptable, on a scale of 1 to 5
- Any additional comments, as necessary

RESULTS TABLE EVALUATION OF BROWNIES MADE WITH A FAT REPLACER

VARIATION	BAKE TIME, MINUTES	HEIGHT	CRUST COLOR AND APPEARANCE	CRUMB APPEARANCE	TEXTURE	FLAVOR	OVERALL ACCEPTABILITY	ADDITIONAL COMMENTS
Full amount of oil (control product)								
Black bean puree								
Black bean puree with half the amount of egg								
Half oil, half black bean puree with half the amount of egg								

Sources of Error

List any sources of error that might make it difficult to draw the proper conclusions from your experiment. In particular, consider if there were differences in how batters were mixed and handled, how smoothly the black beans were pureed, and any problems with ovens.

_____

_____

_____

State what you could do differently next time to minimize or eliminate each source of error.

_____

_____

_____

Conclusions

Select one from the choices in **bold** or fill in the blanks.

1 Brownies made with black bean puree were **shorter than/taller than/the same height as** those made with the full amount of oil. The difference in height was **small/moderate/large**. Black bean puree contributed to leavening because it contains water that converts in the oven to _____, one of the three main leavening gases in baked goods.

2 Brownies made with black bean puree were more **cake-like/chewy** in texture than those made with the full amount of oil. The difference in texture was **small/moderate/large**, and is partly because black beans are high in **moisture/fat**, which is needed for starch to **gelatinize/coagulate**. Other differences between brownies made with black bean puree and those made with the full amount of oil (control product) were as follows:

_____

_____

_____

3 Halving the amount of eggs in brownies made with black bean puree made the brownies **more/less** like the brownies made with the full amount of oil (control product). That is, lowering the amount of eggs made the brownies more **cake-like/chewy** in texture. Other differences between black bean brownies made with half the amount of eggs and those made with the full amount of eggs were as follows:

_____

_____

_____

4 Brownies made with half the amount of oil, black bean puree, and half the amount of eggs **were/were not** acceptable overall. Compared with brownies made with the full amount of oil (control product), those made with half the amount of oil had the following differences in appearance, texture, and flavor:

_____

_____

_____

Overall, these differences were **small/moderate/large**.

5 What other changes could you make to the brownies made with half the amount of oil, black bean puree, and half the amount of eggs to more closely match the brownies made with the full amount of oil (control product)? Consider changes in the amounts of salt, cocoa powder, baking powder, etc.

_____

_____

_____

6 Did you notice any other differences in the brownies, or do you have any other comments about the experiment?

_____

_____

_____

Equivalencies Between U.S. Common (Imperial) and Metric Units

WEIGHT	
1 ounce (oz)	= 28.4 grams (g)
1 pound (lb)	= 454 grams
VOLUME	
1 teaspoon (tsp)	= 5 milliliters (ml)
1 tablespoon (Tbsp)	= 15 milliliters
1 quart (qt)	= 0.95 liters (l)

Volumetric Conversions for U.S. Common Units

1 tablespoon	= 3 teaspoons
	= 0.5 fluid ounce (fl oz)
1 cup	= 48 teaspoons
	= 16 tablespoons
	= 8 fluid ounces
1 pint	= 16 fluid ounces
	= 2 cups
1 quart	= 32 fluid ounces
	= 4 cups
	= 2 pints
1 gallon	= 128 fluid ounces
	= 16 cups
	= 8 pints
	= 4 quarts

Baumé to Brix Conversions

For the range of sugar solutions used by pastry chefs, the following conversions between Baume and Brix units apply: °Brix = °Baumé ÷ 0.55 and °Baumé = 0.55 × °Brix.

°BAUMÉ	°BRIX
10	18
12	22
14	25
16	29
18	33
20	36
28	50

Celsius to Fahrenheit Conversions

The conversions between degrees Fahrenheit and Celsius are as follows: °F = (°C × 9/5) + 32 and °C = (°F − 32) × 5/9. In the following table, Celsius values for oven temperatures (160°–230 °C) have been rounded to the nearest 5 degrees.

°CELSIUS	°FAHRENHEIT
0	32
10	50
20	68
30	86
40	104
50	122
60	140
70	158
80	176
90	194
100	212
165	325
175	350
190	375
205	400
220	425
230	450

Common Substitutions

U.S. COMMON UNITS	
1 lb all-purpose flour	0.5 lb bread flour + 0.5 lb cake flour
1 lb salted butter	1 lb unsalted butter + 0.4 oz salt (2 tsp)
1 lb shortening	20 oz butter; reduce water by 4 oz
1 lb butter	12.75 oz shortening + 3.25 oz water
1 oz compressed yeast	⅓ oz instant yeast
1 oz active dry yeast	¾ oz instant yeast
1 lb fluid milk	14 oz water (0.88 lb) + 2 oz dried milk solids (0.12 lb)
1 lb egg yolks	1 lb 1.5 oz sugared yolks (1.1 lb); reduce sugar by 1.5 oz (0.1 lb)
1 large egg	1.5 oz whole egg
1 large egg white	1.2 oz egg white
1 large egg yolk	0.55 oz egg yolk
1 lb brown sugar	14 oz granulated sugar + 2 oz molasses
1 lb sugar	1 lb honey; reduce water (or other liquid) by 2.5–3 oz
1 oz powdered gelatin (230 Bloom)	15–18 gelatin sheets
1 lb unsweetened chocolate	10 oz 22/24 cocoa powder + 3 oz shortening
1 lb unsweetened chocolate	2 lb bittersweet dark chocolate (50% cocoa solids); reduce sugar by 1 lb
1 lb cocoa powder	1 lb 9 oz unsweetened chocolate; reduce shortening or other fat by 4.5 oz
1 lb buttermilk	15 oz low-fat milk + 1 oz vinegar

Common Substitutions

METRIC UNITS	
1 kg all-purpose flour	500 g bread flour + 500 g cake flour
1 kg salted butter	1 kg unsalted butter + 25 grams salt
1 kg shortening	1.25 kg butter; reduce water by 250 g
1 kg butter	800 g shortening + 200 g water
30 g compressed yeast	10 g instant yeast
30 g active dry yeast	22 g instant yeast
1 kg fluid milk	880 g water + 120 g dried milk solids
1 kg egg yolks	1.1 kg sugared yolks; reduce sugar by 0.1 kg (100 g)
1 large egg	50 g whole egg
1 egg white	33 g egg white
1 egg yolk	17 g egg yolk
1 kg brown sugar	900 g granulated sugar + 100 g molasses
1 kg sugar	1 kg honey; reduce water (or other liquid) by 160-190 grams
30 g powdered gelatin (230 Bloom)	15–18 gelatin sheets
1 kg unsweetened chocolate	630 g 22/24 cocoa powder + 185 g shortening
1 kg unsweetened chocolate	2 kg bittersweet dark chocolate (50% cocoa solids); reduce sugar by 1 kg
1 kg cocoa powder	1.6 kg 22/24 cocoa powder; reduce shortening or other fat by 300 g
1 kg buttermilk	940 g low-fat milk + 60 g vinegar

Bibliography

This is a list of general references. Web addresses are accurate at the time of publication, but readers should consult a search engine, if necessary.

Atwell, William. A. *Wheat Flour*. St. Paul, MN: Eagan Press, 2001.

Beckett, Stephen T., ed. *Industrial Chocolate Manufacture and Use*. 4th ed. Oxford, UK: Blackwell Publishing, 2008.

———. *The Science of Chocolate*. 2nd ed. Cambridge, UK: Royal Society of Chemistry, 2008.

Belitz, Hans-Dieter, W. Grosch, and P. Schieberle. *Food Chemistry, 3rd ed*. Translated from the fifth German edition by M. M. Burghagen. Berlin and New York: Springer, 2004.

Calvel, Raymond. *The Taste of Bread*. Edited by James J. MacGuire. Translated by Ronald L. Wirtz. Gaithersburg, MD: Aspen Publishers, 2001.

Canada Department of Justice. Food and Drug Regulations (C.R.C., c. 870). http://laws.justice.gc.ca/en/ShowTdm/cr/C.R.C.-c.870.

Canadian Food Inspection Agency. "Food." http://www.inspection.gc.ca/english/fssa/fssae.shtml.

Cauvain, Stanley T., and Linda S. Young. *Baked Products: Science, Technology and Practice*. Oxford, UK and Ames, IA: Blackwell Publishing, 2006.

———. *Bakery Food Manufacture and Quality: Water Control and Effects*. 2nd ed. Chichester, West Sussex, UK and Ames, IA: Wiley-Blackwell, 2008.

———. *Technology of Breadmaking*. 2nd ed. New York: Springer, 2007.

Charley, Helen, and Connie M. Weaver. *Foods: A Scientific Approach* 3rd ed. Upper Saddle River, NJ: Prentice Hall, 1998.

Chen, James C. P., and Chung Chi Chou. *Cane Sugar Handbook: A Manual for Cane Sugar Manufacturers and Their Chemists*. 12th ed. New York: John Wiley & Sons, 1993.

Coe, Sophie D., and Michael D. Coe. *The True History of Chocolate*. 2nd ed. New York: Thames and Hudson, 2007.

Dendy, David A. V., and Bogdan J. Dobraszczyk. *Cereals and Cereal Products: Chemistry and Technology*. Gaithersburg, MD: Aspen Publishers, 2001.

DiMuzio, Daniel T. *Bread Baking: An Artisan's Perspective*. Hoboken, NJ: John Wiley & Sons, 2010.

Edwards, W. P. *The Science of Sugar Confectionery*. Cambridge, UK: Royal Society of Chemistry, 2000.

European Union. EUR-Lex: "The Access to European Union Law." http://eur-lex.europa.eu/en/index.htm.

Damodaran, Srinivasan, Kirk L. Parkin, and Owen R. Fennema, eds. *Fennema's Food Chemistry*. 4th ed. Boca Raton, FL: CRC Press/Taylor & Francis, 2008.

Gisslen, Wayne. *Professional Baking. 5th ed*. Hoboken, NJ: John Wiley & Sons, 2009.

Health Canada. http://www.hc-sc.gc.ca/index-eng.php.

Hoseney, R. Carl. *Principles of Cereal Science and Technology. 2nd ed*. St. Paul, MN: American Association of Cereal Chemists, 1994.

Hui, Yui H., ed. *Bakery Products Science and Technology*. Ames, IA: Blackwell Publishing Professional, 2006.

Jackson, E. B., ed. *Sugar Confectionery Manufacture*. 2nd ed. London and New York: Blackwell Academic & Professional, 1995.

McGee, Harold. *On Food and Cooking: The Science and Lore of the Kitchen*. rev. ed. New York: Scribner, 2004.

Pyler, E. J., and L. A. Gordon. *Baking Science and Technology, 4th ed*. 2 vols. Kansas City, MO: Sosland Pub. Co., 2008.

Reineccius, Gary, ed. *Source Book of Flavors*. 2nd ed. Berlin and New York: Springer, 1998.

Stadelman, William J., and Owen J. Cotterill, eds. *Egg Science and Technology*. 4th ed. New York: Food Products Press, 1995.

University of California Postharvest Technology Research and Information Center. "Produce Facts." http://www.coolforce.com/facts/.

U.S. Department of Agriculture. "USDA Food Composition Data." http://www.nal.usda.gov/fnic/foodcomp/Data/.

U.S. Department of Health and Human Services, U. S. Department of Agriculture. "Dietary Guidelines for Americans 2005." http://www.healthierus.gov/dietaryguidelines.

U.S. Food and Drug Administration. http://www.fda.gov/Food.

Illustration Credits

Figure 1.1   Photo by Ron Manville

Figure 1.3   Photo by Ron Manville

Figure 1.4   Photo by Ron Manville

Figure 1.5   Photo by Ron Manville

Figure 3.1   Photo by Ron Manville

Table 3.2   Source: U.S. Department of Agriculture, Agricultural Research Service

Figure 4.2   Photo by Ron Manville

Figure 4.5   Photo by Ron Manville

Figure 4.7   Photo by Ron Manville

Figure 5.1   Courtesy of Wheat Foods Council

Figure 5.2   Courtesy of Stephen Symons, Canadian Grain Commission

Figure 5.4   Photo by Ron Manville

Figure 5.6   Photo by Aaron Seyfarth

Figure 5.7a   Photo by Ron Manville

Figure 5.7b   Photo by Ron Manville

Figure 6.2   Photo by Ron Manville

Figure 6.5   Photo by Ron Manville

Figure 7.1   Photo by Ron Manville

Figure 7.2   Photo by Ron Manville

Figure 7.3   Photo by Ron Manville

Figure 7.4   Photo by Ron Manville

Figure 7.5   Photo by Ron Manville

Figure 7.7   Photo by Ron Manville

Figure 7.9   Photo by Aaron Seyfarth

Figure 8.5   Photo by Ron Manville

Figure 8.7   Photo by Ron Manville

Figure 8.8   Photo by Ron Manville

Figure 8.9   Photo by Ron Manville

Figure 8.10   Photo by Ron Manville

Figure 8.12   Photo by Ron Manville

Figure 8.16   Photo by Ron Manville

Figure 8.17   Photo by Ron Manville

Figure 9.9   Photo by Ron Manville

Figure 9.10   Courtesy of the U.S. Department of Agriculture, Agricultural Research Service

Figure 9.15   Photo by Ron Manville

Figure 9.16   Photo by Ron Manville

Figure 10.1   Reprinted with permission of John Wiley & Sons, Inc. *Professional Cooking, Sixth Edition,* by Wayne Gisslen, 2007

Figure 10.3   Ron Manville

Figure 10.4   Courtesy of U.S. Department of Agriculture

Figure 10.5   Photo by Ron Manville

Figure 11.2   Courtesy SPL/Photo Researchers

Figure 12.2   Photo by Ron Manville

Figure 12.3   Photo by Ron Manville

Figure 12.5   Photo by Ron Manville

Figure 12.7a   Courtesy of National Starch Food Innovation

Figure 12.7b   Courtesy of National Starch Food Innovation

Figure 12.7c   Courtesy of National Starch Food Innovation

Figure 13.1a   Courtesy of Dr. Alexandra Smith, Department of Food Science, University of Guelph, Guelph, Ontario

Figure 13.1b   Courtesy of Dr. Alexandra Smith, Department of Food Science, University of Guelph, Guelph, Ontario

Figure 14.1   Adapted from USDA Nutrient Database for Standard Reference, Release 21 (2008)

Figure 14.2   Photo by Ron Manville

Figure 14.3   Courtesy of Almond Board of California

Figure 15.1   Courtesy of U.S. Department of Agriculture

Figure 15.2   Adapted from data from the USDA Nutrient Database for Standard Reference, Release 21 (2008)

Figure 15.3   Photo by Ron Manville

Figure 15.4   Photo by Ron Manville

Figure 15.6   Photo by Ron Manville

Figure 15.7   Photo by Ron Manville

Figure 16.2   Courtesy of U.S. Department of Agriculture

Figure 16.3a   Courtesy of the California Raisin Marketing Board

Figure 16.3b   Courtesy of the California Raisin Marketing Board

Figure 17.1   Photo by Ron Manville

Figure 17.2   Photo by Ron Manville

Figure 18.1   Photo by Ron Manville

Page numbers in *italics* indicate figures.

and fat plasticity, 219, 221
and flavor perception, 67
and fruit ripening, 437-440
and nut rancidity, 384
and yeast fermentation, 305
Temperature control
importance of, 11-13
and volume in baked goods, 12-13, 303
and water, 37
Tempering
chocolate, 406-407, 409, 412-414, *414*
eggs into hot mixtures, 12, 270
gelatin into cold mixtures, 11-12, 326
Tenacity, of dough, 136, 138
Tenderizers, 34
in eggs, 136, 266
fats, oils, and emulsifiers, 38, 39, 141, 148, 233
and gluten, 136, 140, 144, 148, 149
leaveners, 39, 312
sugars and syrups, 36, 186, 191
Tenderness, 34, 69, 312
in pie pastry, 37, 233, 235, 242
Texture, 67, 68, 69. *See also* Mouthfeel
Theobromine, 398, *403*
Thermal conductivity, 21, 22
Thickening and gelling agents, 324-325, 337. *See also specific types*
functions, 336, 338
storage and handling, 338-339
Thickness, 8, 69, 324
of chocolate products, 410, 411
of syrups, 173
Tinware, 24
Tofu, 482, 484, 485, 486
Tongue, of supertaster, 62, 71, *62*
Top notes, 454-455, 456, 458, 460, 462
Tortilla dough, 120, 139, 147, 308
Touch, and texture, 68
Tougheners, 34. *See also* Structure builders
Trans fat-free shortenings and oils, 220-221
Trans fats. *See* Trans fatty acids
Trans fatty acids, 215, 217, 219-220, *217*
and healthful baking, 472, 474, 479
Treacle, 176, 178
Trigeminal effects, 61, 62, 65-66, 64, 67, *66*
Triglycerides, 214, 215, 217, 220, 224, 231, 232, *214, 215, 232*
Trinitario beans, 396-397
Triticale, 123
Tropical oils, 214, 216, 221, *216*
Tunnels, in baked goods, 13, 39, 40, 46-47, 145
Turbinado sugar, 172
Turgor pressure, 435

UHT, 356, 360
Ultrapasteurization, 356, 357, 360
Umami, 63, 64, *63*
Unbleached flour, 82, 91, 93, 98

Unsweetened chocolate. *See* Chocolate, unsweetened
U.S. common measurements, 5, 7
USDA, 168, 225, 261-263, 276, 429, 473

Van Houten, C.J., 402, 404
Vanilla
bean, 456, 457-458, 463
bean, dried, 460
extract, pure, 457-458
flavoring (artificial), 460, 462
paste, 461, *461*
Vanillin
and chocolate, 462
in imitation flavorings, 460, 462
in real vanilla, 456, 457, 463
Variety grains, 118-133
Vegetable gum, modified, 330
Vegetable gums, (polysaccharides), 324, 328-330, 336. *See also specific types*
Vegetable oil, 216, 217, 219, 230, 243, 249, 250. *See also* Fats and Oils
Viscoelasticity, 137
Viscosity, 8. *See also* Consistency; Thickness
Vital wheat gluten, 89
Vitamin C, 43. *See also* Ascorbic acid
Volatile oil, 456, 459-460
Volumetric measurements, 5-7

Walnuts, 379, 383, 384, 416, 437, 480, 482, *378*
Wasanbon toh, 172
Water
amount in ingredients, 37
conversion to steam, 300, 301
diffusion into fruit, 431, 440, *431*
distilled, and sugar showpieces, 189
functions, 36-37
and gluten development, 36, 40-143
hardness, 141-143, *142*
heat transfer through, 21, 22, *22*
hydration, 36
and mixing, 36-38
pH, 143, *143*
as plasticizer, 237
and starch gelatinization, 41
Water absorption
of artisan breads, 92
of flour, 82, 97
of milk proteins, 365
and particle size, 84
and potato products, 124
of rye, 119
and soy, 125
of spelt, 122
Water activity, 175-176, 190, 306, 361
Water bath, 21, 22, 270, 274
Waxiness, 68, 69, 216
of margarines, 227-228
Waxy maize starch, 325, 331, 332, 333, 337

Weak flours, 84
Weight measurements, 5-7
Wheat
berry, 84, *84*. *See also* Wheat kernel
bran, 81, 94, 95, *80*
bread, 83, 95-96
classifications, 83-84
cracked, 84, *84*
flour, 83. *See also* Flour, white; Whole wheat flour
germ, 81, 94-95, 98, 147, *80*
germinating, 81, *81*
kernel (grain), 80-81, 83-84, *80*
starch, 333
varieties, 80, 83, 122-123
Whey, 358, 359, 360, 363, 364
Whipped cream, 365, 366
formula, 345-348
stabilized, with gelatin, 11, 12, 326, 336
Whipping cream, 360, 361, 365
White chocolate, 399, 407, 409, 412, 416, 417
White flour. *See* Flour, white
White whole wheat flour, 80, 83, 96, 98
Whole grain products
and health, 80, 98, 475-476, 477
stone-ground, 80, 94, 95
storage, 98
Wholemeal flour, 94. *See also* Whole wheat flour
Whole wheat bread, 83, 95-96
Whole wheat flour, 80, 85, 94-96, 97, 98, *84*
and gluten development, 95, 141, 147
and healthful baking, 475-476
storage, 98
vs. wheat flour, 83
white, 80, 83, 96, 98
Windowpane test, 137
Winterized oil, 231

Xanthan gum, 330
in gluten-free products, 483, *483*

Yeast, 304, *304*. *See also* Yeast fermentation
storage of, 313
types, 306, 307-308
Yeast fermentation, 304-306
and flavor, 40, 305, 307
and gluten development, 146-147
and malted products, 182, 304
and no-time dough, 146, 306, 308
and sugars, 189, 190, 306
and temperature, 39, 145-146, 305
Yogurt, 362-363, 366, 484
Yuca root, 332

Zante currants, 433, *433*
Zymase, 304